Light on the Eternal City

Observations and Discoveries in the
Art and Architecture of Rome

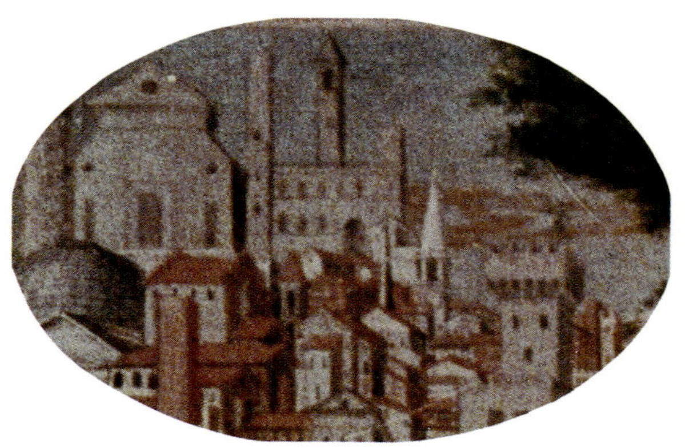

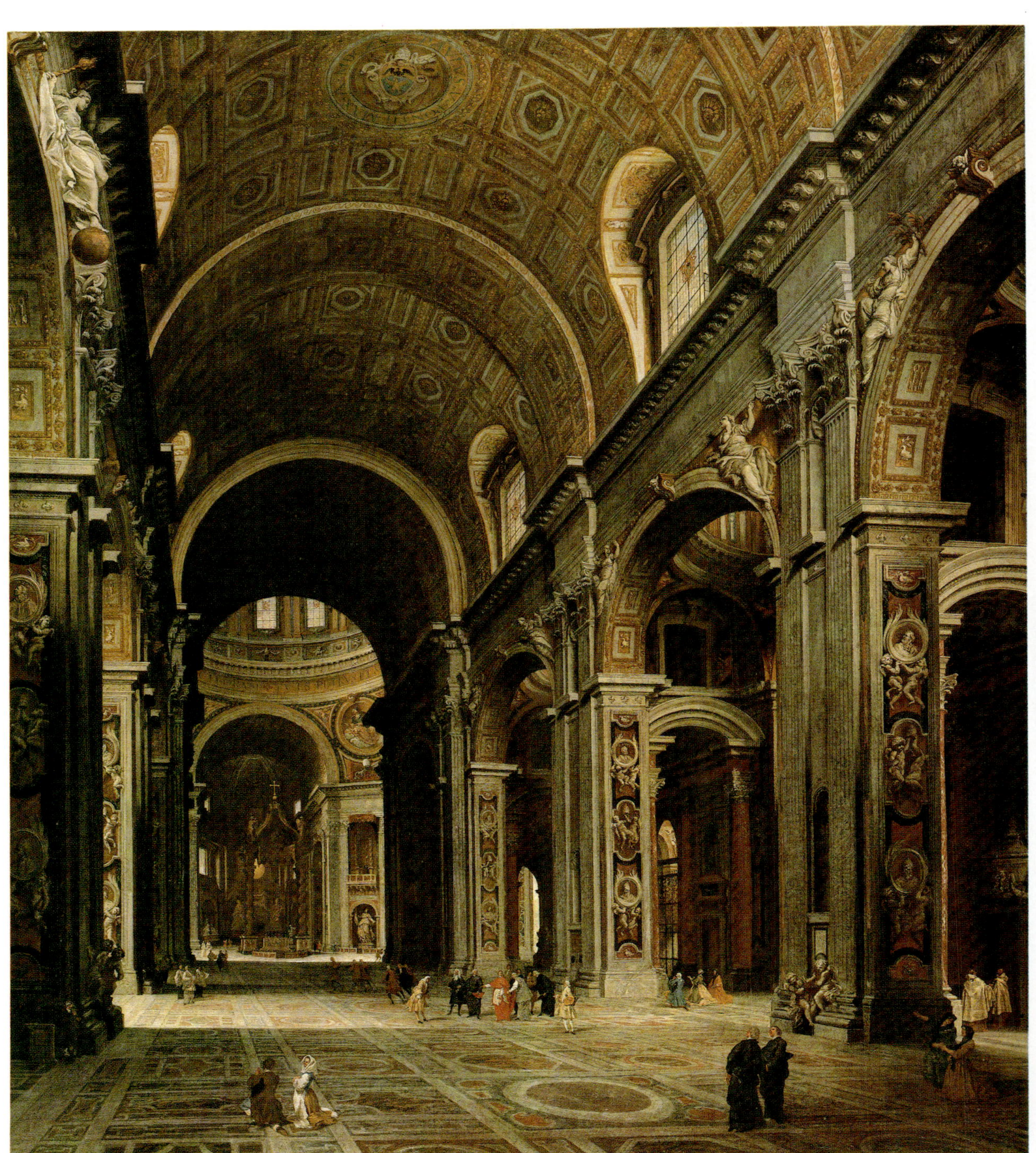

Light on the Eternal City

Observations and Discoveries in the Art and Architecture of Rome

Edited by

Hellmut Hager

and

Susan Scott Munshower

Published with the assistance of the J. Paul Getty Trust

Papers in Art History from
The Pennsylvania State University
Volume II

Library of Congress Catalog Card Number: 86-43122

ISBN: 0-915773-01-5

Cover illustration: Nicola Salvi, *Festival Decoration for the Piazza di Spagna*, Rome, 1728. Rome, Gabinetto Nazionale delle Stampe.

Half-title illustration: *The Departure of St. Augustine from Rome.* Detail of a fresco by Benozzo Gozzoli in the Church of S. Agostino, San Gimignano, showing the Senator's Palace on the Capitoline Hill, Rome (photo: Bibliotheca Hertziana, Rome)

Frontispiece: Giovanni Paolo Pannini, *Interior of St. Peter's Basilica, Rome*, detail (reproduced by courtesy of the Trustees, The National Gallery, London).

Second frontispiece: Giovanni Paolo Pannini, *Pope Benedict XIV Arriving at S. Maria Maggiore*, Rome, Palazzo del Quirinale.

Printed by Thomson-Shore, Inc., Dexter, Michigan.

Again, with gratitude to

William H. Allison

who has been with us from the very beginning,

and to a generous anonymous donor.

Contents

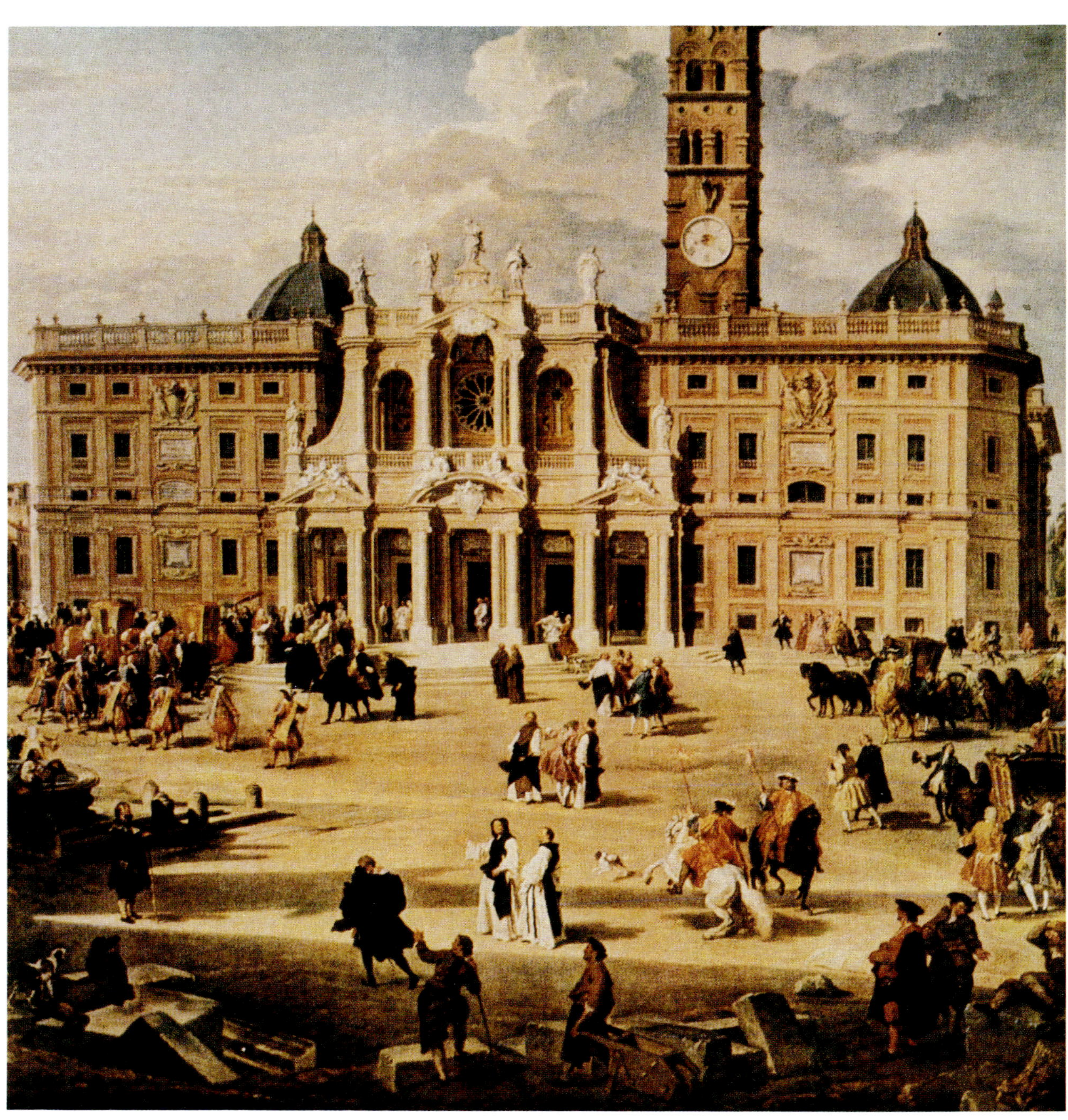

Acknowledgments

The present book, like its predecessor, *Projects and Monuments in the Period of the Roman Baroque,* grew out of a lecture series which gathered some of the most eminent scholars in their fields to share the results of their current research with our university community. Rome, the unifying theme, is approached from a variety of angles, and from numerous points in time. The product of these collective viewpoints is an enlightening view of the artistic, cultural, religious, and practical phenomena of a city and its people; a view that fits new pieces of strategic value into the vast puzzle that is the history of Rome and her art and architecture.

Therefore we owe our greatest debt to the participating scholars for contributing the choicest fruits of their labors to our publication. In addition it is a particular pleasure to convey our expressions of gratitude to the institutions and colleagues who have played a significant role in supporting volume II of our *Papers in Art History* from its earliest planning stages. With deep gratitude we acknowledge the grant received from the J. Paul Getty Trust, without which the publication of our volume would have been impossible. We are also grateful to a private donor — who preferred to remain anonymous — whose contribution was essential for the realization of our book in its present form.

The Director of Penn State's Institute for the Arts and Humanistic Studies, Dr. Stanley Weintraub, and the Associate Director, Professor William H. Allison, have provided generous support for our lecture series, and we are grateful for their continuous encouragement and enthusiasm. Professor Allison made his valuable expertise available throughout each phase of our progress toward publication, and we wish to thank him also for his generous contribution on behalf of the Division of Continuing Education.

Dr. Robert Holmes, former Dean of the College of Arts and Architecture, and Professor Raniero Corbelletti, former Interim Dean, will be gratefully remembered for their warm interest and valuable support of our project. Dean James Moeser, who recently assumed the helm of our College, we acknowledge with special gratitude for his immediate, spontaneous support. A cordial note of thanks is also extended to Dr. Harlan Hoifa, Dean for Graduate Studies and Research.

Among the many friends and colleagues who have encouraged our efforts with active advice and participation are Dr. Henry Millon, Dean of the Center for Advanced Study in the Visual Arts, National Gallery of Art, Washington, D. C.; Allan Braham, Deputy Director of the National Gallery of Art, London; and Professors John Pinto, Smith College, and Dora Wiebenson, University of Virginia at Charlottesville.

The preparation of this volume was also dependent on the technical expertise of a number of talented people. We extend our heartfelt thanks to our computer specialists William Verity, Terri Merdes, Gale Bowman, and Pauletta Leathers. In addition, we greatly appreciate the assistance of James Jamison, who was expert in tracking down essential material at the last minute.

We are also deeply indebted to the colleagues and staff members of our department, whose strong enthusiasm and encouragement have been continuous. We are most grateful to Professor Anthony Cutler for his valuable advice and erudite suggestions; and special mention is also due to Professors Roland Fleischer, Heinz Henisch, and George Mauner, whose inestimable help was always available.

Hellmut Hager
Susan Scott Munshower

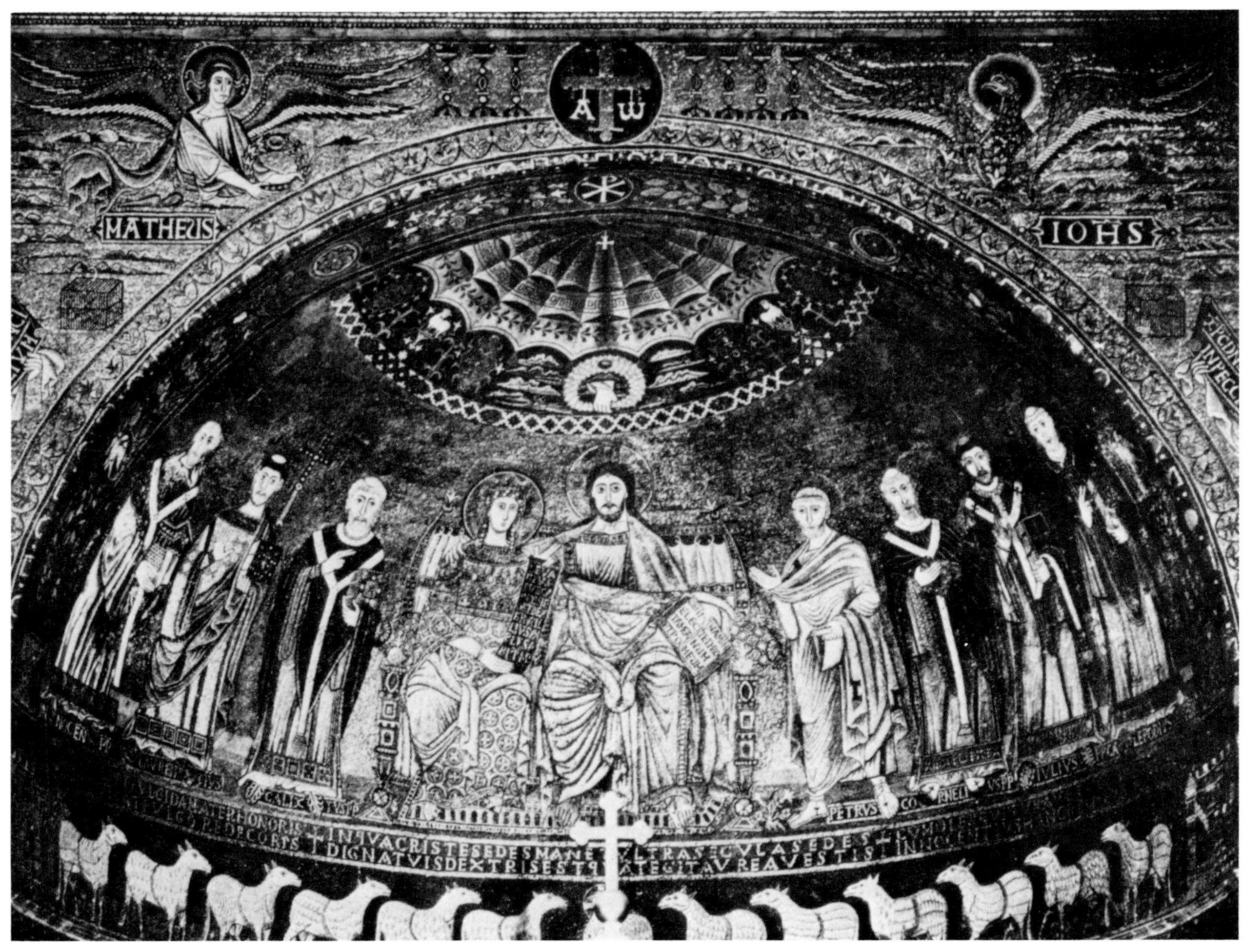

10.   Rome, S. Maria in Trastevere, apse mosaic (photo: author).

Papal Artistic Commissions as Definitions of the Medieval Church in Rome*

1

My topic deals with broad and difficult questions which may be phrased as follows: what made papal programs in Rome particular or singular? What were they meant to tell their audience? Finally, in what way did they differ from each other within different periods of church politics between A.D. 300 (when the pope became a political figure) and A.D. 1300 (when he left Rome for Avignon)?

To create a chronological framework, I propose dividing the millennium I have in mind into five ages or periods with markedly different aspects: (1) the late antique period (4th-6th century) in which the church of Rome struggled for survival in the midst of the collapse of the Roman empire and the migration of the Barbarians, mostly still unbaptised; (2) the age of confrontation with Byzantium (6th-8th century), coinciding with an intensive mission among the Barbarians, many popes being Greek, but with the Greek element eventually being excluded; (3) the age of the origin of the German empire and of the creation of the Church state or *patrimonium Petri*. The situation is characterized by a premature autonomy of the popes (also in terms of the papal coinage, of the right of coronation of the emperor, of undisguised spiritual leadership); (4) the so-called age of investiture, or rather the Age of Church Reform (11th-12th century), when the relations with the emperors produced conflict and the church strived for spiritual as well as temporal autonomy; (5) the climax of the power of the popes in the 13th century, the time of "Rome before Avignon" (R. Brentano),[1] framed by the gigantic figures of Innocent III at the beginning and Boniface VIII at the turn of the century, the age of aspiration toward world leadership, expressed in terms of control of temporal power (the formula of the so-called Two Swords).

To consider these periods, fully, one by one, I would, however, need ten lectures. Instead, I propose to inquire into some types of pictorial programs and to cut across these ages, bearing in mind their well-known differences. All I can do is to distinguish and address the same questions to each successive period.

I.

We first meet papal programs in Roman basilicas; the nave walls carry cycles with the stories from the earthly history of the two Testaments, the main apse an epiphany of the reign of God that will follow the end of history. The eschatological view, an anticipation of what is to come after the present age of dissolution and decay, was an obvious one for Late Antiquity. It is best expressed in St. Augustine's *City of God.* The center of power had shifted to the East. Soon there ceased to be an emperor at all in Rome, at least one relevant to its bishop. There was the need for survival, but survival in what sense and with what destination? Eschatology was the answer to such questions. It was incorporated in a concept of the church of the elect or those to be preserved from catastrophe, a church left to the authority of St. Peter. For the time being, he was the guide of the church on earth. St. Peter was buried in Rome. His successor was bishop of Rome. Thus, the concept of history merged with that of the church of Rome, of the Rome of the apostles Peter and Paul.

Early decorations of Roman church apses such as that of SS. Cosma e Damiano are a visual expression of this view (fig. 1).[2] Christ, in a golden robe, is identified by his imperial gesture as the emperor of the world to come, the eternal emperor. His imperial epiphany takes place before the clouds of the early dawn of the coming age and thus carries a temporal rather than spatial notion, heaven being post-historical rather than extraterrestrial. The triumphal arch elaborates the vision of the "Heavenly Jerusalem" in a strict, literal dependence on the biblical text of the Apocalypse which had received a very specific interpretation appropriate to this age of *fin-de-siecle*. In the same apse, Peter and Paul introduce the Syrian saints Cosmas and Damian into Heaven, or better, into the Church of Christ which will follow the Church of Rome. The role of the pope as participant in this program, will be considered below. The composition which was repeated, three hundred years later, in the 9th-century church of S. Prassede, was a tremendous success (fig. 2).[3]

Another of these early programs, the triumphal arch of the burial church of the martyred San Lorenzo fuori le mura, offers a variant worth considering (fig. 3).[4] Christ, enthroned as the world emperor on the global orb, wears the imperial purple. He is again surrounded by Saints Peter and Paul and this indicates that he qualifies as the lord of the Church in Rome. The pope is recommended and introduced by Lawrence, the patron saint of the basilica. It is too little to say he was the donor. With one exception, he was the only living person ever to appear in a church program in Rome.

In the eye of the public, the pope was left as the only local authority with secular power which, however, in personal union, carried a universal mission by being the representative of Christ on earth. In this capacity, he was the "living St. Peter." St. Peter was also the janitor of Heaven and thus held the keys for admission into a better age. Hence, his tremendous popularity among the barbarian nations, especially the English, in light of their hopes of paradise. Together with his companion, St. Paul, the "Apostle of all nations," he promised security in the midst of what then seemed to be the last days.

Thus, the Roman mosaics show not merely religious programs consisting of theological commonplaces. They view history as a history of salvation leading to an other-than-earthly future; at the same time, they serve to explain the role and mission of the church of Rome, led by the pope, in an eschatological perspective. Christ was the lord of the world and lord of Rome. The programs lend visible expression to the anxieties of the time, but also introduce the pope as the earthly leader of the church and even more, as the only authority in sight after Byzantium had lost its authority.

II.

But Byzantium re-entered the stage when it was no longer welcome in Rome. Its further existence, the continuity of a Roman emperor among Greek-speaking people, came to be a most unwanted problem. The pope of Rome had to define his position not only vis-à-vis Christ, or St. Peter, but vis-à-vis an emperor who also pretended to be Christ's governor or, worse still, the governor of Rome where the pope had become accustomed to the idea of dominating the stage. We enter a second age, the 7th and 8th centuries, which, as far as our topic is concerned, produced what I would like to call the "Battle of Icons." Papal programs adopted a Byzantine iconic language with, however, a reversal of meaning and intention. The cult of icons had become an affair of the Byzantine court in the second half of the 6th century, as Averil Cameron has proved convincingly in several studies.[5] The court took the lead in the official, organized cult of heavenly authorities, bodily present on earth in their likenesses and tangible as well as transportable on such panels. The emperors sometimes expressed their dominion over a Christian empire through the cult or propagation of icons which related their own portraits to the heavenly authorities.

It is, therefore, of some significance that Rome adopted this cult of icons, perhaps beginning with the re-dedication of the Pantheon in 609 as a church of all saints: the new 'temple image' which the church was to shelter is the well-known panel of the Virgin with the golden hand.[6] It became fashionable for the popes to use icons to convey their message to the people. Well known is the case of John VII (705-707), a Greek by birth, whose artistic commissions made him a pontiff of great influence despite his all too short reign. In the mosaics of his chapel in St. Peter's, he appears in front of an orant figure of the Virgin still understood as an icon even in the 17th century when it was transferred to a baroque frame in S. Marco in Florence (fig. 4).[7] Two features distinguish this program from others. The first one is an empress wearing the *insignia* of temporal power (which she never was at Byzantium). Fully in accord with this change is the fact that the pope decided to call himself "Servant of the Mother of God." The implication is: servant of no one else on earth. The positive message is exclusive, that is, all alternatives are excluded.

Recipients of this message included the Byzantine emperor. The hidden tension came into the open when Iconoclasm erupted, the pope soon opposing Byzantium.[8] The formula employed in this mosaic proved successful several times in the following centuries. When Paschal I (817-824) became tired of, or self-protective against, the newly crowned German emperor, he consciously "quoted" a similar icon in his mosaic of S. Maria in Domnica.[9] It is the so-called 'Madonna della Clemenza,' a panel from S. Maria in Trastevere with John VII in proskynesis (fig. 5).[10] Callixtus II (1119-1124) "quoted" the very same icon once again when decorating the chapel of St. Nicholas in the Lateran.[11] By then the popes had finally turned their backs on the German emperors. It is possible that Callixtus II referred to his namesake, Callixtus I, when reproducing the icon, since S. Maria in Trastevere, its home, was considered to be the 'titulus' of that first Callixtus; such a retrospect would agree with the then prevalent ideals of the reform movement.

When such icons refer to heavenly authority clad in the full apparatus of earthly majesty and directly relate the local (as well as the ecclesiastical) authority to it in an act of submission, there is, of course, more to this phenomenon than a striving for independence from temporal power. Though it is true both that the pope used the icon as an instrument of his politics, and that he insisted on leadership in a temporal sense (his spiritual leadership being defined by his role of a living St. Peter); we may nonetheless ask ourselves why it it is the Virgin (*Maria Regina*) to whom he submits. Some possible answers come to mind (including a reference to the Byzantine cult of the Virgin). But I should like to defer the question for a while, suggesting at this point that an initial re-interpretation of the Virgin as a *typos*, or semblance, of the Church might have taken place.[12] Since her earthly rule is so clearly expressed in these formulas, she seems also to claim the very same rule for the church and its leader, the pope, on earth.

III.

We come now to a critical moment in the history of papal art commissions in medieval Rome. A third age triumphantly opened with the coronation of

Charlemagne by Leo III on Christmas day, 800. It was this same Leo III, an unusual personality with great aspirations, who became an outstanding patron of the arts in medieval Rome and devised ambitious decorations for secular buildings. Thus, we are no longer dealing with church decorations alone. Two rather general remarks may be appropriate to emphasize the basic nature of the change: 1) the message of papal programs, is now directed to the Franks rather than to Byzantium, and 2) the programs are located in and related to a new context: three giant palace halls with clear imperial connotations.

Nothing visible remains of one of them, the triconch hall *in Acoli* near St. Peter's. The next, the *Aula Leonina*, was one of two *triclinia* which transformed the Lateran *patriarchium* into a kind of imperial residence for the pope. It was the site of church assemblies, and the triconch plan of the building carried imperial connotations, like its parallel, the *Aula* in Charlemagne's palace at Aachen.[13] The third hall, another *triclinium* in the Lateran, with its eleven conches and two floors, perhaps referred to the "chamber of the 19 divans" at the imperial residence of Constantinople which as a building type is matched by the Lausos palace, recently excavated in Istanbul.[14] The Lateran hall was the site of the pope's state banquets and general councils. The lateral conches had sigma-shaped tables for the banquet guests and a porphyry basin in the middle.

The apse mosaic of the first Lateran *triclinium* or *Aula Leonina*, has been less studied than the two famous investiture scenes flanking it on either side (fig. 6). The mosaic, commissioned about 798, represents Christ among his apostles, as did the 5th-century apse of S. Pudenziana.[15] But the earlier composition represents the council of Christ, in the heavenly Jerusalem, and thus offers a vision of the eternal church. The medieval composition, however, is no longer a static vision of final rest. Instead, it is a narrative: as such, it relates the biblical mandate to St. Peter and all apostles to go out and baptize the people, i.e., to erect the church of Christ on earth. A narrative in an apse is a novelty. In this particular case, it requires us to ask two important questions. First, in what sense does a post-antique decoration adopt late antique models and how does it differ from such precedents? Second, is such a program in a secular building, to be distinguished from church programs, properly speaking?

In our case, the apse mosaic adopts, and transforms, a *traditio legis*, i.e., the appointment of St. Peter to handle the new law of Christ's church on earth.[16] Such a composition was commonplace. It also decorated the front of a sarcophagus at St. Peter's (fig. 7) which sheltered the remains of Leo's famous namesake, Leo the Great (later on, Leo III was buried in the same sarcophagus). A major change in the medieval replica of the old composition is the shift of St. Peter, who originally approached Christ, to the other side. When assigned to the right side of the central figure, the same figure now departs from Christ. In carrying out Christ's order, he begins his mission in the world.

The early sarcophagus, itself only a reflection of a pre-existing monumental image, such as the apse of St. Peter's, could not have been the actual model of the mosaic, but represents the type on which was imposed an entirely new message, when transformed into the medieval version. The antique motives were re-structured in order to serve a new political purpose. Why political? Already the inscription, again a novelty in quoting a biblical text, hints at a political meaning by implying that the mission of Christ was a mission to erect the church of Rome among the new nations of the medieval West.[17]

The clue to the political content is given by the two scenes of investiture, flanking the apse on either side (fig. 6). One, with Christ presiding over Silvester and Constantine, in its present form, is a 17th-century fabrication. But there is evidence for an original image of Constantine, however different it may have looked, like the one once evident on the triumphal arch of St. Peter's. The corresponding image shows St. Peter handing over the *pallium* (the sign of pontifical power) to Leo III, and a *vexillum* (a flag signifying a military function) to King Charlemagne. The head and protector (not lord!) of the Roman church jointly receive the symbols of their appointment from the hand of St. Peter who in turn received their authority from Christ himself. The flanking scenes develop the content of the apse composition (the origin of the church) and project it into the present, thus characterizing the Carolingian king as an instrument in the service of Peter's church. A second inscription, running around the arch of the apse, argues in St. Luke's words for peace on earth in terms of a *Pax Augusta* or a new age of peace (i.e., for the mission of the church) which the Frankish king would guarantee.[18]

The second *triclinium* in the Lateran, the so-called Council Hall has gone, and we are left with only a few descriptions and a clumsy drawing (fig. 8).[19] What this scanty information yields is the impression of a program equally skillfully devised, if not superior, in terms of political content. The main apse contained an image of the church of Rome, reshaped after the model of the apse of St. Paul's. The ten lateral conches, according to the *Liber Pontificalis*, contained fresco paintings representing "the preaching of the apostles in front of the peoples." Why only ten and not twelve? Because the Roman "dioscuri" Peter and Paul, expanding the ten to a full twelve, presided over the others in the main apse. This is a plea for the hegemony of the Church of Rome (symbolized by the elevated main apse with the throne of the bishop of Rome) over the other churches of the world. The statement is carried out in terms of both architecture and painted decoration. The eleven conches make sense only when the painted program is considered.

The mosaic of the main apse refers to the early Christian decoration of St. Paul's. This is quite clear for the 24 elders and the medallion of Christ on the triumphal arch, and it can also be demonstrated for the apse. The reference matches the one to St. Peter's in the other council hall. St. Paul, the apostle of all nations, helps to identify the church of Rome as fountain-head of the churches on earth. It may be significant that the very same Leo III undertook a thorough restoration of St. Paul's, including the upper parts of the mosaic of the triumphal arch. And it is even more telling that Leo, shortly thereafter, restored the ancient church of S. Apollinare in Classe near Ravenna, by replacing the pre-existing uppermost mosaic zone with the composition borrowed from St. Paul's (fig. 9).[20] The early Apostolic basilicas obviously offered convenient symbols of a new, and strongly political, conception of the church of Rome.

IV.

The later history of the papal commissions in Rome proves that the concept of the church of Rome remained the key element in all deliberations as to what papal programs should convey to the people. A prominent and truly novel program of the Age of Reform or Investiture, was the apse mosaic of S. Maria in Trastevere (the former *titulus Callixti* and home of the Virgin's icon, discussed above), a work commissioned by Innocent II and to be dated in the 1130s (fig. 10).[21] The most novel feature is the center of the apse which, for the first time, displays the coronation of the Virgin in Heaven. It is not actually a coronation, but the image of a couple, sharing the throne of the Lord, expressing their mutual affection and protection with gestures and quotations from the Song of Songs: the Lord loves the Woman, the Woman feels, as she says, protected by her lover and Lord. The woman, of course, is the Virgin, the titular saint of the building. But she must also be the Church, *Maria Ecclesia,* and in the context of my argument and the program's intentions, she is above all the Church. This is confirmed by St. Peter, the third active figure in the apse. The figure itself is a quotation from the 5th-century apse mosaic of S. Andrea in Catabarbara, with Christ in the middle of the college of apostles.[22]

The meaning, however, has changed altogether. In the Trastevere mosaic, St. Peter testifies to what happens to Mary, the model of the church. The earthly representative of the church (i.e., of Rome) announces and comments on the queen as the personification and model of the church, the honor conferred on her and the protection offered her by the Lord himself. She is his *synthronos.* In an age when the Church felt threatened by the temporal power of the German emperor but escaped from this danger by striving for autonomy, no better formula could have been found to express its triumph and supreme rank on God's throne. *Maria Regina* is the Virgin Queen who reigns in Heaven and on Earth. We are offered a reformulation of the institution of the church of Rome in terms of scholastic theology, a new formulation by a new age.

If this is political in nature, as I believe it to be, then it is almost disguised in theological formulas, in the language of the age of Scholasticism. The assumption that there were revisions in the concept of the church is not too far-fetched. If we compare this with other papal commissions, it becomes obvious how very much they differ from each other, despite the limited range of visual formulas available to the artists. The latter-day eschatology of the early programs was followed by reactions against temporal power, directed first against Byzantium and then addressed to the Franks. The world continued to exist, and the church of Rome was forced to define its position in it, whether as an independent bishopric or state church or the head of all churches on earth. The relation to temporal power proved to be another infinite issue. The painted programs are the visible expressions of all these conflicts, defeats and triumphs. The church, after all, *was* sent *into* this world, but it was believed to have its past as well as its future in Heaven. The scholastic

formula of the Trastevere basilica places the Church, as the immaculate and immortal protégeé of God himself, at a safe distance, in a literal and metaphorical sense, in Heaven.

V.

But the history of official art in medieval Rome had not yet come to an end. In a fifth age of the millennium under consideration, Ecclesia finally appears in her own right and under her own name: *Ecclesia Romana.* She is no longer the Virgin with the added connotation of *Ecclesia,* but the Roman Church in person. This change again occurred during a program of restoration, and all major commissions were restorations or substitutions for earlier ones. In the apse mosaic of old St. Peter's, renewed by Innocent III (1198-1216), the upper part more or less repeats the pre-existing composition as it has been reconstructed by Tilman Buddensieg (fig. 11).[23] This lower frieze, is however, modified by the insertion of a new triad of figures: the lamb of God, in a eucharistic formula, is flanked by both Innocent and the *Ecclesia Romana*, the latter being the universal church, and a kind of baptized daughter of the deity *Roma.* The body of Christ, administered as a sacrament by the church, is related to the mystical body of the church. The office of the pope who for the first time makes a pair with the personified church, is related to the people of God which is identical with the church of Rome. In the apse of St. Peter's, two formulas are superimposed, an old scheme of antique origin and timeless nature (the all-ruler Christ with his twin representatives, Peter and Paul) and a new one, quite up-to-date in eliminating any temporal leadership other than that of the church's institution. The pope no longer appears as a disguised donor or bishop of Rome, but as the temporal ruler or administrator of *Roma Christiana.* The double reference to the *cathedra,* the seat of the teacher or shepherd, is reinforced by the inscription's emphasis on the "summa sedes" (cf. *Petri*) which is also the "mater cunc*tarum . . . ecclesiarum.*"

In the meantime, decorations in the St. Nicholas chapel in the Lateran (already referred to) and in the meeting rooms of the *curia* in the Lateran had brought into focus, the controversies of the age of church reform, the polemical confrontation of popes and anti-popes, the triumph of the one over the other, and the definition of the pope's right to crown the emperor.[24] The accompanying inscriptions were protested by Barbarosa when he came to Rome. The frescoes in SS.

Quattro Coronati (1246), like their predecessors in the Lateran entrance hall, strengthened the claims of the "Donation of Constantine" and its contrasting description of the relation of pope and emperor.[25]

My final example is again a novel type of commission and connected with the last powerful figure of the medieval papacy, Boniface VIII. It is a balcony structure from which Boniface, in the year 1300, promulgated the first *anno santo* thus making a new attempt to center Western Europe in Rome and the opportunities it offered for salvation (fig. 12). A fresco, painted on the back wall of the upper floor, not only duplicated (or better, portrayed) the loggia as the site of the event, but also commemorated the event itself: it placed the pope in the center of a real *historia* (narrative) which also resulted in a monument to his glory.[26] What is rarely mentioned is the fact that the so-called Jubilee fresco once was only the central protion of three frescoes, the other two representing the baptism of Constantine and the construction, on behalf of Constantine, of the Lateran basilica. These additional subjects stem from the "Donation of Constantine" or the legend of St. Silvester. According to the legend, Constantine had accepted the Christian faith from the hands of the pope and had executed the cathedral of the pope in his own palace. Here again the location of the image and the site of the historical event coincided. In this neighborhood, Boniface appeared as the new lord of the Lateran palace and, indeed, as a new Constantine. The typology offered by the two Constantine scenes served this new and surprising self-understanding of the pope who, according to the inscription, carried the crown of the *Urbs*. The tiara he wears was traditionally part of the imperial insignia transferred by Constantine. The surrounding curia and militia accept and transmit the implication of an imperial court. Here we have arrived at an extreme interpretation of papal power. I should like to add that the loggia of benediction is nothing other than an addition to the Council Hall of Leo III mentioned above (p. 4). Thus, the two structures, whatever their difference in function and meaning, enter into a surprising connection. Their imperial overtones are undeniable. The Council Hall of Leo and the Loggia of Boniface, the one Constantinian in shape and the other Constantinian in meaning, were the prelude and *finale* to the Constantinian setting of the Lateran palace in the Middle Ages.

The popes, who had successfully restricted imperial power to its proper realm, ended up by claiming for themselves world leadership in terms of imperial office. One recalls the many honorific statues, erected in several towns of Guelf orientation, representing larger than life "the most holy father the pope, lord Boniface."[27] At Bologna a statue which was once completely gilded and "erected on the façade of the new town hall so that it may be seen by many people," had originally been planned in marble as one of three statues of the pope in this city. Boniface himself had insisted on having a silver statue, worth a thousand pounds, in the cathedral of Amiens. In the tribunal in which the French king Philippe le Bel posthumously indicted the dead Boniface, the pope was accused of idolatry. He was reported to have said that all rulers on earth should bow in front of a statue of a new pope. Whatever the truth, the glory of the Roman papacy was over. The Holy See was transferred to Avignon. There began an era later called the Babylonian captivity of the Church.

In the following year commissions in Rome also came to an end. There is only one monumental exception with a telling subject. The indefatigable Cardinal Stefaneschi, a truly patriotic Roman, commissioned Giotto's *Navicella* mosaic in the atrium of St. Peter's (fig. 13).[28] It is described as "the story when Christ took Peter's hand to prevent his sinking into the water." A very appropriate subject, appropriate for a crisis when the main concern was the survival of the church. The *Navicella* became famous because it was Giotto's work. But I am sure the people at Strassburg did not think of Giotto when, shortly after the completion of the original, they had a replica painted in the Strassburg church of St. Peter.[29] The mosaic proved to be a perfect symbol of the new crisis, an expression of scarcely concealed fears and stubborn hopes. Cola di Rienzo was impressed by the *Navicella* when, in 1346, he devised a secular paraphrase for the façade of the palace on the Capitol: the widow Rome threatened by the stormy sea of the perils of the age. The Roman people, we are told, preferred the crisis to be solved by something more potent than pictures.[30]

Hans Belting
University of Munich

Notes

*   The text represents the version of a lecture given in 1980 during the symposium on "Church and Cosmos in the Middle Ages" in

Atlanta, Georgia. Titles which are frequently quoted in the following notes are: Christa Ihm, *Programme der christlichen Apsismalerei vom 4. bis zur Mitte des 8. Jahrhunderts*, Wiesbaden, 1960, as: Ihm, 1960. Gerhard B. Ladner, *Die Papstbildnisse des Altertums und des Mittelters* I, Rome, 1941; II *von ·Innozenz II zu Benedikt XI*, Rome, 1970, as: Ladner, I, II. Guglielmo Matthiae, *Mosaici medioevali delle chiese di Roma*, Rome, 1947, as: Matthiae, 1947; same author, *Pittura romana del Medioevo*, vol. I, Rome, 1965, vol. II, Rome, 1966, as: Matthiae, *Pittura* I, II. Walter Oakeshott, *The Mosaics of Rome from the 3rd to the 14th Centuries*, London, 1967, as: Oakeshott, 1967. *Roma e l'età carolingia. Atti delle Giornate di Studio* (3-8 maggio 1976), a cura dello Istituto di Storia dell'Arte dell'Università di Roma, Rome 1976, as: *Roma carolingia. Roma anno 1300. Atti della IV settimana di studi di storia dell'arte medioevale dell'Università di Roma 'La Sapienza'* (19-24 Maggio 1980), a cura di Angiola Maria Romanini, Rome, 1983, as: Roma anno 1300.

1. Robert Brentano, *Rome Before Avignon. A Social History of Thirteenth-Century Rome*, London, 1974.

2. Ihm, 1960, pp. 137-138 and pl. XII, 2; Matthiae, 1967, pp. 135-142 and figs. 78a, 80-85.

3. Per Jonas Nordhagen, "Un problema di carattere iconografico e tecnico a S. Prassede," *Roma carolingia*, pp. 159-166.

4. Ihm, 1960, pp. 138-140; Matthiae, 1967, pp. 149-168 and figs. 89, 91-97; Oakeshott, 1967, pp. 145-146 and fig. 77.

5. Averil Cameron, *Continuity and Change in Sixth-Century Byzantium*, London, 1981.

6. Carlo Bertelli, "La Madonna del Pantheon," *Bollettino d'Arte del Ministero della Pubblica Istruzione*, nos. I-II, 1961, pp. 24-32.

7. Ihm, 1960, 156-157; and Per Jonas Nordhagen, "The Mosaics of John VII (705-707 A.D.). The Mosaic Fragments and their Technique," *Acta ad archeologiam et artium historiam pertinentia*, 2, 1965, pp. 121-166. Cf. Matthiae, 1967, pp. 215-224, figs. 132-135.

8. For the iconoclasm cf. André Grabar, "L'iconoclasme byzantin," (Paris), and the volume of collected studies: *Iconoclasm. Papers given at the Ninth Spring Symposium of Byzantine Studies*, University of Birmingham March, 1975, ed. Anthony Bryer and Judith Herria (Birmingham, 1977).

9. For S. Maria in Domnica, cf. Matthiae, 1967, pp. 235-237, figs. 170-175; and Oakeshott, 1977, pp. 203-204, Pl. xx, figs. 114-118.

10. Carlo Bertelli, *La Madonna di S. Maria in Trastevere*, Rome, 1961.

11. Ladner I, pp. 202-218 and Pl. xx.

12. For the type of S. Maria Regina, cf. Ursula Nilgen, "Maria Regina - Ein politischer Kultbildtypus?," *Römisches Jahrbuch für Kunstgeschichte*, 19, 1981, pp. 1-33.

13. The material has been discussed by the author in the two articles, "Die beiden Palastaulen Leos III. im Lateran und die Entstehung einer päpstlichen Programmkunst," *Frühmittel-alterliche Studien*, 12, 1978, pp. 55-83; 'I mosaici dell' aula Leonina come testimonianze della prima 'renovatio' nell'arte medioevale di Roma," *Roma carolingia*, pp. 167-182, figs. 173-175.

14. Richard Krautheimer, "Die Decannacubita in Konstantinopel. Ein kleiner Beitrag zur Frage Rom und Byzanz," *Tortulae. Studien zu altchristlichen und byzantinischen Monumenten*, 30. Suppl.heft der *Römischen Quartalschrift für christliche Altertumskunde und Kirchengeschichte*, 1966, pp. 195 and figs. 46-47.

15. Ihm, 1960, pp. 130-132, Pl. iii, 1, 2.

16. Walter N. Schumacher, "Dominus legen dat," *Römische Quartalschrift für christliche Altertumskunde und Kirchengeschichte*, 54, 1959, pp. 1-39; Walter N. Schumacher, "Eine römische Apsiskomposition," *ibidem*, pp. 137-202.

17. The inscription is quoted from Giovanni Giustino Ciampini, *Vetera monimenta*, Rome, 1599, II, pl. xxxix and xl.

18. The second inscription: Nicolaus Alemannus, *De Lateranensibus parietinis ab . . . Domino D. Francesco Cardinale Barberino restitutis*, Rome, 1625, pl. II-III.

19. Belting, 1978 (cf. note 13 above).

20. Belting, 1978 (cf. note 13 above).

21. Ernst Kitzinger, "A Virgin's Face: Antiquarianism in Twelfth-Century Art," *Art Bulletin*, 62, 1980, pp. 6-20. Cf. also Matthiae, 1967, pp. 305-314, figs. 260-264; and Oakeshott, 1967, pp. 250-255, pl. XXV and fig. 18; as well as Ladner II, pp. 9-16.

22. Ihm, 1960, pp. 154-155 and pl. VIII, 1.

23. Tilmann Buddensieg, "Le coffret en ivoire de Pola, St. Pierre et le Lateran," *Cahiers Archéologiques*, 10, 1959, pp. 157-195; cf. Ladner II, pp. 56-68.

24. Ladner I, pp. 195-201 and pl. XIX.

25. Matthiae, *Pittura* II, pp. 146-153, figs. 128-137.

26. For the Lateran Loggia della Benedizione and its frescoes: Charles Mitchell, "The Lateran Fresco of Boniface VIII," *Journal of the Warburg and Courtauld Institutes*, 14, 1951, pp. 1-5, Ladner II, pp. 288-296.

27. Ladner II, pp. 296-302, especially p. 300.

28. W. Paeseler, "Giottos Navicella und ihr spätantikes Vorbild," *Römisches Jahrbuch für Kunstgeschichte*, 5, 1941, pp. 49-162 W. Kemp, "Zum Programm von Stefaneschi-Altar und Navicella," *Zeitschrift für Kunstgeschichte*, 30, 1967, pp. 309-320.

29. Werner Körte, "Die 'Navicella' des Giotto," *Festschrift Wilhelm Pinder zum 60. Geburtstag*, Leipzig, 1938, pp. 223-263.

30. Philippe Sonnay, "La politique aristique de Cola di Rienzo (1313-1354)," *Revue de l'art*, 55, 1982, pp. 35 ff.

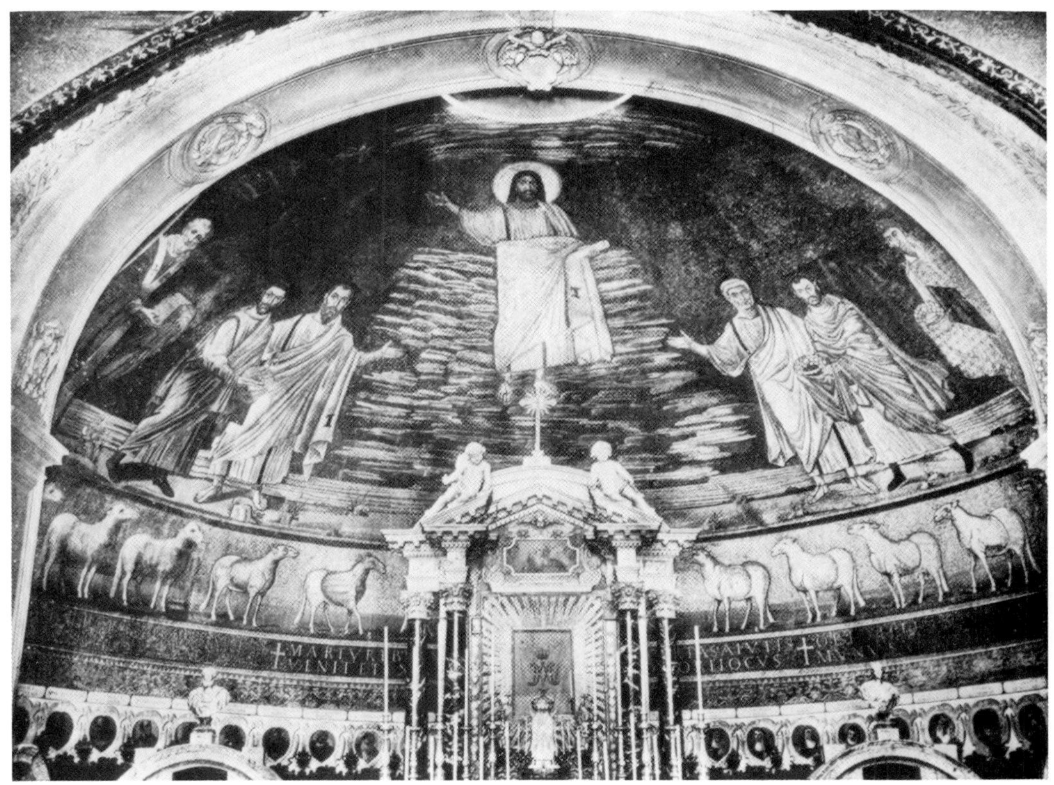

1.   Rome, SS. Cosma e Damiano, apse mosaic (photo: author).

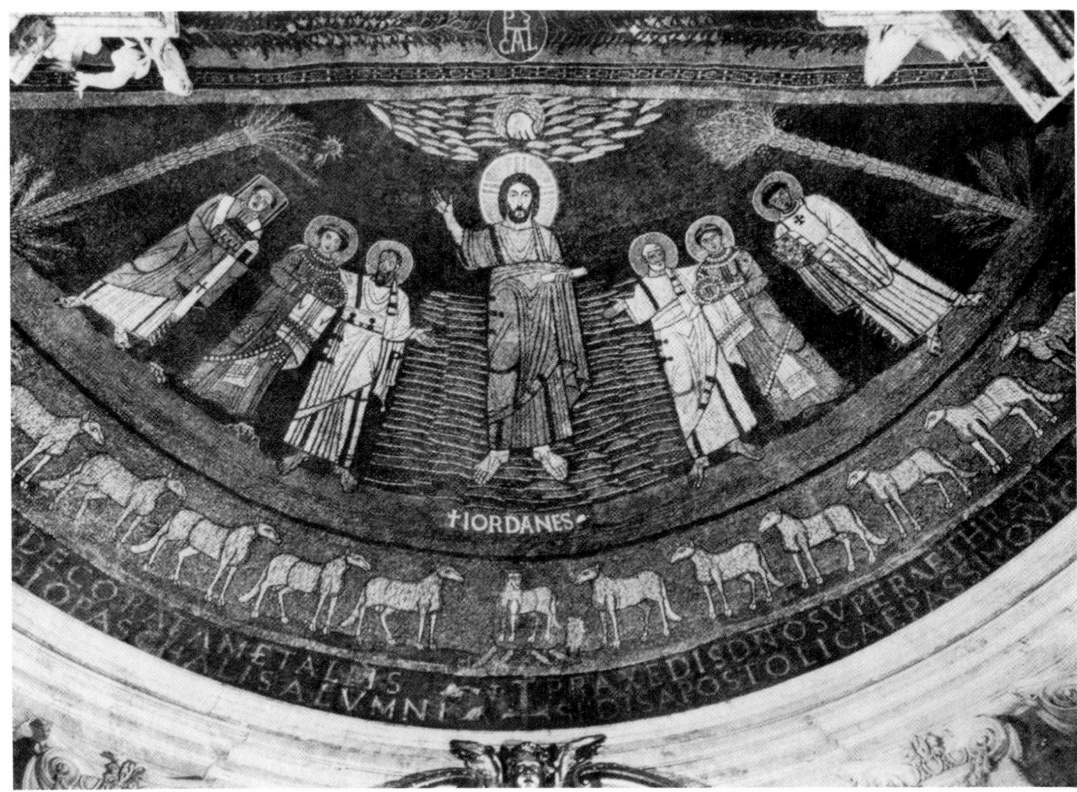

2.   Rome, S. Prassede, apse mosaic (photo: author).

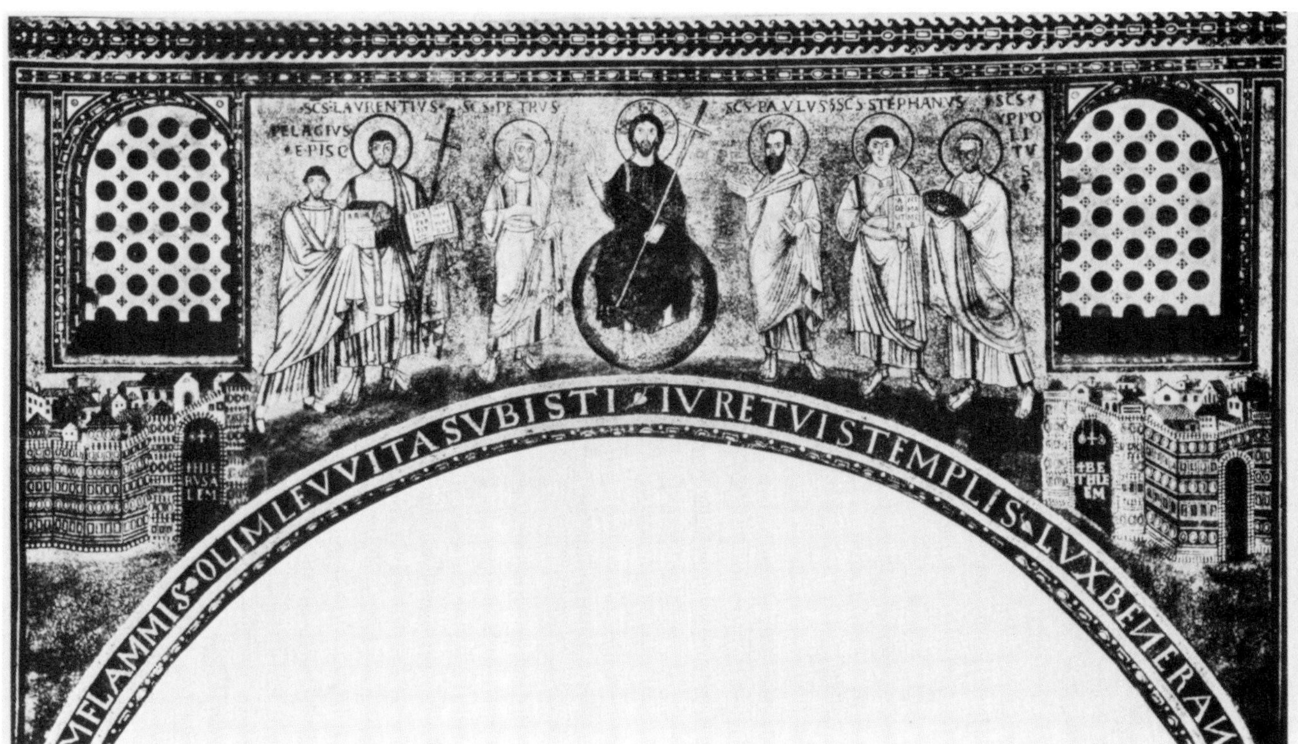

3.   Rome, S. Lorenzo fuori le mura, triumphal arch mosaic (photo: author).

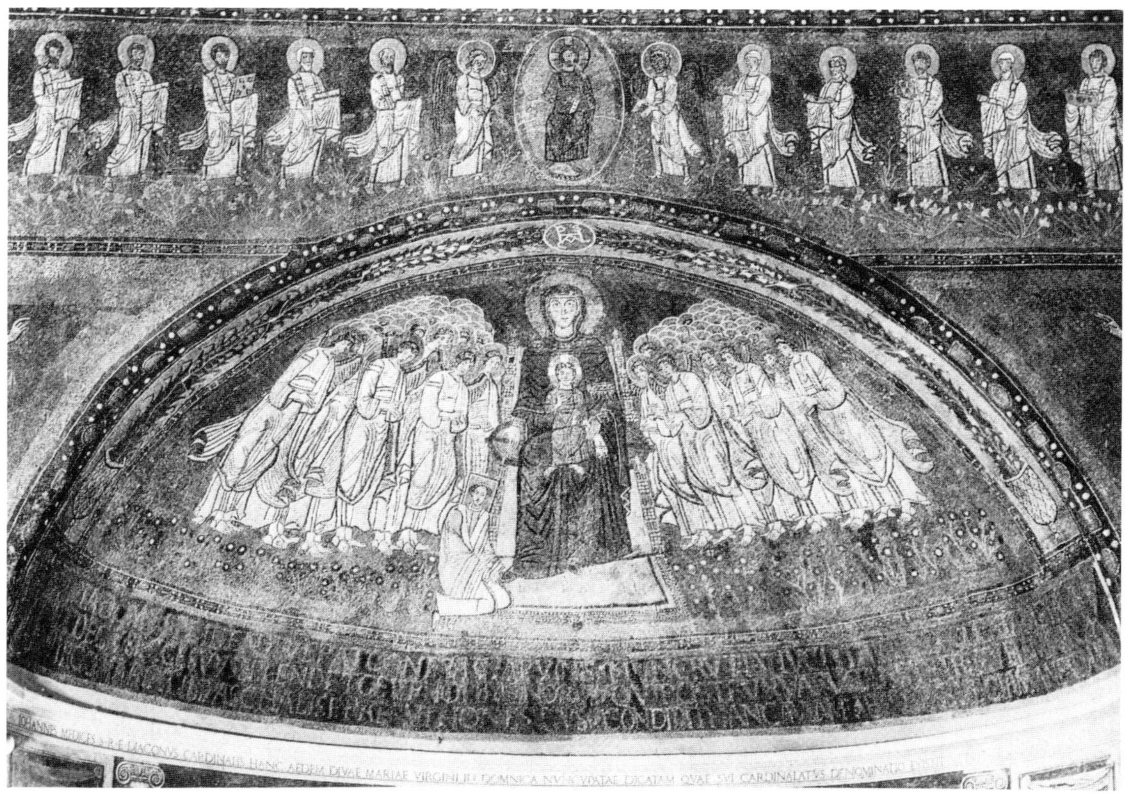

5.   Rome, S. Maria in Domnica, mosaics of apse and triumphal arch (photo: author).

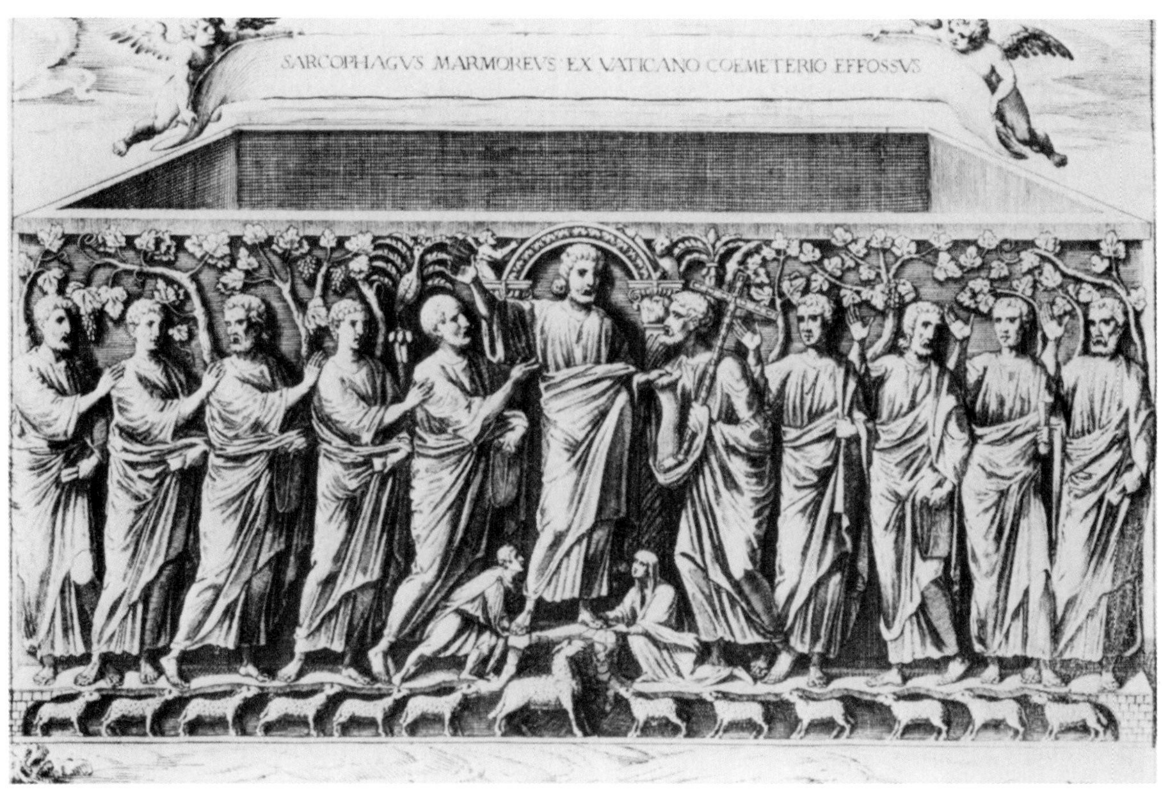

7.   Rome, St. Peter's, sarcophagus of St. Leo (photo: author).

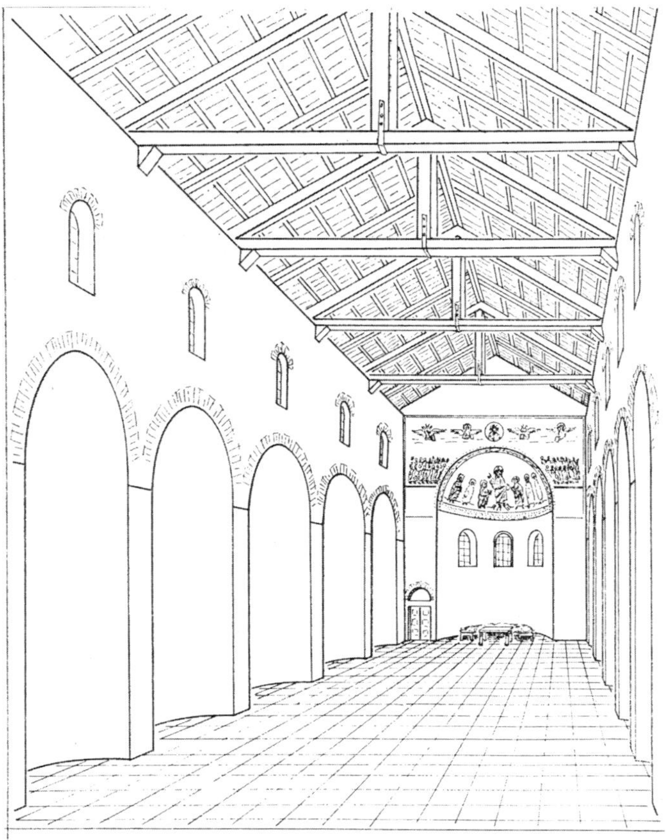

8.   Rome, Lateran, Sala del Concilio,
reconstruction (photo: author).

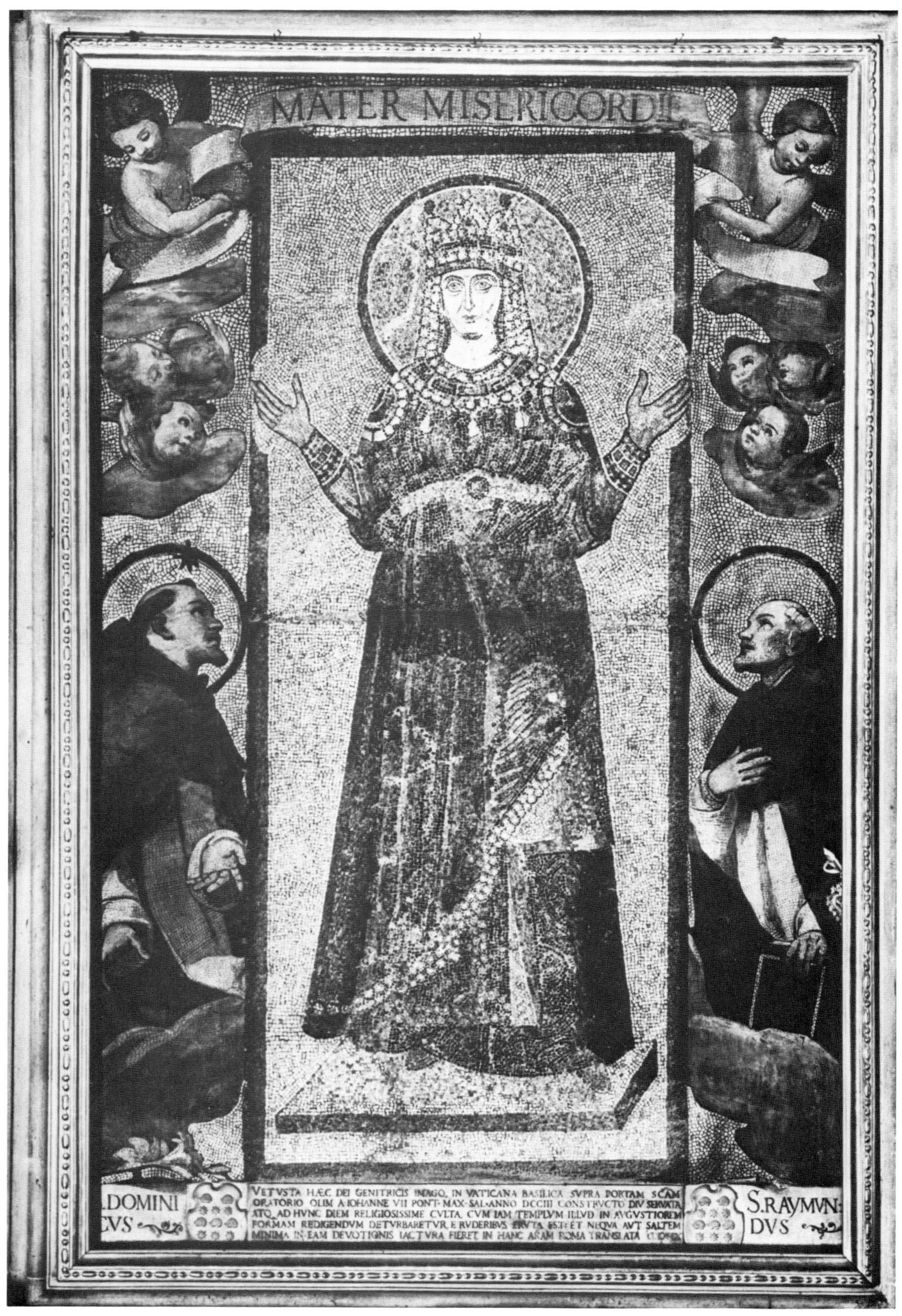

4a.   Mosaic from the Chapel of John VII from Old St. Peter's, now in S. Marco, Florence, (photo: author).

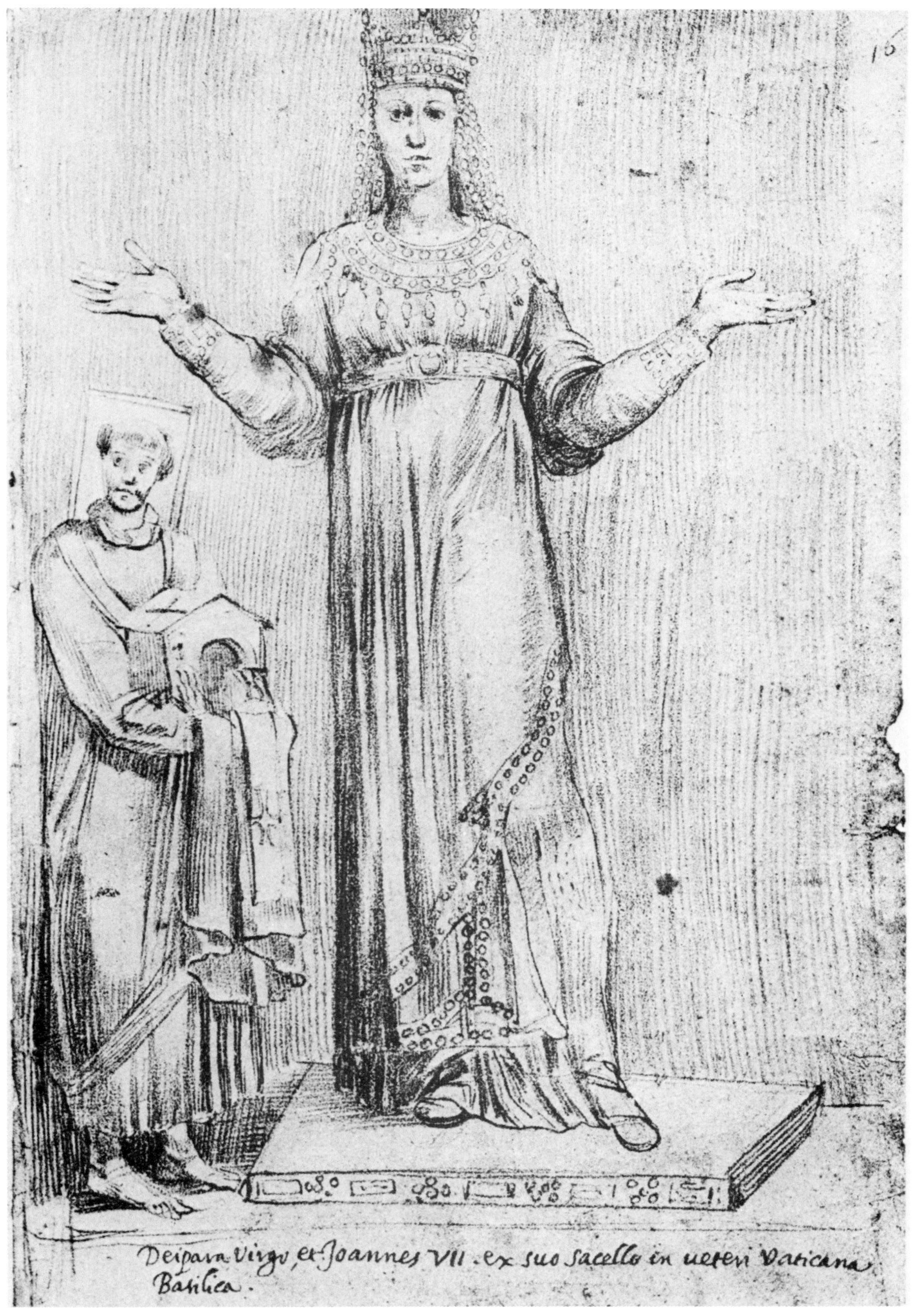

4b.   Maria Regina and John VII; drawing (fol. 49) in Album Arch. Bas. S. Pietro, Biblioteca Apostolica Vaticana.

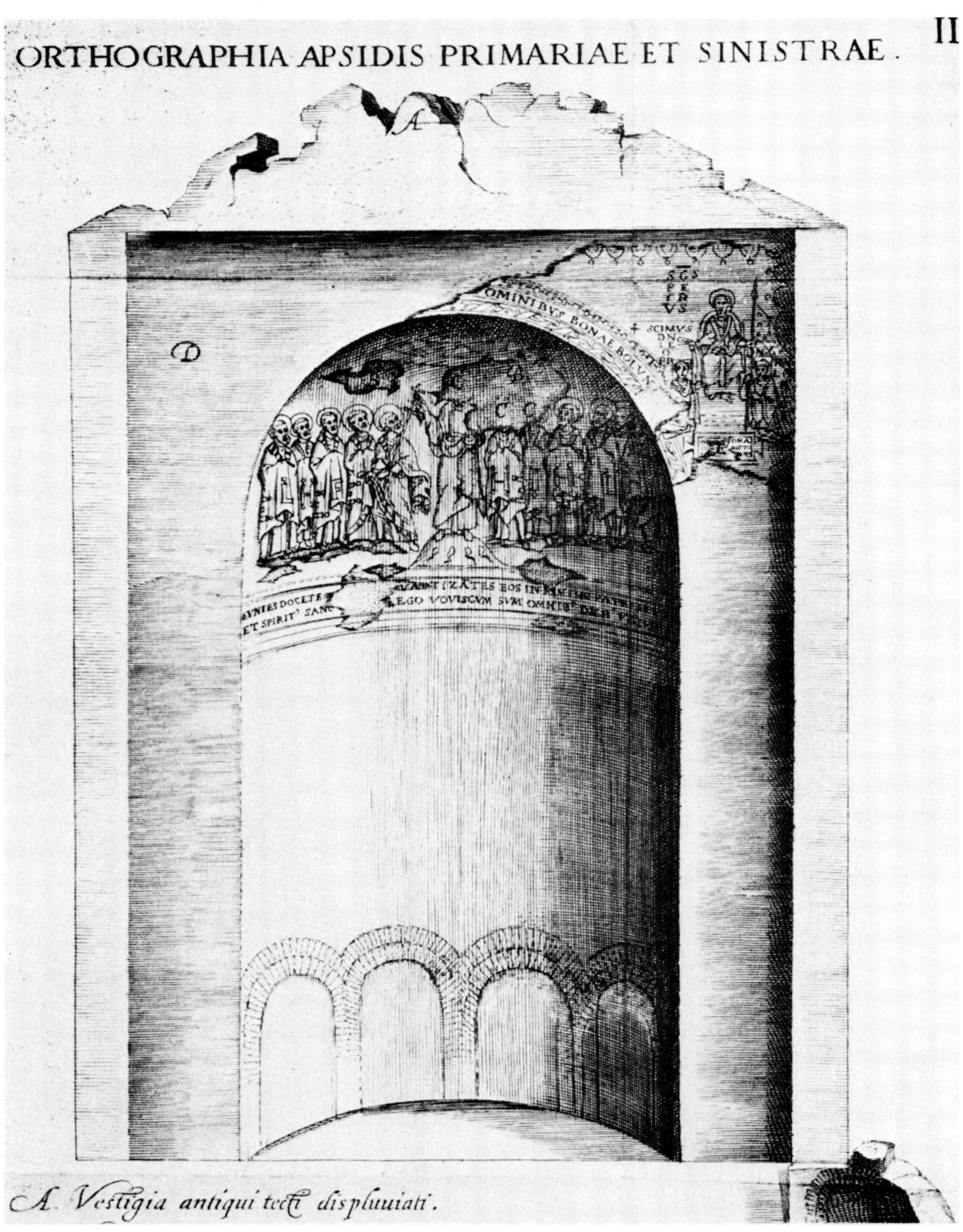

6a.   Rome, L'Aula Leonina, apse before restoration (photo: author).

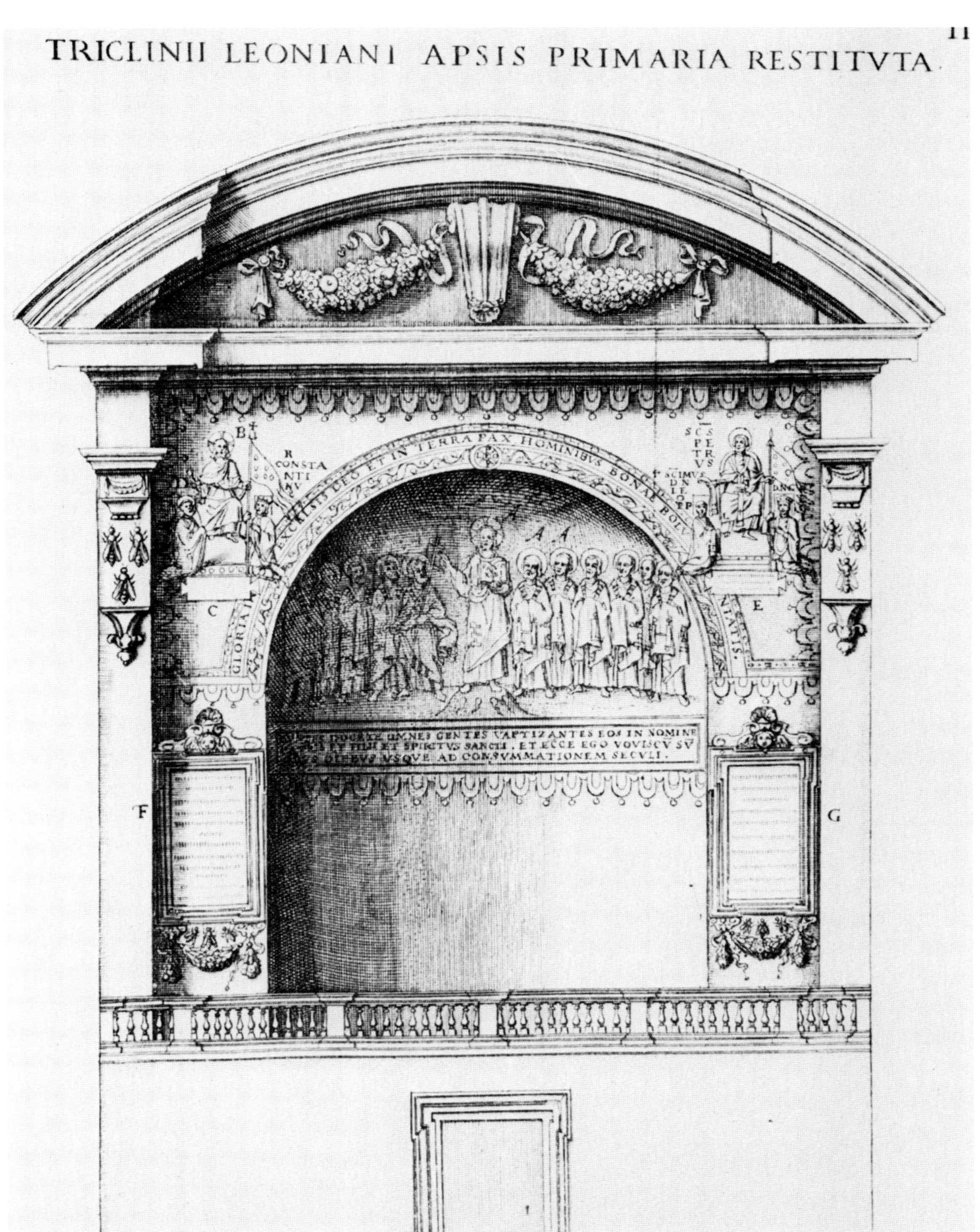

6b.   Rome, L'Aula Leonina, apse after restoration (photo: author).

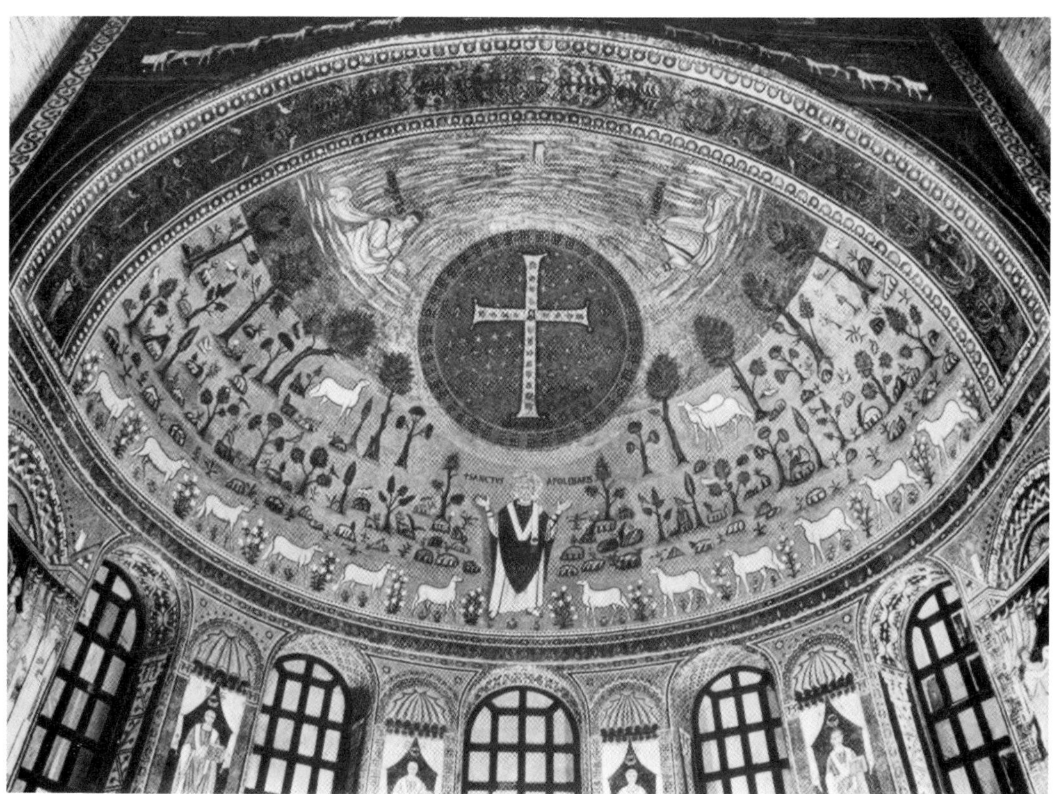

9.   Ravenna, S. Apollinare in Classe, apse mosaic (photo: author).

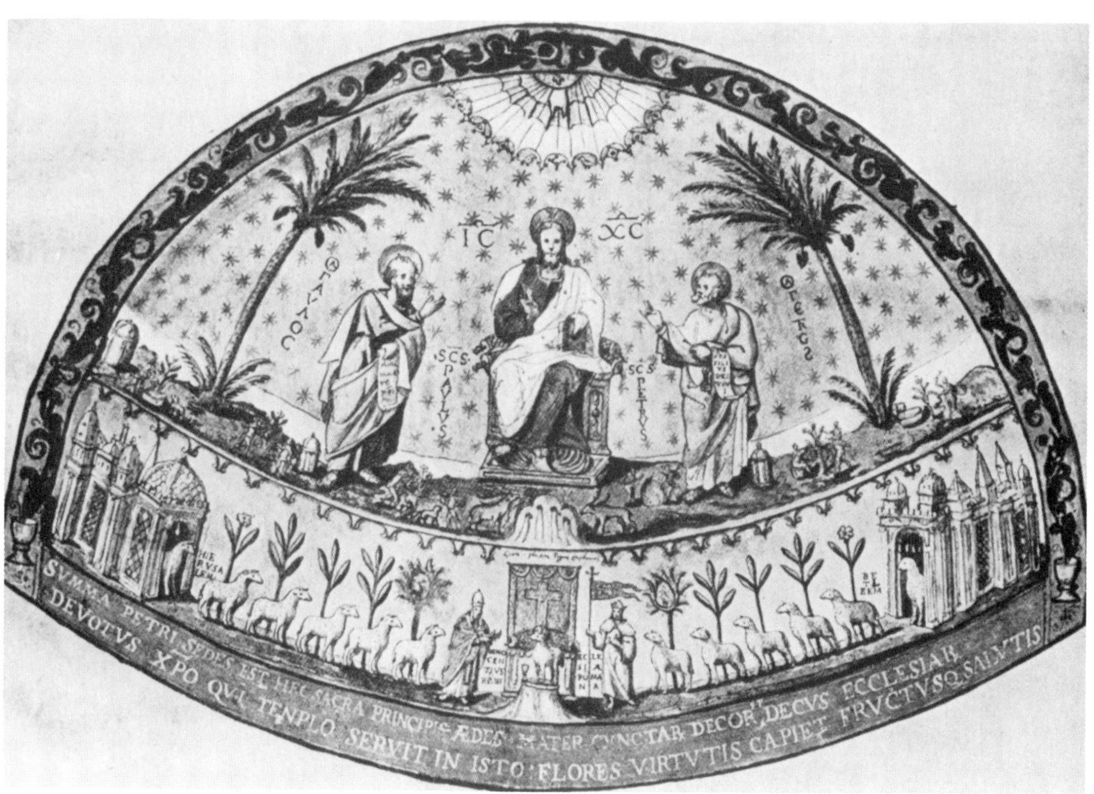

11.   Rome, St. Peter's, fresco representing the Constantinian apse mosaic in the old basilica (photo: author).

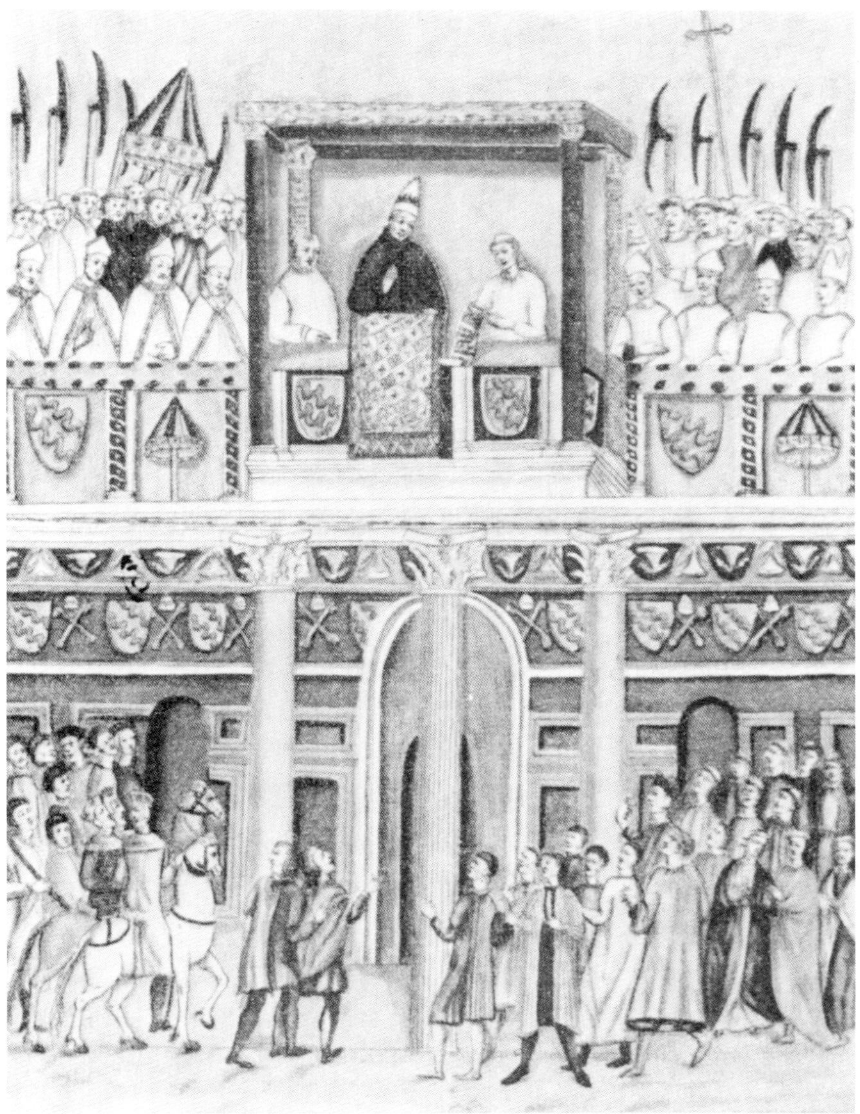

12. Rome, S. Giovanni in Laterano, benediction loggia, fresco (photo: author).

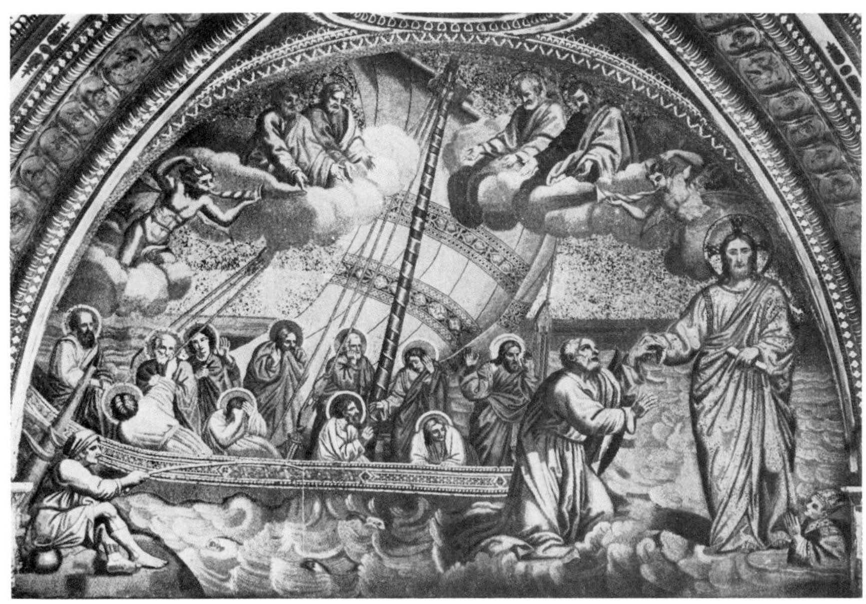

13. Rome, St. Peter's, Giotto's *Navicella* (photo: author).

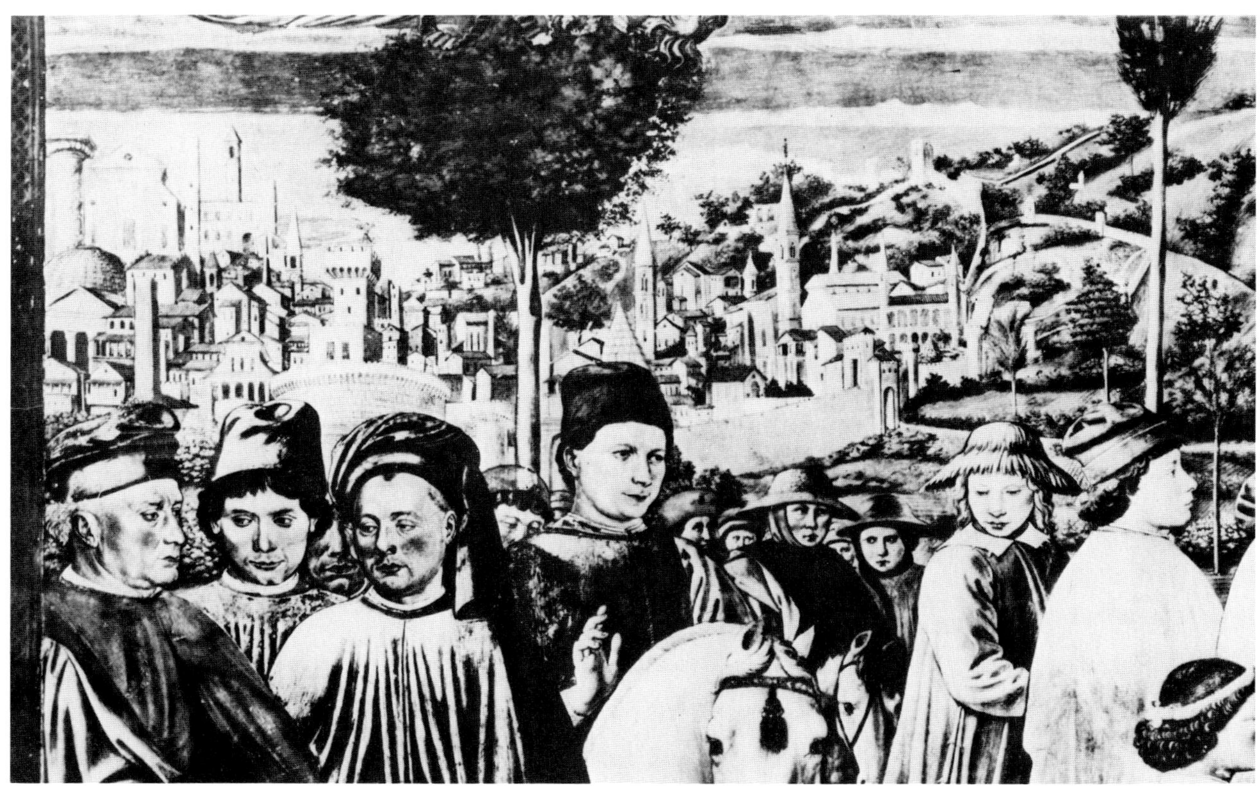

21.   San Gimignano, Sant'Agostino, fresco of the *Departure of St. Augustine from Rome* (detail) by Benozzo Gozzoli, showing loggias of Vatican Palace (right) and the Senator's Palace on the Capitoline Hill (left). (photo: Bibliotheca Hertziana)

Nicholas the Fifth and the Rebuilding of Rome: Reality and Legacy*

2

In Memory of Harold E. Dickson

It was getting on toward afternoon when, on Wednesday, the 21st of February 1459, the papal party arrived before the little tuscan hilltown of Corsignano.[1] The travelers had covered some two dozen miles that day from Sarteano on their five-month progress from Rome to Mantua where the Pope had convened a conference to lay plans for a new crusade against the Turks. Aeneas Silvius Piccolomini, the newly elected Pope Pius II, had been born in Corsignano in 1405 and this was his first recorded return since he had left the town in 1423 to pursue his notably successful career as scholar, author, diplomat and, most recently, cleric. In all probability, he had revisited Corsignano before this, on his frequent travels between Germany and Rome or later during the nine years he had served as Bishop and then Cardinal of nearby Siena. This, however, was his first entry into the town as Pope. What an occasion it must have been for the modest community of little more than three-hundred houses and fifteen-hundred inhabitants! The citizenry of Corsignano did all they could to make their Papal visitor welcome. As Pius himself recorded in his memoirs, the celebrated *Commentarii*: "The town was wonderfully decorated. The people were excited and in holiday mood over the presence of the Pope, who they boasted had been born among them, and they could not look at or cheer him enough."[2] Despite the festivities and the genuine outpouring of affection shown him by the townsfolk, the 54-year-old Pontiff was less than thrilled by his visit. "He was disappointed," says the *Commentarii*, "for most of his own generation had died and those who were left kept their houses, bowed down with old

age and illness, or, if they showed themselves, were so changed as to be hardly recognizable, for they were feeble and crippled and like harbingers of death." The gout-stricken Pope went on to add that "at every step the Pope met with proofs of his own age and could not fail to realize that he was an old man who would soon drop...." He also must have found not only the citizens "bowed down with old age," but the town as well. Physically, the medieval village would have seemed unworthy of its sudden historical importance as the birthplace of the Vicar of Christ. Pius spent only two nights in Corsignano, perhaps in a tent or lodged in uncomfortably cramped quarters in one of his family's old dwellings. On Thursday, he celebrated the Mass of Saint Peter's Chair in the 14th-century Church of San Francesco and, on the next morning, left Corsignano to push on with his party along the road to Siena. It was a stay long enough, however, to determine in his mind to make a glorious example of Corsignano. As he later wrote, "He decided to build there a new church and a palace, and he hired architects and workmen at no small expense, that he might leave as lasting as possible a memorial of his birth." This natal monument, once the humble hamlet of Corsignano, is one of the most impressive and complete examples of Quattrocento architecture and city-planning in Italy. To honor its papal patron, the name of the town was changed in June 1462 to Pienza—the city of Pius.[3]

The initial plans of Pope Pius II Piccolomini for the redevelopment of Corsignano/Pienza called for the creation of a monumental area in the center of town.[4]

This new complex of religious and secular buildings was to be located in the middle of the community and was to be composed of a great cathedral (Pius elevated the town to the rank of a bishopric), an impressive palace for the Piccolomini family, a canon's house, a bishop's palace, a town hall, and other residences grouped about a spacious square. The architectural program was entrusted to Bernardo di Matteo Gamberelli, called Rossellino, who then headed the largest sculptural and architectural firm in Florence.[5]

Bernardo Rossellino began his work at Pienza in May of 1459. Work went rapidly. When Pius again passed through the town in September of 1460 on his return from Mantua, he was, as he wrote, "highly delighted to see rising in his native place buildings which seemed likely to equal any in Italy."[6] When the Pope visited Pienza once again in the late Summer of 1462, he found that the two principal buildings, the Cathedral and the Piccolomini Palace, were all but completed. Considerable space in the *Commentaries* is devoted to the Pope's lengthy and loving description of what he saw. What Pius saw also must have reminded him of what an earlier Pope had envisaged for the pontifical city of Rome.

The humanist scholar Tommaso Parentucelli had been crowned Pope Nicholas V in 1447.[7] He had ascended the throne of Saint Peter with the dream of bringing to Rome a new sense of physical majesty worthy of its role as the seat of a reinvigorated papacy.

One must remember that, while we tend to think of Rome and the papacy as being inextricably linked, that was not necessarily the prevailing view in the early years of the 15th century. The so-called "Babylonian Captivity" had dislodged the popes from Rome for a seventy-two year residence in Avignon, France. Even after the papal return to Italy in 1377, Rome's role as the permanent home of the popes was less than assured. The period of Schism, not finally resolved until 1417, found rival claimants to the Holy See establishing papal seats in such places as Pisa, Florence, and Avignon. Then, too, the Romans themselves had mixed feelings about the blessings of close papal attention. They had enjoyed their freedom during the years of absence and did not relinquish it readily. The Romans, in fact, had chased Nicholas' predecessor, Eugenius IV, from the city in 1434, and it was not until 1443 that he was able to return. Nicholas V, thus, began his reign none too certain about the roof over his head.

We must also remember that Rome was not what it once was in the glorious days of Imperial splendor.[8] From a bustling metropolis of over two million, adorned with columned temples and porticos and the vaulted halls of great basilicas and palaces, it had shrunk to a sprawling but thinly populated city of some 50,000—1/40th its ancient population. The reduction in inhabitants during the Middle Ages was matched by a marked decline in appearance. One could easily describe the city as being in a state of ruinous neglect. The ancient monuments were, of course, true ruins and most of the area within the circuit of the third century wall was given over to pasturage and farm land or covered in briars. Streets, little more than paths, linked the great pilgrimage churches and holy shrine. Little communities clustered about them, but most of the citizens dwelt in the bend of the Tiber northwest of the Capitoline Hill and across the river in Trastevere and in the area before the Basilica of Saint Peter's known as the Borgo.

Nicholas V's immediate predecessors, Martin V and Eugenius VI, had attempted to revitalize the city and its most important Christian monuments but had been so bedeviled by strife and controversy that little beyond some essential repair had been accomplished. Nicholas now determined to do far more.

Shortly after Nicholas V died in 1455, a record of his life was composed by one of his secretaries, the Florentine humanist Giannozzo Manetti.[9] Manetti devoted a substantial part of the biography to a description of the Pope's building and restoration projects in the city of Rome and in the towns of the papal territories. As an astute politician, Nicholas had realized the importance of symbolic display. As part of his program of consolidation and expansion, Nicholas determined to give to his possessions an appearance suitable to the vision he had of what the temporal majesty of the papacy ought to be. In his deathbed "oration," the Pope is reported by Manetti to have dwelt extensively upon his architectural projects. Taking his lead from the Pontiff, Manetti stressed this symbolic aspect of Nicholas' reign. His account, or portions of it, was picked up by other fifteenth-century authors and, in the next century, was given wide circulation in Giorgio Vasari's *Lives of the Artists*.[10]

Manetti divided his description of the works initiated during the reign of Pope Nicholas into two major categories—those carried out in Rome and those undertaken in the papal territories. In Rome, Manetti wrote, Nicholas had concentrated his early efforts upon the repair of the city's fortifications, the renovations of its principal churches, and the restoration of aqueducts and bridges. This work was related directly to preparations for the Jubilee Year of 1450 and for the visit of emperor Frederick III in 1452. Later on, according to Manetti, the Pope had shifted his interests from refurbishing the city to certain never-to-be-completed plans involving a truly palatial Vatican Palace, a reorganization of the Borgo district between the Tiber and Saint Peter's, and, finally, as the *pièce de résistance*, the massive rebuilding of the hallowed old basilica itself. Outside Rome, Nicholas' biographer said that the Pope had directed his attention to various projects in the towns of Fabriano, Gualdo, Assisi, Civitavecchia, Civita Castellana, Narni, Orvieto, Spoleto, and Viterbo.

Manetti insisted that the designing and supervision of all these far-ranging architectural projects was in the hands of the Florentine, Bernardo Rossellino, the very same architect who later worked for Pope Pius II at Pienza. Vasari repeated the attribution of the entire program to Rossellino, saying: "This Bernardo was highly valued as an architect by Pope Nicholas V, who thought much of him, and employed him on many of the works carried out during his pontificate," and later, after describing the work done, adding that, "in all these designs Nicholas employed the abilities and industry of Bernardo Rossellino, as well as others."[11] The important role accorded to Bernardo by Manetti and Vasari generally has been accepted by later commentators. In fact, so closely has Rossellino's name been associated with Nicholas' programs that the new apse begun for Saint Peter's even has entered the literature as the "Rossellino Choir."[12] If Manetti was telling the truth, then, considering the enormous scope of the work reportedly involved, it would establish Bernardo Rossellino as the most active architect of his century.

At first glance, there seems little cause to question the tradition. Manetti was, after all, a contemporary, a member of the papal court, and an intimate of Nicholas V; he certainly was in a position to know and to record the truth. Although a few have challenged the prominent role he gave to Rossellino, almost no one has doubted the actual scope of what was undertaken.[13] There is, however, good cause to disbelieve Manetti's veracity in both cases.

The records of the Vatican Treasury during the years of the reign of Nicholas V are fairly complete.[14] They are filled with numerous entries relating to the ambitious architectural program of the Pope. These entries provide an accurate account of the chronology of the projects undertaken, what they really entailed, and serve as a good indicator of the men who worked on them and the extent of their involvement.

If we compare the documented expenditures with Manetti's description, it becomes clear that Bernardo Rossellino could have had nothing to do with the majority of the programs claimed for him by Manetti. Since it is known that Rossellino did not arrive in Rome before the middle of August 1451 and probably did not enter the papal service until December of that year, his connection with those projects that are documented as being underway or completed prior to that time should be rejected.[15]

The papal documents reveal that, of the projects which Manetti said Rossellino directed outside of Rome, the work at Fabriano, Gualdo, Assisi, and Orvieto already had been begun before the summer of 1451. This evidence is corroborated by references in the local archives. Furthermore, there is no record of his involvement in the undertakings at any of the remaining locations outside of Rome nor at other sites not included on Manetti's list but noted in the papal records.[16] Bernardo Rossellino's participation in this portion of Nicholas' schemes should be discounted. Those involved seem instead to have been either local builders or masons from the Lombardy region of northern Italy.

Bernardo Rossellino's role in the specific architectural programs begun in the city of Rome, itself, is a bit more difficult to sort out; yet, once again, a similar pattern, based upon the date of his entering the service of the Pope, does emerge. A large number of the Roman projects, including several mentioned in the documents but not listed by Manetti, must be immediately removed from consideration; they either were completed or started prior to Rossellino's appearance in the city. Of the remaining dozen or so projects in Rome with which he could have been involved, his name is connected in the documents with only two—the great tower at the Vatican (but only in the limited capacity of designing two hoists used in the final phases of its construction) and, in a substantially more architectural way, in the modernization of the church of San Stefano Rotondo on the Caelian Hill.[17] In no other instance does his name appear in connection with any of the other possible projects. In most cases other masons are mentioned, often as the actual directors of the work. Again the conclusion, based upon the known factual evidence, must be that, aside from the two works mentioned, Rossellino was not involved in any of the projects actually undertaken in Rome for Nicholas V.

What inferences, therefore, may be made concerning the reliability of Manetti's report? First of all, we must recognize what the author's purpose really was. His primary intent was to glorify the dead Pope. Accordingly, Manetti, without compunction, exaggerated the facts, turning simple repair jobs into extensive and often original projects and giving plans and dreams the weight of an almost physical existence. Art historical accuracy was not Manetti's aim.

Neither was accuracy his goal when he grouped all of the many projects under Rossellino's name. Doing so gave the impression of greater cohesiveness to the activities and was a literary convenience as well. Manetti, no doubt, had frequently met with Rossellino while they both served the Pope and was pleased to bestow credit upon a fellow Florentine at the expense of the 'foreign' Lombards, Romans, and other non-Florentines who really had done the bulk of the labor.[18]

Given the arbitrary nature of Manetti's choice, one might ask why he did not give the honor of being Nicholas' architect-in-chief to his fellow Florentine humanist, the celebrated Leon Battista Alberti. It might seem that mention of a significant role for Alberti, true or not, would have given an added luster to the projects. Yet, by associating Alberti with them, Manetti would have detracted from the impression that he wished to give of the Pope's personal responsibility for many of the plans. It was easier to play up this side of the story when the less well-known Rossellino (after all, only a craftsman and not an intellectual) was designated as the architectural executor. In actuality, there was hardly a single project carried out either in Rome or in the Papal States that demanded the attention of an Alberti or even of a Rossellino. Most of the work could have been performed by simple building contractors, stonemasons, or, often, by mere carpenters.

Let us pause for a moment to consider just a few of those projects carried out in Rome under the sponsorship of Pope Nicholas. They will serve to indicate both the range and type of work involved. I must add that the extent of the restoration and building activity during the reign of Nicholas is demonstrated by the fact that the names of 65 stonemasons and other architectural artisans are specifically mentioned in the official records. Most of these held supervisory positions as "maestri" and "soprastanti" and, no doubt, had a number of laborers working under them; the work crew was an extensive one. During the early years of Nicholas' reign considerable attention was given to the repair and rebuilding of the ancient walls about the city. Traces of Nicholas' work are still to be seen in several places including the rebuilt wall bordering the English Protestant Cemetery west of the Porta San Paolo and in the round towers added to the Leonine Walls around the Vatican (fig. 14).

The Torre Nova formed a strong point in the new system of walls which Nicholas ordered for the defense of the Vatican and Saint Peter's (fig. 15).[19] Situated at the western end of the Passato Vaticano (part of Leo X's old wall about the Borgo), the Torre Nova, thus, formed a pendant to the great mole of the Castel Sant' Angelo. It anchored one end of Nicholas V's circuit walls around the Vatican, protected the northeastern slope of the Vatican Hill and guarded one of the chief gates into the Borgo, the Porto San Pietro. Although similar in form to other such towers of the period, it was distinguished by its massive size. The Torre Nova has a diameter of forty meters and a height of nineteen meters and may well have been much higher when first completed. Its enormously thick walls, designed to resist the pounding of cannon fire, are battered for four-fifths of their present height. The interior consists of a great circular room, vaulted *a cresta e vela* with a dome.

Vasari attributed the construction of this impressive tower to Bernardo Rossellino, saying: "he had...made the round tower still known as the tower of Nicholas."[20] That the tower generally has been associated with Rossellino rests not only upon the word of Vasari but also upon the fact that his name figures in payments related to the tower.[21] There were four such entries in the papal accounts, dated between May and November 1452, relating to two hoists "to lift things up into the tower" and to some work done on an adjoining stretch of wall.

Do such mentions of Rossellino's involvement with the tower entitle him to be called its architect? Probably not. Strangely enough, no other mention of the tower beyond those passages cited here is to be found in the existing record books.[22] There are, however, other sources to which we might turn. Giuseppe Brippi, in a polemical poem against the insurrectionist Stefano Porcari, spoke of: "Arces fortificat muris, turrimque stupendam/Extruit, alto animo prudenteque..."[23] Porcari was executed in January 1453, and the poem was composed either before or shortly after that event. While not specifically mentioning the tower, two other poems, also written in 1453, do allude to it.[24] It thus seems certain that the "stupendous tower," as Brippi called it, was substantially complete by the beginning of 1453. There is even good evidence that it already was standing a couple of years earlier. Stefano Infessura's diary said that the Pope "fece lo muro intorno allo palazzo con una rocca tonda, appresso porta Viridaria" and indicated that the work had been carried out in 1451.[25] Indeed, that year had witnessed a flurry of activity involving the renewal of Rome's fortifications. The Emperor Frederick III had stated his wish to come to Rome in 1452 to be crowned. Nicholas was panicked, not so much out of fear of the imperial escort, but out of anxiety about a possible demonstration of Ghibelline sentiment among the populace. There was, consequently, a redoubled effort at strengthening the city's defenses. The Torre Nova was the crowning achievement of that aim.

It seems reasonably certain that Bernardo Rossellino had nothing to do with either the design or the actual construction of the Torre Nova. This job, probably, went to the Lombard builder Beltrame di Martino da Varese, who, in the years 1451 and 1452, was in charge of work undertaken at other points along the wall around the Vatican City. To credit Rossellino with the tower actually would do him no honor as an engineer. In September 1454, part of the Torre Nova collapsed, killing several persons and, in 1463, a portion of the wall next to the tower also gave way.

The fifth-century church of San Stefano Rotondo standing on the Caelian Hill was another target for Nicholas' workers (fig. 16). San Stefano had been subjected to the vicissitudes common to many of Rome's most hallowed shrines. Its circular walls had undergone several depredations and restorations down through the years.[26] In 1446, Flavio Biondo had described it as being in a roofless state with ruined mosaics and cracked marble panels.[27] Four years later, Pope Nicholas set aside an initial sum of 500 florins to start a thorough renovation of the old structure as part of his program of refurbishing the forty station churches in Rome.[28] The extant payment records pertaining to this project all date to the years 1453 and 1454. From the nature of the work carried out at this time, it is evident that the bulk of the restoration must have been undertaken during the two previous years. The fabric

probably was repaired, a new wooden roof installed, an area adjoining the martyr's chapel set apart for a sacristy and the anteroom between the porch and the church proper vaulted.[29] To increase the illumination of the interior, thirty-six round windows were inserted in the arcades walled up in the twelfth century.[30] In the clearstory of the tambour, eight *bifore* windows of the Florentine variety were installed within the old fifth-century openings, while the remainder of the twenty-two original windows were bricked up. Much of Nicholas V's repairs to San Stefano should be termed a beautification project. Apparently, few structural changes were made and, once the essential repairs were undertaken, attention was turned to embellishments.[31] The bulk of the work must have been carried out under the direction of Bernardo Rossellino, whose name figures prominently in the payment records. These accounts are clear concerning his supervision of the repairs; the basic work may have been included in a substantial payment of 700 ducats for five months' labor given to him in March 1453.

One of the account entries, dated 25 June 1453, demonstrates not only Rossellino's principal role in the renovation of the church but also provides a listing of some of the architectural elements he furnished. He was given 1000 ducats "for pavement of Santo Stefano Rotondo and for the plastering of the same, for the altars of marble and doors of marble and windows of marble made in the said church." Although paving and altars have disappeared, the other items remain. The windows are the *bifore* already mentioned, and three of the original marble door frames may be identified by inscriptions and the stemma of Pope Nicholas. One of these is the main portal to the church (fig. 17); another the double doorway leading into the annular nave from the anteroom (fig. 18); the third gives access to the sacristy (fig. 19).[32] A final element, not mentioned in the records, must also be attributed to Rossellino; it is the handsome *lavacro* within the sacristy.[33]

The church of San Stefano Rotondo has a somber and solemn character about it. The work executed there by Bernardo Rossellino for Pope Nicholas well suits this atmosphere. The building, one must remember, was regarded with great respect not only as a sacred Christian shrine, but as an architectural remnant of ancient Rome. Accordingly, it was to be treated with an especial degree of awe and caution.[34] Credit must be given to Rossellino for the care he took in designing the specific architectural features installed under his direction. He clearly recognized that the highly decorative and basically light style common in the vocabulary of Florentine architecture would have been out of place here. Instead, the style with which he rendered doorframes and windows is of a severe nature and harmonizes with the rest of the building. A new Roman Renaissance style was in the process of creation, a manner which ultimately would lead to the High Renaissance forms of Donato Bramante.

Conceptually and physically, the most substantial project in this phase of Nicholas' renewal program for Rome took place on the Capitoline Hill.[35] There, on the traditional site of the Roman *caput et umbilicus mundi*, Nicholas proposed to create an architectural complex to house the civil administration of Rome. Since that administration depended upon his authority, the project also would demonstrate, architecturally, the Pope's secular power over the unruly city. That Nicholas' main objective in his governance of Rome was to establish a sense of order and civic discipline is made explicitly clear in his work on the Capitoline. Already on the hill and utilized as a governmental center for the city during the Middle Ages was a building called the Palazzo del Senatore. This palace housed the Senator, sort of a city manager through whom the Pope ruled the commune. When Nicholas became Pope in 1447, the Senator's Palace consisted of a long and narrow three storied structure flanked by two towers. Across its front, the building was penetrated by superimposed arcades and entered by a ramp leading up to the second story, or *piano nobile*. Under Nicholas, the Senator's Palace was considerably enlarged and given a thorough face-lift. The loggias were closed up and a line of cross windows inserted. The palace also was expanded toward the brow of the hill overlooking the Roman Forum. Three wings were, thus, added to the Senator's Palace to enclose a courtyard. The newly created rear wing was erected on the solid foundations of the ancient Tabularium and two towers were built at its corners to match the older ones at the front. All this work would appear to have been undertaken in anticipation of Emperor Frederick's visit to Rome and carried out by a variety of stonemasons, including the Lombard Beltrame di Martino Varese and the Roman sculptor, Paolo di Mariano da Seze (called Paolo Romano). The latter had the special responsibility, according to the records, for furnishing the marble cross windows. These windows were among the first of their type to be used in Rome.[36] Cross windows are apparently of French origin and made their way into Italy via Lombardy. The presence of a number of Lombard stonemasons, such as Beltrame, on Nicholas' architectural staff suggests that the window design came to Rome with them. It was to become a popular form

in Rome where it was associated primarily with ecclesiastically related palace projects, just as it is here. Cross windows also provide the dominant leitmotiv for the Palazzo dei Conservatori, intended to house the city council of Rome, the Conservators. This new building was placed, for some still uncertain reason, at an oblique angle to the Senator's Palace. Like the revamped Senator's Palace, it was a large block containing a central courtyard. The Conservators' Palace was fronted by a portico above which was placed a row of cross windows flanked by paired arched openings. We have here two secular buildings, but ones which prominently display the sign of the cross. The cross window, with its four separate openings, makes functional sense but it also makes an iconographic impact. Can it be totally accidental that one of its first uses was at the old Papal Palace in Avignon and that, in Italy, the very name by which this form of window is known—*finestra a croce guelfa*—allies it with the papal Guelph party? That the Church was the real authority in Rome would have been visibly clear to civic administrator and citizen alike. One might imagine that Nicholas had intended for the space in front of these buildings to be formalized into an actual piazza with even, perhaps, a building complementary to the Conservator's Palace erected across from it. That, however, would have to wait for another century, for Pope Paul III and Michelangelo.[37]

Such restorations and modifications of the Roman environment are, however, not the projects for which the Rome of Nicholas V is most famed. There remain to be considered those celebrated works which Manetti said were planned but never effected (and thus, of course, never documented in the official records). So far, in his work to restore Rome, Nicholas had aimed at reestablishing a grandeur befitting the capital of the Christian Church and of the Papal States. He, also, was determined to give to the Head of that spiritual and secular power a permanent and suitably splendid headquarters within the Eternal City. Until Nicholas' day, the Lateran Basilica and its palace had served, more often than not, as the center of church affairs and as the principal papal residence in Rome.[38] It was Nicholas who was to firmly establish the primacy of Saint Peter's and the Vatican. With regard to this phase of Nicholas' program, one wonders if the Pope had been inspired to fulfill the prophecy of the widely read, late 14th-century mystic Saint Birgitta of Sweden. In her *Book of Revelations*, Saint Birgitta had described a vision in which she had "beheld the Pope's palace in Rome [stretching] to Castel Saint Angelo and from that to the hospital of Santo Spirito and back again to Saint

Peter's as if it were a wide plain, and the plain was surrounded by a very strong wall. And," she added, "I heard a voice that said, 'The Pope who loves the Bride with the love of Christ and his holy friends shall live here with his counsellors and shall rule the Church of God in freedom and peace.'"[39] Birgitta clearly had dreamt of the Vatican and the Borgo and had seen it as becoming, once and for all, the established home of the Papacy.

Eight decades later, Nicholas justified his commitment to this more ambitious phase of his architectural program, according to Manetti, by asserting that "to create solid and stable convictions in the minds of the uncultured masses, there must be something that appeals to the eye; a popular faith, sustained only on doctrines, will never be anything but feeble and vacillating. But if the authority of the Holy See were visibly displayed in majestic buildings, imperishable memorials and witnesses seemingly planted by the hand of God Himself, belief would grow and strengthen like a tradition from one generation to another, and all the world would accept and revere it. Noble edifices combining taste and beauty with imposing proportions would immensely conduce to the exaltation of the chair of St. Peter. If," Nicholas went on, "we had been able to accomplish all that We wished, our successors would find themselves more respected by all Christian nations, and would be able to dwell in Rome with greater security both from external and internal foes. Thus, it is not out of ostentation, or ambition, or a vainglorious desire of immortalizing Our name, that We have conceived and commenced all these great works, but for the exaltation of the power of the Holy See throughout Christendom, and in order that future Popes should no longer be in danger of being driven away, taken prisoners, and besieged, and otherwise oppressed."[40]

If death had not intervened, or so Manetti claimed, the Pope would have pushed along three great projects.[41] Firstly, we are told that Nicholas intended to reorganize the district of the Borgo, creating order out of its confusion of tiny streets by laying out three loggia-lined avenues leading into the piazza in front of St. Peter's.[42] In this intention, we likely find not only a revival of the porticos of ancient Rome, but a reminiscence of the years Nicholas had spent in Bologna, first as a student, then as secretary to the city's bishop, Nicholas Albergatti, and finally as bishop of Bologna, himself. The use of arcades is a dominant feature of the Bolognese cityscape, as it also is of several northern Italian towns. One should note that it

was also in Bologna that the future pope had gained his first architectural experience. According to one of Nicholas' 15th-century biographers, Vespasiano da Bisticci: "When Pope Eugenius left Florence [1436], he went to Bologna where the Cardinal [Nicholas Albergatti] had his bishopric; and the episcopal residence being in very bad condition, the cardinal, as soon as Maestro Tommaso [Parentucelli—later Pope Nicholas V] arrived in the city began to confer with him as to the rebuilding of it. He gave him a commission to carry out the work, and in a very short time the bishop's home was rebuilt from the foundations."[43]

Secondly, Manetti says that Nicholas wished to convert the Vatican Palace into an enormous complex resplendent with gardens, loggias, aqueducts, fountains, chapels, libraries, a theater, and a new conclave hall.[44] Of this visionary, almost Hadrianic, scheme only a new wing for the palace itself was realized. Actually, since the work on that structure is documented as already having been begun by 1447, what was done may have been part of a 'pre-grand design' program and not related to the papal plan as given by Manetti. In any case, the actual construction work was under the direction of a Florentine stonemason named Antonio di Francesco, unknown except for his involvement here as "ingegniere di palazo." Strangely, despite Antonio's origins, this addition to the Vatican does not show Florentine characteristics, but illustrates the emergence of a Roman "composite" type of palace, a style of architecture which it helped to popularize. The Vatican Palace wing of Nicholas V consisted of a long, three-storied building, one room deep (fig. 20). At its western end, it abutted a tower topped by a belvedere loggia; this tower actually was not completed until the reign of Alexander VI Borgia. Rows of five cross windows emphasized the *piano nobile* and the floor above it (now occupied by the famous Stanze di Raffaello). This architectural composition, of a rectangular block and belvedere tower first appeared with the palace of the influential Cardinal Domenico Capranica (incidentally, the first patron of the future Pius II) and would be further developed, through the model of the Vatican example, in a host of other Roman palaces of which the Palazzo Venezia is the most prominent example.[45] At the end opposite the belvedere tower, the wing of Nicholas V joined an earlier north-south wing of the palace which overlooked a garden through two stories of loggias. These loggias are plainly shown in a fresco painted in San Gimignano by Benozzo Gozzoli between 1463-65 but, evidently, utilizing a view of the Vatican drawn while the artist was working in Rome from 1447 to 1449 (fig. 21). Whether or not these loggias date from the time of Nicholas V or from the late 13th century, as is generally supposed, is not absolutely clear.

Thirdly, the Pope's most ambitious dream of all entailed the total rebuilding of the ancient Basilica of Saint Peter's itself.[46] In short, according to Manetti's biography, if the Pope had had his way and if time had been more accommodating, the seat of the papacy would have been given a magnificence not seen in the cityscapes of Western Europe since the days of Imperial Rome or until the time of Julius II. It is with these intentions and not with the earlier renovation projects that a consideration not only of Bernardo Rossellino's possible role but also that of Leon Battista Alberti becomes particularly cogent. An Albertian presence behind these ideas has been the subject of much scholarly discussion. Recently, one authority has stated that "here Alberti's theory of architecture and Nicholas' program for papal government flow together...."[47] Most scholars now tend to assume that Alberti was the man responsible.

Manetti, of course, had made no mention of Alberti. But Giorgio Vasari did. In writing Alberti's "life," Vasari said that the humanist "became intimate with the Pope, who had hitherto been advised in architectural matters by Bernardo Rossellino...who, having begun to restore the Pope's palace and to do some things in S. Maria Maggiore in conformity with the Pope's wishes, always previously took the advice of Leon Battista. Thus, the Pope, by following the advice of one of them and the execution of the other, carried out many useful and praiseworthy things..."[48] The facts belie much of Vasari's tale. The records prove, for instance, that Rossellino could have had nothing to do with either Santa Maria Maggiore or with any significant part in the work carried out in the Vatican Palace. In addition, it is improbable that he had had any but a passing acquaintance with Alberti prior to his arrival in Rome. Yet the essence of the story may be true. There may have been a change in the Pope's plans, one which might well have involved both Rossellino and Alberti in the drafting of a set of designs for the sort of grand scheme described by Manetti.

From the early 1440s on, Alberti was writing his monumental *De re aedificatoria* which he presented to Pope Nicholas in 1452.[49] In it may be found glimpses of some of the ideas which Manetti said the Pope wished to accomplish. It was through the seemingly plentiful treasury of the Vatican that Alberti may have

seen the possibility of putting his antiquarian researches, architectural theories, and 'life-style' ideas into practice. His presentation of the treatise on architecture to the Pope in 1452 probably was meant to whet Nicholas' appetite for the elaborate proposals of its author. If this suggestion is correct, then it would have been at this point that Rossellino would have become involved—after Alberti had presented the general concepts for the new palace, Borgo, and basilica to the Pope. Alberti was a humanist theoretician and brilliant dilettante of the arts, but not yet a professional architect. The experienced Florentine stonemason, thus, was brought into the inner planning circle. One proof of his important role on the Pope's architectural staff is found in the amount of his monthly retainer. From December 1451 to December 1453, Rossellino received a base salary of 15 ducats per month, 5 ducats more than the next highest paid architect then working for the Pope.[50] Rossellino's yearly retainer of 180 ducats, by the way, was almost twice that received by the great Brunelleschi while working on the Florence Cathedral and equalled that given to the painter Andrea Mantagna for his services as court artist to the Marquis of Mantua in 1458.[51] Rossellino's salary was four times that earned by the average skilled stonemason in contemporary Florence and was a princely sum at a time when one could live quite comfortably on between 100 and 150 ducats a year.[52] Such a sum would not have been given to a man solely involved in the two relatively minor projects at the Torre Nova and San Stefano. Certainly, a protracted contact with Alberti and even a familiarity with the theories contained in the *De re aedificatoria* is indicated by Rossellino's later design for the buildings at Pienza.

Did any of this collaboration between the Pope, Alberti, and Rossellino go beyond the stage of discussion in a Renaissance version of a 'think tank'? Probably not, although the concepts which were projected continued to be mentioned and came to achieve an almost mystic yet misty fame enduring to this day. The single exception may have occurred at Saint Peter's.

The documents involving work on St. Peter's show that, in 1450 and 1451, efforts had been directed toward refurbishing the decaying Constantinian structure—windows, paving, roofing — these were the main items in the entries.[53] Suddenly, however, in June 1452, work began "a la tribuna di san Piero" which continued on through 1455.[54] A change in plan away from a simple restoration of the old structure toward a rebuilding of at least a part of it would seem to be indicated. Is it to be assumed that this tribune represented part of the grand plan outlined by Manetti for rebuilding the church? Did the tribune evolve from the ideas of Alberti given substance by Rossellino?

It is possible, but there is also evidence that the tribune was part of an intermediate project which went beyond the stage of renovation but did not aspire to the total effort at reconstruction recorded in Manetti's manuscript. In the same year in which the tribune was begun, Alberti presented his *De re aedificatoria* to Nicholas, and it contained no hint of any vast project for St. Peter's. On the contrary, Alberti gave advice for restoring the fabric of the old basilica. The great plan given in Manetti must, therefore, have been devised after the completion of Alberti's manuscript. In 1453, in a poem which celebrated the accomplishments of Nicholas V, Pietro de Godi wrote only of the "magnificant and sumptuous tribune of the Basilica of Saint Peter's" and made no mention of any more extensive enterprise.[55] Neither did Mattia Palmieri's chronicle which said: "Since the Pope wanted to build a more beautiful church for St. Peter's, he laid powerful foundations and built the walls up to thirteen ells high. But this great work, equal to any of the antique world, was first interrupted after the advice of Leon Battista and then came to a halt through the death of the Pope."[56]

Stylistic evidence also tends to disassociate the tribune from Alberti and from Rossellino (despite the fact that it got to be called the "Rossellino Choir"). The groundplan of the tribune appears in the famous Uffizi drawing of Bramante's project for St. Peter's and its elevation may be seen in a fresco by Giorgio Vasari in the Cancelleria Palace. Its aspect is quite unlike what would be expected from either Alberti or Rossellino. It is, in fact, most comparable to church apses in northern Italy, an argument supported in the documents which record that the man most actively engaged at the tribune was the Lombard Beltrame di Martino da Varese. The tribune project, it would seem, was the product of the second of three programs for St. Peter's. Since the tribune was worked on continuously until the death of Pope Nicholas, it was, perhaps, intended to incorporate the structure somehow into the third plan for which Alberti and, maybe, Rossellino were responsible—or maybe that third plan was never intended to be implemented.

Manetti has provided us with a lengthy, detailed, but perplexingly complicated description of this impressive design for a totally new St. Peter's. The most recent interpretations of Manetti's description have postulated a nave with paired side aisles bordered by chapels recessed into the walls. This reconstruction is supported by a comparison with other Quattrocento churches in Rome whose plans were derived, perhaps, from this great proposal.[57]

This elaborate third plan for Saint Peter's was never even commenced, much less realized. It all seems so tangible in the accounts of Manetti, yet nothing ever came of it. And that raises another point which I should like to consider. Was any of the grand design for palace, Borgo, and basilica, so painstakingly described by Manetti, ever intended for building? On his deathbed, Nicholas is reported to have said that, in order to solidify his papacy and the authority of the Church, he had found it necessary to "conceive such buildings in mind and spirit."[58] Based upon that proclaimed intention, I should like to suggest that the Pope had never seriously proposed to actually erect much or even any of this. Quite frankly, the papal treasury could not have covered the costs, even after the replenishments of the Jubilee Year of 1450. Rather, is it not more probable that Manetti's description is just sort of an utopian dream, a parallel or sequel to Alberti's architectural treatise?

Admittedly, Manetti's own contemporary biographer, Vespasiano da Bisticci, claimed that "so great was Manetti's integrity that he would never exhibit one thing for another or dissimulate. I do not believe that he ever spoke falsely."[59] Yet, here, he would appear to have done just that. However, it was but a 'white' lie and a literary artifice to extoll the memory of his papal patron and to announce what his master could have done if time and fortune had been more kind. Perhaps, this part of Nicholas' biography had even been composed in consultation with the Pope and his architectural advisors as a written blueprint of what ideally could be achieved.

Nicholas' grand design for the Vatican district and Saint Peter's may well have been a figment of the imagination and, perhaps, even more Manetti's figment than Alberti's or the Pope's. Yet clear traces of the concepts it embraced did materialize in miniature, I believe, a half decade later in the actual constructions undertaken at the little village of Corsignano/Pienza. There, another great humanist Pope, Pius II Piccolomini, directed a personal project aimed at creating a sort of second Vatican, a country curia. The great Piccolomini Palace, the lesser but substantial residences of his cardinals and staff, the little city hall, and the magnificent cathedral—the entire urban scheme for Pienza—have their source in the dreams of Nicholas and his biographer. I find it curious that few have paid much attention to the connection, especially since Nicholas had been Pius' mentor and Pius' architect was the same Bernardo Rossellino who had worked for Nicholas. Nicholas' dream of rebuilding the physical glory of Rome was an impossibility due to the enormity of the concept and the restrictions of time and finances. As Pius, himself, wrote in his memoirs concerning the architectural intentions of Nicholas: "He erected magnificent buildings in his city, though he began more than he finished."[60] Pienza was another matter. The Piccolomini were major property holders; Pius could and did exert enormous pressures on the town's Sienese overlords to compel the sale of properties for his use; and Pius had sufficient Papal resources (soon to be enriched by the discovery of alum near Rome) for such a limited task. It was at Pienza, then, and not in Rome that Rossellino succeeded in living up to the position accorded him by both Manetti and Vasari. In truth, it is in the Pienza of Pius that the Rome of Nicholas came alive.

And that brings us once again to the little Tuscan hilltown of Pienza with which this discussion began. Many features of the individual buildings erected there remind us of elements found in the envisaged Rome of Pope Nicholas or in the antique monuments which Bernardo Rossellino would have seen there during his stay (fig. 22). In the apse of Pienza's new cathedral, we find, for instance, more than a trace of the Tribune commenced by the Lombard Beltrame da Varese during what I have described as "Phase Two" of the rebuilding of Saint Peter's. The form is quite unFlorentine, but Rossellino had been directed by the Pope to make the interior according to the Germanic *hallenkirche* pattern.[61] It was only natural, consequently, that he would sieze upon a design inspired by a northern model.[62] It was a design which he had known from his days in Rome on the building staff of Pope Nicholas V.

Elements of the Piccolomini Palace, built for the Pope and his relatives, also recall features carried over from Rossellino's Roman activities. The articulation of the exterior represents a "first" in Renaissance domestic design and illustrates the increasing sophistication of the fifteenth-century life-style, a life-style that placed a new emphasis upon comfort, elegance, grace, and, not the least, upon tasteful ostentation.[63] The use of superimposed pilasters on the exterior of the Piccolomini Palace was based upon the architectural ordering of such ancient examples as the Theater of Marcellus or the Colosseum or, as is most probable, the so-called Villa of Le Mura di Santo Stefano near Rome.[64] The exterior of the palace tells us that this is not the dwelling of a mere banker or of some petty tyrant, but of a scholarly prince well versed in the learning of the ancients and receptive to progressive ideas.[65] In its antique modernity, it actually goes beyond the Vatican Palace plans of Nicholas V as presented in Manetti. As innovative as the public façades of the Piccolomini Palace are, they are surpassed by the revolutionary character of the southern or garden front of the building. There, three stories of loggias rise the entire height of the building in a manner which recalls the loggias once attached to the Vatican Palace of Nicholas V.[66] In both cases, these walkways provided a view into the secret "paradise" gardens laid out below and of the vista beyond.

Across the street from the papal palace is the palace of one of Pius' most loyal supporters, Giacomo Ammannati, Cardinal of Pavia. This palace, with its cross windows and high belvedere tower is an obvious quotation from Rome, from the completed Vatican Palace wing of Nicholas V (fig. 23). It was a type unfamiliar in Tuscany and put a decidedly Roman stamp on Pienza.

So, too, did the palace prepared for the Bishop of Pienza by Cardinal Rodrigo Borgia across the piazza from the Piccolomini Palace. Its dominant cross window motif also was emphatically Roman and pontifical in appearance. The cross windows used at Pienza mark the first certain use of the type in Tuscany.

Nicholas intended that his cardinals and other officials of the curia live close to him in the Vatican district. The same intention was Pius' for the mini-Rome of Pienza. It appears that the chief prelates and other important papal officials were to build personal residences in Pienza in specific locations as part of the 'master plan.' Several of these palaces actually were brought to completion prior to Pius' death in 1464, enough so that we might even call one block leading away from the town square a veritable 'curial row' (fig. 24). Pius, as had been Nicholas, was quite aware of the importance of establishing a visual dependency for his prelates and for creating an architectural ordering which would reflect the actual organization of the church's hierarchy. We hear about it from Pius, himself, who described a papal audience which he had attended in 1457 while a member of the court of Pope

Calixtus III: "If you once saw the Pope celebrating Mass, or assisting in the Divine Office, you would confess that there is no order of pomp, or splendor save with the Roman pontiff. You would see the Pope sitting high upon his throne, the Cardinals on his right, and the great prelates on his left. Bishops, Abbots, Protonotaries, Ambassadors, all have their place. Here are the Auditors, there the Clerks of the Camera; there the Procurators, there the Subdeacons and Acolytes. Below them are the multitude. Surely you would recognize that the Papal Court resembles the celestial hierarchy, where all is fair to the eye, and all is done according to rule and law."[67] Practicality at Pienza prevented, as it would have done in Nicholas' Rome, the imposition of such a specific residential ordering, but the concept is there. Coming up the street toward the square, we build toward the authority of the papal palace; proceeding in the opposite direction, we feel the power which eminates from the pontifical presence.

As had Pope Nicholas, Pope Pius determined to develop an urban plan which would embrace the spiritual, civic, and domestic concerns of the city; church, communal hall, papal palace, palaces for bishop, canons and prelates—they all are there carefully sited within the predetermined scheme. Contextually, the major buildings of Pienza seem but key words in a new and broad statement of Renaissance harmony. Throughout the town, on buildings large and small, similar architectural and decorative features provide unifying elements giving to Pienza an unusual sense of visual homogeneity. The focal point of this rebuilt and revitalized community is the beautiful piazza. It is around this square that the important religious, civic, and residential buildings of the town are situated. The functional relationships existing between the various buildings receive their visual expression through common decorative leitmotivs and in the organization of the piazza which brings the separate architectural units into cohesive totality.

On my last visit to Pienza, as I sat in front of the little bar (once, some believe, the home of the papal secretary and humanist Gregorio Lolli) and watched the people of the town taking their evening stroll about the spacious piazza in front of Rossellino's great cathedral, I was struck with how perfectly this setting related to those moving through it. The space of the piazza and the backdrop of the noble buildings set about it is a concrete illustration of the humanist principle of rational thought and reasoned living, designed both for individual reflection and group discourse. The impact of the 15th-century architectural environment continues to be felt by those who live in Pienza today. A careful balance is struck between the desire for individuality and the demands of communal life. Somehow, the citizens of Pienza seem different from those of other communities; they are the inheritors of generations reared in this harmonious surrounding. The people of Pienza display a sense of personal and civic pride, a sense of 'decorum' unique even in the hilltowns of Italy.[68] This lasting lesson in urban planning is the most significant contribution which Pienza makes, and it was a lesson learned from those never-realized plans for the Renaissance Rome of Pope Nicholas V.[69]

Charles R. Mack
University of South Carolina

Notes

* Portions of this paper are based upon materials explored in a chapter of my doctoral thesis ("Studies in the Architectural Career of Bernardo di Matteo Ghamberelli Called Rossellino," diss. Univ. of North Carolina at Chapel Hill, 1972). That work, supported by grants from the Samuel H. Kress Foundation, has been augmented and revised by new researches conducted in Italy in 1978, while on sabbatical leave from the University of South Carolina. For their assistance I am grateful to the directors and staffs of the Biblioteca Vaticana, the Bibliotheca Hertziana, the Kunsthistorisches Institut in Florenz, and the State Archives of Rome, Florence, and Siena. A preliminary and much abbreviated version of this paper was presented in October 1979 at the 13th Annual Conference of the Center for Medieval and Early Renaissance Studies (Rome in the Renaissance: The City and the Myth) in Binghamton, NY, and later published as "Bernardo Rossellino, L. B. Alberti and the Rome of Pope Nicholas V," in the *Southeastern College Art Conference Review*, X, 2, 1982, pp. 60-69. My dedication of the present paper to Dr. Harold E. Dickson, Professor Emeritus of The Pennsylvania State University, recalls his class on Renaissance architecture, taught in Chapel Hill in 1967, in which I first acquired my interest in the study of this material and in fifteenth-century Italian architecture in general. This paper also owes

much to the labors of a number of scholars for whom the Rome of Nicholas V has held especial fascination; they include Torgil Magnuson, Charles Burroughs, Christoph Frommel, Eugenio Battisti of the Penn State faculty, and C. William Westfall, whose illuminating book on the subject was published by The Pennsylvania State University Press a decade ago.

1. Details of the trip of Pius II to Manuta and of his visit to Corsignano are found in the Archivo di Stato di Roma (ASR), Camerale I, *Spesi minute di palazzo* (1458-59), reg. no. 1473, c. 21^v; in Aeneas Silvius Piccolomini (Pius II), *Commentarii* (Rome: Domenici Basa, 1584, reprinted Frankfurt/Main: Minerva, 1974), pp. 78-79; and in a contemporary letter of Niccolò Severini published in C. Ugurgieri della Berardenga, *Pio II Piccolomini* (Florence: Olschki, 1973), p. 240, n. 215 and Giovanni Battista Mannucci, *Pienza: arte e storia* (Siena: 1937), pp. 25-26.

2. Pius' description given in the *Commentarii* is available in English translation in *Memoirs of a Renaissance Pope: The Commentaries of Pius II*, trans. Florence A. Gragg, ed. Leona C. Gabel (New York: Capricorn Books, 1962), p. 102, from which these quotations are taken.

3. Pius, *Memoirs*, p. 259.

4. The rebuilding of Pienza is discussed by the Pope in his *Memoirs*, pp. 281-91 and in Flavio Biondo's *Italia Illustrata* (ca. 1462), published in *Scritti inediti e rari di Biondo Flavio*, ed. Bartolomeo Nogara (Rome: Tipografia Poliglotta Vaticana, 1927, reprinted by Anastatica, 1973), pp. 235-39. Recent studies have included: Nicholas Adams, "The Acquisition of Pienza 1459-1464," *Journal of the Society of Architectural Historians*, XLIV, 1985, pp. 99-110; Enzo Carli, *Pienza, la città di Pio II* (Rome: Editalia, 1966); Giancarlo Cataldi, "Pienza e la sua piazza: nuova ipotesi tipologica di lettura," *Studi e documenti di architecttura*, VI, 1978, pp. 73-116; Ludwig Heydenreich, "Pius II als Bauherr von Pienza," *Zeitschrift für Kunstgeschichte*, VI, 1937, pp. 105-46; Mannucci, *Pienza: arte e storia*; D. Ivo Petri, *Pienza: storia breve di una simbolica città* (Genoa: Edigraphica, 1972); Armando Schiavo, *Monumenti di Pienza* (Milan: Alfieri and Larcroix, 1942); and Piero Torriti, *Pienza: la città del rinascimento italiano* (Genoa: Sagep, 1980). A thorough study by the author of the creation of Renaissance Pienza is forthcoming from Cornell University Press.

5. For the architectural career of Bernardo Rossellino and a bibliography, see Mack, "Studies."

6. Pius, *Memoirs*, p. 161.

7. For a convenient and still valuable history of the reigns of Nicholas V and other late medieval and Renaissance popes, consult Ludwig Pastor, *The History of the Popes* (London, Kegan Paul, Trench, Trubner and Co., 1938).

8. A good description of fifteenth-century Rome prior to Nicholas V is presented in Carroll William Westfall, *In This Most Perfect Paradise: Alberti, Nicholas V, and the Invention of Conscious Urban Planning in Rome, 1447-55* (University Park and London: The Pennsylvania State University Press, 1974), pp. 1-16 and 63-84.

9. Giannozzo Manetti, *Vita Nicolai V summi pontificis nunc primum prodit ex manuscripta codice Florentino*. Manetti's life of Pope Nicholas was published in *Rerum italicarum scriptores*, ed. Ludovico Muratori (Milan: 1734), III, 2, pp. 907-60, while those portions of his biography specifically dealing with Nicholas' architectural projects were published in Eugène Müntz, *Les Arts a la Cours des Papes pendent le XV et le XVI Siecle*, I (Paris: Ernest Thorin for the Bibliothèque Écoles Francaises d'Athènes et de Rome, 1878; reprinted Hildesheim/Zürich/New York: Georg Olms, 1983), pp. 339-51 and as an appendix to Torgil Magnuson, "Studies in Roman Quattrocento Architecture," *Figura*, IX, 1958, pp. 351-62. My references to Manetti are taken from this latter source. An excerpt from the will of Pope Nicholas which describes his building program is given in Müntz, *Les Arts*, pp. 337-39. Also consult Massimo Miglio, "Una vocazione in

progresso: Michele Canensi, biografo papale," *Studi medievale*, XII, pp. 463-524, esp. pp. 516-17.

10. For these accounts, see Mack, "Bernardo Rossellino, L. B. Alberti and the Rome of Pope Nicholas V," p. 67, n. 1 and 5.

11. Giorgio Vasari, *The Lives of the Painters, Sculptors and Architects*, ed. William Gaunt (London: J. M. Dent, 1963), II, p. 30.

12. Mack, "Bernardo Rossellino, L. B. Alberti, and the Rome of Pope Nicholas V," p. 67, n. 6. Luciana Finelli's *L'Umanisimo giovane: Bernardo Rossellino a Roma e a Pienza* (Rome: 1985) has come to my attention too late for her observations to be considered in this paper.

13. For a bibliography of the discussions of Nicholas V's program see Mack, "Bernardo Rossellino, L. B. Alberti, and the Rome of Pope Nicholas V," p. 68, n. 16 and Westfall, *In This Most Perfect Paradise*, pp. 185-214. Also see the description in Pastor, *History*, III, pp. 167-85 and the recent discussion in Kunibert Bering, *Baupropaganda und Bildprogrammatik der Frührenaissance in Florence-Rom-Pienza* (Frankfurt/ Bern/New York/Nancy: Peter Lang, 1984), pp. 43-72.

14. On these documents, consult Mack, "Bernardo Rossellino, L. B. Alberti, and the Rome of Nicholas V," p. 67, n. 7.

15. *Ibid.*, p. 67, n. 8.

16. For a summation of the work undertaken in the Papal States during the reign of Nicholas V, see Appendix I to *Ibid.*, pp. 64-65.

17. These documents are presented as an appendix to this paper.

18. A list of workers and the projects upon which they were engaged is given as Appendix II in Mack, "Bernardo Rossellino, L. B. Alberti and the Rome of Pope Nicholas V," pp. 66-67.

19. This tower also has gone under the names Turris Nova, Torrone, Torrione, Torrione degli Svizzeri, Propugnacolo di papa Niccolò V, Torre di Niccolò, and Torre Grande. It has been the subject of a detailed monograph by Amato Pietro Frutaz, *Il Torrione di Niccolò V in Vaticano* (Vatican City: Tipografia Poliglotta Vaticana, 1956). The Torre Nova also was discussed in Magnuson, "Studies," pp. 115-18 and in Redig di Campos, *I Palazzi Vaticani* (Rome: Cappelli, 1967), pp. 43-44, and in Mack, "Studies," pp. 170-73.

20. Vasari, *Lives*, II, p. 31.

21. See documents in Appendix, below.

22. The records kept prior to 1450 are rather confused and incomplete. Payments for repairs on the wall around the city for the years 1450-52 were noted throughout ASR, Camerale I, *Fabbriche* (1450), no. 1502. Work done on the fortifications of the Vatican City for the period 1450-53 were recorded in ASR, *Tesoreria segreta*, no. 1284, c. 159^v; no. 1285, c. 103; no. 1286, c. 52^v, 78, 144, 216, 259; and no. 1287, c. 1, 2, 3, 6, 7, 10, 11, 116, 146, 179, and 201. Many of the documents from the *Tesoreria segreta* were published in Eugène Müntz, *Les Arts*, pp. 159-160.

23. Biblioteca Vaticana, Codex Vaticano latina, no. 3618: *Ad S.d. Nostrum Pontificem Maximum Nicolaum V. conformatio Curie Romane loquentis edita per E.S. oratorem Joseph B. doctorem etc. cum humili semper recommendatione*, c. 4, verses 111-12. The poem is more readily accessible in O. Tommasini, "Documenti relativi a Stefano Porcari," *Archivio di Società Romana di storia patria*, III, 1880, pp. 63-133. The pertinent passage was printed in Frutaz, *Torrione*, p. 18, n. 3.

24. The poems were written by the Roman poet Orazio and by Pietro de' Godi Vicentino. They were published in Horattii Romani, *Porcarii carmen cum aliis eiusdem quae inveniri potuerunt carminibus accedit* and in Petri de Godis Vicentini, *De coniuratione Porcaria dialogus e codice Vaticano erutus*, ed. Maximilian Lehnhardt (Leipzig: 1907), pp. 4 and 64. The extracts also appeared in Frutaz, *Torrione*, p. 18, n. 3.

25.   Stefano Infessura, *Diario dell città di Roma di Stefano Infessura scribasenato*, ed. O. Tommasini (Rome: Fonti per la storia d'Italia, 5, 1890), p. 49. The passage also was published in Frutaz, *Torrione*, p. 18. Westfall (*In This Most Perfect Paradise*, p. 67, n. 4) has pointed out that Infessura mistakenly identified the Porta di San Pietro as the Porta Viridaria when giving the location of the villa owned by Tommaso Spinelli (see, in addition, his discussion of the tower on pp. 144-145).

26.   On the history of San Stefano Rotondo, consult Flavio Banfi, "La Chiesa di Santo Stefano sul monte Celio in Roma," *Annuario dell' Istituto Ungherese di Storia dell' Arte di Firenze*, I, 1947, pp. 3-21; "La Chiesa di Santo Stefano e il monastero dei frati Paolini al Monte Celio in Roma," *Capitolium*, XXVIII, 1953, pp. 289-300; "Santo Stefano Rotondo," *L'Urbe*, XV, 1, 1952, pp. 3-9; Luigi Benedetti, *Santo Stefano Rotondo* (Rome: Quarderni dell' alma Roma, XII, 1962); Spenser Corbett, "Santo Stefano Rotondo," *Rivista di archeologia cristiana*, XXXVI, 1960, pp. 249-61; Ladislao Gero Jun., *Santo Stefano Rotondo, la chiesa nazionale degli ungheresi a Roma* (Budapest: Magyar Tudományas Akadémia Rómaí Történati Bizottsága, 1944); Richard Krautheimer, "S. Stefano Rotondo a Roma e S. Sepolcro a Gerusalemme," *Rivista di archeologia cristiana*, XII, 1-2, 1935, pp. 52-102; Angelo Lipinsky, "Santo Stefano Rotondo sul Monte Celio a Roma," *Arte cristiana*, LIII, 1965, pp. 289-98; G. B. Rossi, "La basilica di Sto. Stefano ed il monastero di S. Erasmo," *Studi di diritto e storia* (Rome: 1886); Sara Rossi, "S. Stefano Rotondo a Roma," *L'Architettura, cronache e storia*, IV, 1959, pp. 774-79; Ritz Sándor, "La Nuova Gerusalemme dell' apocalisse e Santo Stefano Rotondo," *L'Urbe*, XXX, 4-5, 1976, pp. 12-26 and 14-27; and Antonio Thierry, "Il restauro di Santo Stefano Rotondo," *Italia nostra*, XLIX, 1966, pp. 15-21.

Although the church of San Stefano Rotondo was believed, during the Renaissance, to have once formed a part of the Markets of Nero, recent investigations have shown that the building was erected during the reign of Pope Symplicius (468-83). Its plan was in keeping with the symbolism of the period. The structure, as built, consisted of a series of three concentric circles, upon which was inscribed a Greek cross. A high tambour surrounded a central altar. The walls of the tambour rose from an architrave carried on twenty-two Ionic columns. The wall of the tambour was pierced by twenty-two round-headed windows. Encircling this area was an annular nave borded by an arcade of thirty-six Corinthian columns. The four arms of the Greek cross radiated from this second circle. Four separate atriums occupied the spaces between the protruding arms of the cross. The third circle was a solid wall which both formed the outer walls of the arms of the cross and enclosed the atriums between them. In the centuries subsequent to its completion, several restorations were carried out at San Stefano-restorations which significantly altered the character of the early Christian structure. A century after the church was erected, the eastern arm of the cross was converted into a chapel dedicated to the martyr saints, Primus and Felicianus. Here, Pope Theodore I (642-49) built a small apse decorated with mosaics. By the eighth century, the fabric of the tambour was in danger of collapsing and was buttressed by Pope Adrian I (772-95) with a transverse wall across the altar area. The depredations wrought by the followers of the antipope Anacletes II (1130-38) so ruined the church that Pope Innocent II (1130-43) was forced to undertake a drastic program of renovation. This project reduced the church to its present dimensions. The net effect of the work done was that the outer circle was eliminated. The exterior wall (already partially destroyed) was detached from the building and converted into a perimeter wall around the remaining core of the church. this meant the elimination of all but the eastern arm (the Chapel of Saints Primus and Felicianus) of the cross. The middle colonnade, thus, became the new external wall and the arcades, accordingly, were bricked up. A section of the old outer annular wall was retained next to the martyrs' chapel and an entrance portico attached to it. This consisted of five arches resting upon columns with simple beveled capitals. One of the eight original gates led from the portico through part of the old northeastern atrium into the body of the restored church. This alteration in the design of the church often has been attributed to the restorations carried out at the time of

Nicholas V. Francesco di Giorgio Martini is partially responsible for this notion. His treatise on architecture described an "hedifitio ruinato le cholonne et circulatione dele volte di fore el qual fu ornatissimo. Rafationallo papa Nichola. Ma molto piu lo ghuasto. Dicesi Scto. Stefano Ritondo." See Francesco di Giorgio Martini, *Tratatti di architettura ingegneria e arte militare*, ed. Corrado Maltese and Livia Maltese Degrassi (Milan: Edizioni di Polifilo, 1967), I, p. 283. Francesco di Giorgio's opinion was echoed and elaborated upon by Andrea Fulvio, who wrote: "Andandasene in verso san Giovanni Laterano si fa incontro di man destra il Tempio di santo Stefano rotondo…il quale rovinato fu restaurato da Nicolao quinto, pochi anni innanzi, et ridotto in quella forma, che hoggi si vede, hauendo ristretto la sua larghezza di prima, come si vede per il titolo che e posto alla entrare del tempio." See R. Lanciani, *Storia degli scavi di Roma e notizie intorno le collezioni romane di antichità* (Turin: Loescher, 1902), I, p. 57. The error of this view, repeated by some modern authorities, is demonstrated by an examination of the fabric of the church and by Giovanni Rucellai's mid-fifteenth century description of San Stefano (see note 28, below) which indicated that only the innermost circle of columns was visible when he visited the church.

27. "Ecclesia sancti Stephani rotunda, de ipso monte Coelio cognomen habens, quam tecto nunc carentem, marmoreis columnis et crustatis varii coloris marmore parietibus musivoque opere inter primas urbis ecclesias ornatissimam fuisse judicamus, eaque in Farini aede prius fundata fuit" from Flavio Biondo da Forli, *Roma instaurata*, I, 8 as quoted in Müntz, *Les Arts*, p. 141. Four years later, the Florentine banker Giovanni di Paolo Rucellai, in Rome for the Jubilee Year, spoke of "la chiesa di Sancto Stefano ritondo, tempio d'idoli, tondo in su 20 colonne con architravi aperto per tutto et da torno uno andito con tetto serrato di mattoni con una capella antica dellato con musaico e con tavolette e tondi di porfido et serpentino . et con foglaimi di nachera et grappoli d'uve et tarsie et altre gentileze." See Eugène Müntz, *Les Arts a la cours des papes: nouvelles recherches* (Paris: Mélanges d'archeologie e d'histoire, 1884), p. 141.

28. For this and other documents pertaining to the Nicholas V restorations to San Stefano Rotondo, see the Appendix to this paper. The most recent consideration of the Renaissance renovation is that of Erminia Gentile Ortona, "Santo Stefano Rotondo e il restauro del Rossellino," *Bollettino d'arte*, LXVII, 1982, pp. 99-106, which only came to my attention after the writing of this paper.

29. The wooden ceiling which was installed during the restoration of Pope Nicholas is still largely preserved. The wooden consoles are particularly noteworthy. Traces of paint on the beams give but a shadowy hint of the sumptuous decoration. The center of the vault of the anteroom contains the painted stemma of Nicholas V. The corbels supporting the vault of the anteroom are of the plain, triangular variety with budded tips.

30. Most of the "ochi," as they are called in the documents, are still in place. Two, however, were removed when a chapel was added at the southern side of the martyrs' chapel and others were walled up when the adjoining convent was built (see note 31, below).

31. The complex of buildings for the convent which abuts the northern side of the church apparently is of later date than the time of Pope Nicholas. This is demonstrated by the fact that two of his round windows were walled up when a wing of this establishment was attached to the annular wall of the church, by the character of the corbels in the convent's cloister, and by the decoration of the walls around the cloisteryard. A well in the yard bears the stemma of Pope Leo X (1513-21) and the convent buildings would appear to date from his papacy.

32. The design of the entrance portal to San Stefano is rather ponderous due to the heavy frame of the lunette which is not set back from the ends of the cornice. The turned-in cyma and fillet are typically Florentine, but the entablature lacks the trim of dentil, ovolo or astragal common to Rossellino's usually decorative manner. In fact, the severe form of this doorframe, as well as other details of the restoration of the church, would seem to reflect Roman rather than Tuscan taste. From the

anteroom, the annular nave is reached via two doors flanking an encased fifth-century column. These doors are linked into a *bifore* arrangement by a common entablature. An inscription in the frieze over the doorway reads: +ECCLESIAM HANC PROTOMARTIRIS STEPHANI DIVANTE COLLAP-SAM / -NICOLAVS V PONT MAX: EX-TINTEGRO INSTARAVIT MCCCCLIII. The third marble doorway installed by Rossellino provides access to the sacristy from the Chapel of Saints Primus and Felicianus. Its lintel displays the simply carved arms of the Pope and the inscription: P^AP. N.V.

33. The frame of this *lavacro* is visually and stylistically connected with the door to the sacristy. The only difference is the insertion of a frieze area carrying the inscription: NICOLAVS. PAPA. V. M. CCCC. LIII. Although not mentioned in the accounts, the *lavacro* must be attributed to Rossellino. It may be compared to the closet well in the courtyard of the Palace of Tommaso Spinelli built in Florence by Bernardo Rossellino between 1458-65. See Charles Mack, "Building a Florentine Palace: The Palazzo Spinelli," *Mitteilungen des Kunsthistorischen Institutes in Florenz*, XXVII, 3, 1983, p. 279.

34. See, for instance, the Bull of Nicholas V in Biblioteca Vaticana, *Bullarium Vaticanum*, II, pp. 146-47 (published in Müntz, *Les Arts*, p. 141.

35. On the Capitoline Hill projects of Nicholas V, see Carlo Pietrangeli, "I Palazzi Capitolini nel Rinascimento," *Il Campidoglio* (Rome: Edizioni di Capitolium, 1965), pp. 21-28; "Il Palazzo Senatorio nel Medioevo," *Capitolium*, XXXV, 1, 1960, pp. 3-19; and *Le primi fasi architettoniche del Palazzo Senatorio* (Rome: Edizioni di Capitolium, 1959). Also consult the summary in Westfall, *In This Most Perfect Paradise,* pp. 92-100. The pertinent documents relating to the work carried out were published in Müntz, *Les Arts*, pp. 146-50.

36. On the development of the cross window in Italy, see Frederico Hermann, *Il Palazzo di Venezia* (Rome: Libreria dello Stato, 1948), pp. 21-25; Charles Mack, "Notes Concerning an Unpublished Window by Bernardo Rossellino at the Badia Fiorentina,"

Southeastern College Art Conference Review, V, 1, 1970-71, pp. 2-3; Vincenzo Golzio and Giuseppe Zander, *L'Arte in Roma nel Secolo XV* (Bologna: Cappelli, 1969), pp. 59-104; and Natale Rauty, "Le finestre a crociera del Palazzo Panciatichi a Pistoia" in *Atti del 2 Convegno Internazionale di Studi: Il gotico a Pistoia nei suoi rapporti con l'arte gotica italiana* (Pistoia: Centro italiano di studi e d'arte Pistoia, 1966), pp. 93-101. Paolo Romano's career is examined in Anna Maria Corbo, "L'atività di Paolo di Mariano a Roma," *Commentari*, XVII, 1966, pp. 195-226.

37. For Michelangelo's Capitoline Hill, see James S. Ackerman, *The Architecture of Michelangelo* (Harmondsworth, Baltimore, Ringwood: Penguin, 1971), pp. 139-73. Work on the Palazzo Nuovo, across from the Palazzo dei Conservatori, although planned by Michaelangelo, did not actually get under way until 1603.

38. On this, see Westfall, *In This Most Perfect Paradise*, pp. 5-7.

39. See Anthony Butkovich, *Revelations: Saint Birgitta of Sweden* (Los Angeles: Ecumenical Foundation of America, 1972), p. 24.

40. Published in Pastor, *History*, II, pp. 166-67.

41. These great architectural programs have been the subject of several important researches. All of the proposed projects were considered in G. Dehio, "Die Bauprojecte Nicolaus des Fünften und L. B. Alberti," *Repertorium für Kunstwissenschaft*, III, 1880, pp. 241-57; in Magnuson, "Studies," pp. 55-214; and in Westfall, *In This Most Perfect Paradise*, pp. 103-84.

42. The Borgo received separate treatment in Torgil Magnuson, "The Project of Nicholas V for Re-Building the Borgo Leonino in Rome," *The Art Bulletin*, XXXVI, 1954, pp. 89-115 and, again, in his "Studies," pp. 68-97. Westfall, *In This Most Perfect Paradise*, devoted pp. 103-16 to this topic. See also S. Tadolini, "Il piano per i Borghi di Nicolò V e L.B. Alberti," in *Strenna dei Romanisti* (Rome: 1971), pp. 357-64.

43.   Vespasiano da Bisticci, *Renaissance Princes, Popes and Prelates*, trans., William George and Emily Waters, ed., Myron P. Gilmore (New York: Harper and Row, 1963), p. 35.

44.   The most extensive reconstruction of the plans for rebuilding the Vatican Palace is to be found in Magnuson, "Studies," pp. 98-162; in Westfall, *In This Most Perfect Paradise*, pp. 129-165, and in that same author's "Alberti and the Vatican Palace Type," *Journal of the Society of Architectural Historians*, XXXIII, 1974, pp. 101-21.

45.   On the belvedere tower type, see Christian Elling, *Function and Form of the Roman Belvedere* (Copenhagen: I Kommission Has Ejnar Munkgaard, 1950). For the Palazzo Capranica, also consult Prospero Simonelli and Giuseppe Fratadocchi, *Almo Collegio Capranica: lavori di restauro anno mariano* (Rome: Angelo Belardetti, 1955) and for the most recent of several studies of the Palazzo Venezia, see Christoph Frommel, *Der Palazzo Venezia in Rom* (Opladen: Westdeutscher Verlag, 1982).

46.   Those publications containing studies specifically devoted to the work planned for Saint Peter's have included: Luciana Finelli and Sara Rossi, "San Pietro come Team-work," *L'Architettura*, XXII, 1977, pp. 721-27; Constantine Jovanovits, *Forschungen über den Bau der Peterskirche zu Rom* (Vienna: 1877); Magnuson, "Studies," pp. 163-214; Frans Graf Wolf Metternich, "Gedanken zur Baugeschichte der Peterskirche im 15. und 16. Jahrhundert," in *Festschrift für Otto Hahn zum 75 Geburtstag* (Göttingen: 1954) and "Bramantes Chor der Peterskirche," *Römische Quartalschrift*, LVII, 1962, pp. 271-91; Armando Schiavo, "Il San Pietro del Rossellino e il monumento di Giulio II," *Studi romani*, XI, 1963, pp. 693-95; Gunter Urban, "Zum Neubau-Projekt von St. Peter unter Papst Nikolaus V," in *Festschrift für Harald Keller* (Darmstadt: Eduard Roether, 1963), pp. 131-73; and Westfall, *In This Most Perfect Paradise*, pp. 117-27.

47.   Westfall, *In This Most Perfect Paradise*, p. 62.

48.   Vasari, *Lives*, I, p. 350.

49.   On the date of the completion of the manuscript, see Mattia Palmieri, "De temporibus suis ab anno MCCCXLIX," in *Rerum italicarum scriptores*, ed., G.M. Tartini (Florence: 1748), I, p. 241. The date also is discussed in Richard Krautheimer, *Lorenzo Ghiberti* (Princeton Univ. Press, 1956), pp. 268-70, n. 28. The most up-to-date publications of Alberti's treatise are *L'Architettura (De re aedifcatoria)*, trans., Giovanni Orlandi, ed., Paolo Portoghesi (Milan: il Polifilo, 1966) and *Zehn Bücher über die Baukunst*, trans. and ed., Max Theuer (Darmstadt: Wissenschaftliche Buchgesellschaft, 1975).

50.   See Mack, "Bernardo Rossellino, L. B. Alberti and the Rome of Pope Nicholas V," Appendix II, p. 66.

51.   Michael Baxandall, *Painting and Experience in Fifteenth Century Italy* (London, Oxford, New York: Oxford University Press, 1972), p. 12.

52.   Richard A. Goldthwaite, *The Building of Renaissance Florence: An Economic and Social History* (Baltimore and London: The Johns Hopkins Univ. Press, 1980), pp. 321 and 435-39 and Pastor, *History*, II, p. 199.

53.   Mack, "Bernardo Rossellino, L. B. Alberti and the Rome of Pope Nicholas V," p. 68, n. 21.

54.   *Ibid*, n. 22.

55.   Godi, *De coniuratione Porcaria*, p. 21.

56.   See Mack, "Bernardo Rossellino, L. B. Alberti and the Rome of Pope Nicholas V," p. 68, n. 24.

57.   Santa Maria del Popolo and Sant' Agostino are good examples.

58.   Manetti, *Vita Nicolai V*, p. 950 quoted in Westfall, *In This Most Perfect Paradise*, p. 33.

59.   Vespasiano da Bisticci, *Renaissance Princes, Popes and Prelates*, p. 373. On the "artistic license" of Renaissance writers, see the valuable comments of John Onians in

"Brunelleschi: Humanist or Nationalist," *Art History*, V, 1982, pp. 259-60.

60. Pius, *Memoirs*, p. 68.

61. *Ibid.*, p. 287.

62. For northern protypes, see Richard Kurt Donin, *Österreichische Baugedanken am Dom von Pienza* (Vienna: Erwin Müller, 1946). For the appearance of the type in Italy in such buildings as the Cathedral of San Lorenzo in Perugia and San Fortunato in Todi, see W. Krönig, "Hallenkirchen in Mittelitalien," *Römisches Jahrbuch für Kunstgeschichte*, II, 1938, pp. 1-142. The shape of the apse of the Pienza Cathedral also may be related to that of the tribunes of the Florence Cathedral.

63. The Piccolomini Palace usually has been regarded as having been designed in imitation of Giovanni Rucellai's palace in Florence, but see Charles Mack, "The Rucellai Palace: Some New Proposals," *The Art Bulletin*, LVI, 1974, pp. 517-29 and "The Palazzo Rucellai Reconsidered," in *Actas del XXIII Congresso internacional de historia del Arte (1973)*, II, Granada, 1977, pp. 344-50. Precedence for the Rucellai Palace recently has been reasserted by Brenda Preyer, "The Rucellai Palace," in F. W. Kent, et al., *Giovanni Rucellai ed il suo Zibaldone II: A Florentine Patrician and his Palace* (London: The Warburg Institute of the Univ. of London, 1981), pp. 179-84.

64. On the Villa of Le Mura di Santo Stefano, drawn by Pirro Ligorio in the late 1540's, see Margaret Lyttelton and Frank Sear, "A Roman Villa Near Anguillara Sabazia," *Papers of the British School at Rome*, XLV, 1977, pp. 227-51 and T. F. C. Blagg, A. G. Luttrell and M. B. Lyttelton, "Ligorio, Palladio, and the Decorated Roman Capital from Le Mura di Santo Stefano," *Papers of the British School at Rome*, XLVII, 1979, pp. 102-16. The now-vanished Septizonium of Emperor Septimius Severus at the foot of the Palatine Hill in Rome also could have served as an inspiration.

65. As his Christian names (Aeneas Silvius) would indicate, the Pope's family placed considerable emphasis upon the antique connections of the Piccolomini. For the legendary Roman heritage of the family, see Pius, *Memoirs*, p. 29. The Pope's easy familiarity with the classics is demonstrated by his almost playful use of Virgil when he chose the name of Pius at his election to the papacy, thus putting his worldly life firmly behind him to become the "pius Aeneas."

66. See Westfall, *In This Most Perfect Paradise*, pp. 148-149.

67. This description comes from Pius' *De ritu, situ, moribus et conditione Germaniae*, as quoted in Cecilia M. Ady, *Pius II (Aeneas Silvius Piccolomini): The Humanist Pope* (London: Methuen, 1913), p. 255.

68. One is reminded of a statement made by the fourteenth-century French humanist, Petrus Berchorius: "Since piazzas are areas...arranged for the purpose of providing space or set up for the meetings of men, it should be remarked that in general through piazzas the condition of man in this world can be discovered." See William S. Heckscher, *Sixtus IIII Aeneas insignes statuos romano populo restitudendas ensuit* (Hague: 1955), n. 67 and, again, in Westfall, *In This Most Perfect Paradise*, p. 98.

69. Other fifteenth-century urban schemes stimulated, in part, from the examples set by Nicholas V and Pius II may be found in the projects carried out in Mantua, Urbino, and Ferrara and reflected in the treatises of Antonio Filarete and Francesco di Giorgio Martini.

APPENDIX

Documents Concerning Bernardo Rossellino's
Work for Pope Nicholas V

The majority of the documents published here,
found in the Archivio di Stato di Roma (ASR), have
appeared previously in Adamo Rossi, "Spogli
Vaticani," *Giornale di erudizione artistica*, VI, 1887,
pp. 129-228; Eugène Müntz, *Les Arts a la cours des
papes* (Paris: Ernest Thorin for Bibliothèque des
Écoles Français, 1898), and *Les Arts a la cours des
papes: nouvelles recherches* (Paris: Mélanges
d'archeólogie e d'histoire, 1884); Maryla Tyszkiewicz,
Bernardo Rossellino (Florence: Stamperia Polacca,
1929); and Amato Pietro Frutaz, *Il Torrione di Niccolò
V in Vaticano* (Vatican City: Tipografia Poliglotta
Vaticana, 1956). The documents presented below deal
solely with matters directly involving Bernardo
Rossellino or with those projects upon which he is
documented as having been at work. Documents nos.
16, 17, 18, 19, 20, 24, 25, 26, 27, and 28 are
published here for the first time. In other cases, the
previously published texts have been revised after
comparison with the original entries. It should be noted
that, in several instances, two entries for a single
payment are given or otherwise indicated. This is due
to the fact that double notations often appear in the
account books. I have divided the documents into three
categories dealing with: 1) general payments to
Rossellino during the time he was in the papal employ
in Rome, 2) payments relating to the Torre Nova at
the Vatican and the hoists which Rossellino furnished
for that project, and 3) entries dealing with the
restoration of the Church of Santo Stefano Rotondo.
All documents that have been published previously are
so indicated.

General Payments:

Doc. 1. 31 December 1451. A M° Bernardo da
Fiorenze ingegniere in palazo furono pagati ducati
15, bol. 10 per suo salario fino a questo dì.
ASR, *Tesoreria segreta*, 1285, c. 273ᵛ
(Rossi, p. 200; Tyszkiewicz, p. 116)

Doc. 2. 26 March 1452. A M° Bernardo da Fiorenze
ingegniere di palazo ducati 30 di camera al lui per
resto sua provisione fino a dì ultimo del presente

mese di marzo.
ASR, *Tesoreria segreta*, 1286, c. 109ᵛ
(Rossi, p. 201; Tyszkiewicz, p. 116)

Doc. 3. 9 April 1452. A Bernardo di Matteo da
Firenze ingegniere di palazzo ducati 15 simili per
sua provisione del mese daprile.
ASR, *Tesoreria segreta*, 1286, c. 153ᵛ
(Rossi, p. 201; Tyszkiewicz, p. 116)

Doc. 4. 27 September 1452. A Bernardo da Firenze
ingegniere di palazo ducati 15 simili al lui in ne le
stanze del agnolo dove si e amalato per sua
provisione del mese di luglio a ducati 15 il mese.
ASR, *Tesoreria segreta*, 1286, c. 206
(Rossi, p. 201; Tyszkiewicz, p. 116)

Doc. 5. 15 October 1452. A Bernardo da Firenze
ducati 30 simili al lui de le stanze del agnolo per
sua provisione dagosto e settembre a ducati 15 il
mese.
ASR, *Tesoreria segreta*, 1286, c. 206
(Rossi, p. 201; Tyszkiewicz, p. 116)

Doc. 6. 6 May 1453. A Bernardo di Matteo da
Firenze ingegniere in palazo ducati 15 di camerali
contanti per sua provisione del mese daprile.
ASR, *Tesoreria segreta*, 1287, c. 78
(Tyszkiewicz, p. 117)

Doc. 7. 26 May 1453. M° Bernardo di Matteo da
Firenze ingegniere di palazo di dare 50 di pappi
contanti al lui...
ASR, *Tesoreria segreta*, 1287, c. 126
(Rossi, p. 201)

Doc. 8. 3 June 1453. ducati 50. Coupled with Doc.
27, below.
ASR, *Tesoreria segreta*, 1287, c. 105
(Rossi, p. 201)

Doc. 9. 20 June 1453. Di altri ducati 40 contanti i
quali li presto per suoi bisogni. Coupled with Doc.
7 above.
ASR, *Tesoreria segreta*, 1287, c. 126
(Rossi, p. 201)

Doc. 10. 29 December 1453. Ducati 41, bol 8 da
conti. Coupled with Doc. 9, above.
ASR, *Tesoreria segreta*, 1287, c. 126ᵛ
(Rossi, p. 201)

The Hoists and the Torre Nova:

Doc. 11. 6 May 1452. M° Bernardo di Matteo da Firenze ingegniere di palazzo ducati 25 di papa conti a lui i quali gli do per parte di 1° defizio da tirare roba in su la tore per prezo di ducati 100 di camera a tutte sue spese di chonsentimento di Nostro Signore.

> ASR, *Tesoreria segreta*, 1286, c. 168
> (Rossi, p. 201; Tyszkiewicz, p. 116;
> Frutaz, p. 17, n. 3)

Doc. 12. 12 June 1452. Ducati 25 simili per parte del edifizio facto a la tore. Coupled with Doc. 11, above.

> ASR, *Tesoreria segreta*, 1286, c. 168
> (Rossi, p. 201; Tyszkiewicz, p. 116)

Doc. 13. 7 July 1452. Ducati 15 simili. Coupled with Doc. 11, above.

> ASR, *Tesoreria segreta*, 1286, c. 168
> (Rossi, p. 201)

Doc. 14. 9 November 1452. A Bernardo di Matteo da Firenze ingegniere di palazo ducati 65 simili per uno defizio fornito e uno non fornito per lo lavoro de la tore et del muro grosso a tutte sue spese de legname infuore e choxi siamo questo di dinanzi dachordo e disobrigha noi e noi lui con questo che tutte le chose apartenenti al detto edifizio s'intenda et deba rimanere a la chasa.

> ASR, *Tesoreria segreta*, 1286, c. 225
> (Rossi, p. 201; Tyszkiewicz, p. 116;
> Frutaz, p. 17, n. 3)

Doc. 15. 4 September 1454. A Nichola da Fabriano sopra la Monitione de la fabricha di palazo ducati uno di papali contanti a lui per comprare carne per dare manzare a li manoali che cavavanola domenica matina homini che morino quando cade lo fondamento de la torre nova.

> ASR, *Spese Minute*, 1469
> (Müntz, *Les Arts*, p. 85, n. 3)

Doc. 16. 31 December 1463. Ducati 50 dati di comandamento di Sua Santita a M° Gilio Romano per parte di lavoro di uno muro caduto della Vigna a presso alla Torre Grande.

> ASR, *Tesoreria segreta*, 1289, c. 116

Doc. 17. 24 January 1464. Ducati 25 dati di comandamento di Sua Santita a M° Giglio d'Andrea Toccho muratore per parte di denari d'uno muro fa della Vignia a presso alla Torre Grande.

> ASR, *Tesoreria segreta*, 1289, c. 118

Doc. 18. 3 February 1464. Ducati 50 dati di comandamento di Sua Santita a M° Gilio de Toccho da Roma per parte del mura fa a presso la Torre Grande.

> ASR, *Tesoreria segreta*, 1289, c. 119

Doc. 19. 29 February 1464. Ducati 50 dati di comandamento di Sua Santita a M° Gilio de Toccho per lo muro della vigna del palazo a presso la Torre grande li quali denari lefer dare per mani del bancho d'Ambruogio Spannocchi in Roma.

> ASR, *Tesoreria segreta*, 1289, c. 123$^\mathrm{v}$

Doc. 20. 16 March 1464. Ducati 77 pagare di comandamento di Sua Santita a M° Gilio de Toccho da Roma per resta del muro a fatto nella vignia a presso la torre grande di Roma.

> ASR, *Tesoreria segreta*, 1289, c. 126$^\mathrm{v}$

S. Stefano Rotondo:

Doc. 21. 4 November 1450. Item. Florenos similes 500 pro totidem solutis fratri Nicolao bullator, exponendos in fabrica pro ecclesia Santi Stefani in Celio Monte de mandato di Nostrae Papae.

> ASR, *Mandati camerale*, 831, c. 178
> (Müntz, *Nouvelles Recherches*, p. 140)

Doc. 22. 6 March 1453. M° Giovanni d'Andrea e chonpagni maestri di finestre di vetro deno dare . . . ducati 40 di camera cont. a loro cioe a M° Giovanni detto per parte dele finestre fa a santo Stefano Ritondo . . . .

> ASR, *Tesoreria segreta*, 1286, c. 104
> (Müntz, *Les Arts*, p. 142)

Doc. 23. 14 March 1453. M° Bernardo di Matteo da Firenze abitante a Roma de dare . . . ducati 700 di camera e quali a auti cont. per me da Alesandro Mirabelli e Anbruogio Spanochi e comp$^\mathrm{a}$ di corte in 5 partite da di 14 Novembre 1452 a questo presente di sono . . . deloro . . . e quali ducati 700 nostro Signore a fatti dare al detto maestro Bernardo per parte de lavoro fa a santo Stefano Ritondo . . . .

> ASR, *Tesoreria segreta*, 1287, c. 105
> and 2$^\mathrm{v}$

(Müntz, *Les Arts*, p. 142; Tyszkiewicz, p. 118).

Doc. 24. 10 April 1453. Da Nostro Signore fino ad x aprile ducati 30 . . . a M° Giovanni chi fa le finestre di vetro a Santo Stefano Ritondo.
ASR, *Tesoreria segreta*, 1287, c. 4 and 104

Doc. 25. 23 April 1453. Da Alesandro Mirabelli e Ambrogio Spanochi conp. di corte . . . ducati 100 M° Bernardo da Firenze iso indebito a lui [c. 105] per lo lavoro di Santo Stefano ritondo i quali Alesandro e conp. pagano . . . .
ASR, *Tesoreria segreta*, 1287, c. 4^v

ducati 100 per detta cagione.
ASR, *Tesoreria segreta*, 1287, c. 105
(Rossi, p. 201; Müntz, *Les Arts*, p. 142)

Doc. 26. 12 May 1453. Da Nostro Signore . . . ducati 50 . . . a M° Giovanni da Firenze per lo finestre del vetro di Santo Stefano Ritondo.
ASR, *Tesoreria segreta*, 1287, c. 5^v

Doc. 27. 3 June 1453. Da Alesandro Mirabelli e Ambrogio Spanochi conp. di corte . . . ducati 200 . . . a M° Bernardo da Firenze per lo lavoro di Santo Stefano Ritondo . . . debito a lui c. 105.
ASR, *Tesoreria segreta*, 1287, c. 6

200 florins per resto e saldo d'achordo con Nostro Signore de lavore che il detto Maestro Bernardo a fatto a santo Stefano Ritondo. Coupled with Doc. 8.
ASR, *Tesoreria segreta*, 1287, c. 105
(Rossi, p. 201; Müntz, p. 142)

Doc. 28. 22 June 1453. Da Nostro Signore . . . ducati 25 . . . per dare i quali dela finestre del vetro di Santo Stefano Ritondo.
ASR, *Tesoreria segreta*, 1287, c. 7

Doc. 29. 25 June 1453. A M° Bernardo di Matteo da Firenze maestro di muro . . . ducati 1000 di camera . . .sono per lo palmentato di santo

Stefano Ritondo e per entonichatura d'esso per li altari di marmo e porte di Marmo e fenestre di marmo a fatte in detta chiesa a tutte sue spese d'ogni e ciaschuna chosa e choxi e rimasto d'achordo cho Nostro Signore.
ASR, *Tesoreria segreta*, 1287, c. 143
(Müntz, *Les Arts*, p. 142; Tyszkiewicz, p. 118)

Doc. 30. 10 July 1453. Ducati 36 cont. a Charlo suo [Giovanni d'Andrea] conpagno per resto e saldo d'achordo de lavoro di santo Stefano . . . .
ASR, *Tesoreria segreta*, 1287, c. 104
(Müntz, *Les Arts*, p. 142)

Doc. 31. 10 July 1453. A Maestro Giovanni d'Andrea e li conpagni dipintore di finestre di vetro . . . ducati 236 di camera . . . per 8 finestre grande e 2 ochi grande e 2 finestre picole e 36 ochi picoli a fatte a santo Stefano Ritondo a fighure e a ochi.
ASR, *Tesoreria segreta*, 1287, c. 143 and 104
(Müntz, *Les Arts*, pp. 142-43)

Doc. 32. 15 July 1453. Ducati 26 di camera cont. a M° Nicholo da Firenze m° di legniame sono per sue manifatture di una porta fe ale chamare di mis. Ghottifredi. 2 porticelle fe ale chapele del ponte e per 15 tavole di nocie e per una porta fatta a santo Stefano Ritondo . . . .
ASR, *Tesoreria segreta*, 1287, c. 147
(Müntz, *Les Arts*, p. 117)

Doc. 33. 31 December 1453. 1000 ducati per lo lastricho e incholatura di santo Stefano Cielimonte 236 ducati per le finestre del vetro di detto luogho.
ASR, *Tesoreria segreta*, 1287, c. 33
(Müntz, *Les Arts*, p. 39)

Doc. 34. 27 April 1454. A maestro Domenico da Montelupo fabro . . . ducati 28, bologni 51 di camera per libre 827 di fero lavorato dato a santo Stefano Ritondo cioe 4 finestre e una catena per la volta e arpioni e grapi per tutto d'achordo.
ASR, *Spese minute*, 1469, c. 81^v
(Müntz, *Les Arts*, p. 143)

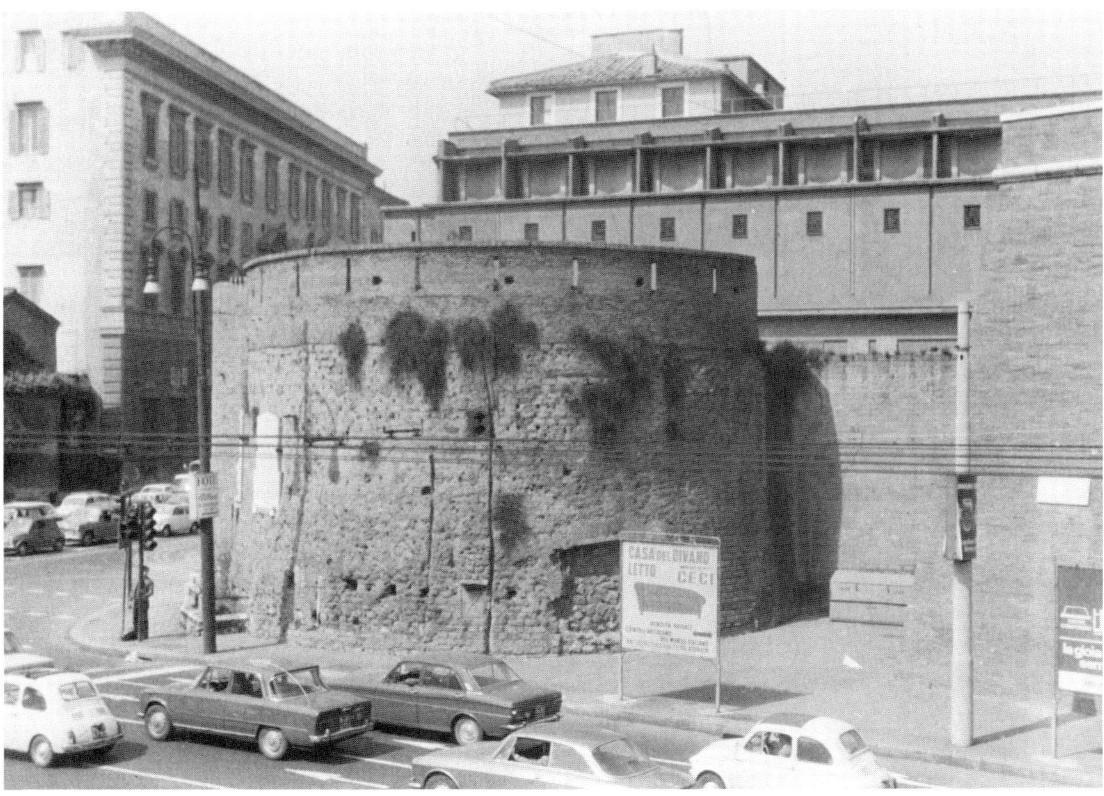

14.   Rome, round tower of Nicholas V added to the Vatican walls at the Porta Cavalleggeri (photo: author).

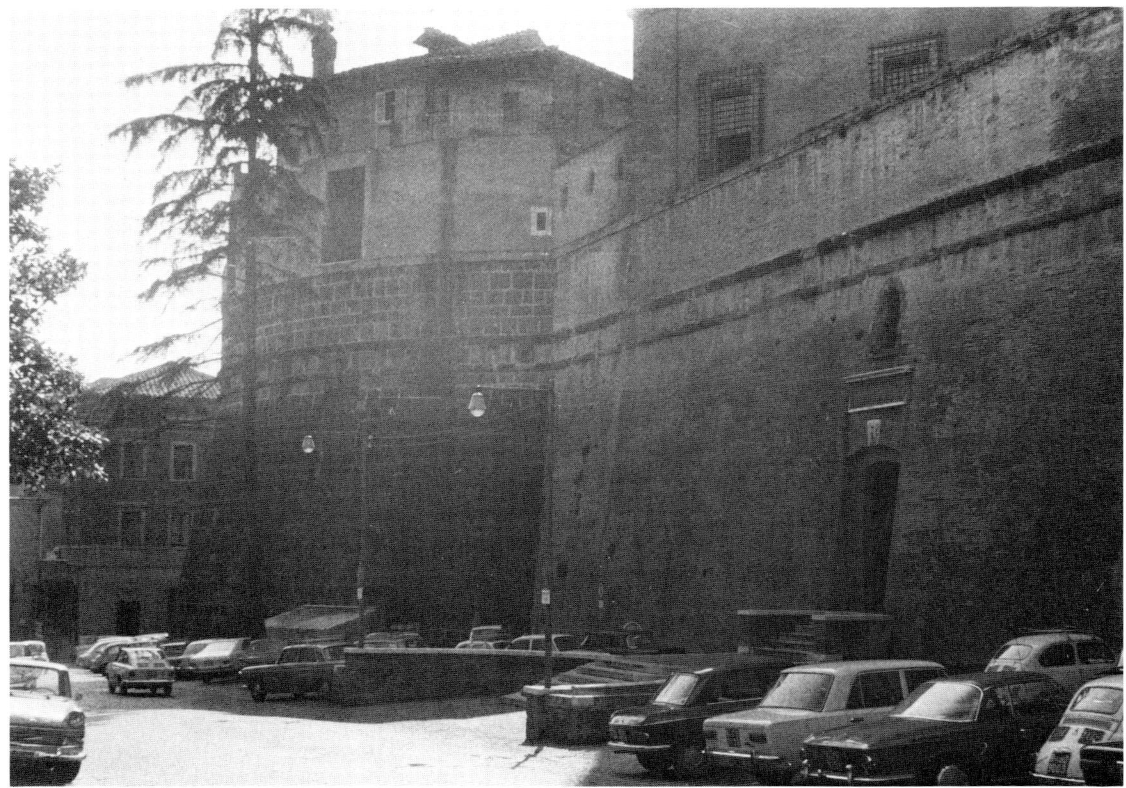

15.   Rome, the *Torre Nova* built by Nicholas V near the Porta San Pietro of the Vatican (photo: author).

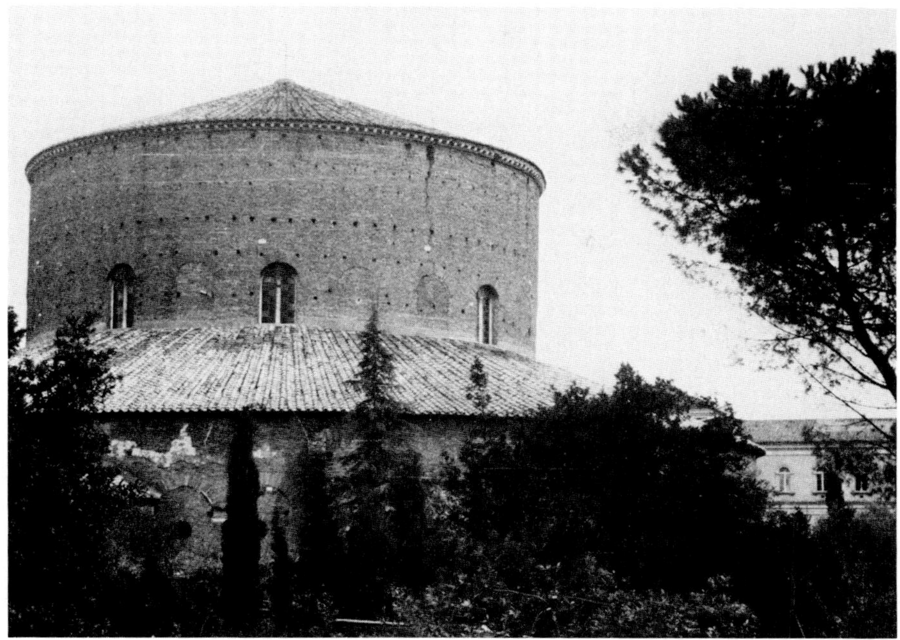

16.   Rome, Early Christian church of S. Stefano Rotondo, restored under Nicholas V, showing *bifore* and *occhi* installed by Bernardo Rossellino (photo: author).

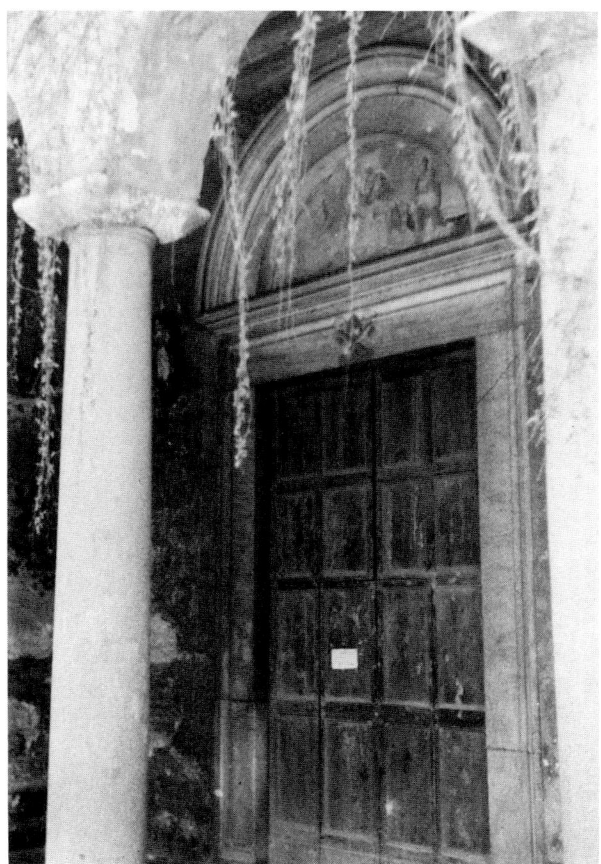

17.   Rome, S. Stefano Rotondo, main portal installed by Bernardo Rossellino (photo: author).

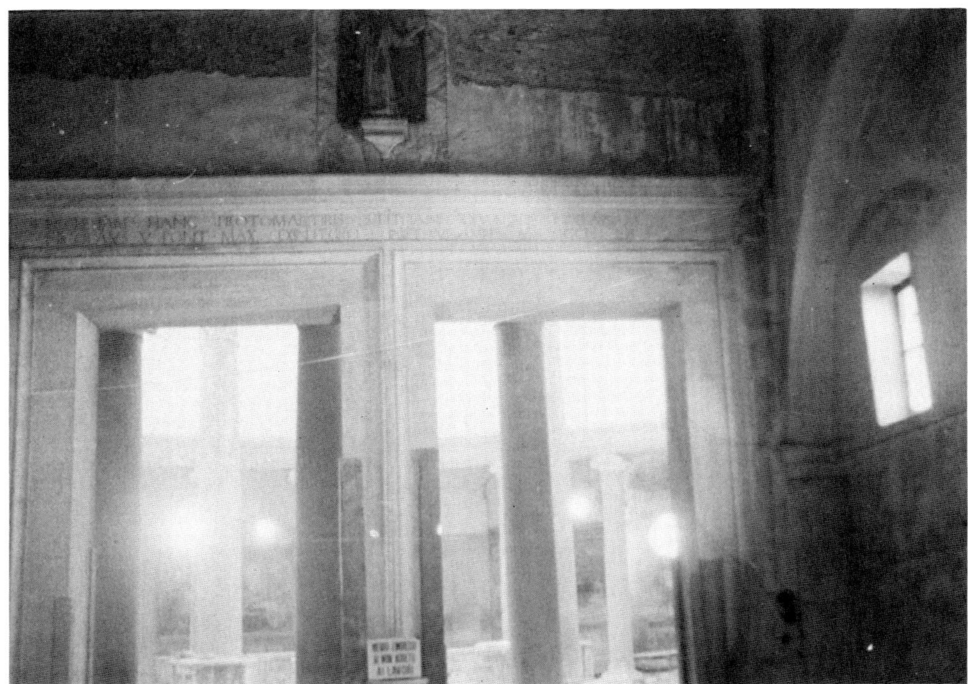

18.   Rome, S. Stefano Rotondo, marble double doorframe of Bernardo Rossellino leading from anteroom to annular nave (photo: author).

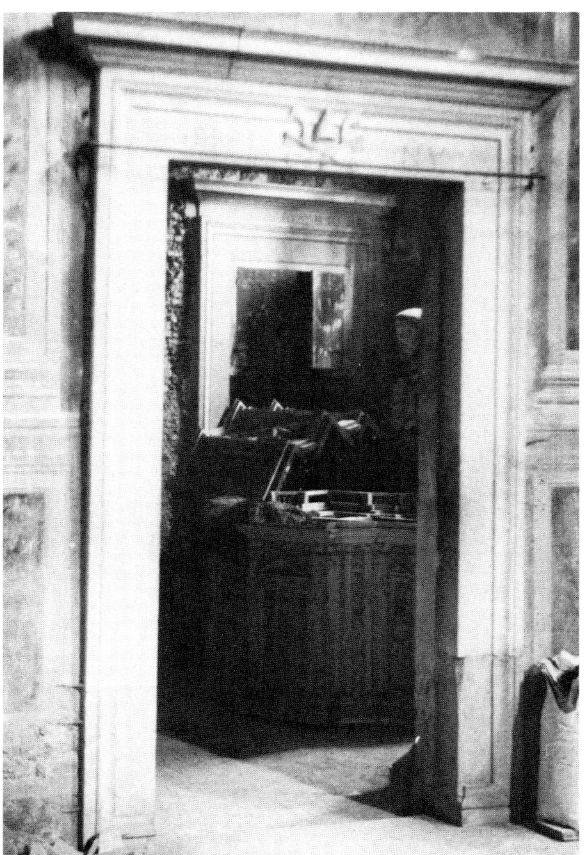

19.   Rome, S. Stefano Rotondo, doorway to sacristy, installed by Bernardo Rossellino with his *lavacro* shown beyond (photo: author).

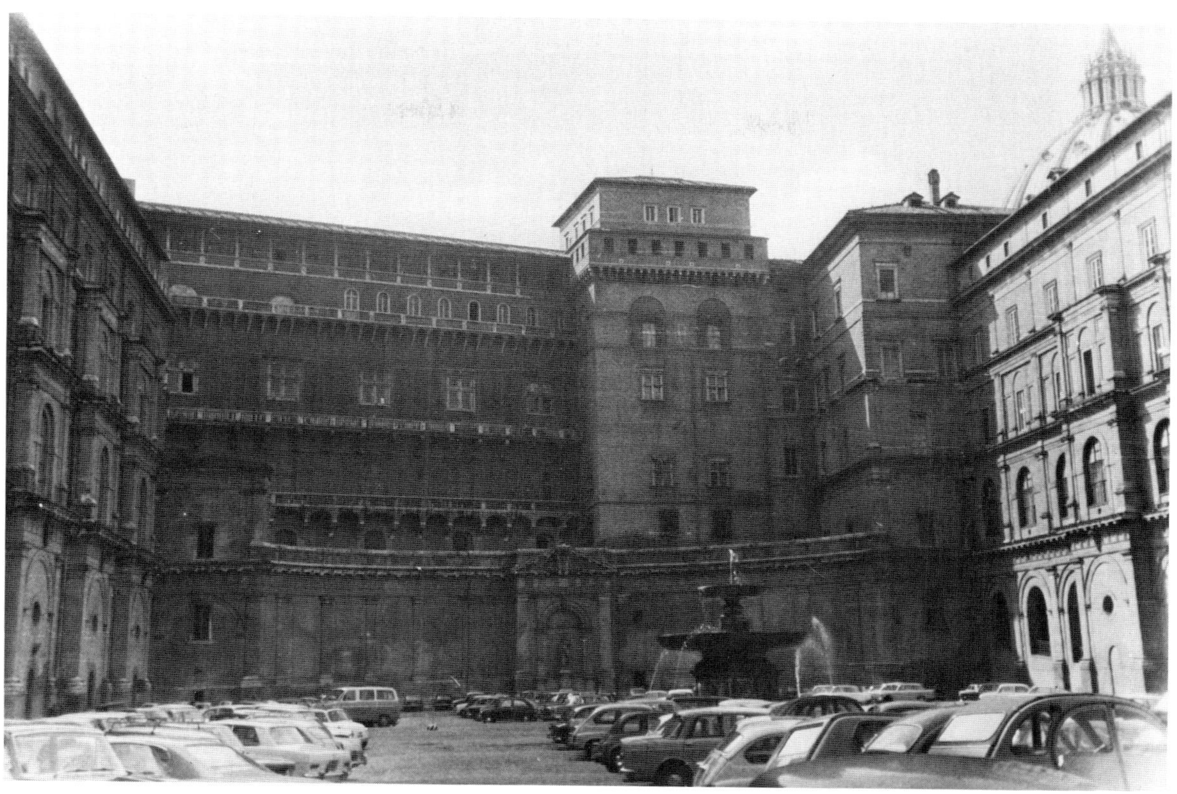

20.   Rome, Vatican Palace with the wing of Nicholas V built by Antonio di Francesco and the Borgia Tower (photo: author).

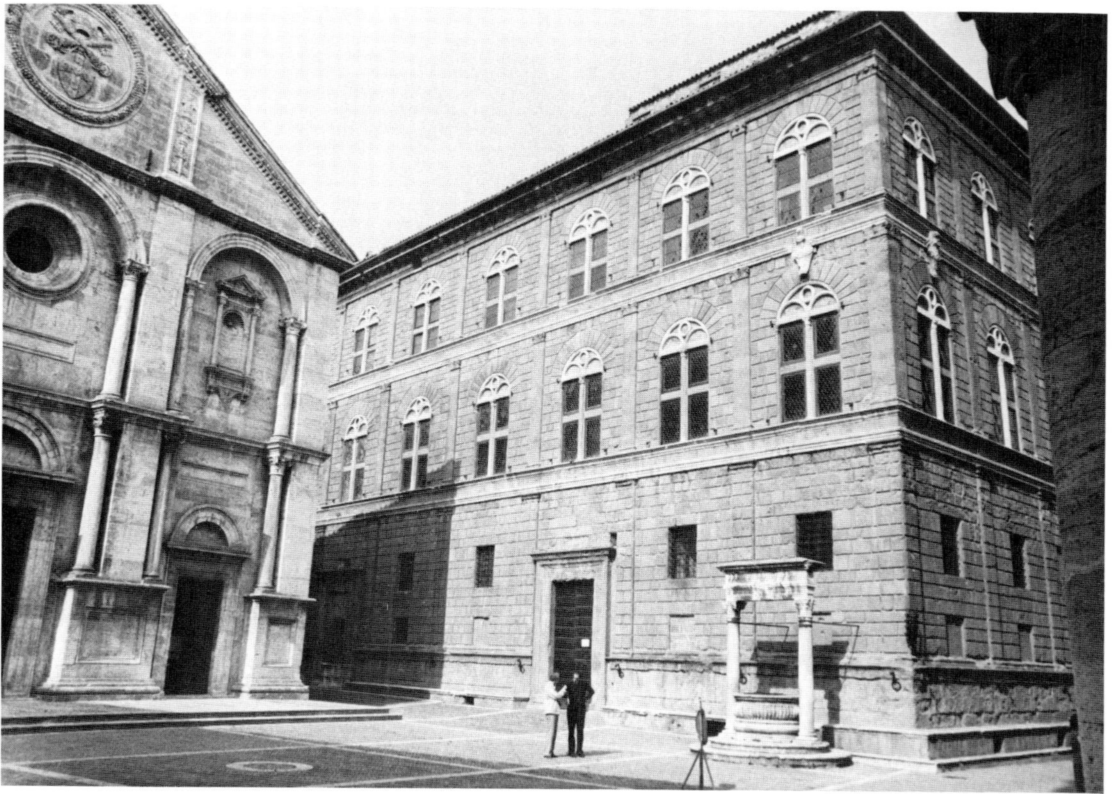

22.   Pienza, showing the Piazza Pio II with the façades of the Cathedral and the Palazzo Piccolomini (photo: author).

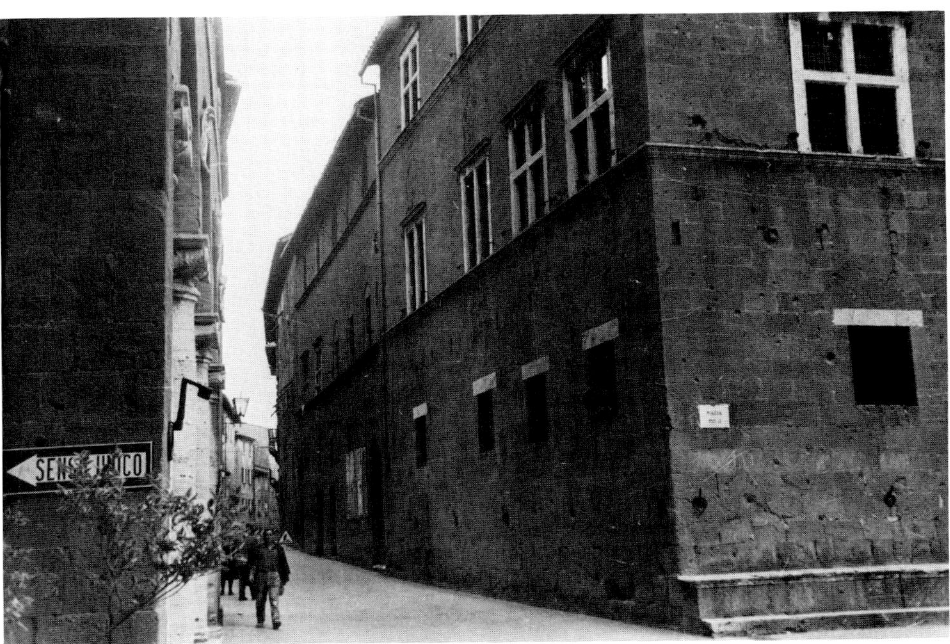

24.   Pienza, row of palaces of cardinals and other papal officials (photo: author).

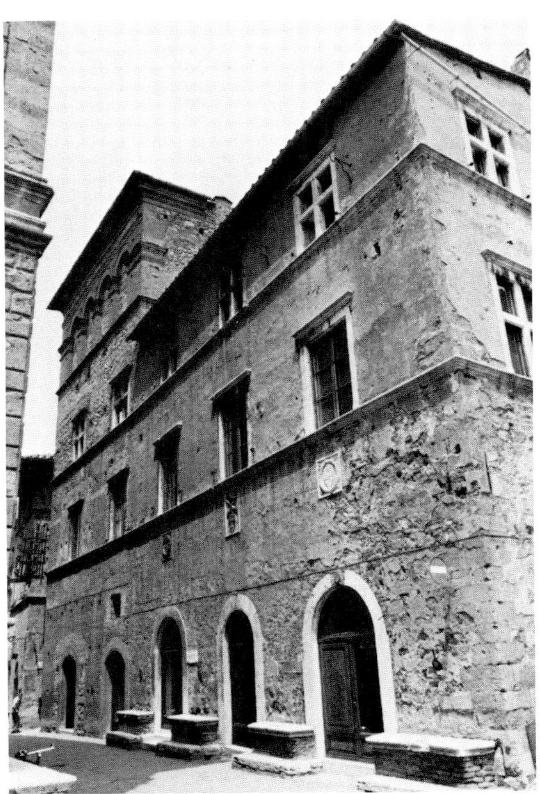

23.   Pienza, The Palazzo Ammannati (photo: author).

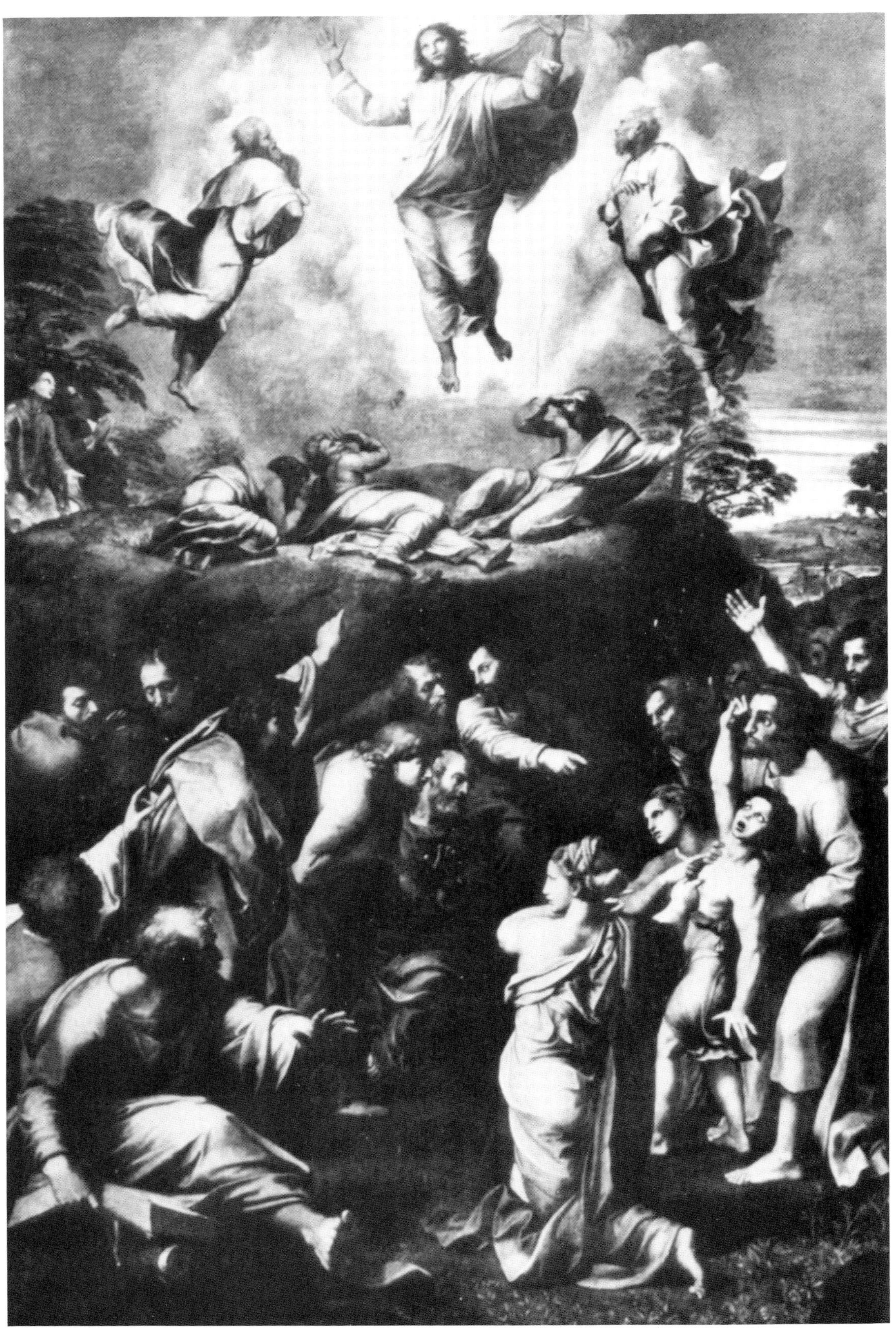

50.   Raphael, *Transfiguration*, Rome, Vatican (from Oskar Fischel, *Raphael*).

Leonardo, Raphael, and Caravaggio

3

In memory of Howard Hibbard

The rather unexpected topic of this paper[1] would have puzzled me until recently, when I travelled to Milan to study Leonardo's *Last Supper* being cleaned, and then within Lombardy. I did so specifically to consider the works of certain Lombard painters of the later sixteenth century, because I had the relationship between Leonardo and Caravaggio than generally has been recognized. From Northern Italy I travelled to Rome; and, with a different purpose altogether in mind, I returned to the Vatican to see Raphael's work again. It is probable that if that itinerary, which was Caravaggio's own, had been reversed, I would not have been stimulated to consider this topic, which was formulated by two specific encounters. The first was upon seeing Paolo Cavagna's *San Rocco* in Bergamo (fig. 41), which led me to review and expand the basis of Roberto Longhi's persuasive argument that Caravaggio was essentially a Lombardic painter. The second encounter was with Raphael's *Transfiguration* (fig. 50), when I realized that Raphael's art had played a significant role in Caravaggio's development, and why.

*   *   *   *   *

If one posits that Caravaggio's work should be understood as inseparable from a North Italian, and more particularly Lombard, sense of picture-making, it is not necessary to rely exclusively upon those well-known and repeatedly cited compositional motifs that Caravaggio may have remembered by artists such as Lorenzo Lotto, Antonio Campi, Figino, Moretto, and the like.[2] Longhi perceptively discussed most of them fifty years ago,[3] even though his further, polemical insistence on Caravaggio's Lombardic roots has fared less well in the later scholarship, which has tended to emphasize Venetian or Central Italian factors instead.[4] Those motifs are valuable indicators, particularly because they can direct us toward an understanding of Caravaggio's ideas on art, not in the sense of a systematically developed theory, but of how his North Italian training helped form his conception of the art of painting.

The currents running through Lombard art during the decades preceding Caravaggio's youth were so complex that only certain salient points can be emphasized here. Foremost, perhaps, is the need to recognize that *two* highly compatible, cross-fertilized strains should be outlined. One, which has been neglected and to which I will return in more detail, is Leonardo's, specifically the legacy of his dark mode of painting as a means of achieving *rilievo* and expression.[5] The other is what Longhi stressed in his analysis of Lombard Cinquecento painting:[6] *veracità pittorica*, pictorial truthfulness, which he traced through the art of Foppa, Borgognone, Lotto, Moretto, Moroni, and Savoldo, down to the Campi and Peterzano. Longhi stressed that despite, or even due to, the Venetian-Brescian currents that merged with this Lombard tradition, a combination of objective naturalism and emphasis on light are cornerstones of the Lombard way of thinking about, and making, form. As Sydney Freedberg aptly characterized this pictorial conceptualization in Lombardy, "its main constituent was mimesis, bound to an idea of art . . . that preceded the aesthetic factor of artistic style." Hence, his analysis of artists from Bramante and Gaudenzio to those working at the century's end relies on characterizations such as "acute sensibility to light," "sharp in rendering form," "versim," "rigor of structure and description," etc.[7]

Various Lombard painters seldom discussed in the context of Caravaggio's origins, but whose works ultimately fed the formation of Simone Peterzano, Caravaggio's teacher, could be cited in support of Longhi's ideas, including even Andrea Previtali, who, as early as 1517, developed an extraordinary clarity and isolation of naturalistically modelled forms in strong light (fig. 25)[8]; Nicola Moietta, who was from the small town of Caravaggio itself, and whose figures in the *Madonna of the Rosary* of 1521 (fig. 26) rightly have been characterized as "quasi di statue dipinte"[9]; or Fermo Stella, who probably was from Caravaggio, too, who worked with Gaudenzio, and whose polyptych of 1547 is unmittigatingly naturalistic (fig. 27), almost like a Zurbarán *avant la lettre*.[10] Peterzano, whose *Pietà* and *Sts. Paul and Barnabas at Lystra* (figs. 28, 29) stress the hard tactility and presence of forms, certainly should be understood as integral in this heritage.[11]

In her essay in *The Age of Caravaggio*,[12] Mina Gregori rightly has stressed the significance of our finally knowing that Caravaggio was over twenty years old when he left his native region for Rome, i.e., that he must have been very well steeped in the Lombard tradition of painting. That tradition was significantly based on the ideas of the greatest resident Lombard, Leonardo da Vinci. In his excellent monograph, Howard Hibbard recently outlined many of the most revealing formal links between Caravaggio and Leonardo.[13] Caravaggio's *St. John the Baptist* (fig. 30), if that actually is its subject,[14] could have conceptual affinities with the naked, quasi-androgynous *St. John* in Paris by Leonardo, and more so with other Leonardesque paintings of the Baptist, such as from the circle of Cesare da Sesto (fig. 31). Leonardo, we read in Vasari,[15] planned an unfinished Medusa head in oil on panel, as Caravaggio did. And how we are reminded of Caravaggio when Vasari further writes that Leonardo painted a picture of "a vase filled with water and some flowers in it, where, besides the marvelous vividness, he had imitated the dewdrops so that it seemed more real than life"![16] The angel in the *Sacrifice of Isaac* (fig. 32) is entirely Leonardesque,

regardless of whether its pointing gesture may or may not also be indebted to the *Madonna of the Rocks*. Paintings by Bernardino Luini and others from Leonardo's circle (fig. 33) are strikingly similar to Caravaggio's late design of *Salome Receiving the Head of the Baptist* (fig. 34). James the Less in the *Last Supper* (fig. 35) I believe inspired Caravaggio's apostle at the right of the *Supper at Emmaus* in London (fig. 36), not only in formal ways, but because the eucharistic meanings of the two images are so closely linked. Moreover, the modelling of Christ's head in Caravaggio's *Emmaus*, not just his unusual beardlessness, is thoroughly Leonardesque, as Marco d'Oggiono's more youthful *Christ* indicates (fig. 37). And now that the *Last Supper* is being restored and can be reassessed in terms of its initial appearance, it is clearer than ever how truly fundamental Leonardo's still life must have been for the Lombard tradition of still-life painting leading to Caravaggio by way of artists such as Figino, Lomazzo's student, whose *Still Life with Peaches* (fig. 38) might be compared with a cleaned lunette above the *Last Supper* (fig. 39), and then with Caravaggio's own *Still Life* in the Ambrosiana (fig. 40).

These parallels are a reminder that the clues are right there in Caravaggio's pictures, which, on a more profound level, also mirror Leonardo's determined interest in establishing the relief of images. For the Renaissance master, that was the fundamental end of painting because he considered its goal to be the illusionistic imitation of nature. The means to achieve it was chiaroscuro. "The primary purpose of the painter is to make a plane surface display a body in relief, detached from that plane," he wrote. Then follows a passage that Caravaggio would have cherished: "he who in that art most surpasses others deserves most praise, and this concern, which is the crown of the science of painting comes about from the use of shadows and lights, or, if you wish, brightness and darkness. Therefore whoever avoids shadows avoids what is the glory of art for noble minds." And again, "an object represented in black and white will display stronger relief than in any other way." Or, to cite one more passage from the so-called *Trattato*, "the form of any body will seem to be in greater relief and more detached from the backgrounds when the borders between the form and background are of the greatest possible contrast of bright or dark color."[17]

It is essential to recognize that Caravaggio would have felt less sympathy with Leonardo's deep interest in reflected lights and his famous mistiness, or *sfumato*, which Leonardo refers to in his exhortation, "you must not make shadows sharp or definite lest your work should have a wooden effect."[18] That which we generally call Caravaggesque lighting relies on the structure, but not the surface refinements, of Leonardo's chiaroscuro. Perhaps equally relevant to an understanding of Caravaggio's Lombardic inheritance is Leonardo's equation of seeing with understanding, his conception of art as gifted transcription. Thus, we have his statement that, "the mind of the painter must resemble a mirror," and his warning that, "the painter will produce pictures of small merit if he takes for his standard the pictures of others. But if he will study from natural objects he will bear good fruit."[19]

Two of Caravaggio's own views could not seem more Leonardesque: that "a painter is a *valentuomo* is he knows how to paint well and to imitate well natural things," and, in Van Mander's report completed as early as 1603, that "all art is nothing but a bagatelle . . . unless it is done after life."[20] Nor could Caravaggio's avowed rejection of the Old Masters as necessary models be more in keeping with Leonardo's dictum just cited. As a youth in Milan, Caravaggio would have absorbed such ideas naturally from his teacher, Peterzano (whose role in Caravaggio's formation is too often minimized today), and from the artist-theoretician, Gian Paolo Lomazzo. Lomazzo's theory is deeply steeped in Leonardo's ideas,[21] yet his art and writings are not even mentioned in the most thorough, excellent catalog of Caravaggio's work recently published by Mia Cinotti, though, with her characteristic perceptiveness and deep familiarity with Lombard art, Mina Gregori has emphasized Lomazzo's importance for our understanding of Caravaggio.[22] In particular, she calls attention to Lomazzo's neo-Leonardesque views on the emotions and strong, contrasted psychological reactions, and their relevance to Caravaggio's mimetic intentions. Later we will return to the role of the *moti*, as Lomazzo called them, but it is crucial to emphasize as well that, in his *Trattato* of 1584, Lomazzo first dealt with light as an artistic means separable from color. He discussed, if not very consistently, the differences between "primary" and "secondary" lights; and he singled out in the first category a *lume divino*, a type of primary light, which, he says, is found in Correggio's *La Notte* and Raphael's *Transfiguration* (fig. 50) and is particularly suited to religious subjects.[23] Caravaggio himself first used what Lomazzo might have called a *lume divino* in the *Ecstasy of St. Francis*, which, perhaps not by coincidence, was one of Caravaggio's earliest religious paintings. What is more, a consistent

change occurred — from a light to a dark palette — as Caravaggio's iconography generally shifted from genre to Christian themes. Lomazzo, in fact, voicing views that Caravaggio would have supported, said that Leonardo's chiaroscuro in particular allowed the artist "to do everything that nature herself can do," and that oil painting is the finest medium, superior even to fresco, because its effects are more naturalistic.[24]

During the last quarter of the century, when Caravaggio was growing up and studying in Milan, Leonardo's legacy unquestionably remained alive, but was frequently reinterpreted by those artists, such as Peterzano, who recognized an incompatibility between subtly graded chiaroscuro on the one hand, and strong colors and hard surfaces on the other, which were desired by those seeking an aggressively plastic style. Various painters who stayed on in Lombardy after Caravaggio's departure explored the potential that he had seen in the art of his day, albeit with less consequence.[25] Artists such as Cerano, Giulio Cesare Procaccini, and Morazzone, the leaders of the Lombard school during the 1590s, at times seem to have been as convinced as Caravaggio was of the efficacy of dramatic chiaroscuro for formal and psychological effects. Their work, like Francesco del Cairo's shortly later, which can be seen as the epitomization of the Leonardesque strain of painting in Lombardy, depends at times almost exclusively on achromatic *chiaro* and *scuro*. The visitor to Bergamo should be no less struck by the style of Gian Paolo Cavagna, a painter of modest talent who nonetheless developed a style, surely independent of Caravaggio's, that rightly has been compared with the work of Tristan and Borgianni,[26] two artists actually influenced by Caravaggio. Cavagna's *San Rocco* (fig. 41) is signed and dated 1591, i.e., about a year before Caravaggio reached Rome.

Vasari already had made a related and important observation that few historians could have recognized so easily today: "to the art of painting," he wrote, "Leonardo contributed a certain darkness to the style of oil painting [*una certa oscurità*], which has enabled the moderns to give great vigor and relief to their figures."[27] Lomazzo, whose *Self Portrait* as a melancholic Bacchus I believe influenced the conception of Caravaggio's *Bacchino malato*,[28] surely agreed with Vasari. Writing just at the time of Cavagna's altarpiece, he made an astute remark. Stressing the necessity in painting of a dominant light, "which gives force and liveliness to all the others," he praised four masters who, "with great shadow on their figures," understood the effect of "a principal light," and hence created scenes with "un rilievo mirabile." Lomazzo named Leonardo da Vinci, Gaudenzio Ferrari, and Cesare da Cesto, i.e., three artists working within the Lombard tradition. Then he added a surprising fourth, not only through uncritical admiration, I believe: "Raffaello d'Urbino."[29]

*   *   *   *   *

The path I have taken from Lombardy to Rome has been a long one, but that was necessary because the role of Leonardo's legacy in Caravaggio's art has been unappreciated, and because it is essential for the second portion of this paper to understand Caravaggio within his North Italian context. For, it is with Lombard eyes that I propose he looked carefully and admiringly at the late works of Raphael. Giulio Carlo Argan's paper of 1974, entitled "Caravaggio e Raffaello,"[30] is the sole study directed to this topic, though in fact Argan's theoretical interests are entirely different from those I am raising. Moreover, his discussion of *furor poeticus* versus *praxis*, poetic inspiration versus acquired practice or making, is based on a very tenuous connection between a Raphaelesque *St. Luke Painting the Virgin* in the Accademia di San Luca in Rome and Caravaggio's second design for the Contarelli Chapel altarpiece. Other proposals regarding Raphael's direct influence on Caravaggio are more persuasive, and almost embarrassing in light of Bellori's words. Caravaggio, he tells, "despised the superb statuary of antiquity and the famous paintings of Raphael; he considered nature to be the only subject fit for his brush."[31] Undoubtedly such an assessment, however exaggerated it might have been, lent real authority to the commonly held view that Caravaggio rejected wholesale the authority of the Old Masters.

It nonetheless has been persuasively argued that Caravaggio's initial design of the *Martyrdom of St. Matthew* as known through x-rays (fig. 42) — it must be stressed that this was the artist's first ambitious history painting and his first public commission — relied in part on Raphael's *Battle of Ostia* (fig. 43), from which a principal figure in profile in the foreground with a sword in hand was quoted, and whose orchestration of movements seems to have influenced Caravaggio's approach to disposition of figures.[32] Likewise, the first *St. Matthew* for the Contarelli Chapel (fig. 44) almost surely pays homage to Raphael's inventions, whether his *Jupiter and Cupid* in the Farnesina, or the engraved *St. Matthew* (fig. 45).[33] A third likely connection links the basic conception of the first

version of the *Conversion of St. Paul* for the Cerasi Chapel with Raphael's tapestry design.[34] Any other formal borrowings are problematic, though Wagner perceptively compared Caravaggio's *Medusa* with the possessed boy in the *Transfiguration*,[35] which will concern us shortly.

First, certain general observations are in order. Caravaggio's attraction to Raphael's art consistently points to Raphael's late style, since even the *St. Matthew* engraving, excerpted from the *School of Athens*, conveys the plastic forms of the late 'teens, when it was engraved. That is, Caravaggio, no less than an artist like Domenichino, seems to have disregarded Raphael's earlier work in favor of those rhetorically dramatic late narratives. Secondly, Caravaggio's thinking turned to Raphael precisely when his lighter, early style, which had been developed solely for non-narrative subjects and had relied heavily on a Venetian-Lombardic genre tradition, became unsuited to the demands of his commissions when, ca. 1600, he was faced with the task of inventing *istorie* for the Contarelli and Cerasi Chapels. Thirdly, in each instance wherein Caravaggio apparently took Raphael as an initial guide, something went wrong. All three of the designs just cited were replaced with other, less Raphaelesque ideas. This indicates that during the biennium 1600-02 Caravaggio's art passed through what Hibbard perceptively called "a kind of High Renaissance crisis,"[36] when the painter struggled, not successfully at first, to reconcile his Lombard vision and still-limited experience with Central Italian principles of monumental history painting. To put it another way, for the first time, Caravaggio had to find a path to tempering mimesis with art.

Whether consciously or not, Caravaggio must have sensed the problem inherent in his earlier work, most of which contained no more than a single figure, and most of which represented half-lengths. The Bolognese painter Francesco Albani later put his classicizing finger on the problem when he said that he could not suffer Caravaggio's followers (astutely, he distinguished them from the master), because "although the mere imitation of nature is partly commendable . . . they present to our view a half-length figure and pass it off as a complete picture, thereby freeing themselves from the obligation of painting the thighs, the legs, and the floor on which it stands . . . and dispensing with perspective, with thoughts, with expression and — what I should have mentioned before — with invention."[37] By using the term invention, Albani evokes the Aristotelean notion of Imitation, that its first function is to convey a story with universal patterns of significant human thought, feelings, and action. This is what Poussin meant when he said that action "is by itself so valuable and efficacious that Demosthenes gave it the first place in all rhetorical devices . . . without action . . . lines and colors are useless."[38]

Such ideas had become commonplace in artistic thinking of the time, but certainly that does not mean that they were unimportant. Of further relevance for this inquiry is the critical-historical view of Michelangelo and Raphael that was forming in the later sixteenth century. In his dialogue of 1557, Lodovico Dolce has the Venetian, Aretino, tell the Florentine, Fabrini, "first, as to Invention, whoever pays good attention, and minutely considers the paintings of [Raphael and Michelangelo], will find Raphael to have most admirably observed every thing relative to this . . . and Michelangelo little or nothing." While conceding that "in the nude . . . Michelangelo is stupendous . . . no master ever excelled him," Dolce, like others, increasingly admitted that Michelangelo was a more limited artist than Raphael, particularly because he was wanting in action or, in literary terms, in plot.[39]

Caravaggio would have been familiar with such critical distinctions, and, in practical terms, I believe that he learned from the works of those Renaissance masters in distinctly different ways. Some of Caravaggio's evident borrowings from Michelangelo are worth recalling[40] — for instance, the influence of one of the Sistine *Ignudi* (fig. 46) on the *Victorious Love* (fig. 47), or Michelangelo's *Pietà* (fig. 48) on the Christ of the *Entombment* (fig. 49) — because they typically were emulations of isolated nudes. However, those models by Michelangelo, like Nature herself, could not have opened a path for Caravaggio to expressive *dispositio*, which, by later Renaissance standards, was embodied only in those examples of history paintings that had surpassed created nature in pursuit of higher truths. Faced with the task of designing *istorie*, yet unwilling to give up essential components of his Lombard training, Caravaggio attacked the problem of narrative art. He discovered a solution to the impass not only by studying Michelangelo, whose art, like that of Annibale Carracci, he surely admired and wanted to challenge;[41] but also by understanding the later Stanze and, above all, the *Transfiguration* (fig. 50), in a way that no Central Italian had done: more specifically, by seeing with a Lombard's eyes how Raphael himself, as

Kathleen Weil Garris most fully demonstrated, had met the challenge of Leonardo's art by adopting a late dark manner.[42]

Lomazzo, it will be recalled, grouped Raphael with three Lombards when praising strong shadows and relief in art. Already by 1518, in fact, Sebastiano del Piombo had singled out in Raphael's final paintings "figures as if they had been in the smoke . . . figures of shiny metal, all dark and all light . . . designed in Leonardo's manner."[43] Bellori relates that he and Carlo Maratta often heard Andrea Sacchi tell of how, after a trip to Venice and Lombardy, he feared returning to the Stanze, expecting not to like Raphael's color any longer; but that as Sacchi stood in the doorway looking at the *Attila* fresco — one of the paintings of the later Stanze — he was overwhelmed, finding there the perfect union of Titian and Correggio, and "il più degno colore di pennelli lombardi."[44]

It should be recognized that in the seventeenth century "Lombard" could mean anyone from the Carracci to Correggio to Titian and Giorgione, to those whom we now would designate as real Lombards geographically, i.e., that it could have the generic meaning of "North Italian," though always carrying with it the dual sense of naturalism and an art that addresses the relationship between chiaroscuro and *colore*.[45] This is what Federico Zuccaro probably meant to evoke when he remarked in the Contarelli Chapel that all he could see were "the ideas of Giorgione." Vasari himself claimed that Giorgione imitated oils by Leonardo that were terribly dark, and Zuccaro probably believed that such really was Giorgione's manner.[46] For our purposes, what matters is that Raphael's late style could have been understood by subsequent generations, from Lomazzo's to Sacchi's, as paradigmatically successful in preserving action and expression *without* sacrificing chiaroscuro, color, and the semblance of truthfulness by Lombard standards. Therein lies a key to Caravaggio's mature style.

If the historical circumstances have been sketched with sufficient care, it should be evident that the lower half of Raphael's *Transfiguration* (fig. 50), its classicizing structure notwithstanding, was the most significant pre-Caravaggesque painting in Rome. This is because there Raphael renewed in Central Italian painting "both Leonardo's structural and expressive innovations in the depiction of *historia* and his invention of the 'certa oscurità'."[47] Photographs cannot convey what now is so evident in the cleaned original, that the forcefulness of the Apostles, the possessed boy, and his family and friends is overwhelming, precisely because of the plasticity borne by the chiaroscuro. A series of comparisons between the way form is conveyed in the *Transfiguration* and in Caravaggio's mature works, particularly in the first *St. Matthew* (figs. 44, 51), the second *Conversion of St. Paul* (figs. 51, 52), the *Entombment* (figs. 53, 54), and the *Doubting Thomas* (figs. 55, 56), is striking. It cannot be a coincidence that every one of those pictures by Caravaggio was painted within a short span of time, from ca. 1601 to 1603, or 1604 at the latest, *and* that Caravaggio's most Leonardesque pictures — the Capitoline *St. John*, the London *Supper at Emmaus*, and the *Sacrifice of Isaac* — can be dated in precisely the same period of his career, just after 1600.

These evocations of High Renaissance models indicate that Caravaggio's Lombard background led him to discover in Raphael's art, despite its vast conceptual differences from his own, an unusual path to bringing *idea* to *natura*, which in turn reinforced in him Leonardo's heritage. Some of Leonardo's precepts still prevailed, however much Raphael's more modern prototypes interested him. One thinks, for instance, of Leonardo's notation, "historical pictures ought not to be crowded and confused with too many figures."[48] In certain regards, Caravaggio must have seen the *Transfiguration* as compatible with Leonardo's and his own ideas on conveying human drama. One recalls Vasari's words that Raphael, "after seeing the works of Leonardo da Vinci, who had no peer in the expression of heads of men and of women, and surpassed all other painters in giving grace and movements to his figures, was left marvelling and amazed."[49] Leonardo stressed in writing, and demonstrated in the *Last Supper*, the importance of forceful, unambiguous gestures, as Raphael did in the *Transfiguration* and other late works. Leonardo even called attention in his notes to the efficacy of showing a man "with his arms flung out towards the listener" (figs. 35, 36); "light and shadow," he wrote, "together with foreshortening, constitute the ultimate excellence in the science of painting." He recommended showing still other figures who are "silent and attentive, all looking at the orator's face with gestures of admiration, and . . . some old men in astonishment . . . with the corners of their mouths pulled down and drawn in, their cheeks full of furrows, and their eyebrows raised, and wrinkling the forehead where they meet" (figs. 56, 57).[50]

From their perspective of Renaissance studies, Kathleen Weil Garris and David Brown have both referred to the influence on Caravaggio's art of Raphael's renewal of Leonardo's style.[51] The common argument in our points of view is that in the *Transfiguration* and other dark-manner pictures by Raphael, Giulio Romano, and their circle, Caravaggio was forcefully shown how light can be used not only in the service of isolating beautiful parts of bodies and significant gestures, in the way Leonardo had done so seductively; but, more importantly, of how in history paintings light can simultaneously achieve realistic effects and dramatic unity.

On the basis of this historical and pictorial evidence, it can be shown that what we call Bolognese classicism and Caravaggesque naturalism had similar catalysts in crucial stages of their formations, despite their well-known theoretical differences, which in this paper I am accepting as understood. That parallel occurred because Caravaggio and Annibale Carracci each arrived in Rome steeped in North Italian traditions, one more Lombard, one more Venetian, and each then sought to temper a naturalistic vision through Central Italian models. While Raphael's importance for Bolognese art has been widely recognized, Caravaggio's encounter with Raphael has not, though it would be mistaken to give the narrow impression that Raphael was an exclusive formative source for Caravaggio by emphasizing here what has been neglected. Vincenzo Giustiniani, that perceptive collector and humanist, concluded that Annibale's *and* Caravaggio's mature achievements represented "the most difficult" of all styles, for in his letter to Dirck van Amayden of ca. 1620, he cites "Caravaggio, the Carracci, and Guido Reni and others" as practioners of "the most perfect method," which he praises and defines as that which "combines style with nature." Some artists, he writes, "stressed naturalism more than style, others style more than naturalism, without however neglecting the one or the other, as well as insisting on good design, true coloration, and appropriate and realistic lighting."[52]

Giustiniani was not insensitive to what modern historians emphasize as a Caravaggio-Carracci dichotomy, nor do I believe that he simply was promoting his protégé, Caravaggio, by assigning him to the highest ranks along with the Carracci. Giustiniani must have sensed in paintings such as those by Annibale and Caravaggio in the Cerasi Chapel (figs. 58, 59) comparable responses to problems of formal disposition, despite Caravaggio's obvious rejection of a classicizing *idea del bello*; and that, in profoundly important ways, both pictures couple North and Central

Italian attitudes. Like Raphael's late works, they seem timeless and placeless, despite Caravaggio's refusal to generalize from the particular, because actions in both paintings are symbolically, more than naturalistically, ordered. Certainly, this does not mean that Caravaggio shared Annibale's attitude toward Raphael in terms of classical imitation. Caravaggio's views must have been very different, and they indicate how he might have claimed to have rejected the Old Masters but at the same time been indebted to them.

It must suffice in this context to recall that a combination of Aristotelean and Hellenistic-Roman attitudes in rhetoric led to a Renaissance practice whereby praiseworthy models frequently were chosen to imitate. As Petrarch had written, "a proper imitator should take care that what he writes resemble the original without reproducing it . . . the similarity should be planted so deep that it can only be extricated by quiet meditation. The quality is to be felt rather than defined . . ."[53] That is, imitation is not copying, and it presupposes a disposition to conscious emulation. Throughout the Renaissance, as often has been noted, the issue was not whether to imitate, but rather who, and how. First, one typically selected the best models, then one reinterpreted them, and finally, if successful, one improved upon them. This is the method, or artistic attitude, that underlies the practice of painters of such leanings as Domenichino, whose *Last Communion of St. Jerome* was consciously designed in imitation — in the laudable, classical sense of the term — of Agostino Carracci's *Last Communion of St. Jerome*.[54] It is this artistic relationship, this tradition of imitation, that Caravaggio could have had in mind when he said, at least according to Bellori, that it was "the highest achievement in art not to be bound by the rules of art."[55] While we never can be sure of the precise meaning of that assertion, it would explain why one does not find Caravaggio deliberately using Raphael in the referential, apparent manner that Annibale or Domenichino did.

The modern formalist tendency to stress stylistic categorizations has thwarted discussion of Caravaggio and Raphael together, but such would not have been the case for Giustiniani, whose cultural matrix allowed him to see their works in a different light. It is worth citing the most germane statement I know by another Caravaggesque artist of the period, even though the specific words of the quotation, but not its meaning, are probably a later recollection. The Aragonese painter Jusepe Martinez visited his compatriot Ribera in Naples in 1625, when Ribera still retained strong

Caravaggesque strains in his tenebristic and naturalistic style. Martinez later wrote this about his interview with Ribera: "I asked him if he wanted to return to Rome to see again in the original the pictures that he had previously studied. He sighed a great sigh, saying, 'Not only do I wish to see them again, but also to study them again. For those works need to be studied and meditated on over and over again. Even though we are now painting differently, anyone who does not take these works as a foundation will end in ruin, above all in history paintings, which are the acme of perfection. The paintings of the immortal Raphael in the Vatican Palace teach us; he who studies these works will be a history painter tried and true'."[56]

*   *   *   *   *

Caravaggio's much-publicized wish to reject artistic authority could be explained simply through his interpretation and emulation of Leonardo's ideas on art and nature, combined with a strain of rebelliousness that seems to have been a part of the painter's personality. But perhaps Caravaggio's position can also be understood in the much wider context of the history of cultural ideas, since his rebellion against the necessity of subordinating the observation of nature to the imitation of preexisting models was provocatively echoed in arguments articulated by writers and scientists of his time. To put the matter another way, this raises the issue of Caravaggio's apparent wish to escape from what we call the Academic Tradition, though in deference to historical fact one should say from Aristotelean authority, or from the classical method of Imitation as practiced by the Bolognese painters and others, since the actual Academic Tradition was only then being institutionalized.

That wish was also at the core of contemporary literary and scientific controversy. As students of literary criticism know well, it was precisely during Caravaggio's youth that the first salvos were fired in Italy in what later, particularly in France and England, would be called the "Quarrel of the Ancients and Moderns."[57] Numerous interrelated factors stimulated heated debates over what constitutes legitimate genres in writing and their consequent forms, that is, to what degree ancient authority *must* determine modern practice. Caravaggio's boastful dismissal of classical statuary and Raphael evokes a view such as that expressed by Giuseppe Malatesta, who, in 1589, wrote this about modern practice in his *Della nuova poesia* . . .: "I should much marvel at you, that you should wish to attribute so much to the authority of the ancients, were it not that I see almost everybody lost in a similar error . . ."[58] Compare this view with one expressed about sixty years earlier by Marco Girolamo Vida in his *De arte poetica* (1527): "Hence on the ancients we must rest alone/ And make their golden sentences our own . . . Come then, ye youths, and urge your generous toils; / Come, strip the ancients, and divide the spoils / Your hands have won — but shun the fault of such / Who with fond rashness trust themselves too much."[59] Malatesta's modern rejection of such an attitude springs in part from his conviction that Nature changes, and hence that so, too, must the rules of art, since what pertained in ancient Greece no longer was necessarily relevant to later sixteenth-century Italy. For, if Nature did not change, if she were uniform and fixed, then the forms of the moderns could not improve on, indeed should not deviate from, those antique paradigms. However, if Nature changes, then the way was open to new forms, even to a notion of "artistic progress." A corollary of this literary debate, as Bernard Weinberg has written, is the placement of precepts in opposition to Nature, rules against talent and genius, mind and theory against the senses.[60] In each of these three pairings, the so-called "moderns" chose the latter alternatives: Nature, talent and genius, and the senses. And so, too, would have Caravaggio.

In 1581, eight years before Malatesta penned what has been quoted, Robert Norman published one of the most advanced views of his day by opposing ancient scientific authority.[61] Foremost, that meant Aristotle's *Physics*, which he found to be entirely incompatible with what has come to be called the inductive method. Francis Bacon's role in developing and establishing that view shortly later is much better known, and it is worth noting that Bacon's rejection of an unchanging universe was tied to a belief, not unlike Descartes', that man knows only what he does and makes; and that Bacon rejected the value of the imagination, scorning as "verbal philosophy" what for long had been the very heart of epistemological methods.[62]

Caravaggio maintained that art springs from similarly acquired data. "He never made a single brushstroke that he called his own," Bellori understood, "but [he] said rather that it was nature's."[63] Giustiniani reported that "Caravaggio said it was as much work for him to make a good painting of flowers as of figures."[64] And, in a passage already cited, Van Mander related Caravaggio's belief that "all art is nothing but a bagatelle . . . unless it is done after life . . . we can do nothing better than to follow Nature."

Viewed in these broader terms, Caravaggio's "High Renaissance crisis" can be seen as more than a simple challenge from artists such as Leonardo and Raphael, and as more than a struggle toward reconciling principles of Lombard and Roman attitudes. Caravaggio's uneasy confrontation was with the very premises of history painting and its close relationship with ancient authority and moral philosophy. His personal "quarrel with the ancients" went neither as far, nor as fast, as that of the writers and scientists of his time, even though he repeatedly transgressed basic standards of history painting, most notably the rules of decorum.

That the Renaissance tradition is essential to an understanding of Caravaggio's art is evident in his greatest pictures after ca. 1600, most apparently the *Entombment* (fig. 49), which the classicist Bellori liked most,[65] and some modern viewers tend to like least, because its disposition and demonstrative pathos seem to upset the attractive if misleading notion that Caravaggio's originality and reliance on nature are incompatible with a deep debt to earlier masters. The *Death of the Virgin* (fig. 60), completed in 1606, and the *Resurrection of Lazarus* (fig. 61), painted in 1609, are carefully built on classic, Central Italian principles of design, yet they ultimately depend on Lombard chiaroscuro for their relief and dramatic unity. As Caravaggio retreats from visual reality in order to transcend the incidental, a vocabulary of primary signs supports his momentous staging. In these and other late works, the emotive content is borne by highly calculated formal dispostion. In his last years, Caravaggio, like Ribera, became "a history painter tried and true."

Richard E. Spear
Oberlin College

Notes

1.   In order not to falsify the initial character of this essay, which was conceived and written as an illustrated lecture, it has been altered only slightly for publication, primarily through the addition of notes. Unfortunately but unavoidably, the visual evidence will be difficult to assess from small black and white illustrations.

2.   For the most thorough review of all formal borrowings, see Mia Cinotti, *Michelangelo Merisi detto il Caravaggio*, Bergamo, 1983. Additional links proposed by Alfred Moir, *Caravaggio*, New York, 1982, tend to be problematic (see Richard E. Spear, "Stocktaking in Caravaggio Studies," *The Burlington Magazine*, CXXII, 1984, p. 163).

3.   Roberto Longhi, "Quesiti caravaggeschi," *Pinacotheca*, I, 1928-29, pp. 17-33, 258-320 (reprinted in *"Me Pinxit" e Quesiti caravaggeschi, 1928-34*, Edizione delle opere complete di Roberto Longhi, IV, Florence, 1968).

4.   See A. Berne Joffroy, *Le dossier Caravage*, Paris, 1959, for an excellent compilation of the attitudes of Kallab, Lionello Venturi, Marangoni, Voss, etc.

5.   This was "his most striking legacy...to later Cinquecento painting" (Kathleen Weil Garris Posner, *Leonardo and Central Italian Art: 1515-1550*, New York, 1974, p. 31).

6.   Roberto Longhi, "Cose bresciane del Cinquecento," *L'arte*, XX, 1917, pp. 99-114 (reprinted in *Scritti Giovanili, 1912-1922*, Edizione delle opere complete di Roberto Longhi, I, pt. 1, Florence, 1961). Also, see Berne Joffroy, pp. 124-29.

7.   S. J. Freedberg, *Painting in Italy: 1500 to 1600* (The Pelican History of Art), Harmondsworth, rev. ed., 1979, pp. 359-81, 583-99.

8.   On Previtali, see Pietro Zampetti and Ileana Chiappini, in *I Pittori bergamaschi dal XIII al XIX secolo*, ed. G. A. Dell'Acqua, Bergamo, *Il Cinquecento*, I, 1975, pp. 87 ff.

9.   On Moietta, see Pietro Tirloni, in *I pittori bergamaschi . . .*, I, 1975, pp. 539 ff.

10.   On Stella, see Zeno Birolli, in *I pittori bergamaschi . . .*, II, 1976, pp. 173 ff.

11.   On Peterzano, see Edi Baccheschi and Maurizio Calvesi, in *I pittori bergamaschi . . .*, IV, 1978, pp. 473 ff.

12.   "Caravaggio Today," *The Age of Caravaggio* (exhibition catalogue), The Metropolitan Museum of Art, New York, 1985, p. 28.

13.   Howard Hibbard, *Caravaggio*, New York and London, 1983.

14.   In a forthcoming article that summarizes the iconographic problem and various earlier interpretations, Creighton Gilbert argues that the subject is the shepherd Paris.

15.   Giorgio Vasari, *Le vite . . .*, ed. G. Milanesi, Florence, 1906, IV, pp. 25-26.

16.   Vasari-Milanesi, IV, p. 25.

17.   Leonardo da Vinci, *Treatise on Painting*, ed. A. P. McMahon, Princeton, 1956, I, p. 161, no. 434; *The Literary Works of Leonardo da Vinci*, ed. Jean Paul Richter, 3rd ed., London, 1970, I, p. 229, no. 285; and *Treatise on Painting*, I, p. 75, no. 152. Also, see John Shearman, "Leonardo's Colour and Chiaroscuro," *Zeitschrift für Kunstgeschichte*, XXV, 1962, pp. 13-47.

18.   *The Literary Works . . .*, I, p. 213, no. 236. Also, see Moshe Barasch, *Light and Color in the Italian Renaissance Theory of Art*, New York, 1978, pp. 44-76, on Leonardo's interests in reflected lights and *sfumato*.

19.   *The Literary Works . . .*, I, p. 310, no. 506, and p. 371, no. 660.

20.   Cinotti, p. 242 (with further references), and Hibbard, p. 344.

21.   See Barasch, p. 194, n. 37.

22.   In *The Age of Caravaggio*, pp. 36-39.

23.   On Lomazzo's views on light, see especially Barasch, pp. 140-58.

24.   See especially Weil Garris Posner, pp. 13; 50, n. 8; and 71, n. 172, with further references; and Barasch, p. 164.

25.   Mina Gregori, "Note storiche sulla Lombardia tra cinque e seicento," in *Il seicento lombardo*, Milan, [1973], I, pp. 19-46 (with further references).

26.   On Cavagna, see Luisa Bandera, in *I pittori bergamaschi* . . ., IV, 1978, pp. 131 ff.

27.   Vasari-Milanesi, IV, p. 50. On Vasari's remark and Lomazzo's poem on Leonardo's chiaroscuro, see Weil Garris Posner, p. 50, n. 8.

28.   Spear, "Stocktaking in Caravaggio Studies," p. 165, and *The Age of Caravaggio*, pp. 60-62, cat. no. 5.

29.   Gian Paolo Lomazzo, *Trattato dell'arte de la pittura*, Milan, 1584, p. 237 (bk. IV, ch. xx).

30.   Giulio Carlo Argan, "Caravaggio e Raffaello," in *Colloquio sul tema Caravaggio e i Caravaggeschi*, Accademia Nazionale dei Lincei, Rome, 1974, pp. 19-28.

31.   Reprinted and translated in Hibbard, p. 362.

32.   See Cinotti, pp. 527, 530-31, and 596 for discussion and illustrations of the x-ray evidence. A less convincing source for the profile figure, a lost painting by the Cavaliere d'Arpino, has been proposed by Herwarth Röttgen, *Il Caravaggio, ricerche e interpretazioni*, Rome, 1974, p. 231 and pl. 64.

33.   Hibbard, p. 142, pls. 89-90.

34.   Hibbard, pp. 124-27, pls. 75, 77.

35.   Hugo Wagner, *Michelangelo da Caravaggio*, Bern, 1958, p. 25.

36.   Hibbard, p. 257.

37.   Carlo Cesare Malvasia, *Felsina pittrice*, Bologna, ed. 1841, II, p. 163 (transl. in R. Goldwater and M. Treves, *Artists on Art*, New York, rev. ed., 1947, p. 127).

38.   Reprinted and translated in Anthony Blunt, *Nicolas Poussin*, New York, 1967, I, pp. 362-63.

39.   Lòdovico Dolce, *Dialogo della pittura intitolato l'Aretino*, Venice, 1557 (anon. transl., London, 1770, excerpted and reprinted in R. Klein and H. Zerner, *Italian art: 1500-1600, Sources and Documents*, Englewood Cliffs, N.J., 1966, pp. 61, 65).

40.   Among other discussions, see Hibbard, pp. 149-63 *et passim*.

41.   For two very different views on Annibale's and Caravaggio's relationship, see Donald Posner, *Annibale Carracci*, London, 1971, I, pp. 134-38 (Caravaggio "forced Annibale into a polemical position from which there was no retreat," p. 138), and Charles Dempsey, *Annibale Carracci and the Beginnings of Baroque Style*, Glückstadt, 1977, pp. 85-86, n. 59 ("the mature style of Caravaggio is unthinkable without the precedent of Annibale . . . Caravaggio is the first, Ludovico only excepted, to have completely grasped the implications of the Carracci reform and then gone on to create his own new style from the basis of that understanding"). I do not mean to deny Caravaggio's probable benefit from the study of Annibale's art when I lessen its importance as seen by Dempsey and introduce Raphael's models as well.

42.   Weil Garris Posner (p. 51, n. 14, for a resumé of the earlier literature).

43.   *Il carteggio di Michelangelo*, ed. G. Poggi (with P. Barocchi and R. Ristori), Florence, 1965-73, II, p. 32, no. CCCIV. Also, see Weil Garris Posner, p. 14, for discussion of Sebastiano's remark.

44.   Giovan Pietro Bellori, *Le vite de' pittori, scultori e architetti moderni*, ed. E. Borea, Turin, 1976, p. 558.

45.   See the important discussion in Dempsey, pp. 25 ff. *et passim*.

46.   Hibbard, p. 112 and n. 8.

47.   Weil Garris Posner, p. 6 (with further discussion of Raphael's specific indebtedness to Leonardo).

48.   *The Literary Works* . . ., I, p. 340, no. 578.

49.   Vasari-Milanesi, IV, p. 373.

50. *The Literary Works . . .*, I, p. 344, no. 593, and p. 345, no. 594; and *Treatise on Painting*, p. 282, no. 840.

51. Weil Garris Posner, p. 42 and David Alan Brown, "Leonardo and Raphael's *Transfiguration*," Raphael conference, Bibliotheca Hertziana and Musei Vaticani, Rome, March 1983 (in press).

52. Reprinted and translated in Hibbard, p. 346.

53. Reprinted and translated by Thomas M. Greene, "Petrarch and the Humanist Hermeneutic," in *Italian Literature, Roots and Branches. Essays in Honor of Thomas Goddard Bergin*, New Haven and London, 1976, pp. 211-12. The bibliography on this tradition, especially in literature, is vast. Most recently, see Terence Cave, *The Cornucopian Text*, Oxford, 1979; Thomas M. Greene, *The Light in Troy*, New Haven and London, 1982; and David Quint, *Origin and Originality in Renaissance Literature*, New Haven and London, 1983, all with copious references.

54. See Richard E. Spear, *Domenichino*, New Haven and London, 1982, I, pp. 34-36, and Spear, "Plagiary or Reinterpretation?", *Art News*, LXXXII, 1983, no. 9, pp. 121-23; and Elizabeth Cropper, *The Ideal of Painting: Pietro Testa's Düsseldorf Notebook*, Princeton, 1984, pp. 122-28.

55. Reprinted and translated in Hibbard, p. 371.

56. Excerpted and translated by Brown in R. Enggass and J. Brown, *Italy and Spain: 1600-1750, Sources and Documents*, Englewood Cliffs, N.J., 1970, p. 180.

57. The classic studies include John B. Bury, *The Idea of Progress*, London, 1924, and Richard Foster Jones, *Ancients and Moderns*, St. Louis, 1961.

58. Cited and translated by Bernard Weinberg, *A History of Literary Criticism in the Italian Renaissance*, Chicago, 1961, II, p. 662.

59. *The Art of Poetry*, ed. A. S. Cook, New York, 1926, pp. 131, 133.

60. Weinberg, II, p. 988.

61. See the discussion of Norman in Jones, pp. 14 ff.

62. See the essay by Paolo Rossi, "Hermeticism, Rationality and the Scientific Revolution," in *Reason, Experiment, and Mysticism in the Scientific Revolution*, eds. M. L. Righini Bonelli and W. R. Shea, New York, 1975, pp. 247-73.

63. Reprinted and translated in Hibbard, p. 371.

64. See Hibbard, pp. 83-84 on interpretation of this passage, with further references.

65. Reprinted and translated in Hibbard, p. 366.

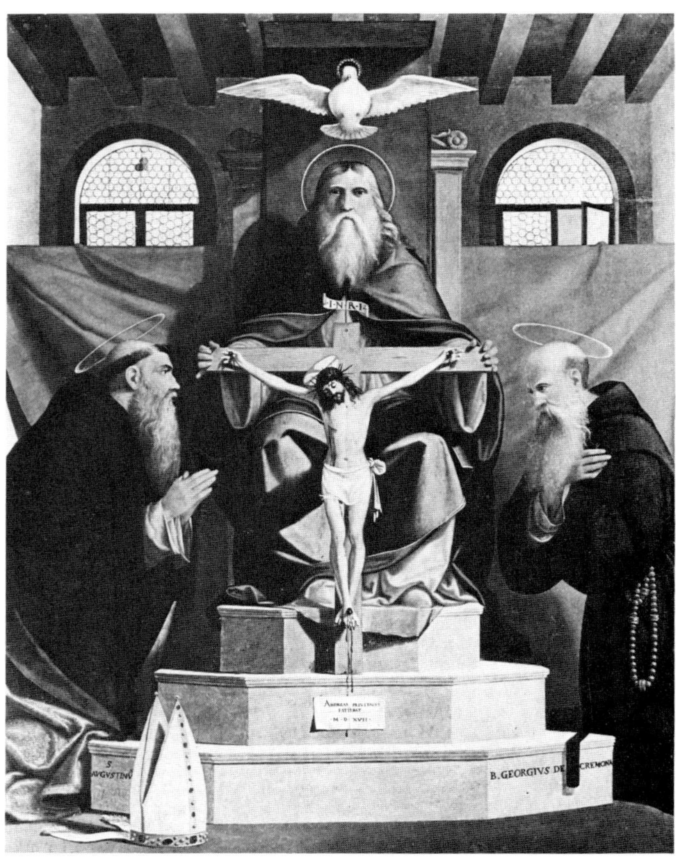

25.   Andrea Previtali, *The Trinity*, S. Nicola, Almenno San Salvatore (from *I pittori bergamaschi*, vol. I).

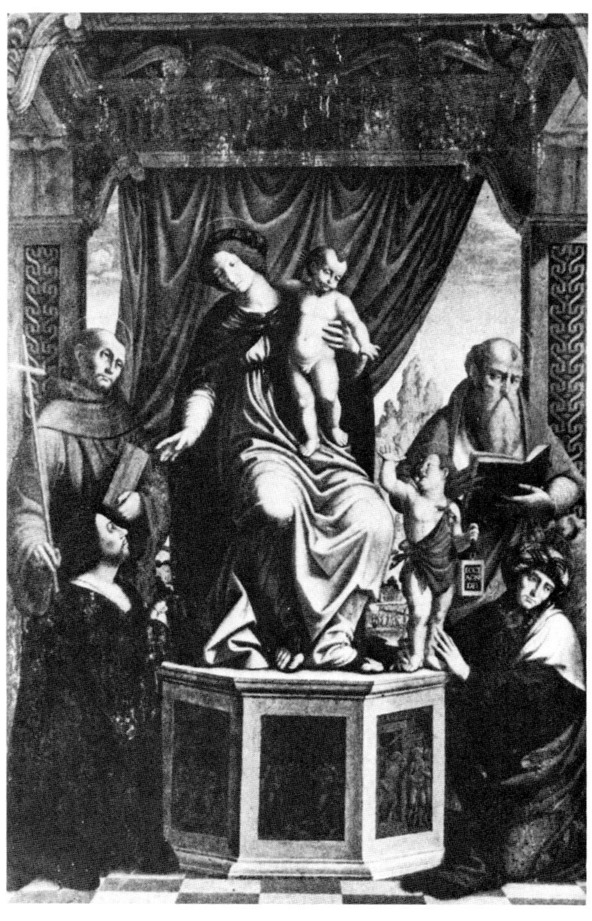

26.   Nicola Moietta, *Madonna of the Rosary*, Hospital, Caravaggio (from Moir, *Caravaggio*).

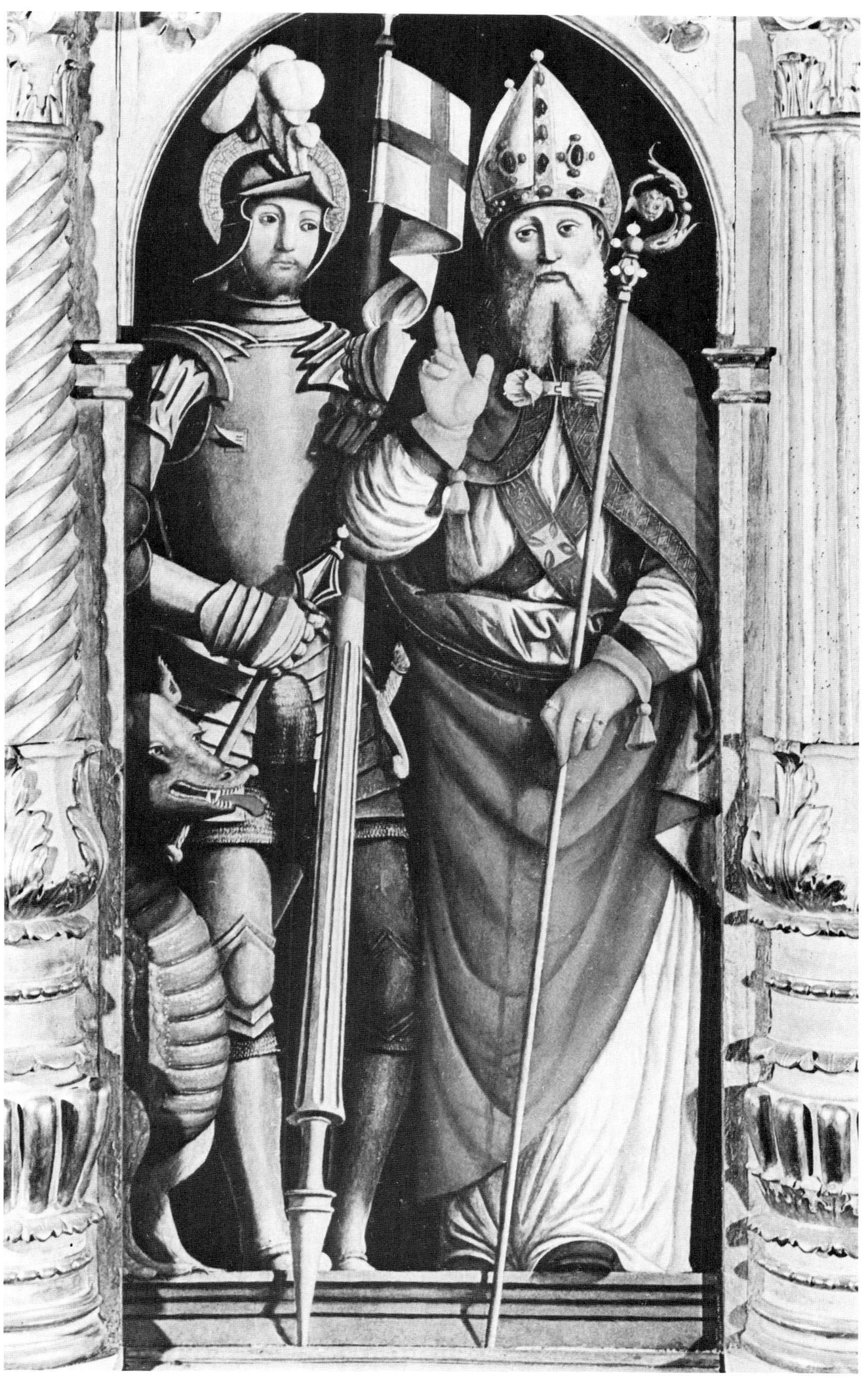

27.   Fermo Stella, *Polyptych of S. Ambrogio*, Omegna, S. Ambrogio (*I pittori bergamaschi*, vol. II).

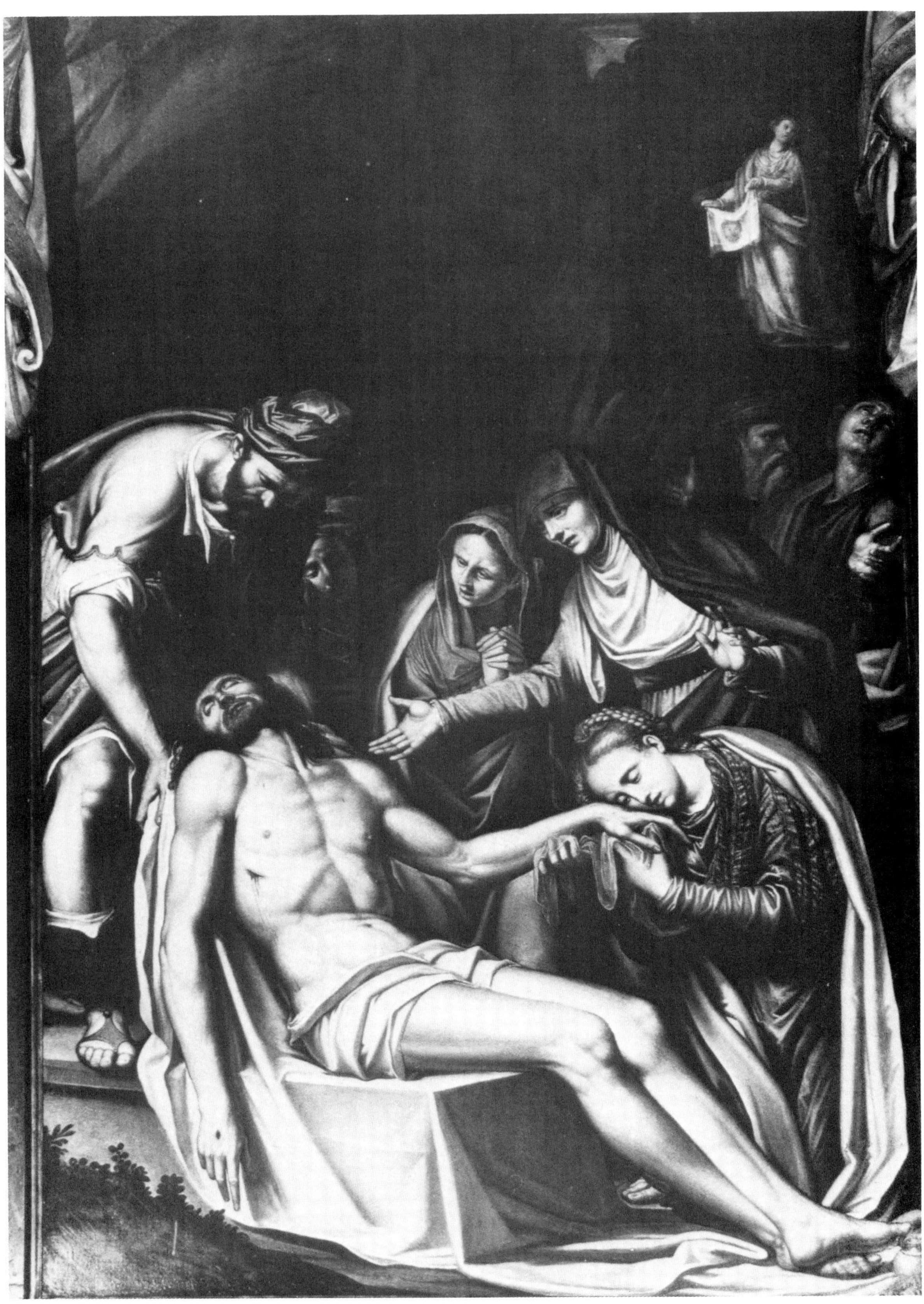

28.   Simone Peterzano, *Pietà* (from *I pittori bergamaschi*, vol. IV).

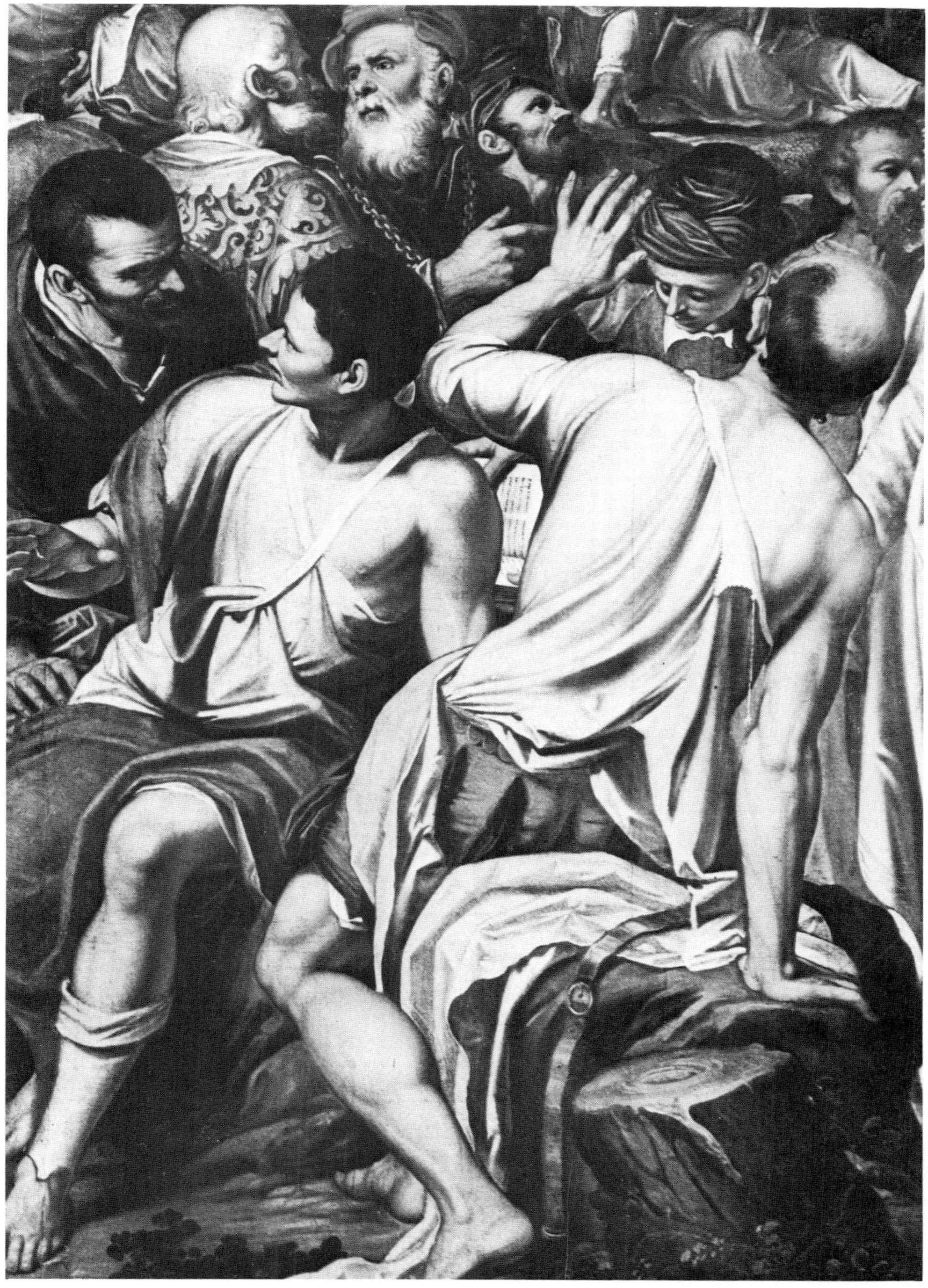

29.   Simone Peterzano, *Saints Paul and Barnabas at Lystra*, detail, Milan, Church of SS. Paolo e Barnaba (*I pittori bergamaschi*, vol. IV).

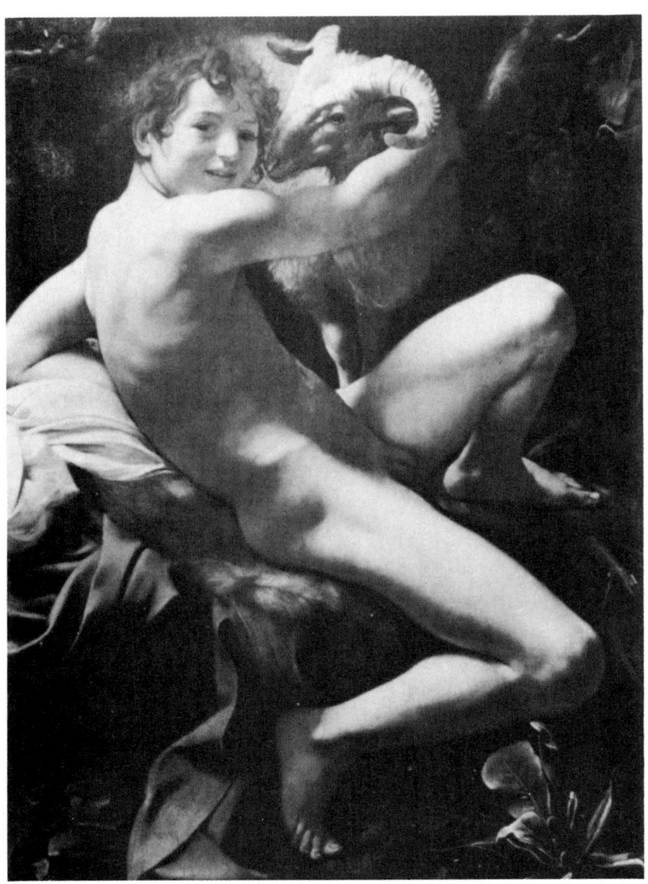

30.   Caravaggio, *St. John the Baptist*, Capitoline Museum, Rome (from Hibbard, *Caravaggio*).

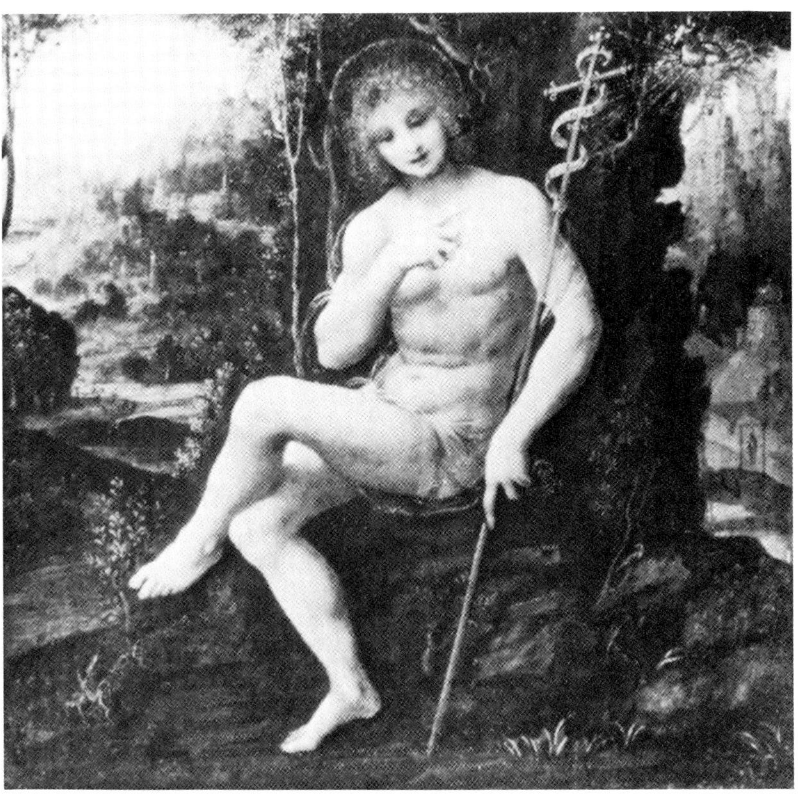

31.   Cesare da Sesto, *St. John in the Wilderness*, Edinburgh, National Gallery (loan; from Hibbard, *Caravaggio*).

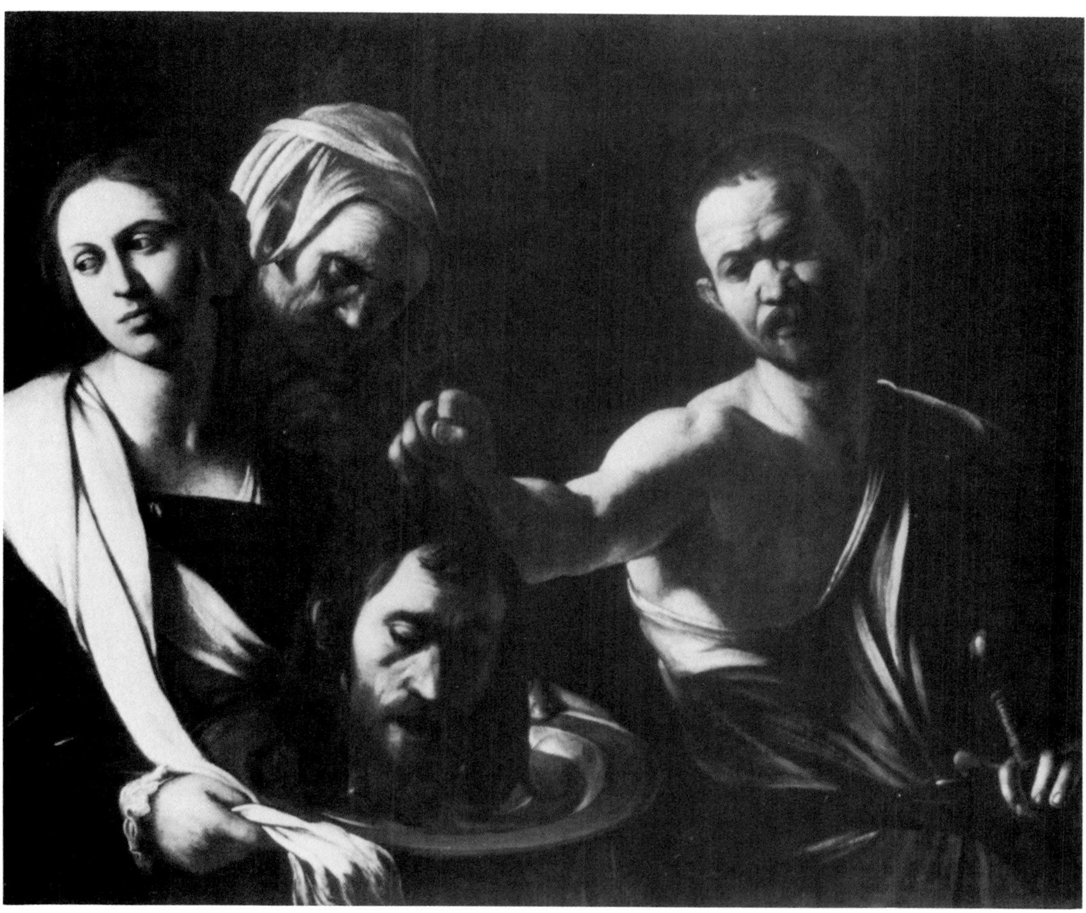

34. Caravaggio, *Salome Receiving the Head of John the Baptist*, London, National Gallery (from Hibbard, *Caravaggio*).

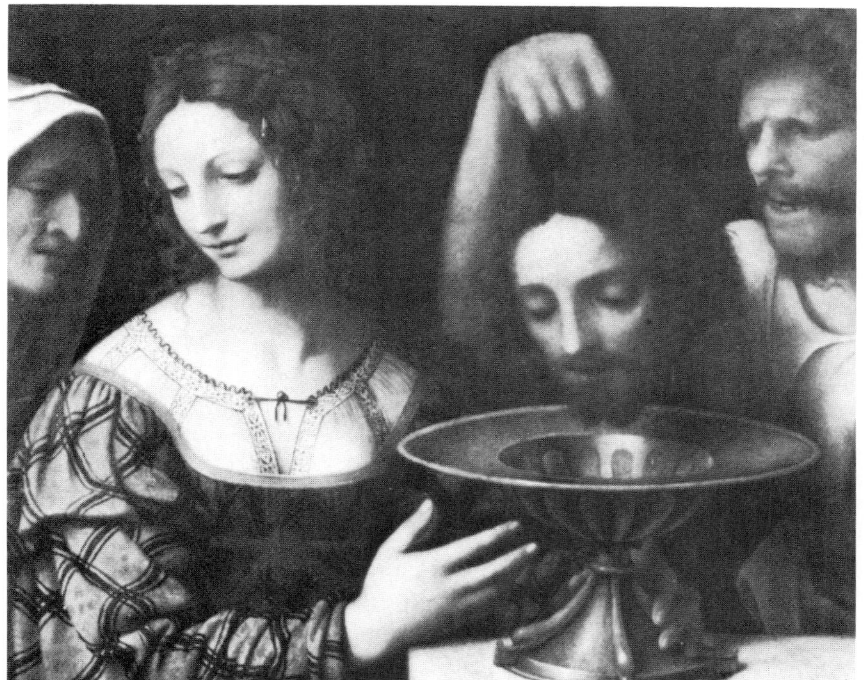

33. Bernardino Luini, *Salome Receiving the Head of John the Baptist*, Florence, Uffizi (from Hibbard, *Caravaggio*).

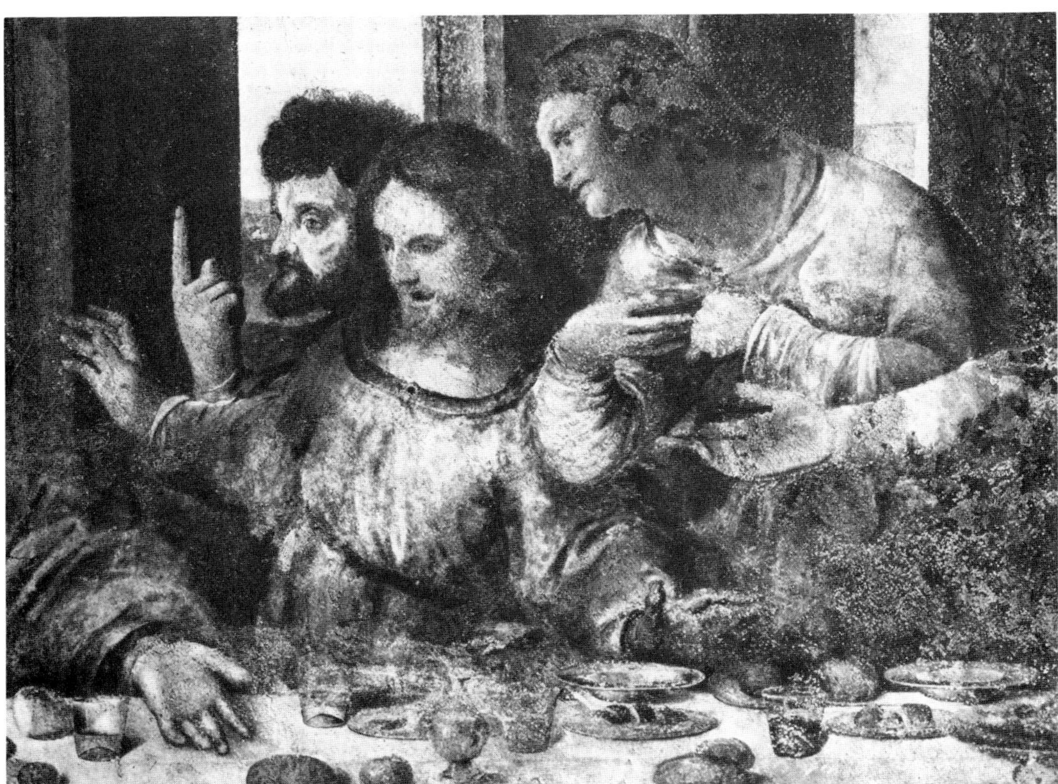

35.   Leonardo, *The Last Supper*, detail (from L. Goldscheider, *Leonardo da Vinci*).

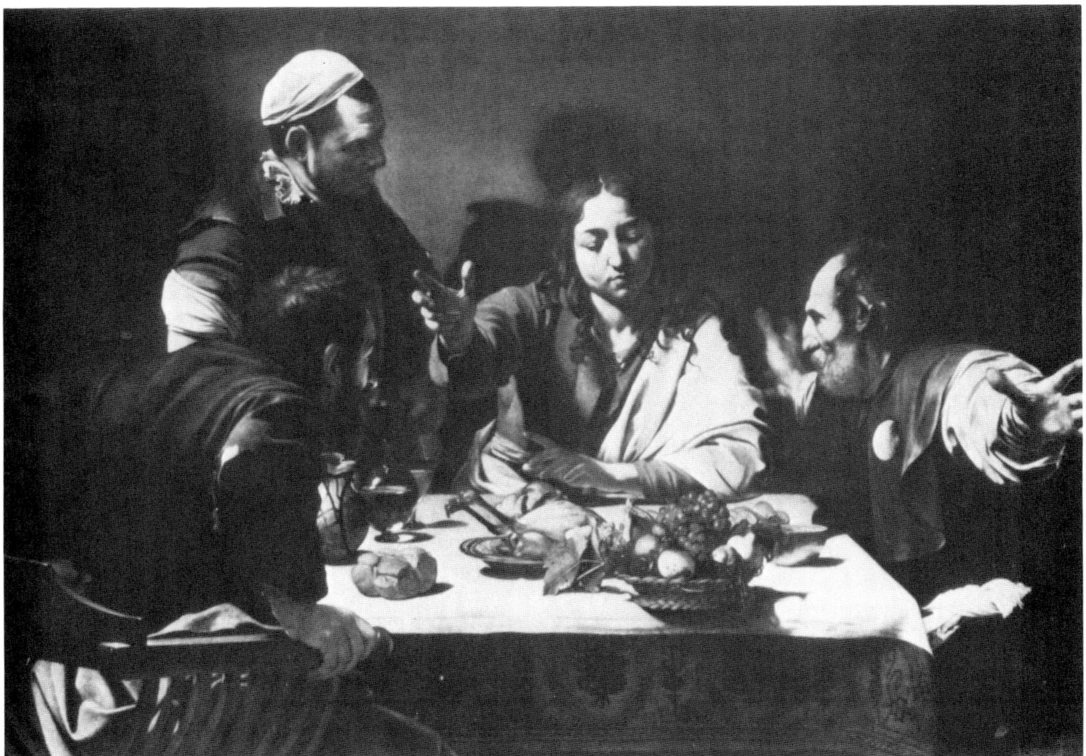

36.   Caravaggio, *Supper at Emmaus*, London, National Gallery (from Hibbard, *Caravaggio*).

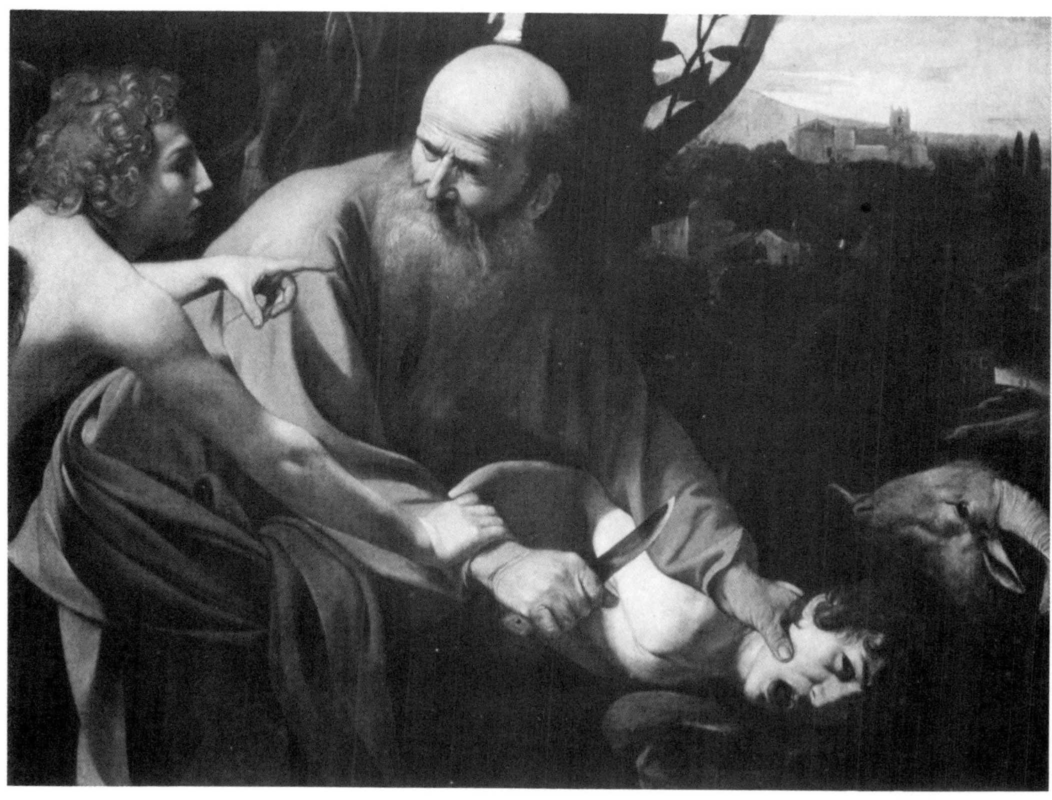

32.   Caravaggio, *Sacrifice of Isaac*, Florence, Uffizi (from Hibbard, *Caravaggio*).

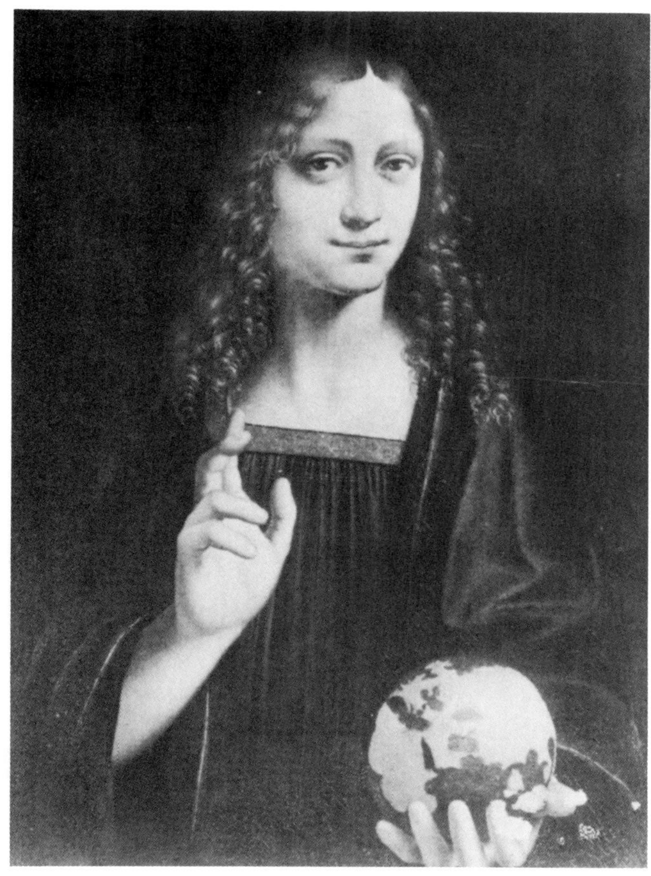

37.   Marco d'Oggiono, *Salvator Mundi*,
        Rome, Galleria Borghese (from
        Hibbard,   *Caravaggio*).

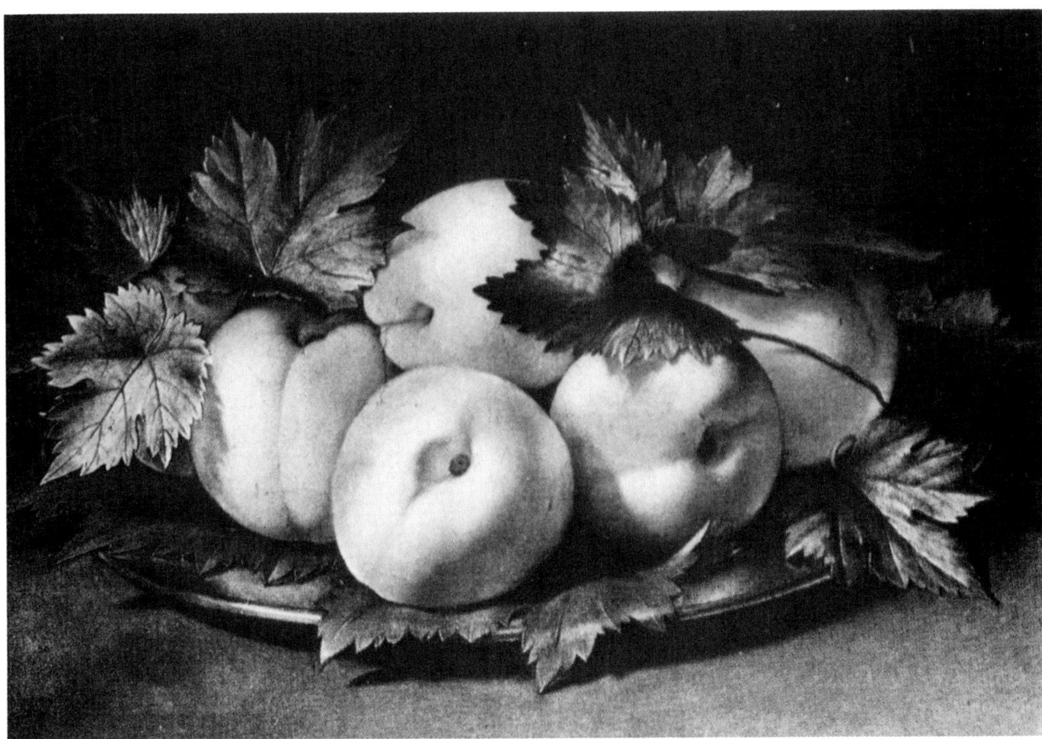

38.   Ambrogio Figino, *Still Life with Peaches*, Lorenzelli Collection (from J. Spike, *Italian Still Life Painting*).

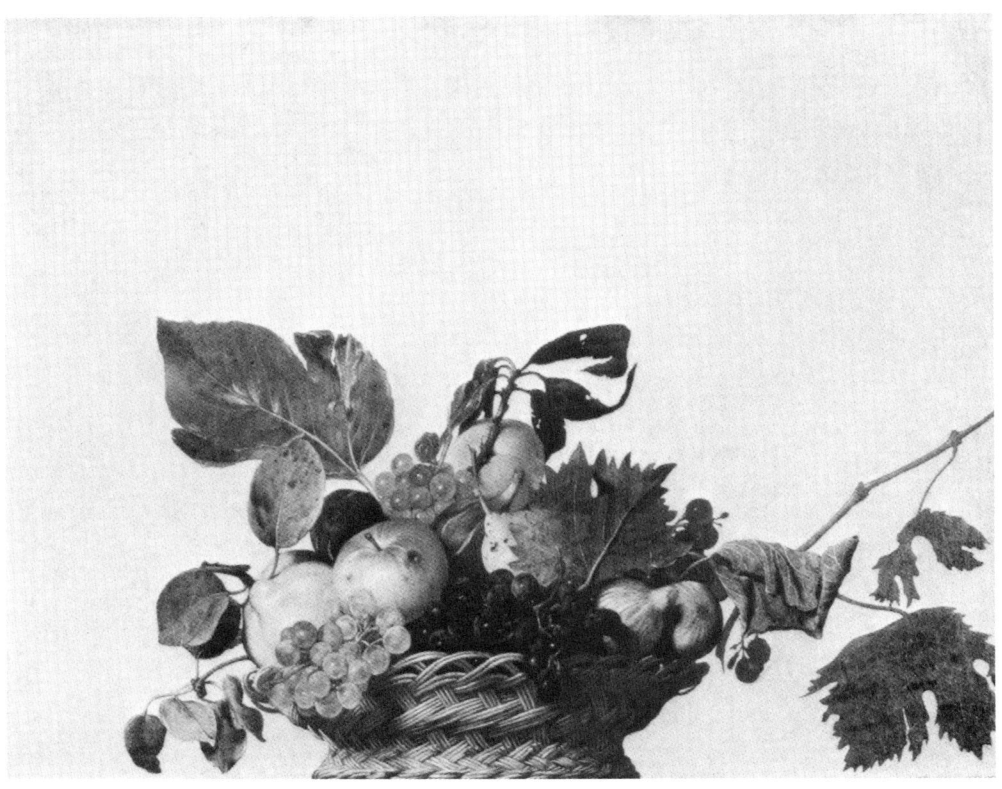

40.   Caravaggio, *Still Life*, Pinacoteca Ambrosiana, Milan (from *The Age of Caravaggio*).

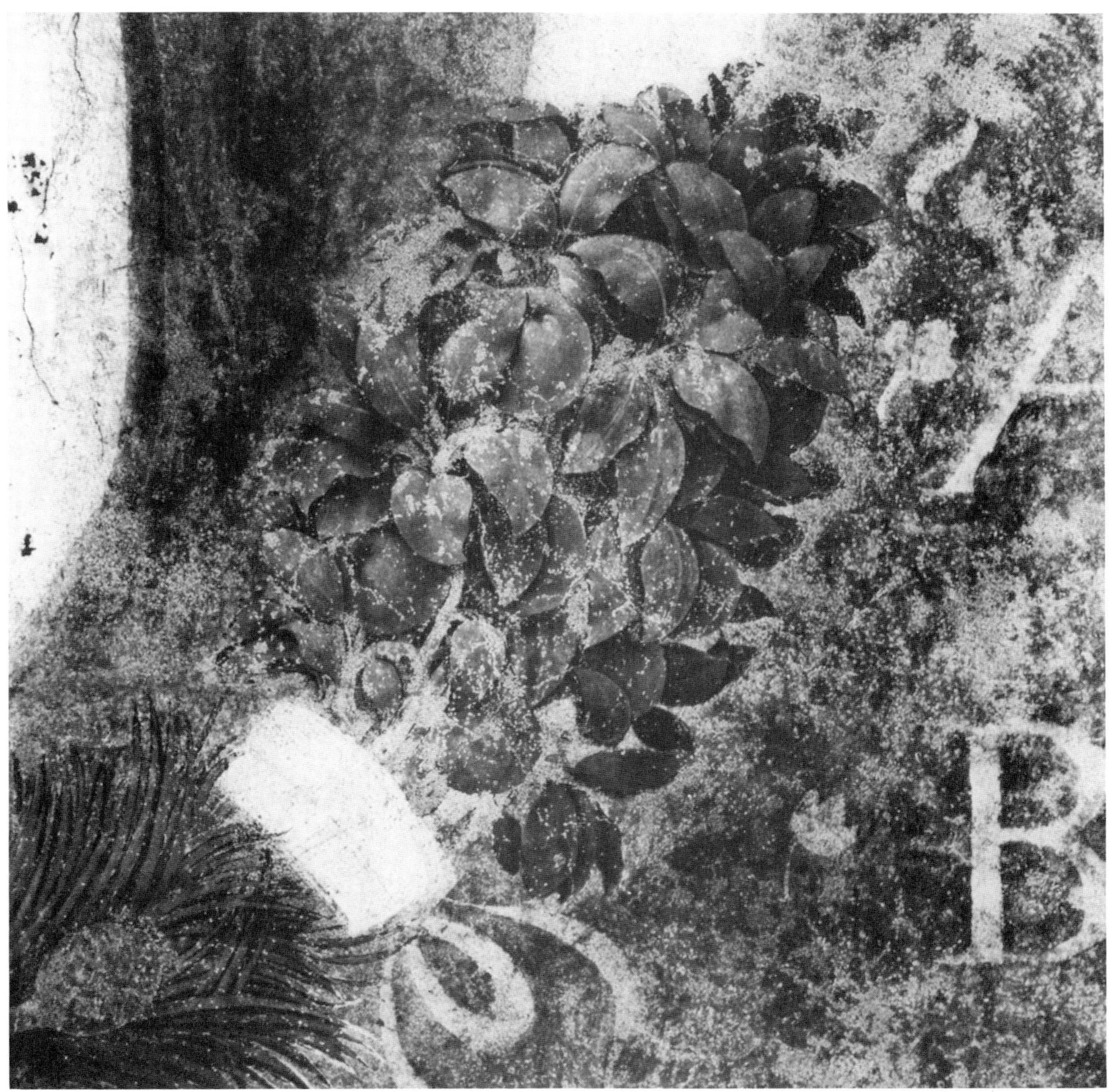

39.   Leonardo, *Last Supper*, detail of lunette on the right above the painting, (from D. A. Brown, *Leonando's Last Supper: The Restoration*).

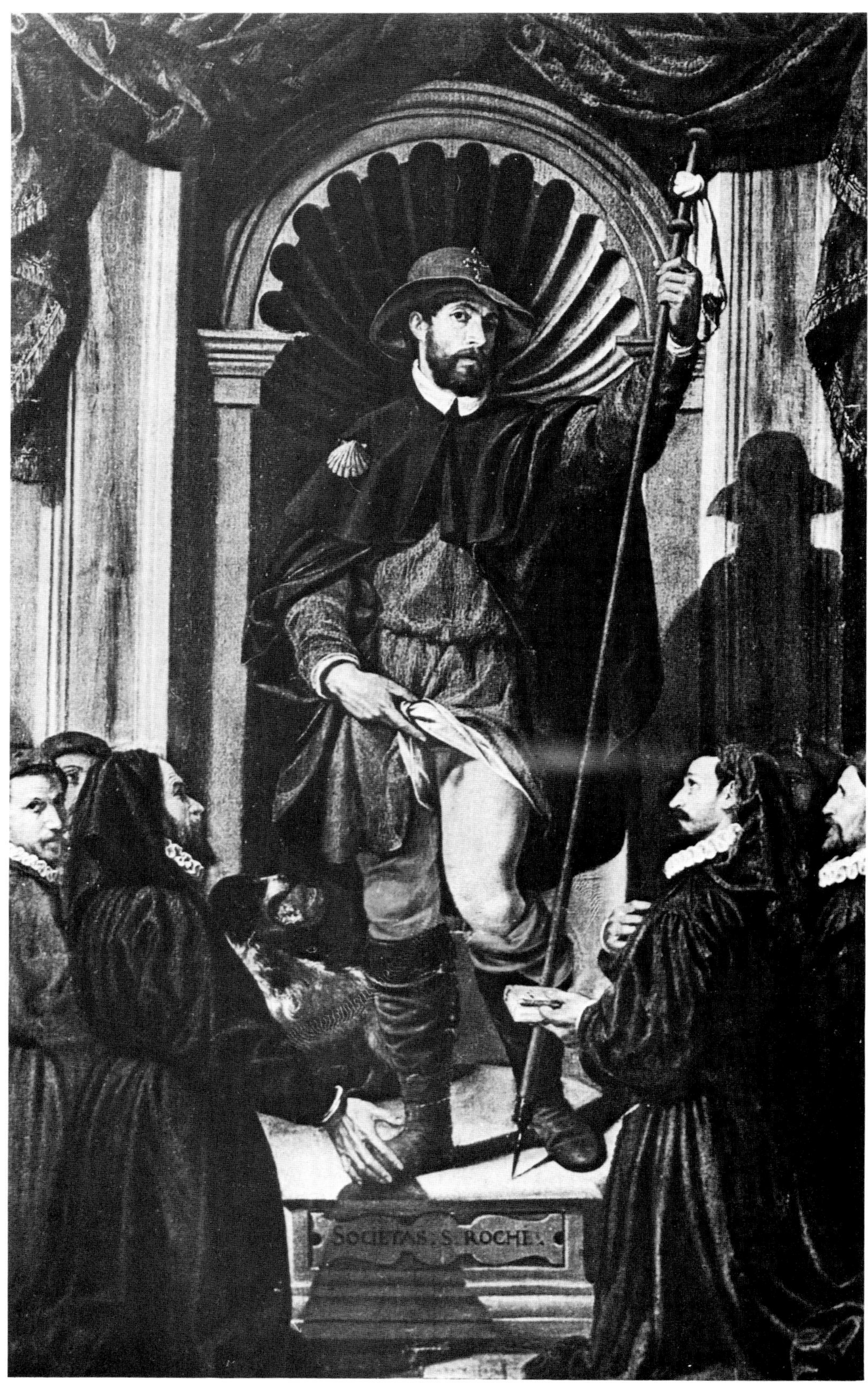

41.   Paolo Cavagna, *San Rocco*, Church of S. Rocco, Bergamo (*I pittori bergamaschi*, vol. IV).

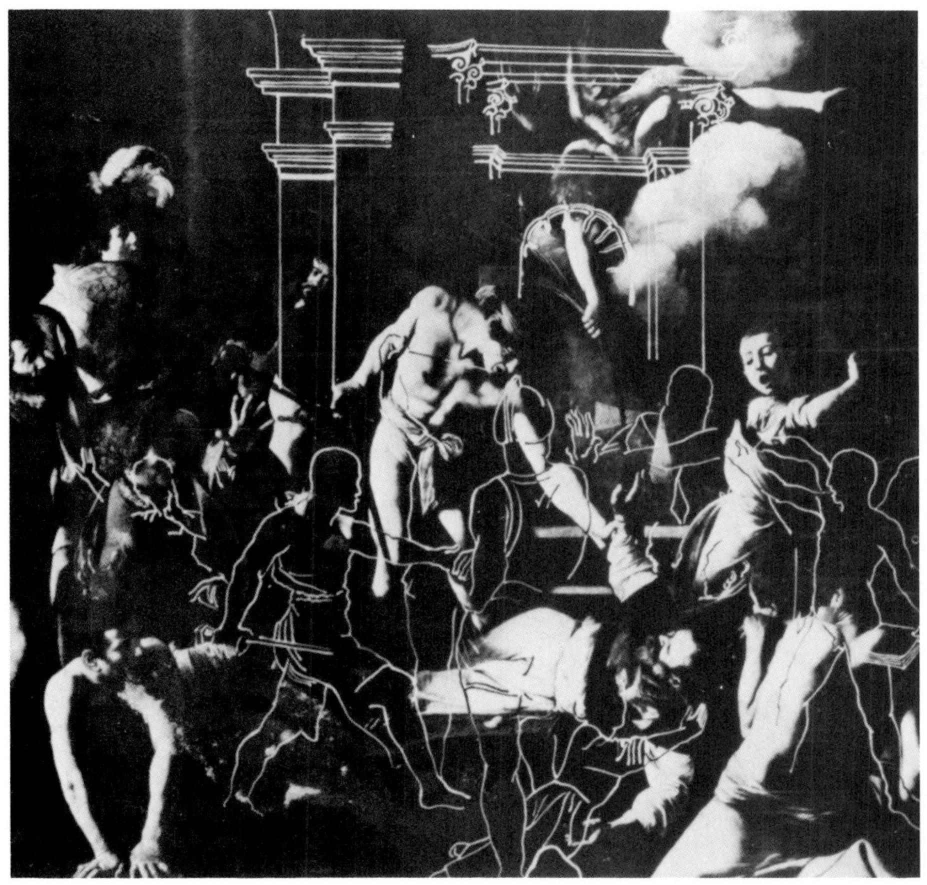

42.   Caravaggio, X-Ray of the *Martyrdom of St. Matthew,* Contarelli Chapel, S. Luigi dei Francesi, Rome (from Hibbard, *Caravaggio*).

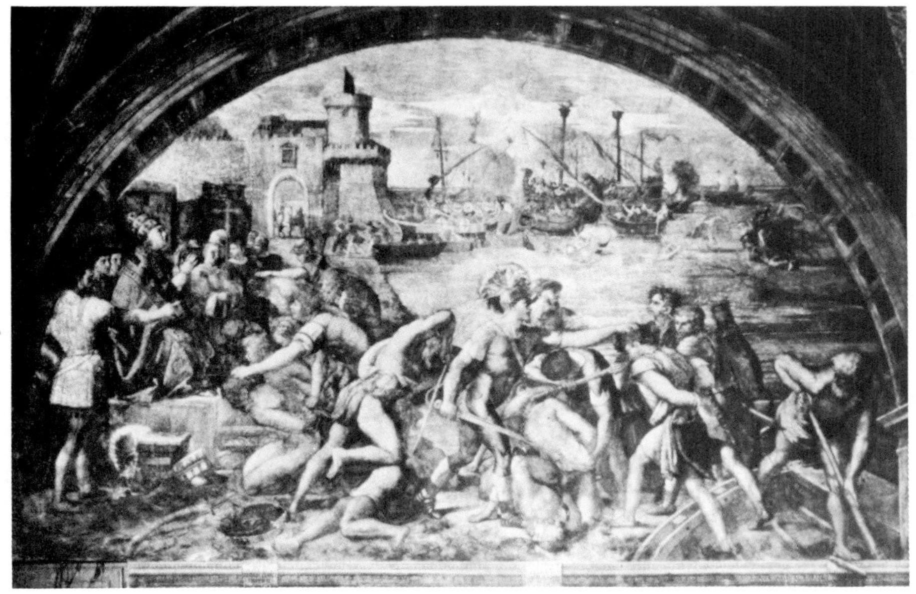

43.   Raphael, *The Battle of Ostia*, Vatican, Stanza dell' Incendio (from Dussler, *Raphael*).

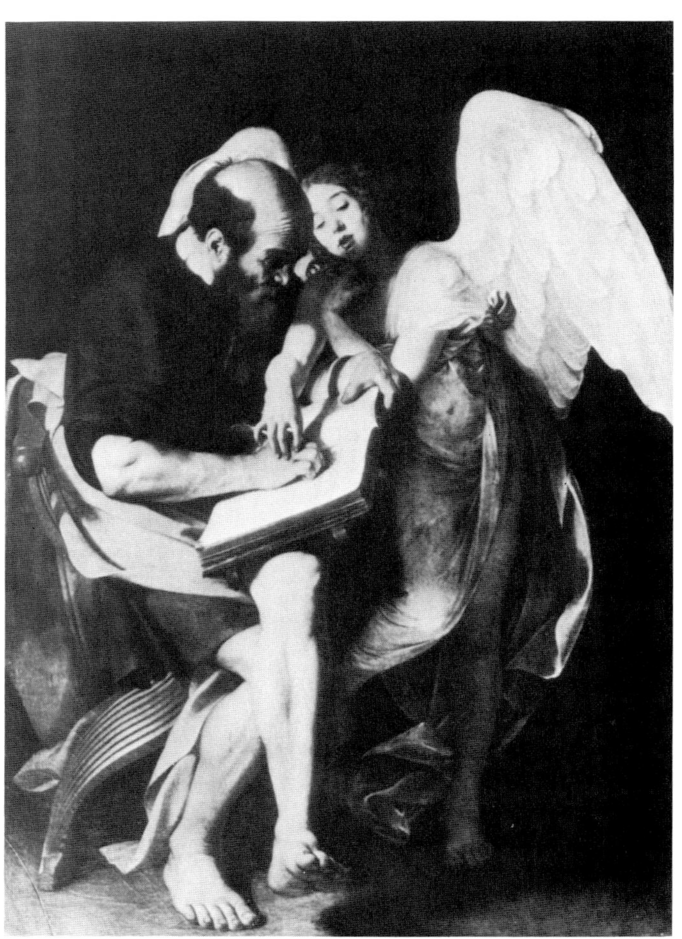

44.   Caravaggio, *St. Matthew and the Angel*, destroyed
(from Hibbard, *Caravaggio*).

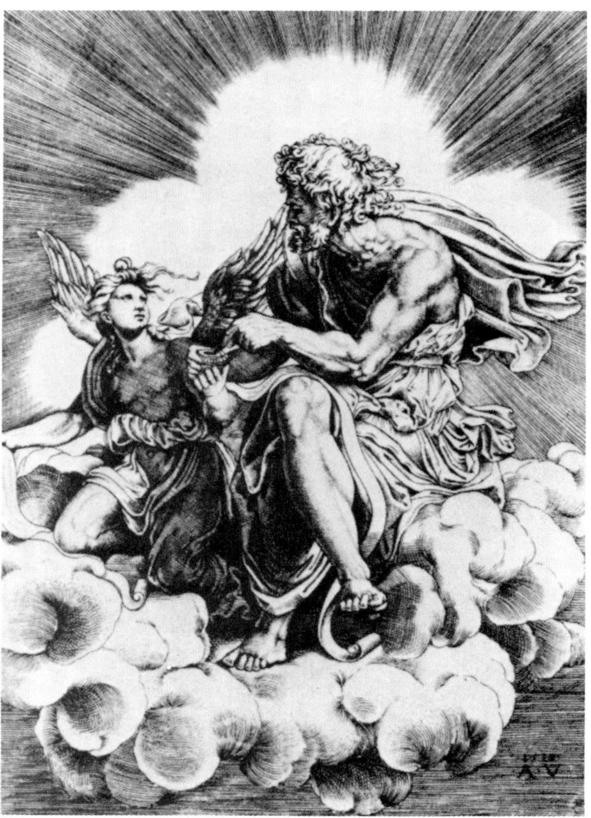

45.   Agostino Veneziano after Raphael, *Inspiration of
St. Matthew*, 1518 (from Hibbard, *Caravaggio*).

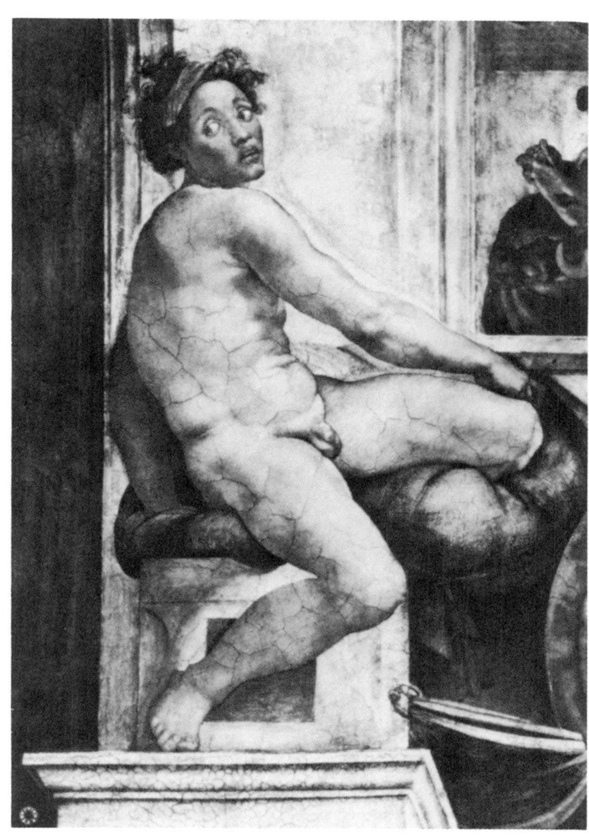

46.   Michelangelo, *Ignudo,* Sistine Chapel Ceiling, Rome (from Hibbard, *Caravaggio).*

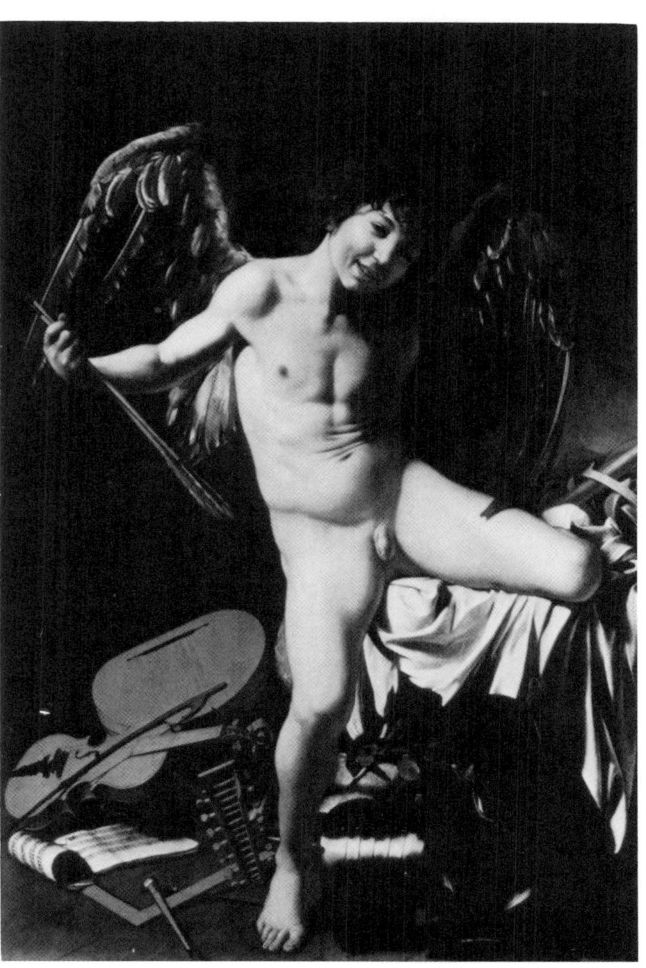

47.   Caravaggio, *Victorious Love*, Berlin, Staatliche Museen (from Hibbard, *Caravaggio*).

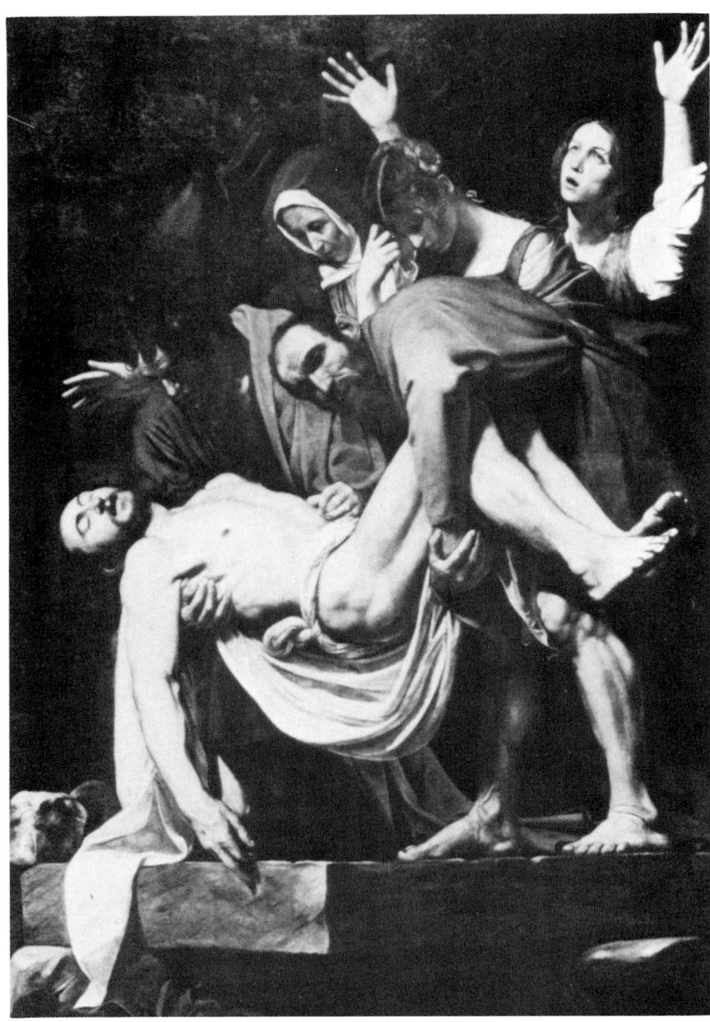

49.   Caravaggio, *Entombment of Christ*, Rome, Vatican Museums (from Hibbard, *Caravaggio*).

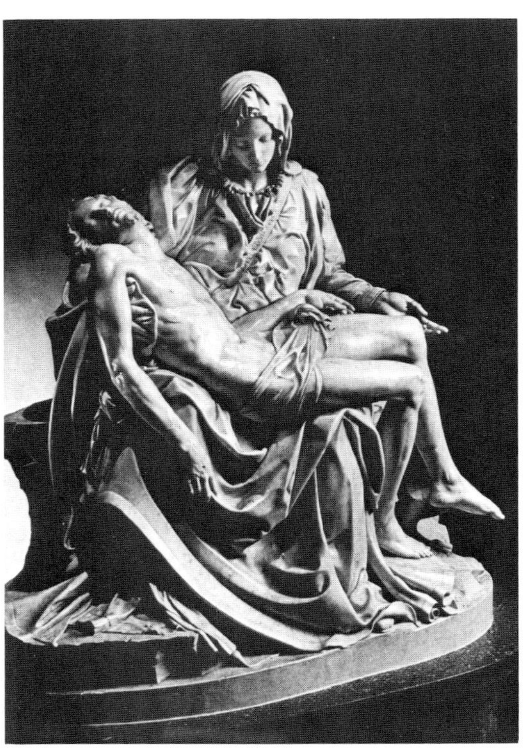

48.   Michelangelo, *Pietá*, Rome, St. Peter's (Alinari).

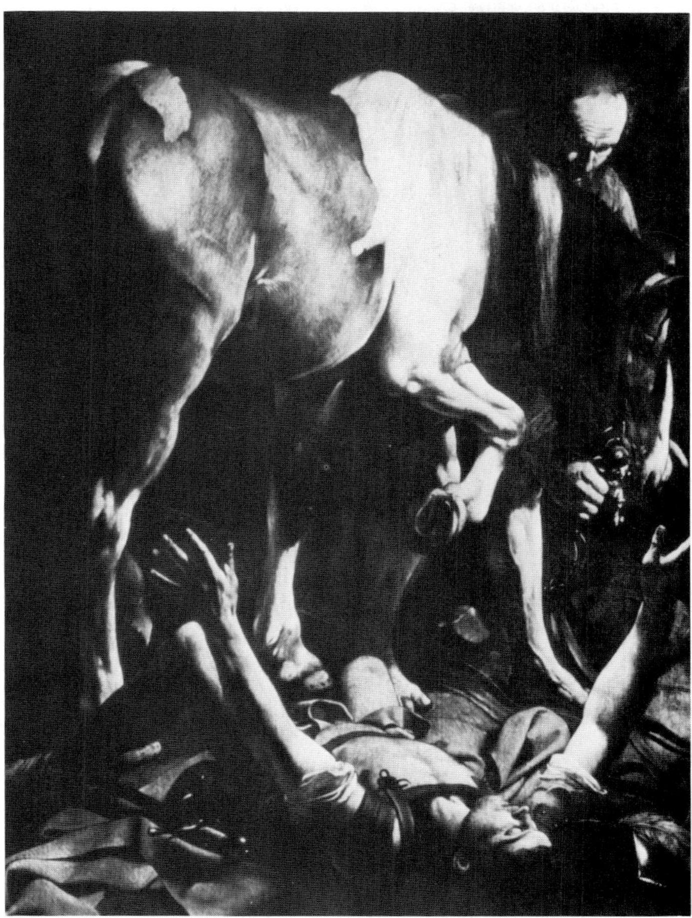

52.   Caravaggio, *Conversion of St. Paul*, Rome,
S. Maria del Popolo, Cerasi Chapel (from
Hibbard, *Caravaggio*).

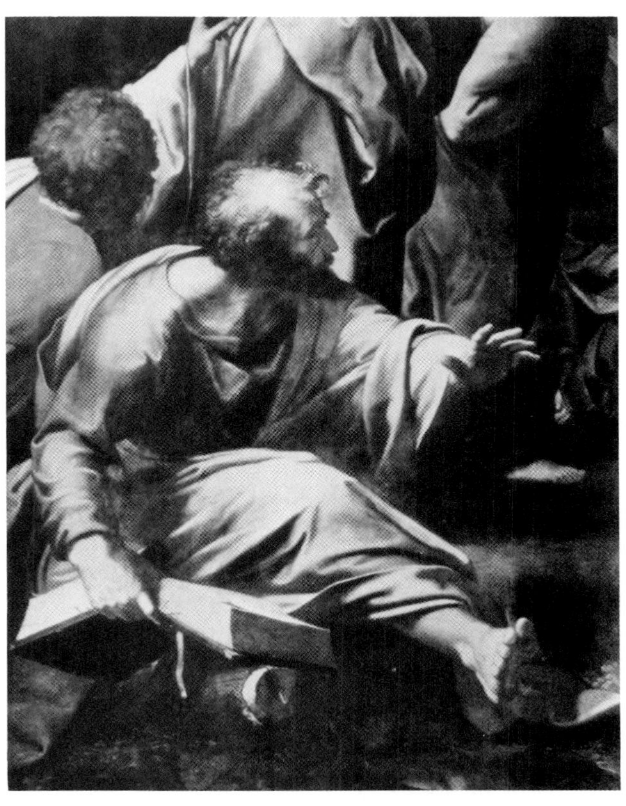

51.   Raphael, *Transfiguration*, detail.

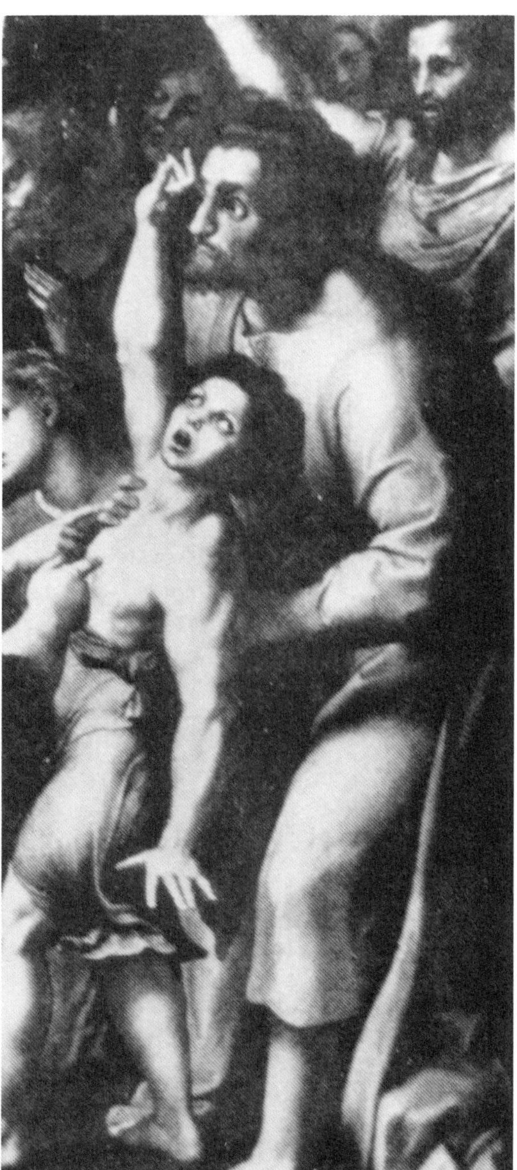

53.   Raphael, *Transfiguration*, detail.

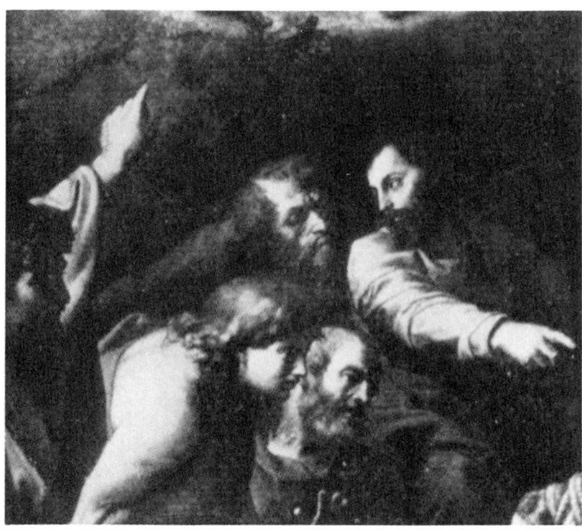

55.   Raphael, *Transfiguration*, detail.

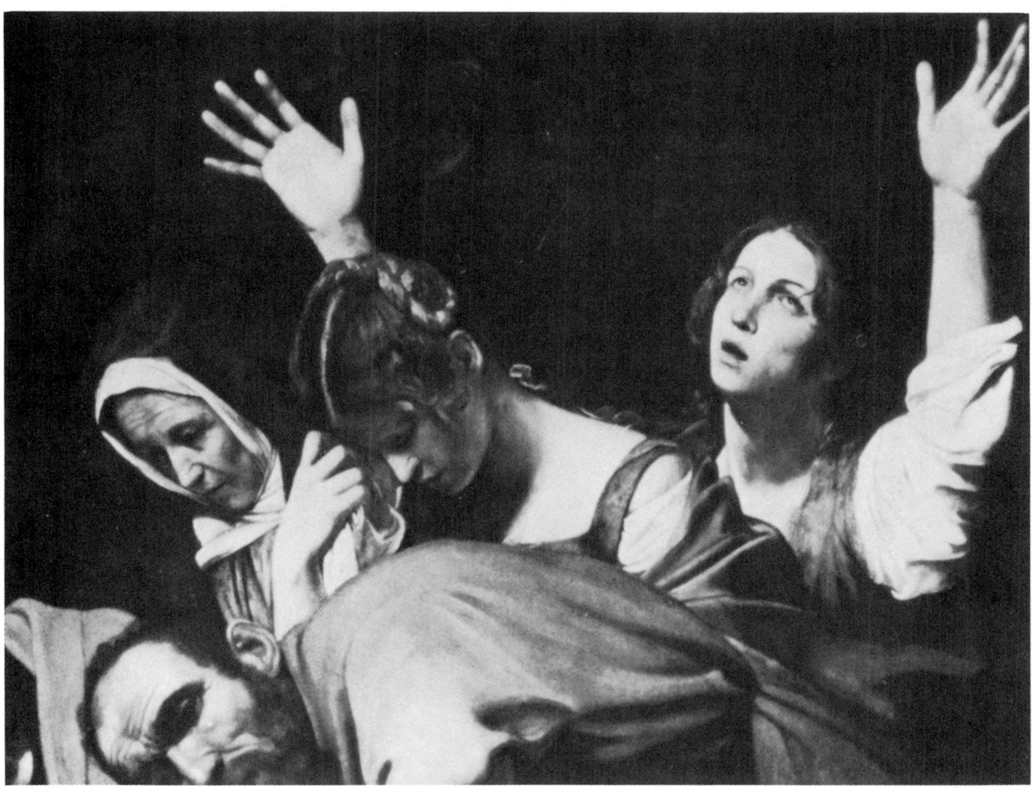

54.   Caravaggio, *Entombment of Christ*, detail, Rome, Vatican Museums (from Hibbard, *Caravaggio*).

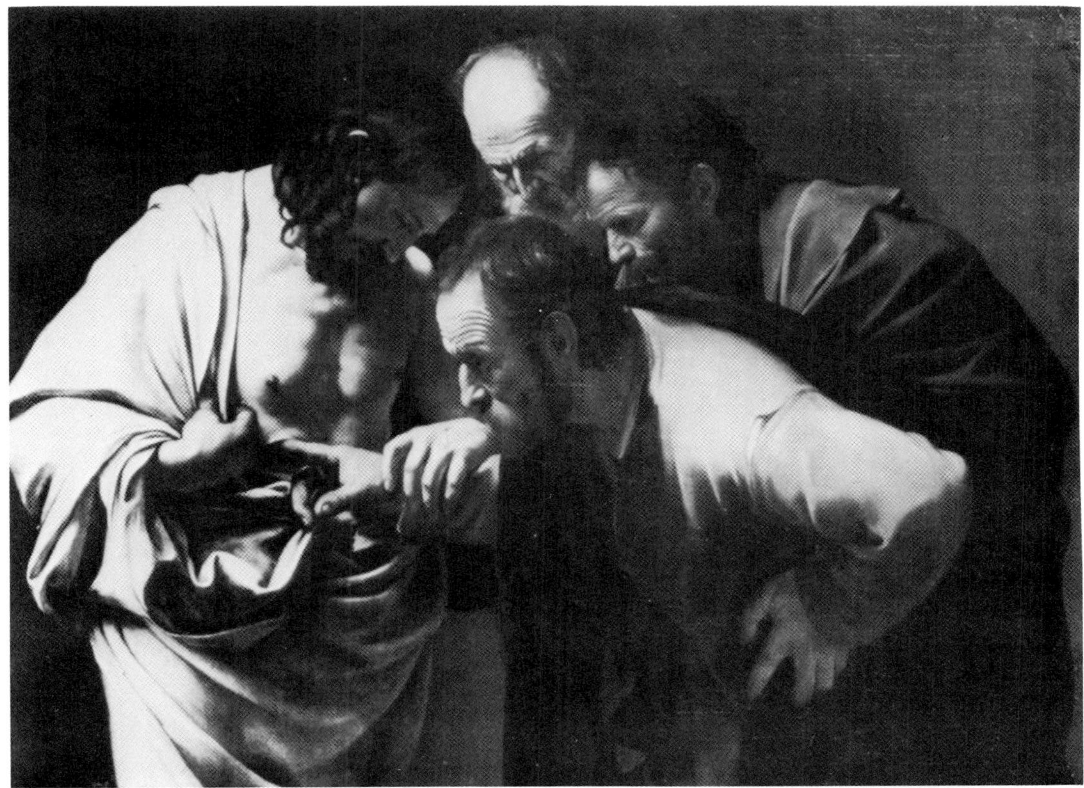

56.   Caravaggio, *Doubting Thomas*, Potsdam, Staatliche Schlösser und Garten (from Hibbard, *Caravaggio*).

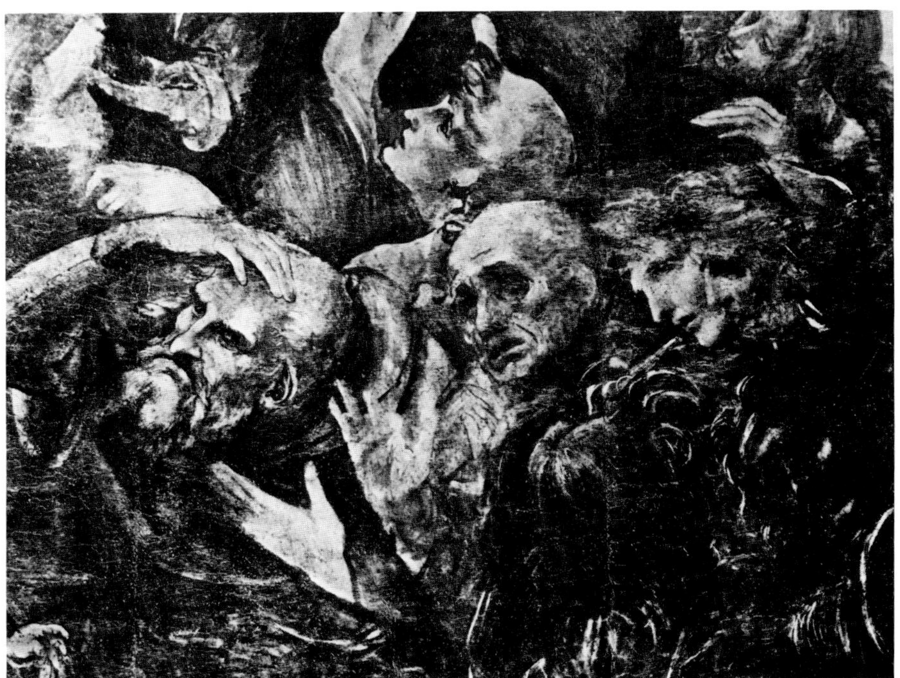

57.   Leonardo, detail from the *Treatise on Painting* (from L. Goldscheider, *Leonardo da Vinci*).

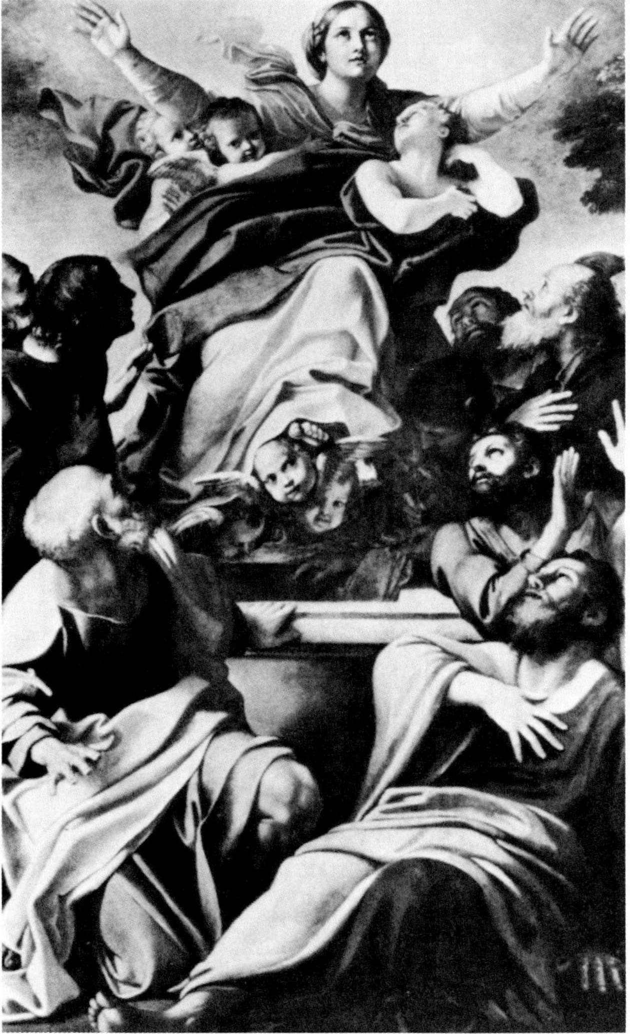

58.   Annibale Carracci, *Assumption of the Virgin*, Rome, S. Maria del Popolo, Cerasi Chapel (from Hibbard, *Caravaggio*).

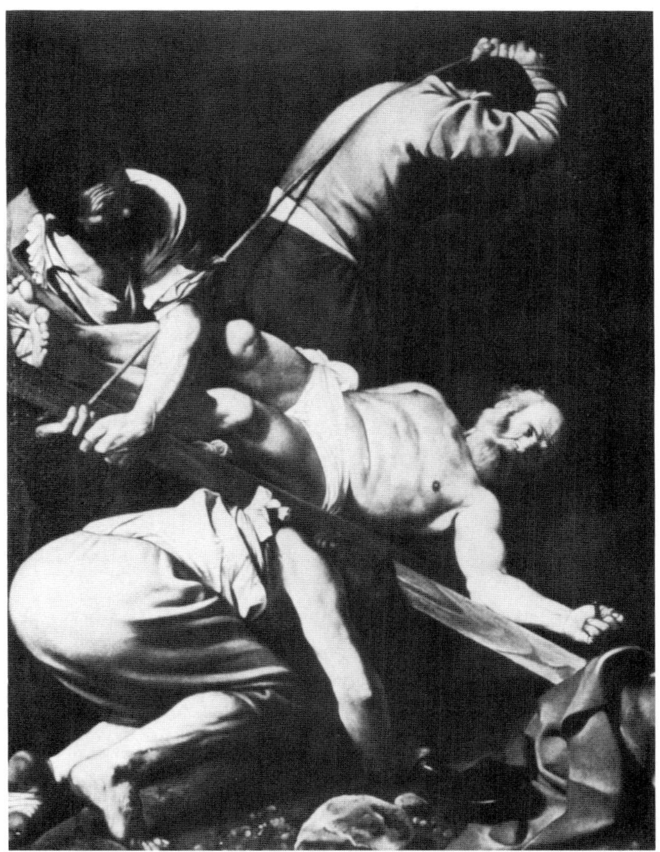

59.   Caravaggio, *Crucifixion of St. Peter*, Rome,
       S. Maria del Popolo, Cerasi Chapel (from
       Hibbard, *Caravaggio*).

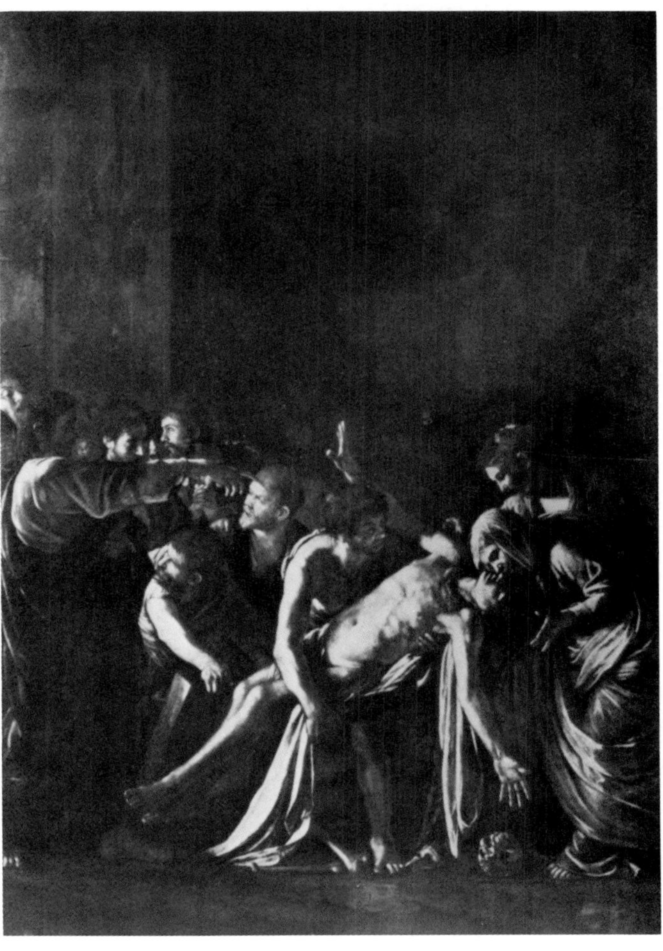

61.   Caravaggio, *Resurrection of Lazarus*, Messina,
       National Museum (from Hibbard, *Caravaggio*).

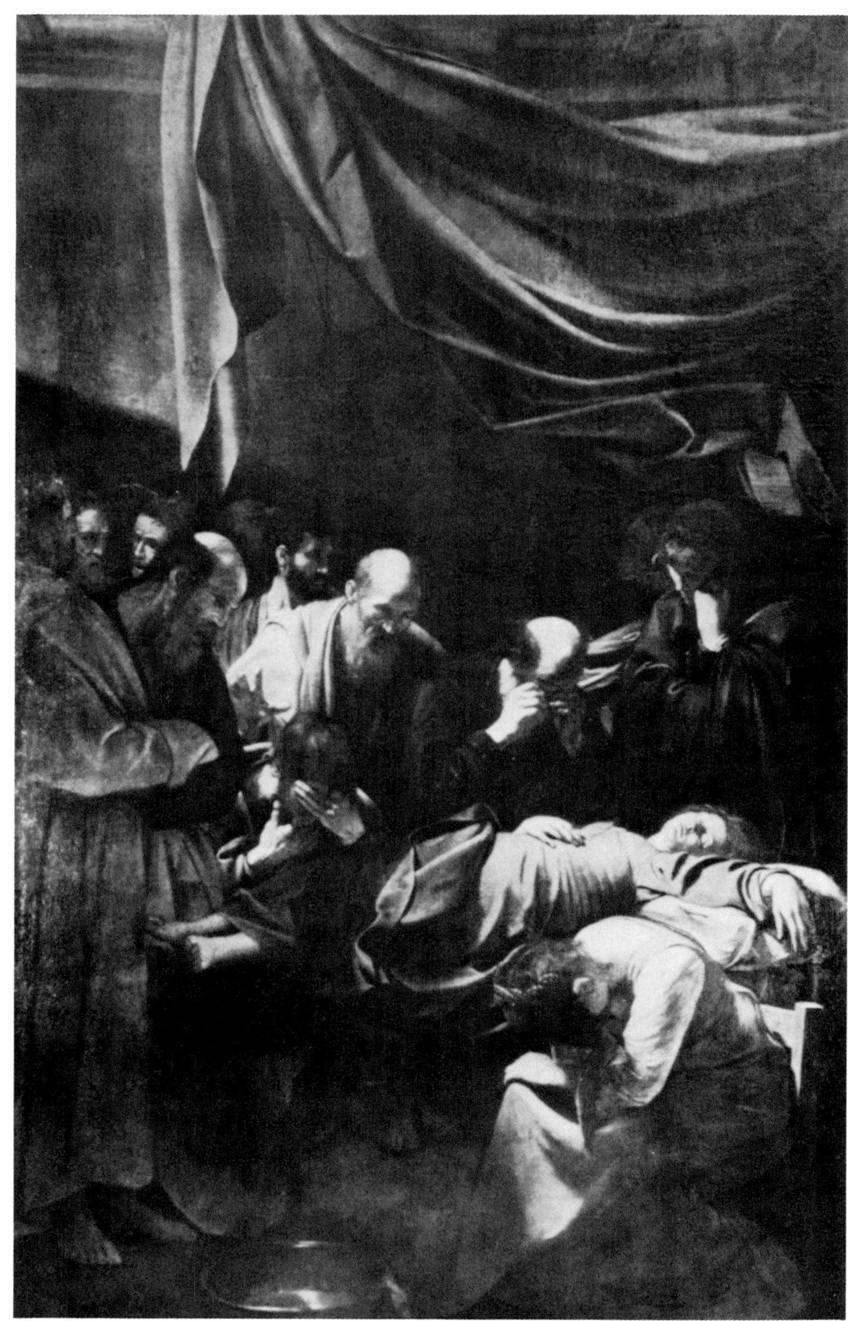

60.   Caravaggio, *Death of the Virgin*, Paris, Louvre (from Hibbard, *Caravaggio*).

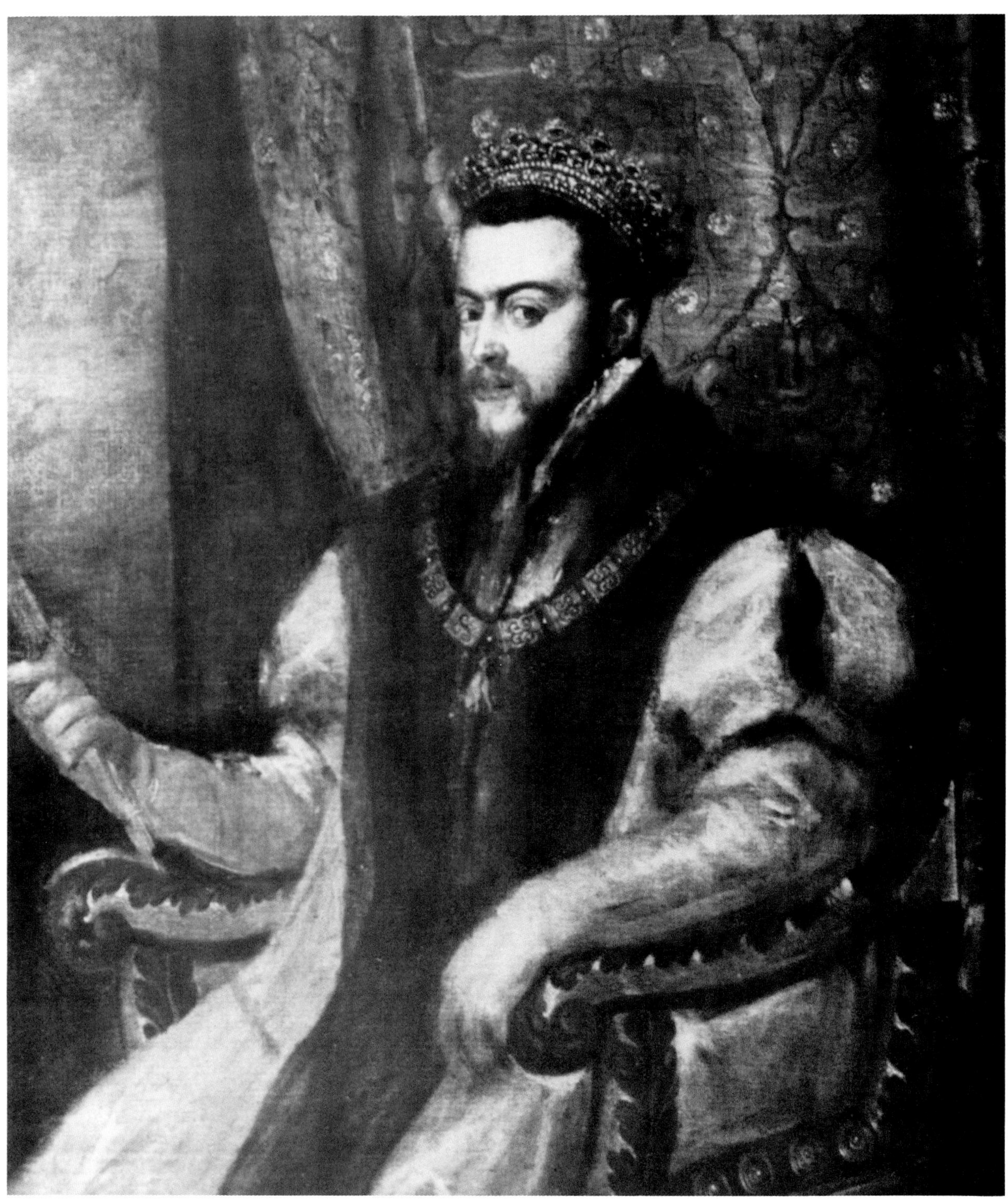

62. Titian (?), *Portrait of Philip II*, Cincinnati (Ohio), Museum of Art.

Oil Sketches, Unfinished Paintings, and the Inventories of Artists' Estates

4

Although a great deal is now known about the working practices of sixteenth and seventeenth century artists, there is much that remains obscure, particularly with regard to the history and development of the oil sketch. When and why oil sketches came to be used, what part they played in the execution of a painting, and even how they can be recognized are all questions for which we have no satisfactory answers or, more accurately perhaps, for which we have a multiplicity of often competing and ill-assorted ones. No small part of this problem lies in the evidence offered by the works remaining in an artist's studio on his death, when these are known. The peculiar attraction of such material was already noticed by Pliny, who wrote that "the latest works of artists and the pictures left unfinished at their death are valued more than any of their finished paintings . . . [because] in these we see traces of the design and the original conception of the artists."[1] This tendency to imbue an artist's unfinished pictures with the record of his creativity has commonly expressed itself in two ways: firstly, in a general temptation to seek personal or technical idiosyncracies in an artist's studio properties; and secondly, in a ready inclination to identify these small and often not so small paintings with oil sketches, where we likewise hope to surprise the artist in the act of creation.

The conjunction suggested here of studio properties with working practices on the one hand, and oil sketches on the other, appears clearly in the interpretation of Titian's estate. Although after Titian died in 1576 many valuable paintings were stolen from his house and others were sold, Ridolfi[2] and most later authors imply that when Cristoforo Barbarigo bought the artist's house in 1581, he acquired with it the paintings by Titian later known to be in his family's collection.[3] Still in the hands of a descendant in the late nineteenth century, one group of these paintings[4]— all portraits, all of famous men, and all evidently unfinished—was subjected to an interpretation derived from their provenance. Introducing them into a discussion of Titian's pictorial technique, Pietro Selvatico noted, as Ridolfi had done, that many versions of the pictures were known and that (although executed at different times) they had been kept by the artist until his death; he then concluded that the paintings were not unfinished replicas, but studies or sketches made from life for the production of copies or variant pictures.[5] This idea, apparently stated for the first time by Selvatico in 1875, was given wider currency two years later by Crowe and Cavalcaselle in their authoritative monograph on Titian, where it was extended to include one of the religious paintings that had also belonged to the Barbarigo.[6] And even today, when no one would maintain that the pictures attributed to Titian formerly in the Barbarigo collection represent an artistically coherent group,[7] a number of individual paintings are still called studies and oil sketches.[8]

In ways not dissimilar, the practice of using oil sketches in the design of a painting has been ascribed to artists other than Titian on the basis of the inventories of their estates. In this case, such a conclusion has been facilitated by the ambiguity arising from the lack of a fixed artistic vocabulary during the sixteenth and seventeenth centuries. The following study, by examining artists' inventories and related materials, therefore seeks to establish what kinds of studio properties were likely to be found in an artist's workshop, to explain why they were there, and to determine what they can tell us about an artist's use of oil sketches.

The inventory of 1529 enumerating the studio properties left by Palma Vecchio is especially important for these purposes.[9] It exactly describes the various states at which work on 28 unfinished paintings had been interrupted, and provides in its detail a standard of comparison for later inventories. There were canvases only covered by gesso priming and a few with charcoal underdrawing; more numerous were the compositions that had been blocked out or underpainted (*bozado*), some with the addition of color (*bozada e colorida in parte, bozado poco più*); finally there were paintings described as a third or half finished, as well as almost complete (*terzo fato, mezo facto, quasi finido*).

Although the detailed descriptions of this inventory were rarely duplicated, later inventories show the same kind of distinctions among the sequential stages of unfinished paintings. In some cases the distinctions are elementary, as in the inventories of the properties of Marcello Venusti (1579)[10] and Tomaso Laureti (1602),[11] in which canvases with underdrawings (*disegnato, disegnato solamente*) were differentiated from those on which an underpainting had been laid (*sbozzato, abbozzato*). In other cases, such as the 1629 inventory of the effects of the little-known Antonio Pomarancio, there is the same kind of descriptive clarity found in the Palma inventory: primed canvases again are distinguished from those with underdrawings (*disegnato solamente, profilato*) and those with underpaintings (*abbozzato*) from pictures that were apparently more complete (*non finito, quasi finito*).[12]

If the distinctions made among paintings left incomplete in these inventories may be traced to pecuniary motives, their objective value as categories is confirmed by some wills, where the same terms are used to qualify the class of unfinished pictures. In Paul Brill's testament of 1626, for example, the class of unfinished paintings is specified as follows: *quadri, imprimiti, abbozzati, cominciati et non finiti.*[13] However tentatively, therefore, the inventories enable us to identify the several stages of execution recognized during the period, while confirming the fact that sizable numbers of unfinished paintings—often far more than can be reasonably thought to be "in progress" at the time of the artist's death—were normally to be found in artists' studios. Thus the inventory of 1592 drawn up after the death of Jacopo Bassano lists some 60 incomplete pictures and, as in the case of the Barbarigo paintings, many already were old (*sbozzato vecchio*) at the time the inventory was made.[14]

The presence of large numbers of unfinished pictures in an artist's studio can be explained in part by Renaissance workshop practices. This is especially clear in the case of the *abbozzo* or underpainting, which accounts for the largest number of unfinished pictures. The *abbozzo* has been described as a point of arrival in the conception and progress of a painting, and it was therefore a relatively autonomous stage in the execution of the work.[15] Typically, the *abbozzo* differed in color from the succeeding layers of paint,[16] and it was evidently allowed to dry before the painting was finished. "Asciutti che erano quegli abbozzi," wrote Boschini,[17] and Pietro da Cortona in a letter of 1645 to a patron explained that "la tela con l'abbozzo si vada asciugando acio restino i colori più vivaci e meglio condizionati."[18] Consequently it was a natural point at which to interrupt the work on a painting.

This practice, however, also encouraged a division of labor, which further increased the likelihood that an artist would have *abbozzi* on hand in his studio. Although it scarcely needs repeating that the artist responsible for laying down the underpainting of a picture was not necessarily the same one who completed it, the relatively independent character of the respective shares may be worth emphasizing here. For a head of Cosimo Vecchio de' Medici, Vasari noted in his *Ricordanze* that he had had it roughed out (*feci bozzare*) by Beschieri, who received 2 scudi, while Vasari, who finished the painting received 4.[19] The same procedure was followed for two painted copies of Michelangelo's *Leda* cartoon. For the first Vasari actually received the lesser amount; for the second, when he did all but the underpainting (*eccetto che bozzata*), he claimed two-thirds of the final price.[20] Similarly, Benedetto Caliari, brother of Paolo Veronese, described the execution of a painting whose program was supplied by the patron: "Dunque come da me dissegnato, da Carlo abosiato, e da Gabriel finito."[21] Sometimes paintings were blocked out in groups of more than one. On 15 December 1554, during a stay in Arezzo, Vasari recorded that he had roughed out several paintings ("io abbozzaj molti quadrj").[22] And this practice could also pertain to multiples of the same subject as, in fact, Cristofano Allori indicated in a letter of 6 August 1619 in which he directed his assistant to block-out those Judiths that he had to do ("quelle Giuditte come l'ho fatto fare").[23]

Subject of course to individual variations conditioned by personality or style, workshop practices of this kind must be one reason why so many paintings at this stage of execution are found in artists' estates. Another consideration, however, arises from the subjects of these unfinished paintings, and in both regards the canvases left by Titian on his death may be taken as typical. According to the testimony of Palma Giovane, Titian frequently set aside the pictures he had begun, then later returned to rework them.[24] As we have seen, this pratice conforms with the handling of their *abbozzi* by other artists, and it can have been idiosyncratic only in the extent to which Titian may have been accustomed to use it. It would, however, account for the fact that a number of the compositions represented by the paintings attributed to the artist in the Barbarigo collection originated at different moments of his career.

No more unusual are the subjects of the unfinished Barbarigo paintings, since most were portraits and since portraits, in many cases only begun, are commonly found in artists' estates. Twenty unfinished portraits, for example, were grouped together ("biente retratos enpezados") in the inventory drawn up after the death of the Venetian-trained El Greco on the occasion of his son's marriage,[25] and six of unidentified sitters ("retrati . . .cominciati et non finiti") were likewise grouped in the estate of Sebastiano del Piombo, inventoried in June of 1547.[26] A seventh unfinished portrait by Sebastiano depicted Clement VII and was one of three representations of the Medici Pope listed in the inventory.

Elsewhere too in the estates of artists we regularly meet with multiple versions of the same sitter. The will (October 1606) of Nicolas Breul, the first husband of Adam Elsheimer's wife, refers to five portraits in varying sizes for different patrons of the then reigning pope, Paul V.[27] And in the 1633 inventory of the painter Jean Lhomme's estate (in addition to as many as 25 portraits of unidentified sitters among 178 paintings) Urban VIII and his family were represented by 12 portraits, most depicting the Cardinal brother and nephews of the pope.[28] Similarly, in 1621, Gerolamo Bassano, the youngest son of Jacopo, bequeathed to his nephew the most complete ("il più finito") of the portraits he had made of the then recently canonized Carlo Borromeo.[29]

In these, and often in other instances, the number of paintings with the same likeness is readily explained by the importance or topicality of the persons portrayed, which must have led to portraits being made or only begun in anticipation of multiple sales. Even leaving aside the numerous replicas and copies of portraits made inside and outside Titian's shop, we know that the demand for likenesses of this kind was widespread. During four months in 1534, for example, Vasari received payment for four portraits of Duke Alessandro de' Medici,[30] while in 1531, Sebastiano's letters showed him trying to satisfy a lively demand in Rome for paintings of Clement VII,[31] and a document of 1547 indicates that the artist continued to supply portraits of the pope, dead since 1534, and of Giulia Gonzaga, first painted in a much lauded version of 1532, until just before his death.[32]

But only an enormous market for effigies of the fashionable or famous, which might be compared to the official photographs of presidents and popes common today, could account for the inventory of pictures owned by the now totally unknown painter Nicolao Ventura, whose possessions were sequestered in Rome in 1616.[33] Of the 767 paintings summarily described, 324 were portraits or heads, 110 were figures of popes, princes, cardinals, philosophers and saints, and 128 represented princes, turks, and poets. Some fifty years later, with buyers of more modest means in mind, the publishing firm of Giovanni Jacopo de' Rossi began issuing a series of engraved portraits of living cardinals,[34] but the inventory of Mario de' Fiori indicates that the market for painted portraits continued unabated. Prepared after the death of the artist in 1673, the inventory lists almost 800 paintings, and 100 of these – some described as old – are called unfinished. By no means all, or even most, were the flower paintings or still lives for which the artist is now best known. Indeed more than 500 of the paintings were portraits. A few represented monarchs and princes; others, which punctuate the inventory singly and in groups of 10 and 20, are designated "diversi cardinali e personaggi," while still others, including one group of 235, are simply described as "ritrati diversi."[35] More important, however, than the sheer quantity of portraits and the investment in effort and materials they suggest, are five unfinished portraits of cardinals. Since all are described as without heads (*senza testa*)[36] and were surely intended to be completed with whatever likeness a buyer desired, we have here explicit evidence for what can only be surmised from the number and repetition of likenesses elsewhere – that portraits were frequently painted or only blocked out on speculation and all too often were still on an artist's hands at his death.[37]

The Barbarigo portraits attributed to Titian (Paul III, Philip II, Francis I, etc.) therefore fit readily with these portraits, old and new, finished or not, left in large numbers by other painters, and it seems more reasonable to see them too as potentially marketable replicas (some unfinished) rather than original sketches or models. This conclusion is in no way vitiated by the remaining pictures known to have been in Titian's estate, which conform on one hand with the pattern traced for the portraits and on the other with the evidence of the inventories. Four paintings, for example, were sold to Tintoretto by Pomponio Vecelli after his father's death. From the ways in which they are described by the sources, these paintings were certainly not finished.[38] Yet it would perhaps be hasty to conclude that Titian was actually working on them at the time of his death, since three of the pictures—a *Flagellation of Christ*, a *Venus and Adonis*, and a *Tale of Callisto*—were evidently replicas or variants of compositions known in other examples,[39] and as in the case of the portraits, the repetition of subjects is a recurrent feature in artists' inventories.[40]

In the inventory of Palma's effects there are three unfinished heads of Christ, two female nudes, and two paintings of the Madonna and Child with St. John the Baptist, along with other variants of the then popular *sacra conversazione*.[41] The Bassano inventory of 1592 repeats subjects even more insistently and confirms the observation of W. R. Rearick that to "meet the rising demand for these genre-like pictures Jacopo established a programme for their mass production in which sons and assistants were set to duplicating compositions *seriatum*."[42] The inventory of Girolamo Muziano's estate (1592) shows the same situation within a different range of works. Among the many examples of duplication, there were three paintings depicting Christ washing the feet of the Apostles and no fewer than seven devotional pictures of St. Jerome.[43]

In the Muziano inventory a few of the entries indicate the destination or patron of the works, but the number of those which do not suggests that, like the portraits of famous men, popular subjects in replica or variant versions must often have been painted or blocked out as a kind of studio stock without a buyer at hand. Indeed the bleak picture of unending difficulties that emerges from the daily accounts in Lorenzo Lotto's *Libro di spese diverse* indicates just how many uncommissioned works he was forced to execute. He sent paintings to Venice to be sold, and to Rome; he gave paintings to Jacopo Sansovino to sell; he held a sale of his own; all with little success. He also made or

had made replicas of some of these paintings. For example, in an entry for May 1544, Lotto records that he had sent two paintings, a night Nativity and a Baptism of Christ, from Treviso to a "gilder" and evidently middleman in Venice. He also adds to the entry that replicas of these pictures ("doi altri quadri simili ali sopra diti, recavati et imitato") were made for further commerce ("da farne più derata") and valued at half the originals' price. Although the primary versions were to return to him unsold in 1545, we learn that in December, 1544 the replicas had been taken to Sicily by the Venetian jeweler Lauro Orso and sold in Messina.[44]

Uncommissioned, and therefore saleable, work of this kind, though without the connotations it had for the hapless Lotto, was a natural concomitant of an artist's activity, and it was undoubtedly the rare master who could not produce on demand, as Rubens did, something "trovato in casa."[45] That Titian too disposed of some such stock appears from a letter of 1548 written by Aretino. He reports that when it became known that Titian would go to Augsburg, people flocked to the artist's studio and bought out everything to be found there.[46] For those artists, like Lotto, who could count on neither public commissions nor regular patronage, commerce in uncommissioned paintings would have been staple fare and explains the contents of their estates. Thus the inventory of Antonio Pomarancio cited earlier lists ten Madonna paintings of various sorts, seven of which were unfinished and two "dell' istessa maniera." Of the four *Assumptions of the Virgin*, two were finished, and three had the same dimensions. Two unfinished paintings of Venus and Cupid also had the same dimensions. That these pictures, which can only have been replicas or copies, as well as nearly all the other works listed, formed a stock of uncommissioned paintings can be confirmed in this case by the fact that during the settlement of the estate most were sold, in bulk, for the modest sum of 30 scudi.[47]

The actual role of unfinished paintings in this rudamentary art market is revealed by evidence of a more narrative sort. Malvasia, for example, reports that Guido Reni was approached by an emissary of Cardinal Francesco Barberini after he had failed to furnish a promised picture. Turning around the various "bozze" leaning against the walls of his studio (therefore unfinished paintings, not oil sketches) and deciding on a half-length Christ Child, Guido completed it for the Cardinal in a few hours.[48] Similarly, during the trial of Don Fabrizio Valguarnera, the Sicilian diamond thief arrested in Rome who had been converting gems into paintings, the Veronese painter Alessandro Turchi testified that he had shown the defendant those paintings that he had in his studio. Valguarnera liked an "abbozzo" of Adam and Eve mourning Abel and had ordered Turchi to finish it for him.[49] Unfinished pictures, including replicas, also formed a part of the group of works that Rubens had in his house ("ch' io ritrovo in casa") in 1618, when he offered to exchange paintings by his hand for a collection of ancient sculptures belonging to Sir Dudley Carleton.[50]

Thus in the interests of economy and in keeping with common workshop practices, uncommissioned paintings, whether originals, replicas, or copies, would be brought to a convenient level of finish and then completed on demand. That this pragmatic approach to the art market was already a longstanding tradition by the sixteenth century can be inferred from the description in Sacchetti's *Novelle* of a painter of crucifixes, who always had four to six finished and unfinished works on hand.[51] It therefore follows that many of the *sbozzi* and *abbozzi*, the works *abbozzati* and *principati*, *non terminati* and *non finiti* listed in the inventories of artists' estates during the Renaissance and Baroque periods must have been made on speculation. And since a good number of these in turn were likely to have been done at different stages of an artist's career—as the inventories sometimes specify—or were copies and replicas blocked out by someone other than the artist, they can have had little value in revealing those "secrets of art" ascribed by Boschini to Titian's unfinished paintings[52] or that avenue into an artist's mind sought by Pliny in the paintings left incomplete because of death.

Equal caution must be observed in attributing the use of oil sketches to an artist on the evidence of an inventory, since neither terminology nor size is a sure guide to identifying painted preparatory works. Although a model by Rubens is described as a "disegno o sbozzo" by 1606,[53] and such examples multiply as the century advanced,[54] the metaphorical application of terms derived from *abbozzare* or *sbozzare* to artistic ideas in the process of formation originated in the actual roughing out of a composition in paint or stone, and this original usage is not entirely superceded. In all those instances in the *Vite* in which the sense can be precisely determined from the context, when Vasari used the word "bozza" in reference to a painting, he intended a roughed-out picture, not a sketch, and this seems typical of the sixteenth century.[55] Armenini, an

imitator of Vasari in many respects, repeated the latter's complaint that Tintoretto left his "bozze per finite" and elucidated what was meant in his discussion of technique, where the *bozza* is associated with the broadly executed underpainting.[56] Similarly, Aretino admired the "bozze de le istorie" by Schiavone, but counseled the artist to be sure that "la fretta del farle si convertisse ne la diligenza del finirle."[57] The descriptive terminology of these writers, if not their judgments, continues into the seventeenth century. Both Ridolfi and Boschini use the words "abbozzi" and "abbozzature" for unfinished paintings, and in 1648 Pietro da Cortona called one of his own, unmistakably incomplete paintings an "abbozzo."[58] Moreover, the "sbozzo" of Sant' Andrea led to martyrdom and another of Cato listed in the inventory of the contents of Sacchi's house taken in 1661 are probably the same pictures later owned by Carlo Maratta and inventoried in 1712, where however they are described respectively as an "abbozzo" and "non terminata."[59] Similar problems of meaning arise even when actual preparatory works are involved, as may be illustrated by two roughly contemporary accounts of painted sketches by Ciro Ferri and Luca Giordano. From the contexts in which they appear, Ferri's "bozzetto colorito" for the dome of Sant' Agnese in Rome was clearly what would now be described as a modello, whereas the "modello" made by Giordano was just as clearly a real "bozzetto," though the artist himself called it a "macchia."[60]

Thus, unless it can be otherwise controlled, the ambiguity of these terms makes it impossible to determine exactly what is being described when they appear in the inventories. In the case of Andrea Camassei, for example, who has acquired a certain reputation as an early practitioner of the oil sketch, there is no way to be sure that the several "abbozzi" listed in his inventory of 1649 refer to oil sketches rather than paintings that had been begun but not finished. Significantly, perhaps, four of these were portraits—including two of the Principessa de Rossano[61]—although there were other "abbozzi" of mythological and religious subjects and at least one composition Camassei is known to have treated on another occasion.[62]

If, in this and other instances, the terminology used to describe an artist's effects offers no certainty with regard to his use of oil sketches, neither does the diminutive size of the works listed, although large size is a plausible criterion of exclusion. The distinction emerges from the fact that the expanding role of painted preparation in the seventeenth and eighteenth centuries coincided with a growing demand for small-sized pictures. Often these small paintings were reduced replicas, frequently of paintings in another medium and sometimes unfinished.[63] In the inventory of Carlo Maratta (1712), where the *abbozzi* ranged in size to up to two meters square, one is listed as "copiato dal quadro che andiede in Palermo."[64] Therefore it is at least as likely that a small "abbozzo" or "sbozzo" of a subject known in another size was an unfinished, reduced replica as that it was an oil sketch used to prepare its larger counterpart.

The fact that preparatory oil sketches, should any be present, cannot readily be distinguished from small, unfinished originals, replicas, or copies, reveals once again the evidential limitations of the inventories of artists' estates. Inevitably, an inventory of an artist's studio properties records not only the rupture caused by death or circumstance, but carries forward and incorporates the detritus of the past. It represents not a specific practice of the moment, but the cumulative effects of past practices. It therefore tends to document generalized norms rather than individual idiosyncracies and tells us more about the times than the artist. In Sacchi's estate, there were numerous replicas, including two small versions in oil of the frescoed *Divine Wisdom* and a "sbozzo" of Hagar, the Angel and Ismael, the latter one of two depictions of this subject listed in the inventory and like several by Sacchi pertaining to a composition known in multiple versions.[65] Thus if, as has been suggested, the many replicas in Sacchi's oeuvre signify a creative crisis, this manifested itself only as an exaggeration of a typical procedure. In the same way, the seemingly anomalous or personal features of such an inventory as that prepared after Elsheimer's death in 1610 become more explicable. Although Elsheimer's uncompromising critical standards could account for some of the small paintings on copper left incomplete, at least the ten unfinished paintings on canvas—a support used for just one surviving autographic and atypical picture by the artist— should probably be explained as the stock of roughed out, and usually less important works by a painter or his assistants, seen elsewhere.[66]

Yet, if with respect to an artist's use of oil sketches or Pliny's high hopes for learning the secrets of an artist's creativity, the inventories must be regretfully set aside, they nevertheless offer an insight of another kind, for they enable us to glimpse those common practices and procedures that represented the everyday life of an artist.

Linda Freeman Bauer
University of California, Irvine

Notes

1. The Elder Pliny's Chapters on the History of Art, trans. by K. Jex-Blake, with commentary by E. Sellers [1896], Chicago, 1967, chapt. 35, 145, cited by Julius S. Held, *The Oil Sketches of Peter Paul Rubens*, Princeton, 1980, p. 12.

2. Carlo Ridolfi, *Le maraviglie dell' arte* [1648], ed. by Detlev von Hadeln, Berlin, 1914, 1, p. 200.

3. The only exception is Charles Hope (*Titian*, London, 1980, p. 167, n. 2), who argued on the basis of a partial transcription of Cristoforo Barbarigo's will, published by Giuseppe Cadorin (*Dello amore ai Veneziani di Tiziano Vecellio*, Venice, 1833, p. 113) and containing a bequest of paintings to Cristoforo's natural son, Andrea, that only the four paintings listed in the excerpt were acquired with Titian's house. However, Cadorin's comments elsewhere (pp. 43 and 77, n. 97)—and he must have seen the entire document—do not support this restriction. Even in its fragmentary form the document suggests that a conditional bequest of the paintings ("li quali vadino de herede in herede primo geneto") had been made to Andrea, who was not the primary heir but who also received the house. Since the latter passed from Andrea's wife to his daughter (Cadorin, pp. 31, 113) it seems likely that the four paintings returned to the family when Andrea died without male issue and that the remaining paintings listed by Ridolfi, including the portraits discussed below, had been left by Cristoforo to his brother and universal heir, Domenico (ibid., p. 113).

4. Most of the pictures are included in Harold E. Wethey, *The Paintings of Titian, II, The Portraits*, London, 1971: *Francis I* (Leeds, Harewood House, Earl of Harewood), cat. no. 36; *Doge Andrea Gritti* (New York, Metropolitan Museum), cat. no. 51; *Paul III* (Leningrad, Hermitage), cat. no. 74; *Philip II* (Cincinnati, Art Museum), cat. no. 81. For the

last, a portrait of Doge Antonio Grimani now apparently lost, see G. B. Cavalcaselle and J. A. Crowe, *Tiziano la sua vita e i suoi tempi*, Florence, 1977, 1, p. 212.

5. Pietro Selvatico, *Di alcuni abbozzi di Tiziano e di altri dipinti nella galleria del Conte Sebastiano Giustinian Barbarigo in Padova*, Padua, 1875, esp. pp. 9-10.

6. Cavalcaselle and Crowe, *Tiziano*, esp. 2, pp. 156-60 (*Philip II*), but also I, pp. 268-69 (*Doge Andrea Gritti*), and p. 358 (*Francis I*); for their suggestion that the late, unfinished *St. Sebastian* (Leningrad, Hermitage) may have been a "primo modello," see 2, p. 429. Cf. too Luigi Lanzi's discussion of the Barbarigo "abbozzi" in the context of Titian's unfinished, roughed out paintings (*Storia pittorica della Italia*, 5th ed., Florence, 1834, 3, p. 95), which became in translation (by Thomas Roscoe, London, 1872, 2, p. 165) "rough drafts" and "first sketches."

7. The quality of the paintings is uneven and ranges from the generally admired *Magdalene* (Leningrad, Hermitage) to the *Doge Andrea Gritti* considered by most to be the work of an assistant and today in storage in the Metropolitan Museum. The subjects were also ones treated by Titian on more than one occasion (*Paul III* and *Philip II*) and at different moments in his career (for example, the *Doge Andrea Gritti* and *Francis I* have been dated to the 1530s, the *Paul III* and *Philip II* to the 1540s). Some of the paintings are clearly finished; others, especially those discussed by Selvatico, display a rough, unevenly developed surface.

8. This position was developed most fully by E. Tietze-Conrat, "Titian's Workshop in His Late Years," *The Art Bulletin*, 28, 1946, pp. 80ff., who argued that all of the Barbarigo portraits but that of Doge Antonio Grimani are sketches. She has been followed by Wethey (portraits of Philip II, Francis I, and, on the basis of its provenance, possibly Paul III) and most recently by Wolfgang Braunfels (*Philip II*; "I quadri di Tiziano nello studio a Biri Grande [1530-1576]," *Tiziano e Venezia convegno internazionale di studi, Venezia, 1976*, Vicenza, 1980, p. 408).

9. Gustav Ludwig, "Archivalische Beiträge zur Geschichte der venezianischen Malerei," *Jahrbuch der königlich preussischen Kunstsammlungen*, 24, Beiheft, 1903, pp. 76-79.

10. Rome, Archivio di Stato, Collegio de' Notari Capitolini, Not. Curzio Saccoccia, vol. 1552, 28 October 1579, fols. 463r-469v (cited by A. Bertolotti, "Giunte agli artisti lombardi in Roma," *Archivio storico lombardo*, 10, 1883, p. 106).

11. St. Peter's, Archivio della Reverenda Fabbrica di San Pietro, 1 Piano, Serie 2, vol. 7, fols. 69r-71r; this inventory was kindly brought to my attention by Morton Abromson.

12. Linda Freeman Bauer, "L'inventario dei beni di Antonio Pomarancio e alcune note sulla vita e l'opera del pittore," *Bollettino d'arte*, 68, 1983, 19, pp. 31-34. Cf. too in this regard the richly detailed inventory (15 March 1627) of Giovanni Battista Paggi's estate (Genoa, Archivio di Stato, Not. Borsotto Bartolomeo, filza 29, scansia 968); this inventory was kindly brought to my attention by Timothy Standring.

13. Didier Bodart, "Les tableaux de la succession de Paul Bril," *Mélanges d'archéologie et d'histoire de l'art offerts au professeur Jacques Lavalleye, Université de Louvain Recueil de travaux d'histoire et de philologie*, ser. 4, 45, 1970, p. 9.

14. Giovanni Battista Verci, *Notizie intorno alla vita e alle opere de' pittori, scultori, e intagliatori della città di Bassano*, Venice, 1775, pp. 91-100.

15. Luigi Grassi, "I concetti di schizzo, abbozzo, macchia, 'non finito' e la costruzione dell' opera d'arte," *Studi in onore di Pietro Silva*, Florence, 1957, pp. 97-106 and esp. p. 99.

16. Cf., for example, Giorgio Vasari, *Le vite de' più eccellenti pittori, scultori e architettori [nelle redazioni del 1550 e 1568]*, ed. by R. Bettarini and P. Barocchi, Florence, 1966, 1, p. 134 (1550 ed.) and commentary, 1, p. 209; Filippo Baldinucci, *Vocabolario toscano dell' arte del disegno*, Florence, 1681, s.v. *abbozzo*; and the summary of Venetian techniques by

Marco Boschini in the *Breve instruzione*, preface to the *Ricche minere della pittura veneziana* [1674], ed. by A. Pallucchini with *La carta del navegar pitoresco*, Venice and Rome, 1966, pp. 752-53. A practical expression of the same point may be found in such a payment as that to Andrea Camassei for "Colori diversi p[er] abbozzare, et finire detti quadri" (Marilyn Aronberg Lavin, "A Seventeenth-Century Painter's Supplies: Document of Payment to Andrea Camassei," *The Art Bulletin*, 52, 1970, p. 193).

17.   Boschini, *Breve instruzione*, p. 753; cf. similarly Giorgio Vasari, *Le vite de' più eccellenti pittori, scultori ed architettori* [1568], ed. Gaetano Milanesi, 3, Florence, 1878, pp. 573-74, who described how, in the early days of oil painting, Perugino did not allow the layers of paint in an altarpiece to dry sufficiently; or conversely Giovanni Battista Armenini, *De' veri precetti della pittura* [1587], with notes by Stefano Ticozzi, Milan, 1820, p. 173, who recommended a remedy for "bozze" which were overly dry and repelled the color.

18.   Vincenzo Ruffo, "Galleria Ruffo nel secolo XVII in Messina," *Bollettino d'arte*, 10, 1916, p. 44, letter of 19 March 1645 to Don Antonio Ruffo.

19.   *Il libro delle ricordanze di Giorgio Vasari*, ed. Alessandro Del Vita, Rome, 1938, p. 37, 15 October 1541; I am most grateful to Charles Davis for calling my attention to this item and those cited in n. 20. Likewise, Armenini, *De' veri precetti*, p. 335, related that during his youthful travels he arrived in Milan and was employed by Bernardino Campi to rough out a picture using Campi's cartoon ("io abbozzai una tavola col mezzo di un suo cartone"); on the success of this work, he stayed some months in Campi's employment.

20.   *Il libro delle ricordanze*, p. 35, 25 June 1541, and p. 36, 15 August 1541.

21.   E. Cicogna, *Delle iscrizione veneziane*, Venice, 1834, 4, p. 177.

22.   *Il libro delle ricordanze*, p. 72, 15 December 1554.

23.   Letter of 6 August 1619 to Jacopo Jacopi in Claudio Pizzorusso, *Ricerche su Cristofano Allori*, Florence, 1982, pp. 50-51 and 114-15 for the entire letter. The pertinent passage reads: "Mi raccomandi a ms. Zanobi e di gratia quando ha finito la sua opera mi compiaccia di tirare innanzi le cose mie, e vorrei che facesse i campi a quelle Giuditte come l'ho fatto fare all' anconetano." Cf. too the list of unfinished works offered in 1620 during Allori's last illness to the Grand Duke as repayment for a debt, ibid., pp. 116-18, and subsequently pp. 120-23.

24.   Boschini's account of Titian's working method in the *Breve instruzione*, pp. 711-12, was based on information provided by Palma Giovane.

25.   F. de B. San Román, "De la vida del Greco," *Archivo espanōl de arte y arqueologia*, 3, 1927, pp. 285ff. for the inventory; the portraits are item 209.

26.   Benvenuto Gasparoni, "Il testamento e l'inventario di Sebastiano del Piombo," *Arti e lettere*, 2, 1865, appendix, pp. 163-67; for the portraits, p. 164. The portions of the inventory pertaining to art have now been reprinted by Michael Hirst, *Sebastiano del Piombo*, Oxford, 1981, pp. 154-56.

27.   Rome, Archivio di Stato, 30 Notari Capitolini, Ufficio 19, vol. 71, Not. Petrus Martinus Trucca, fols. 435r-436r; cited by Keith Andrews, "The Elsheimer Inventory and other Documents," *The Burlington Magazine*, 114, 1972, p. 596, n. 7.

28.   Jacques Bousquet, "Un compagnon des caravagesques français a Rome Jean Lhome," *Gazette des beaux-arts*, ser. 6, 53, 1959, pp. 88, 89-92.

29.   G. d. B., "I testamenti di Francesco il giovane e di Gerolamo da Ponte," *Bollettino del Museo Civico di Bassano*, 2, 1905, p. 110; "un San Carlo di queli ho qui in Venetia, fatti di mia mano, il più finito;" cf., for example, in the 1629 inventory of paintings deriving from the estate of Paul Brill, "Due quadretti di testa di San Carlo" (Bodart, "Les tableaux de la succession de Paul Bril," p. 12).

30. *Il libro delle ricordanze*, p. 21, 8 January, 4 February, 13 March, and 9 April.

31. Hirst, *Sebastiano del Piombo*, p. 110; these included originals, a replica, and a head with an up-to-date likeness sent to Bugiardini for use in making others.

32. Ibid., pp. 115-16 and nn. 110, 111.

33. A. Bertolotti, "Inventari di sculture, pitture ed oggetti di belle arti," *Giornale di erudizione artistica*, 5, 1876, pp. 285-86.

34. Ellis Waterhouse, "A Note on Giovanni Maria Morandi," *Studies in Renaissance and Baroque Art presented to Anthony Blunt on his 60th birthday*, London and New York, 1967, pp. 120. For a bourgeois collector, who owned 18 portraits of cardinals and one of Innocent X, see Milton J. Lewine, "An Inventory of 1647 of a Roman Art Collection," *Arte antica e moderna*, 1962, pp. 310-15. Cf. too Wolfram Prinz, *Die Sammlung selbstbildnisse in den Uffizi: Geschichte der Sammlung*, Berlin, 1971, pp. 17-22, for the background to this kind of collection.

35. O. Montenovesi, "Il pittore Mario de' Fiori, Documenti," *Archivio della società romana di storia patria*, 73, 1950, pp. 225-35; for example, p. 227: "ventinove ritratti di cardinali e prencipi, in tela, di palmi 3;" p. 230: "trentasei ritratti di diversi cardinali e personaggi;" p. 233: "sessanta uno ritratti di diversi personaggi, in tela, di 3 palmi" and the "diocento trenta cinque ritratti diversi, tra buoni e cativi, in tela, di palmi 3." Cf. now the Sustermans inventory (1681) published by Alessandro Guidotti in *Sustermans: sessant' anni alla corte dei Medici*, Florence, 1983, for example, no. 285: "cinque *ritratti* non finito;" no. 420: "quattro quadretti . . . entrovi *ritratti* non finiti;" and no. 230: "dodici quadri . . . non finiti, entrovi *ritratti*."

36. Ibid., for example, p. 233: "due altri retratti de cardinali, senza testa, non finiti, della medema grandezza [6 x 9 palmi]." Two of the portraits measured 6 x 8 palmi, the fifth 7 x 5 palmi (p. 233).

37. Although French artists fall outside the scope of this study, it is worth observing that their inventories confirm the practice described here. Among the works of Simon Vouet and his shop (Gaston Brière, "Inventaires du logis de Simon Vouet dans la Grande Galerie du Louvre [1639 et 1640]," *Fédération des sociétés historiques et archeólogiques de Paris et de l'Ile-de-France, Mémoires*, 3, 1951, pp. 129-153, and esp. 142-45) were inventoried 22 or 23 portraits—originals and copies, finished and not—such as "huict coppies de portraictz, . . . achevez et non achevez" (p. 144), or "six portraitz non achevez" (p. 145). In the estate of Mathieu Le Nain (Georges Wildenstein, "L'inventaire après décès de Mathieu Le Nain 1677," *Gazette des beaux-arts*, ser. 6, 45, 1955, pp. 200-10) were recorded at least 89 generally small and mostly inexpensive portraits, for example, "douze autres portraits . . . tants faits que non achevez" (p. 206), or "douze petits tableaux représentans des portraits de mareschaux de France et autres seigneurs" (ibid.). See too the inventories of the estates of Philippe de Champaigne (1674) and especially that of Jean-Baptiste, his nephew (1681), in J. Guiffrey, "Les peintres Philippe et Jean-Baptiste de Champaigne nouveaux documents et inventaires après décès," *Nouvelles archives de l'art français*, ser. 3, 8, 1892, pp. 172-201. Similarly, large numbers of originals and copies were listed in a register kept by Hyacinthe Rigaud for the years 1681-1698, in which the name of the sitter, price, and status as original or copy were included. For example, in 1682 there were 32 portraits and 5 copies, whereas in 1692 there were 36 originals and 32 copies, of which 19 were "retoucheés." For the collection of portraits during this period, see Edmond Bonnaffé, "Notes sur les collections des Richelieu," *Gazette des beaux-arts*, ser. 2, 26, 1882, pp. 9-11.

38. See Ridolfi, *Le maraviglie dell' arte*, 1, p. 207, where the paintings were called "abbozzature," and cf. Boschini, *Breve instruzione*, pp. 711-12.

39. The theme of Callisto may have been nearly as popular in Titian's shop as the much reproduced Venus and Adonis, since in

addition to the famous painting of the subject owned by Philip II, there seem to have been others. Charles Hope, *Titian*, p. 127 and n. 14, has observed that beyond the *favole*—one a Diana and Callisto—offered to Maximilian II in 1568, another series was probably offered to Albrecht V, Duke of Bavaria. Hope also argued that for less important clients Titian's shop worked primarily from a repertoire of extant pictures (pp. 154, 158-59). With respect to the portraits, see Benedetto Agnello's letter of 8 February 1549: "ma io per me credo che [Titian] non voglia dare [a portrait] finchè non habbia finita la copia che ha da mandare al Re di Romani, la qual apena è cominciata" (in Alessandro Luzio, "Altre spigolature tizianesche," *Archivio storico dell' arte*, 3, 1890, p. 210, repeated by Tietze-Conrat, "Titian's Workshop," p. 80, n. 36).

40.   In addition to the examples discussed below, see in particular the inventory of Giacinto Gimignani's estate in Ursula Verena Fischer [Pace], *Giacinto Gimignani (1606-1681): Eine Studie zur römischen Malerei des Seicento*, Diss. Albert-Ludwigs-Universität, 1973, pp. 126-31. She remarks (pp. 69-70) on the number of paintings in the inventory that repeated earlier subjects and concludes that Gimignani often must have executed several versions "gleichzeitig oder später, unabhängig von einem bestimmten Auftrag-, die möglicherweise zum freien Verkauf bestimmt waren." See likewise the inventories of Giacinto Brandi, Rome, Archivio di Stato, Not. AC, vol. 4282 (20 March 1691), fols. 298r-312v, cited and discussed in this regard by Antonella Pampalone, "Per Giacinto Brandi," *Bollettino d'arte*, 58, 1973, pp. 138 and esp. 140, and that of Lazzaro Baldi (1703) in Antonella Pampalone, *Disegni di Lazzaro Baldi nelle collezioni del Gabinetto Nazionale delle Stampe*, Rome, 1979, pp. 147-65. Finally, it might be noted that the same kind of extensive repetition was remarked by Wildenstein, p. 199, in the case of Le Nain's inventory, and by Brière, p. 122, in the case of Vouet's.

41.   Ludwig, "Archivalische Beiträge," pp. 76-79.

42.   "Jacopo Bassano's Later Genre Paintings," *The Burlington Magazine*, 110, 1968, p. 242; cf. the prominence of copies in Jacopo's last testament (Livia Alberton Vinco da Sesso and Franco Sartori, "Il testamento di Jacopo dal Ponte detto il Bassano," *Arte veneta*, 33, 1979, pp. 163-64).

43.   Ugo da Como, *Girolamo Muziano 1528—1592: Note e documenti*, Bergamo, 1930, pp. 193-96.

44.   *Il "Libro di spese diverse" (con aggiunta di lettere e d'altri documenti)*, ed. by Pietro Zampetti, Venice and Rome, 1969, pp. 96, 97, 124, 125; see too p. 339.

45.   See below, and note 50.

46.   *Lettere sull' arte di Pietro Aretino*, ed. by Ettore Camesasca with commentary by Fidenzio Pertile, Milan, 1957, 2, pp. 192-93, letter of January 1548 to Nicola Perrenot de Granvelle.

47.   Bauer, "L'inventario dei beni di Antonio Pomarancio," pp. 31-34. For similarities in subject cf. the "Tre *Madonne con il puttino in braccio*, dal mezzo in su" in the estate (1626) of Guglielmo Caccia (Alessandro Baudi di Vesme, "L'arte negli stati sabaudi di tempi di Carlo Emanuele I, di Vittorio Amedeo I e della reggenza di Cristina di Francia," *Atti della società piemontese di archeologia e belle arti*, 14, 1932, p. 123) or the "altre Madonne bozzate" in the estate (1577) of Orazio Samacchini (summarized by M.-A. Gualandi, *Memorie originali italiane risguardanti le belle arti*, ser. 3, Bologna, 1842, p. 179). For the value of such stock cf. the request in 1767 of Urbano Vanvitelli for a license to send 189 paintings to Naples "quali sono la più parte di Mon.r Gasparo Vanvitelli [his father, d. 1736], detto degli Occhiali, parte studi e li altri abbozzati e il resto copie di Autori inferiori, in tutto del valore di Scudi 300" (in Giorgio Morelli, "Appunti bio-bibliografici su Gaspar e Luigi Vanvitelli," *Archivio della società romana di storia patria*, 92, 1969, p. 131; this notice was kindly brought to my attention by Charles Davis).

48.   *Felsina pittrice vite de' pittori bolognesi*, ed. by Giampietro Zanotti, Bologna, 1841, 2, p.

28: "voltando varie bozze poggiate a' muri, si consigliò con lo stesso di quella, fosse stata più a proposito, ed ambidue conclusero in una mezza figura d'un Signorino, . . . Raccomandatolo dunque allo trepiedi, in poche ore il diede finito."

49. Jane Costello, "The Twelve Pictures Ordered by Velasquez and the Trial of Valguarnera," *Journal of the Warburg and Courtauld Institutes*, 13, 1950, p. 279, deposition of 16 January 1632; see also the testimony of Lanfranco, 27 July 1631, pp. 274-75, and that of Poussin, 28 July 1631, p. 275. The use of blocked-out pictures as a stock was noted by Costello and by Francis Haskell, *Patrons and Painters*, London, 1963 p. 15. With respect to the inventories cf., for example, the "Sei tavole di tella con sopra bozi de quadri da principiare" recorded in 1630 among the goods of Daniele Crespi (Giorgio Nicodemi, *Daniele Crespi*, Busto Arsizio, 1930, p. 50).

50. Max Rooses and Charles Ruelens, *Correspondance de Rubens*, Antwerp, 1898, 2, letters from Rubens to Sir Dudley Carleton of 17 March 1618, p. 130; 28 April, pp. 135-38; 20 May, pp. 161-62; 26 May, p. 170-71; and 1 June, p. 181. Although Rubens wrote in the margin of his letter of 28 April that the greater number of paintings was finished, the remaining letters show how much he had exaggerated. It can also be inferred that at least two of the paintings were reduced, unfinished replicas—a *Last Judgment* (see letter of 28 April, p. 137) and a *Hunt* (see letter of 25 November from Toby Mathew to Sir Dudley Carleton, p. 261). Moreover, the same practice was subsequently indicated in a letter from Rubens to Valguarnera written just before the latter's arrest (*Correspondance*, Antwerp, 1907, 5, letter of 20 June 1631, p. 382).

51. Sacchetti, *Novelle*, no. 84; see too Peter Burke, *Culture and Society in Renaissance Italy 1420-1450*, London, 1972, pp. 105-106: "The demand for Virgins, Crucifixions or St. John the Baptist was sufficiently great and sufficiently standardized for workshops to produce them before the customer turned up, but they might be left unfinished in case the customer had some special demand."

52. *Breve instruzione*, p. 712.

53. Michael Jaffé, "Peter Paul Rubens and the Oratorian Fathers," *Proporzioni*, 4, 1963, p. 212.

54. Eg. Filippo Baldinucci, *Vocabolario toscano dell' arte del disegno*, Florence, 1681, s.v. *bozza*.

55. Vasari-Milanesi, lives of Raphael (4, 1879, p. 328), Andrea del Sarto (5, 1880, pp. 52-53), Rosso (5, p. 157), Battista Franco (6, 1881, p. 587, with reference to Tintoretto), Vasari (7, 1881, p. 667; the painting had been roughed out by his cousin Cristofano Gherardi as indicated in the latter's life, 6, p. 221). Here, as with the other examples, the word *bozza* has often been translated "sketch" in English and German editions of Vasari. The meaning of *bozza* in connection with an apparatus designed by Vasari in Venice is unclear to me (6, p. 225).

56. *De' veri precetti della pittura*, Ravenna, 1587, pp. 116, 126.

57. *Lettere sull' arte*, 2, p. 221.

58. See p. 2, and nn. 17, 18, and 38.

59. For the inventory of Sacchi's estate, see Ann Sutherland Harris, *Andrea Sacchi*, Oxford, 1977, pp. 119-22; the Maratta inventory was published with omissions and minor inaccuracies by Romeo Galli, "I tesori d'arte di un pittore del Seicento (Carlo Maratta)," *L'Archiginnasio*, 22, 1927, pp. 231-38, and 23, 1928, pp. 59-79. Although certain connections between entries are precluded, they are suggested, as in the case of the *Sant' Andreas* (Harris, no. 136 ; Galli, no. 428) or the *Catos*, where the dimensions of the painting on *tela d'imperatore* (6 palmi, or 54") in Sacchi's estate (Harris, no. 320) would have corresponded roughly to the "mezza figura grande al naturale" that Maratta owned (Galli, no. 312). Cf. too the "tela disegnata con il transito di S[ant'] Anna" by Sacchi listed in 1661 (Harris, no. 224) with the "abbozzo del Transito di Sant' Anna" ascribed to him in 1712 (Galli, no. 317).

60. For the contract of 11 September 1670 binding Ferri to make a "bozzetto" from which, once approved, he could not deviate without express permission, see Vicenzo Golzio, "Notizie sull' arte e gli artisti, tratte da archivi privati," *Archivi d'Italia*, ser. 2, 1, 1933-34, pp. 300-302; for Giordano's "modello" also for a cupola, see the letter of 7 February 1682 from Andrea del Rosso to Apollonio Bassetti in F. Büttner, *Die Galleria Riccardiana in Florenz* (Kieler kunsthistorische Studien, 2), Frankfurt and Bern, 1972, p. 229 (and cf. Bernardo De Dominici, *Vite dei pittori, scultori ed architetti napoletani* [1742], Naples, 1846, 4, pp. 144-45.

61. The inventory was published by Ann Sutherland Harris, "A Contribution to Andrea Camassei Studies," *The Art Bulletin*, 52, 1970, pp. 69-70; the other portraits depicted Urban VIII and Taddeo Barberini. A final portrait depicting a son of Taddeo and not designated an "abbozzo" was like the others on *tela da testa*. Cf., in addition to the portraits discussed above, those listed in the 1664 inventory of the artistic goods of Francesco Raspantino, Domenichino's student and heir of his artistic properties, in Richard E. Spear, *Domenichino*, New Haven and London, 1982, p. 340: "Un Ritratto di Papa Innocenzo, D. Olimpia, la Prpessa Giustiniani, e due della Prpessa Ludovisi, e Card^e Panfilio, in tutto n sei, di

tela da Testa, senza Cornice mia mano."

62. Cf. the "abbozzo" depicting one of the Seasons and painted on *tela d'imperatore* (6 palmi) with the three *Seasons* (5-1/2 x 7-1/2 palmi) that appear in Barberini inventories (Marilyn Aronberg Lavin, *Seventeenth-Century Barberini Documents and Inventories of Art*, New York, 1975, pp. 271, 364, 369, 376, 399, and 400.

63. See too, for example, above, note 50.

64. The *abbozzo*, Galli, no. 432, measured 5 palmi.

65. Versions of the *Divine Wisdom* are recorded in nos. 297 and 327 of the 1661 inventory; for others that had already been given or sold by that time, see Harris, cat. no. 17. For the *Hagar and Ismael in the Wilderness*, see nos. 23 and 132 and cat. no. 22.

66. Keith Andrews, *Adam Elsheimer*, Oxford, pp. 48-49; the painting on canvas is a self-portrait (Florence, Uffizi).

67. A number of the inventories of artists' estates along with other inventories, published before 1895, are listed in Fernand De Mély and Edmund Bishop, *Bibliographie générale des inventaires imprimés*, 3 vols., Paris, 1895.

Handlist of Inventories Consulted
for Artists Working in Italy[67]

Abbreviations for frequently cited sources

Bertolotti—A. Bertolotti, "Inventari di sculture, pitture ed oggetti di belle arti," *Giornale di erudizione artistica*, 5, 1876.

Gualandi—M.-A. Gualandi, *Memorie originali italiane risguardanti le belle arti*, ser. 2-3, Bologna, 1841-42.

Masetti Zannini—G. L. Masetti Zannini, *Pittori della seconda metà del Cinquecento in Roma*, Rome, 1974.

Milanesi—G. Milanesi, *Documenti per la storia dell' arte senese*, 3, Siena, 1856.

1500   Neroccio di Bartolommeo Landi. Milanesi, pp. 7-8; see now Gertrude Coor, *Neroccio de' Landi: 1447-1500*, Princeton, 1961, pp. 152-59.

1506   Lorenzo Lotto. G. Bampo, "Spigolature dall' archivio notarile di Treviso," *Archivio veneto*, 32, 1886, pp. 173-74.

1516   Fra Bartolommeo. Vicenzo Marchese, *Memorie dei più insigni pittori, scultori e architetti domenicani* (4th ed.), Bologna, 1879, 2, pp. 176-86.

1516   Mariotto Albertinelli. Ludovico Borgo, *The Works of Mariotto Albertinelli*, New York and London, 1976, pp. 553-55.

1524   Girolamo di Benvenuto. Milanesi, pp. 78-79.

1524   Giulio Romano. Paolo Mazio, "Particolari della famiglia e della vita di Giulio Romano ricavati da carte autentiche ed inedite," *Il Saggiatore*, 1, 1844, pp. 67-68.

1529   Palma Vecchio. Gustav Ludwig, "Archivalische Beiträge zur Geschichte der venezianischen Malerei," *Jahrbuch der königlich preussischen Kunstsammlungen*, 24, Beiheft, 1903, pp. 75-79.

1529   Giovanni Antonio Sodoma. Milanesi, pp. 110-12 (see also 1548-49).

1533   Zuan Maria di Zuan Battista a Zudaica. Gustav

Ludwig, "Archivalische Beiträge zur Geschichte der venezian-ischen Malerei," *Jahrbuch der königlich preussischen Kunstsammlungen*, 24, Beiheft, 1903, p. 25.

1547   Sebastiano del Piombo. B. Gasparoni, "Il testamento e l'inventario di Sebastiano del Piombo," *Arti e lettere*, 2, appendix, 1865, pp. 163-67; entries pertaining to art published by Michael Hirst, *Sebastiano del Piombo*, Oxford, 1981, pp. 154-56.

1548-1549   Giovanni Antonio Sodoma. Milanesi, pp. 181-82 (see also 1529).

1564   Michelangelo. Aurelio Gotti, *Vita di Michelangelo Buonarroti*, Florence, 1875, 2, pp. 148-51.

1566   Daniele da Volterra. B. Gasparoni, "La casa di Michelagnolo Buonarroti," *Il Buonarroti*, 1, 1866, pp. 178-80.

1573   Zenobio Camei. Masetti Zannini, p. 20.

1574   Giorgio Vasari. Alessandro Cecchi in *Giorgio Vasari*, Florence, 1981, pp. 30-32 (the Aretine house) and pp. 42-43 (the Florentine house).

1575   Girolamo Sicciolante, di Sermoneta. Masetti Zannini, pp. 103-108.

1577   Orazio Samacchini. Summarized by Gualandi, 3, pp. 178-79.

1578   Giulio Clovio. A. Bertolotti, "Don Giulio Clovio: Principe dei miniatori," *Atti e memorie delle deputazioni di storia patria per le provincie della Emilia*, new ser., 7, pt. 2, 1882, pp. 273-76.

1579   Marcello Venusti. Rome, Archivio di Stato, Collegio de' Notari Capitolini, Not. Curzio Saccoccia, vol. 1552 (28 October 1579), fols. 323r-325v and esp. 463r-469r; cited with extract by A. Bertolotti, "Giunte agli artisti lombardi in Roma," *Archivio storico lombardo*, 10, 1883, p. 106.

1580   Arcangelo Salimbeni. Milanesi, pp. 225-226 (extracts).

1583   Domenico Tibaldi. Gualandi, 2, pp. 30-40.

1584   Pietro Antonio Alciati. Masetti Zannini, p. 4.

1592   Girolamo Muziano. Ugo da Como, *Girolamo Muziano 1528-1592: Note e documenti*, Bergamo, 1930, pp. 193-196.

1592   Pietro Ximenez, di Cabreda. Masetti Zannini, p. 130.

1592   Jacopo Bassano. Giovanni Battista Verci, *Notizie intorno alla vita e alle opere de'pittori, scultori e intagliatori della città di Bassano*, Venice, 1775, pp. 91-100.

1599   "N." Masetti Zannini, pp. 130-31.

1602   Tommaso Laureti. St. Peter's, Archivio della Reverenda Fabbrica di San Pietro, 1 Piano, Series 2, vol. 7, fols. 69r-71r; cited by Morton Colp Abromson, *Painting in Rome during the Papacy of Clement VIII (1592-1605): A Documented Study*, New York and London, 1981, p. 68, n. 77.

1609   Annibale Carracci. Roberto Zapperi, "L'inventario di Annibale Carracci," *Antologia di belle arti*, 3, 1979, pp. 62-63.

1610   Federico Zuccaro. Bertolotti, pp. 284-85.

1610   Adam Elsheimer. Keith Andrews, *Adam Elsheimer*, Oxford, 1977, pp. 48-50.

1612   Federico Barocci. *Studi e notizie su Federico Barocci*, Florence, 1913, pp. 75-85.

1614   Carlo Sellitto. Museo e Gallerie Nazionali di Capodimonte, *Mostra didattica di Carlo Sellitto primo caravaggesco napoletano*, Naples, 1977, pp. 149-51, 151-52.

1615   Bernardino Baldi. Gualandi, 3, p. 186.

1616   Nicolao Ventura. Bertolotti, pp. 285-86.

1626   Guglielmo Caccia. Alessandro Baudi di Vesme, "L'arte negli stati sabaudi ai tempi di Carlo Emanuele I, di Vittorio Amedeo I e della reggenza di Cristina di Francia," *Atti della società piemontese di archeologia e belle arti*, 14, 1932, pp. 123-24.

1626   Cristofano Roncalli. Rome, Archivio di Stato, 30 Notai Capitolini, Ufficio 11, vol. 125, fols. 369r-373r; cited by W. Chandler Kirwin, "The Life and Drawing Style of Cristofano Roncalli,"

Paragone, 29, 1978, 335, p. 48, n. 18.

1627   Giulio Cesare Procaccini. Summarized by Vittorio Caprara, "Nuovi reperimenti intorno ai Procaccini," *Paragone*, 28, 1977, 333, p. 98, n. 10.

1627   Giovanni Battista Paggi. Genoa, Archivio di Stato, Not. Borsotto Bartolomeo, filza 29, scansia 968 (15 March 1627), cited with extracts mostly pertaining to the artist's library by Venanzio Belloni, *Caröggi, Creûze e Möntae*, Genoa, 1975, pp. 191-197.

1629   Antonio Pomarancio. Linda Freeman Bauer, "L'inventario dei beni di Antonio Pomarancio e alcune note sulla vita e l'opera del pittore," *Bollettino d'arte*, 68, 1983, 19, pp. 33-34.

1629   Paul Brill. Didier Bodart, "Les tableaux de la succession de Paul Bril," *Mélanges d'archéologie et d'histoire de l'art offerts au professeur Jacques Lavalleye, Université de Louvain recueil de travaux d'histoire et de philologie*, ser. 4, 45, 1970, pp. 10-12 (see also pp. 12-14).

1630   Daniele Crespi. Giorgio Nicodemi, *Daniele Crespi*, Busto Arsizio, 1930, pp. 43-56.

1633   Jean Lhomme. Jacques Bousquet, "Un compagnon des caravagesques français a Rome Jean Lhomme," *Gazette des beaux-arts*, ser. 6, 53, 1959, pp. 89-92 (French translation).

1633   Antonio Zelli. Bertolotti, p. 286.

1649   Andrea Camassei. Ann Sutherland Harris, "A Contribution to Andrea Camassei Studies," *The Art Bulletin*, 52, 1970, pp. 69-70.

1654   Baccio Ciarpi. Adelaide Pescatori, "L'inventario della dimora di un pittore del Seicento a Roma," *Rivista d'arte*, 33, 1958, pp. 65-72.

1656   Michele Pietra. C.-A. Levi, *Le collezioni veneziane d'arte e d'antichita dal secolo XIV ai nostri giorni*, Venice, 1900, 2, pp. 19-24; see now Simona Savini Branca, *Il collezionismo veneziano nel '600*, Padua, 1964, pp. 134-40.

1660   Michelangelo Cerquozzi. Giuliano Briganti, Ludovica Trezzani, and Laura Laureati, *I bamboccianti*, Rome, 1983, pp. 381-85.

1661   Andrea Sacchi. Ann Sutherland Harris, *Andrea Sacchi*, Oxford, 1977, pp. 119-22.

1664   Francesco Raspantino. Richard E. Spear, *Domenichino*, New Haven and London, 1982, pp. 338-46.

1665   Francesco Cairo. Silvano Colombo in *Francesco Cairo 1607-1665*, Milan, 1983, pp. 241-49.

1665   Nicolas Poussin. F. Boyer, "Les inventaires après décès de Nicolas Poussin et de Claude Lorrain," *Bulletin de la société de l'histoire de l'art français*, 54, 1928, pp. 146-49.

1667   Cornelius De Wael. Maurice Vaes, "Corneille De Wael (1592-1667)," *Bulletin de l'institut historique belge de Rome*, 5, 1925, pp. 224-34.

1669   Pietro da Cortona. Karl Noehles, *La Chiesa dei SS. Luca e Martina nell' opera di Pietro da Cortona*, Rome, 1969, pp. 364-65 (extracts).

1673   Mario de' Fiori. O. Montenovesi, "Il pittore Mario de' Fiori, Documenti," *Archivio della società romana di storia patria*, 73, 1950, pp. 225-35.

1675   Gaspard Dughet. Marie-Nicole Boisclair, "Documents inédits relatifs a Gaspard Dughet," *Bulletin de la société de l'histoire de l'art français*, 99, 1973, pp. 83-84.

1681   Giacinto Gimignani. Ursula Verena Fischer [Pace], *Giacinto Gimignani (1606-81): Eine Studie zur römischen Malerei des Seicento*, Diss. Albert-Ludwigs-Universität, 1973, pp. 126-31.

1681   Justus Sustermans. Alessandro Guidotti in *Sustermans: Sessant' anni alla corte dei Medici*, Florence, 1983, pp. 123-131.

1682   Claude Lorrain. F. Boyer, "Les inventaires après décès de Nicolas Poussin et de Claude Lorrain," *Bulletin de la société de l'histoire de l'art français*, 54, 1928, pp. 156-59.

1682   Francesco Cozza. Luigi Cunsolo, *Francesco Cozza pittore ed acquafortista*, Cosenza, 1966, pp. 296-99.

1682   Heirs of Paolo Veronese. Gregorio Gattinoni, *Inventario di una casa veneziana del secolo XVII (La casa degli eccellenti Caliari eredi di Paolo il Veronese)*, Mestre, 1914.

1687   Pietro Liberi. Silvio de Kunert, "Notizie e documenti su Pietro Liberi," *Rivista d'arte*, 13, 1931, pp. 560-67.

1691   Giacinto Brandi. Rome, Archivio di Stato, Not. AC, vol. 4282 (20 March 1691), fols. 298r-312v, cited by Antonella Pampalone, "Per Giacinto Brandi," *Bollettino d'arte*, 58, 1973, p. 156.

1693   Ermanno Stroiffi. C.-A. Levi, *Le collezioni veneziane d'arte e d'antichità dal secolo XIV ai nostri giorni*, Venice, 1900, 2, pp. 77-78.

1703   Lazzaro Baldi. Antonella Pampalone, *Disegni di Lazzaro Baldi nelle collezioni del Gabinetto Nazionale delle Stampe*, Rome, 1979, pp. 147-56 (with reference to other inventories).

1712   Carlo Maratta. Romeo Galli, "I tesori d'arte di un pittore del Seicento (Carlo Maratta)," *L'Archiginnasio*, 22, 1927, pp. 231-38; 23, 1928, pp. 59-78; and David L. Bershad, "The Newly Discovered Testament and Inventories of Carlo Maratti and his Wife Francesca," *Antologia di belle arti*, 25-26, 1985, 68-84.

1713   Stefano Maria Legnani. Vittorio Caprara, "Nuovi documenti su Stefano Maria Legnani, il Legnanino," *Paragone*, 31, 1980, 363, pp. 97-101 (extracts).

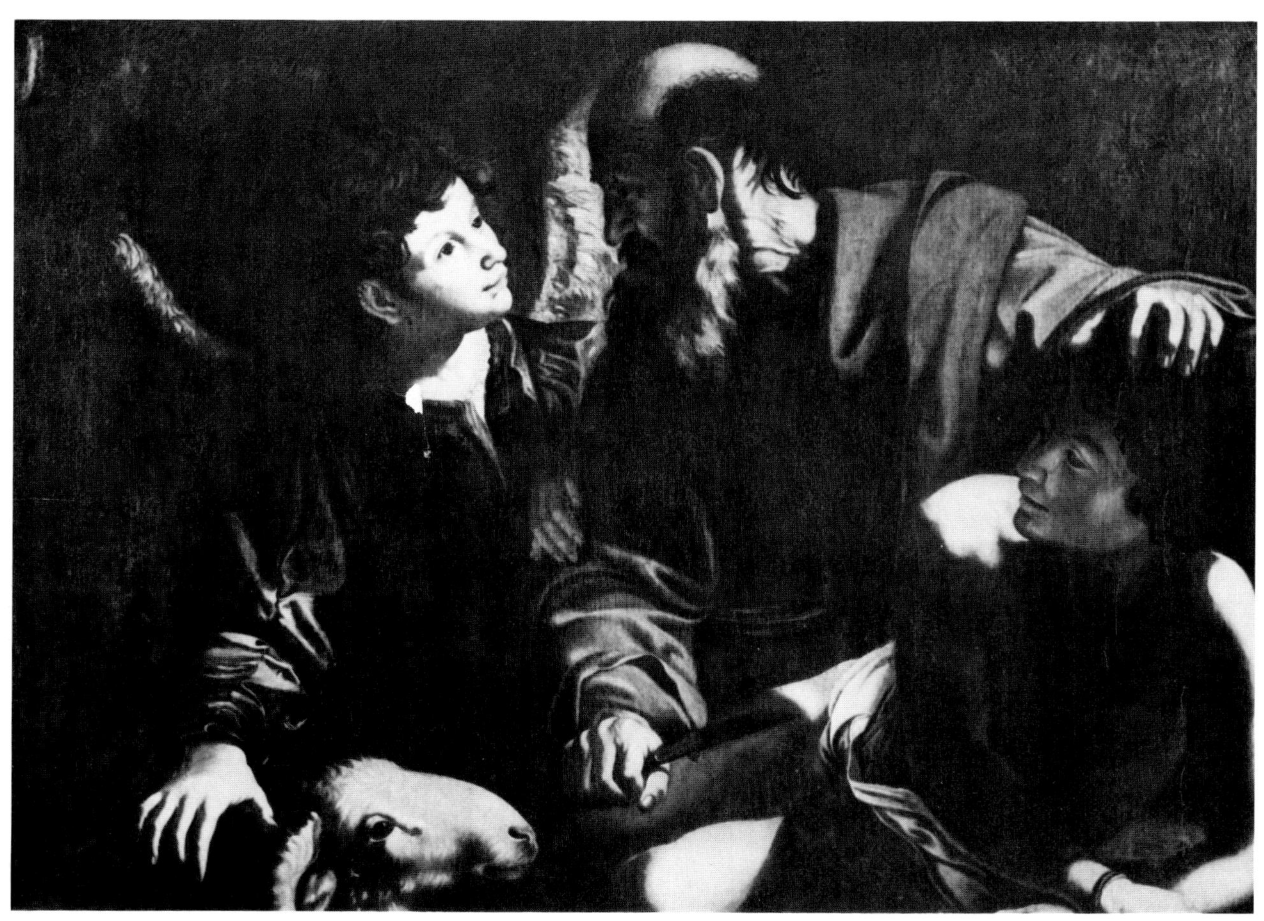

63.   Anonymous artist, *Sacrifice of Isaac*, Boal Collection, Boalsburg, Pennsylvania.

A Caravaggesque *Sacrifice of Isaac:* Multiple Versions, Multiple Problems*

Since antiquity, the cultural heritage of Italy has inspired artists from other countries. There were revivals of Roman antiquity throughout the Middle Ages and, from the period of the Renaissance on, an influx of foreigners came to see both the country and its art. Major painters arrived including, in the fifteenth century, Van der Weyden from Flanders and Jean Fouquet from France: in the sixteenth century, Dürer and El Greco; and in the seventeenth, Poussin and Rubens. After the turmoil associated with the Reformation and the Sack of Rome, relative peace and prosperity reigned in Italy during the Seicento, the age of the Church Triumphant, and it was during the 1600s that the greatest number of artists from all over Europe travelled to Italy and, especially, Rome. Even more attractive than the pageantry of Venice, reflected in its sumptuous painting, were the artistic traditions of the Eternal City.[1] Of major importance was the art of antiquity, the Italian Renaissance, represented primarily by Raphael and Michelangelo, the Academies, in particular the Accademia di San Luca, founded in 1593 by Federigo Zuccari, and finally the recent and revolutionary painting of Michaelangelo da Caravaggio.[2]

According to Alfred Moir, the greatest period of activity for these "Caravaggeschi" or unofficial followers of Caravaggio, was circa 1610-1640.[3] During the first six years of the seventeenth century when Caravaggio was still in Rome, the jealous and hot-blooded painter, threatening artists who imitated his style, `had discouraged to a great extent its dissemination in that city.[4] Just after his death in 1610, the Caravaggeschi in Rome were at a peak of activity,

although the Caravaggesque style of painting was short-lived there and no longer in vogue after circa 1620, having been replaced almost immediately by the exuberant High Baroque of Giovanni Lanfranco. Its popularity continued until a later date elsewhere: about 1630 or after in Spain and through the middle of the century in provincial France.[5]

Problems concerning the Caravaggeschi are challenging and numerous.[6] Confusion arises over the many unknown or anonymous Caravaggeschi as well as the scores of unattributed paintings and multiple versions. Moir identifies these anonymous, unofficial followers of Caravaggio as students, provincials, professionals, and travellers producing copies which served as studies, souvenirs, replacements, substitutes, duplicates, and fakes.[7] In many cases, even the country from which the artist originates is debated.[8] Sometimes an attempt is made to assign to a painting an artist so obscure that his name is not known. Such an attribution was made for the famous *Still Life* in the National Gallery in Washington, once given to Caravaggio himself, but now, along with a few other paintings, to the obscure "Pensionante del Saraceni," the French roommate of Carlo Saraceni.[9] There are also many excellent Caravaggesque paintings for which no artist at all can be identified.[10]

Moir divided this "potpourri" of paintings, related stylistically to those of Caravaggio, into four basic categories: (1) Compositions, (2) Versions, that is, other paintings of the same composition and of equal quality, (3) Variants, similar in format but with different additions and arrangements, and (4) Copies, inferior versions.[11] With Caravaggio, as with other artists of the period, there are sometimes more than one painting of the same subject and composition, and both of equally fine quality. In other words, there is more than one "signature" painting.[12] Moir has analyzed data concerning the physical aspects of such Caravaggesque multiples with the following conclusions: as a rule, variants outnumber copies; although some copies are larger, most are smaller and shorter, less vertical, than the original; and finally, the scale of the copy seems to depend upon the importance of the original.[13] Despite these statistics, there are still many unanswerable questions related to their overall significance within the artistic context of the Seicento. For example, it has yet to be determined why two paintings by the same artist, equal in quality and access and often within close proximity, will receive such different responses.[14] There is not only the problem of multiple versions, but of multiple copies, and to complicate matters further, these are not only of originals by Caravaggio,[15] but of originals by other hands working in the style of Caravaggio. Moir refers to these as "fraudulent originals," that is, paintings which are original in conception but a recreation of Caravaggio.[16]

He believes that this term is applicable to a famous *Sacrifice of Isaac*, well represented by a painting in the Columbus Chapel of Boal Mansion in Boalsburg, Pennsylvania (fig. 63).[17] Altogether, there are possibly as many as nineteen examples of this composition, an unusually large number even for Caravaggesque multiples, although no prints or drawn copies are known. Moir does not consider even the composition to be by Caravaggio, but it has been published elsewhere as part of the corpus of Caravaggio's paintings and as a copy of a lost original by Caravaggio.[18]

Whatever the tenebrist painting in Boalsburg may be, its composition, executed in the style of Caravaggio, was undeniably very popular in the Seicento (and perhaps subsequent centuries as well).[19] Copies, probable versions, or possible originals of this particular *Sacrifice of Isaac* can be associated with Spain, Italy, Peru, Portugal, and, more recently, the United States. The provenance of the Boalsburg painting is Spanish.

The Columbus Chapel (figs. 64, 65, 66), which dates from the seventeenth century, was brought to America in about 1919 or possibly earlier.[20] The Chapel's original name was Our Lady of the Pastures (Senõra de Branãs).[21] It was located in the Palacio de

Colón in Llamas del Mouro, near Oviedo, in northern Spain (figs. 67, 68). The Chapel was dedicated on February 1, 1612, in accordance with a decree of the Bishop of Oviedo.[22] Although it is not possible to prove that the paintings in the Chapel, several of which date from the early seventeenth century, came with the Chapel, it is probable that most or all were inherited from the Sierra family (figs. 69, 70).[23]

As far as can be determined, Caravaggio painted only one *Sacrifice of Isaac*, that of 1603, now in the Uffizi Gallery in Florence (fig. 71).[24] The work displays several remarkable qualities: for this late date, there is no tenebrist light; the inclusion of a vast landscape is unusual for an artist who almost never painted it even in minimal form; and the composition is rather retardataire and contrived, somewhat Mannerist, as is the motif of the stiffly gesturing angel. Moir, while doubting that the Boal composition is by Caravaggio, sees this tenebrist interpretation as "improved":

> The anonymous inventor reduced the compelling melodrama of the Uffizi original, but he also replaced Caravaggio's friezelike arrangement of the figures, with a more modern, three-dimensional grouping of the figures around the spatial center of the knife and Abraham's foreshortened arm, the result producing a composition like that of Roman Caravaggesque paintings of ca. 1610-1620.[25]

Moir is uncertain as to whether any of the paintings in this Boalsburg group, that is, with this particular tenebrist composition, could be the original. In his references to other versions, he proposes that the *Sacrifice of Isaac* in the Bona Collection in Como (fig. 72), said to have been stolen in 1949,[26] and that in Castellamare di Stabia outside Naples (fig. 73),[27] are seventeenth century copies.[28] About the Boalsburg painting, the obviously inferior copy in the Convent of St. Ursula in Alcalá de Henares (fig. 74), and another fine example in a savings bank in Madrid, the Confederación de Cajas de Ahorros (fig. 75), he is noncommittal.[29] The latter along with the one in Pennsylvania, is superior, and both of these could be versions, as defined by Moir, if not originals. It is difficult if not impossible, for anyone to dismiss problems of relative quality or attribution without seeing all of the paintings,[30] and added to the problem of accessibility is that of the poor condition of some.[31]

All of the paintings of this composition, with the exception of a smaller one in Lima,[32] are of approximately the same size: ca. 1.2 meters x 1.78 meters, or about 42 x 63 inches. None are signed or dated.[33] In light of Moir's conclusions about the scale and proportions of copies, that they are often smaller and less vertical than the original, this could indicate that all extant canvases, the Lima painting being the smallest, may be copies of a larger, possibly more vertical, lost original. The idea of the scale of the copy being dependent upon the importance of the original is, perhaps, more applicable. All of the versions, except for the one in Lima, are typically large-scale Baroque and, if not originals in themselves, then must make reference to a major painting.

This composition has several interesting features. The angel, with reddish highlights on his ears reflecting flames of the external sacrificial fire below, is very portrait-like. Such an anthropormorphic angel is, in itself, typical of the period and can be found in paintings such as the *Santa Francesca Romana* of Giacomo Galli ("Lo Spadarino") in the Collection of Dr. Edoardo Almagiai in Rome.[34] In our painting, the angel not only has short cropped hair, but is in contemporary dress, a detail unusual, but not totally without parallel, in the early seventeenth century.[35] The portrait-like face and the suit of the angel in the Boalsburg painting, as well as the other versions and/or copies, indicate that the artist probably used an actual model in contemporary dress.[36] The identity of the angel, especially portrait-like in the Boalsburg painting, is unknown, but his tangible quality and physical presence recall the popularity of stage plays and masques held not only in the Church, but in the Spanish court.[37]

A variant of Caravaggio's *Sacrifice of Isaac* of 1603 is provided by an engraving of Jean Charles Le Vasseur (1734-1816; fig. 76), a print of which is in the Boston Museum of Fine Arts.[38] It has been repeatedly and erroneously linked to the Boalsburg composition.[39] With it can be associated instead a different composition represented by a *Sacrifice of Isaac* in the Rapp collection in Stockholm (fig. 77), and another variant, a vertical painting in the Ramirez collection in Jaen, Spain (fig. 78).[40] There are still other Caravaggesque compositions of the *Sacrifice of Isaac* to which the composition of the Boalsburg group could be compared. An anonymous example, which was for sale in Spain during the early 1980s (fig. 79) is somewhat related to the Le Vasseur print in the figure of Isaac.[41] The French painter, Valentin, although one of the Caravaggeschi, created an interpretation (fig. 80) which

bears little resemblance to any of the preceding compositions except to recall, in the closeness and planar arrangement of the figures, the Caravaggio of 1603. A little later in the century the Neapolitan, Francesco Guarini, offers much more violence (fig. 81) with true Baroque emphasis upon the momentary action, but once again, an entirely different composition. Still another variation which was at Bonham's Auction House in London (fig. 82) is like the Jaen painting in its verticality but, despite a similarity between the figure of Isaac and that of Caravaggio's David in the Villa Borghese, bears the least formal resemblance to any of the previously cited examples. Such comparisons underscore the existence of other Caravaggesque paintings of the *Sacrifice of Isaac* which are not of the same tradition.[42]

A more pertinent comparison for the Boalsburg painting and its group is a *Sacrifice of Isaac* in the Colegio de Corpus Christi in Valencia (fig. 83). It has, very recently, been attributed convincingly to the Spanish painter, Pedro Orrente (1570-1645) and should probably be dated from about 1616.[43] The figure of Abraham in the Orrente, in both physiognomy and pose, with profile facing toward the left, is remarkably like that of Abraham in the Boalsburg composition. Both figures of Abraham are Caravaggesque types and comparable to one of the apostles in his famous *Death of the Virgin* of 1606 (fig. 84). Orrente's painting is, without doubt, closest to the version represented by the Boalsburg painting, primarily in the almost identical figure of Abraham.

The implications provided by analysis of geographic distribution of paintings of the Boalsburg version have direct bearing upon the problem of attribution. Moir maintains with logic that "a concentration of copies of a lost painting in a country or area of region may offer some evidence as to the location of the original...whereas the lack of any copies of a lost original in a country or a region is strong evidence of the original's having been unknown there."[44] If we recall both present and previous locations of all nineteen versions and copies, we can notice a concentration of paintings in both Italy and especially Spain, the central region in particular.[45]

Spain

1) Llamas del Mouro (Asturias), Spain (now in Boalsburg, Pennsylvania, U.S.A.).

2) Peñãfiel (Valladolid)

3) Madrid-Barcelona dealer

4) Confederación de Cajas de Ahorros, Madrid (formerly private collection, Madrid).

5) Museum of San Carlos, Valencia*

6) La Guardia, Toledo*

7) Parish Church, Torrijos, Toledo

8) Parish Church, Torrijos, Toledo

9) Ermita del Cristo, Toledo

10) Convent of St. Ursula, Alcalá de Henares

11) Cathedral, Zamora

12) S. Roque, Seville

13) Private collection

14) Dowry of Donã Antonia Cecilia Hernandez de Hijar (early 18th Century).

15) Saragossa (see note 19)

Italy

16) Varese, (Como), Prof. Luciano Bona*

17) Castellamare di Stabia, Naples

Portugal

18) Museum of Art, Lisbon*

Peru

19) Lima

*These have been reported missing.[46]

The distribution is significant in light of the fact that, during the early seventeenth century, very few Italian painters visited Spain,[47] whereas many Spanish artists came to Italy. Conversely, almost no paintings travelled from Spain to Italy, although numerous canvases were sent from Italy to Spain. Since both Naples and Sicily were at this time under Spanish dominance and governed by Spanish Viceroys, the major part of the traffic of paintings from Italy to Spain was through the port of Naples. Needless to say, paintings sent to Spain from Italy were not always by Italian artists.[48] The locations of paintings with our composition imply that it had its origins in a painter of any nationality who was working in Italy.

This geographical survey underscores a stylistic evaluation of the Boalsburg version of the *Sacrifice of Isaac*. Even without such information, and using the best paintings of this group as a basis for judgements, they would appear to be either Italian (Roman or Neapolitan) or Spanish, and dating from about 1610-1620. This is, however, a matter of opinion.

Anthony Blunt, who visited the Columbus Chapel during the 1960s, made associations between the style of the Pennsylvania *Sacrifice* and the French painter, Simon Vouet.[49] Yet, even the closest comparison to Vouet's early Caravaggesque period in Rome, represented by paintings such as the *Birth of the Virgin* of ca. 1620 in S. Francesco a Ripa, emphasizes the differences more than the similarities between Vouet and the Boalsburg composition. The French painting is much more sophisticated and skillful with a far more interesting and complex spatial articulation. A letter written in 1963 by Pierre Boal, grandfather of the present Director of Boal Mansion, mentions that "a great English professor and connoisseur who has just visited," (probably, again, Anthony Blunt), suggested the name of Orazio Gentileschi, the Pisan-born Roman follower of Caravaggio and one of the few Caravaggeschi who had known Caravaggio personally, as a possible artist for the painting.[50] Once again, the closest type of comparison, Gentileschi's *Judith and Holofernes* of ca. 1610-20 in the Wadsworth-Atheneum, with typical Gentileschi elegance, is as radically different from the Boalsburg painting as it is from Caravaggio's own *Judith and Holofernes* in the Coppi Collection in Rome. Stephen Pepper, who saw the painting in Boalsburg during the 1970s, has proposed an attribution to the Neapolitan painter, Giovanni Battista Caracciolo.[51] If we compare the detail of the Boalsburg figure of Isaac (fig. 85) to that of Adam in Caracciolo's *Immaculate Conception* of ca. 1610 in Santa Maria della Stella in Naples (fig. 86), there is certainly a similarity of pose, as well as technique of lighting with typical Caracciolesque pools of light falling over the figure placed before a chiaroscuro background, but whether such motifs are sufficient for final attribution is doubtful.[52] The pose of Isaac alone is not that unusual as it recalls not only Caracciolo's *Adam*, but the figure of St. Paul the hermit in what is now thought to be an early work by the Spanish Baroque painter, Jusepe de Ribera in the Meadows Museum at Southern Methodist University (fig. 87).[53] Caracciolo's *Salome* (of around 1615-20) in the Uffizi is also somewhat similar in its effect of light bathing the figures but, again, the overall effect is not that close to our *Sacrifice of Isaac*. Although Caracciolo is a better attribution than Vouet or Gentileschi, there are other Neapolitans who have only recently received attention and who might be more relevant. There is Carlo Sellitto, whose *St. Cecilia* in the Capodimonte in Naples bears some resemblance in its figure types to those of Zurbarán, to whom the Peru copy of our painting was attributed.

Jusepe de Ribera, from Valencia in the eastern part of Spain, might be called a Spanish-Neapolitan Caravaggesque painter. There is dispute as to the date of his arrival in Italy, but he settled in the Spanish-dominated city of Naples in 1616, if not before.[54] After travelling through northern Italy, he came to Rome and joined the Accademia di San Luca probably in the preceding year.[55] According to recent but unfounded interpretations by Craig Felton, Ribera's arrival in Naples could have been as early as 1607, and he could have been a pupil of either Carlo Sellito or Caracciolo.[56] Family archives in Boalsburg maintain that their painting of the *Sacrifice of Isaac* is by the same Jusepe de Ribera. Unfortunately, the earliest datable document to this effect, from the will of Mme. Maria Victoria Montalvo, the "widow of Colón," is recent, dated May 6, 1906,[57] but the attribution to Ribera has been a tradition in the family over the centuries. Sixteenth and seventeenth century records of the Sierra family, which pertain to the Chapel, are of little use. They describe in great detail jewelry, furnishing, and business transactions but refer to the paintings collectively. There are no references whatever to particular painters or paintings.[58]

The Boalsburg *Sacrifice of Isaac* does not resemble closely the few early Riberas we know: the *Sense of Taste* which may date from ca. 1615 and be one of the earliest extant Ribera paintings, the *St. Jerome* of ca. 1620 in the Capodimonte, the *Drunken Silenus* of 1626, or the *Crucifixion*, ca. 1620-6 painted for the Duke of Osuna, who was Viceroy of Naples from 1616-20 (fig. 88).[59] By 1626, when accepted

into the Order of Christ, Ribera was referred to as "pittore eccelente."[60] Today, we have only a handful of paintings and prints by him from between about 1616 and 1626, and probably none before 1615. It is, therefore, extremely difficult to judge his very early style which is, for the most part, unknown. I think we can conclude from these examples of his early efforts that, at least by 1620, Ribera was a far more sophisticated and independent painter, less tied to a strict Caravaggesque tradition, than is the artist who executed our painting of the *Sacrifice of Isaac*. The Boalsburg painting is, nevertheless, of fine quality if eclectic, and probably a very early work of one of the more distinguished Caravaggeschi.

We might digress for a moment and consider some of the theoretical aspects of such stylistic analysis. The relationship between the early and mature modes of an artist varies greatly according to the individual. Dürer and Picasso were highly precocious, producing remarkable drawings at the age of about thirteen, and although their styles were not yet mature, their extraordinary talent is evident. The opposite is true of the Spanish Baroque painter, Francisco Ribalta, a Valencian and possible teacher of Ribera.[61] Ribalta's *Decapitation of St. James* in the church of Algemesí, Valencia, of 1603 is a timid adaptation of that in the Escorial painted in 1571 by his teacher, El Mudo. His *St. James Killing the Moors*, also in Algemesí and from this same early period, is poorly drawn with an awkwardness that is the result of more than its Mannerist heritage. With Ribalta, however, there is a drastic change from the early works to the late. One could hardly believe that his *St. Bernard Embracing the Crucified Christ* of 1620 in the Prado is by the same artist. It is Caravaggesque painting of the highest quality—dramatic, concentrated, naturalistic, and well conceived. A radical change in style between the early and late works can be seen as well in the works of the already-mentioned Pedro Orrente, although the level of quality is more consistent than in the case of Ribalta.[62] His early *Supper at Emmaus* in the Budapest Museum from the late sixteenth century, which is in the tradition of Venetian painting of the period (he was called "the Spanish Bassano"), bears little or no resemblance to his *Sacrifice of Isaac* of ca. 1600-10 (fig. 83) which is in his mature Caravaggesque style. Although one might conclude that the greatest artists, such as Velazquez and Rembrandt, consistently produced excellent works from the outset of their career,[63] artistic development is an individual problem and one about which it is impossible to make sweeping generalizations.

We must now evaluate and summarize the information available concerning the Boalsburg group as a whole and that *Sacrifice* in particular which is a superior example of this composition. From purely visual analysis, we would probably place the painting from about 1610-20. If Italian, it could well have been painted in Rome or Naples. Since most of the versions of this *Sacrifice of Isaac* are in Italy and Spain, they are probably by an artist who was working in Italy. The concentration in Spain of this particular composition would indicate that for some reason it was extremely important, especially for the Spanish and for the city of Toledo. Family tradition of the present owners maintains that the painting is by Jusepe de Ribera, but Ribera's early years, especially before 1615, are unknown to us. We do have, however, a letter written by Ludovico Carracci in 1616 which mentions a great Spanish painter, almost certainly Ribera, who had been in Parma at this early date and who worked in the style of Caravaggio.[64] For example, we know that Ribera did a drawing of the famous *Crucifixion of St. Peter* in Santa Maria del Popolo.[65] Furthermore, we know that one painting in the Boalsburg group, the *Sacrifice of Isaac* in the Parish church in Peñafiel (Valladolid), was done for the dukes of Osuna, one of whom was Viceroy of Naples from 1616-1620 and an important early patron of Jusepe de Ribera. Paintings which Ribera executed for the Duke of Osuna were often sent back to Spain, an example being the famous *Crucifixion*, already mentioned, of ca. 1620-26 painted in Naples but sent almost immediately to the Colegiata in Osuna. The date on which the Boalsburg Chapel was dedicated and probably decorated, 1612, coincides with the early career of Ribera. Finally, and of vital importance, is the fact that Ribera did paint a very famous *Sacrifice of Isaac* which is no longer extant but known to us through description. It is mentioned by the eighteenth century Neapolitan biographer, Bernardo de Dominici, as one of the major attractions in the city of Rome:

> Moltissime se ne veggono nella famosissime gallerie di Roma. Nella villa Savelli è sacrifico di Abramo, opera molto lodata: e dicesi che il Ribera dipingendola, forte biasimava coloro che avean dipinto in mano ad Abramo uno spadone, laddove il coltello (com'egli fece) era proprio per il sagrifici, come a nostri giorni egregiamente ha fatto il celebre Carlo Maratta.[66]

It is interesting that Moir, like de Dominici, has commented primarily upon the central knife in our *Sacrifice of Isaac*, without in any way being dependent upon the earlier writer's observation.[67] One wonders whether de Dominici was careless in his reference to the Villa, rather than the Palazzo, of the Savelli.[68] There were a number of palaces in Rome which were associated with the family, the most famous of which was in the ancient theatre of Marcellus (fig. 89) and had already, since the fifteenth century, been the palace of the Orsini family.[69] It was in this particular palace that the Savelli had housed a famous art collection, and it is known that they owned other paintings by Ribera.[70]

In the final analysis, our *Sacrifice of Isaac* does not truly resemble the works of any known painter. The question remains as to whether or not circumstantial evidence is sufficient for an association with the famous one by Ribera.[71] If ours is, indeed, the same, it would fill an important gap in our knowledge of the Spaniard's early career. The most conservative solution would be to let it remain in the realm of the anonymous Caravaggeschi.

Jeanne Chenault Porter
The Pennsylvania State University

Notes

*   I wish to thank the following people for their assistance and encouragement: the late Francis Hyslop, George L. Mauner, Christopher Boal Lee, Richard L. Garner, Donald C. Henderson, Grace R. Perez, and James A. Jamison.

1.   Venice, which had been a major artistic center in the sixteenth century, ceased to be in the Seicento. Nevertheless, most seventeenth-century painters continued to visit it, and it is thought that both Caravaggio and Ribera were probably there at some time. Few painters from other regions settled in Venice, an exception being the Ligurian, Bernardo Strozzi.

2.   Some foreign painters, such as Peter Paul Rubens and Adam Elsheimer, arrived before the death of Caravaggio in 1610, but many arrived after. There was also the confluence of Italian painters from other cities who came to study Caravaggio's paintings in Rome: Saraceni from Venice, Orazio Gentileschi from Pisa, Borgianni from Sicily, Manfredi from Mantua, etc. Caravaggio himself was from

Lombardy; the Carracci and their followers, some of which were influenced by Caravaggio, were from Bologna. Most of the Neapolitan painters, such as G. B. Caracciolo, were in Rome breifly.

3. Alfred Moir, *Caravaggio and His Copyists*, New York, 1976, p. 4. See note 5. In Naples, Artemisia Gentileschi continued to paint in the Caravaggesque mode well into the middle of the century.

4. *Ibid.*, p. 4. Especially after 1603, Caravaggio discouraged imitators. Because of his adaptation of Caravaggio's *Crucifixion of St. Peter* in S. Maria del Popolo, Guido Reni was in danger for his life. G. Honthorst's drawing after the same painting was done after 1610. Despite earlier protestations, the *Crucifixion* was copied frequently after the death of Caravaggio by painters such as Francisco Ribalta, who sent a signed copy back to Spain. Moir, pp. 92-93. Caravaggio was in Naples twice, before and after his visits to Malta and Sicily. The Neapolitan school of painting emerged shortly after his first departure from Naples in 1607.

5. *Ibid.*, p. 5, states that by the middle of the seventeenth century, Caravaggesque painting was out of style. There are, nevertheless, adaptations later in the century by painters such as the French provincial master, Georges de la Tour.

6. *Ibid.* Also of value is the Benedict Nicolson, *The International Caravaggesque Movement*, Oxford, 1979.

7. Moir, *op. cit.*, pp. 11-12.

8. Examples of such Caravaggesque paintings about which there is confusion concerning their national origin include *The Guardroom* (Dresden, Gemäldegalerie), attributed to both Manfredi and Tournier; *The Carpenter's Shop* (Hartford, Wadsworth Athenaeum), originally thought to be by Carlo Saraceni, but now given to Guy François. For an analysis of the French Caravaggeschi, as they are related to the Italian, see: (Catalogue), *Valentin et les Caravaggesques français*, Grand Palais, Paris, 1974, pp. 108; Pierre Rosenberg, *France in the Golden Age* (Seventeenth Century French Paintings in American Collections), The Metropolitan Museum of Art, New York, 1982, pp. 63, 197-199.

9. Rosenberg, *Ibid.*

10. Examples in major museums of such fine Caravaggesque paintings, for which an attribution is still in question, include the *Death of Adonis* (Cleveland, Museum of Art), and the *St. Agatha* (Naples, Capodimonte). Craig Felton, *Jusepe de Ribera* (Ph.D. thesis, University of Pittsburgh, 1971), has confused matters further by stating that the *St. Agnes* in the Dresden Gemäldegalerie is a studio attribution. Such erroneous attributions have, unfortunately, been recorded by other writers. Although Felton corrects this particular misattribution in his more recent catalogue (Craig Felton and William B. Jordon, *Jusepe de Ribera, lo Spagnoletto*, Kimbell Museum, Fort Worth, 1982), there are several other examples of faulty judgment in his inclusion of paintings, particularly some in galleries and on the art market, which are surely not originals by Ribera.

11. Moir, *op. cit.*, p. 2.

12. Such multiple originals include the two paintings of *John the Baptist* by Caravaggio, one in the Capitoline and the other in the Doria-Pamphili Collection in Rome. In the sixteenth century, Titian did multiple originals of *Danae*, *Venus and Adonis*, etc.

13. Moir, *op. cit.*, pp. 3, 26, 27.

14. This could be due to the subject itself. See note 19. Moir, *ibid.*, p. 20. For some reason, perhaps the complexity of the composition or the rarity of the subject, Caravaggio's *Seven Acts of Mercy*, still in the Pio Monte della Misericordia in Naples, was never copied. Gian Pietro Bellori's criticism of Caravaggio's *Conversion of St. Paul* in the Cerasi Chapel was surely not responsible for the dearth of painted and drawn copies. The *Crucifixion* opposite (see notes 4, 65) was both adapted and copied frequently. Moir, *ibid.*, p. 34. There are neither extant copies of Caravaggio's *Conversion* nor literary references to copies,

(there are both for his *Crucifixion*). *Ibid.*, p. 22: "This multiplication must be indicative of some penchant for the original, . . . or perhaps the influence of a single copyist . . . or finally of the practice of making copies of copies . . ."

15. Bartolomeo Manfredi from Mantua often forged paintings by Caravaggio, especially after the latter's death in 1610. *Ibid.*, p. 35, is extremely conservative in his acceptance of only one extant painting, the *Mary and Martha* in the Detroit Art Institute, as a copy of a lost autograph Caravaggio.

16. *Ibid.*, pp. 18, 36.

17. The painting in Boalsburg (105 C, Fig. 87 in Moir, p. 117) is 41-3/4 in. x 63 in. It is not signed or dated. The condition is poor, with the top of the head of Abraham retouched and the knee of Isaac over-painted. It seems that the painting was not cut down on the sides or top. The hands of Isaac might have been cut off or rolled under, since they appear as complete in other versions of the composition. The angel has auburn hair and wears a dark jacket with purple sleeves. His ears are reddish. Abraham has a red robe and brown cloak.

18. Moir, *op. cit.*, p. 117. Moir publishes the Boalsburg painting as in Boalsbury. He believes that it is not a composition by Caravaggio. Moir has not seen the painting, but acquired a photo of it in the files of the Courtauld Institute in London. The photo was supplied by Anthony Blunt, who had seen the painting in Pennsylvania during the 1960s. Michael Kitson, *The Complete Work of Caravaggio* (Classics of Art), London, 1969, no. 30, includes the version in the Bona Collection in Como (see fig. 72). "To judge from the photograph, the rather slack linear figure style, scattered pools of light and totally undramatic treatment of the subject, seem more typical of a follower of Caravaggio, possibly Caracciolo himself." Kitson states in a letter of Nov. 15, 1977, that he doubts that the composition is by either Caravaggio or Caracciolo. Renato Guttuso, in his Italian edition of the *Classici dell'arte (L'Opera completa)*, Milan, 1967, p. 92, no. 35, includes the Como painting as among those of Caravaggio. Nicolson, *op. cit.*, lists a number of variants under "Caravaggesque Unknown" (Roman-based), but adds that this specification is "unsettled." See pp. 30, 31, 37. Nicolson mentions six types of compositions for the *Sacrifice of Isaac* (the first and third are virtually the same. See figs. 76, 77). He includes other examples in Verona (attributed to Saraceni), in Glasgow (to Loeweehns), Vienna (Dorotheum), and a private collection in Naples, none of which are illustrated. Nicolson concludes that the composition of the Boalsburg *Sacrifice* is by Caravaggio and mentions three copies of it after a lost original. Maurizio Marini, *Io, Michelangelo da Caravaggio*, Rome, 1974, cited by Nicolson, reproduces the paintings in Como, Castellamare di Stabia, and the Confederación in Madrid (figs. 72, 73, 74), all of which be believes are copies of a lost Caravaggio. Valentin (Catalogue), *op. cit.*, p. 178; the author believes that the Boalsburg composition is by Caravaggio and known through copies (Como, Castellamare di Stabia). Neither is close to the *Sacrifice* by Valentin in Montreal (fig. 80).

19. It is uncertain whether the composition or the subject matter account for the large number of similar paintings in "the Boalsburg group." See note 24. There is no apparent association with Maffeo Barberini. There is the question why this Old Testament theme was so much in demand during the period of the Counter-Reformation, when, following upon the dictates of the Council of Trent, subjects of Christ, the Madonna, and the Saints were preferred. Many Old Testament subjects were important for their roles as precursors of the New Testament. Paintings depicting *Judith, Esther and Hasueras, David and Goliath*, etc., were also very popular during the Seicento. Gian Pietro Lomazzo, *Trattato dell' arte della pittura, scoltora et architettura*, Milan, 1584, gives numerous references to Abraham and Isaac, as well as many other Old Testament heroes. He mentions Abraham as a symbol of Faith, virtue, etc. For other interpretations of the subject during the early Seicento, see note 18. The seventeenth-century biographer, José Martinez, *Comprenda noticias curiosas de Algunas colecciones de Pitturas que hubo en*

Zaragoza, 1866, mentiones a *Sacrifice of Isaac* painted in the Caravaggesque style. It is impossible to determine whether it belongs to the Boalsburg group or is a completely different composition. Francisco Ribalta (see note 61) did a print of the *Sacrifice of Isaac* which was signed and dated 1599. Delphine Darby, *Francisco Ribalta and His School*, Cambridge, Mass., 1938, p. 286. Fenellosa Mingarro, *El pintor Francisco Ribalta, estudio critico*, Castellon, 1901. The print cannot be located, and there is some debate as to whether it ever existed. Attempts to trace it through an early writer on Ribalta, D. Juan de la Cruz Martí, have been unsuccessful. Ribalta is a painter often associated with both Pedro Orrente and Jusepe de Ribera. Mina Gregori, etc., (Catalogue), *The Age of Caravaggio*, The Metropolitan Museum of Art, New York, 1985, pp. 282, 284, mentions the *Sacrifice of Isaac* as a prefiguration of Christ's sacrifice in accordance with the writings of St. Paul and St. Augustine. There is also Federigo Borromeo's *De pictura sacra* and the *De civitate Dei*. See M. Calvesi, "Caravaggio o la ricerca della salvazione," *Storia dell'arte*, no. 9-10, pp. 93-142.

20. Richard L. Garner and Donald G. Henderson, *Columbus and Related Family Papers, 1451-1902* (An Inventory of the Boal Collection), The Pennsylvania State University, University Park, Pennsylvania, 1974. There is some confusion concerning the dates of importation and reconsecration of the chapel. The exterior was made of Pennsylvania limestone with a façade designed by Theodore D. Boal. Documents of 1876 indicate that at that time, the chapel was in such poor condition that services had to be held at the local church. *Ibid.*, p. 35.

21. The Iglesia de Neustra Senõra de Branãs is the official name of the chapel at Llamas del Mouro.

22. *Boal Archives* (microfilm), Library of The Pennsylvania State University, Item 25, Reel 161. Garner and Henderson, *op. cit.*, p. 35. The chapel was dedicated at the expense of Capt. Diego Garcia de Siena and his wife, Donã Magdalena de Valdes. Here it states that the chapel was an annex of the parish church of S. Martin of Siena. In 1777, there was a license issued for the re-dedication and repair of the Branãs Chapel (here called S. Martin of Siena), in the house of Llamas del Mouro. It was at that time re-dedicated to the Columbus family. *Boal Archives, Ibid.*, Item 161, Reel 62.

23. For the relationship of the Sierra family to the Colón, see figs. 69 and 70. Many paintings which are now at Boal Mansion were probably inherited from the Sierras. It cannot be proven, however, that the *Sacrifice* was theirs. Several other paintings in the chapel date from the late sixteenth or early seventeenth century; *St. John, St. Bartholomew* on either side of the altar which are derived from Goltzius prints; a *Holy Family* which is a copy after Giulio Romano. See F. Russel, "Spinola *Holy Family* of Giulio Romano," *The Burlington Magazine*, 124, May 1982, pp. 297-298.

24. Due to recent archival discoveries, Caravaggio's *Sacrifice of Isaac*, long considered a work of the 1590s, can be given this late date. M. Aronberg Lavin, "Caravaggio Documents from the Barberini Archives," *The Burlington Magazine*, CIX, 1967. Bellori mentions that it was done for Cardinal Maffeo Barberini. There is no apparent connection between the patron and the subject of the painting (see note 19). Most scholars now agree that the Uffizi *Sacrifice of Isaac* is the only painting of this subject by Caravaggio (see note 18). Catalogue, Giuseppe Scavizzi, *Caravaggio e i caravaggeschi*, Naples, 1963, p. 19, no. 6, published the Castellamare di Stabia *Sacrifice of Isaac* as a copy after a lost Caravaggio (see note 27). Gregori, *Op. Cit.*, p. 284 presents the *Sacrifice of Isaac* in Castellamare di Stabia, as a possible copy after Caravaggio, and related to Caravaggio's Uffizi *Sacrifice*. There is, however, little similarity between them.

25. Moir, *op. cit.*, pp. 42, 43. See note 18.

26. Kitson, *op. cit.*, no. 30, says it is greatly overpainted. See also Guttuso, *op. cit.*, no. 35; Juan Ainaud, "Ribalta y Caravaggio," *Anales y Boletín de los Museos de Arte de Barcelona*, 1947, p. 14, etc. Roberto Longhi, "Siu Margini Caravaggeschi," *Paragone*, 21,

1951, pp. 20-34, refers to Le Vasseur's print (fig. 76); also mentions the Como painting as by Caravaggio. Berne Joffroy, *Le Dossier Caravage*, Paris, 1959, p. 325, states that the painting of the *Sacrifice* and the Le Vasseur print (fig. 76, note 38) do not tally. Moir, *op. cit.*, belives the Como painting, that in Castellamare di Stabia, Penãfiel, and the Museo di S. Carlos, Valencia, are all seventeenth-century copies. He is noncommital about the other versions. Kitson and Guttuso repeat Longhi's provenance of Queen Christina of Sweden, the Odescalchi, and the Dukes of Orleans for the supposed original. In a letter of Oct. 25, 1977, Prof. Luciano Di Bona of Varese, the previous owner, states that the painting was stolen in 1949. It measures ca. 160 cm. x 110 cm. and was neither signed nor dated.

27.   Moir, *op. cit.*, p. 117. Moir, p. 44, "In this context, it is conceivable that the Spanish copyists of the Castellamare-Di Bona variant of the *Sacrifice of Isaac* would have preferred the variant over the original composition, if the choice had been offered to them, or actually did so; for this modernized version presumably would be more appealing to their taste than Caravaggio's own, becoming slightly archaistic by 1610." The quality of the *Sacrifice* in the duomo in Castellamare di Stabia is inferior. Located between the sacristy and ambulatory of the cathedral, it measures ca. 128 cm. x 155 cm. See note 24 (Scavizzi). Felton (Ph.D. thesis, *op. cit.*) cites a version of an *Entombment* by Jusepe de Ribera in the same cathedral, p. 302, A-102. He enters the original as in an unknown location in the United States.

28.   Moir, *op. cit.*, p. 117, calls all the versions mentioned "painted copies." (See note 26.)

29.   Moir, *op. cit.*, p. 117. The painting in the Confederación comes from a private collection in Madrid. Further information about its provenance is unavailable. It is ca. 100 cm. x 160 cm. and neither signed nor dated. Marini, *op. cit.*, p. 122 includes it, along with the paintings in Como and Castellamare di Stabia, as a copy after Caravaggio. A. E. Perez-Sanchez, *Caravaggio y el naturalismo espanõl*, Seville and Madrid, 1973, judges it

to be "one of the best of a composition of Caravaggio (done) probably well after the painting in the Uffizi." He states that it was engraved by Le Vasseur (fig. 76); see note 38. Ainaud, *op. cit.*, p. 386. Juan A. Gayo Nunõ, *La Pintura espanõla en los museos provinciales*, Madrid, 1964. In April 1960, Gayo Nunõ issued a certificate to the Confederación which refers to the painting as an old copy of a lost original by Caravaggio. Another name suggested by Gayo Nunõ was Cavarozzi. See note 34. No measurements are available for the painting in the Convent of St. Ursula in Alcalá de Henares. It is an inferior copy. Moir, p. 118.

30.   Moir has not seen the Boalsburg painting; Kitson has not seen the one in Como which was stolen in 1949. Both have relied on photographs to analyze these difficult problems of attribution and condition. Perez-Sanchez, *op. cit.*, cites eight. All but the one in Lisbon are "inferior." Moir, p. 118.

31.   The *Sacrifice* in Boalsburg, which is in poor condition, was touched up by a local restorer during the 1950s. See note 17.

32.   The National Institute of Culture in Lima has no knowledge of this painting. The *Sacrifice* was seen in a private collection in Lima during the 1930s by Pierre Boal, then owner of the Boalsburg painting. He remembered it as being considerably smaller than his own version and was told that the Lima canvas was attributed to Zurbarán. Since Mr. Boal was a member of the United States Foreign Service, it is possible that the collection was that of the President of the State. Another famous collection in Lima was that of Genevieve Thorndike, who owned many fine Spanish paintings, including some by Jusepe de Ribera (see fig. 87).

33.   See note 17. It is uncertain as to whether the bottom of the Boalsburg painting has been cut down, but seems doubtful that a signature would have been lost from any of the versions.

34.   Richard Spear, *Caravaggio and His Followers*, The Cleveland Musium of Art, 1971, and Icon Eds., New York (revised edition), pp. 94-95. Spear has mentioned that the angel in the Boalsburg painting is reminiscent of those of

Bartolomeo Cavarozzi of Viterbo (1590-1625). See note 29. Gregori, *op. cit.*, p. 284 mentions the youth in the guise of an angel instructing an old man as it appears in Caravaggio's *Rest on the Flight into Egypt* and first *St. Matthew*. See G.C. Argan, "Caravaggio e Raffaello," *Colloquio sul tema Caravaggio e i Caravaggeschi*, Rome, Feb. 12-14, 1973; pp. 19-28. Gregori discusses the relationship between Abraham and the angel in Caravaggio's Uffizi *Sacrifice* as "human" rather than "supernatural."

35. Adam Elsheimer, *Tobias and the Angel*, National Gallery in London.

36. Caravaggio would undoubtedly have used a model but wrapped him in a "sheet."

37. Marin Hume, *The Court of Philip IV*, Brentano's, New York, 1927. The angel in the *Sacrifice* recalls, perhaps, the nine-year-old Prince Philip (later Philip IV of Spain), who, in a gossipy letter written in 1614, describes his performance as cupid in a room of the palace devoted to such events. Although he performed his part "most prettily," he had become seasick from riding in the highly ornamented chariot. Gregori, *op. cit.*, p. 284 tries to relate the figure of the angel in Caravaggio's Uffizi *Sacrifice* to his young *John the Baptist* and the *Amor Victorious* and questions whether the model could be the "vago Giulietto" praised in a madrigal. See M. Cinotti, *Il Caravaggio e le sue grandi opere da San Luigi dei Francesi*, Milan, 1971.

38. Jean Charles Le Vasseur (1734-1816). Figure 76. See Ainaud, GREGORI, *OP. CIT.*, P. 284 TRIES TO RELATE THE FIGURE OF THE ANGEL Kitson, Guttuso, etc., and note 26. Longhi, *op. cit.*, plate 23. Since the Le Vasseur print is from the eighteenth century, it could have been influential only from that period on. Its composition is close to that of the *Sacrifice* in the Rapp Collection in Stockholm (fig. 77) and the Ramirez Collection in Jaen (fig. 78). It is not related to the composition of the Boalsburg group.

39. Joffroy, *op. cit.*, maintained that the print and the painting do not correspond. See note 26.

40. Nicolson, *op. cit.*, considers the composition of the Rapp painting and that of the Le Vasseur print to be different. See p. 37. Gregori, *op. cit.*, p. 284 attributes the painting in the Rapp Collection, Stockholm, to the Lombardian painter, Giuseppe Vermiglio, on whom she is preparing a monograph.

41. Ampliaciones y Reproducciones, MAS, Barcelona (photograph and information).

42. See note 18.

43. David Kowal, "El Sacrificio de Isaac: Una obra inédita de Pedro Orrente," *Archivo espanõl*, October, 1977, pp. 429-432, pl. 21. The painting reproduced is in the Museo de Bellas Artes, Bilbao. Fig. 83 is of the same composition. Pedro Orrente (1580—1645) may have been El Greco's oldest pupil and was in Toledo with him. His work is often confused with that of Estebán March and J. J. Espinosa. There are many works by Orrente in both Valencia and Toledo, and he is linked artistically with Francisco Ribalta as well. See note 19. He was in Italy from 1604 to 1612. See Nigel Glendinning, Catalogue, *The Golden Age of Spanish Painting*, Royal Academy of Arts, London, 1976, p. 44. It is interesting that paintings in the Boalsburg group are (or were) associated with both Valencia and, especially, Toledo. Orrente finally came under the influence of the Caravaggesque style, and Glendinning describes his "biblical canvases treated like genre scenes."

44. Moir, *op. cit.*, p. 23.

45. There is undoubtedly some reason why four paintings of this composition were in Toledo. See note 43. Perez-Sanchez, *op. cit.*, mentions the version in a private collection.

46. Moir, *op. cit.*, pp. 117-118. There may, of course, be some repeats when only a literary reference is given, as in the case of the Hijar dowry. The Lisbon painting is apparently missing. Moir does not specify which of at least twenty museums in Lisbon once owned it. It is not at the Museo nacional de arte antiga. See note 30. The painting in Como was stolen in 1949. See note 26. The Penãfiel *Sacrifice* is still in situ. The versions in the Museum of

San Carlos, Valencia and La Guardia, Toledo disappeared in 1936. The former (Moir, p. 117, 105g) might have been the same composition as fig. 83. The Lima painting cannot be located. The painting in the major sacristy of the cathedral in Zamora is in situ (1.60 cm. x 1.10 cm.). Gregori, *op. cit.*, p. 284 discusses versions, copies, and interpretations of Caravaggesque paintings of the *Sacrifice of Isaac*.

47. One exception would be Orazio Borgianni (1578-1616), an Italian follower of Caravaggio who travelled twice to Spain.

48. Jusepe de Ribera, a Valencian who settled in Naples, sent many paintings from Naples back to Spain. Moir, *op. cit.*, mentions that the great influx of paintings from Italy to Spain began in 1615 (there were, of course, many sent by Titian in the sixteenth century). The followers of Caravaggio working in Rome during the early years of the Seicento were from all over Italy and Europe.

49. Anthony Blunt made such a statement to the Director of Boal Mansion.

50. Letter from Pierre Boal, August 10, 1963 (*Boal Archives*, The Pennsylvania State University). Orazio Gentileschi was one of the few Caravaggeschi who knew Caravaggio personally.

51. Statement made by Stephen Pepper to Director of the Boal Mansion. See note 18. Michael Stoughton does not associate the composition of the Boal painting with Caracciolo (letter, Jan. 10, 1986).

52. Moir, *op. cit.*, p. 158, note 277.

53. This painting, which is a recent acquisition of Southern Methodist University, Dallas, may be an early work by Ribera. Similar in composition to the late painting of the same subject in the Prado, it is in the tenebrist tradition. See note 32.

54. Chenault, Jeanne, "Ribera in Roman Archives," *The Burlington Magazine*, III (September 1969), pp. 561-562.

55. *Ibid.*

56. Felton and Jordan, *op. cit.*, propose an earlier date for Ribera's arrival in Italy: 1607-14. Unfortunately, this is pure speculation and not based on fact. See pp. 29, 49.

57. *Boal Archives,* The Pennsylvania State University.

58. *Boal Archives*, *op. cit.*, Reels 3, 6.

59. *Sense of Taste*, (Hartford, Wadsworth Athenaeum) was originally attributed to Pietro Novelli. *Drunken Silenus* (Naples, Capodimonte); *Crucifixion* (Osuna, Colegiata).

60. Chenault, Jeanne, "Jusepe de Ribera and the Order of Christ: New Documents," *The Burlington Magazine*, 118 (May, 1976), pp. 304-307.

61. See notes 19 and 43. There is no documentary evidence to indicate that Ribera was the pupil of Ribalta, although both were Valencian, may have arrived in Italy at about the same time, and studied the works of Caravaggio. Ribalta did a copy of Caravaggio's *Crucifixion of St. Peter* in the Cerasi Chapel. See note 4. Darby, *op. cit.*, p. 70.

62. See note 43.

63. This is hardly the case for the late style of Picasso.

64. Elizabeth de Gué Trapier, *Jusepe de Ribera*, New York, 1952, p. 7. The letter of December 11, 1618, reads as follows: "painters of excellent taste, especially that Spanish painter who follows the school of Caravaggio. If he is the man who painted a St. Martin at Parma, and was with Signor Mario Farnese, I need to be clever" (not to be surpassed by him).

65. Moir, *op. cit.*, p. 92, no. 24-d.

66. Bernardo de Dominici, *Vite dei pittori, scultori ed architetti napoletani*, Naples, edition 1844, p. 133. August L. Mayer, *Jusepe de Ribera, lo Spagnoletto*, Leipzig, 1923, does not include a *Sacrifice of Isaac* in his section of lost paintings by Ribera, despite its mention by de Dominici. Francesco Scannelli, *Il microcosmo*

della pittura, Cesna, 1657, states that "in Rome around this time (ca. 1610-1620) rather mannered subjects painted by the artist called "lo Spagnoletto" imitated truth successfully, but were as yet weak in technique and invention. The paintings are nearby, especially in Rome; the best are in the Palace of Prince Giustiniani where there are several works."

67.   Moir, *op. cit.*, pp. 42-43.

68.   The major Villa Savelli was in Ariccia and became the Villa Chigi in 1661. See Isa Barsali, *Ville della campagna romana*, Milan, 1975, p. 244.

69.   Johannes A. F. Orbann, *Documenti sul barocco in Roma*, Rome, 1920, p. 259, 101 note; 237, 32-33, etc., mentions several palaces owned by the Savelli, the most important being in the Theatre of Marcellus. The palace continued to be called the Palazzo Savelli long after it was taken over by the Orsini. See fig. 89. Georgina Masson, *Italian Villas and Palaces*, New York, 1966, p. 207. Alessandro Marabottini, *Theatrum Marcelli (El Quilseo de' Savelli)*, Rome, 1973, includes many sixteenth and seventeenth century prints of the palace, still frequently referred to as the Palazzo Savelli. Since the Palazzo Savelli in the Theatre of Marcellus housed a huge and famous art collection, it is highly probable that Ribera's *Sacrifice of Isaac* was located there.

70.   Trapier, *op. cit.*, p. 249, mentions a *St. John with a Lamb* and a *St. Athanasius*, both by Ribera, which were owned by the Savelli in Rome.

71.   Pedro Orrente is another painter who could be linked to the Boalsburg group through circumstantial evidence. There is, however, more evidence to indicate that the artist might have been Ribera.

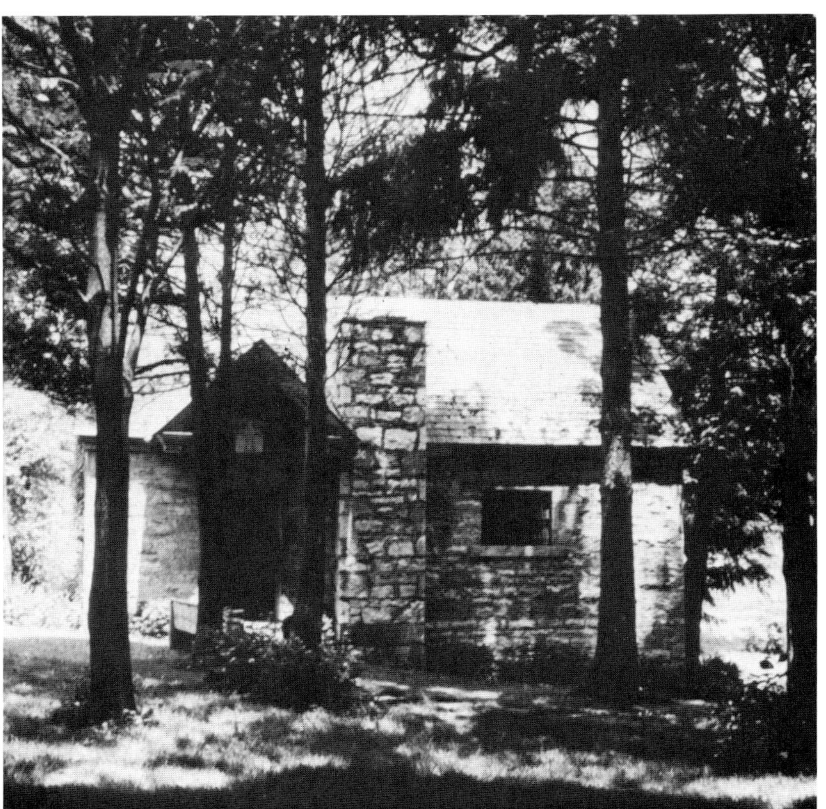

64.   Columbus Chapel, exterior. Boal Mansion, Boalsburg, Pennsylvania.

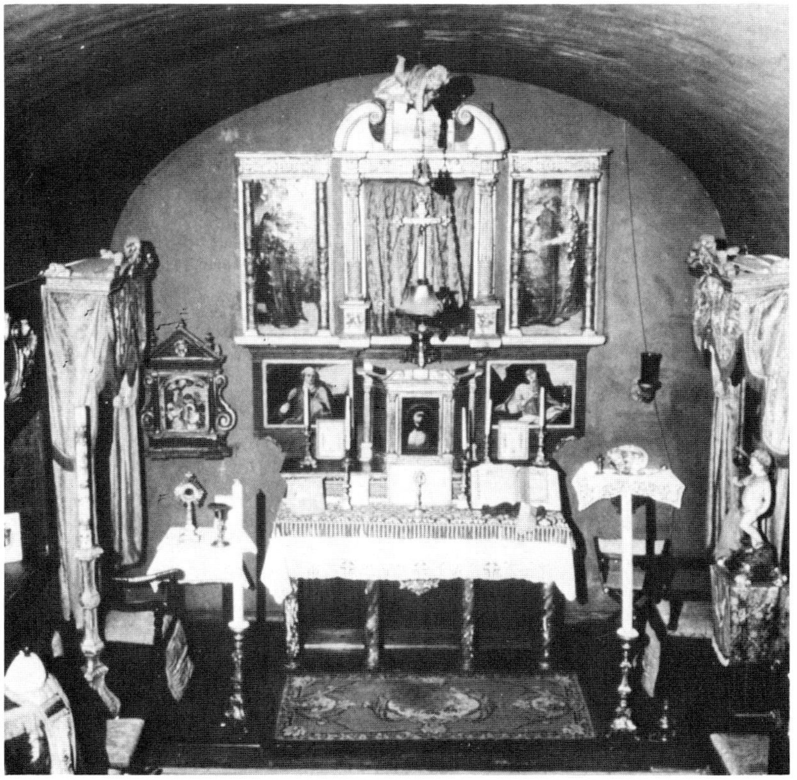

65.   Columbus Chapel, interior. Boal Mansion, Boalsburg, Pennslvania.

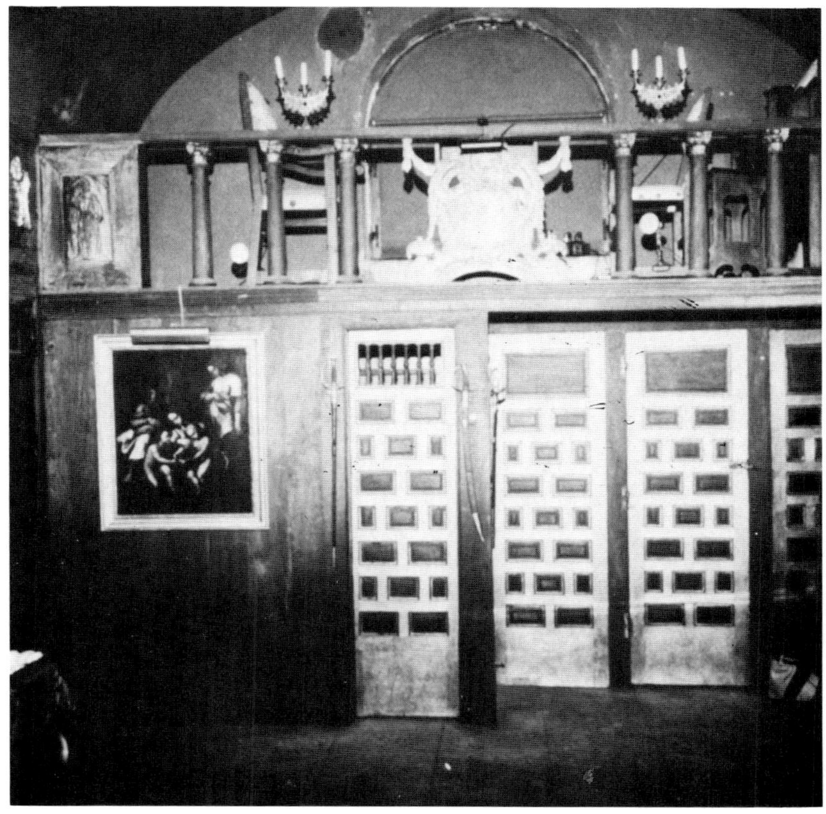

66.   Columbus Chapel, interior. Boal Mansion, Boalsburg, Pennsyslvania.

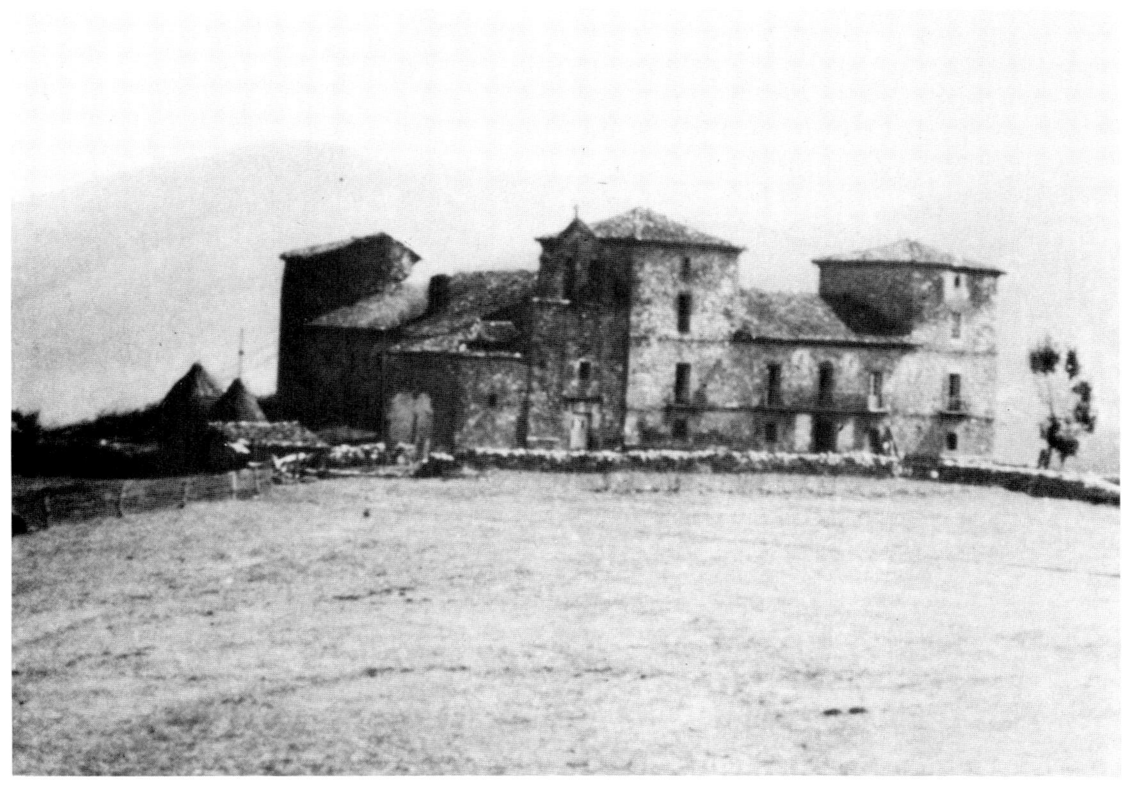

67.   Palacio de Colón, Llamas del Mouro (Asturias), Spain.

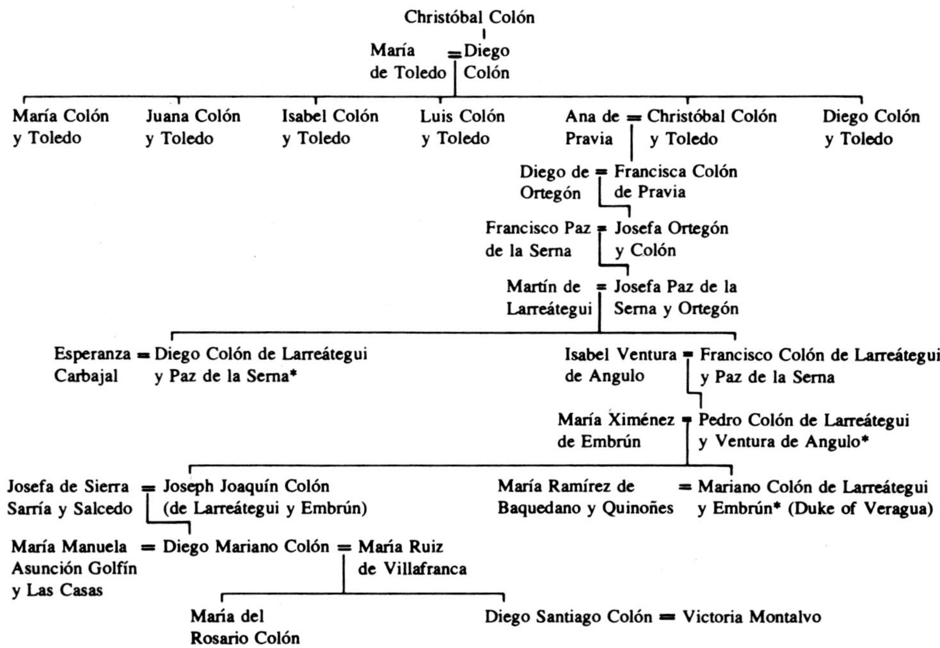

Based upon family tree now hanging in the Boalsburg Chapel. See also John Boyd Thatcher, *Christopher Columbus* (New York, 1904); Rafael Nieto y Cortadillas, *Los descendientes de Cristóbal Colón* (Havana, 1952); Otto Schoenrich, *The Legacy of Christopher Columbus* (Glendale, Calif., 1949).

*Litigants for title.

69. Colón Family Tree (after Garner and Henderson, *Columbus and Related Family Papers*).

SIERRA SARRIA SALCEDO FAMILY TREE

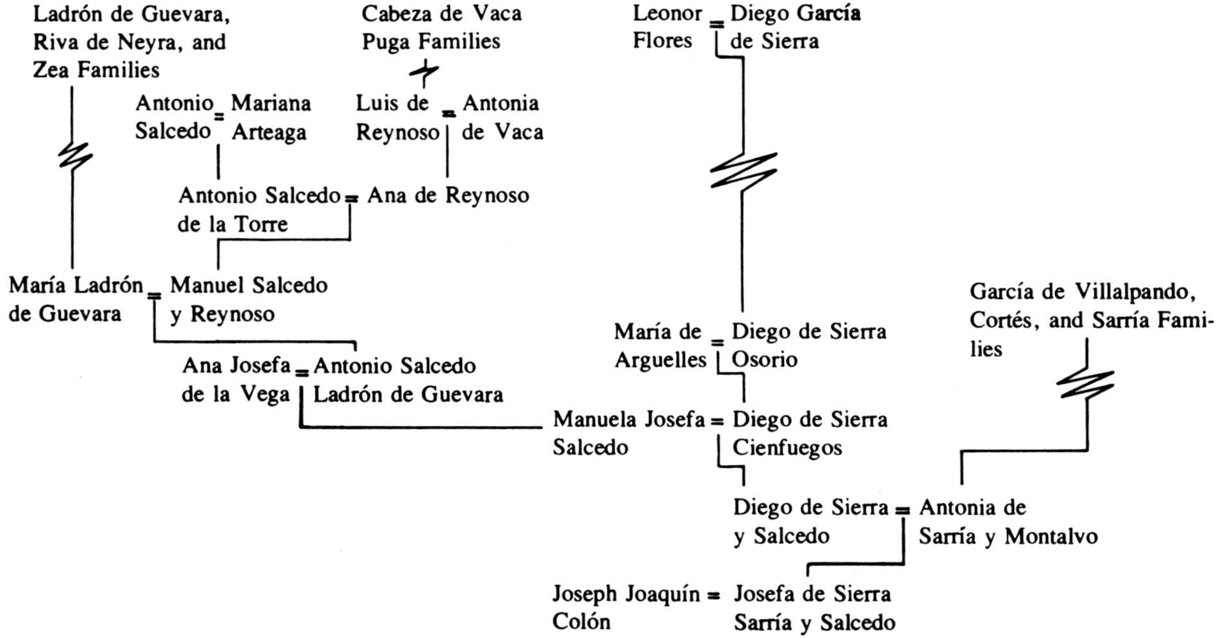

70. Sierra Sarria Salcedo Family Tree (after Garner and Henderson, *Columbus and Related Family Papers*).

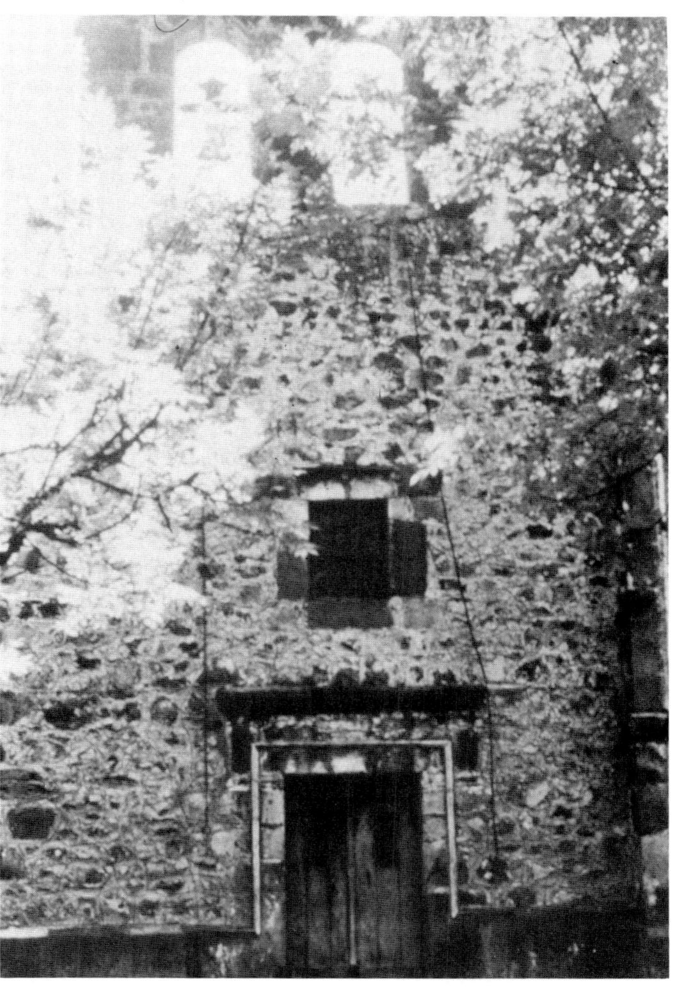

68.   Palacio   de   Colón,
       exterior   of   chapel.
       Llamas   del   Mouro
       (Asturias), Spain.

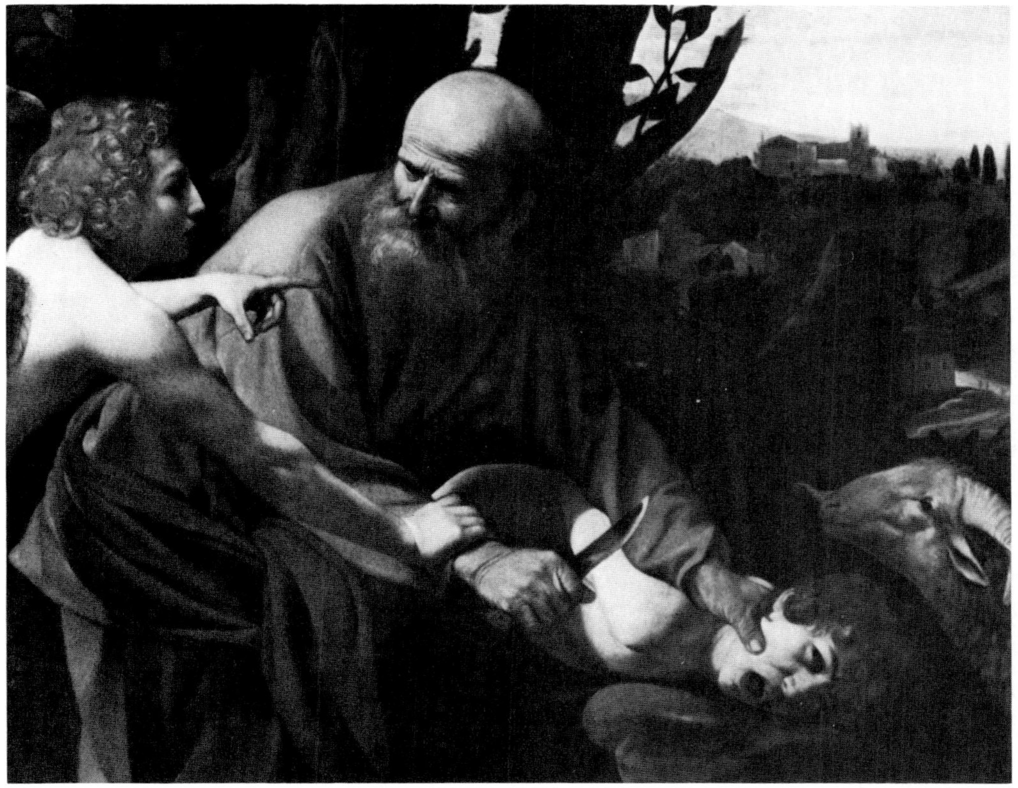

71.   Caravaggio, *Sacrifice of Isaac*, 1603 (Florence, Uffizi).

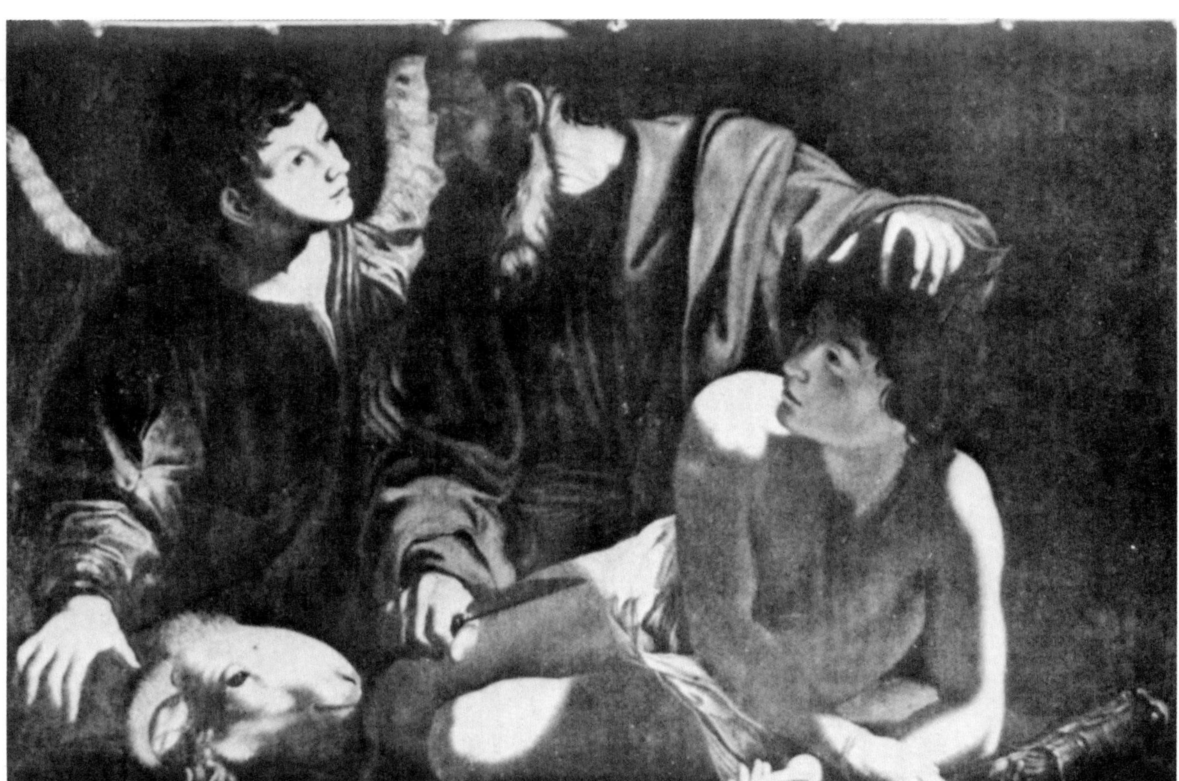

72.   Anonymous artist, *Sacrifice of Isaac* (Formerly Como, Italy: Collection of Prof. Luciano di Bona).

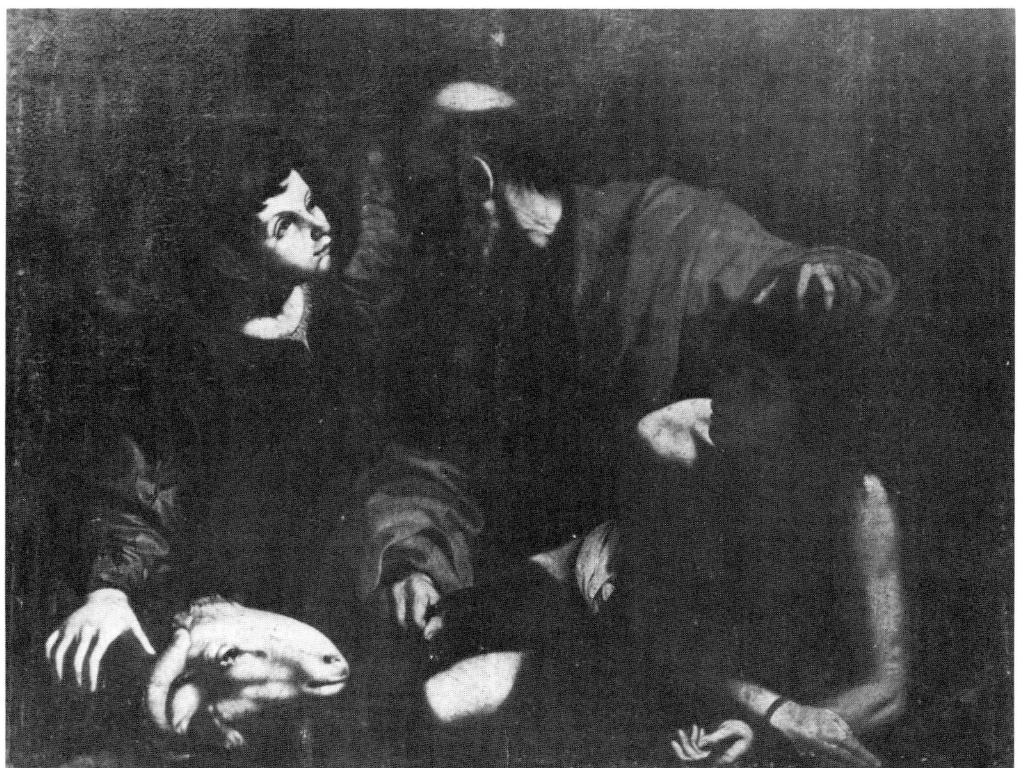

73.   Anonymous artist, *Sacrifice of Isaac* (Duomo, Castellamare di Stabia).

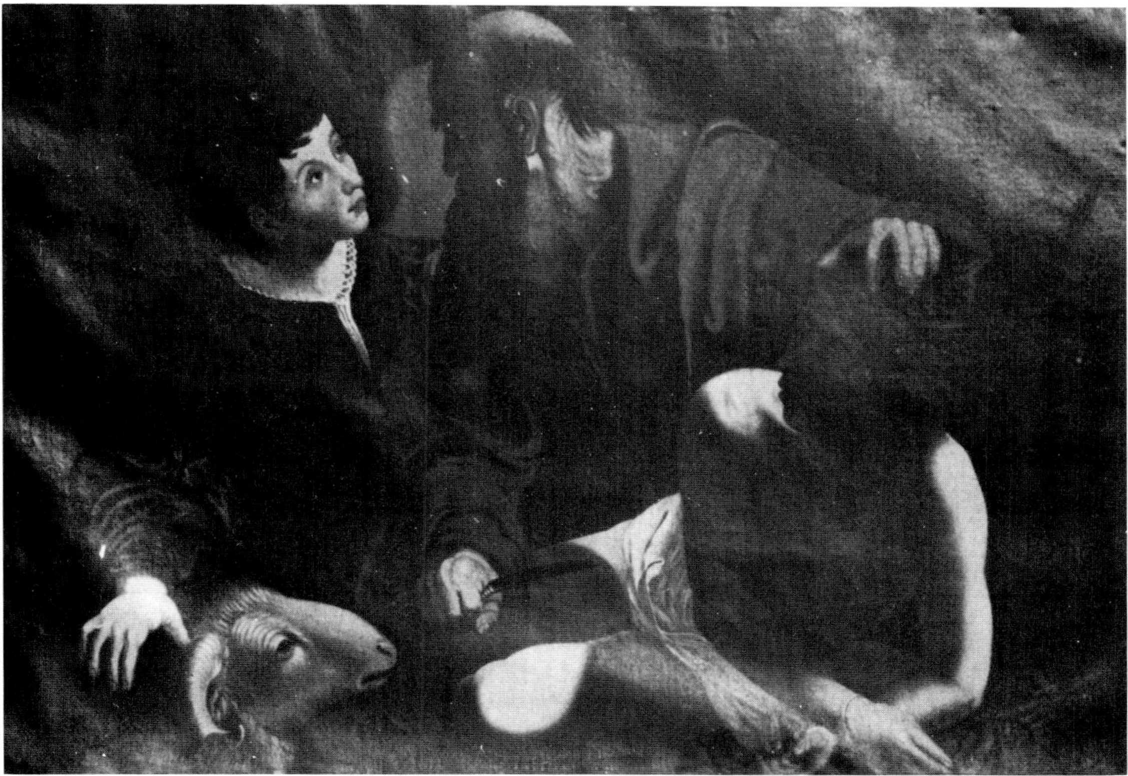

74.   Anonymous artist, *Sacrifice of Isaac* (Alcalá de Henares, Convent of St. Ursula).

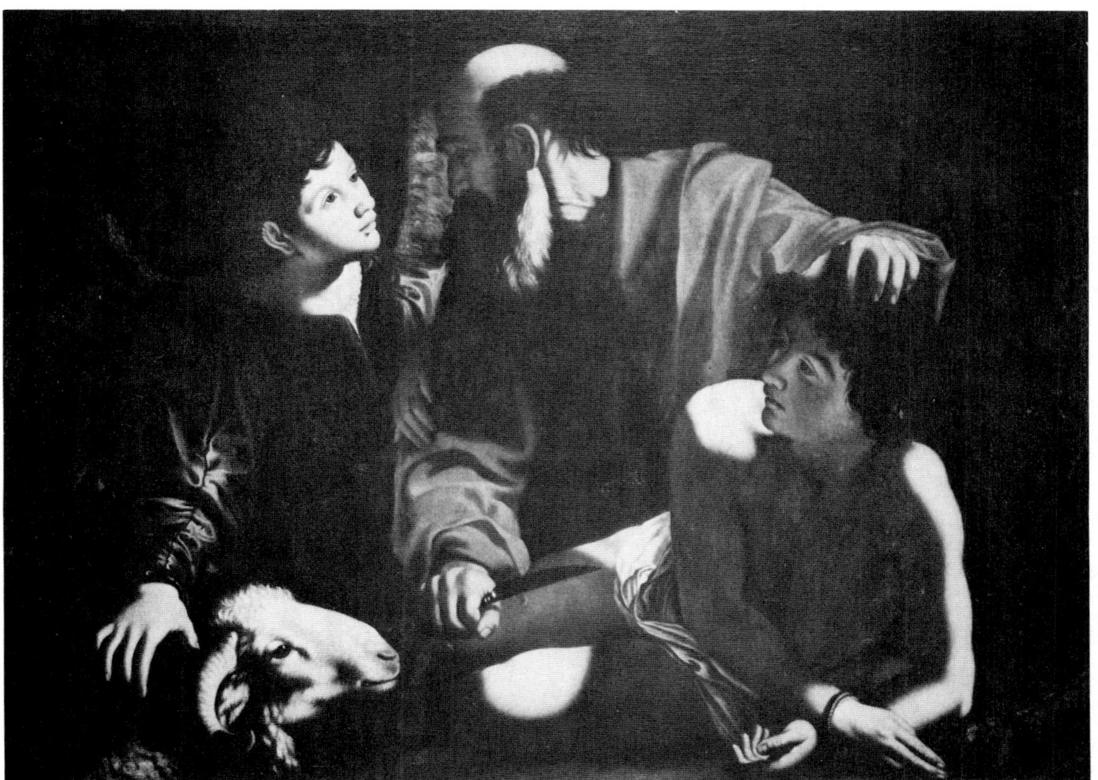

75.   Anonymous artist, *Sacrifice of Isaac* (Madrid, Confederación de Cajas de Ahorros).

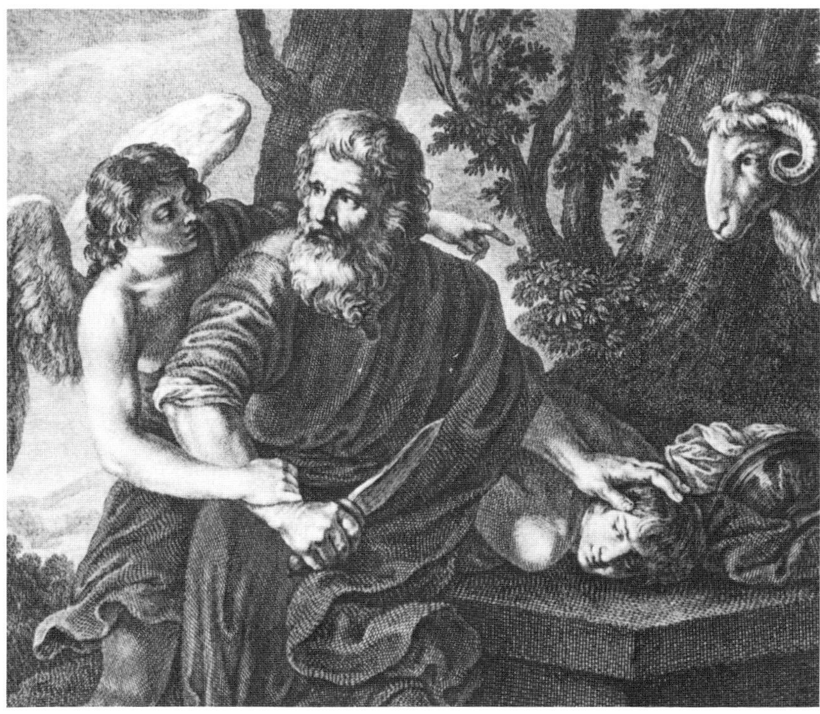

76.   Jean Charles Le Vasseur, copy of lost *Sacrifice of Isaac* attributed to Caravaggio (Boston, Museum of Fine Arts).

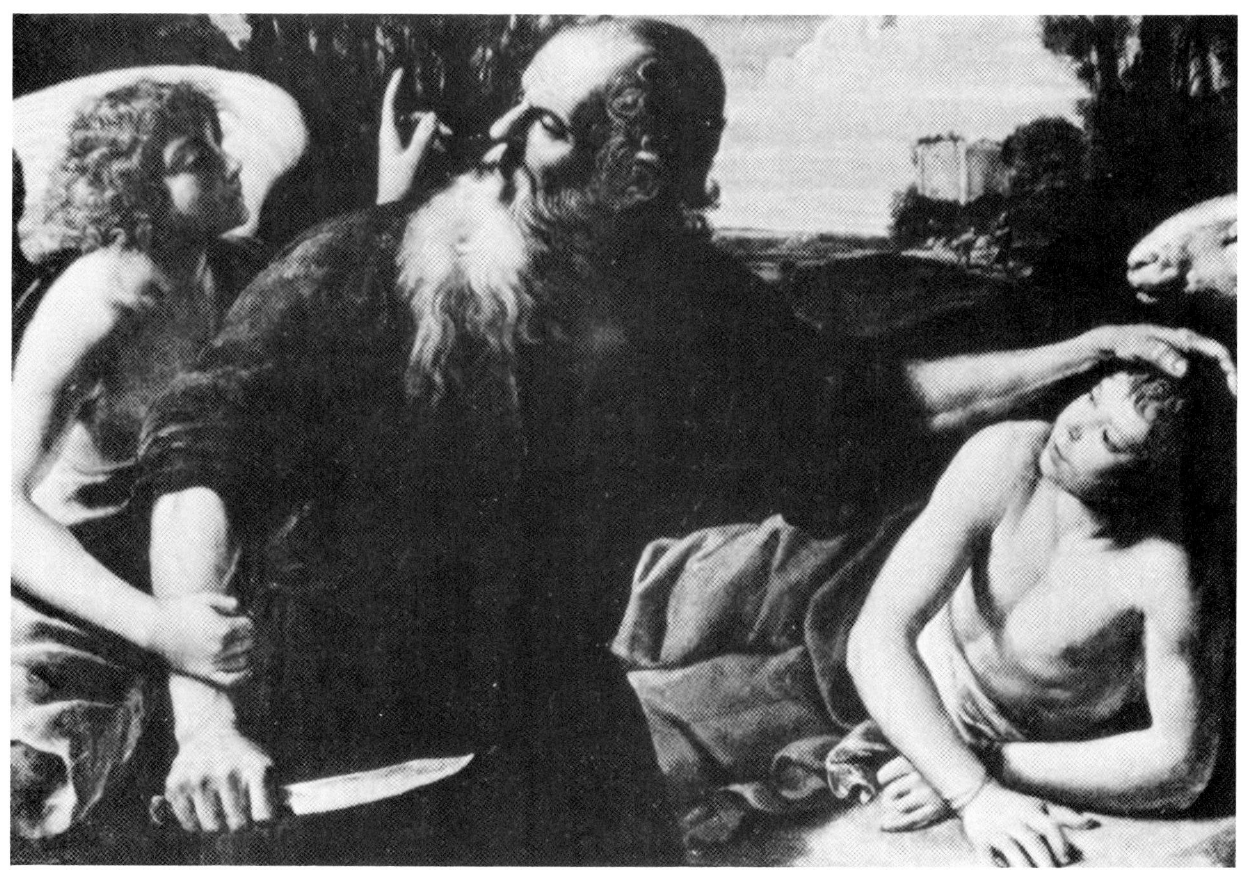

77.   Anonymous artist (Giuseppe Vermiglio?), *Sacrifice of Isaac* (Stockholm, Rapp Collection).

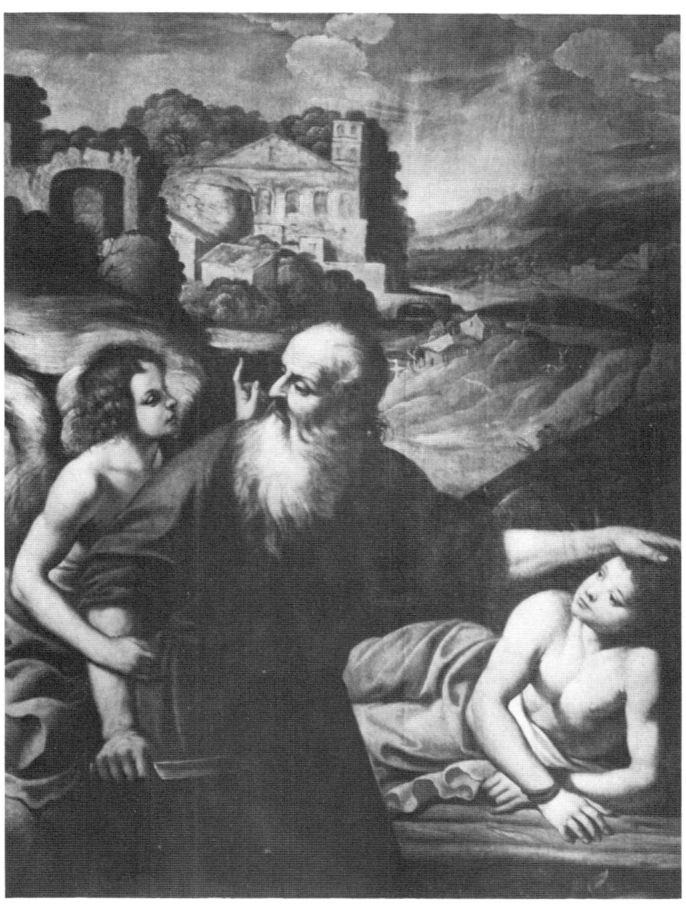

78.		Anonymous artist, *Sacrifice of Isaac* (Jaen, Collection Ramirez).

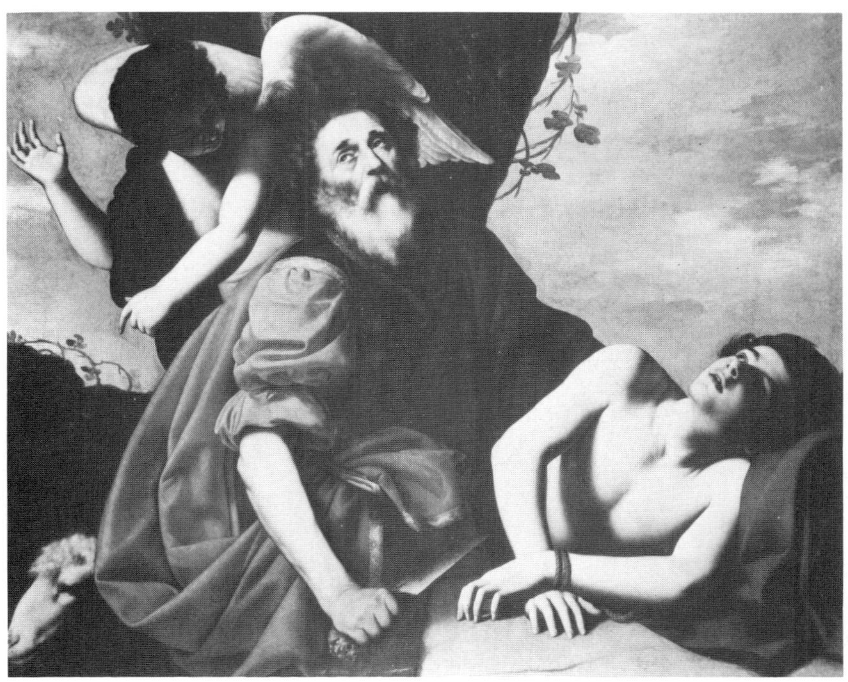

79.		Anonymous artist, *Sacrifice of Isaac* (Madrid, En Comercio, M. Gonzalez).

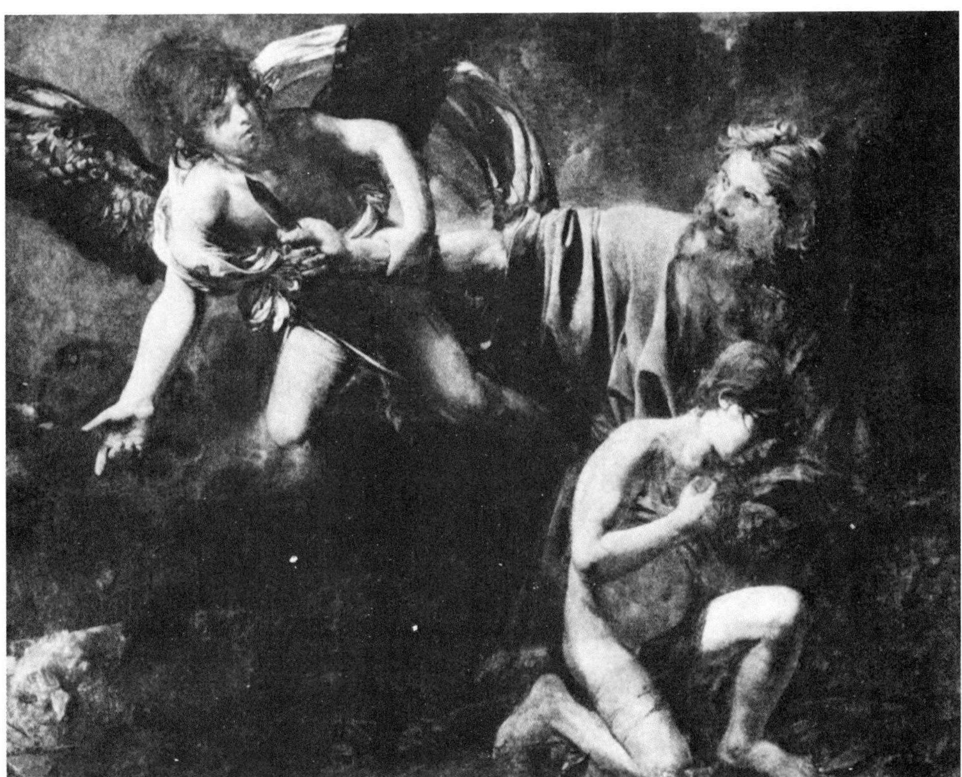

80.   Valentin de Boulogne, *Sacrifice of Isaac* (Montreal, Museum of Fine Arts).

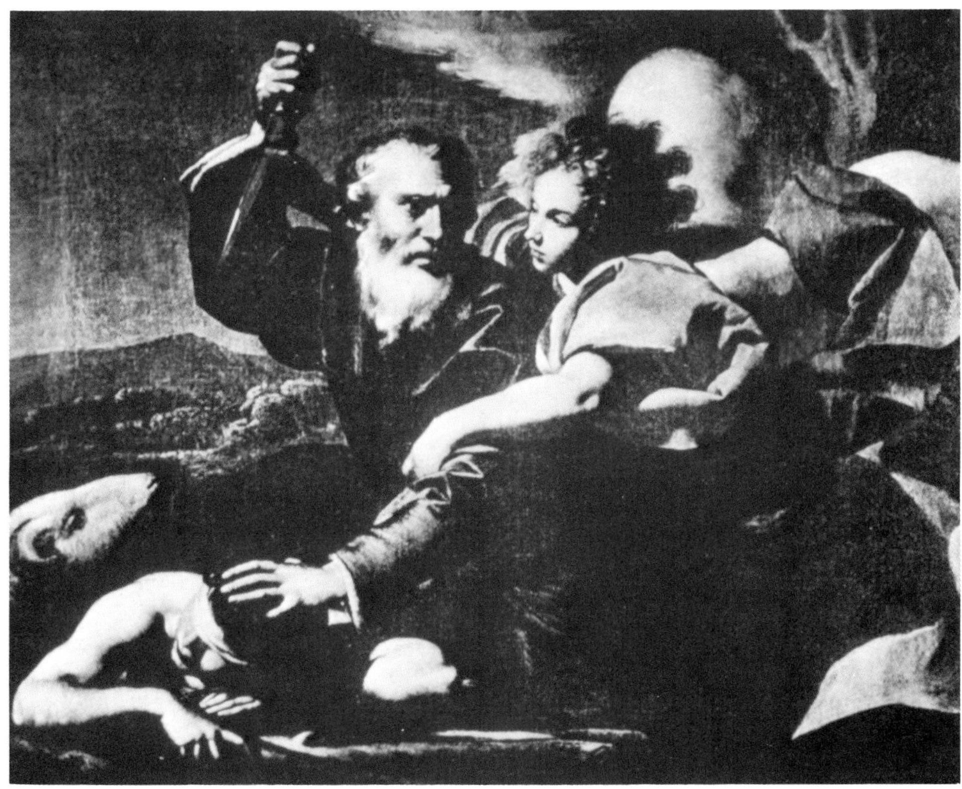

81.   Francesco Guarino (attributed by G. Ortolani), *Sacrifice of Isaac* (Salerno, Private Collection).

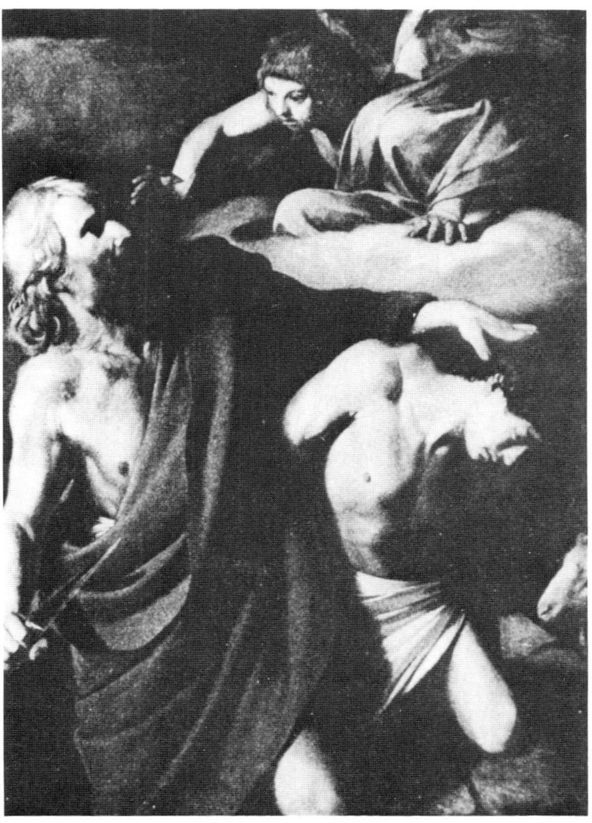

82.   School of Caravaggio, *Sacrifice of Isaac*
(London, Bonham's, 1974).

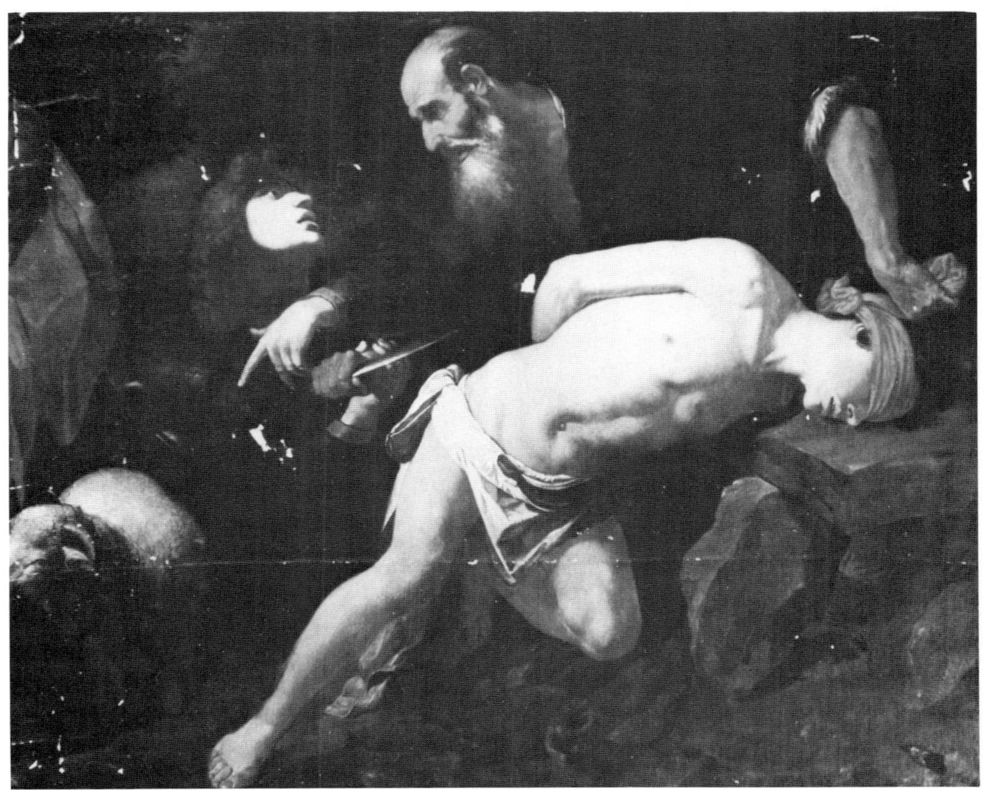

83.   Pedro Orrente (formerly attributed to Espinosa, Jeronimo Jacinto), *Sacrifice of Isaac* (Valencia, Ayuntamiento).

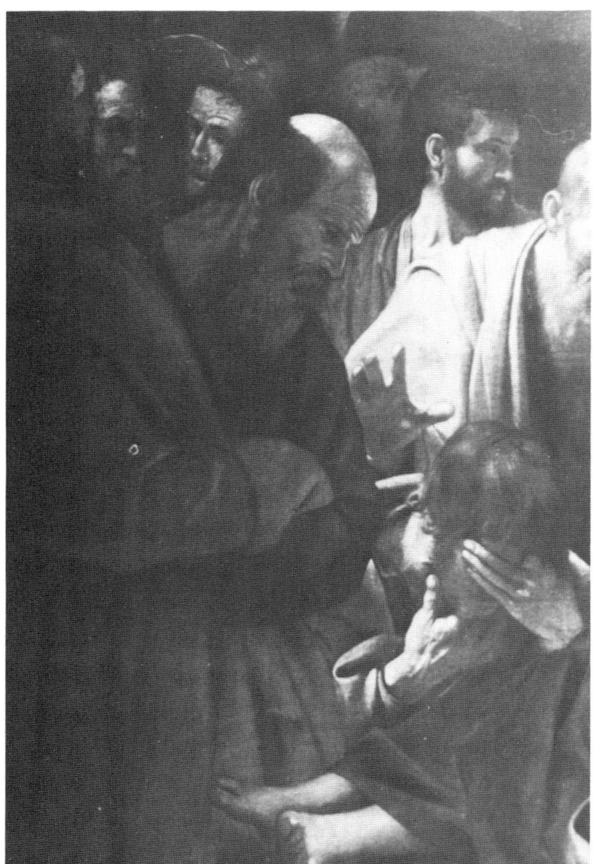

84.   Caravaggio, *Death of the Virgin*, detail (Paris, Museé National du Louvre).

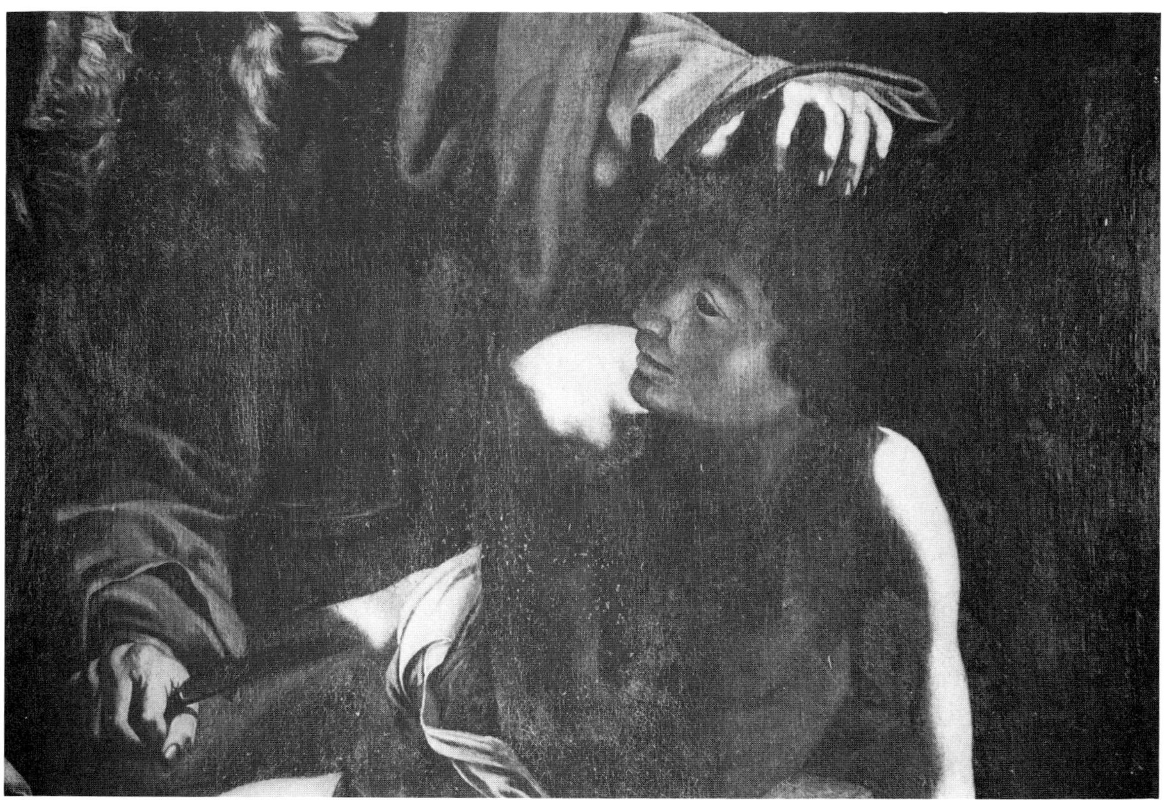

85.   Anonymous artist, *Sacrifice of Isaac*, detail of fig. 63 (Boal Collection, Boalsburg, Pennsylvania).

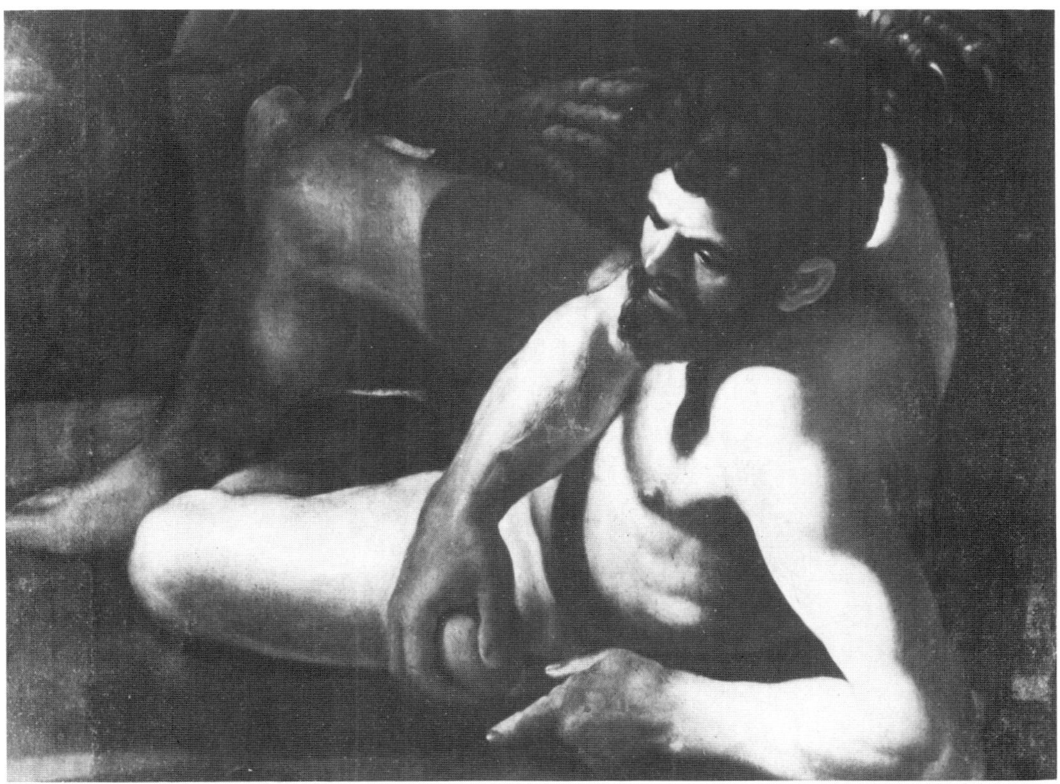

86. Giovanni B. Caracciolo, *Immaculate Conception with Saints Dominic and Francis*, detail (Naples, S. Maria della Stella).

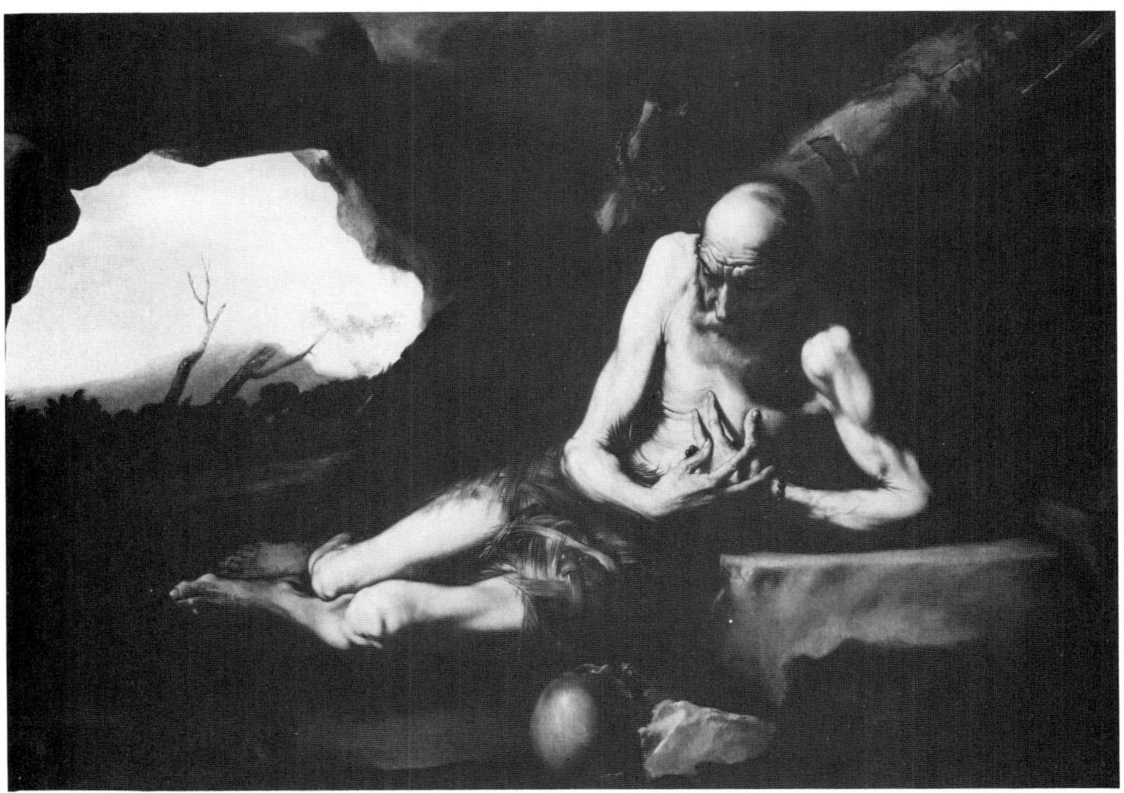

87. Jusepe de Ribera, *St. Paul the Hermit,* 1620-1625 (Dallas, Texas, Meadows Museum and Gallery, Southern Methodist University).

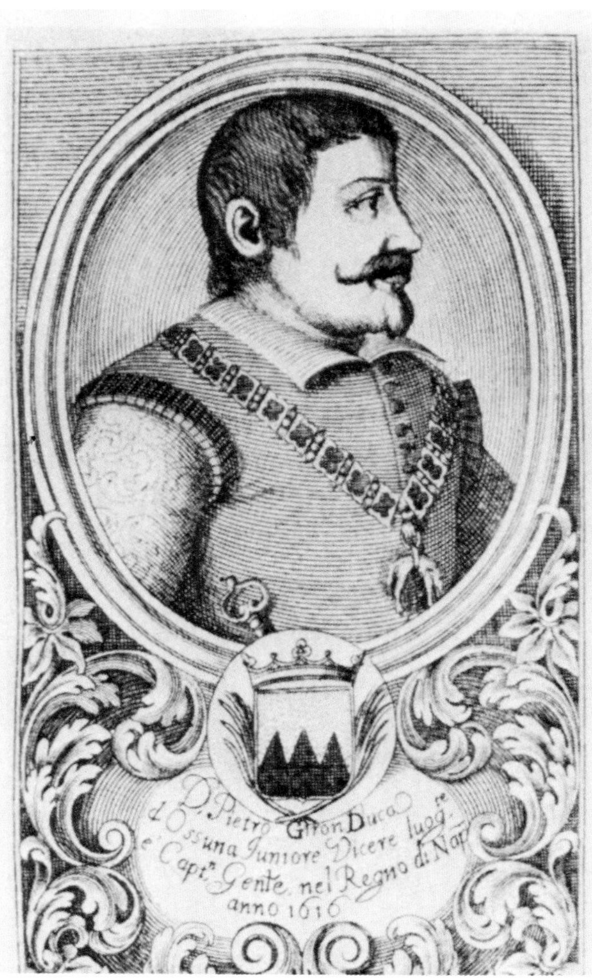

88.   Anonymous artist, *Don Pietro Girón, Duke of Osuna, Viceroy of Naples*, 1616-1620 (engraving).

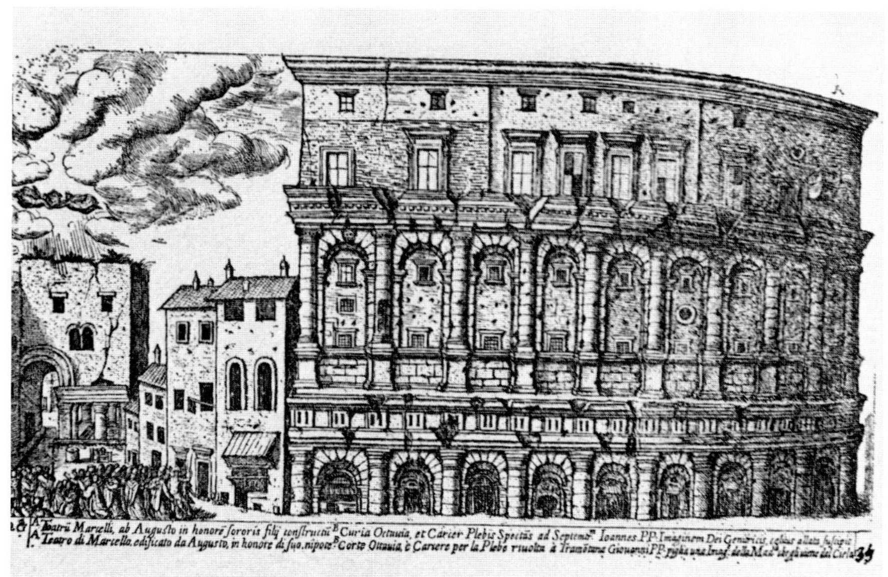

89.   Theatre of Marcellus (Palazzo Savelli), engraving by Alò Giovannoli, *Vedute degli Antichi Vestigi di Roma*, early 17th century.

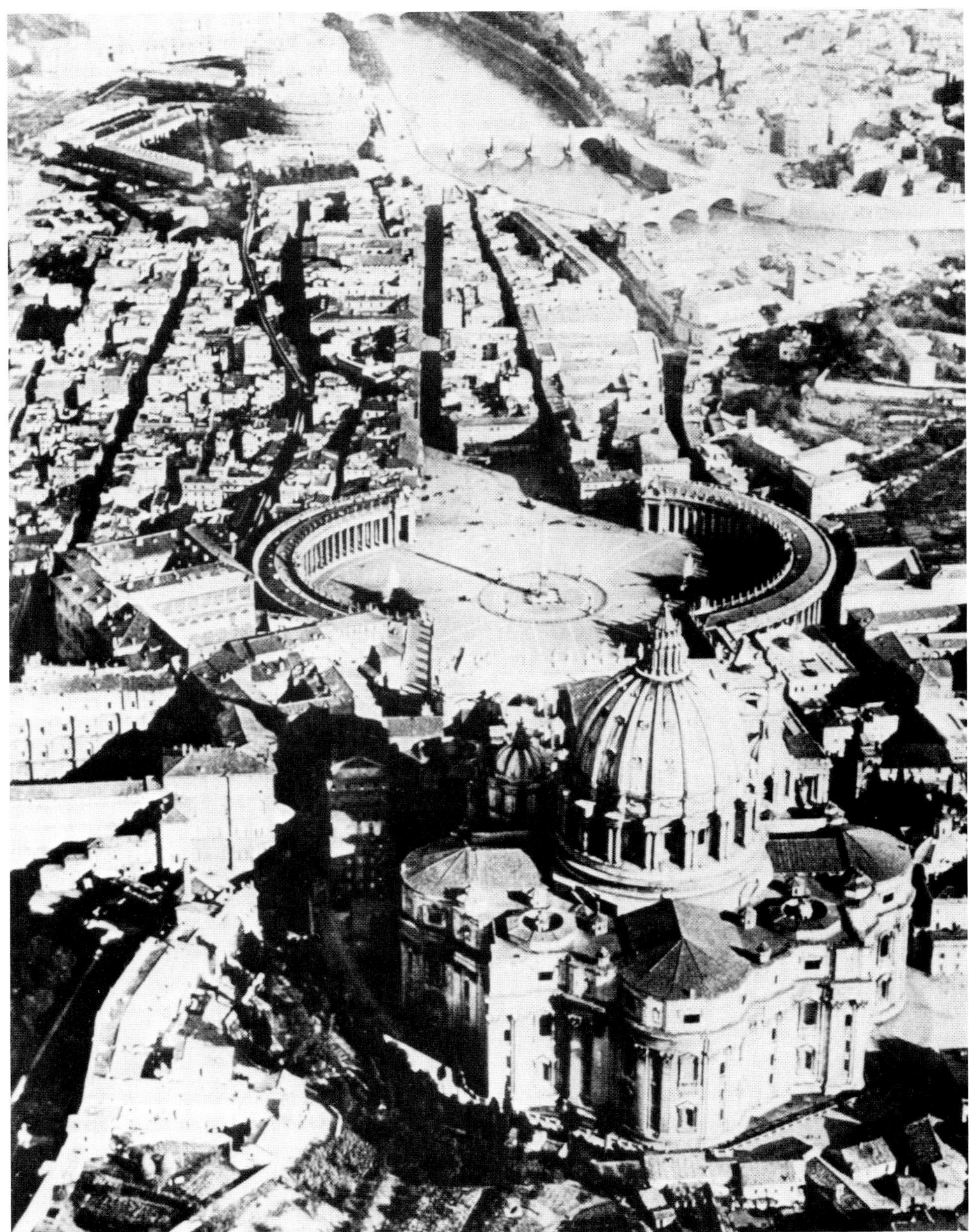

90   Rome, Piazza S. Pietro, aerial view (Birindelli, *La macchina heroica*)

The Fortune of Bernini's Colonnaded Piazza San Pietro and the City Frontispiece in Urban Planning*

6

In 1656 Alexander VII announced his intention to complete the square of St. Peter's, and shortly thereafter the *Sacra Congregazione della Reverenda Fabrica* assigned the task to Gianlorenzo Bernini.[1] Site clearance began the following year and the definitive project drawings were completed as early as 2 September, 1657.[2] Finished by 1667, the monumental construction of the piazza was Bernini's most conspicuous, and to a degree the most controversial of his accomplishments. Therefore it was criticized by many of his contemporaries who had offered alternatives to the Pope,[3] and was carefully studied by later architects traveling to Rome or who were otherwise familiar with the architectural situation of the Vatican complex. The colonnaded piazza (fig. 90) is usually considered Gianlorenzo's most memorable design. This paper seeks to investigate the influence of Bernini's oval court on projects of the period and after the seventeenth century. Since its completion, the piazza as the city's major "scenographic frontispiece" attracted the attention of French and Italian urban planners. By the second half of the eighteenth century, the colonnades served as inspiration for many ambitious building programs, some of which were aimed towards the creation of a "New Rome" and intended to rival the pre-eminence of the Eternal City.

The resemblance Wittkower noted of the cathedral of the Virgin of Kazan in Leningrad, for example, and the piazza in front of the church of San Francesco di Paola in Naples, reflects these ambitions to emulate Bernini's square.[4] The former was connected with the development of the city's beginning in 1703 and continued by Emperor Paul I into the nineteenth century,[5] and the latter part of the revitalization of Naples by Bourbon King Ferdinand I when he returned in 1815.[6] Both building campaigns were launched to focus foreign attention on the capital cities as well as to stress the authority of the sovereigns and their abilities to plan on an urban scale. Although Wittkower argued that the "aftermath" of the colonnaded piazza — as in Leningrad and Naples — continued for two and a half centuries,[7] he somewhat underestimated the need for further discussion. No comprehensive study of these and earlier adaptations of the Roman square have been published. Wittkower added to the just-mentioned examples only the proposal for the chapel and forecourt of the Royal Naval Hospital established in 1694 at Greenwich by William and Mary.[8] It is intended that the present examination of the fortune of Bernini's square of St. Peter's will also broaden our understanding of the relationships between the French and Roman academies and of their influence[9] — which extended as far as Leningrad.

In addition to Wittkower, Oechslin and others have tried to follow the course of Bernini's piazza in later architecture. At the *Corso Internazionale di alta Cultura: Bernini e l'universo barocco* (Rome, 1980), Oechslin presented two still unpublished lectures,[10] the first of which studied the piazza's appearance in European architecture of the eighteenth century. Orefice's recent article[11] and Cousins' unpublished dissertation[12] also make significant contributions to the research. Orefice drew together a range of important sites of the late seventeenth and eighteenth centuries which transfer the geometry of the court to public square planning. Despite the wide range of examples, her discussion tends to be brief and largely undocumented. Cousins examines how the young architectural students at the Roman Accademia di San Luca made use of the oval piazza in drawings for the *concorsi* of 1728, 1732 and 1738 for prescribed waterfront projects.

The research of these scholars will serve as a point of departure for this study, which will consider the scenographic aspects of the oval court in urban planning. We shall approach the topic in five stages, beginning with a brief summary of the evolution of Bernini's projects and a discussion of the essential characteristics of the Piazza San Pietro, to provide a basis for our later consideration of projects demonstrating a kinship with St. Peter's square. We will then focus on projects of the third quarter of the seventeenth century executed by Louis XIV's architects, the first group of protagonists to advance the oval court in city planning. An examination of architectural fantasies and theatrical design will follow, where the scenic potential of the piazza first explored by the *architects du roi* was realized by both French and Italian architect-scenographers. In the fourth section we shall consider a number of French and Italian projects which integrated the oval court into plans for refurbished and newly built cities as the central public square. Finally, the development of the Nevsky Prospekt — the last great experiment in classical urban planning which merged the French and Italian ideals into one vast building program— will serve as a terminus.

Brauer and Wittkower[13] and Kitao[14] agree that Bernini's singular manipulation of well-known architectural devices helped create for Rome a public space considered the *teatro* of the Christian universe.[15] As is generally accepted, the piazza's unprecedented monumental curved colonnades were not yet present in the architect's first project. Bernini first planned a trapezoidal court with covered loggias, yet the experimental wooden construction models proved the inadequacy of the project.[16] It was essential that the Pope be visible from both the loggia above the entrance for the special *Urbi et Orbi* Easter blessing as well as his window of the Vatican apartment to the south for the regular blessing of the pilgrims during the year.[17] In addition, the obelisk erected in 1586 and Maderno's fountain placed to the right in 1613 had to be considered.[18] In his *giustificazione* Bernini argued for an oval scheme since it made the Pope visible from both points and allowed for increased spaciousness.[19] Eventually, Bernini chose to shape the piazza (fig. 91) as an *ovato tondo*, a construction of circles first published over a century earlier by Peruzzi's Bolognese pupil, Serlio, in his *Il primo libro d'architettura* (Paris, 1545).[20] Finally, the covered loggias for the square plan that were first transformed into open, single-aisled arcades eventually became trabeated colonnades to alleviate the visual discrepancy caused by the curve of the arches (fig. 92).[21]

Although the piazza could not have been conceived without Bernini's consideration of a number of building types, particularly the ancient ampitheatre,[22] the monumental porticoes are immediately related to and probably dependent upon Palladian scenic devices and theatre design. It is often suggested that Palladio's reconstruction of classical monuments such as the theatre at Pola,[23] as well as the Teatro Olimpico in Vicenza might well have served Bernini in his concern for a calculated allusion to theatrical architecture.[24] All three arenas are surrounded by an inner, curving colonnade oramented with a balustrade and a row of statues. Wittkower pointed to scenic motifs pictured in Palladio's first volume of the *Quattro libri dell' architettura* (Rome, 1570) that may also have provided an impetus for Bernini's plan.[25] The twin, single colonnades at the Villa Tressino at Meledo, for example, extend laterally from the stepped entrance,[26] and embrace the beholder in fashion comparable to that of the colonnades which symbolically encompass the pilgrim like the arms of the church.[27]

Later architects who further developed the theatrical colonnade would have been well known to Bernini. The façade of S. Maria della Pace by Pietro da Cortona erected in Rome the same year Alexander VII announced his project for the Piazza San Pietro is often quoted for its scenographic qualities.[28] The architect introduced a curved story of double, rather than Bernini's later choice of single, columns to enclose the portico.[29] This system was adopted by Cortona for an actual theatre planned for the Palazzo Pitti in Florence.[30] Campbell describes it as a "scenographic ensemble,"[31] where an open court was framed on one side by a curved, colonnaded belvedere. He rightly argues that the spectator would have experienced "a full articulation of the design"[32] as a theatrical device as he passed through the entrance portal, an effect that anticipated the drama of embracing colonnades in the Roman piazza. Cognizant of this exceptional quality, Bernini's principal student, Carlo Fontana, described it in the first publication devoted to the Vatican complex (Rome, 1694).[33]

Le quali, dilatandosi per l'aria l'acque a cagione del loro potente decliuio, apportano tanto godimento, insieme con la vista di quelle verdure de' Giardini, che si riceue per gl'Intercolonnij di quei Portici, che si riconosce per somma marauiglia una si vasta, e maetosa vnione di quegli ornamenti, e Portici.

It is precisely this aspect of the piazza that is its singular feature: Bernini drew together Palladian scenic devices, creating a "dramatic narrative"[34] where "the composition encompasses an angle of vision that is just a little excessive for comfort but only so much that the strain properly enhances the breathtaking magnitude of the piazza . . . and the temple fronts of the colonnades, frame the ensemble like a picture, hold the panorama together."[35] That Bernini simultaneously retained the purity of the ancient amphitheater did not go unnoticed and was voiced as early as 1656 by the building committee,[36] and was later fully discussed by Fontana in his treatise.[37] The piazza was considered the foremost public arena where pilgrims entering the court enjoyed a simultaneous view of its features, which were achieved by Bernini's use of open, monumental colonnades, and offered an unobstructed view of the Pope on certain occasions.

The inspiring facility of Bernini's solution became apparent within a generation of the piazza's completion. It served directly or indirectly as a source for a number of *places royales* in Paris and elsewhere later in the reign of Louis XIV relative to the monarch's extensive building program for the creation of handsome, efficient cities. Two public squares by Jules Hardouin-Mansart — the *Place des Victoires* in Paris and the *Place des Etats* at Dijon — were mentioned by Lavedan[38] and later Zucker,[39] where the circular or hemispherical scheme was planned as a setting for a statue of the sovereign. The *Place des Victoires* is germane to this study because of its kinship with the open, embracing qualities of the piazza at St. Peter's. However, two features of the *Place* (fig. 93) in J. H. Mansart's project must be mentioned, which depend in part on practices established earlier by Louis' court architects. First, rather than using free-standing colonnades, palaces[40] recalling the façade of Versailles have enclosed courts.[41] Furthermore, they were ornamented with colossal pilasters and set on arcaded rusticated foundations. Second, the plan of the *Place des Victoires* indicated that the view towards the statue from points along the main avenue was of prime concern to Mansart. Emphasis on a principal approach and axial perspective was also precedented at

Versailles, where the *avenue de Paris* extended to the Cour d'Honneur.[42] This deviated from Bernini's projects to enclose the piazza with a colonnaded propylea — the *terzo braccio* (figs. 90 and 91) — blocking the view of the church from the Borgo.[43] In this regard, the *Place des Victoires* is decidedly French, although it may be suggested that proposals to clear the *spina* and provide a direct approach to the Piazza San Pietro did not go unnoticed by J. H. Mansart when he executed the project drawing in 1684-85.[44]

Although the *Place des Victoires* exhibits the French preference for an axial symmetrical layout, the round shape formed by two separate enclosures radiating from the building opposite the main approach could not have been imagined without considering projects for the Piazza San Pietro.[45] However, it is not surprising that Mansart preferred the open, circular arrangement, as it agrees with the rationalist doctrine promoted by the Royal Academy dictating that a statue of the king be consistently in view from all sides. Colbert's theories, advanced by Blondel in his *Cours d'architecture* (Paris, 1675), specified that this effect could be best achieved with a circular or octagonal *place*.[46] That Bernini had observed earlier in his *giustificazione* the advantage of the oval over the trapezoidal shape for similar reasons[47] can only serve to underscore Mansart's debt to the Roman architects responsible for the projection of the square of St. Peter's.

The *Place des Victoires* was praised well into the eighteenth century for its openness,[48] yet it is quite orthodox when compared with the plans for the court in front of the *Dôme des Invalides*, where J. H. Mansart attempted to approach the monumental scale of St. Peter's for Louis XIV[49] with a project containing a hemicycle court shaped by curved wings.[50] The first proposal seems to have been submitted in 1676, shortly after he became *Architecte des Bâtiments du Roi* (1675), and is known to have been favorably received by the head of the Academy, Louvois, who requested its development in 1678.[51] For unclear reasons, perhaps owing to the priority of finishing the building proper, Mansart's idea was not immediately realized. Interestingly, he was requested to re-introduce his plan in 1698 — perhaps pressed by his brother-in-law and pupil Robert de Cotte, who may have prepared the second project drawing.[52] The published engraving of the second proposal (fig. 94)[53] shows that the wings terminating in pavilions were covered loggias rather than free-standing colonnades, but their ample, monumental proportions and decorated balustrade derived from Bernini's piazza. Furthermore, the intent to recall the Vatican complex at the *Invalides* has been readily observed in the chapel's façade and massive dome set on a prominent drum.[54]

Patterning the forecourt as well as the *dôme* after St. Peter's was altogether a suitable and natural solution for several reasons. First, its Roman origin would have found favor with Colbert despite his previous inability to reconcile Bernini's exuberant designs for the Louvre with the prevailing taste for strict classicism. On more than one occasion Colbert recognized Rome as the most illustrious city in the world and respected Bernini as its leading decorator.[55] Moreover, it reflects Mansart's regard for the Italian architecture and scenography he intensely studied between 1675 and 1681.[56] By 1698, the impact of these efforts coupled with Bernini's presence at the French court between 1665 and 1667 to participate in redesigning the Louvre,[57] is effectively expressed in J. H. Mansart's chapel at Versailles, referred to as an "explosion of Berninism on French soil."[58] In addition, the resemblance may relate to the special public function of the *Invalides*. Like the chapel at Versailles, it was intended as an demonstration of Louis' piety and, as an urban monument that provided for military pensioners, it emphasized his magnanimous character.[59] This was stressed as early as 1683 in the first exposition on the complex, ordered by the monarch to advertise it, in which Le Jeune de Boulencourt fully discussed Louis' plans for a handsome site.[60]

Although it is true that the complex represented the religious zeal and magnanimity of the King, some scholars argue a less unmitigated reason for its commission that may account for the resemblance to St. Peter's. Braham and others rightly contend that it was "to represent the military prowess and glory of the Bourbon dynasty and reaffirm Louis' status as absolute sovereign."[61] Braham further argues that moving the customary burial site to the *Invalides* from St. Denis — the traditional resting place for French kings — paralleled the monarch's compulsive exertion of authority when he shifted the court from Paris to Versailles in 1677.[62] Braham also proposes that the principal reason for J. H. Mansart's departure from the traditional layout of dome and choir to an inverted plan was to provide adequate space for a new funerary chapel for the family.[63] That the monarch chose the veterans' complex rather than Versailles for the Bourbon burial spot may well have been a calculated effort to advance his military achievements among the public and the pensioners.[64] However, the desired

separation between areas accessible to the pensioners and those used by the court[65] was sustained by the soldiers' entrance from the *cour d'honneur*, and although the hemicycle of arcades served to hide the barracks from general traffic, its purpose seems to have been outweighed by the more important spectacle of the entry of Louis and the French court.[66]

Following the tradition established in France, similar purposes gave rise to the constuction of the state hospitals in London at Chelsea and Greenwich.[67] Shortly after drawings of the *Invalides* were forwarded by Louvois to the Duke of Monmouth — who visited the building in 1672 and again in 1677[68] — Charles II founded a hospital for soldiers at Chelsea in 1682.[69] There, Christopher Wren's use of paired columns for the portico[70] recalls Perrault's project of 1667 for the east front of the Louvre,[71] and the plan to dispose them on either side of the entrance is indebted to Bernini.

These ideas, most likely introduced to Wren while he was in Paris in 1665,[72] came to fruition at Greenwich when he became Surveyor of the project in 1695.[73] At the site of two royal residences outside London overlooking the Thames, the hospital for seamen was founded by William and Mary in 1694 as the counterpart to the one in Chelsea.[74] Wren had to consider first the extant west wing of Charles II built between 1662 and 1669.[75] A perspective view shows a series of symmetrical blocks (fig. 95)[76] (arranged like those of the *Invalides*) flanking the main axis which culminates in the view of a central, domed vestibule with adjacent hall and chapel (fig. 96).[77] Single storey colonnades radiate from the vestibule entrance curving to connect the east and west blocks. Perhaps inspired by the drawings forwarded by Louvois and Boulencourt's publication,[78] Wren paraphrased the Piazza San Pietro by attaching modest quadrant colonnades to the chapel and, similar to Bernini's arrangement of double columns for the passages along the transverse axis (fig. 91), enriched them with two oval-pedimented portals at the cross-entries.[79]

Wren's proposal was rejected, however, because he failed to consider the Queen's request that the view remain clear from the riverfront to her residence directly south,[80] and it was not until the first decade of the eighteenth century that the matter was taken up again. In 1705, after he succeeded Wren as Deputy-Surveyor, Nicolas Hawksmoor revived the plans for an oval court.[81] A compromise seemed imminent when he suggested moving the monarch's residence further south to higher ground for a panoramic view of the river.[82] His daring idea, distinguished by its domed, centralized church with eastern apse, was thoroughly dependent upon St. Peter's.[83] Like Wren's project, the court linked the east and west blocks, but the colonnades, visible in a reconstruction by Downes (fig. 97),[84] were transformed into monumental arcades housing wards and offices. The court was approximately half the size of the Roman piazza, yet the extant drawing fragment of the ground plan discloses Hawksmoor's dependence on the Roman prototype.[85]

It is not surprising that such a bold proposal was reintroduced at this time. The publication of Mansart's second project in 1702[86] and Hawksmoor's own anticipation of extra revenue available at the projected completion of St. Paul's in 1711[87] encouraged an elaboration of Wren's plan. Like the precedent set at the French court, the architects for Greenwich prepared to exploit the scheme of the Piazza San Pietro in order to emphasize sovereign policy for state supported pensioners.[88] Although Downes suggests that the limited funds available to a constitutional monarchy resulted in a solution more judicious than the one in Paris,[89] the adoption of the Roman plan was nevertheless considered by Hawksmoor worthy of a Queen with a "fixt Intention of Magnificence."[90]

It is equally significant that the riverfront perspective was stressed; Greenwich was most easily accessible by river and in full view of London, factors emphasized by Hawksmoor in his descriptive pamphlet on the hospital complex when he remarked: " . . . the principal front of the Great Building lies open to the Thames, elevated upon a terrace . . . in view of all the world . . . and . . . in the sight of (the Grand Emporium) London."[91] Moreover, it is notable that efforts to explore the oval piazza architecturally coincided with the rising interest in waterfront development. Certainly this was a concern since the rebuilding of London after the devastating fire of 1666. For example, a semicircular court was among Wren's first proposals for rebuilding the Thames riverbank, which was accompanied by John Evelyn's suggestion for a similar scheme to articulate the quay in front of the avenue to St. Paul's.[92]

That a corresponding policy found special expression during the reign of Louis XIV need not be recounted here, although it was the Sun King who devoted exceptional energy to this area.[93] For example, Louis intended to extend his sphere of influence by advancing maritime trade and naval operations.[94] Germane to this study is the special promotion of Marseilles to the principal commercial port city, since the project for the *place* proposed by Pierre Puget only a year after Mansart's *Place des Victoires* was created in Paris, included the enlargement of the piazza to monumental dimensions.[95] The *place* was to be located above the quay and, as the setting for an equestrian statue of the monarch, was the climax to a series of improvements for the growing city.[96] In the 1680s — perhaps shortly after Colbert's death — the first proposals for a harborfront piazza were submitted to the Academy.[97] Puget developed the eastern section of the port with an oval court framed by a two-storied palace set on a lofty arcaded, rusticated foundation (fig. 98).[98]

The impressive piazza planned for Marseilles followed a series of presentations of waterfront structures along the heavily travelled Seine.[99] Earlier, for example, LeVau emphasized the riverfront perspective of the *Collège des Quatre Nations* begun in 1662,[100] followed shortly after by Perrault's colonnaded façade of the Louvre.[101] However, that Puget found his inspiration in the Piazza San Pietro appears to indicate the proclivity of the planners to live up to their assertion that Marseilles was the *fameuze soeur de Rome*.[102] Until Louis XIV, no one dared to challenge the firmly established status of Rome as the pre-eminent cultural and artistic center,[103] and, as if following the initiative of the monarch when he attempted to supercede Rome with the new city of Versailles, the magistrates of Marseilles in collaboration with the Academy, prepared an engaging waterfront of monumental proportions that depended upon a Roman design.[104]

For the young students at the Roman Accademia di San Luca, Bernini's piazza was also the emulated model for the first class competition of 1728, which specified a design for an attractive piazza for a coastal harbor.[105] The assignment is testament to the primacy of establishing a papal port and, as Cousins suggests, served as a vehicle for publically advancing the idea to develop Civitavecchia, a project in which Bernini and Carlo Fontana had once been involved.[106] Current efforts stressed developing the waterfront side of Civitavecchia's harbor, which was to be accented with buildings of commanding presence and grandeur.[107] In a like manner, the language of the students' *soggetto* emphasized that "la grandezza e misura della Piazza" be considered.[108] Seeming to hint at the Piazza San Pietro, the author of the *soggetto* — perhaps on the advice of the Pope[109] — further stipulated that this was to be achieved by designing a piazza surrounded by a palace crowned with a belvedere and flanked by two porticoes. The students responded by planning a semi-oval piazza and, as Cousins observes (except for Issachi) "the contestants followed Bernini's scheme of a corridor flanked on either side by a corridor of lesser width."[110] Notable are the entries by Guagli and Marchionni (fig. 99)[111] for piazzas animated by open arcades extending from the corner pavilions of the two-storied semi-oval palace.[112] Marchionni distinguished his entry by freely interpreting Bernini's projects for the *terzo braccio* (fig. 91) as a breakwater to protect the harbor.[113] Nicoletti's third prize entry (fig. 100) also borrowed from the Roman square,[114] his palazzo was enlivened with wings of quadruple colonnades ending in two-storey tetrastyle gateways resembling those at each terminus of the basilica's porticoes, and noting a further likeness to Bernini's work, Cousins observes that the transverse extended oval palazzo attached to a court depends on the Italian architect's first Louvre project.[115]

Although both imitated Bernini's scheme, the Accademia students can be distinguished from their conservative French predecessors by their keen use of scenic devices. The projecting oval in Nicoletti's plan functioned as a focus accented both by the laterally extended porticoes and the colonnaded belvedere above. Also, the vast space set above the quay guaranteed an uninterrupted, panoramic view of the continuous colonnades. The openness of the design markedly contrasted with the fixed perspectives preferred by the French as we find in J. H. Mansart's *Place des Victoires*. By stressing the view from the water, where no single point of reference could be commanded of the beholder, the seemingly staggered colonnades convey a sense of rhythm and movement. The resulting *vedute per angolo* could be described as a "swift dramatic movement into space which leaves the viewer with the impression that the buildings . . . extend into infinity."[116]

The scenographic system adopted by the young architectural students was precedented in theatrical architecture, such as Cortona's Pitti Palace project mentioned above, and reached monumental dimensions at St. Peter's. Although the open colonnade as an effective illusionistic device was discovered during the sixteenth century by architects such as Peruzzi and Palladio, it had yet to be exploited to the gigantic proportions of the Piazza San Pietro. Peruzzi rendered a diagonal twin colonnade in the frescoes of Roman landscape at the Villa Farnesina to suggest receding planes.[117] At the Villa Chiericati in Vicenza (fig.

101), Palladio — whose impact on Bernini has been strongly emphasized — bundled together at right angles a triad of columns at each end of the porch to accent its depth.[118] The axial arrangement was considered mandatory by those who inherited the Renaissance tradition of balanced, symmetrical composition. Conversely, Bernini's crescents of multiple colonnades predict the novel use of oblique rather than symmetrical stage sets by the end of the seventeenth century.[119] The oblique design was presented by Sabbattini in *Practica di fabricar scene* (Ravenna, 1638),[120] yet it was not until the beginning of the Settecento that the *scena per angolo* was fully developed by the great families of Italian scenographers. Ferdinando Galli-Bibiena, Bolognese founder of the celebrated dynasty of court scenographers, is credited with the perfection of the *vedute per angolo*, a system which he published in *L'architettura civile* in 1711, and was frequently practiced in Rome by Filippo Juvarra at the beginning of the century.[121] Bibiena transformed Bernini's quadruple colonnades into exuberant stage designs by using multiple vanishing points and eliminating the proscenium arch common to Renaissance sets. The oblique perspective is "not dependent upon great stage depth, . . . and, inasmuch as the spectator sees only a portion of the scene, he is stimulated to supplement it with an imagined expanse beyond the given stage picture."[122] Likewise, the architectural students at the Accademia, well-trained in matters of perspective already in use by the seventeenth century, added a measure of depth and scenographic quality to the waterfront ensemble by planning an open colonnade that could be viewed from any angle.

The freedom given to the competing students could not compare with the creative imagination of the scenographers, who came closest to capturing Bernini's intent to shape an area closed by a colonnaded propylea which, when approached, opened swiftly and dramatically to the vistor. A stage set for an unidentified port (!) scene by Ferdinando Bibiena's son Giuseppe depicts a gently curving colonnade to the right (fig. 102).[123] The piazza recedes to the left and depth is accented by columns. The Piazza San Pietro is again echoed in a theatre sketch (fig. 103) by Fabrizio Galliari — the youngest and most innovative member of that family of scenographers succeeding the Galli-Bibiena — for a play performed in Turin in 1762.[124] To the left, a curved, free-standing colonnade is set on a high stylobate; each portico terminates in a pedimented entry, and, as at St. Peter's, the balustrade is ornamented with sculpture. In addition, the resemblance to, if not outright imitation of, the Roman piazza is made obvious both by the obelisk at the epicenter of the curve and the juxtaposition of a second colonnade to the right, which lends a distinctly ellipsoidal shape to the set. The view towards the harbor is something akin to looking northeast towards the Borgo from the *piazza retta* of St. Peter's.

Despite the increasing influence of classical models during the decades of the 50s and 60s, the scenic aspect of Bernini's monumental colonnades was explored by the French students of the Académie Royale d'Architecture.[125] Charles de Wailly's elevation of a palace that won first prize in 1752 (fig. 104), and opened to him the avenue for further study in Rome at the French Academy,[126] features an elaborate triumphal arch set between quadrant porticoes of multiple colonnades articulated with pedimented pavilions surmounted by low domes.[127] It is true that Wailly's solid palace acts as a barrier and the resulting reduced perspective is less scenic than the perforated assembly of buildings and unlimited vistas staged by his Italian counterparts. Nevertheless, the dramatic mood of Wailly's architecture is communicated by his "expressive use of light and shade" and "receptivity to the visual grandeur of the seventeenth-century tradition."[128]

A spectacular reference to Bernini is vigorously demonstrated by an architectural fantasy that may be connected with de Wailly's activity as a theatre designer (fig. 105), and conveys his affection for the monumental splendor of the Roman tradition.[129] Twin colonnades attached to a centrally planned building sweep to the right in pronounced arcs, ending in a richly decorated enormous triumphal arch. The dramatic recession into space *per angolo* heightened by the cast light admirably compares to the projects of his Italian contemporaries and depends upon practices evolved from the workshops of the Galli-Bibiena, as well as the teaching of Filippo Juvarra during his Roman years.

Likewise, the architect Marie-Joseph Peyre, prize winner of the preceding year who accompanied de Wailly to Italy, was equally affected by the scenic tradition of the Roman architects and architect-scenographers. His entries for the *concorsi* held at the Accademia di San Luca in 1753 and 1756 are often cited as illustrations of the deep impressions Bernini's piazza made on the young architect.[130] Peyre's inventive cathedral for the competition of 1753 is framed by a pair of quadruple colonnades attached to matching palaces, and is testament to the growing

influence of classical models.[131] But especially interesting is Peyre's solution for the competition of 1756, a design for a structure to house three academies which is bi-axially organized with a balustrade broken only by the presence of austere domes (figs. 106 and 107).[132] Although his extensive commentary on the academy and other projects published in his *Oeuvres d'architecture* (Paris, 1765) disclose Peyre's regard for ancient architecture[133] — certainly reflected in the severity of his design — the semicircular porticoes attached to opposite elevations of the main structure restate the Piazza San Pietro in a manner that imparts a measure of scenographic quality through sheer magnitude of proportion and visionary character.[134]

The appreciation of both the scenic aspect and geometry of the Piazza San Pietro as a model for large-scale urban projects was precedented by Filippo Juvarra, who during his years in Rome, as Millon has established, occasionally prepared designs connected with competitions at the Accademia in which he did not compete. A case in point is a drawing related to the *Concorso Clementino* of 1706, a project for a church and hospital complex.[135] His perspective sketch (fig. 108) shows an ellipsoidal court enclosed by a curving arcaded exedra terminating in domed pavilions.[136] In much the same fashion as Wren's proposal for Greenwich, open porticoes screen the lower level of the hospital façade and serve to focus one's vision on the dome, supported by a high drum enriched with columns.

While it is true that the immediate visibility of Bernini's piazza would have impressed the students directly, it was probably Juvarra, documented to have taught at the Academy in 1707, 1708, 1711 and 1712,[137] who brought to life the project's finer points which he most likely learned during his collaboration with Carlo and Francesco Fontana between 1704 and 1706.[138] Furthermore, Juvarra's model for the competition of 1715 for the new sacristy, with its curved, colonnaded inner court attached to the south apse of St. Peter's, attracted considerable attention.[139] As Millon points out, it was exceptional to be advanced so quickly to instructor at the Accademia di San Luca, and the appreciation of Juvarra's talents is attested to by the permanent display of his *concorso* drawings in the Academy building.[140] Coupled with his status as an accomplished scenographer who was familiar with the Bibiena *scena per angolo*, Juvarra seems to have artfully relayed the merits of Bernini's solution to numerous students, including Juvarra's principal pupil Luigi Vanvitelli, who was to play so prominent a role in the evolution of the Berninesque oval court in urban planning.[141] One can only speculate if the lost "Disegno di piazza ovale con colonnato ed arco trionfale del re Luigi XIV" mentioned in Giovanni Sacchetti's list of Juvarra's drawings under the year 1732[142] — re-incarnated Bernini's ideas.[143]

It is significant, however, that Juvarra's vision for this *place* followed the course of events seen earlier at the court of Louis XIV and later that of William and Mary in London. For unknown reasons the project was abandoned, and it may be possible that Juvarra's design conflicted with the *noble simplicité* observed earlier in the work of de Wailly and Peyre that would pervade the spirit of French architecture at mid-century.[144] For example, when the project was revived in 1748 by the Paris merchants to honor Louis XV, the winner of the competition, Ange-Jacques Gabriel,[145] proposed an octagonal court bisected by a central axis opening to the Seine and linked by avenues with the old city of Paris.[146] The *place* was enclosed by corner pavilions opposite two loggias that evoke the Louvre with their colossal order and elevated, rusticated foundation (fig. 109).[147] Now the *Place de la Concorde*, the square is often cited as it was in 1765 by Patte (*Monumens érigés en France à la gloire Louis XV*) as a paragon of public planning characterized by unlimited vistas and openness, fully integrated into the city environment.[148] Just as his predecessor, Louis XV was preoccupied with presenting a resplendent yet functional urban environment designed to enhance the *gloire* of his reign, and continued the tradition established by the Sun King of embellishing Paris with a number of *places royales* viewed from the riverfront.[149] And, like Puget's project for Marseilles, it has been rightly recognized as a "monumental entrance to the town" and therefore affiliated with the aesthetic function of the Piazza di San Pietro.[150] Akin to Bernini's square, Gabriel's project was ornamented with a central monument and was planned to provide a principal view from the river past twin buildings towards the proposed church of the Madeleine.[151]

Allied with Gabriel's system was the public square built between 1752 and 1755 at Nancy also dedicated to Louis XV, where the influence of the Piazza San Pietro was equally decisive.[152] Architect Emmanuel Héré de Corny utilized Bernini's scheme in an unprecedented form by axially aligning three courts (fig. 110). These linked the new city with the old section refurbished by its commissioner, Stanislaus Lezcyznski of Lorraine, deposed King of Poland and father-in-law to the French monarch.[153] The sequence

began with the great court embellished with a statue of Louis XV by Lemoyne, followed by a bridge above the moat leading to the medieval fortifying wall; immediately past the wall Héré distinguished the entry to the *Place Carrière* with a triumphal arch.[154] Following was a promenade lined with ornamental trees and grillwork culminating in a view of the ellipsoidal court attached to the *Hôtel de l'Intendance* (fig. 111). Héré's plan is dependent upon Bernini's conception with regard to the shape of the court, and indebted to Carlo Fontana for its sequence of individual spaces to direct the flow of movement.[155] Its distinctly axial compostion appears to be closely related to Fontana's published solution for a triumphal arch and trapezoidal court as a visual prelude to the *piazza obliqua* (fig. 112).[156]

The emphasis placed on natural ornament and the special consideration given to the inter-connecting streets by Gabriel and Héré illustrates the importance attached to the setting of the public square within the urban landscape; consequently, the oval court takes on new meaning in eighteenth-century city planning.

Again a previously unknown sensitivity to city topography was demonstrated in the design of *places royales* by the concern for linking isolated sections by means of a central axis punctuated by open spaces to express progression through space.[157] At Nancy, the visitor moved through a series of "visual arrests" — an arrangement Zucker identifies conclusively as Italian, epitomized in Bernini's design.[158] Spatial suspense is generated by the "rhythmical alternation of smaller and larger, higher and lower structures in their relative proportions to the framing façades and of the perforation of grilles, triumphal arch and colonnades . . . "[159] While it is true that the *place royale* at Nancy exemplifies both the growing interest in classical models reinforced by the conservative tradition of Colbert and Blondel, and the need for uncluttered traffic patterns to relieve urban chaos, it strongly reflects the appeal of the Roman predilection for scenic effects.[160]

At the same time, the *place royale* continued to be emphasized as an "architectural showcase" dedicated to the monarch.[161] In his *Traité de la police* (Paris, 1738), de la Mare carefully distinguished the *place royale* from the commercial or administrative square as the pre-eminent public setting;[162] he was followed by Patte, who gave special praise to the expansive vistas and spaciousness of squares dedicated to Louis XV.[163] Perhaps it can be suggested here that during the eighteenth century the *place royale* was transformed into the city frontispiece as a solution to the problem of providing healthy, agreeable surroundings that simultaneously reinforced the autonomy of the monarch and championed his role as an urban planner.[164]

These ideas found consummate expression at the Neapolitan capital of Caserta, where the scheme of the transverse ellipse bisected by a central axis was intimately related to projects for the Piazza San Pietro.[165] There, even though issues of topography and interfering buildings were altogether unique for this newly built city, the plan functioned as the frontispiece to this autonomous administrative center. The arrangement was presented in 1752 by Luigi Vanvitelli for the monarch Charles II, Bourbon King of Naples, and although it would be Charles' successor, Ferdinand IV, who witnessed its completion in 1774,[166] the first project was made public in 1756 (fig. 113).[167] The rectangular palace followed the style of baroque classicism, and the impact of French models on the vast system of geometric gardens and central axis connecting Caserta with Naples was decisive (fig. 114).[168] But the intersecting streets and passage encircling the court of assembled wards was contingent upon current experiments in urban planning. The resulting perspectives *per angolo* and fragmented views of the sprawling complex of buildings beyond, for example, document Vanvitelli's debt to Juvarra and the collaborators of the Galli-Bibiena in Naples.[169]

Over and above these attributes is the marked revival of the Piazza San Pietro, which may be evidence of an ideological concern transcending the broader interest in practicing modern city planning. While it is true that Vanvitelli would have become familiar with the geometry of the Roman square as *Architetto della Fabrica di S. Pietro* in 1750,[170] the project for Caserta is now known to be related also to a drawing which could have been visible only at the Spanish court of Charles' father, Philip V.[171] The project visualized Robert de Cotte's autonomous setting of 1714-1715 for the royal palace at Buen Retiro (fig. 115).[172] Both Caserta and the Spanish complex are characterized by a logical layout of gardens around a geometric palace and, although the French architect planned a circular, rather than oval, court, the perpendicular extensions joining the palace and square shape an area corresponding to the *Piazza retta*.

It has been argued that the resemblance of the two plans indicates Charles' intervention in the project for Caserta, where the monarch seems to have explicitly advanced the idea of the French *palace royale* as a setting for himself and court spectacles.[173] However, because he simultaneously evoked the foremost Roman site by reviving the Piazza San Pietro's special *teatro* shape as a prelude to his palace,[174] it may be further suggested that the Neapolitan king also emulated the urban situation in front of the chateau of Versailles. Charles not only promoted Caserta as the cultural and social center of the kingdom but also perceived himself as the benevolent heir to Europe's exemplary administrations, modelling his own after that of Louis XIV.[175] New publications such as Vasi's *Delle magnificenze di Roma (Rome 1758)*.[176] and studies of Rome's urban design by Nolli (Rome, 1748)[177] may have stimulated him to associate himself with the celebrated tradition of the Roman High Baroque.

Coupled with these concerns was a desire to create a city unmatched in beauty and engineering perfection. Although this idea can also be traced to Versailles — the city Charles admired most — it became a special feature of urban planning by the middle of the eighteenth century.[178] For example, monarchs succeeding Charles hoped to make Naples the first city of Europe,[179] an idea that continued into the nineteenth century when Ferdinand I built his oval court in front of San Francesco di Paola (fig. 116),[180] whereas French architect-planners maintained their vision of Paris as the world's capital.

The building campaigns proposed during the eighteenth century for cities such as Paris and Caserta, which aimed towards creating the most beautiful city in the universe, could hardly compare in scale with the redesign of St. Petersburg soon after it was designated capital of the empire in 1703.[181] The entire city was redeveloped and a special emphasis was placed on the Neva riverfront. There, "an architectural sequence building up to a climax in the space of the five central squares was superbly accomplished by the manipulation of the architectural character and the spatial hierarchy of the various projects flanking the boulevard . . . ."[182]

The first among the visual ensemble of squares bisecting the boulevard — designated the "Great Perspective Road" in 1788[183] —followed the tradition of positioning a semi-circular court opening on the waterfront (fig. 117). The crescent shaped court was to be complemented by a matching structure attached to the south portico of the building it embellished, the new cathedral of the Virgin of Kazan (fig. 118),[184] and therefore was directly related to Peyre's competition project of 1756 (figs. 106 and 107).[185] The French design was probably introduced to the church's Russian architect Andrew Voronikhin during his student years at the academy in St. Petersburg, at that time directed by Peyre's collaborator and companion in Rome, Charles de Wailly.[186] Also linked with French taste and, ultimately, Palladian classicism, was the severity of Voronikhin's conception, reflected in the austerity of the pedimented façade, the slender, Neo-classical dome, and the plain balustrade above the colonnade.[187]

The desire of both the architect and the commissioner Emperor Paul I for an entirely Roman plan, however, reinforced by their separate sojourns to the continent,[188] is visible in the Latin cross scheme.[189] Furthermore, the "silhouette" of St. Peter's is patently echoed by the rows of columns and tetrastyle gateways, and the similarity was even closer with the presence of the obelisk once standing in the square."[190] Evidence that Paul I sought to restate the grandeur and beauty of Rome may be found in the significance the emperor attached to his position as grand master of the Knights of St. John of Jerusalem. The cathedral commemorated his recent election to the office and, encouraged by his special role as the Order's first non-Catholic administrator (as Hamilton observes) he even entertained the desire of becoming Pope.[191] The building quite literally reproduced the papal atmosphere in the Russian capital.

More broadly, Voronikhin's cathedral project of 1801 was an integral part of a larger, expansive program representing an active desire for the architect-planners and commissioners of Leningrad to build the universal capital. The foresight given to the plan superceded earlier experiments and resulted in a city environment highlighted by buildings unique in character yet fully integrated by the three-pronged layout of the main avenues. Moreover, although the channels and waterways of the Neva were interconnected with the overall scheme, the Nevsky Prospekt itself maintained a special focus. Notably articulated by the semi-oval square in front of the Kazan cathedral, the banks of the river were referred to as "the window looking into Europe" and virtually functioned as the city frontispiece of Leningrad.[192]

It has been argued that the cathedral of the Virgin of Kazan and its open square set along the main vista of Leningrad was connected with one of the last great efforts in urban planning.[193] The three-pronged network of streets depended upon the French practice of axial alignment that provided a deep perspective along a main artery. the reqularly shaped squares, on the other hand, are firmly indebted to Bernini, and the scheme of the semi-oval square derives from his Piazza San Pietro. Because the cathedral and many of the connecting buildings along the quay were erected during the first half of the nineteenth century, they reflect the current fashion for Palladian structures. However, the integration of streets with open squares and continued emphasis on presenting a handsome waterfront was linked to the changing aesthetic in urban design during the eighteenth century, where health, efficiency, and beauty were of prime concern.

In this study, the Russian square represents primarily the final stage in the evolution of the transverse oval courtyard, from architectural traditions established during the latter part of the seventeenth century, to its prominent role as the city frontispiece. Unlike the earliest experiments by the architects to the Sun King, where the curved embracing qualities of Bernini's piazza found its greatest appeal, Voronikhin's court was surrounded by monumental, free-standing colonnades.

However, it was the geometry of the Piazza San Pietro that transferred most readily. It was revived once again in the nineteenth century not only in Naples, but also when Valadier transformed the Piazza del Popolo in Rome (fig. 119). There, the motif of the two exedrae, which expand Rainaldi's originally wedge-shaped square in the transverse direction, restate the idea of the hemi-cycle oval.[194]

Pamela S. Hemzik
The Pennsylvania State University

Notes

*   This paper developed out of a seminar taught at The Pennsylvania State University by Professor Hellmut Hager, who encouraged me to pursue the study of Bernini and was my advisor on this topic. I am grateful to Professor Anthony Cutler who cheerfully and carefully edited the text, although I am solely responsible for errors. Very special thanks are extended to Cynthia Odell for her expert and speedy typing of the manuscript and Susan Munshower for her assistance with the photographs.

1. L. von Pastor, *History of the Popes*, XXXI, London, 1940, pp. 291-299; and F. Baldinucci, *Vita di Gian Lorenzo Bernini: scultore, architetto, e pittore*, Florence, 1682, ed. S. S. Ludovici, Milan, 1948, pp. 109-110.

2. This date has been established by Richard Krautheimer (*The Rome of Alexander VII, 1655-1667*, Princeton, 1985, pp. 63-73, 169-175). Basic for all studies concerning the evolution of the projects for the Piazza di San Pietro: H. Brauer and R. Wittkower, "Petersplatz," in *Die Zeichnungen des Gianlorenzo Bernini*, I, Berlin, 1931, pp. 64-102; and T. Kitao, *Circle and Oval in the Square of St. Peter's: Bernini's Art of Planning*, New York, 1974; M. Birindelli, *La macchina heroica: il disegno di Gianlorenzo Bernini per Piazza San Pietro, Rome, 1980*; see further, Christof Thoenes, "Studien zur Geschichte des Petersplatzes," *Zeitschrift für Kunstgeschichte*, 26, 1963, pp. 97-145.

3. Alternate schemes are discussed by A. Busiri-Vici, *La piazza di San Pietro nei secoli III, XIV, XVII*, Rome, 1893; and R. Wittkower, "A Counter-Project to Bernini's 'Piazza di San Pietro'," *Journal of the Warburg and Courtauld Institutes*, III, 1939-1940, pp. 88-106. See note 33 below and fig. 28 for Carlo Fontana's proposed triumphal arch entry published in his *Templum Vaticanum* (1694).

4. R. Wittkower, *Art and Architecture in Italy, 1600-1750*, 3rd edition, Baltimore, 1980, p. 196.

5. I. Egorov, *The Architectural Planning of St. Petersburg*, Athens Ohio, 1969, passim; and notes 181 and 185 below.

6. G. Alisio, *Siti reali dei Borboni: Aspetti dell' architettura napoletana del Settecento*, Naples, 1976, p. 62, and note 179 below.

7. R. Wittkower, *Art and Architecture*, p. 196.

8. *Ibid.*, 196. A brief summary of projects dependent upon the hemicycle scheme is given by J. J. Bishop in "The Role of the Circus and Crescent in 18th and 19th Century British Town Planning," published dissertation, Boston University, 1962, pp. 1-27.

9. H. Hager, "The Accademia di San Luca in Rome and the Académie Royale d'Architecture in Paris: A Preliminary Investigation," *Projects and Monuments in the Period of the Roman Baroque. Papers in Art History from The Pennsylvania State University*, vol. I, 1984, pp. 129-141; especially note 2 for bibliography relevant to the history of academies of art and architecture; and note 126 below.

10. W. Oechslin, "La fortuna del colonnato fino al '900," and "Il colonnato di San Pietro: echi nel '700 francese," papers presented at the *Corso internazionale di alta cultura: Bernini e l'universo barocco*, Rome, 1980.

11. G. Orefice, "La diffusione dei 'modelli' romani degli spazi urbani," *Gian Lorenzo Bernini architetto e l'architettura europea del Sei-Settecento*, II, Rome, 1984, pp. 599-609.

12. W. F. Cousins, Jr., "The Ideal Port and the *Concorsi Clementini* of 1728, 1732, and 1738 at the Accademia di San Luca in Rome," unpublished dissertation, The Pennsylvania State University, University Park, Pa., 1982.

13. See note 2 above.

14. See note 2 above.

15. Brauer and Wittkower, "Petersplatz," passim; Kitao, *Circle and Oval*, pp. 10-11, 25-26; see also R. Bernheimer, "Theatrum mundi," *The Art Bulletin*, XXXVIII, 1956, pp. 225-247, where the idea of the piazza as a theater is given critical attention, and in particular, R. Krautheimer, op. cit., Chapter IV.

16. Bernini stated in his *giustificazione* that the oval plan was chosen immediately after the installation of the wooden construction (Brauer and Wittkower, "Petersplatz," p. 71; Kitao, *Circle and Oval*, pp. 1-14). For the full scale models, see George C. Bauer, "From Architecture to Scenography: the Full-scale Model in the Baroque Tradition," *Comité International d'Histoire de l'Art, Atti del XXIV Congresso Internazionale de Storia dell' Arte*, 5, Bologna (1979), 1982, pp. 141-149.

17. Kitao, *Circle and Oval*, pp. 23-24.

18. *Ibid.*, p. 5.

19. Bernini remarked that the square plan would not only greatly reduce the size of the piazza but also interfere with the view of the Pope on Holy Days. (Brauer and Wittkower, "Petersplatz," pp. 69-71, 76-78; and Kitao, *Circle and Oval*, pp. 10-11).

20. See Kitao, *Circle and Oval*, pp. 71-73, for his discussion of Serlio's use of the oval and his fig. 41 where the *ovato tondo* can be seen inscribed in a diagram of the piazza. Further study was made by H. Kruft, "The Origin of the Oval in Bernini's Piazza S. Pietro," *The Burlington Magazine*, CXXI, 1979, pp. 796-800.

21. Brauer and Wittkower, "Petersplatz," pp. 71-76; and Kitao, *Circle and Oval*, pp. 7, 15-16.

22. Brauer and Wittkower, "Petersplatz," passim; Kitao, *Circle and Oval*, pp. 22, 26.

23. Kitao, *Circle and Oval*, p. 26, fig. 33 (London, RIBA, vol. X, fol. 3). See also R. Wittkower, "Palladio e Bernini," *Bollettino del Centro Internazionale di Studi di Architettura: Andrea Palladio*, VIII, 1966, p. 15. For a more restrained assessment of Palladio's influence on Bernini see Christof Thoenes, "Bernini architetto tra Palladio e Michelangelo," in: *Gian Lorenzo Bernini Architetto e l'architettura europea del Sei-Settecento*, a cura di Gianfranco Spangnesi e Marcello Fagiolo, Rome, 1983, pp. 105-134.

24. Wittkower, "Palladio e Bernini," figs. 2 and 3.

25. Wittkower, "Palladio e Bernini," p. 15, proposes that Bernini was familiar with the north Italian architect through Cortona. See also H. Hager, "Puntualizzazioni su disegni scenici teatrali e l'architettura scenografica del periodo barocco a Roma," *Bollettino del centro internazionale di studi di architettura: Andrea Palladio*, XVII, 1975, pp. 119-129, where the author provides a definition for scenographic architecture and examines its origins in set design.

26. A. Palladio, *I quattro libri dell'-architettura*, II, Cap. XIV, Rome, 1570, pl. XXXI.

27. Kitao, *Circle and Oval*, p. 14.

28. Wittkower, *Art and Architecture*, p. 242, fig. 147; and Hager, "Puntualizzazioni su disegni scenici teatrali," p. 120.

29. Wittkower, *Art and Architecture*, p. 242, did observe, however, "as early as 1657 Bernini made an intermediary project with double columns for the colonnades of St. Peter's, and his final choice of a Doric order with Ionic entablature was here anticipated by Cortona."

30. That Bernini was indebted to Cortona's projects for the Pitti Palace was first observed by Wittkower, *Art and Architecture*, p. 246; and idem, "Palladio e Bernini," p. 15, where he suggested that these and related proposals were known through published engravings.

31. M. Campbell, *Pietro da Cortona at the Pitti Palace: A Study of the Planetary Rooms and Related Projects*, Princeton, 1977, pp. 157-164, esp. p. 161, fig. 187.

32. *Ibid.*, pp. 161-162.

33. C. Fontana, *Il Tempio Vaticano e sua origine con gl'Edifittii più cospicui antichi, e moderni fatti dentro, e fuori di` Esso*, Rome, 1694, p. 184; cf. Christof Thoenes, "Studien zur Geschichte des Petersplatzes," *Zeitschrift für Kunstgeschichte*, 1963, pp. 125 ff.

34. Wittkower, "Palladio e Bernini," p. 23.

35. Kitao, *Circle and Oval*, p. 53.

36. See *ibid.*, p. 7, note 12, where the *avviso* of 19 August 1656 is cited.

37. Fontana, *Il Tempio Vaticano*, IV, cap. 2, esp. pp. 183-184 (Brauer and Wittkower, "Petersplatz," p. 77; and Kitao, *Circle and Oval*, p. 21).

38. P. Lavedan, *Histoire de l'urbanisme*, II, *Renaissance et temps modernes*, Paris, 1941, pp. 134-135, 285-287. Although it is not within the scope of this paper to study the

German descendants of Bernini's scheme, Lavedan comments briefly on the association of the Zwinger at Potsdam and Dresden with the Roman courtyard (*Ibid*, p. 189). See also note 156 below.

39. P. Zucker, *Town and Square from the Agora to the Village Green*, New York, 1959, p. 179.

40. See Lavedan, *Histoire de l'urbanisme*, II, p. 135 and L. Hautecoeur, *Histoire de l'architecture classique en France*, II, Paris, 1948, pp. 603-607, fig. 476 for perspective engravings of the site.

41. A. Blunt, *Art and Architecture in France 1500-1700*, 4th edition, Harmondsworth, 1982, fig. 276.

42. *Ibid.*, fig. 276.

43. R. Wittkower, "Il terzo braccio del Bernini in Piazza S. Pietro," *Bollettino d'arte*, XXIV, 1949, pp. 129-134; and H. Hager, "Progetti del tardo barocco romano per il terzo braccio del colonnato della Piazza S. Pietro," *Commentari*, XIX, 1968, pp. 303-334.

44. Pope Sixtus V's plan to clear the *Spina* was first revived by Urban X and supervised by Cardinal Spada, a member of the building committee until 1662 (Kitao, *Circle and Oval*, pp. 9-10, 61-66). See R. Krautheimer, op. cit., pp. 91 ff.

45. See for example the plan published by Brauer and Wittkower (*Die Zeichnungen*, II, pl. 192a) which is attributable to Carlo Rainaldi.

46. The argument for this topic as it was advanced by Colbert and Blondel at the Royal Academy is outlined by Lavedan, *Histoire de l'urbanisme*, II, pp. 239-243, 284 and fig. 105 A and B. See also L. Hautecoeur, *L'architecture classique en France*, II, pp. 462-491 for an examination of these theories.

47. See note 19 above.

48. Pierre Patte, *Monumens érigés en France à la gloire de Louis XV*, Paris, 1765, pp. 99-105.

49. P. Reuterswärd, *The Two Churches of the Hôtel des Invalides*, Stockholm, 1965, pp. 9-13. A comprehensive study of the history of the complex as well as an extensive bibliography of the documents and secondary sources was published in connection with the exhibition at the Museé de l'Armée, Paris, under the direction of R. Ballargeat (*Les Invalides: trois siècles d'histoire*, Paris, 1974).

50. Reuterswärd, *The Two Churches of the Hôtel des Invalides*, p. 13.

51. *Ibid.*, pp. 15-16, and 28.

52. *Ibid.*, pp. 28-29, fig. 4.

53. The engraving by Pierre Lepautre, based on de Cotte's project drawing, was published in Pierre de Bellocq's *L'église des Invalides, Poème*, 1702 (*Ibid.*, pp. 28-29).

54. The kinship of the courtyard with Bernini's piazza has been observed, but without further discussion, by Anthony Blunt (*Art and Architecture in France*, pp. 364-365, note 9; see also P. Bourget and G. Cattaui, *Jules Hardouin Mansart*, Paris, 1956, pp. 34-38, 64-66; and L. Hautecoeur, *L'architecture classique en France*, II, p. 581.

55. C. Gould, *Bernini in France: An Episode in Seventeenth-Century History*, Princeton, 1982, p. 45.

56. Bourget and Cattaui, *Jules Hardouin Mansart*, p. 10, note the French architect's interest in Alberti, da Vinci, and Scamozzi; moreover, they suggest that Serlio's oval constructions were known to Mansart when he planned the forecourt of the hospital.

57. Baldinucci, *Vita di cavaliere Gio Lorenzo Bernino*, pp. 111-126. Paul Freart de Chantelou, *Diary of the Cavaliere Bernini's Visit to France*, edited and with an introduction by Anthony Blunt, annotated by George C. Bauer, translated by Margery Corbett, Princeton, 1985.

58. Gould, *Bernini in France*, p. 135.

59. *Les Invalides: trois siècles d'histoire*, pp. 139-146.

60. Le Jeune de Boulencourt, *Description générale de l'hostel royal des Invalides, établi par Louis le Grand dans la plaine Grenelle...avec les plans, profils et élévations de ses faces, coupes et appartemens*, Paris, 1683.

61. A. Braham, "L'église du dôme," *Journal of the Warburg and Courtauld Institutes*, XXIII, 1960, p. 216; and R. Neuman, "Robert de Cotte, Architect of the Late Baroque," 2 vols., Ph. D. diss., University of Michigan, Ann Arbor, 1978, p. 151.

62. Braham, "L'église du dôme," p. 216.

63. *Ibid.*, passim. See also B. Jestaz, "Ancien membre de l'Ecole français de Rome: Jules Hardouin-Mansart et l'église des Invalides," *Gazette des Beaux-Arts*, LXV, 1965, pp. 59-74.

64. Perhaps it can be suggested here that the building of the Invalides may have been in celebration of the recently successful Dutch Wars of the 1670s, largely the result of new strategies implemented by Vauban and Louvois. Louis XIV was not an especially remarkable or courageous soldier, and would certainly have realized the advantage of publicizing his triumphs, however infrequent. See J. B. Wolf, "Louis XIV, Soldier King," in *Louis XIV and the Craft of Kingship*, ed. J.C. Rule, Columbus, Ohio, 1969, pp. 196-226 for his discussion of military tactics during the administration of the monarch.

65. Without comment, Reuterswärd (*The Two Churches of the Hôtel des Invalides*, pp. 95-105) suggests that J. H. Mansart may have planned a waterfront entrance to the Bourbon Chapel when the architect altered the traditional layout. However, the diagram published by Orefice (*Gian Lorenzo Bernini architetto*, p. 610, fig. 5) as a reproduction of the first project by Mansart for the square in front of the Invalides is a design for a "Place Louis XV" which Pierre Contant d'Jury submitted in 1748 for the Quai Malaquet (see E. A. Gutkind, *Urban Development in Western Europe: France and Belgium*, vol. V, New York, 1970, pp. 273 ff., pl. 193).

66. *Les Invalides: trois siècles d'histoire*, pp. 42-44.

67. See B. Sevestre, "Un modèle pour l'Europe," in *Les Invalides: trois siècles d'histoire*, pp. 338-350, esp. 348-350.

68. D. Ascoli, "The Royal Hospital of Chelsea (1681-1794)," in *Les Invalides: trois siècles d'histoire*, p. 371.

69. A discussion of the hospital at Chelsea is included in *The Nineteenth Volume of the Wren Society*, 1942, eds. A. T. Bolton and H. D. Hendry, Oxford, 1942, pp. 61-86, and pls. XXX-XLVII.

70. J. Summerson, *Architecture in Britain 1530 to 1830*, 4th edition, *Harmondsworth*, 1963 (reprint, Baltimore, 1969), pls. 96b and 97.

71. Blunt, *Art and Architecture in France*, p. 332, fig. 274. The link with French architecture was observed by K. Downes, in *English Baroque Architecture*, London, 1966, p. 33.

72. Blunt, *Art and Architecture in France*, pp. 115-116; and K. Downes, *The Architecture of Wren*, London, 1982, pp. 8-9.

73. See *The Architecture of Wren*, pp. 107-110, for Downes's chronology of the building campaign.

74. *Ibid.*, pp. 16-17.

75. J. H. V. Davies, "The Dating of the Building of the Royal Hospital at Greenwich," *Archaeological Journal*, CXII, 1956, pp. 126-136.

76. G. Beard, *The Work of Christopher Wren*, Edinburgh, 1982, pl. 45. Many of the project drawings are reproduced in *The Sixth Volume of the Wren Society, 1929*: *The Royal Hospital for Seamen at Greenwich, 1694-1728*, Oxford, 1929.

77. Beard, *The Work of Christopher Wren*, pl. 46. Both the perspective and plan are preserved in the Sir John Soane's Museum, London.

78.   Downes, *The Architecture of Wren*, pp. 83-84.
C. I. A. Ritchie ("The Hostel of the Invalides
by Thomas Povey (1682) Lambeth Palace
Library MS. 745," *Medical History*, X, 1966,
pp. 1-2), remarks that it was Charles II's
interest in the Invalides that motivated Louis
XIV to charge Boulencourt with writing an
exposition on the French Hospital. In addition,
Ritchie concludes that Wren seems to have had
access to an unpublished commentary on the
Invalides composed by the Englishman Thomas
Povey.

79.   The project elevation for the church, also
located in the Sir John Soane's Museum, is
reproduced in *The Sixth Volume of the Wren
Society*, pl. XXI.

80.   Beard, *The Work of Christopher Wren*, p. 43;
and Downes, *The Architecture of Wren*, p.
107.

81.   Downes, *The Architecture of Wren*, p. 110 and
idem, *Hawksmoor*, Cambridge, Mass., 1959,
p. 89.

82.   Downes, *Hawksmoor*, p. 91. Nicolas
alternatively proposed raising the Queen's
residence one story higher in order to provide
for an uninterrupted vista (Downes, *English
Baroque Architecture*, p. 52).

83.   Downes, *Hawksmoor*, pp. 91-93.

84.   Downes, *English Baroque Architecture*, fig. 22
center. Downes (*Hawksmoor*, p. 93, notes 28
and 29) argues against Bolton's attribution of
the drawing to Vanbrugh (*The Sixth Volume of
the Wren Society*, p. 86) and, furthermore,
considers his reconstruction erroneous in the
light of a number of newly-discovered
drawings connected with the Greenwich
project.

85.   The fragment showing the ground plan (*The
Sixth Volume of the Wren Society*, pl. XXVII)
was drawn out by Downes, *Hawksmoor*, fig. 6.

86.   See note 53 above.

87.   Downes, *English Baroque Architecture*, p. 52;
see also *idem, Hawksmoor*, p. 106, where the
author discloses "..some time after 1702 a
number of schemes were devised in the Office
of Works for enlarging Greenwich Hospital;
unfinished and in debt as it was, there were
ideas of making it even bigger, prodigiously
expensive and on a scale to dwarf not merely
Chelsea but the stillborn Whitehall and the
Invalides."

88.   See *The Sixth Volume of the Wren Socity*, p.
21, where we find Hawksmoor's laudatory
remarks concerning the hospital benefactors'
unselfish provision for the well-being of the
veterans.

89.   Downes, *Hawksmoor*, p. 91.

90.   See *The sixth Volume of the Wren Society*, p.
20, where this extract from Hawksmoor's
*Remarks on the Founding and Carrying on the
Building of the Royal Hospital at Greenwich*,
London, 1728, are published.

91.   *Ibid.*, pp. 20-21. See Downes, *English
Baroque Architecture*, fig. 91 for a waterfront
prospect of the hospital from the Isle of Dogs.

92.   Lavedan, *Histoire de l'urbanisme*, II, pp.
367-373, fig. 183. See also T. F. Reddaway,
The Rebuilding of London after the Great Fire,
London, 1940; and Bishop, "The Role of the
Circus and Crescent," pp. 24-26.

93.   This topic was most recently examined by D.
Rabeau, "Monumental Art, or the Politics of
Enchantment," in *The Sun King: Louis XIV
and the New World*, ed. R. Macdonald,
exhibition   catalogue,   Louisianna   State
Museum, New Orleans, 1984, pp. 122-135.

94.   Full treatment of this subject is found in J.
Konvitz's dissertation "New Port Cities of
Louis XIV's France: Brest, Lorient, Rochefort
and Sète, 1660-70," Princeton, 1973, later
encapsulated in "Grandeur in French City
Planning Under Louis XIV," *Journal of Urban
History*, II, 1975, pp. 3-42. Much of his
material is included in his *Cities and the Sea:
Port City Planning in Early Modern Europe*,
Baltimore, 1978, pp. 73-147.

95.   Puget's commission is analysed by K. Herding
(*Pierre Puget: Das bildnisches Werk*, Berlin,

1970, pp. 92-94, 115-124), R. Plovin ("Les projets de Place Royale à Marseille," *Provence historique*, XXII, 1972, pp. 93-105) and F. Tavernier, ("Project de Place Royale," *Arts et Livres de Provence*, LXXVIII, 1971, in *Pierre Puget: Pour le troiscentcinquantième anniversaire de sa naissance à Marseille le 16 octobre 1620*, pp. 115-122).

96.   C. Carrière and R. Pillorget, *Histoire de Marseille*, Toulouse, 1973.

97.   Konvitz, "Grandeur in French City Planning," p. 22.

98.   Marseilles, Museé des Beaux Arts, Inv. Nr. D 74 (Herding, *Pierre Puget*, pp. 119-121, 188-196, fig. 252).

99.   Hautecoeur, *L'architecture classique en France*, II, pp. 429-432, describes Colbert's plan to develop the Seine riverbanks and its role in the King's building campaign as it was treated by Blondel, in his *Cours d'architecture*; there, the academician devotes an entire section to riverfront projects and the importance of the waterfront perspective (Pt. IV, Liv. XII, Ch. 1, pp. 603-604).

100.   Blunt, *Art and Architecture in France*, pp. 326-327, fig. 269. Interestingly, LeVau planned to connect the forecourt of the Collège with the Louvre by a bridge undoubtedly meant to rivet the attention of the approaching vistor on the sweeping curve of the lateral wings unfolding from the domed church.

101.   See note 71 above.

102.   Herding, *Pierre Puget*, p. 188, refers to the magistrate Chalvet's speech before one of Louis' adminstrators where he compared the French port with the antique city.

103.   A succinct profile of Rome's role as the "most important diplomatic center in the Christian world" with an artistic heritage that was continually reinforced by each pope is given by J. A. Hook, "Urban VII: The Paradox of a Spiritual Monarchy," in *The Courts of Europe: Politics, Patronage, and Royalty 1400-1800*, ed. A. G. Dickens, New York, 1977, pp. 213-232.

104.   Cousins points out that the importance attached to the waterfront perspective is precedented in Puget's *oeuvre* for the shipyard at Toulon, where the architect's aerial prospect shows a semicircular arcade enclosing the harbor promenade ("The Ideal Port," p. 45, note 35, fig. 36). The curved wings are exceptional, however, in that they frame the entrance to the city and therefore anticipate the emphasis given to the city frontispiece during the eighteenth century. Puget continued to experiment with this scheme at Marseilles where variations on the idea of crescent wings to embellish a waterfront were presented in a group of drawings associated with the project. Konvitz ("Grandeur in French City Planning," p. 30, fig. 14) reads one alternative design as a longitudinal setting shaped by triple colonnades, "involv(ing) water as dramatic, integral elements."

105.   Cousins, "The Ideal Port," pp. 1-5. See also his discussion of the *Concorso Clementino* of 1738, which required the design of a large piazza in a city on a river, especially Carlo Mondelli's First Class, first prize entry featuring two courtyards aligned on separate levels (*Ibid.*, passim; and *Architectural Fantasy and Reality. Drawings from the Accademia Nazionale di San Luca In Rome, Concorsi Clementini 1700-1750*, exhibition catalogue, Museum of Art, The Pennsylvania State University, University Park, Pennsylvania, 1982 ("*Concorsi Clementini* of 1728, 1732, and 1738," *idem*, pp. 123-130, fig. XI-67).

106.   *Ibid.*, pp. 87-89, and note 109 below.

107.   M. Fagiolo dell'Arco and M. di Macco, "Bernini e Carlo Fontana i l'Arsenale di Civitavecchia," *Arte Illustrata*, XLIII-XLIV, pp. 26-39.

108.   The text of the *soggetto* of 1728 is cited by Cousins, "The Ideal Port," pp. 176-177.

109.   Cousins suggests that the author of the text may have been the French architect Derizet who became a member of the Accademia in 1728, and had visited Civitavecchia before arriving in Rome. Cousins further hypothesizes "that since Civitavecchia and Ancona were of current papal concern the suggestion of the port as a

competition topic originated with the Pope himself or his counselors" ("The Ideal Port," p. 78, note 8, and p. 123, note 74).

110. *Ibid.*, p. 69.

111. The competition drawings were published by P. Marconi, A. Cipriani, and E. Valeriani, in *I disegni di architettura dell'Archivio storico dell'Accademia di San Luca*, II, Rome, 1974, numbers 322-328 (Marchionni), 329-331 (Guagli), 332-335 (Nicoletti), 336-339 (Barca), and 340-344 (Isacchi). Additional biographical information on the prize-winners is given by Cousins, "The Ideal Port," p. 14, note 3.

112. Cousins, "The Ideal Port," 69-70, pp. 74-75.

113. Likewise, the third prize winner, Nicoletti, manipulated the theme of the *terzo braccio*, in the free-standing structures flanking the palace. Cousins describes the "perforated, screen-like connecting units in Nicoletti's elevation" as "reminiscent of the two storey propylaeum envisaged by Bernini as his final design for the piazza's *terzo braccio*, a design elaborated upon by Carlo Fontana in engravings illustrating his 1694 book on the Basilica." ("The Ideal Port," p. 70).

114. *Ibid.*, 73.

115. "What Nicolleti did, in effect," Cousins explains, "was to extrude the central oval and combine it with a version of the Piazza S. Pietro porticoes in place of the two-story wing arcades for the Louvre project." See Blunt, *Art and Architecture in France*, fig. 271, where Bernini's project of 1664 is reproduced.

116. See the introduction by D. Kelder in *Drawings by the Bibiena Family*, exhibition catalogue, Philadelphia Museum of Art, Philadelphia, 1968, for her observations on Baroque scenography.

117. In addition to C. Frommel, "Baldassare Peruzzi als Maler und Zeichner," *Römisches Jahrbuch für Kunstgeschichte*, XI 1967-1968, see the recent study by S. Ray, "Peruzzi architetto e l'ambiguità della prospettive," *Architettura*, XXVII, 1981, p. 791.

118. R. Wittkower, "Palladio e Bernini," p. 16, fig. 23.

119. M. Bauer-Heinhold, *The Baroque Theatre: A Cultural History of the 18th and 19th Centuries*, New York, 1967, pp. 123-124. See also M. Bates Lowry, *Renaissance Architecture*, New York, 1962, p. 43, where he argues for the origin of the scenic use of the column in Peruzzi's work.

120. N. Sabbattini, *Pratica di fabrica scene e machine ne'teatri*, Ravenna, 1638, caption 25 ("Come si segni una Piazza una facciata sfuggita"), and caption 26 ("Come si debba segnare una Strade, che mostri andare per dritto in una facciata sfuggita").

121. F. Galli-Bibiena, *L'architettura civile preparata su la geometria e ridotta alle prospettive*, Parma, 1711, IV, pp. 129-141, operazione 69. Galli-Bibiena's method for designing a scene viewed on an angle is cited in translation by D. H. Ogden (*The Italian Baroque Stage*, Berkeley and Los Angeles, 1978, pp. 60-64, figs. 23 and 24). In addition to the studies by A. Hyatt Mayor (*The Bibiena Family*, New York, 1945) and F. Hadamowsky, *Die Familie Galli-Bibiena in Wien*, Vienna, 1962), see *Dai Parigi ai Bibiena: bozzetti scenografici nelle collezioni del Museo Teatrale alla Scala*, exhibition cataloque, Museo Teatrale, Prato, 1979, for extensive bibliography.

122. Odgen, *The Italian Baroque Stage*, p. 46l and M. Viale Ferrero, *Scene e scenografici del Settecento*, Turin, 1964.

123. Cagli, Biblioteca Civica.

124. The drawing, now preserved in Turin (Bibl. Reale, Album con Rilegatura in Pelle Marrone, tom. VII (1), MS. Varia 327, fol. 203) is a preliminary sketch for Scene VI, Act III of "Demetrio" and carries an inscription reading "Gran piazza di Selucia" (M. Viale Ferrero, *La scenografici del '700 e i fratelli Galliari*, Turin, 1963, no. 56, pp. 155, 41, 43, 271-273; see also the recent monograph *I Galliari, primi scenografi della Scala. A cura di S. Anguisani*, Milan, Museo Teatrale alla Scala, 1983). Its similarity to the Piazza San Pietro

was mentioned by Hager, "Puntualizzazioni su disegni scenici teatrali e l'architettura scenografica," p. 123, notes 23 and 24.

125.   Hager, "The Accademia di San Luca in Rome and the Académie Royale d'Architecture in Paris," p. 129; and N. Pevsner, *Academies of Art: Past and Present*, Cambridge, 1940, pp. 82-100, esp. 98-100.

126.   A. Braham, *The Architecture of the French Enlightenment*, Berkeley and Los Angeles, 1980, pp. 89-90, pl. 113. An appendix of the *Grand Prix* assignments, their winners and patrons is given by D. D. Egbert, *The Beaux-Arts tradition in French Architecture Illustrated by the Grand Prix de Rome*, Princeton, 1980, p. 171. See also *Charles de Wailly, peintre architecte dans l'europe des lumières*, Caisse nationale des monuments historiques et des site, exhibition catalogue, Paris, 1979, pp. 18-19; fig. 16, p. 79.

127.   H. Hager ("The Accademia di San Luca and the Académie Royale d'Architecture in Paris," p. 131), advanced Braham's observation that de Wailly's scheme recalls the Piazza San Pietro by noting that " . .De Wailly attempted quite successfully to revive the scenography of the *terzo braccio* of St. Peter's colonnades with a new version of Bernini's and Carlo Fontana's triumphal arch motifs in the center." Braham's ideas concerning this analogy were published earlier in "Charles de Wailly and Early Neo-Classicism," *The Burlington Magazine*, CXIV, 1972, pp. 670-685.

128.   A. Braham, *The Architecture of the French Enlightenment*, p, 90.

129.   *Charles de Wailly, peintre architecte dans l'europe des lumières*, op cit., pp. 38-40, fig. 84. See also *Piranese et les Français 1740-1790*, Rome, Académie de France, exhibition catalogue, Rome, 1976, no. 66, p. 134, where the drawing is dated after de Wailly's return from Rome in 1756. See also S. Erikson, *Early Neoclassicism in France*, London, 1974, p. 345.

130.   A. Braham, *The Architecture of the French Enlightenment*, p. 90; and L. Hautecoeur, *L'architecture classique en France*, IV, pp. 225-232.

131.   *Ibid.*, pp. 84-85, fig. 104; and E. Kaufmann, *Architecture in the Age of Reason: Baroque and Post Baroque in England, Italy, and France*, Cambridge, 1955, pp. 143-144, figs. 100-101.

132.   Kaufmann, *Architecture in the Age of Reason*, p. 143, figs. 98 and 99.

133.   M. J. Peyre, *Oeuvres d'architecture*, Paris, 1765.

134.   See note 127 above; and H. Hager, "The Accademia di San Luca and the Académie Royale," p. 132, especially note 37, where he comments on the relationship of Peyre's entry to the Piazza San Pietro.

135.   H. Millon, *Filippo Juvarra: Drawings from the Roman Period, 1704-1714*, Rome, 1984, xx, note 57, xxxi notes 114, 71, 80, 221-222. Millon argues that at least ten drawings by Juvarra's hand can be linked with the *concorso* for a "large public forum with church and hospital" executed early in 1706 while the architect was in Naples. It may be mentioned here that the scheme of the Piazza San Pietro was evoked by Pierre de Villeneuve in his first-prize entry for the First Class *concorso* of 1708 to design an academy of fine arts (*Architecural Fantasy and Reality*, s.v. "Concorso Clementino of 1708," by Christine Challingsworth, pl. VI-31). This topic will be treated extensively in her dissertation ("The 1708 and 1709 *Concorsi Clementini* at the Accademia di San Luca in Rome and the Establishment of the Academy of Arts and Sciences as an Autonomous Building Type," The Pennsylvania State University, University Park, Pa.)

136.   The drawings are preserved in Turin, in the collection of Adriano Tournon (Millon, *Filippo Juvarra*, no. T009).

137.   H. Millon, "Filippo Juvarra and the Accademia di San Luca in Rome in the Early Eighteenth Century," *Projects and Monuments in the Period of the Roman Baroque. Papers in Art History from The Pennsylvania State*

University, vol I, 1984, pp. 14-15; and idem., *Filippo Juvarra*, idem., p. XXV.

138. Millon, *Filippo Juvarra*, passim.

139. H. Hager, *Filippo Juvarra e il concorso di modelli del 1715 bandito da Clemente XI per la Nuova Sacrestia di S. Pietro*, Rome, 1970, fig. 15. In addition to R. Pommer, *Eighteenth-Century Architecture in Piedmont: The Open Structures of Juvarra, Alfieri, and Vittone*, New York, 1967, pp. 24-25, 141-143; and L. Rovere V. Viale, and A. Brinckmann, *Filippo Juvarra*, Milan, 1937, pp. 60, 128-129, see W. Cousins, "The Ideal Port," 73-74, for his discussion of Juvarra's impact on the competition drawings.

140. Millon, *Filippo Juvarra*, p. xix.

141. See V. Viale, ed., *Catalogo della Mostra di Filippo Juvarra architetto e scenografo*, Messina, 1966; M. Viale Ferrero, *Filippo Juvarra scenografo e architetto teatrale*, Turin, 1970; and M. Myers, *Architectural and Ornament Drawings: Juvarra, Vanvitelli, the Bibiena Family and other Italian Draughtsmen*, exhibition catalogue New York, 1975.

142. G. B. Sacchetti, "Catalogo dei disegni fatti dal signor cavaliere ed abate don Filippo Juvara dal 1714 al 1735 compilato dal suo discepolo G. B. Zaccheti," *Giornale di erudizione Artistica*, ed. A. Rossi, Perugia, 1874. Cited after Vittorio Viale, *Catalogo della Mostra di Filippo Juvarra*, p. 93.

143. For Juvarra's project for a monumental mausoleum for Louis XIV which was never executed, although a number of developed project drawings for an interior colonnade remain, see S. Jacob, *Italienische Zeichnungen der Kunstbibliothek Berlin: Architektur und Dekoration 16. bis 18. Jahrhundert*, Berlin, 1975, nos. 753-755.

144. Kaufmann, *Architecture in the Age of Reason*, p. 131.

145. The construction was sponsored to recognize the king's recent Peace of Aix-la-Chapelle and the project's status as the leading architectural campaign stimulated numerous responses (W. Kalnein and M. Levey, *The Art and Architecture of the Eighteenth Century in France*, Baltimore, 1972, p. 279); see also A. Braham, *Histoire de l'urbanisme*, II, pp. 310-315; and C. Tadgell, *Ange-Jacques Gabriel*, London, 1978, passim.

146. Braham, *The Architecture of the French Enlightenment*, pp. 39-40.

147. Kalnein and Levey, *Art and Architecture of the Eighteenth Century in France*, pp. 279-280.

148. Patte, *Monumens érigés en France à la gloire Louis XV*, pp. 119-121; see also Zucker, *Town and Square*, p. 186.

149. Patte provides an aerial plan of Paris in his book (see note 48 above) identifying the *places royales* of Louis XV; the *places* dedicated to Louis XV are fully discussed by Lavedan (*Histoire de l'urbanisme*, II, pp. 301-323).

150. Zucker, *Town and Square*, pp. 180—181.

151. The first project was not submitted until 1763 by Conant d'Ivry (Braham, *The Architecture of the French Enlightenment*, pp. 50-51, fig. 58).

152. Hautecoeur, *L'architecture classique en France*, III, Paris, 1950, pp. 66-73, 488-495; Kalnein and Levey, *Art and Architecture of the Eighteenth Century in France*, pp. 276-278; Lavedan, *Histoire de l'urbanisme*, II, pp. 315-319; and C. Pfister, *Emmanuel Héré et la Place Stanislas*, Nancy, 1905-1906.

153. Kalnein and Levey, *Art and Architecture of the Eighteenth Century in France*, p. 276. See especially P. Marot, *La place royale de Nancy: Image de la reunion de la Lorraine à la France, du monumen du Bien-Aimé à la statue du Bienfaisant*, Paris, 1966, for his discussion of the political relations between the monarchy and the independent province of Lorraine. Other projects executed by Héré in that area were published by the architect in his *Plans et élévations de la place royale de Nancy & des autres edifices à l'environment bâtis par les les ordres du Roy de Pologne duc de Lorraine*, Paris, 1753.

154. Hautecoeur, *L'architecture classique en France*, IV, fig. 410; and A. Brinckmann, *Platz und Monument als künstlerlisches Formproblem*, Berlin, 1963, pp. 148-153, fig. 78.

155. Zucker, *Town and Square*, Berlin, 149, pp. 150-152.

156. See note 33 above. A similar layout appeared within two decades in a design of 1777 by P. M. D'Ixnard for the palace of Clemens Wenzeslaus, Prince Bishop of Trier, at Koblenz, where the architect planned a triumphal entry to a transverse, ellipsoidal court (Pierre du Columbier, *L'architecture français en Allemagne au dixhuitième siècle*, Paris, 1956, fig. 68. About Michael d'Ixnard's projects which were superseded by A. F. Peyre the Younger's reduced plans see Ernst Hager, *Die Coblenzer Residenz, Ein Schlossbau des Klassizismus*, Munich, 1927, pp. 5-9, 23-29 and 31 ff, pls. 3-6 (with documents).

157. Zucker, *Town and Square*, pp. 179-181; and Brinkmann, *Platz und Monument*, pp. 136-166. A similar project attributable to Phillip Gerlach was proposed two decades earlier, between 1734-1737, for the Belle Alliance Square in Berlin. There, recalling Mansart's *Place des Victoires*, a triad of buildings forming an oval was planned to open up the area of the new Friedrichstadt (Orefice, *Gian Lorenzo Bernini architetto*, p. 601, pl. 2). For the square in Berlin see also W. Hager, *Die Bauten des deutschen barocks*, 1942, p. 358, pl. 162.

158. Zucker, *Town and Square*, 145, pp. 150-153; and Lavedan, *Histoire de l'urbanisme*, p. 190. See also R. Kain, "Classical Urban Design in France: The Transformation of Nancy in the Eighteenth Century," *Connoisseur*, CCII, 1979, pp. 190-197.

159. Zucker, *Town and Square*, pp. 235-236.

160. *Ibid.*, p. 179.

161. Rabreau, "Monumental Art," pp. 134-135.

162. R. de la Mare, *Traité de la police*, IV, Paris, 1738, p. 390 (Kalnein and Levey, *Art and Architecture of the Eighteenth Century in France*, p. 273, note 33).

163. Patte, *Monumens érigés en France à la gloire Louis XV*, passim.

164. Kalnein and Levey, *Art and Architecture of the Eighteenth Century in France*, p. 273; and H. M. Apostolides, *Le roi machine: spectacle et politique au temps de Louis XIV*, Paris, 1981, where the public celebrations of the monarch's arrival in Paris and the provincial capitals are discussed.

Perhaps it may be suggested here that the noteable independence of William II and his proclivity towards absolutism may have contributed to the idea to revive the Piazza San Pietro at Greenwich as a setting for court spectacles. William's administration is considered by R. M. Hatton, "Louis XIV and his Fellow Monarchs," in *Louis XIV and the Craft of Kingship*, pp. 155-195; and analysed by M. A. Thompson in *Some Developments in English Historiography During the Eighteenth Century*, London, 1957, p. 5.

165. In addition to R. de Fusco, *Luigi Vanvitelli*, Naples, 1973, pp. 101-167, see the recent monograph on Caserta by G. L. Hersey, *Architecture, Poetry, and Number in the Royal Palace at Caserta*, Cambridge, Mass., 1983. Both authors provide extensive bibliography and documentation.

166. Hersey, *Architecture, Poetry, and Number*, pp. 64-72.

167. The project engravings were published in a splendid exposition by Vanvitelli in *Dichiarazione dei disegni del reale palazzo di Caserta*, Naples, 1756.

168. Hersey, *Architecture, Poetry, and Number*, pp. 45-51, 104; and de Fusco, *Luigi Vanvitelli*, pp. 24-27.

169. See F. Mancini, M. T. Muraro, E. Povoledo, et al., *Illusione e pratica teatrale: proposte per una lettura dello spazio scenico dagli Intermedi fiorentini all'Opera comica veneziana*, Venice, 1975, pp. 97-101. In addition to F. Mancini, *Scenografia napoletana nell'eta barocca*, Naples 1964, see U. Giurleo, "I Bibiena a Napoli," *Partenope*, I, 1960, p. 175.

170. De Fusco, *Luigi Vanvitelli*, p. 101; and G. Nicolosi, "Luigi Vanvitelli architetto della Reverenda Fabrica di S. Pietro in Vaticano," in *Atti dell'VIII Congresso Nazionale di Storia dell'Architettura*, Rome.

171. Hersey, *Architecture, Poetry, and Number*, p. 109.

172. Paris, Bibliothèque Nationale (Y. Bottineau, *L'art de cour dans l'Espagne de Philippe V, 1700-1746*, Bordeaux, n.d., pp. 258-280, pl. XVIII).

173. Hersey, *Architecture, Poetry, and Number*, pp. 72-82.

174. De Fusco, *Luigi Vanvitelli*, pp. 103-104, points out that in his *Dichiarazione* Vanvitelli stressed Caserta's link with historical antecedents of Rome, citing the Temple of Jove, S. Angelo in Formis, and St. Peter's.

175. De Fusco, *Luigi Vanvitelli*, 26, pp. 101-102.

176. In addition to many of the Italian texts, French architects published the antiquities of Rome (Hautecoeur, *L'architecture classique en France*, IV, pp. 5-12; and Kaufmann, *Architecture in the Age of Reason*, pp. 201-204) and at least three studies of the Vatican complex appeared during the eighteenth century: J. de Tarade, *Desseins de Toutes les parties de l'Eglise de Saint Pierre de Rome*, Paris, 1713; G. M. Dumont, *Détails des plus intéressantes parties d'architecture de la Basilique de St. Pierre de Rome*, Paris, 1763; J. G. Soufflot, *Plans et déscriptions de l'Eglise de Saint Pierre de Rome et de la colonnade de la place antérieure*, Lyone, n.d. ("Piazza S. Pietro come modello da Carlo Fontana al Letarouilly," *Gian Lorenzo Bernini architetto*, pp. 411-440).

177. G. B. Nolli, *Nuova pianta di Roma data in luce da Giovanbattista Nolli l'anno MDCCXLVII* ("Piazza S. Pietro come modello da Carlo Fontana al Letarouilly," *Gian Lorenzo Bernini architetto*, pp. 428 and 430).

178. See note 175 above.

179. Hersey (*Architecture, Poetry, and Number*, p. 68, note 13), comments that Ferdinand IV's desire to make Naples the pre-eminent European city was put forth by V. Ruffo in his *Saggio sull' abbellimento*, Naples, 1789. This idea was advanced by the later Neapolitan administrators such as Ferdinand I who, as part of his revitalization program, built an oval court in 1817 (fig. 32) decorated with pendant equestrian statues of Charles III and himself opposite the Palazzo Reale in Naples (N. P. Faraglia, "Il largo di palazzo," *Napoli nobilissima, rivista di topografia ed arte napoletana*, II, fasc. X, n.d., especially pp. 158-159).

180. *Napoli e il suo Golfo*, pl. 9. See also note 179 above.

181. Egorov, *The Architectural Planning of St. Petersburg*, fig. 45.

182. *Ibid.*, p. 206, fig. 44 and 45.

183. *Ibid.*, p. 31, note 5.

184. L. Reau, *L'architecture russe de Pierre le Grand à nous jours*, Paris, 1922, p. 91. Exhaustive bibliography for Voronikhin and the cathedral is provided by I. Grabar, W. Lasarew, and W. Kemenow, in: *Geschichte der russischen Kunst*, VI, Dresden, 1976.

185. Reau, *L'architecture russe*, pp. 90-92.

186. See note 181 above.

187. Several studies devoted to Palladianism in the development of Russian achitecture are included in the *Bollettino del centro internazionale di studi di architettura: Andrea Palladio*, IX, 1967.

188. Reau, *L'architecture russe*, p. 91.

189. G. Hamilton, *The Art and Architecture of Russia*, 2nd edition, Baltimore, 1975, pp. 221-222.

190. *Ibid.*, pp. 221-222, note 301.

191. *Ibid.*, pp. 221-222.

192. Egorov, *The Architectural Planning of St. Petersburg*, p. xvii.

193. Konvitz, *Cities and the Sea*, passim.

194. For Valadier's project, see Paolo Marconi, *Giuseppe Valadier*, Città di Castello, 1964, p. 186, fig. 107, and *Valadier, segno e architettura*, catalogo a cura di Elisa Debenedetti (Exhibition, 1985-1986, Rome), Ministero per i beni culturali e ambientali Istituto Nazionale per la Grafica, Rome, 1985, no. 141, pp. 75 ff; fig. on p. 177, (Rome, Gabinetto Nazionale delle Stampe, F.N. 3596).

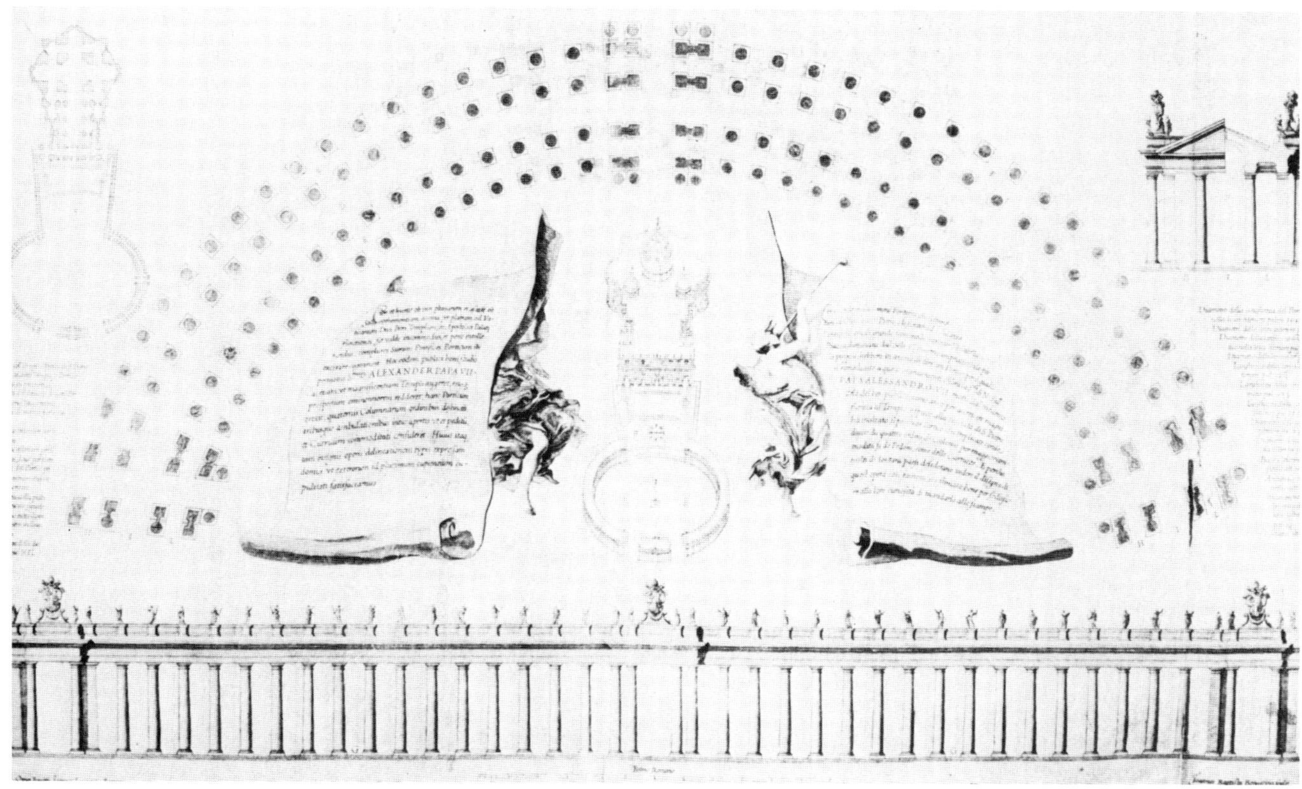

91.   Rome, Piazza S. Pietro, plan, engraving by Bonacina, 1659. Rome, Vat. Chigi P VII 9, fol. 19v-20 (Kitao, *Circle and Oval*).

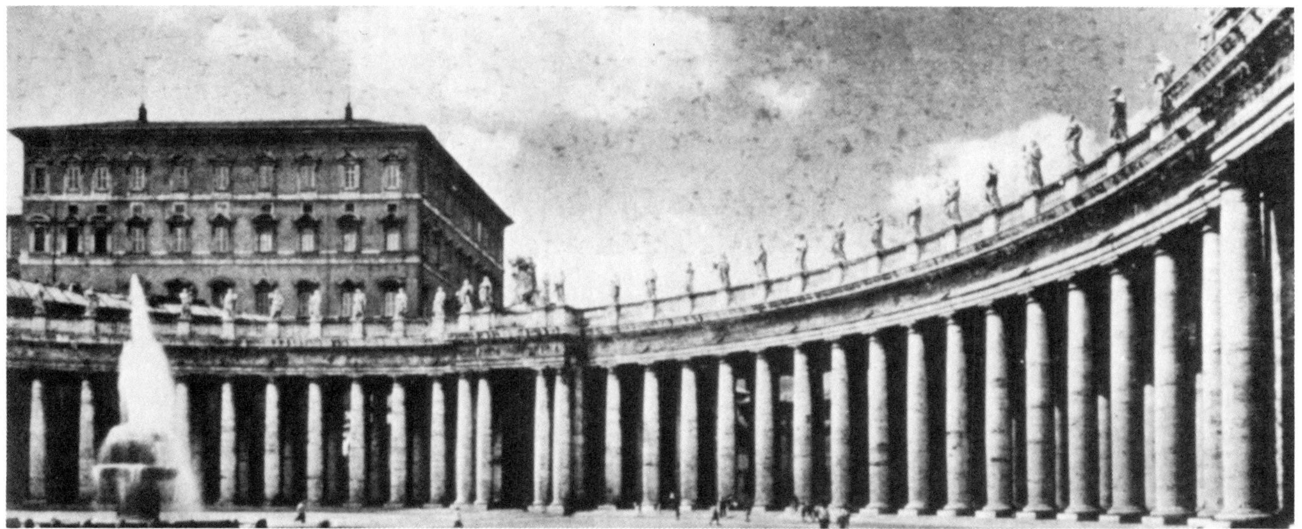

92.   Rome, Piazza S. Pietro, View of right colonnade (Fagiolo dell' Arco, *Bernini*).

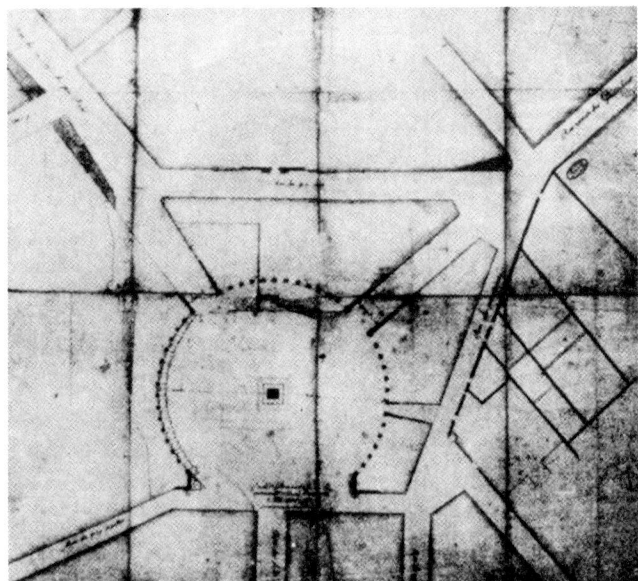

93.   Jules Hardouin Mansart, project plan for the *Place des Victoires*, Paris. Paris, Archives Nationales, Q^1 1191. (Lavedan, *Histoire de l'urbanisme*).

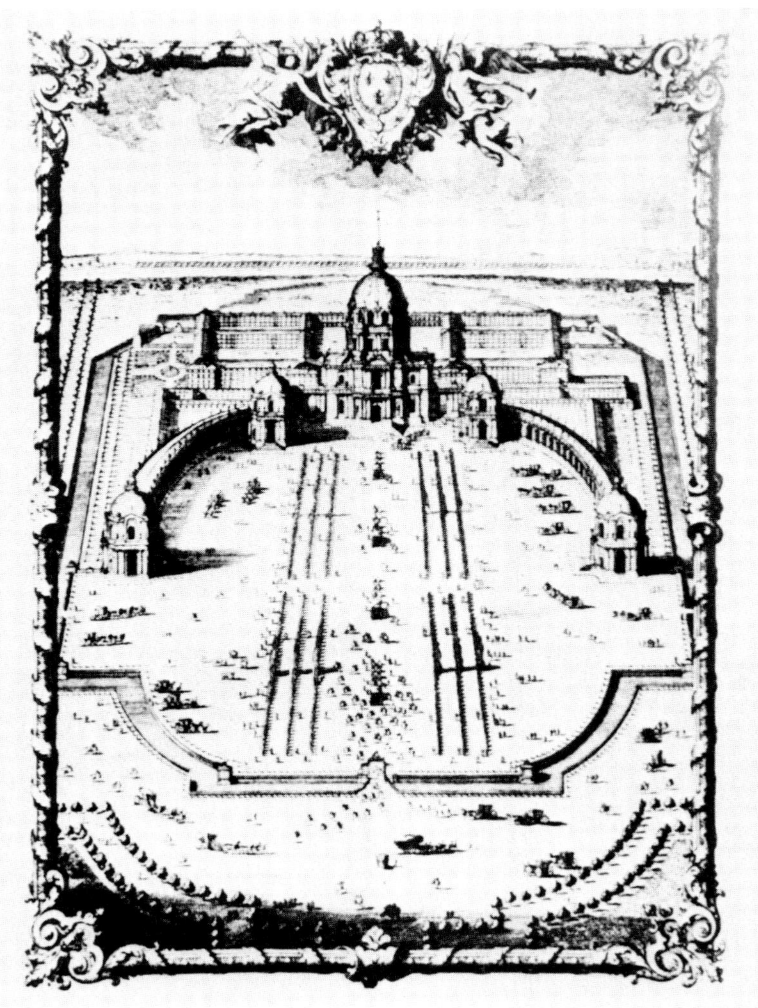

94.   Paris, Church of the Invalides, project by Jules Hardouin Mansart, engraving by Jacques LePautre (Lavedan, *Histoire de l'urbanisme*).

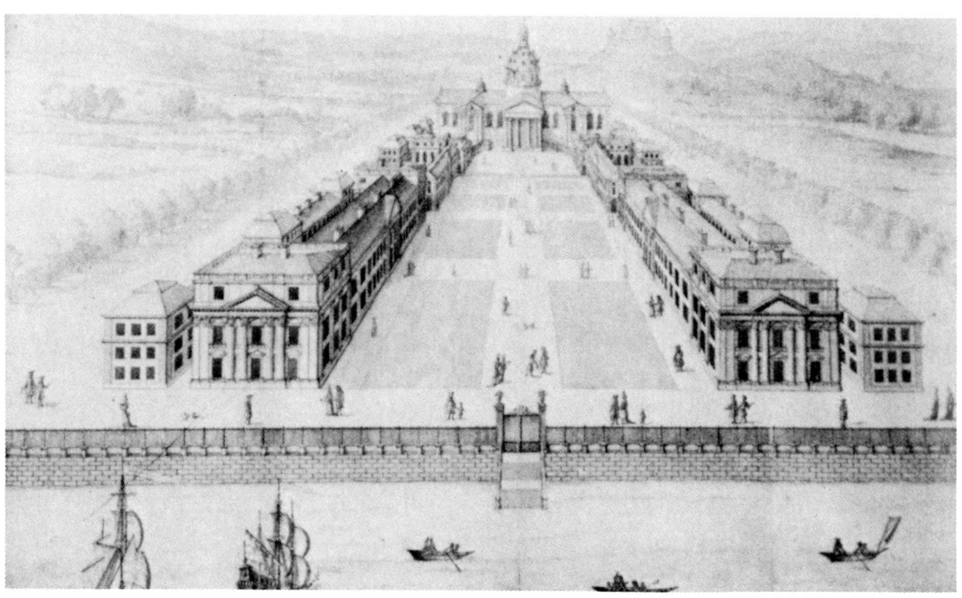

95.   Christopher Wren, project perspective for the Royal Hospital, Greenwich, London, Sir John Soane's
Museum (Beard, *The Work of Christopher Wren*).

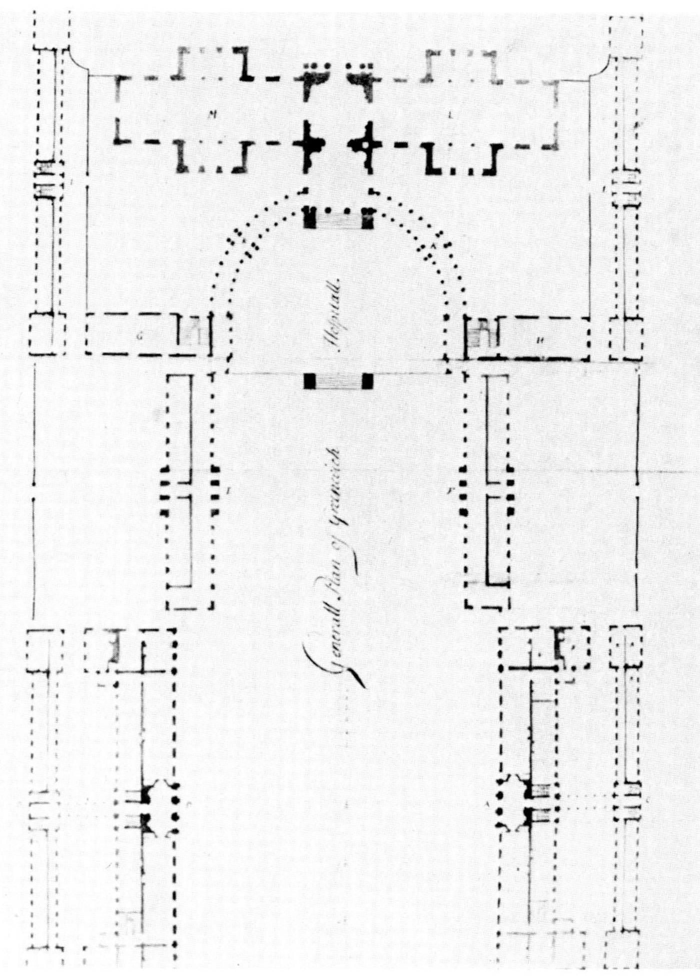

96.   Christopher Wren, project plan for The Royal Hospital, Greenwich.
London, Sir John Soane's Museum (Beard, *The Work of Christopher
Wren*).

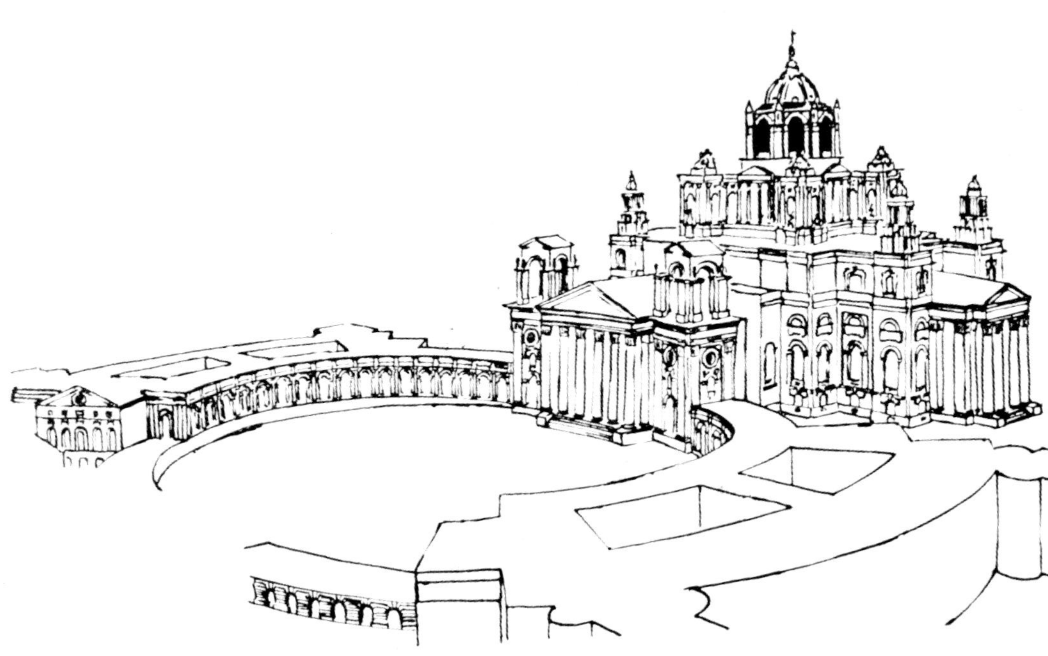

97.   Nicolas Hawksmoor, reconstruction by Downes of project for The Royal Hospital, Greenwich (Downes, *English Baroque Architecture*).

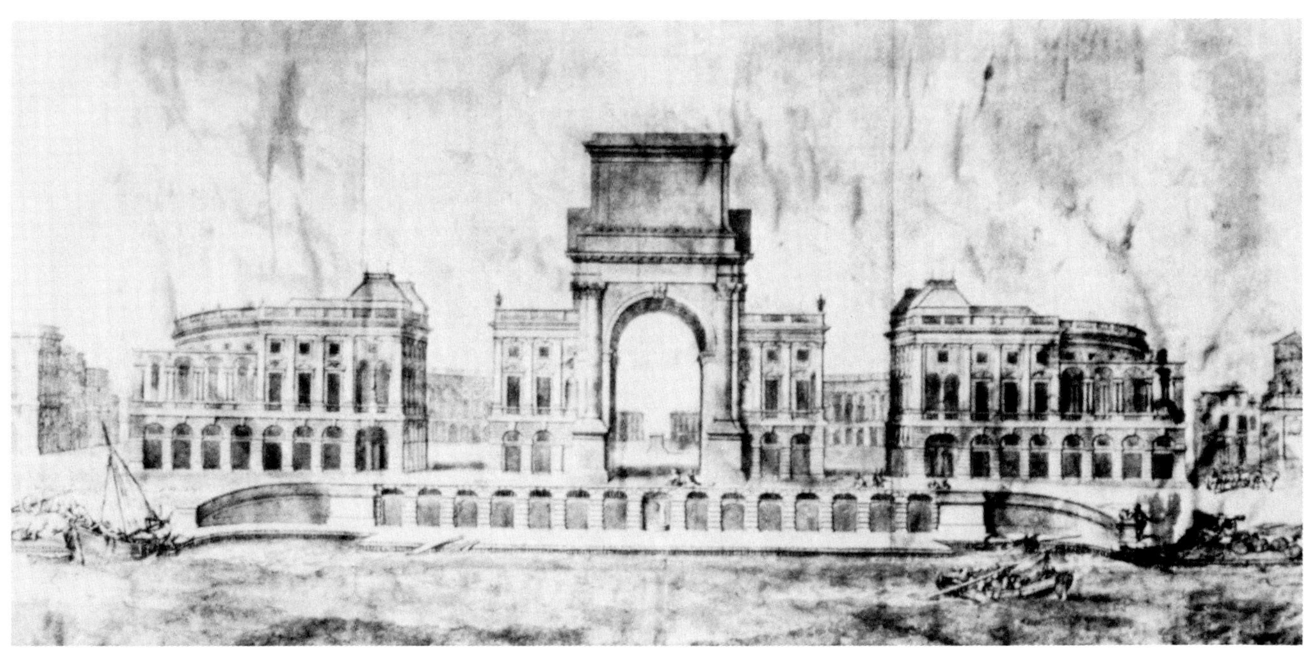

98.   Pierre Puget, project drawing for the *Place Royale*, Marseilles (Herding, *Puget*).

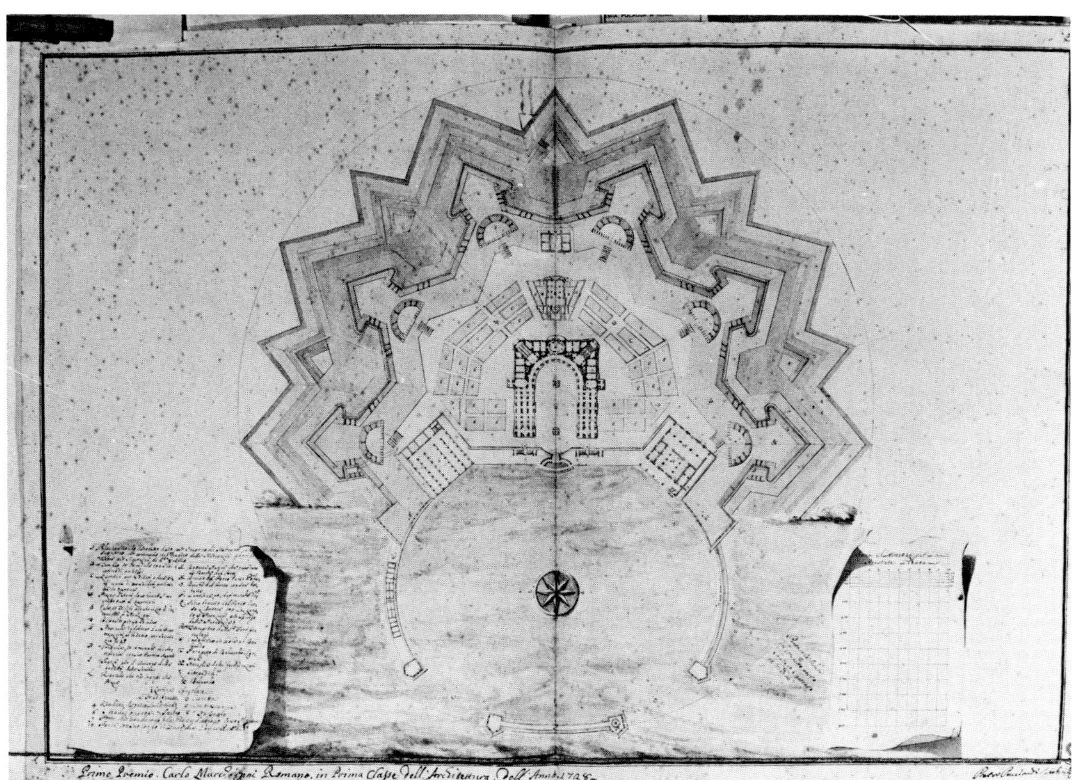

99.   Carlo Marchionni, project for a piazza connected with a harbor, plan. *Concorso Clementino* 1728, First Class, first prize. Rome, Accademia di S. Luca (Marconi, et al., *I disegni di architettura*).

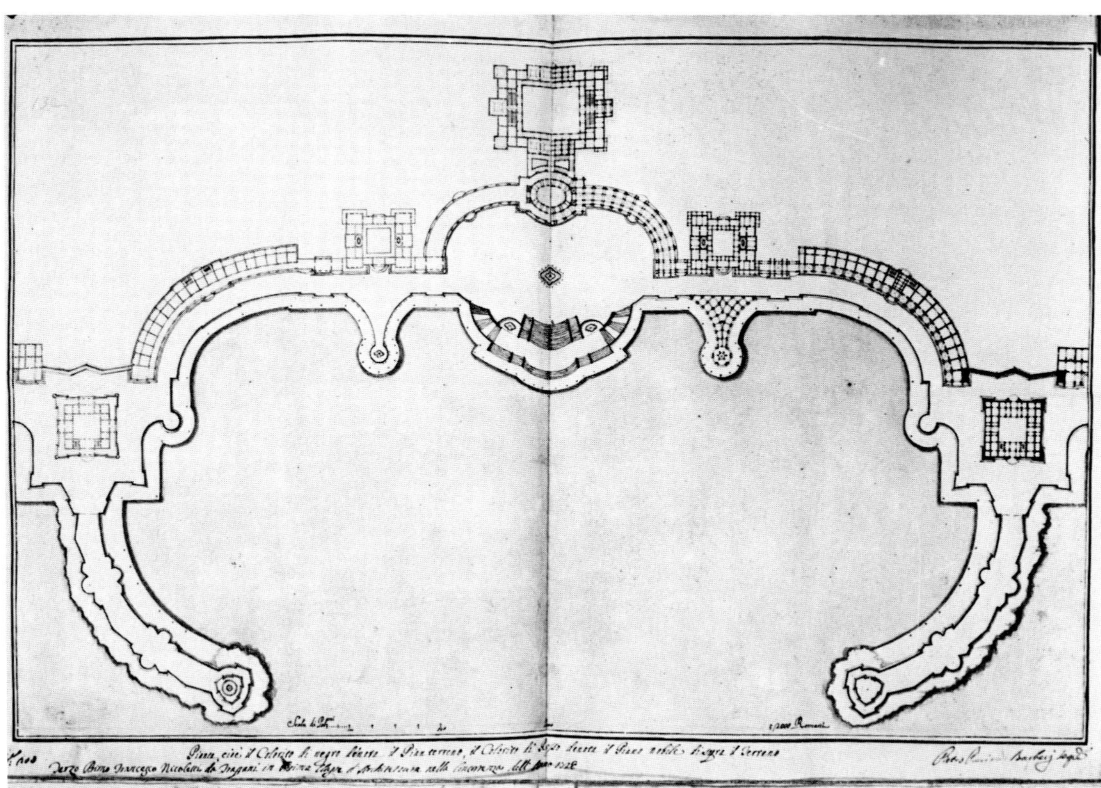

100.   Francesco Nicoletti, project for a piazza connected with a harbor, plan. *Concorso Clementino 1728*. First Class, third first prize. Rome, Accademia di S. Luca (Marconi, et al., *I disegni di architettura*).

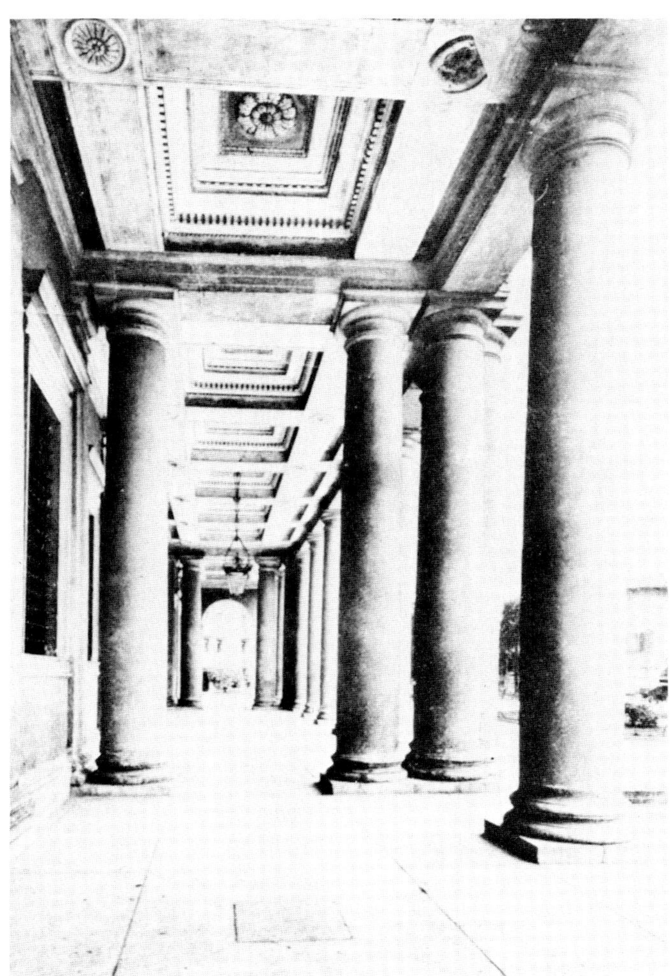

101.   Vicenza, Villa Chiericati, view of portico (Wittkower, "Palladio e Bernini").

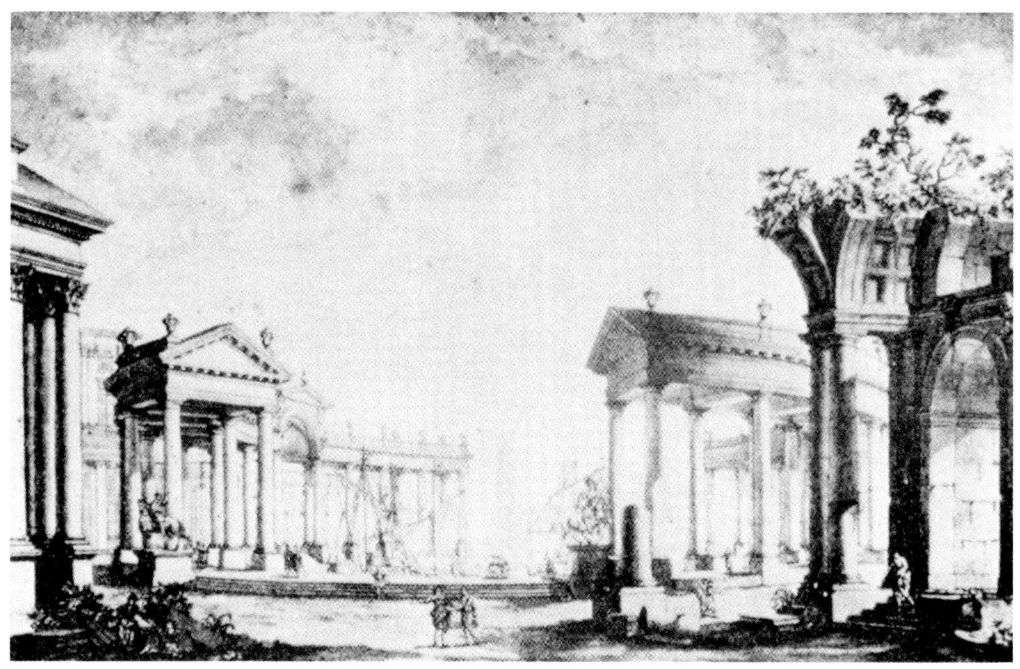

102.   Giuseppe Galli-Bibiena, theatre design of a port. Cagli, Biblioteca Civica.

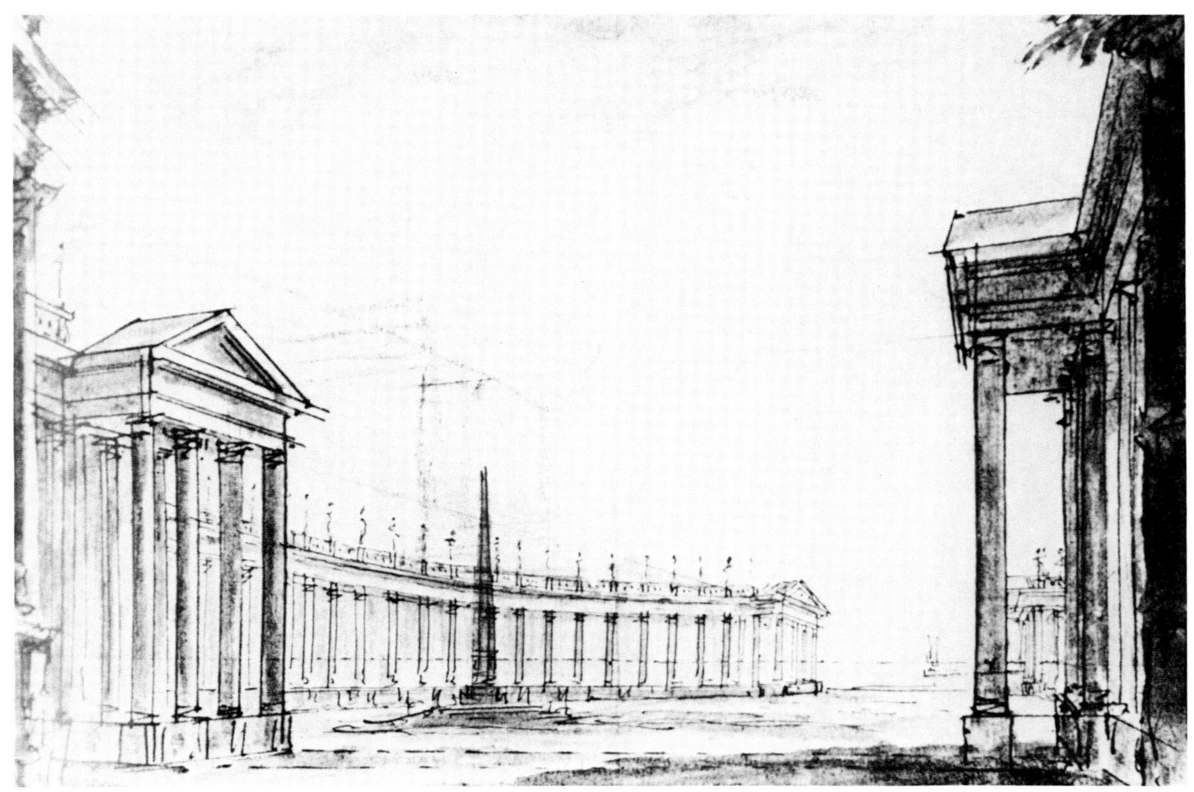

103. Fabrizio Galliari, preliminary sketch for a theatre set. Turin, Biblioteca Reale, Album con Rilegatura in Pelle Marrone (Viale Ferrero, *La scenografici del '700*).

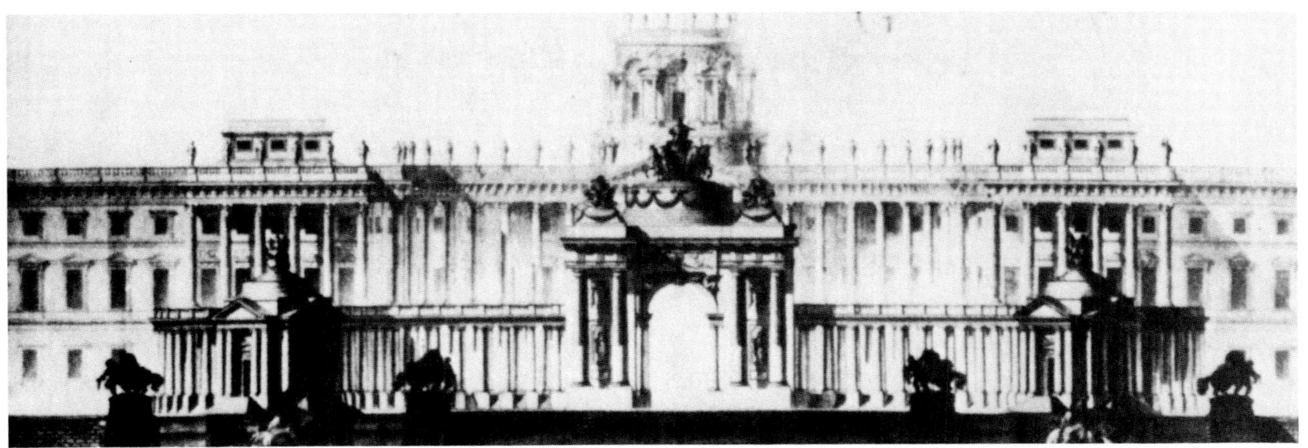

104. Charles de Wailly, project for a palace, elevation. Concours 1752, first prize. Paris, Ecole Nationale Supérieure de Beaux-Arts (Braham, *The Architecture of the French Enlightenment*).

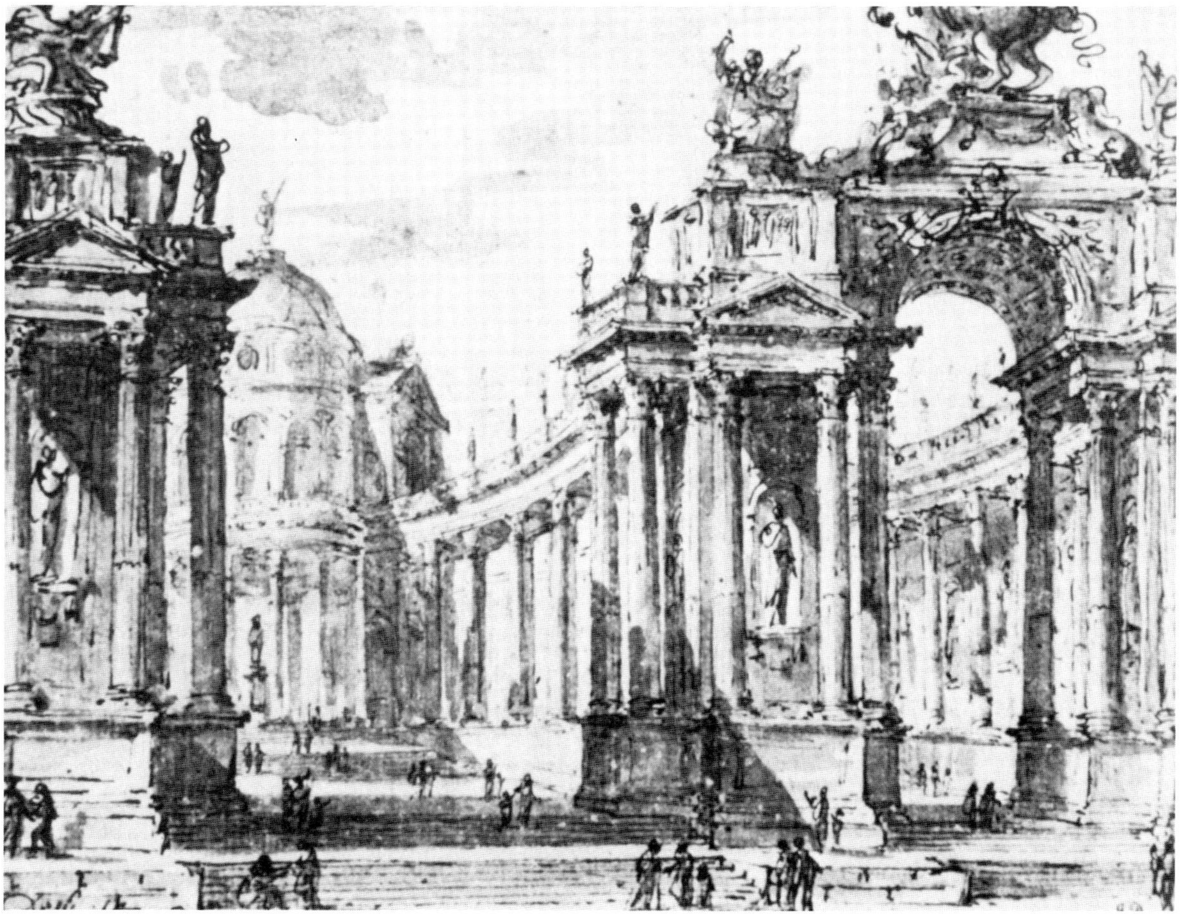

105.   Charles de Wailly, architectural fantasy with double portico. Paris, Ecole Nationale Supérieure de Beaux-Arts (*Piranèse et les français*).

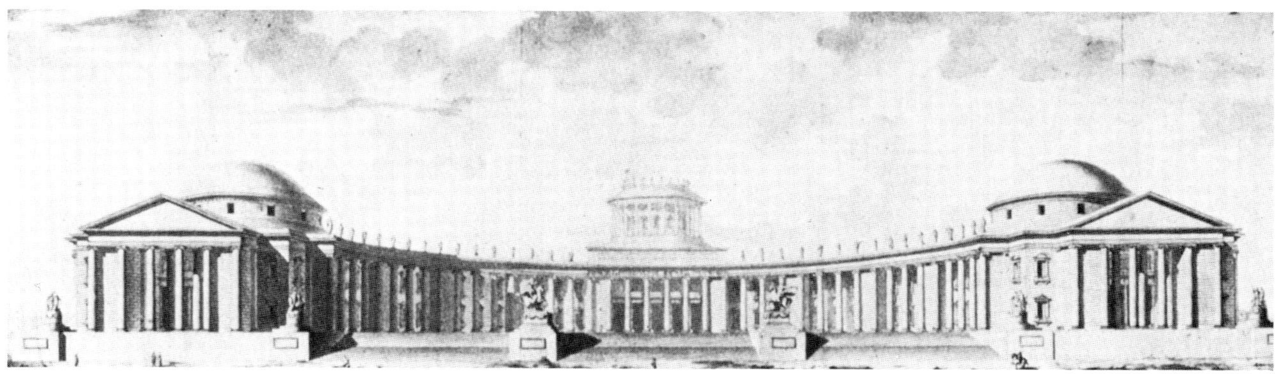

106.   Marie-Joseph Peyre, project for a building for three academies, elevation. *Concours* 1756, first prize (Peyre, *Oeuvres d' architecture*, 1765.

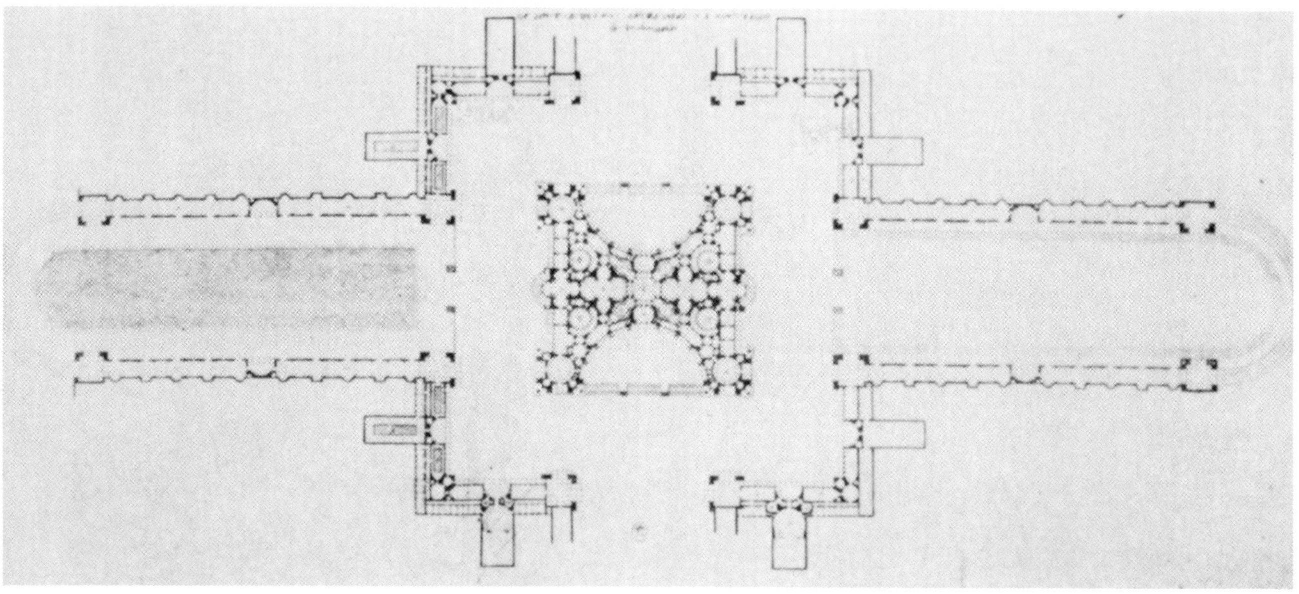

107.   Marie-Joseph Peyre, project for a building for three academies, plan. *Concours* 1756, first prize (Peyre, *Oeuvres d' architecture*).

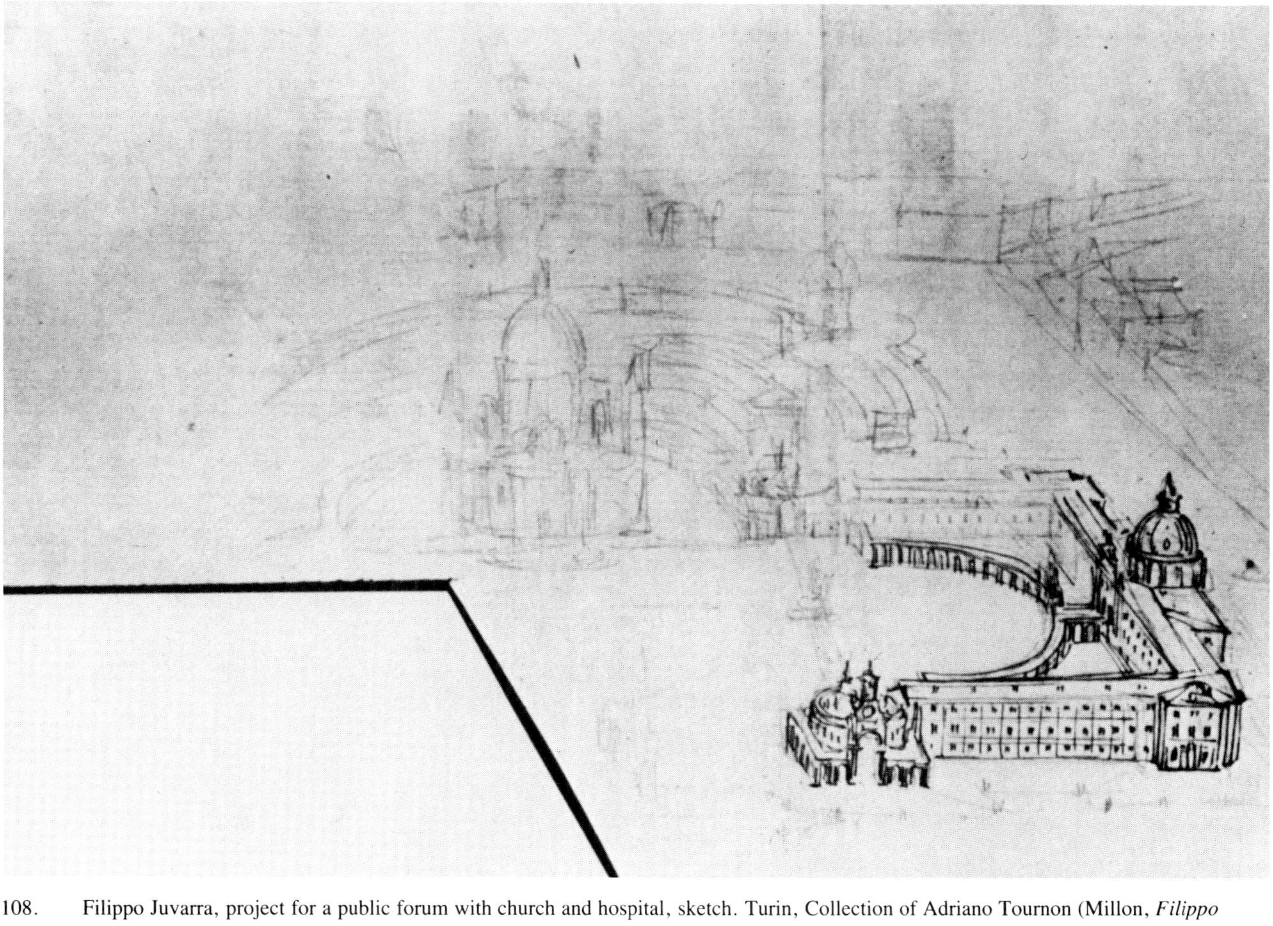

108.   Filippo Juvarra, project for a public forum with church and hospital, sketch. Turin, Collection of Adriano Tournon (Millon, *Filippo Juvarra*).

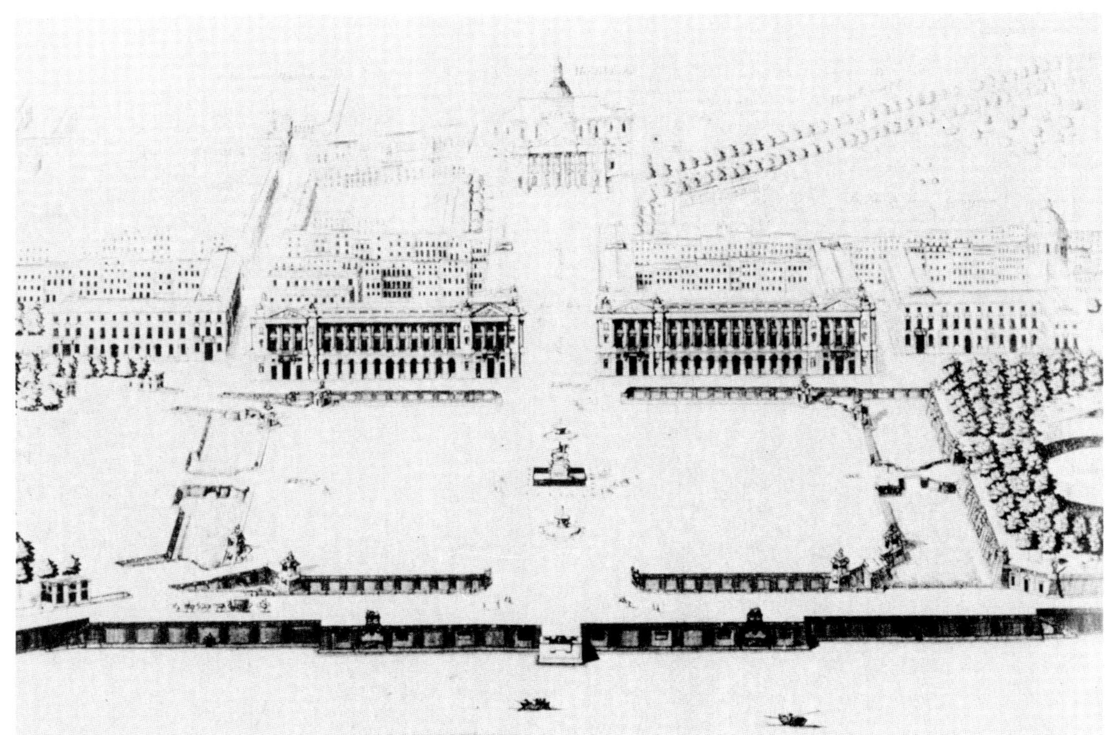

109. Ange-Jacques Gabriel, project perspective for *Place Louis XV* (now *Place de la Concorde*), engraving. Paris, Bibliothèque Nationale (Kalnein and Levey, *Art and Architecture of the Eighteenth Century in France*).

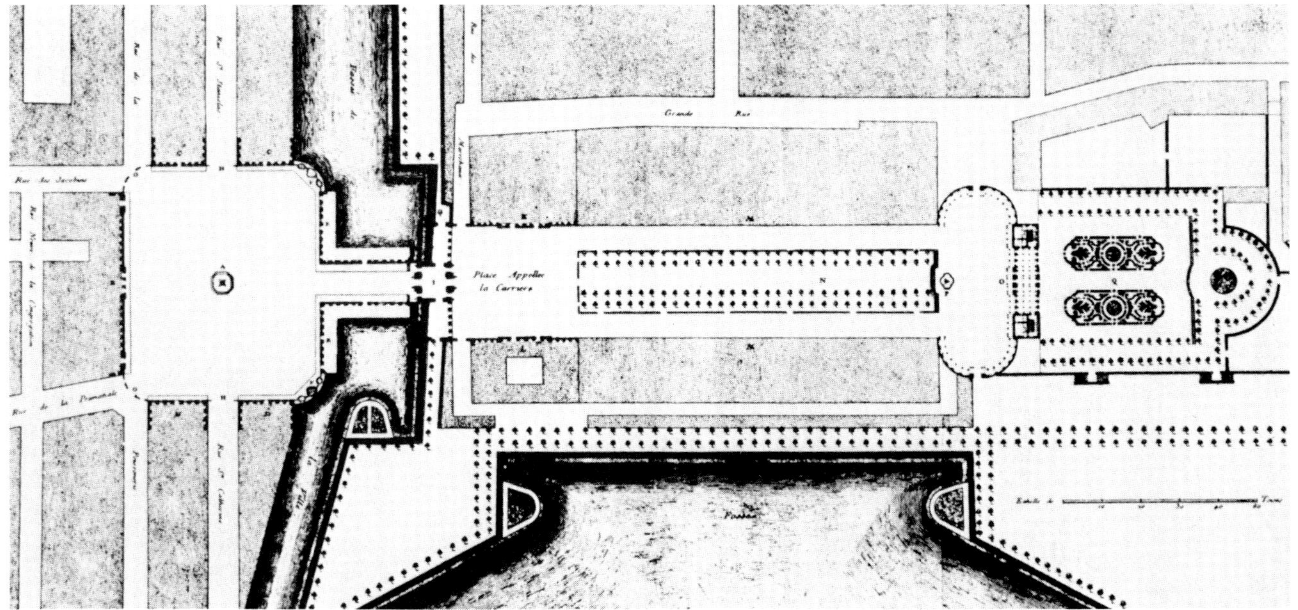

110. Emmanuel Héré de Corny, project plan for the *Place Royale*, Nancy (Patte, *Monumens érigés en France à la gloire Louis XV*, 1765).

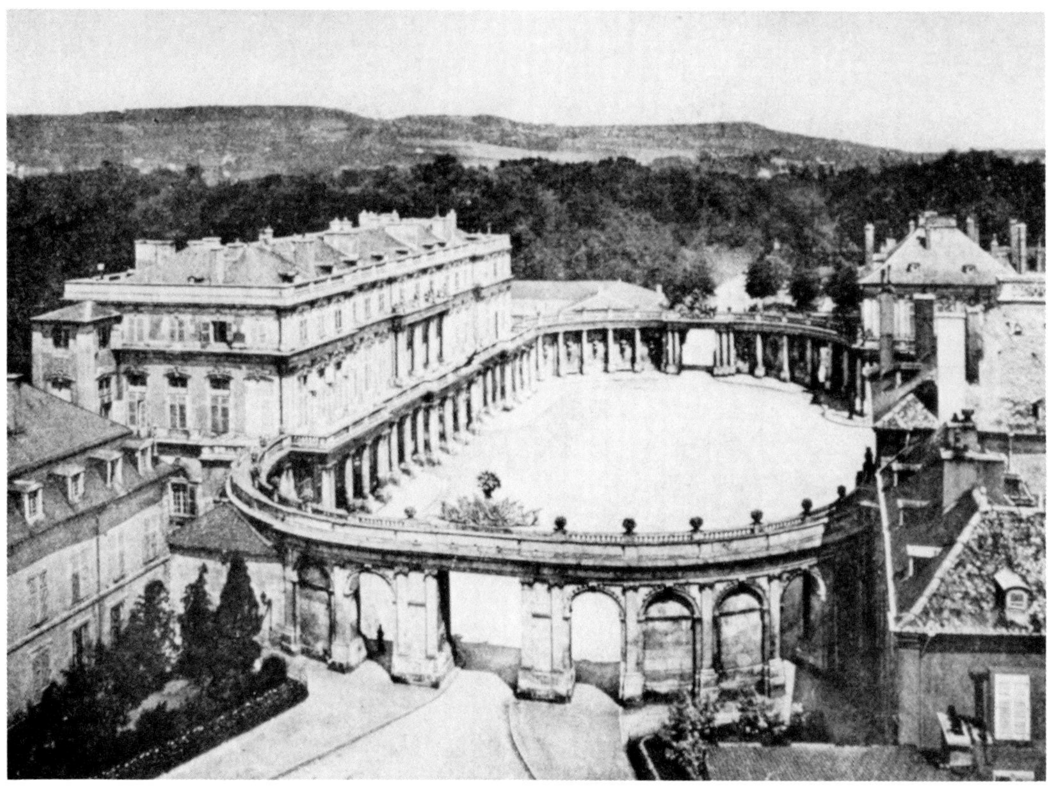

111. Nancy, Place du l'Intendance (now Palais du Gouvernement), view (Brinckmann, *Platz und Monument*).

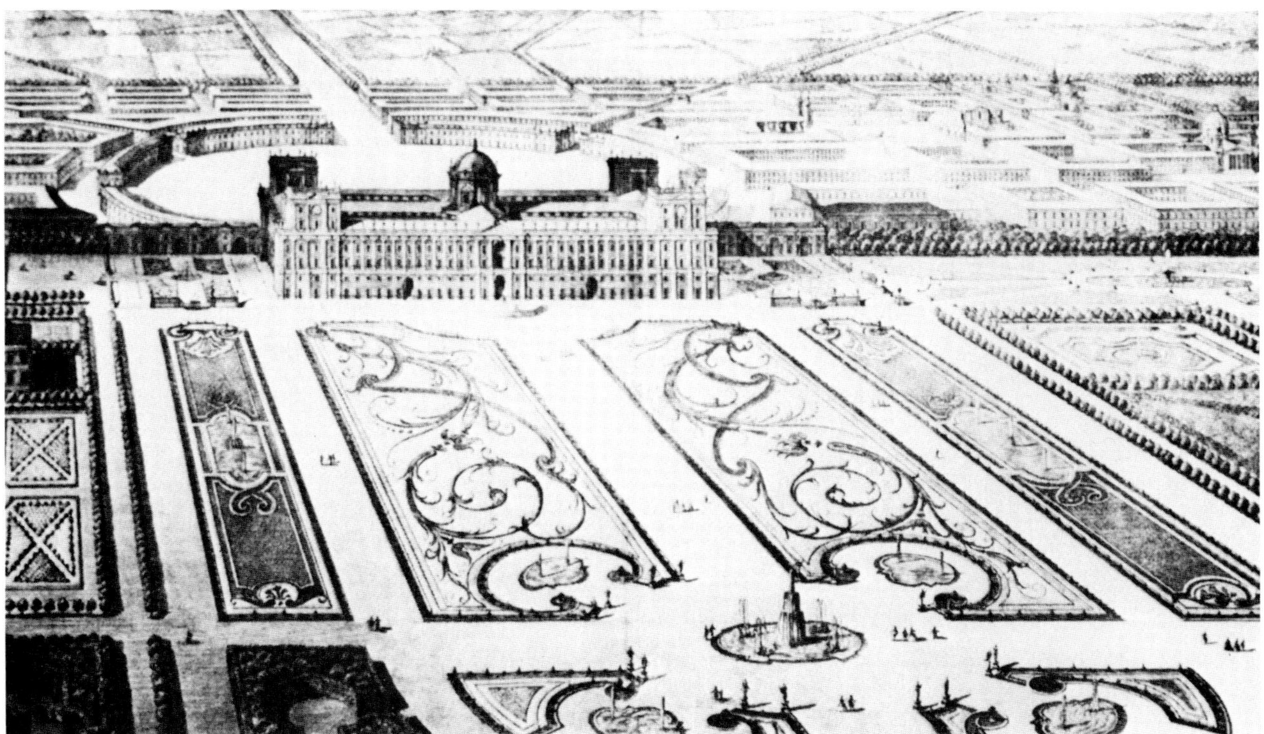

114. Luigi Vanvitelli, project perspective for the Palazzo Reale, Caserta (Vanvitelli, *Dichiarazione dei disegni del real palazzo di Caserta*, 1756).

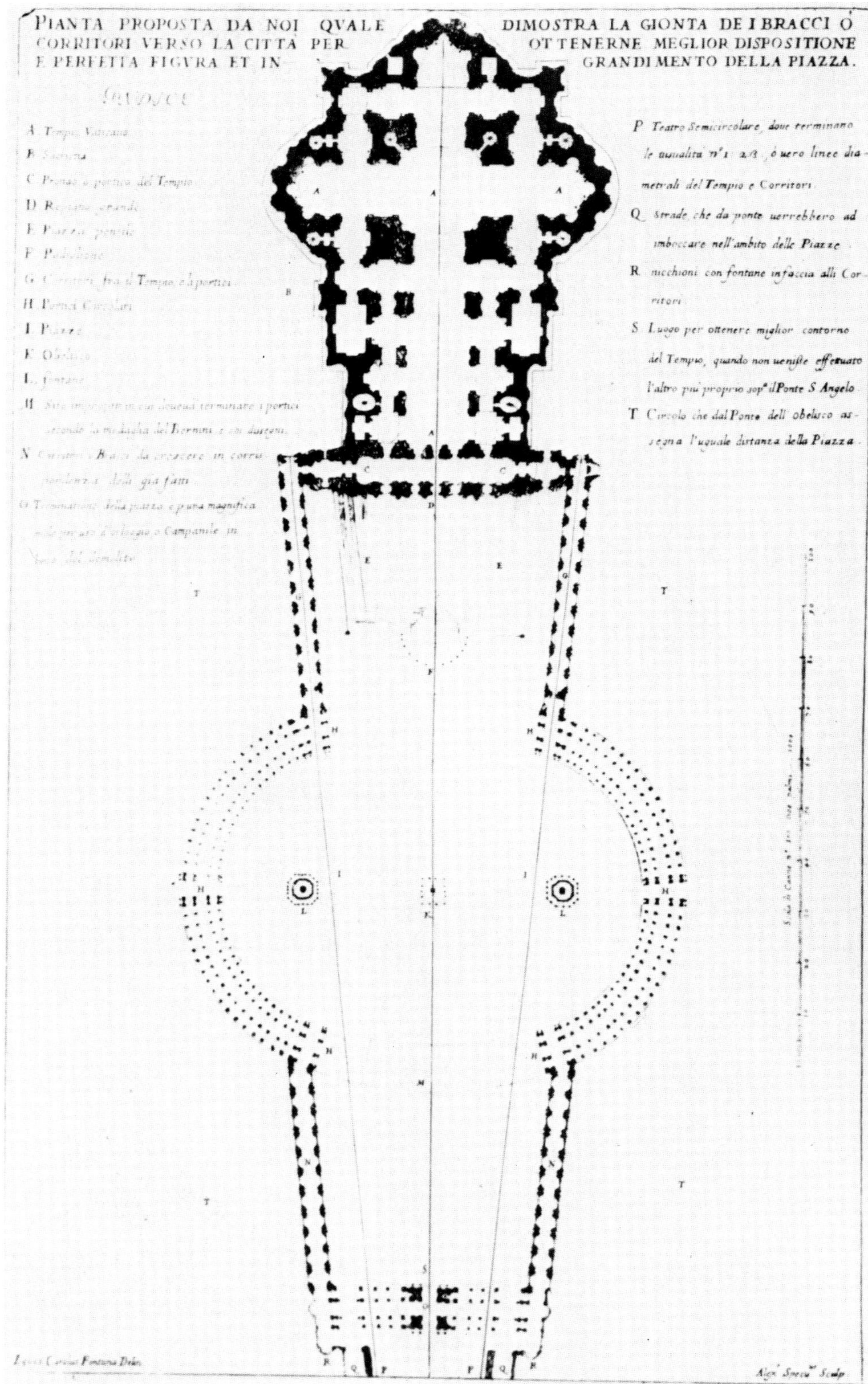

112.   Carlo Fontana, project plan for the Piazza S. Pietro, Rome (Fontana, *Il Tempio Vaticano*, 1694).

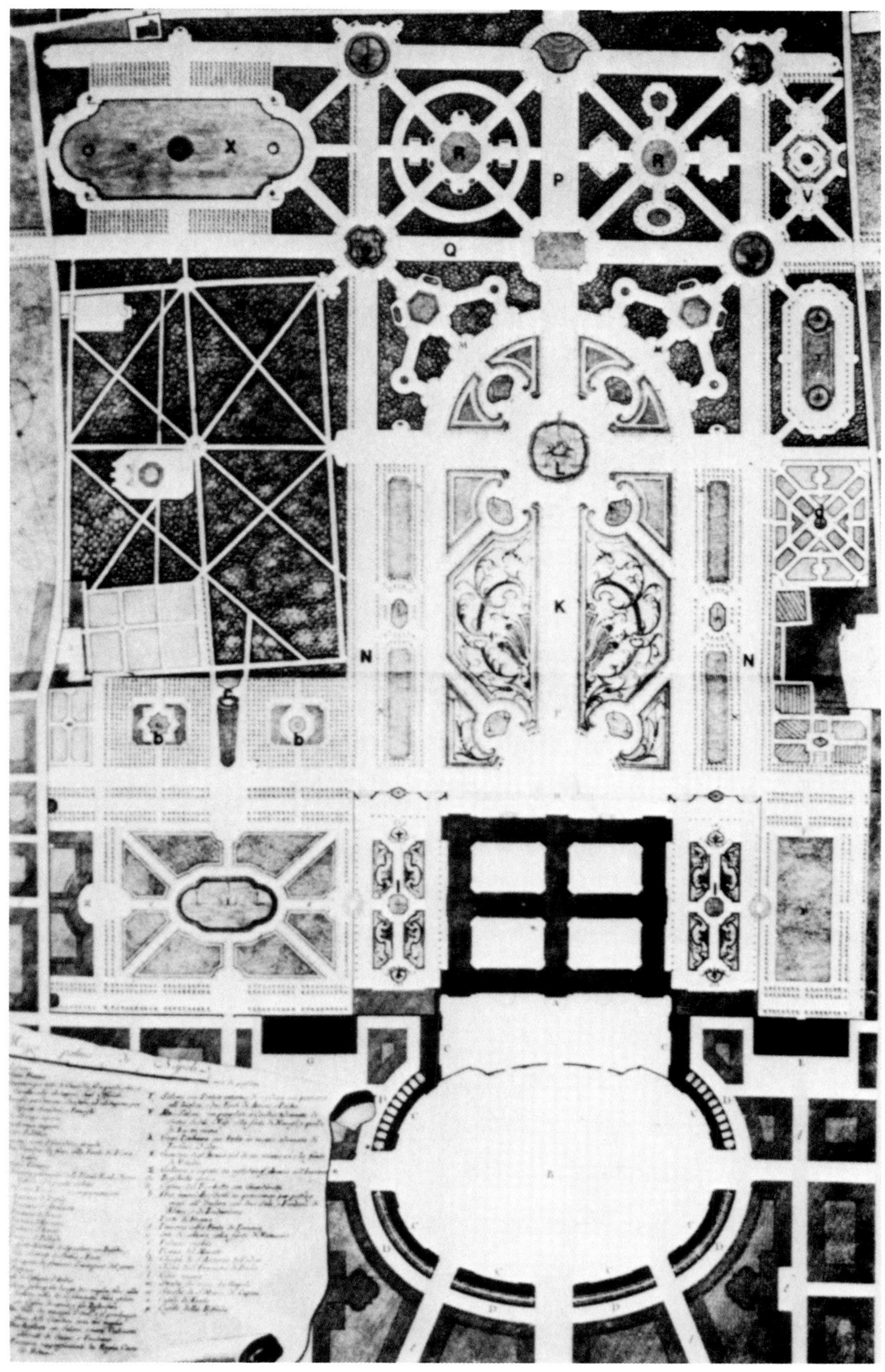

113.   Luigi Vanvitelli, project plan for the Palazzo Reale, Caserta (Vanvitelli, *Dichiarazione dei disegni del real palazzo di Caserta*, 1756).

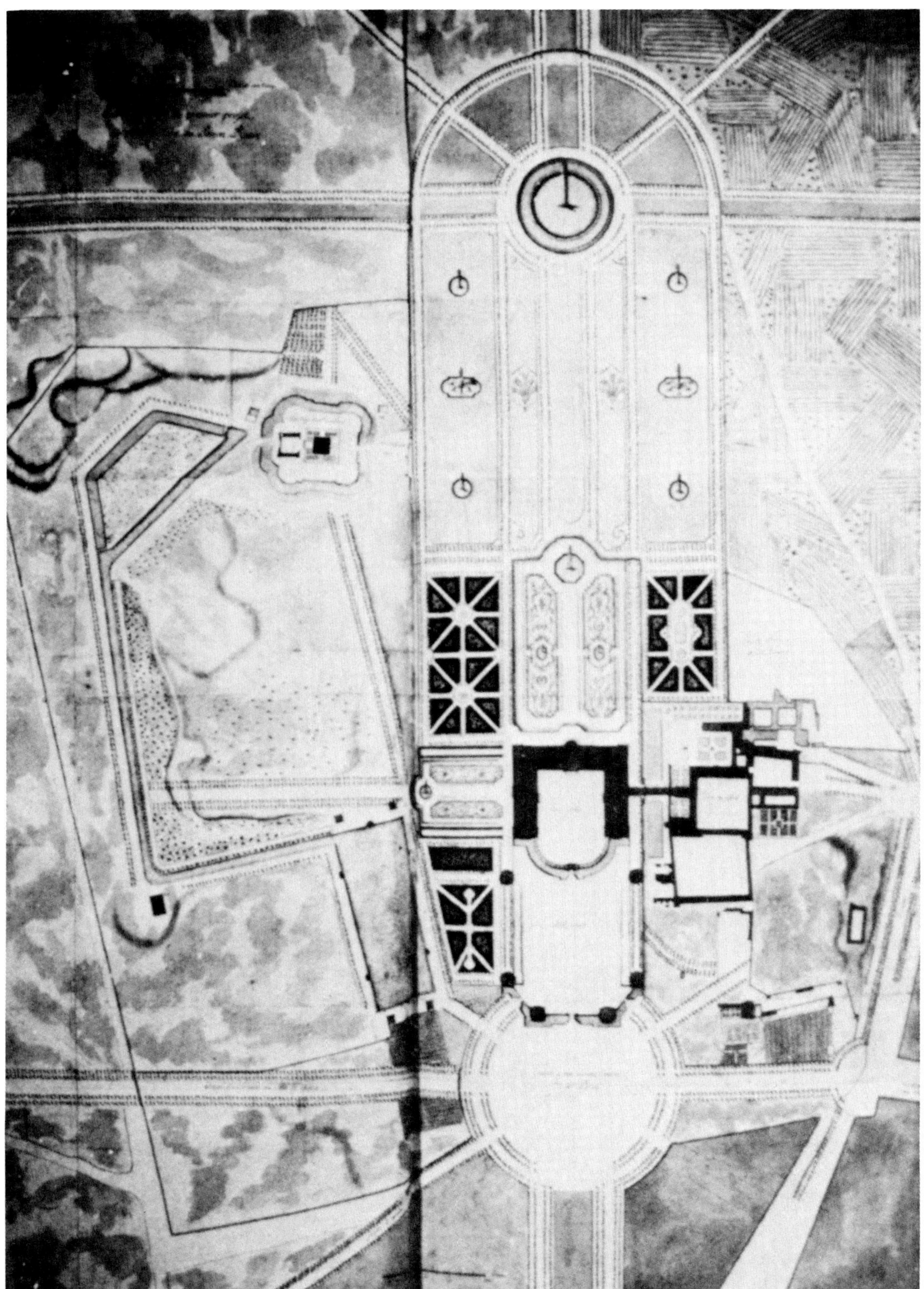

115.   Robert de Cotte, project plan for Buen Retiro. Paris, Bibliothèque Nationale (Bottineau, *L'art de cour dans Espagne de Philippe V*).

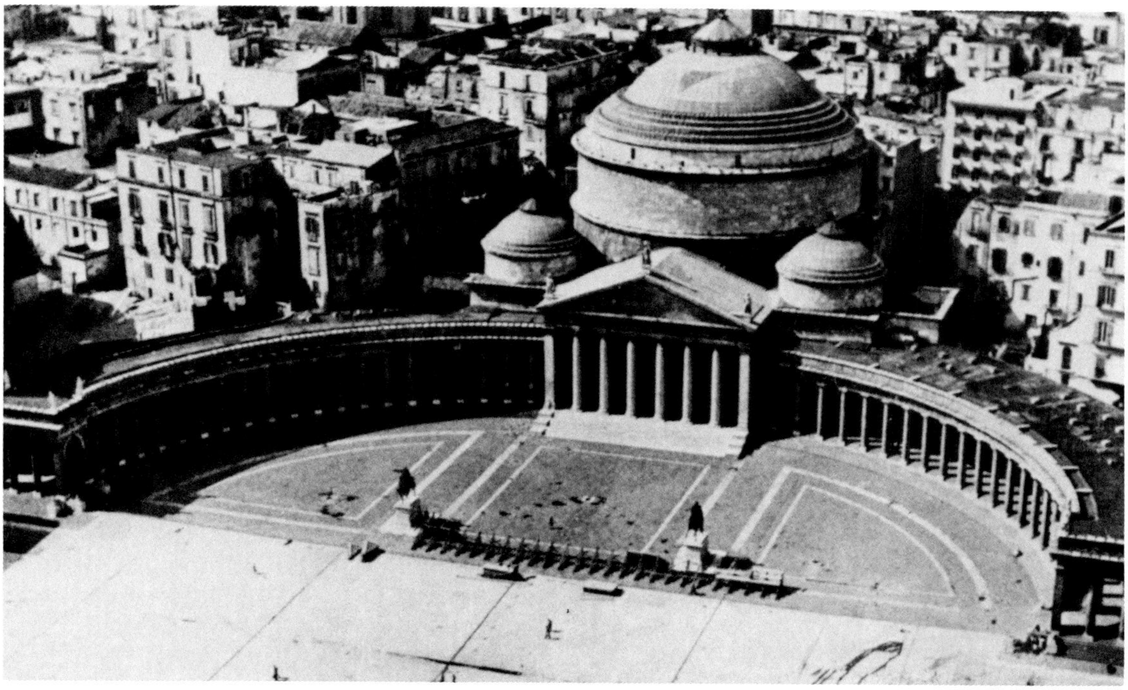

116.   Naples, San Francesco di Paola, aerial view (*Napoli e il suo Golfo*).

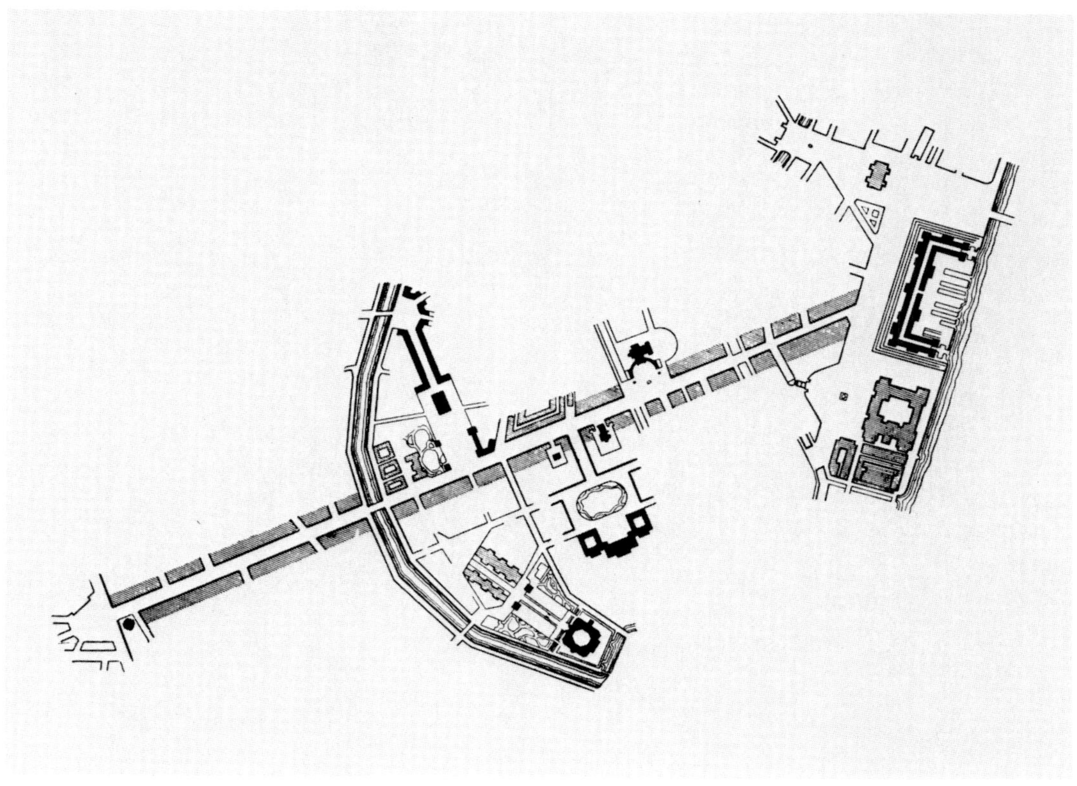

117.   Leningrad, plan of Nevsky Prospekt (Egorov, *The Architectural Planning of St. Petersburg*).

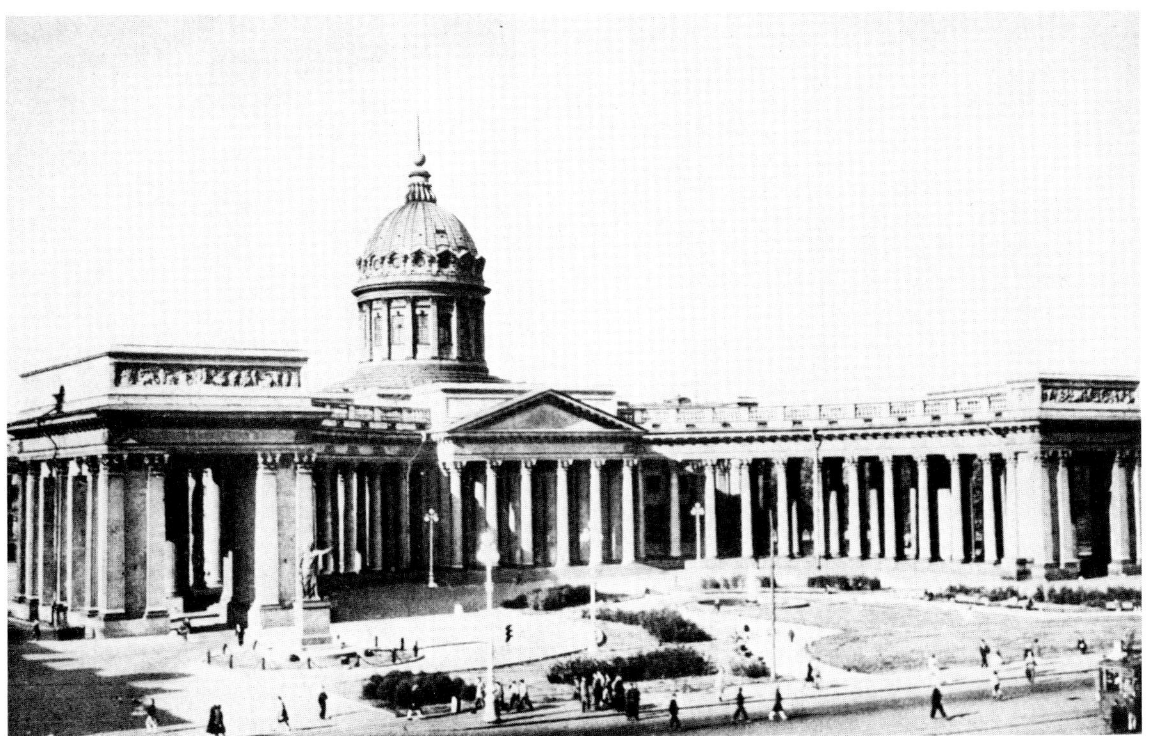

118.   Leningrad, Cathedral of the Virgin of Kazan, view from the north (Hamilton, *Art and Architecture of Russia*).

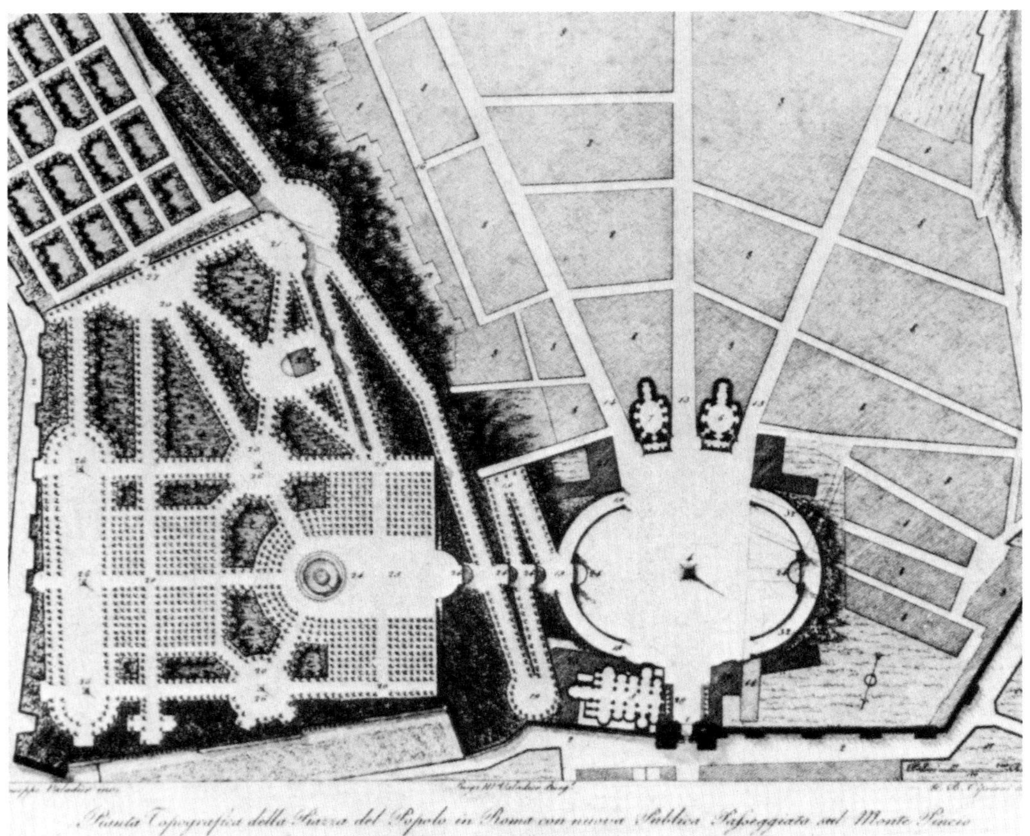

119.   Giuseppe Valadier, project for the Piazza del Popolo, ca. 1815. Rome, Gabinetto Nazionale delle Stampe
(*Valadier, segno e architettura*, Rome, 1986).

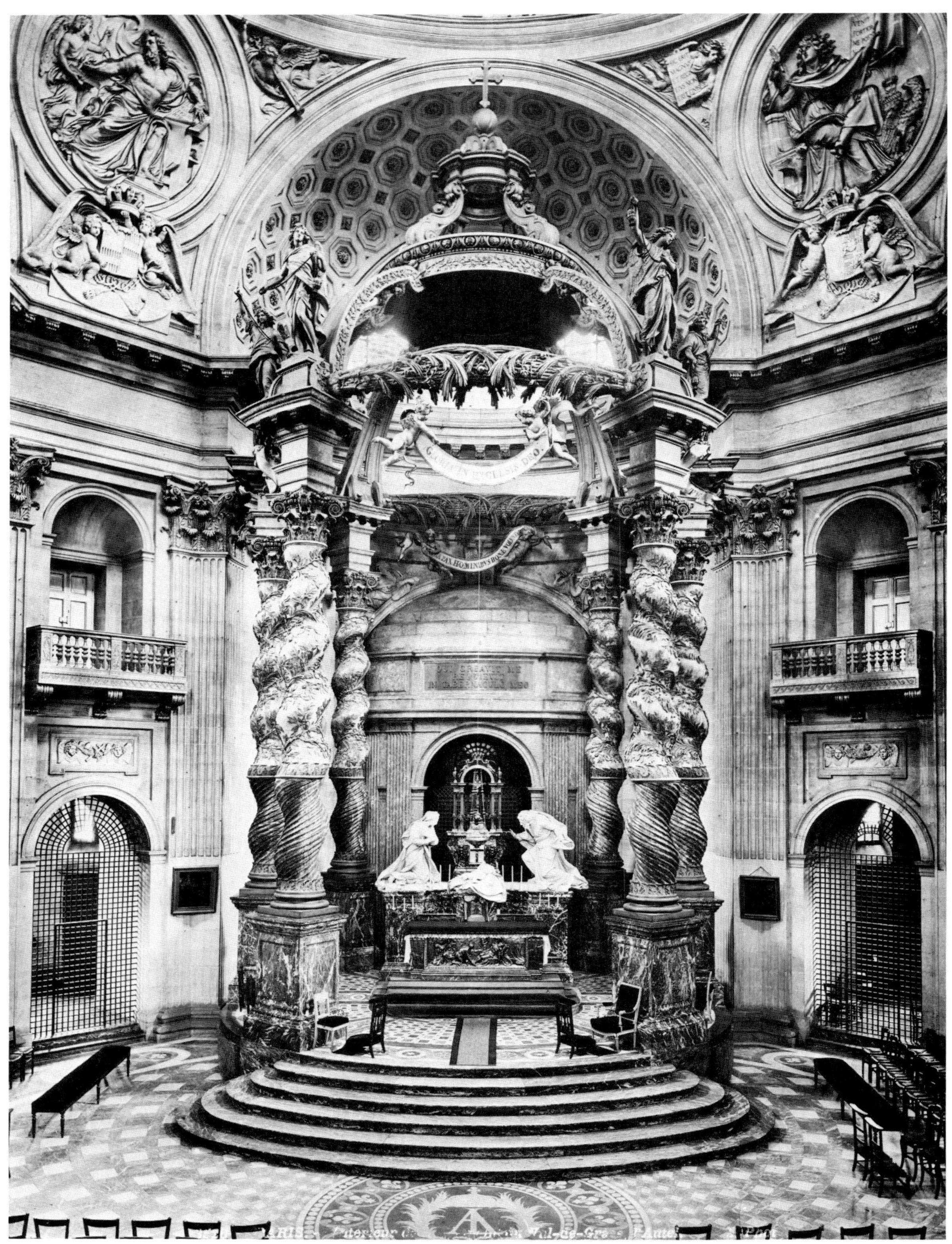

121.   The Val-de-Grâce, Paris. High Altar (photo N. D. Roger-Viollet).

Bernini's Altar for the Val-de-Grâce*

7

In the Spring of 1665, when Bernini arrived in Paris to prepare his plans for the Louvre, the church of the Val-de-Grâce in Rue St. Jacques (fig. 120) was nearing completion, although its final consecration would not take place until 1710.[1] The church was commissioned by Anne of Austria for the convent she had founded in the early 1620s of Benedictine nuns who came from the Abbaye du Val-de-Grâce de Notre-Dame de la Crèche at Val-Profond, a few leagues from Paris. Having been without child since her marriage to Louis XIII, the Queen had vowed that, were she to conceive, she would build a magnificent temple in this new Val-de-Grâce. When, after twenty-three barren years, she bore Louis XIV in 1638, rumor attributed this unexpected event to one of those fateful accidents that confirm the workings of Divine Providence. The King, it was said, on his way to Fontainebleau, had been forced to pass the night in the convent where the Queen was then living, because his bed had been left behind at St. Germain and so prevented his sleeping at the Louvre as he had intended.[2]

Appropriately, perhaps, the church built by the Queen Mother to commemorate the birth of Louis XIV was a chief locus for the birth pangs accompanying the parturition of seventeenth-century French art. In 1646, François Mansart, the first architect of the church, was abruptly dismissed for reasons not yet clear.[3] Later, Pierre Mignard and Dufresnoy used the commission for the decoration of its dome as an excuse for not joining the newly reformed Academy of Painting and Sculpture;[4] and in 1665, Bernini's design for its high altar played out in miniature, as it were, the fate of his plans for the Louvre.

Although it is now certain that Reymond[5] erred in attributing to Bernini the high altar presently in the Val-de-Grâce (fig. 121), the artist's project, his approach to its design, and the conditions leading to its rejection can all be reconstructed to varying degrees.

Bernini first saw the church on June 13th, when he inspected Mignard's work in the dome and examined a model for the high altar as it appears today, which was almost certainly designed by Gabriel Le Duc.[6] When Jacques Tubeuf, the Superintendent of the Queen Mother's Works, asked his opinion of the altar, Bernini laconically replied that Michelangelo used to say that the money one spent on designs paid interest of one-hundred percent. Subsequently, the artist explained to Chantelou that he had refrained from commenting on the altar because he realized Le Duc was not pleased by what he said. In order not to offend anyone, he had said nothing about the ornaments of the church nor its other defects.[7]

On June 21st, Bernini returned to the Val-de-Grâce in search of a suitable piece of marble for his bust of Louis XIV.[8] It was on this visit that he must have discussed the altar with the spiritual director of the nuns and given vent to his criticisms, because four days later he was asked to prepare a new design.[9] This Bernini did with great dispatch in two days on July 3rd and 4th.[10] On the 5th of July, the design was presented to the Queen Mother, who was reportedly pleased with it, although there was evidently some concern over the suitability of its location.[11] These doubts must have grown, because by the 22nd of July Bernini apparently knew that his design would never be executed.[12] Then on August 1st, new contracts were let for completing the altar as originally planned.[13]

The high altar designed by Bernini was intended, like his plans for the Louvre, to solve what James Ackerman has called "universal formal problems," problems, that is, which are defined in terms of symmetry and proportion, vocabulary and syntax, and which are considered solved when the resulting design expresses generally recognized values. Thus Chantelou explained to Colbert that when Bernini examined the church he had not known that the grille screening the nun's choir on the right transept was to be duplicated for the Queen's chapel of Ste. Anne on the left. He had therefore placed the altar where he did in order to obviate this apparent asymmetry.[14] This comment suggests that Bernini's design was for a free-standing altar beneath the dome. Oval in plan, according to Mattia de' Rossi,[15] Bernini's assistant in Paris, such an altar would have consolidated and centralized the lateral axis of the crossing. Moreover, only here would it have made a sight worthy to be seen by those entering the church, as de'Rossi described it,[16] and still be visible from the chapel of Ste. Anne, as Chantelou says it was.[17] At the church of the Sorbonne, where these formal conditions were almost exactly duplicated because the left transept provided access from the college, Bernini also recommended that the altar be placed under the dome.[18]

Unfortunately, little can be said about the actual architecture of Bernini's Val-de-Grâce altar, since it is only known from the brief description written by Mattia de' Rossi. According to de' Rossi, it was to be oval in shape with eight Corinthian columns, an entablature composed of architrave, frieze, and cornice, and above, a frontispiece.[19] However, the disappointingly vague impression left by this description of the altar may be supplemented by what I believe to be a more circumstantial knowledge of its sculptural decoration.

Given the dedication of the Convent and the circumstances leading to the construction of the church, it should come as no surprise that the imagery chosen for representation on the altar was the Nativity. In fact, one of the nuns later wrote that the Queen Mother wanted the church to be both magnificent and sumptuous, so that it would contrast as much as possible with the mean and abject place in which the Eternal Word had become flesh.[20] This notion, if it really reflects the thought of the patron, may explain the simplicity and the austerity of the *Nativity* (fig. 122) commissioned from Michel Anguier two months before

Bernini arrived in Paris and eventually placed on the altar.[21] What Bernini's *Nativity* would have looked like may be gathered from a drawing in Berlin (fig. 123) attributed to the artist by Peter Dreyer.[22] In this drawing the affinities of pose and grouping with Anguier's *Nativity*, which Bernini would presumably have known from Le Duc's model, seem too pointed to be merely fortuitous. The bent posture of Joseph with his hands raised and the kneeling figure of the Virgin are very close, although in contrast to the purely French pathos of Anguier's group, Bernini's is clearly distinguished by that passionate expression with which, de' Rossi said, the Cavaliere was wont to endow his figures.[23] Nor does the character of the drawing argue against the possibility that it reflects a sculptural group.

Few of Bernini's drawings, of course, are pictorial in the strict sense of the word. In most instances, they easily posit translation into three-dimensional form and, except in those cases when they specifically prepared a two-dimensional work, seldom depend on surface relations to effect a sense of space. Even in his presentation drawings, made for their own sakes, such elements are eschewed entirely or reduced to insignificance. The Berlin *Nativity* is no exception to the rule. Each figure displaces an appropriate volume of space and the composition is compact, round, and three-dimensional. Moreover, the long axis of the group running on a shallow diagonal from St. Joseph to the Virgin would fit nicely in an oval space, and the elevated height of the manger, with the Child at an angle and tipped up, would have made Him visible from below, a concern equally apparent if differently resolved in Anguier's work.

Similarly dependent on the spatial conception of Bernini's design is the reversal of the figures as compared to Anguier's group. Anguier's figures are arranged frontally, and the Virgin turns her back on the chapel of Ste. Anne to face and be seen from the nun's choir on the right. The altered position and crossed axes of Bernini's Virgin and Child would have opened up views from both the left and right, and the Virgin, now facing left, would have conformed with what Chantelou said was Bernini's wish to make the altar visible from the Queen's chapel of Ste. Anne.[24]

Indeed, with the two reworkings of the Christ Child on the right, only the wreath of putti behind and the fragment of a dated, autograph letter on the verso, which suggests a date for the sheet of 1667, prevents us from connecting the drawing directly with the altar. But even if the letter and the drawing are contemporary, there would still be good reason to assume that the drawing accurately reflects Bernini's composition for the altar, since there is a definite pattern of repetitions and near replicas in the artist's work during these years. The pose of the Christ Child, for example, closely follows that of the infant held by St. Joseph in an unusual drawing executed on a wall in the Chigi Palace at Ariccia and dated 1663.[25] Similarly, a presentation drawing representing the penitent St. Jerome (Paris, Louvre) done by the artist while he was in Paris and given to Colbert, varies, without major distortions, the motifs and composition of an earlier drawing (Rome, Biblioteca Vaticana).[26] Another, less obvious example also illustrates Bernini's plastic conception of pictorial composition. For if we compare a splendid, autograph brush drawing of the Holy Family (Rome, Rospigliosi-Pallavicini Gallery) with a studio replica of another Bernini drawing representing the same subject (Budapest, Kupferstichkabinett), we quickly realize that we are essentially seeing the same figures from two different points of view.[27]

But if the Berlin drawing, whether or not dated to 1667, preserves the composition of the sculpture on the altar, the *Nativity* was not meant to stand alone. His design, Bernini told Chantelou, would reveal a man who was a painter, a sculptor, and an architect,[28] and Mattia de' Rossi says that the design included a glory of angels and a God the Father in the frontispiece.[29] What part of these additional ornaments would have been painted and how they may have related to the putti in the drawing cannot now be determined, but their presence places the design firmly in the tradition of altars with a painting or statue below and God the Father in a pediment or frontispiece above. Numerous examples of this type from the fifteenth and sixteenth centuries have survived from every part of Italy, and they provide direct prototypes for several mid-seventeenth-century Roman altars. The first of the group is Pietro da Cortona's never executed design of 1634 (Windsor Castle, Royal Library) for the church of S. Giovanni dei Fiorentini (fig. 124).[30] Two more, the major altar of S. Nicola da Tolentino (fig. 125) and another in a chapel at S. Agostino were executed for the Pamphili.[31] And Bernini used the same type for the altar in his church at Castel Gandolfo (fig. 126).[32]

In these seventeenth-century examples it can be argued that what is chiefly represented is the Trinity, with the dove of the Holy Spirit sometimes displaced to the dome or vault above and Christ, as the Second Person, identified with the Holy Sacrament. In its simplest and purest form, this interpretation of the Trinity appears in an altar of 1675 designed by Le Brun, where the tabernacle for the reserved Host was surmounted by the dove and a God the Father with a glory of angels.[33] Le Brun's altar may be compared to Carlo Rainaldi's decorations for the Forty Hours Devotions held at the Gesù in 1650, where the Sacrament tabernacle, the dove of the Holy Spirit, and God the Father likewise form the Trinity,[34] or to the substitution of the consecrated and transubstantiated Host for the presence of Christ at the Last Supper and in the Trinity in an early eighteenth-century monstrance (Kraiburg, Inn).[35]

The relevance of this iconography for Bernini's design appears from the fact that the high altar of the Val-de-Grâce was also its Sacrament altar. Le Duc's altar, pushed back into the apse (fig. 120), gave the nuns, in their Sacrament chapel behind, devotional access to the Host and enabled them to take communion through an opening in the grille without having to enter the church.[36] How Bernini's altar, standing beneath the dome, would have accommodated the cloistered sisters is not known, since the only comment that seems to bear on the issue is the regrettably brief report that François Mansart approved Bernini's idea for the altar of placing it in front of the grille and the little one, "le petit," behind.[37] Nevertheless, the connection of the altar with the Holy Sacrament led Bernini to elaborate its imagery beyond what was present in Le Duc's model. All to no avail, of course, because the design was rejected.

Chantelou, attempting to still troubled waters, rationalized the failure of Bernini's project by attributing it to the poor health of the Queen Mother, who wished to see her church finished before she died and therefore decided to complete the altar already begun.[38] Bernini, responding more personally, variously blamed the fickleness of the French and their lack of taste, the cabal of jealous architects ranged against him, and the wish of people simply to annoy him by asking his advice and then not taking it.[39] What is certainly true is that Bernini's design was clearly admired by those who first saw it.[40] But the trouble with Bernini, Colbert remarked to Chantelou, was that he never bothered to inform himself about anything,[41] and in the end, it must have been the design's uncertain ability to answer the practical demands of the commission that gave scope to his critics and led to its rejection.

In fact, Bernini had envisioned his task and made his design almost exclusively as a self-conscious demonstration of artistic prowess. He carefully adjusted the altar to conform to and correct what he mistakenly took to be the formal conditions of the site, and he expanded the iconography according to a widely accepted tradition in order to enhance its representational value and to show that he was a master of painting, sculpture, and architecture. Nor, as in the case of his plans for the Louvre, could he have been expected to do anything else. For at a time when function was still largely a matter of custom and tradition, considerations of utility tended to follow rather than to precede the formal design. Bernini knew that, in order to be built, the virtues of even beautiful designs sometimes had to be explained.[42] What neither he nor his French patrons yet realized was that without a programmatic approach to design, which could have compensated for his lack of familiarity with French forms and usages, the widely recognized formal beauty of Bernini's Parisian designs would finally be found wanting.

George C. Bauer
University of California, Irvine

Notes

*   A slightly different version of this paper was first read at the Bernini Symposium held at the Institute for Advanced Studies, Princeton, New Jersey, in 1982, and I should like to thank Irving Lavin, as well as Hellmut Hager, for having given me the opportunity to present this material. My thanks are also due to Marilyn Lavin for providing me with information about an earlier *Nativity* in the Capuchin church at Albano, which may be connected with Bernini.

1.   For a chronology of the events concerning the building of the church, see Peter Smith, "Mansart Studies, II: The Val-de-Grâce," *The Burlington Magazine*, CVI, 1964, appendix, pp. 112-115.

2.   See Allan Braham, "Mansart Studies, I: The Val-de-Grâce," *The Burlington Magazine*, CV, 1963, p. 351.

3.   Cf. the discussion in Peter Smith and Allan Braham, *François Mansart*, London, 1972, p. 57.

4.   For this conflict, see Guillaume Janneau, *La peinture française au XVII^{el}siècle*, Geneva, 1965, p. 166.

5.   Marcel Reymond, "L'autel du Val-de-Grâce et les ouvrages du Bernin en France," *Gazette des beaux-arts*, ser. 4, Vol. V, 1911, pp. 367-94. Cf. below, the following note.

6.   The altar presently in the church is a 19th-century reconstruction by Victor Ruprich-Robert of the original one, which with the exception of a part of its sculpture was destroyed during the Revolution (see Pierre Lemoine, "Le maître-autel de l'église du Val-de-Grâce," *Bulletin de la société de l'histoire de l'art français*, 1960, pp. 96-98). The author of its design is still not absolutely certain, since the documents, some of which date to before Bernini's arrival in Paris and therefore exclude his participation, either do not name the designer or cite both of the architects for the church at this time, Pierre Le Muet and Gabriel Le Duc. For these documents, see Pierre Chaleix, "A propos du baldaquin de l'église du Val-de-Grâce," *Bulletin de la société de l'histoire de l'art français*, 1961, pp. 211-214; and Claude Mignot, "L'église du Val-de-Grâce au faubourg Saint-Jacques de Paris: architecture et decor (nouveaux documents 1645-1667)," *Bulletin de la société de l'histoire de l'art français*, 1975, pp. 101-136. Nevertheless, the attribution of the design to Le Duc by Michele Beaulieu ("Gabriel Le Duc, Michel Anguier et le maître-autel du Val-de-Grâce," *Bulletin de la société de l'histoire de l'art français*, 1945-46, pp. 150-161) must surely be correct, because it is to Le Duc that Chantelou attributes it. See Paul Freárt de Chantelou, *Journal de voyage du Cavalier Bernin en France*, ed. by L. Lalanne and cited here in the Pandora edition, Paris, 1981, p. 37.

7.   Chantelou, pp. 37-38.

8.   Ibid., pp. 41-42.

9.   Ibid., pp. 43-44.

10.   Ibid., p. 49.

11. Ibid, p. 50. In letters to Rome of 10 July 1665, both Mattia de' Rossi (Leon Mirot, "Le Bernin en France," *Mémoires de la société de l'histoire de Paris et de l'Ile-de-France*, XXXI, 1904, pp. 226-27, n. 2) and Carlo Roberti de' Vittorj, the papal nuncio (Armando Schiavo, "Il viaggio del Bernini in Francia nei documenti dell'Archivio Segreto Vaticano," *Bollettino del centro di studi per la storia dell' architettura*, X, 1956, p. 33), describe the Queen Mother's pleasure on seeing Bernini's design. But Colbert's conversation with Chantelou three days later on 8 July (Chantelou, p. 54) indicates that the reception given to his project was not all that the artist would have desired. Bernini, however, does not seem to have been upset by whatever was said, and Colbert's curiosity about the artist's reaction may rather reflect his earlier experience of Bernini's response to the criticism of his first design for the Louvre (Mirot, pp. 182-85).

12. This appears from Chantelou, pp. 66-67, for on this date Bernini saw and admired a design for the Val-de-Grâce altar by Pierre Mignard, which evidently had been executed in rivalry with Le Duc. In praising Mignard's design, Bernini contrasts it "à celui que l'on exécute," as the sun to a torch.

13. Lemoine, p. 102.

14. Chantelou, p. 54.

15. Mirot, pp. 226-27, n. 2.

16. Ibid.

17. Chantelou, p. 54.

18. For the church of the Sorbonne, see Anthony Blunt, *Art and Architecture in France 1500 to 1700*, Harmondsworth, Middlesex, 1973, pp. 197-98. Bernini's advice on the placement of the altar is in Chantelou, pp. 261-62, although the situation here may have been more complicated, since it involved coordinating the altar with Cardinal Richelieu's tomb.

19. Mirot, pp. 226-27, n. 2.

20. Quoted in Louis Hautecoeur, *Histoire de l'architecture classique en France*, II, Paris, 1948, p. 51.

21. Anguier's *Nativity*, which was placed on deposit at the Petits-Augustins in 1793 when the original altar was destroyed, later went to Saint-Roch, where it remains today. See Lemoine, pp. 97-98.

22. Peter Dreyer, *Vom späten Mittelalter bis zu Jacques Louis David. Neuerworbene und neubestimmte Zeichnungen in Berlin Kupferstichkabinett*, Berlin, 1973, p. 83.

23. Mirot, pp. 226-27, n. 2.

24. Chantelou, p. 54.

25. For this drawing, see Heinrich Brauer and Rudolf Wittkower, *Die Zeichnungen des Gianlorenzo Bernini*, Berlin, 1931, pl. 115.

26. These two drawings may be compared side by side in ibid., pls. 116 and 117.

27. For the autograph in Rome, see Ann Sutherland Harris, *Selected Drawings of Gian Lorenzo Bernini*, New York, 1977, pl. 85; and for the studio replica, Brauer and Wittkower, pl. 178a.

28. Chantelou, p. 50: "Il avait dit *auparavant* que ce dessin faisait voir qu' un homme était peintre sculpteur et architecte." For Bernini's integration of the three arts, see Irving Lavin, *Bernini and the Unity of the Visual Arts*, New York and London, 1980.

29. Mirot, pp. 226-27, n. 2.

30. This altar, which reached only the stage of a full-scale model that stood in the church for many years, is discussed by Karl Noehles, "Architekturprojekte Cortonas," *Münchner Jahrbuch der bildenden Kunst*, XX, 1969, pp. 183.

31. For these two altars, see Jennifer Montagu, "Alessandro Algardi's Altar of S. Nicola da Tolentino and Some Related Models," *The Burlington Magazine*, CXII, 1970, pp. 282-91; and Rudolf Preimesberger and Mark Weil, "The Pamphili Chapel in Sant' Agostino,"

Römisches Jahrbuch für Kunstgeschichte, XV, 1975, pp. 183-98.

32.   See Vicenzo Golzio, *Documenti artistici sul Seicento nell' Archivio Chigi*, Rome, 1939, pp. 379-407.

33.   For this altar at the Grands-Augustins, see Hautecoeur, II, pp. 825-26 and fig. 655.

34.   Rainaldi's decorations are discussed and illustrated by Per Bjurström, "Baroque Theater and the Jesuits," *Baroque Art: The Jesuit Contribution*, ed. by R. Wittkower and I. Jaffe, New York, 1972, pp. 106-108; and by Mark Weil, "The Devotions of the Forty Hours and Roman Baroque Illusions," *Journal of the Warburg and Courtauld Institutes*, XXXVII, 1974, pp. 234-35.

35.   For this work of 1705 by Gregorius Vaith of Augsburg, see Gertrude Schiller, *Iconography of Christian Art*, New York, 1971, II, p. 40 and fig. 116.

36.   Lemoine, p. 96.

37.   Chantelou, p. 102: "Mansart . . . -approuvait la penseé qu' avait eue le Cavalier pour l'autel du Val-de-Grâce de le faire au-devant de la grille et le petit au fond." This comment suggests that Bernini had worked out some arrangement with two altar tables—one for the public congregation and one for the nuns in their Sacrament chapel, an idea bound to be approved by Mansart, since it seems to have been his preferred solution to the problem when he was the architect of the church. See Braham, "Mansart Studies, I," pp. 352, 357.

38.   Chantelou, p. 81.

39.   Ibid., pp. 66-67, 81, 167.

40.   In addition to the approbation recorded in the letters to Rome of Mattia de' Rossi and the papal nuncio (above, note 11) or Mansart's approval cited above, cf. Chantelou's description of the design as "beau et magnifique," and the opinion of Colbert, who when he first saw the design, said "Je voudrais qu' il eût couté au Roi deux cent mille écus, et qu' il y eût en France un homme capable de faire ces ouvrages," meaning that were there one man in France capable of making such designs, there would be others almost as good (Chantelou, pp. 49-51).

41.   Chantelou, p. 54: "M. Colbert a dit là-dessus que c'était qu' il ne voulait s'informer de rien."

42.   Ibid., p. 50: "il m'a dit qu' il serait bien aise que je parlasse de ce dessin d'autel et disse ce que j'en connaissais; que je savais que les belles choses (quoiqu' il ne sût pas les faire) avaient besoin d'être aideés."

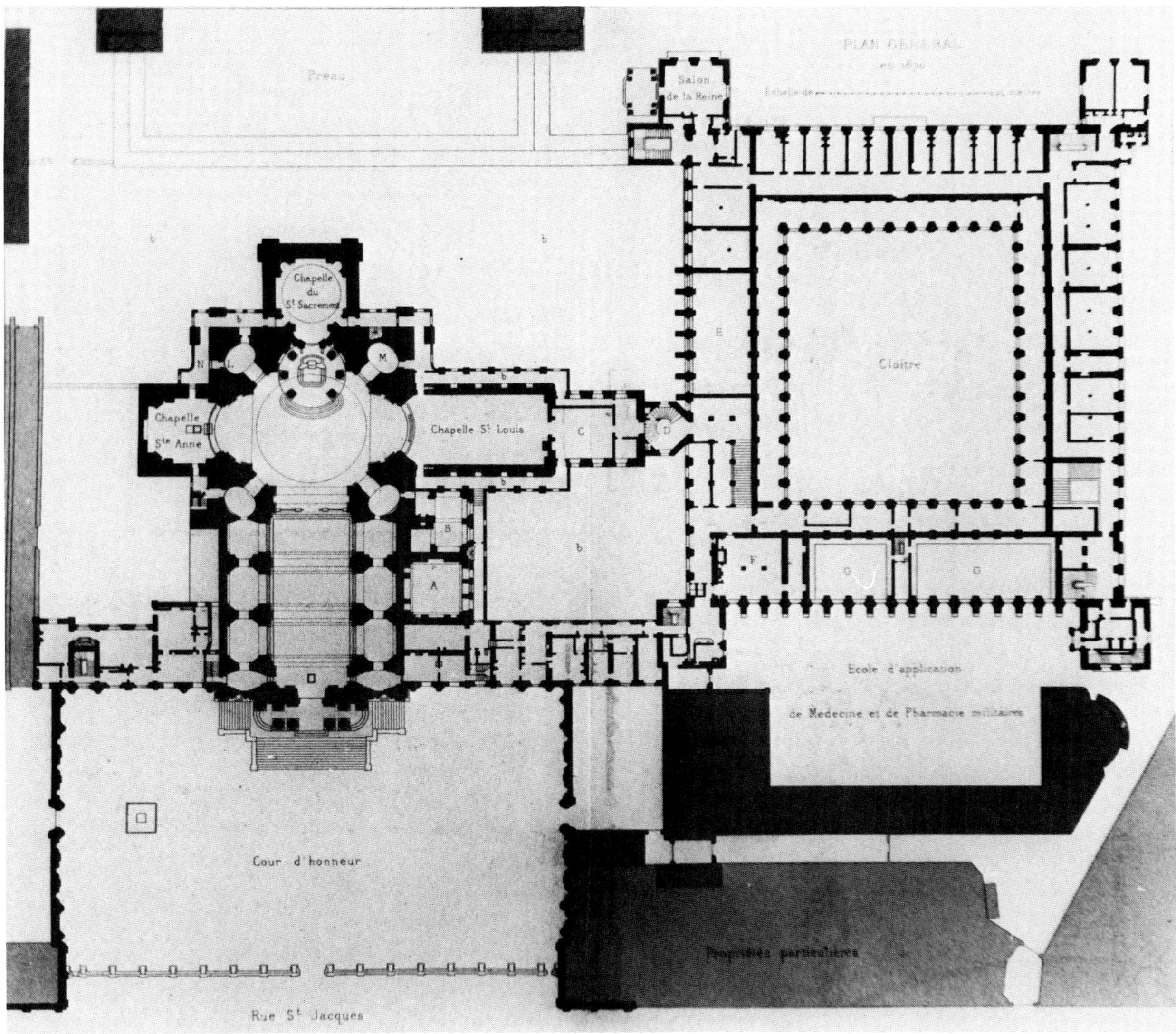

120.   The Val-de-Grâce, Paris. Plan of church and convent (from Ruprich-Robert, *L'Eglise et le monastère du Val-de-Grâce*, Paris, 1875)

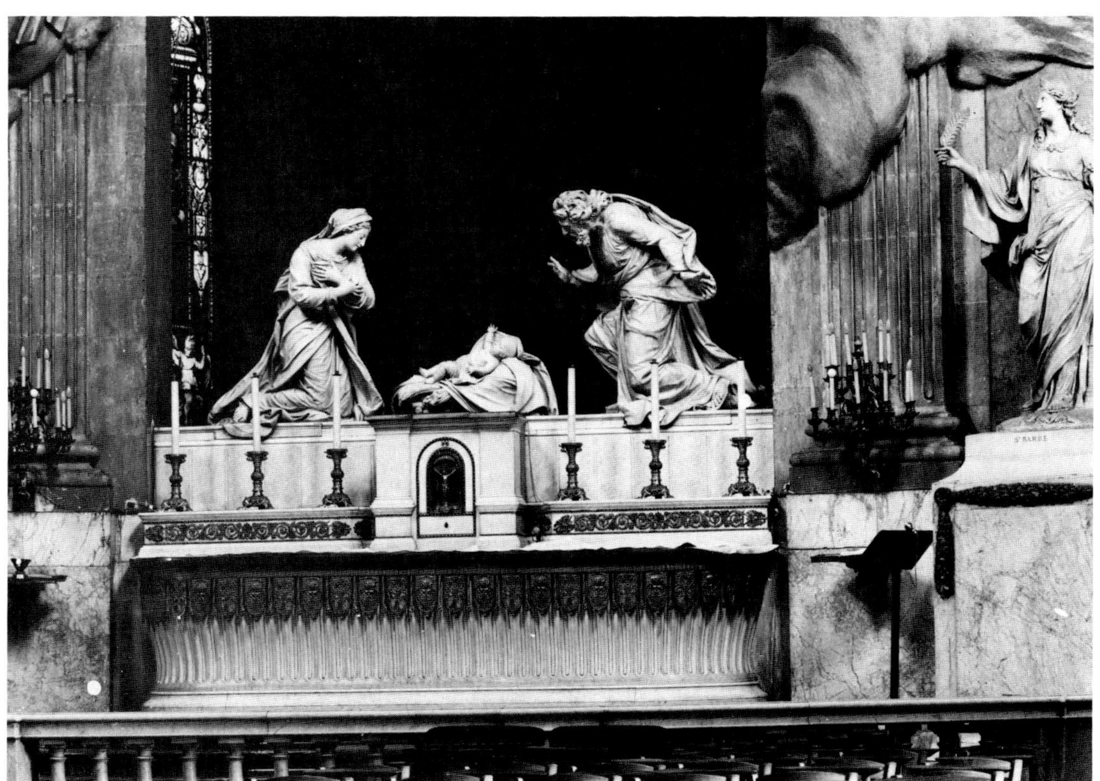

122.   Michel Anguier, *Nativity*. Paris, St. Roch (photo N. D. Roger-Viollet).

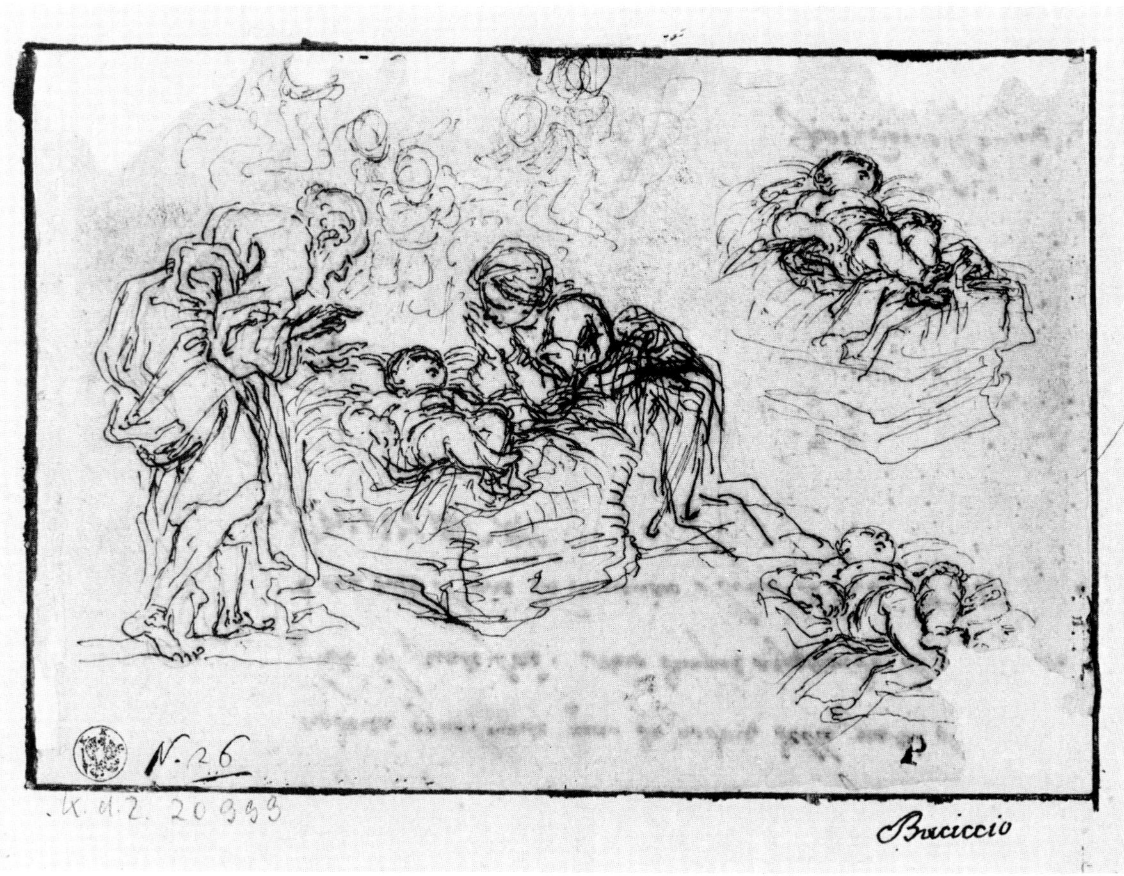

123.   G. L. Bernini, *Nativity*. Berlin, Kupferstichkabinett (museum photo).

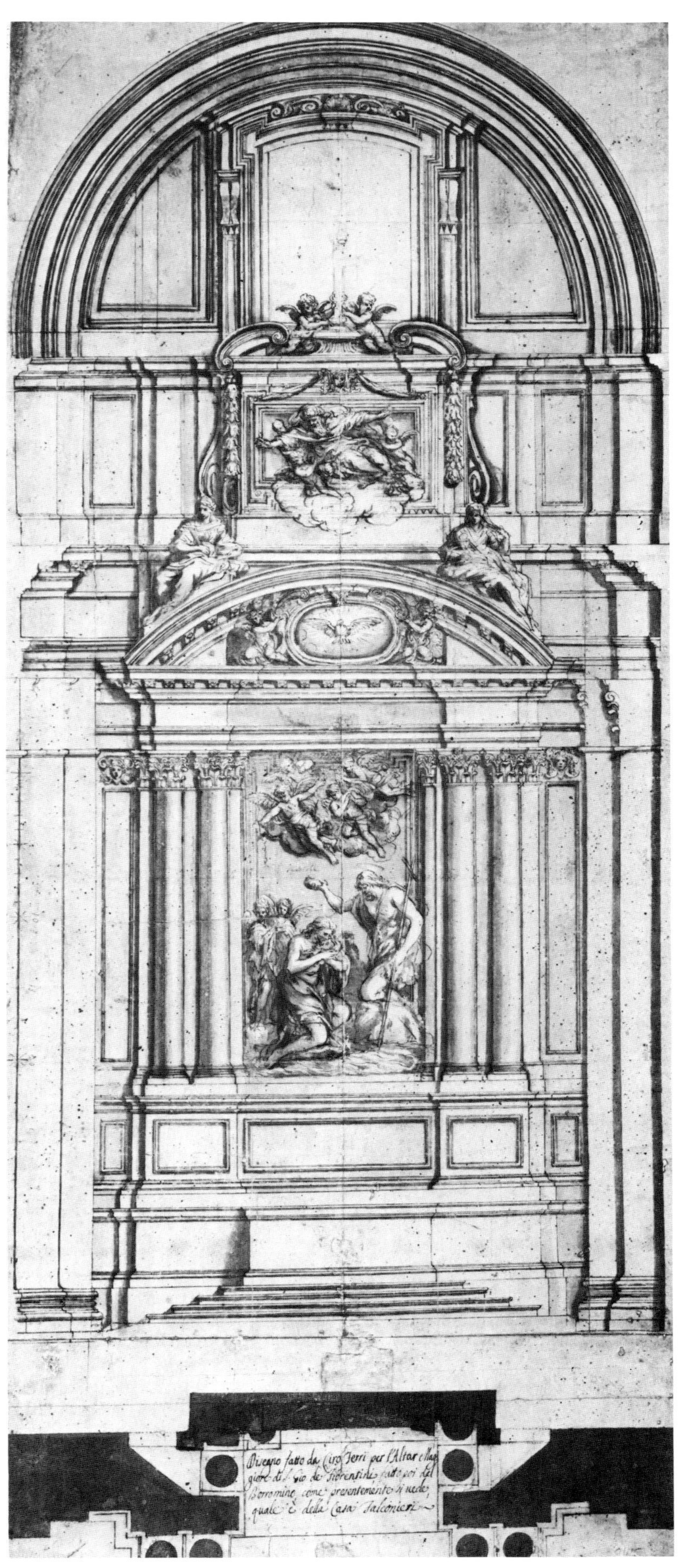

124. Pietro da Cortona, Project for the High
      Altar of S. Giovanni dei Fiorentini,
      Rome. Windsor Castle, Royal Library
      (reproduced by Gracious Permission of
      Her Majesty Queen Elizabeth II).

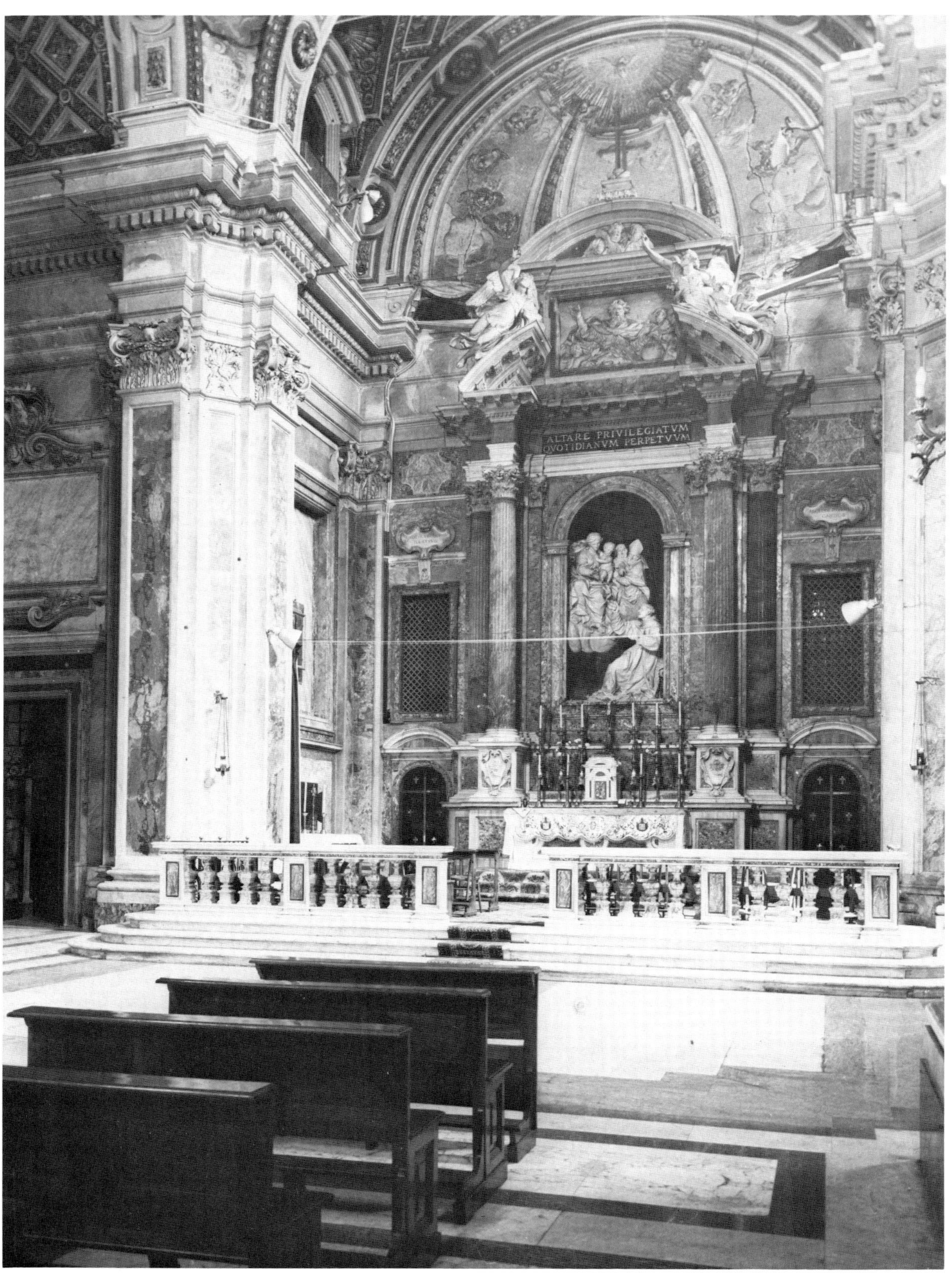

125.   S. Nicola da Tolentino, Rome. High Altar (photo Bibliotheca Hertziana).

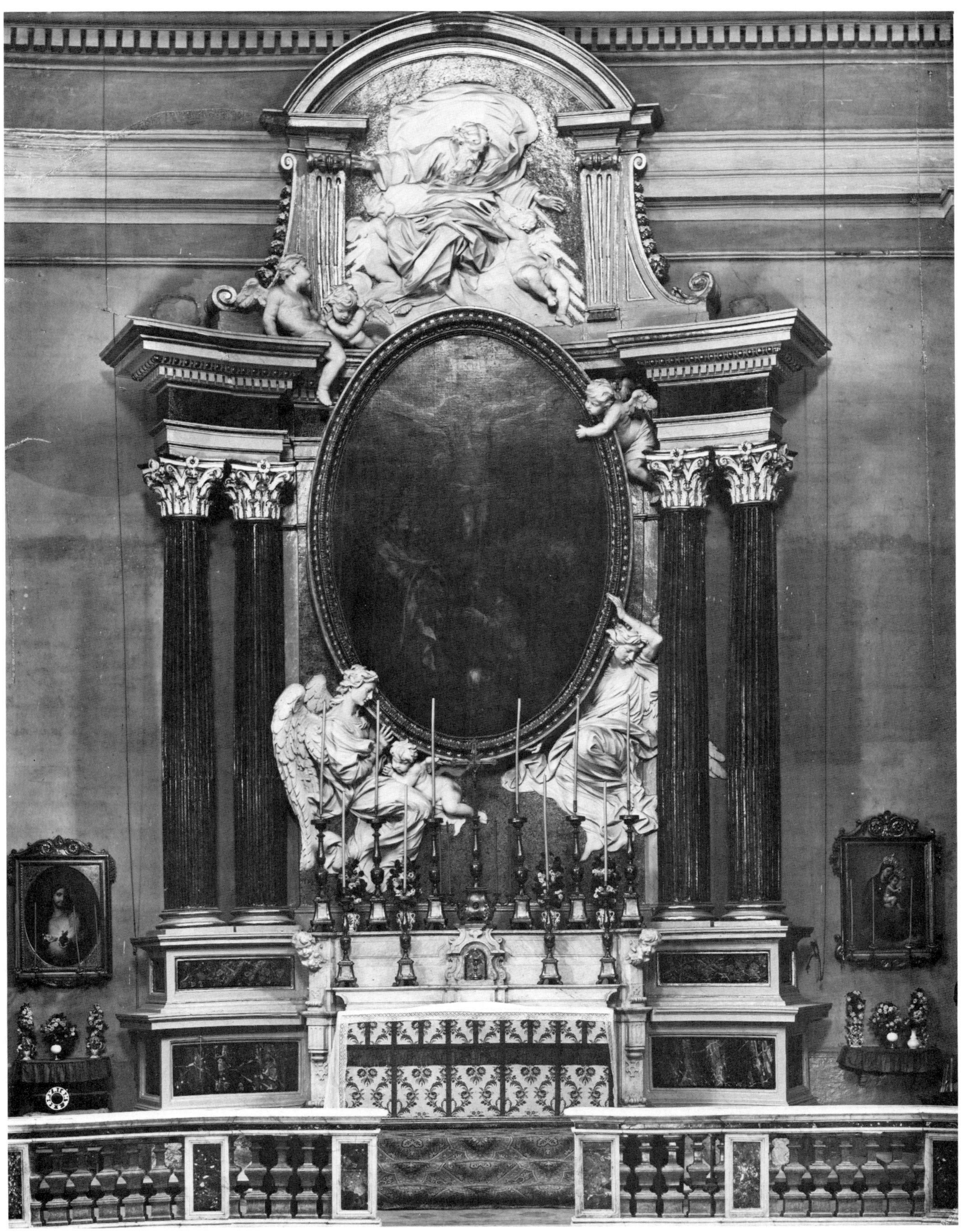

126.   S. Tomaso da Villanova, Castel Gandolfo. High Altar (photo Alinari).

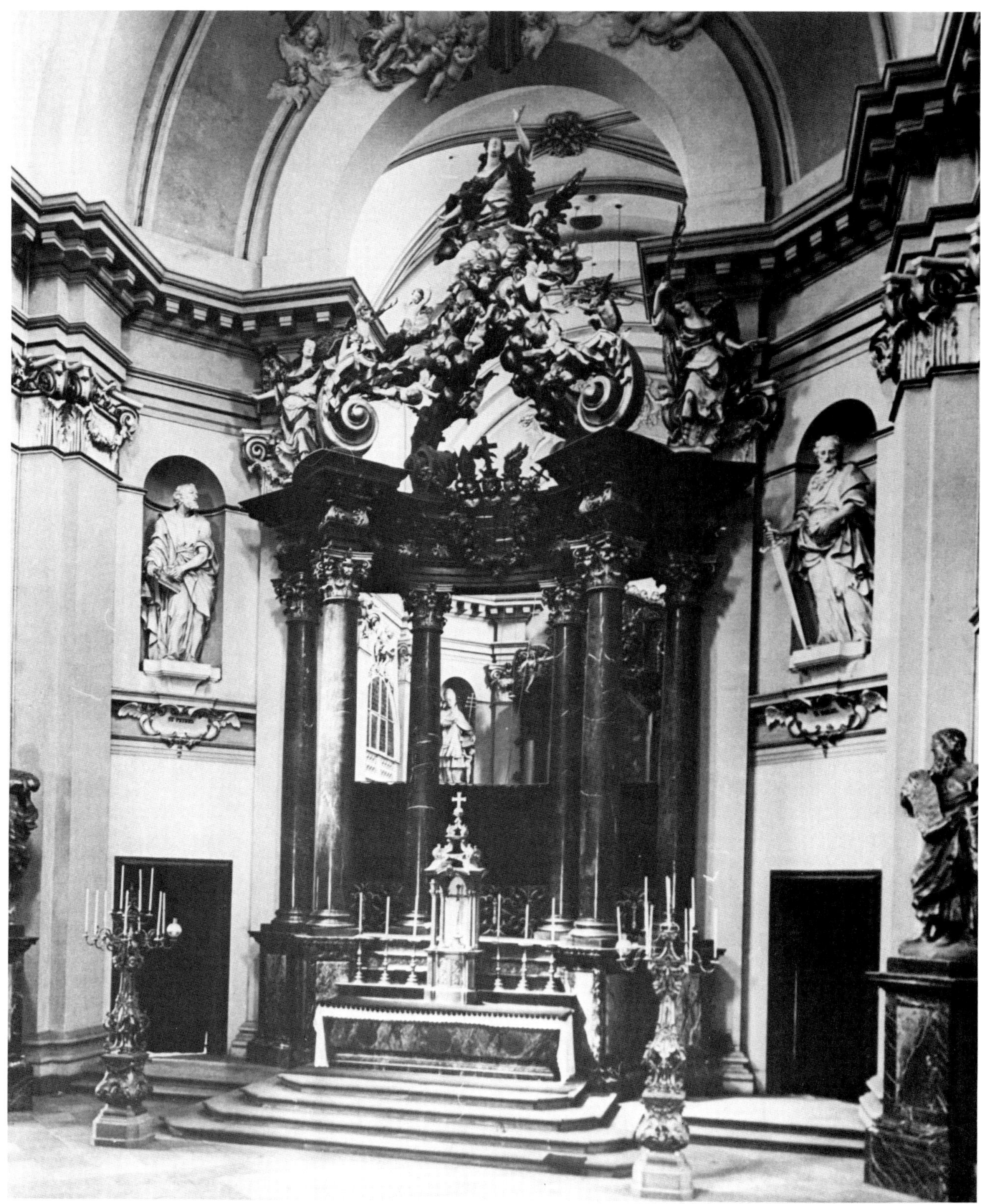

139.   Fulda, Cathedral, oblique view of high altar (Bildarchiv Foto Marburg).

Johann Dientzenhofer's Cathedral in Fulda and the Question of its Roman Origins

8

The rebuilding of the time honored Carolingian basilica above the shrine of St. Bonifatius in Fulda was one of the most prestigious building tasks available in Germany at the beginning of the eighteenth century. The reasons which led Prince Abbot Adalbert von Schleifras to appoint the young Johann Dientzenhofer for so important a commission have been the subject of much speculation. But certainly the fact that Dientzenhofer had completed his architectural education in Rome (supported by the elector in Mainz, Lother Franz Graf von Schönborn) from where he had just returned when he was appointed *Stiftsbaumeister* in Fulda on 4 September, 1700, accounts at least partially for his selection as architect.[1]

The monastery church (fig.128), erected by Dientzenhofer between 1704 and 1712, which is dedicated to the Redeemer and St. Bonifatius, obtained cathedral status in 1752, subsequent to a very eventful and complex planning history. The building has the form of a barrel vaulted basilica with a slightly projecting transept (figs. 129 and 133). The nave is flanked by aisles in the shape of interconnecting chapels with transverse oval domes (fig. 136). But the most salient features are the rhythmic bay system and the dome above the crossing which rests on a high drum (fig. 138). Because of these features which were unusual for the time in the area around Fulda, the church occupies a rather significant position. Questions concerning the origin of its concept have been answered in different or controversial ways, and therefore are still unclarified.

A local tradition which says that Carlo Fontana sent the project, was declined by Hans Bernhard Schlereth, whose investigations of 1826 laid the foundation for all future research concerning the building history of the basilica.[2] It was also rejected by Otto Albert Weigmann, who reviewed the events of the planning and building history at the beginning of our century in his ground-breaking work on the Dientzenhofer family of architects (1902, republished in 1979).[3] Weigmann denied the rumors that Dientzenhofer used plans by Carlo Fontana and insisted that Dientzenhofer made the designs for the church himself.[4]

Karl Freckmann, who devoted a monograph to the building (1928) associated the scheme of its groundplan with the "innumerable" variants of the Roman basilica of St. Peter's, specifically its "followers" in central Europe, the Salzburg cathedral, the church of the Theatines in Munich, and the Hauger Stiftskirche in Würzburg.[5] All of these churches are Latin cross basilicas with domes above the crossing, but beyond these typological generalities, none of them shares the specific features of the ground plan or elevation with the cathedral in Fulda.

Frieda Dettweiler's dissertation of 1927 about the stucco decoration in Fulda cathedral and its authors, published simultaneously with Freckmann's monograph, moved the search for Roman connections a considerable step ahead, because she associated the interior decoration at Fulda with the "more severe style" of Carlo Fontana and his followers.[6] Further, Dettweiler pointed specifically to Francesco Fontana's church of SS. Apostoli in Rome (1702-1714) for the fomation of the nave vault and the shape of the lateral chapels; she observed that SS. Apostoli originated almost simultaneously with Dientzenhofer's church in Fulda. Dettweiler thereby identified a building which, as we shall see below, is of considerable importance for our discussion. She also published a record of payment dated 19 June, 1706, for the transportation of a "Stieftsbauw Model" from Rome, for which the *Canonico* Nicolaus von Hornik in Frankfurt received remuneration.[7] This very illuminating archival contribution, however, remained surprisingly inconsequential for a long period. When Coudenhove-Erthal cited a passage from Lione Pascoli's *Vita* of Carlo Fontana to the effect that the architect had made a design for the cathedral in Fulda which so pleased the bishop there that he commissioned a model from him,[8] he was evidently unaware of Dettweiler's document. Coudenhove-Erthal concluded that Pascoli's statement "must contain some truth" but that it could only relate to certain elements of the interior decoration. He referred to the altar in the chapel of the Holy Virgin, which though executed by local masters, he suggested should be part of Fontana's oeuvre because of the motif of the crown carried by angels, which reminded him of Carlo's altar in S. Maria in Traspontina (1674).[9] The chapel in Fulda extends from the end of the southern aisle as a "mirror image" of the sacristy on the opposite side (fig. 129).

Amazingly little of what was accomplished by scholars before and around 1930, besides the information regarding the bare bone facts of the building history, has found entry into the literature dealing with our monument.

Hans Gerhard Franz, who re-approached the oeuvre of the Dientzenhofer family within the context of his book on Baroque architecture in Bohemia and its impact on Germany (1963), maintained that Johann Dientzenhofer developed the plan for the cathedral in Fulda after the model of Borromini's S. Giovanni in Laterano.[10] The rhythmic bay system of the nave of S. Giovanni is certainly a feature both churches have in common. But the handling is conspicuously different in the Lateran basilica where the niches in tabernacles alternate with the arched openings instead of the trabeated ones in the narrow intervals in Fulda, which occur only in Borromini's projects for S. Giovanni.

For bibliographical material on Fulda, Eberhard Hempel (1965) refers the reader to Max Hauttmann's book on ecclesiastical architecture of the Baroque period in Bavaria, Suevia and Franconia (1921), and also insists that Dientzenhofer was dependent on Borromini's Lateran Basilica.[11]

Hempel was followed by Christian Norberg-Schulz (*Late Baroque and Rococo Architecture*, 1972), who called the cathedral in Fulda rather derogatorily "a somewhat conventional building."[12] Anthony Blunt (1982) mentioned Fulda among the commissions which reached Carlo Fontana from Vienna and Prague, but were not carried out. Concerning the shape of the cathedral, he credited Dientzenhofer with having achieved a "maximum of Roman gravitas" under the constraints imposed by an earlier building. Blunt criticized only the barrel vault which is subdivided by arches that alternate with "the deep penetrations for the clerestroy windows."[13] In his new inventory of monuments in Fulda, Erwin Sturm (1984) passes over the name of Carlo Fontana in silence,[14] and the same was the case in the earlier survey by Ludwig Pralle (1980).[15]

Our brief survey of the literature concerning the cathedral in Fulda can be concluded with a look into the most recent edition of George Dehio's *Handbuch der Deutschen Kunstdenkmäler* (Hessen, 1982), which for the question of typological precedents offers only the familiar reference to the Roman basilicas in the Gesù tradition and St. Peter's.[16] It amazes the reader, however, with the statement that a model of the dome of St. Peter's was received in Fulda, an apparent misunderstanding or arbitrary interpretation of the eighteenth-century sources, possibly the document published by Frieda Dettweiler.[17]

Within this context we observe a considerable variety of answers concerning the origin of the scheme for the cathedral in Fulda. There is not even unaminity about the question whether or not the church can be directly associated with Roman prototypes, or should be linked to the tradition of churches in Germany already dependent on them. This confused situation therefore suggests a re-examination of the material from the beginning. It is convenient to approach first the cardinal question of the model sent from Rome: do the two sources refer to the same model, and if so, what did it represent? What role can be attributed to it within the context of the building history?

Pascoli tells us no more than that subsequent to the submission of drawings for the church in Fulda, Carlo Fontana was commissioned to provide a model for the Prince Abbot.[18] The fact that a model was requested from the architect and about three decades after Fontana's death Pascoli still mentioned it with considerable emphasis, does sound as though he had rather precise information. This might also indicate that it was not only a drawn project which had been submitted before, but a wooden model to be visualized as fairly elaborate and certainly not insignificant in size. However, we cannot be sure whether it represented the entire church or only part of it. The hypothesized "respectable" size alone contains no sufficient clue to the answer to our question. We know, for example, that small scale clay models showing the entire basilica of St. Peter's were made in Michelangelo's time, as well as the famous large scale model for the projected dome.[19]

Models for entire buildings, even for rather extensive groups of structures, were produced by the school and followers of Carlo Fontana during his lifetime and after his death. The most notable example is the competition for the new sacristy of St. Peter's of 1715, in which Filippo Juvarra played the leading role. Actually, the model submitted by Antonio Canevari resembles a church rather than a sacristy.[20] It shows a domed building on the ground plan of a longitudinal oval which, like the cathedral in Fulda, is conceived as a free-standing building that is attached only at the rear to an adjoining building group in the shape of a deep rectangle. To the same category belongs Juvarra's famous model for the Superga in Turin of 1716.[21] Such models were also used in central Europe, and those requested from Balthasar Neumann for the Abbey Church in Münsterschwarzach (1727) and the pilgrimage sancturary of Vierzehnheiligen (1744) are perhaps the best known examples.[22]

Other types of portable models which were in use include wooden projects for the façade, such as Fausto Rughesi's model of 1593 for the front of S. Maria in Vallicella,[23] or closer in date, the façade model of 1696 by Carlo Fontana's nephew Girolamo for the cathedral in Frascati (fig. 127).[24]

In fact, Frieda Dettweiler suggested that the model mentioned in her document of 1706 referred to a dome.[25] This conclusion was based on the relatively advanced construction of the cathedral in Fulda at the time (see below) and also on the fact that Dientzenhofer was then still at the beginning of his career; as mentioned above, structures with a dome above their crossing were still unusual in the area around Fulda when he was appointed *Stiftsbaumeister* in 1700.[26]

Concerning Fulda, the possibility of a model for one of the chapels or altars, as suggested by Coudenhove-Erthal, certainly cannot be ruled out:[27] Fontana's former assistant Nicola Michetti produced one - complete with the altar and interior decoration, including the altarpiece for the Cappella Rospigliosi-Pallavicini at S. Francesco a Ripa in Rome (ca. 1710, fig. 151).[28] A comparable model for a still unidentified chapel or chapel vestibule, apparently of Roman origin, exists in the Cooper-Hewitt Museum of Design in New York (period of Pope Gregory XV, 1621-1623).[29]

The entry of 19 June 1706, in the expense account for the artisans who worked on the cathedral in Fulda, published by Dettweiler, speaks rather unequivocally, however, of a "Stieftsbauw Model" - a model for the monastery church itself - which interpreted literally would be compatible with the passage in Pascoli's *Vita* of Carlo Fontana. Furthermore, as there is only one model from Rome mentioned in the list of expenses, it is most likely that the two sources refer to the same piece, unless evidence to the contrary can be presented. Therefore the account entry and Pascoli's statement seem to be mutually supportive. Finally, the amount spent for its transportation (44 fl. 16 kr. 5 pf.) would exclude a small sketch in wax or clay and speak for a model of considerable dimensions.[30] But again this does not offer the desired criteria for establishing conclusive evidence. To come closer to the heart of the matter we should try to relate the documentary note regarding the model to the well documented chronology of the planning and building history.

The foundation stone was laid as early as 23 April 1704, but on 3 February 1705, the Prince Abbot requested Dientzenhofer to submit new designs.[31] On the other hand, a decision must have been made without delay, as work on the construction proceeded quickly; during the summer of 1707 the level of the main cornice of the nave was reached. As Dettweiler tried to establish from the book-keeping practices at Fulda, a model paid for in June, 1706, would not have arrived before March or April of the same year; too late, she felt, to allow for comprehensive changes with respect to the organization of the building as a whole. She therefore concluded that it could have related to only part of the church, and that Dientzenhofer was asked by his patron to provide himself with advice for the construction of the dome.[32]

The arguments to be gained from a review of the building chronology, however, seem to be almost equally supportive of one of the other possibilitites mentioned: a model for the façade, one of the chapels, or some of the altars. On the other hand, since the model arrived approximately a year and a half before the nave had reached the level of the main cornice, it may not have been too late for such a model to affect the articulation of the interior.

Since the term "Stieftsbauw Model" seems to imply that it represented the entire church rather than only part of it, it must have shown at least enough of the structure to be perceived by the record-keeper as a *pars pro toto*; otherwise he certainly would have entered it in the records under a different title. We might then think of the dome or the façade, the shape of which was determined only about 20 April 1709, after the completion of the roof structures. At that time it was contracted to utilize the inferior parts of the medieval bell towers for those of the new church.[33] The use of the expression "Stieftsbauw Model" in this case would pre-suppose that the portions of the building which were still under debate and required clarification, were for the purpose of clear demonstration connected with the model of the entire church, which at that time was already well underway, but possibly still allowed latitude for substantial modifications.

Since the shipment of a model from Rome implies the possibility of a substantial interference on the part of a Roman architect, we now have to consider the corollary question of the date on which the original plans were submitted to the Prince Abbot. Furthermore, as Pascoli would have it, was Carlo Fontana really the author, and did these plans and the model have any effect on the actual course of events?

Such plans could have been submitted on various occasions. For instance, at the beginning (before 4 September 1700, the date of Dientzenhofer's appointment as the architect), or about a year later when on 18 July 1701, Dientzenhofer's plans were sent to Probst Friedrich von Buttler at Thulba for inspection by the latter's architect, whose name is not mentioned. He is referred to simply as the "Franciscan architect,"[34] and was even considered for the position of director or the construction of the church in Fulda. At that time he was not even the only alternative for the already appointed *Stiftsbaumeister*; other architects are mentioned, evidently rather "unknown quantities" since almost none of them could be identified.

Plans from abroad also could have arrived sometime before the foundation stone was laid, 23 April 1704, but the arrival was most likely before 3 February 1705, the date on which Dientzenhofer was asked to submit new plans. These he presented in four different versions with staggered levels of anticipated costs, varying between 33,000 and 55,200 *Rheintaler*. His projects included options for a wooden dome, a dome of brick masonry, one for a church with increased height and width, and most expensive, one with flanking columns.[35]

It is at this juncture that a plan from Rome might have superseded the long array of earlier projects, none of which seems to have met the expectations of Adalbert von Schleifras. The considerable number of these suggestions, and the number of architects selected for consultations, which included even minor ones, is revealing for the kind of patronage practiced by the Prince Abbot at Fulda. Strangely enough, he seems to have insisted upon consultations with experts whose calibre of judgment was probably much inferior to that of Johann Dientzenhofer, who was already in his service. For the complicated character of his progress regarding decisions, he might best be compared to his peer, the Prince Bishop Johann Philip Franz von Schönborn in Würzburg.[36] Dientzenhofer would later serve him (beginning in 1720, as "Bambergischer Hofbaumeister") as assistant to Balthasar Neumann in the building of the Residenz, and on other projects.[37] But notwithstanding certain inhibitions, both patrons were evidently endowed with sufficient judgment to allow those projects to prevail which we now accept with appreciation.

Now we should respond to our basic question: was the plan realized for the cathedral in Fulda the one which came from Rome, reportedly devised by Carlo Fontana, which seems to have been translated into the model recorded in 1706? Or is the invention of the cathedral as it stands now either entirely or at least partially to be given to Johann Dientzenhofer as the architect responsible for the execution?

To seek for a strictly alternative answer - Carlo Fontana or Johann Dientzenhofer - seems to be hazardous: the very traditional, to a degree even *retardataire* church in Fulda is characterized as a basilica by the rhythmical bay system which is almost as atypical for Fontana as it is for Dientzenhofer. The latter's abbey church at Banz (1710-1716, fig.142), which associates itself with the Guarinesque tradition transmitted to him by Bohemian architects,[38] is absolutely independent from the Italianate basilicas of the corresponding period. One would hardly think of his name in connection with the cathedral in Fulda, had he not been documented as its architect from the beginning to the end of the planning and construction periods. Also, among the numerous drawings and projects by Carlo Fontana that have come to light since earlier scholars on Fulda ruled him out as the possible inventor of the scheme, there is virtually none which shows any affinity with our church.[39]

Does this observation then discredit Pascoli as a source with regard to Fulda? Such a radical, and still premature conclusion, however, would prevent us from recognizing what could turn out to be the identifiable kernel of truth in his statement.

Among all architects active in Rome at the beginning of the *Settecento*, one in particular stands out because of his authorship of a sumptuous basilica in which he once again subscribes to the traditional device of the rhythmic bay system: Francesco Fontana, whose church of SS. Apostoli was already mentioned by Frieda Dettweiler. The planimetric affinity between SS. Apostoli in Rome and the basilica in Fulda becomes even more convincing if one compares the only known plan of the eighteenth century for the church in Fulda (fig. 132),[40] with Francesco Fontana's plan in the Uffizi or its engraved rendering by Domenico de Rossi (fig. 131).[41] Apart from the different spacing of the pilasters, which in Fulda are arranged to allow for the trabeated passages surmounted by Johann Artari's statues in the high niches between them, the configuration is absolutely analogous. Comparable also are the high arches (fig. 130) which open up the access to the side chapels. They are connected with each other by intermediate bays to form aisles that are continued beyond the transept along the choir and lead to the sacristy on the left and to the symmetrically planned chapel of the Holy Virgin on the right (fig. 136). The attached full columns flanking the passages in the intervening spaces between the neighboring chapels which serve as supports for the domes of each of the side chapels, appear individually related to SS. Apostoli (fig. 135).[42] From there also the bridges above these passages (at Fulda, limited only to the junctures of the aisles with the transept) seem to have been carried over. The alignment of the spaces accompanying the nave is particularly effective in Fulda through the perspective effect, which in fact, recalls in general the aisles in S. Giovanni in Laterano[43] even though the use of full columns as well as the elliptical domes distinguish the situation in Fulda from that of the

Lateran basilica. However, in one further respect our church unmistakably reveals a close familiarity with the interior of S. Giovanni: where the corners of the nave next to the interior façade are blunted in a fashion similar to that which we observe in Fulda at the ends of the transept, and where the monks' choir is separated from the nave behind the high altar.[44] The stilted arches which surmount the passages between the side chapels are anticipated in Rainaldi's churches in Rome,[45] whereas the trabeated openings which lead into them from the nave are likely to stem again either from Borromini himself, who employed this device in the Cappella dei Re Magi in the Palazzo di Propaganda Fide,[46] or from Giovanni Antonio de Rossi, who followed Borromini in his church of S. Pantaleo (fig. 134).[47] Above the level of the main cornice, a connection with Fulda might be detectable in the form and arrangement of the windows placed directly beneath the "penetrations" of the barrel vault, but the absence of any decoration or articulation of the vault in Fulda does not suggest further comparisons with the Roman prototype.[48]

The configuration of the inner shell of the dome, which is subdivided by coupled ribs in continuation of the doubled pilasters of the drum, and perforated by oculi of diminishing sizes, echoes the inner dome of Fischer von Erlach's Collegiate church in Salzburg (figs. 137 and 138).[49] The number of circular openings surrounding the oculus in the center is limited there to four. Their increase to sixteen (in a certain way precedented by Enrico Zuccalli's dome of the Theatine church in Munich, 1674-1675)[50] as well as their careful differentiation in size, leave us with the impression that the architect in Fulda elaborated in this respect on prototypes which continued the Roman tradition north of the Alps.

This re-proposes our original question whether or not the scheme of the cathedral in Fulda was originally designed by an architect for whom training in Rome was essential or even indispensable (as it had been for Fischer von Erlach) or by an artist who was Roman himself. This latter observation, as well as the eclectic handling of Roman motifs, which can be traced back to different sources, seems almost to speak for the first possibility, Johann Dientzenhofer. Such a conclusion, however, would disregard some of our earlier observations and negate the possibility of any impact of the well documented project sent from Rome. What should be examined more closely at this point is the circumstance that the material sent from Rome was subjected to modifications, either before or during the construction, a situation that can also be observed elsewhere.[51]

What can be established is the "Roman" character of the planimetric scheme as represented on the ground plan surviving from the building period of the cathedral (fig. 132) and had we no knowledge about its destination, it could almost be mistaken for a design related to the planning history of SS. Apostoli.

It is therefore necessary to consider this plan under the aspect of condition and draughtsmanship to obtain an opinion concerning its author.[52] The project is cut on all sides, drawn with pen on white paper (44,2 x 33,3 cm) and shows rather dark gray wash to indicate the masonry of the wall; pink wash to denote the altars and the pulpit. Why the plan was reduced in such a way that the façade and monks choir, along with the sacristy and chapel of the Holy Virgin were cut off completely, is a question we cannot answer. However, the walls of the chapels flanking the towers seem to have been respected. It is unlikely that this was done when the plan was connected with Schlereth's manuscript, because it could easily have been folded for that purpose. Therefore it must have happened earlier, and the possibility cannot be discarded *a priori* that the cutting took place when modifications for the façade and monk's choir were considered, though it would have been more natural and quite in conformity with the practices of draughtsmanship to paste flaps showing the alternative solutions over those portions that were considered for modification.[53]

The rather dark gray tones of the washes distinguish this drawing from the fairly light ones found on Fontana's plans or those from his studio. Washes of the latter kind were frequent in Rome and elsewhere throughout the first half of the eighteenth century.[54] Therefore Weigmann is probably right in observing not only an affinity of draughtsmanship with Dientzenhofer's plans for the Probstei Holzkirchen but also that the "quality of the paper" is the same.[55]

Does the establishment of Dientzenhofer's authorship of the ground plan in Fulda allow us to credit him with the invention of the scheme? There is still one detail to be considered: the scale of the plan which is indicated in a unit of measurement still to be identified. Assuming hypothetically that the scale is given in *Palmi Romani*, the nave on the plan would measure 110 *palmi* from the interior façade to the crossing, which equals 24,20 m and corresponds rather precisely to the 23,00 m which is the length on the measured plan by Freckmann (fig. 129).[56] Therefore it can be taken for

granted that the plan, if not drawn in Italy (which seems very unlikely after Weigmann's observations) copied or adjusted a no longer extant plan which might have been the project sent from Rome to Fulda initially, as was recorded by Pascoli. Since the planimetric scheme does not relate to any of Carlo Fontana's known buildings or projects, but shows such a close affinity to Francesco Fontana's SS. Apostoli, we have to assume that Pascoli's information is imprecise only so far as his having recorded the name of Carlo instead of Francesco. Furthermore, it is also possible that the original commission had been given to Carlo, who passed it on, as he did on other occasions, to his son Francesco; Pascoli could have been unaware of the situation which had occurred in affiliated studios. All things considered, we can hardly go wrong if we conclude that the basic scheme for the cathedral in Fulda, as represented on the surviving drawing, can be attributed to Francesco Fontana, whose premature death in 1708 put an end to a promising, though fairly conservative development. Furthermore, it is now almost certain that the model ordered from Rome was based on this plan, which is the one that became definitive for the construction.

Therefore Dientzenhofer's role must have been limited to the adjustment of a predisposed plan. We can credit him only with certain modifications, such as the simplified articulation and ornamentation of the interior, and perhaps details such as the trabeated passages and the statuary niches above them, or the treatment of the inner shell of the dome (fig. 138). In their decision to preserve or incorporate the medieval twin towers, the Prince Abbot in Fulda and his architect Dientzenhofer might have received encouragement from Rome, where an analogous procedure had been employed in connection with the façade of the cathedral dedicated to St. Peter in Frascati (fig. 127). Designed by Francesco Fontana's cousin, Girolamo, it was nearing completion when Dientzenhofer was in Italy.[57] The façade articulation in Fulda with its widely spaced columns in both tiers as the support for the concluding pediment (fig. 128) might have been inspired by this "Roman" precedent which was terminated just in time for the Holy Year of 1700. The general scheme also, with the church as the major element projecting forward from a rectangular building block into the open area, connects well with the Roman tradition, even though this situation was preconstituted in Fulda.[58]

* * * * *

Assessing Dientzenhofer's role in Fulda, we are now able to conclude that concerning the church, his position was more or less limited to the adjustment of the project sent from Rome, provided by Francesco Fontana for a building task in Germany. The original project, though in a fragmented state, has survived in Dientzenhofer's copy. No doubt Dientzenhofer handled himself with considerable ease and skill, taking advantage of any leeway as the building construction proceeded.

We can now raise the question concerning the authorship of the major element of the interior decoration, the high altar, which also establishes a clearly discernable connection with Rome (figs. 139, 140a). Did Johann Dientzenhofer's contribution as the *Stiftsbaumeister* in Fulda again exhaust itself in the adjustments of a preconceived scheme sent from Rome? Did he design it, modify it, or simply supervise its construction?

The crowning element of the altar, with the powerful scrolls of the S-curved ribs which in Fulda support a statue of the Assumption of the Virgin by Johann Neudecker the Elder, undoubtedly has its origin in the Baldacchino of St. Peter's.[59] It rests on the heavy entablature of a colonnade which consists of four dark marble columns on high pedestals, receding in conformity to a concave plan (figs. 129, 140b) with a wider interval in the center. Against the lateral intervals of the colonnade two columns, set with their bases diagonally to the altar front, have been positioned in a more forward plane. In this way two groups consisting of three columns each are established to form an architectural frame for the opening in the center.[60] In front of it a spatial enclosure is created by the two columns placed underneath the projections of the entablature which breaks forward like a pair of open tongs.

Coudenhove-Erthal, addressing himself to the question of the authorship, considered an association with Carlo Fontana very questionable.[61] But Carlo's son Francesco had designed a comparable structure for the altar of S. Antonio in SS. Apostoli. Of this project, which recalls the tradition of Palladio's curved colonnade behind the *altare maggiore* of the Redentore, and Bernini's high altar in S. Paolo Maggiore in Bologna (begun 1634), unfortunately nothing more than the ground plan has survived (fig. 131); consonant with the circular form of the still existing apse of the transept of the earlier church, we observe a semicircular colonnade in Francesco's plan which is flanked on the

outer sides by a pair of columns that are attached to piers.[62] But on the whole the affinity is strong enough to suggest at least the possibility that the project for the high altar, as Coudenhove-Erthal assumed was the case for the altar of the Holy Virgin in the chapel dedicated to her, came from Rome, and that Francesco Fontana was its author.[63] On the other hand, a much stronger kinship is to be observed with Jean de Champaigne's high altar of SS. Trinità dei Monti (fig. 146). There the four columns which are engaged to curved walls with flat pilasters attached to them enclose an oval "stage" reminiscent of Bernini's Cappella Cornaro, which was created to enshrine a sculptural group of God the Father and the Man of Sorrows supported by a cloud and surrounded by a group of angels. Instead the space is now occupied by a voluminous tabernacle of the 19th century. For the crowning feature, a group of angels carrying the cross was envisaged.[64]

The altar in SS. Trinità dei Monti had served as a sourse of inspriration on earlier occasions. Sedlmayr pointed out that its construction took place while Fischer von Erlach was in Rome in 1675, and it inspired his idea for the high altar of Mariazell in 1692.[65] Even closer to the prototype is the Mausoleum for Ferdinand II in Graz (1695-1697) which had been commissioned by the Emperor Leopold I.[66] The latter shares with de Champaigne's altar the scenic arrangement of the columns, and directly anticipates the use of the motif in Fulda derived from the Baldacchino in St. Peter's in Rome, as the crowning feature for a colonnade modelled after the high altar in SS. Trinità dei Monti. The altar in Fulda differs in one important respect from the altar in SS. Trinità, as well as from the two designs by Fischer von Erlach which were destined to embrace scuptural decoration displayed in scenographic form. The columns on the rear side of the altars in Rome and Graz are clearly employed as a screening device to enclose the scenic arrangement in the center from behind. In Fulda, however, the spacing is such as to allow for a free view through the superstructure of the high altar (figs. 139 and 140a) right into the monks' choir (and from there back into the church (fig. 140b) where the prospect is terminated at the distance of two and a half bays by the altar painting above the mensa in the apse (a copy after Rubens' *Last Supper* (fig. 141).[67]

The controlled view through the opening of an architectural frame above the altar to a distantly located altarpiece, has again been achieved with an increased degree of complete illusionistic perfection in the monastery church at Banz (fig. 142) of 1710-1716, which Dientzenhofer accomplished subsequent to the church in Fulda.[68] The high altar separates the monks' choir exactly like the one in Fulda and has been erected on the site precisely where it appears on the ground plan of the church, a drawing most likely by Dientzenhofer himself (fig. 145).[69] The high altar was carried out in conformity with a model produced by the sculptor Balthasar Esterbauer, who also executed the altar in the monks' choir, where the painting, as in Fulda, fits perfectly into the frame of the high altar for the spectator entering the church. The contract with the sculptor (27 September 1714) precludes any doubt that these works were realized under the supervision of Dientzenhofer.[70] On the strength of this analogy and because of his position, he is the most likely candidate for the authorship of the high altar in Fulda which was constructed by the sculptor Johann Neudecker the Elder.[71]

Both altars anticipate by several years the famous scenographically conceived altar compositions by the Asam brothers in Weltenburg, begun 1721 (fig. 152)[72] and Rohr, 1719-1723 (fig. 154).[73] About the time of the origin of the altars in Fulda and Banz, Cosmas Damian, who won first prize in the First Class of painting of the *Concorso Clementino* of 1713 at the Accademia di San Luca, was in Rome with his brother Egid Quirin.[74] They were probably studying the same sources which proved crucial for Johann's development after his sojourn in Rome about 1700. One of the major inspriations evidently came from Bernini, whose *Cathedra* in St. Peter's, visible within the "frame" provided by the twisted columns of the Baldacchino, offered a most spectacular example of a controlled view over a long distance which Dientzenhofer certainly could not have missed. But even earlier when Bernini had "removed" from its frame, so to speak, the altarpiece in the Cappella Raimondi at S. Pietro in Montorio to take advantage of laterally displayed light sources, and made it visible through an opening flanked by columns,[75] he had inaugurated a development ready to be used by Johann Dientzenhofer. The German architect did so most successfully by drastically increasing the distance with the help of perspective devices which he probably adopted from Andrea Pozzo. It will be remembered that Pozzo carried Bernini's device to the north at the beginning of the eighteenth century when he remodelled the Jesuit church in Vienna (1703-1709).[76] Finished in 1705, the chapel of the high altar is separated from the nave by two colossal columns. They frame the view towards the altar, above which the painting of the *Assumption of the Virgin* is placed against the wall of a "light box"[77] in the

fashion of the ones used by Bernini in the Cappella Raimondi and for the Cornaro Chapel.[78]

But even with the intermediate step offered by Pozzo in Vienna and through his illusionistic accomplishments elsewhere,[79] the altars in Fulda and Banz are a notable advancement beyond their precursor within the category of altars with perspectively guided vistas. Framed views as such and even those conducted across a considerable distance with or without the employment of flanking columns were customary in Rome throughout the sixteenth and seventeenth centuries. By means of the brilliant employment of foreshortening devices, the Galleria Spada is the most outstanding example (fig. 158).[80] The very common orientation towards a fountain placed at the far end of a courtyard and visible through the entrance arch or along the channel of a corridor, offered analogous visual experiences. The analogy becomes perfect, especially when the fountain is framed like an altar, as is the case in Carlo Fontana's arrangement in the cortile of the Palazzo Massimo (end of the seventeenth century, fig. 148) which resembles the superstructure on his numerous designs for the high altar of S. Spirito dei Napolitani.[81] Carlo Fontana was engaged in the design of perspectively controlled views, for example, when he transformed the small rectangular window in the central niche of the Fontana Paola into a wide arched opening to offer a glance into the botanical garden, as can be verified in Giacomo de Rossi's engraving of 1724.[82]

An optical experiment of a different kind was made by Fontana in the Baptismal Chapel of St. Peter's, where he opened the sail vault with a transverse oval oculus and created the illusion of a drum in which the window is located above the chapel in the outer wall of the church.[83] The high altar in Fulda also brings to mind the project for the Fontana di Trevi in the Kunstbibliothek in Berlin (attributable to Mattia de Rossi rather than to Carlo Fontana) where a colonnade is used in a similar way to screen off an open space which exists there between two palaces. The central interval, however, regardless of the decoration that might have been envisaged behind it, was conceived as a backdrop for the statue of Neptune to be placed in front of the screen, rather than for a specific object to be viewed through the opening in the center.[84]

More conventional, at least in principle, than the "scenic" effect created through the enlargement of the window in the central interval of the Fontana Paola, is his altar in S. Maria dei Miracoli (1677).[85] The structure (fig. 149) consists of full framing columns, and appears at the end of a rather deep choir which might be likened to a visual corridor, in particular since Fontana took special care to emphasize the scenic qualitites of the sculptural arrangement. Raggi's group of angels carrying the miraculous image of the Madonna is indirectly illuminated from above through a carefully devised space left between the pediment and the apse wall.[86] The glory of the Holy Spirit in the vault and the angels holding the cross supplement the scenographic composition very effectively and was a motif copied, for example, in the Asam church in Munich.[87]

One of Carlo Fontana's most successful attempts to employ the device of the conducted view is his Cappella Cybo in S. Maria del Popolo.[88] The field of vision is limited there by means of the coupled columns flanking the crossing to ensure that the attention of the spectator entering the chapel is concentrated on Maratti's altarpiece of the *Immaculate Conception* (fig. 153).

In his altar designs for Mariazell and his altar in the Mausoleum of Ferdinand II in Graz, Fischer von Erlach, as we have seen, followed his Roman precedents rather closely and in principle did not supercede Carlo Fontana's conceptual basis. To so do was left to Johann Dientzenhofer. Encouraged by altars in the tradition of Bernini's Cappella Raimondi and Fontana's experiment with the Fontana Paola on the Janiculcum, he fused what had been successfully attempted there with the powerful experience of the vision of the *Cathedra* appearing behind the high altar in St. Peter's.[89]

Before the Asam brothers arrived on the artistic scene in southern Germany, Dientzenhofer made the audacious experiment of "perforating" the high altars in Fulda and Banz (figs. 139 and 142) to open up the vista towards a distant perspective goal. What seems to have been less important to him was the scenographic reality which Bernini and, on occasion, Carlo Fontana had achieved through sculptural configurations.

The Asam brothers accomplished the complete scenographic illusion by employing the perspectively controlled far distant view realized by Dientzenhofer. In Weltenburg, the structure of the baldachin or tabernacle surmounted by a statue of the *Assumption*, as in Fulda, has assumed the shape and purpose of a screen for the "light chamber"[90] which has the sole and explicit function of housing the equestrian statue of

St. George. It can be perceived underneath the opening between the spiralled flanking columns, which (again like the situation in Bernini's Cappella Raimondi) is ordinarily reserved for an altarpiece. The traditional retable in Weltenburg has been replaced by an object which could be defined as "painterly sculpture" in the Berninian sense (cf. the Cappella Cornaro) or perhaps more appropriately as a "three-dimensional" painting.

Important precedents leading from the Italian tradition directly to the high altar in Weltenburg are Pozzo's *altare maggiore* decoration in S. Francesco Saverio in Mondovi (1676, fig. 150), where the statue of the titular saint visible beneath a tabernacle in the shape of a triumphal arch has been painted on a luminous foil to indicate "openness."[91] Even closer is one of the projects by Pozzo for the high altar in the Gesù in Rome, in which the artist "opened" the apse behind the altar to allow the spectator to look into an adjoining room which seems to exist on a higher level behind the mensa as we can find it in Rohr (fig. 154).[92] The result would have been quite analogous to the situation in Weltenburg, notwithstanding the use of a different medium.

In the Stiftskirche at Rohr, the way is opened towards the attainment of full scenographic reality. What confronts us behind the high altar is a chapel articulated in the customary fashion with full columns.[93] But the level of this space has been raised, as in Fulda and in Pozzo's Gesù project, to that of a stage. It has been prepared for the scene of the *Assumption of the Virgin* realized with lifesize three dimensional statues, which by means of the ecstatic quality of their gestures produce the effect of a spectacle taking place "live." In their apparent animation, the statues of the disciples surrounding the empty sarcophagus which is again elevated on a stepped base, assume the role of living actors. The theatricality of the composition culminates in the respresentation of the Virgin Mary. In her pose ascending toward Heaven, especially from a distance, she appears to be raised by supernatural power rather than lifted by the angels underneath the cloud at her feet.[94]

The degree of reality achieved in this altarpiece is also largely due to the exceedingly well considered contrast between the strongly moving figures and the strictly architecturally conceived sanctuary, which could have been designed in exactly the same fashion for an ordinary chapel independent from any concept of scenic performances. The columns at the entrance, for example, respond to the familiar function like *quinte* of hiding from the spectator what he is not supposed to see — the laterally disposed light sources for indirect illumination.[95] The receding columns at the far end of the space conduct one's attention to the representation in the center. The means employed are quite comparable to those used by Carlo Fontana in his Cappella Cybo (fig. 153), and certainly not by coincidence. Egid Quirin Asam obviously did not fail to study it thoroughly when he was in Rome. Carlo Fontana was still alive when the Asam brothers arrived in 1711, and they could have found in him, as well as in Filippo Juvarra, who had finished his Cappella Antamoro in S. Girolamo della Caritá in 1710,[96] a congenial preceptor for the demonstration of the way in which, after the death of the great master Bernini, the three arts could be interrelated successfully to create a unified effect which had been anticipated by the architect in his designs.

It can also be taken for granted that the Asam brothers were well acquainted with the "complete work of art" predisposed in the above mentioned model by Carlo Fontana's assistant Nicola Michetti of 1710 for the Cappella Rospigliosi-Pallavicini in S. Francesco a Ripa (fig. 151).[97] The arrangement of the double twisted columns engaged to frame the round-headed altarpiece might well have had an impact on the comparable employment of twisted columns in Weltenburg, next to the opening behind the main altar. And it is further probable that during their sojourn in Rome they did not miss the opportunity to observe the Rospigliosi-Pallavicini chapel, under construction at the time in conformity to a somewhat modified plan, which was to become the most luxuriously decorated chapel of its period.

Johann Dientzenhofer, who had been in Rome before the Asam brothers and was equipped with the perspective knowledge obtained from Andrea Pozzo,[98] opened the avenue for their arrival with his experiments at Fulda and Banz. For this kind of anticipatory function he seems to deserve more credit than has usually been granted to him. Whereas for the interior elevation of the cathedral in Fulda only minor modifications were possible, the task of the arrangement of the high altar gave him the scope he needed to break new ground.

But the perspective scenography in the fashion developed by Johann Dientzenhofer which is visible through the opening of the screen was not entirely superseded by the more realistic variant which the Asam brothers and their followers like François Cuvilliés and Joachim Dietrich brought to perfection. Dietrich's high altar in the Priory church in Diessen, perhaps the most spectacular work in the following of the Asam, already manifests a certain fusion of both categories; instead of sculptural decoration "on the stage" the prospect for the spectator entering the church (for most of the year), is again concluded by a painted representation of the *Assumption* (by Balthasar August Albrecht, 1738, fig. 155). However, the fact that the painting can be lowered like a backdrop according to the calendar of liturgical celebrations to change scenes composed of individual figures or representations painted on flat surfaces showing the birth, crucifixion, burial (fig 156), and resurrection of Christ, brings the scenic altar in closest proximity to stage practices.[99] Parenthetically, it also recalls our earlier work in this tradition, Andrea Pozzo's above mentioned altarpiece in S. Francesco Saverio at Mondovi (fig. 150), where a change in representation is possible by simply turning the retable.[100] The potential of this rather rudimentary "invention" — less than a century later — has reached the full climax of its development in Diessen.

François Cuvilliés, who designed the altar in Diessen, was certainly very much aware of Johann Dientzenhofer's experiments. And also an artist like Ferdinand Schor was probably directly indebted to Dientzenhofer for the inspiration for his high altar in S. Maria de Victoria in Prague of 1723. Once again the powerful effect of the spiral columns of the altar structure impresses the spectator, guiding his view upwards, but at the same time focussing his attention on a painted altarpiece set back in the center of the apse and brightly illuminated by laterally disposed windows.[101]

Further south, again in Italy, the scheme of the perspectively controlled view applied to an altar, is once more and very favorably, represented about 1740 in Benedetto Alfieri's *altare maggiore* of the Basilica del Sacro Monte at Verallo Sesia (Piedmont; fig. 157).[102] The central interval of the concave colonnade which consists of four columns, is opened wide to allow a view of the brightly illuminated fresco of the *Dormition of the Holy Virgin* which appears at the far end of the choir. Very congenial to Bernini's creation in S. Andrea al Quirinale, the painted figure of the deceased behind the altar is on a higher level sculpturally "resuscitated" to increase the degree of scenic reality. In direct analogy with Fulda, even though not quite as effectively, the statue of the Virgin Mary (in stucco above the altar) ascending to Heaven is conceived as the culminating feature of the entire structure of the altar. In this case a direct dependency on Fulda cannot be postulated, but without doubt it was the prototype designed by Johann Dientzenhofer for the cathedral in Fulda - distinguished as the burial place of St. Bonifatius - which set the fashion for subsequent monuments.

With his next project, the monastery church in Banz, Dientzenhofer demonstrated to his patrons in Fulda that what was essential to him was not so much (as they seem to have thought) a model from Rome to follow, as the inspirational quality of the Roman experience as such. This was supplemented by that of the Guarinesque structures in Bohemia, which eventually had an even stronger impact on his development, unfortunately cut short by his early death in 1729.[103] Observed in the above context, Dientzenhofer emerges as a major creative force at the beginning of the eighteenth century in Germany, and as an architect whose full potential can only be imagined.

Hellmut Hager
The Pennsylvania State University

Notes

1. Otto Albert Weigmann, *Eine Bamberger Baumeisterfamilie um die Wende des 17. Jahrhunderts. Ein Beitrag zur Geschichte der Dientzenhofer*, Strassburg, 1902 (2nd ed., 1979) pp. 34 ff. For the letter of recommendation see O. A. Weigmann, op. cit., p. 35, note 2. Weigmann (p. 36) assumes that Dientzenhofer's sojourn in Italy lasted between six and eight months, with the date of his appointment in Fulda (4 September 1700) as the *terminus ante quem* for his return.

2. Franz Berhard Schlereth, *Der Dom und die vorigen Hauptkirchen in Fulda, geschichtlich und architektonisch dargestellt*, Ms. Fulda 1826 in the Hessische Landesbibliothek Fulda, 2 B68a; partial publication in: *Buchonia, Zeitschrift für vaterländische Geschichte*, vol. I, part 1, 1826, pp. 85-151; vol. II, part 2, 1827, pp. 148-208. See especially Ms. Fulda, p. 98, note a.

3. O. A. Weigmann, op. cit.

4. O. A. Weigmann, op. cit. pp. 136 ff.

5. Karl Freckmann, *Der Dom zu Fulda*, Augsburg, 1928, p. 14; see also pp. 42 ff.

6. Frieda Dettweiler, *Die Stuckarbeiten im Dome zu Fulda und ihre Meister*, Ph.D. diss. Frankfurt a. M., 1927, Fulda, 1928, p. 45.

7. F. Dettweiler, op. cit., p. 1, note 1; this document (see full citation below, note 30) was first mentioned by F. B. Schlereth, Ms. Fulda, op. cit. p. 98, note a. Nicolaus Hornik (or Horneck) in Frankfurt was employed by the Schönborn on a similar occasion and is mentioned in a letter of 20 January 1720, by Friedrich Karl in Vienna to Johann Philip Franz in Würzburg. Karl Lohmeyer, *Die Briefe Balthasar Neumanns*, Saarbrücken, Berlin, Leipzig, Stuttgart, 1921, p. 183, no. 32.

8. Lione Pascoli, *Vite de' pittori, scultori ed architetti moderni*, II, Rome, 1736, pp. 547 ff. Eduard Coudenhove-Erthal, *Carlo Fontana und die Architektur des römischen Spätbarocks*, Vienna, 1930, pp. 144 ff, pl. 28.

9. E. Coudenhove-Erthal, op. cit., pp. 145 ff. pl. 28. It might be added that the system of the wall articulation marked by an entablature rising to an arch above every second bay derives from Borromini's S. Maria dei Sette Dolori (cf. K. Freckmann, op. cit., pl. 21; E. Hempel, *Francesco Borromini*, Vienna, 1924, pls. 80 ff.). For the original function of the chapel and the date of the altar (1758) see below, note 63.

10. Heinrich Gerhard Franz, *Bauten und Baumeister der Barockzeit in Böhmen*, Leipzig, 1962, p. 162; cf. F. Dettweiler, op. cit., p. 10.

11. Max Hauttmann, *Geschichte der kirchlichen Baukunst in Bayern, Schwaben und Franken, 1550-1780*, Munich, Berlin, Leipzig, 1921, pp. 147 ff, pl. 12, II; Eberhard Hempel, *Baroque Art and Architecture in Central Europe*, Baltimore, Harmondsworth, 1965, pp. 149 ff, 327 note 8.

12. Christian Norberg-Schulz, *Late Baroque and Rococo Architecture*, New York, 1974, pp. 104 ff; 360 note 6.

13.	Anthony Blunt, *Baroque and Rococo, Architecture and Decoration*, New York and Cambridge, etc., 1982, pp. 175 ff, 265.

14.	Erwin Sturm, *Die Bauund Kunstdenkmäler der Stadt Fulda*, Fulda, 1984, p. 74.

15.	Ludwig Pralle, *Fulda Dom und Abteibezirk, Königstein im Taunus*, 1980

16.	George Dehio, *Handbuch der Deutschen Kunstdenkmäler Hessen.* Bearbeitet von Magnus Backes, Munich, 1982, pp. 295 ff.

17.	G. Dehio, ed. M. Backes, op. cit., p. 297.

18.	"Inventò trattando un disegno per la cattedrale di Fulda, e gli fu poi dal vescovo, cui molto piacque, commesso il modello. Altro ne mandò per certe rimesse, e stalle molto prima all' imperador Leopoldo, e gli alzò quando mori il catafalco nella chiesa dell' Anima." L. Pascoli, op. cit., II, pp. 547 ff.

19.	A scene painted by the artist Passignani of Michelangelo presenting his project to Pope Pius IV (about 1620) shows an example of an architectural model which might be classified as an "average size" model for an entire church. In Passignani's painting, only the model's façade is missing, which was probably detachable to allow views of the interior (see J. Ackerman, *The Architecture of Michelangelo* (Text and Plates), New York, 1961, p. 100, pls. 57a, 58a; and Catalogue, London, 1964, p. 100). Comparable was the lost model of Michelangelo's final project for S. Giovanni dei Fiorentini (1560) shown on its stand in the engraving of 1607 by Le Mercier, who also gives us the measurements: 9 1/2 *palmi romani* for the length and width and 7 for the height, which equals 2,03 and 1,54 m respectively (J. Ackerman, op. cit., Text and Plates, pp. 106 ff, pl. 71a). A Model of this size would certainly have been suitable for transportation, even across the Alps; however, one of somewhat smaller dimensions might be more likely for shipment all the way from Rome to Fulda. For architecture models in general, see Ludwig Heydenreich, "Architecturmodell," in *Reallexikon zur Deutschen Kunstgeschichte*, I, 1937, pp. 918-939.

20.	Hellmut Hager, *Filippo Juvarra e il concorso di modelli del 1715 bandito da Clemente XI per la nuova sacrestia di S. Pietro*, Rome, 1970, pp. 39 ff.

21.	Nino Carboneri, *La Reale Chiesa di Superga di Filippo Juvarra*, 1715-1735, Turin, 1979, pp. 8 ff, pls. VII-XI.

22.	Hans Reuther, *Die Kirchenbauten Balthasar Neumanns*, Berlin, 1960, pp. 22, 77, 99 ff; pls. 23, 24, 59; Christian Otto, *Space Into Light: The Churches of Balthasar Neumann*, Cambridge, Mass., 1979, p. 38, figs. 27, 47, 86. The use of wooden models was also well established in Germany by the 16th century. A model for an entire church was presented by Hans Hieber for "Zur schönen Maria" in Regensburg (1519-1521), and the model for his Perlachturm dates 1591. See Henry Russel-Hitchcock, *German Renaissance Architecture*, Princeton, 1981, pp. 26 ff, pls. 23, 25 ff.

23.	For the competition of 1593 won by Fausto Rughesi see Jacob Hess, *Kunstgeschichtliche Studien zu Renaissance und Barock*, Rome, 1967, p. 359: Joseph Connors, *Borromini and the Roman Oratory: Style and Society*, New York, 1980, pp. 10, 27, 162. Figure of Rughesi's model: Eugénie Strong, *La Chiesa Nuova (S. Maria in Vallicella). Guida storico ed artistica con un saggio biografico sopra San Filippo Neri di Piero Misciatelli*, Rome, 1923, pl. VI.

24.	Leonello Razza, *La Basilica Cattedrale di Frascati*, Frascati, 1979, pp. 114-127; H. Hager, "Girolamo Fontana e la facciata della cattedrale di San Pietro a Frascati," *Commentari*, 28, 1977, pp. 273-288. When the decision was made to add the nave to Michelangelo's church of St. Peter's, a model was requested from Carlo Maderno in 1607, although the work on the foundations continued for some months according to a different plan, and had to be interrupted (see Howard Hibbard, *Carlo Maderno and Roman Architecture 1580-1630*, London, 1971, pp. 53, 68, 159, 163 ff). Not without interest for our question is the fact that two models were made for the church of S. Andrea della Valle, one the church and another for the dome, about 1620. In 1628 a model by Orazio Grassi was made for S. Ignazio (H. Hibbard, *Maderno*, pp. 85, 232).

25. F. Dettweiler, op. cit., p. 1, note 1.

26. Models of this kind have survived for the cathedral in Como by Tommaso Rodari (for the apse, 1487), by Rodari and Cristoforo Solari (for the area around the crossing without the dome, 1513) and by Francesco Castelli (for the dome, 1688). The projects for the cathedral are now in the Museo Civico in Como. For the source material see Carlo Francesco Ciceri, *Selva di notizie autentiche riguardanti la fabbrica della cattedrale di Como con altre memorie patrie e analoghe all' argomento*, Como, 1811; cf. D. Santo Monti, *La Cattedrale di Como*, Como, 1897, pp. 80-85; 121-128; pls. 7, 8, 9 and 20. See also Federico Frigerio, *La Cupola della Cattedrale di Como a le sue vicende*, Como, 1935, pp. 10-22; pls. 1, 2, 6, 7, 35, 36. For a model of 1769 to re-model the dome (Giulio Gagliori) see pls. 33 ff. A project for the dome was also submitted by Carlo Fontana (without a model), but the dome remained unexecuted until the commission was given to Filippo Juvarra in 1730 (see D. Santo Monti, op. cit., pls. 21 ff; F. Frigerio, op. cit., pls 8, 9, 10; E. Coudenhove-Erthal, op. cit., pp. 58 ff; for Juvarra: F. Frigerio, op. cit., pls. 12-25; Salvatore Boscarino, *Juvarra Architetto*, Rome, 1973, pp. 350-356, pls. 385-397.

27. E. Coudenhove-Erthal, op. cit., pp. 144 ff.

28. *Altari barocchi a Roma*, a cura di Emilio Lavagnino, Giulio Romano Ansaldi e Luigi Salerno, Rome, 1959, pp. 199-208; pl. on p. 203. Fiorella Pansecchi, "Il modello della Cappella Pallavicini Rospigliosi in S. Francesco a Ripa," *Bollettino dei musei comunali di Roma*, 9, 1962, pp. 21-31. For the dating of the model 1711-1712 and the most recent research on the planning and building history of the chapel, see John Pinto, *Nicola Michetti (ca. 1675-1758) and Eighteenth-Century Architecture In Rome and St. Petersburg*, Ph.D. diss. Harvard University, Cambridge, Mass., 1976 (Ms. Bibliotheca Hertziana, Rome), pp. 40-58.

29. For this model which bears the coat of arms of

Gregory XV (1621-1623) see Richard Wunder, "The Architect's Eye," *The Cooper Union Museum Chronicle*, vol. 3, no. 4, September, 1962, pp. 13 ff, no. 24. It shows a vaulted room, the entrance of which is flanked by doubled full columns. The flanking walls have arched panels for pictorial decoration. As a whole the model looks like an ancestor of Fontana's Cappella Cybo.

30. "44 fl. 16 kr, 5 pf. Hr. Niclaus v. Hornik Canonico in Frankfurt wegen von Rom aus anhero expediertem und überschicktem Stieftsbauw Models auf gdsten Befelch p. Hr. Ziegler intimiert." Quotation checked with the original document in the Staatsarchiv in Marburg (Rechnungen II, Fulda Nr. 240, fol. 177), after F. Dettweiler, op. cit., p. 1, note 1. It is certainly illuminating to note on comparison that the amount paid to Hornik for the transportation of the model exceeds the annual salary of 40 fl. offered to Johann Dientzenhofer when he was appointed architect to the court in Bamberg on 1 September 1711 (see O. A. Weigmann, op. cit., p. 38).
Very informative for our understanding of the value of the currency (fiorino = florin = gulden) used at that time are the wages: a good workman was paid one-half fl. per diem for his services, whereas a workman below the average category received only one-third fl.. See O. A. Weigmann, op. cit., p. 142.

31. O. A. Weigmann, op. cit., pp. 137 ff, 142.

32. F. Dettweiler, p. 1, note 1.

33. O. A. Weigmann, p. 139.

34. O. A. Weigmann, p. 137. According to Anton Schmitt, (*Der Dom zu Fulda, Grabeskirche des Heiligen Bonifatius*, 8th ed., Fulda, 1964, p. 4) his name is Antonius Peyer, who had built the deanery in Fulda (1702-1704).

35. O. A. Weigmann, p. 139 ff. A date early in 1705 for the drawing and the subsequent model would also be in agreement with a certain dating element contained in the passage quoted from Pascoli (see above, note 18) to the effect that "molto prima" Fontana had sent projects "per certe rimesse e stalle" to Vienna for the

Emperor Leopold I, whose death in 1705 provides the ultimate *Terminus ante quem* for the stable projects which, as Pascoli said, preceded the Fulda model considerably. For the stable projects, see Ugo Donati, *Artisti Ticinesi a Roma*, Bellinzona, 1942, p. 282, pl. 295. For their dating there is considerable leeway into the late years of the *Seicento* because the relationship with Leopold I must pre-date by some time the appearance of Carlo Fontana's "trattato delle Acque" of 1696 which mentions him as the Emperor's architect and engineer (E. Coudenhove-Erthal, op. cit., pp. 85 ff).

36.   Christian Otto, *Space into Light*, pp. 29-34, 58-59, 77.

37.   K. Lohmeyer, op. cit., pp. 198 ff, nos. 101, 102, 103, 104, 105, 108; pp. 205 ff, no. 141; p. 215, no. 185; H. Reuther, *Die Kirchenbauten*, op. cit., p. 107; same author, *Die Zeichnungen aus dem Nachlass Balthasar Neumanns, Der Bestand in der Kunstbibliothek Berlin*, Berlin, 1981; H. Hager, "Balthasar Neumann's Schönborn Chapel at Würzburg Cathedral and its Berninesque Prototype," *Architectural History*, Journal of the Society of Architectural Historians of Great Britian, vol 26, 1983, pp. 74-77.

38.   O. A. Weigmann, op. cit., pp. 38, 118, 121 ff; H. G. Franz, op. cit., 161 ff; H. Reuther, *Die Kirchenbauten Balthasar Neumanns*, pp. 11 ff.

39.   Allan Braham and Hellmut Hager, *Carlo Fontana. The Drawings at Windsor Castle*, London, 1977, pp. 19-23.

40.   Hugo Schmerber, *Beiträge zur Geschichte der Dientzenhofer*, Prague, 1900, p. 22, note 1.

41.   Emma Zocca, *La Basilica dei SS. Apostoli in Roma*, Rome, 1959, pls. 15, 28; Domenico de Rossi, *Architettura Civile*, III, Rome, 1721, pl. 19.

42.   For a view from the nave into the side chapels see Giovanni Battista Pannini's representation of the interior of SS. Apostoli in his painting of the consecration of the church by Benedict XIII, in E. Zocca, op. cit., pl. 10; Giulio Magni, *Il Barocco a Roma nella architettura e nella scultura decorativa*, vol. I, *Chiese*, Turin, 1911, pl. 71. Cf. F. Dettweiler, op. cit., p. 10.

43.   Cf. F. Dettweiler, op. cit., p. 12, note 2; K. Freckmann, op. cit., pl. 14; Eberhard Hempel, *Francesco Borromini*, Vienna, 1924, pls. 58 ff; Paolo Portoghesi, *Borromini, Architettura come linguaggo*, Milan, 1967, pls. 96 ff; Anthony Blunt, *Borromini*, London, 1979, pl. 99.

44.   Cf. K. Freckmann, op. cit., pls. 10, 12. E. Hempel, *Borromini*, pl. 55; P. Portoghesi, *Borromini*, op. cit., pl. 93; and especially Anthony Blunt, *Guide to Baroque Rome*, New York, 1982, pl. 98.

45.   *Fulda, aufgenommen von Hans Retzlaff, beschrieben von Ernst Kramer*, Munich, 1953, pl. 4. 23; K. Freckmann, op. cit., pl. 14.

46.   Cf. K. Freckmann, op. cit., pls. 11, 13; P. Portoghesi, *Borromini*, pls. 168, 169.

47.   Gianfranco Spagnesi, *Giovanni Antonio de Rossi, Architetto Romano*, Rome, 1964, pl. on p. 194.

48.   A. Blunt, *Baroque and Rococo*, p. 264, considered the barrel vault the cathedral's "weakest feature." The dome above the crossing, with the diagonal display of windows that alternate with statues in niches, flanked by double pilasters in conformity with the nave decoration also evokes Roman precursors, especially the Gesù with its analogously articulated drum, and its statue of a saint which faces the spectator as the terminal point of his visual axis on the upper level (See Pio Pecchiai, *Il Gesù di Roma*, Rome, 1952, pl. XI).

49.   Cf. H. Retzlaff and E. Kramer, op. cit., pl. 24; Full color view in L. Pralle, *Dom und Abteibezirk* on p. 44; Felicitas Hagen-Dempf, *Die Kollegienkirche in Salzburg*, Vienna, 1949, pl. 15.

50.   *Münchens Kirchen, Mit einem chronologischen Verzeichnis der bestehenden Kirchenbauten herausgegeben von Norbert Lieb und Jürgen Sauermost*, Munich, 1973, pp. 113, 121, pl. 132.

51.   A good example of the period is the Jesuit College at Loyola. Cf. H. Hager, "Carlo Fontana and the Jesuit Sanctuary at Loyola,": *Journal of the Warburg and Courtauld Institutes*, 37, 1974, pp. 280-289.

52.   The plan attached to the manuscript of F. B. Schlereth, op. cit., was first published by O. A. Weigmann, op. cit., pp. 140 ff, pl. 20.

53.   The method of clipping and adding on was of course also customary; one has to think only of the ground plans of Michelangelo's St. Peter's, which were cut down in those places where Maderno's nave projects had to be attached. See H. Hibbard, *Maderno*, pp. 158 ff, pls. 48c, 50, 51b.

54.   For the style of Carlo Fontana's drawings, see A. Braham and H. Hager, *Carlo Fontana*, pp. 19-23.

55.   O. A. Weigmann, op. cit., p. 140, note 1.

56.   K. Freckmann, op. cit., fig. I on p. 15.

57.   Cf. note 24 above.

58.   K. Freckmann, op. cit., pl. 7. Cf. overall plan in L. Pralle, *Dom und Abteibezirk*, p. 82 (inside cover sheet) For the above mentioned tradition of monastery churches, see H. Hager, *Filippo Juvarra*, pp. 34 ff; same author, "Bernini, Mattia de Rossi and the Church of S. Bonaventura at Monterano," *Architectural History*, Journal of the Society of Architectural Historians of Great Britain, 21, 1978, pp. 68-74. The Roman tradition leads from Carlo Rainaldi's earlier plans for S. Maria in Campitelli by way of San Bonaventura at Monterano, realized by Bernini's assistant Mattia de Rossi, to Pozzo's famous engraved project for a circular church which has been related to S. Maria dei Fornaci in Rome, and reaches its culmination in Juvarra's Superga in Turin (Cf. N. Carboneri, op. cit., pls. XXVII-XXVIII). The Stiftskirche in Fulda would thereby occupy a position chronologically between the two last mentioned monuments. This remains true even though the ecclesiastical building itself, which incorporates considerable portions of the earlier structure, returns to the Latin cross Roman basilica style which was re-established as the officially recommended building type during the Counter-Reformation. The connection with St. Peter's in Rome, so strongly manifest in the early medieval basilica, and therefore of necessity close to the mind of Prince Abbot Adalbert von Schleifras throughout all vicissitudes of the planning history, is at least typologically preserved through the employment of a markedly Roman building type. That the configuration of the church as it stands now (as concerns the width of the nave and its aisles as well as that of the transept) was determined by the plan of Ratgarbasilica (791-819) becomes evident in a comparison of their schemes. Cf. Manfred F. Fischer and Friedrich Oswald, "Zur Baugeschichte der Fuldaer Klosterkirchen. Literatur und Ausgabungen in kritischer Sicht," *Rheinische Ausgrabungen*, I, 1968, pp. 268-280 (*Beihefte der Bonner Jahrbücher*, vol. 28). For the preceding churches see also: Helmut Beumann and Dieter Grossmann, "Das Bonifatiusgrab und die Klosterkirchen zu Fulda," *Marburger Jahrbuch für Kunstwissenschaft*, 14, 1949, pp. 17-51; Werner Meyer-Barkhausen, "Die karolingische Klosterkirche in ihren baugeschichtlichen Beziehungen zu Rom," *Hessiches Jahrbuch für Landesgeschichte*, 10, 1960, pp. 1-15; E. Sturm, op. cit., p. 71.

59.   Neudecker's wooden statue of the Holy Virgin is part of a scenic composition which shows the Holy Trinity in a glory of angels under the vault realized in stucco by Johann Baptista Artari from Lugano (Karl Freckmann, *Der Dom zu Fulda*, Augsburg, 1928, p. 35). The statues of God the Father and Christ are shown awaiting the Virgin Mary with a Crown. See L. Pralle, *Das Münster*, 10, 1957, pl. on p. 449, and same author, *Fulda, Dom und Abteibezirk*, op. cit., pl. on p. 39; for a detailed view of the statue of Mary, see also *Reclams Kunstführer*, IV, Stuttgart, 1969, pl. on p. 225.

60.   On the side of the monks' choir the entablature appears to be composed of three convex segments (fig. 140b). K. Freckmann's plan was modified by Hajo Mattern with regard to the position of the foremost columns of the high altar (but without indicating the curve of the colonnade in the center); see L. Pralle, *Fulda*,

op. cit., 1980 (inside of the rear cover). For additional views of the structure of the altar see Joseph Braun, "Altarciborium," in: *Reallexikon zur Deutschen Kunstgeschichte*, I, 1937, p. 483, pls. 11 and 12 on p. 478 (confrontation with Bernini's Baldacchino in St. Peter's); H. Retzlaff and E. Kramer, *Fulda*, op. cit., pl. 21 (view from monks' choir; see fig. 140b).

61. E. Coudenhove-Erthal, op. cit., p. 146.

62. Emma Zocca, *La Basilica dei SS. Apostoli in Roma*, Rome, 1959, pl. 15 on p. 61; for a comprehensive study of the history of the Cappella di S. Antonio see Cathie Cook Kelly, "Ludovico Rusconi Sassi and Early Eighteenth-Century Architecture in Rome," Ph.D. dissertation, The Pennsylvania State University, 1980, Ann Arbor, 1980, pp. 80-103; for Bernini's altar in S. Paolo Maggiore in Bologna, see Irving Lavin, *Bernini and the Unity of the Visual Arts*, New York - London, 1980, pp. 63-65 (with complete bibliography).

63. E. Coudenhove-Erthal, op. cit., p. 145 (pl. 28); L. Pralle, *Fulda*, op. cit., 1980, pl. on p. 51. The altar, however, was executed only after the middle of the 18th century (1758) and the chapel served earlier as a chapter house and burial place for the monks (E. Sturm, op. cit., pp. 126 ff).

64. Domenico de Rossi, *Architettura civile*, III, pl. 52; and for a comparison with the plan of the Cappella Cornaro: same author, *Disegni di vari altari e cappelle nelle chiese di Roma*, Rome, 1713, pl. 21. Irving Lavin, op. cit., pl. 139. For a precise drawing of the ground plan by Nicodemus Tessin the Younger, see Hans Kauffmann, *Giovanni Lorenzo Bernini, Die figürlichen Kompositionen*, Berlin, 1970, pls. 70a and 70b.

65. Hans Sedlmayr, *Johann Berhard Fischer von Erlach*, 2nd edition, Vienna, 1976, pp 66 ff; 251 ff, pls. 45, 82.

66. H. Sedlmayr, op. cit., pp. 109 ff, 262 ff, pl. 83. For a late representative of this type, which had its climax in the high altar of the Jesuit church in Mannheim, designed in 1733 by Alessandro Galli-Bibiena and executed by Verschaffelt in 1758 (damaged in World War II and not yet reconstructed), see J. Braun, op. cit., *Reallexikon zur Deutschen Kunstgeschichte*, I. pl. 14 on p. 479 (St. Peter and St. Ignatius in Mainz, 1786). For the altar in Mannheim (full scale model by P. Egell) see A. Hyatt Mayor, *The Bibiena Family*, New York, 1945, pp. 30f, 36, pl. 32; *Die Kunstdenkmäler des Stadtkreises Mannheim*, Hans Huth, et al., Munich, 1982, p. 644 and pls. 450 ff.

67. K. Freckmann, op. cit., p. 34, pl. 15. Cf. *Reclam's Kunstführer*, op. cit., IV, p. 230, and Pralle, *Fulda*, op. cit., 1980, pp. 41 and 50 with good illustrations of the situation. E. Sturm, op. cit., p. 106, identifies Joh. Ignaz Albin as the author of the copy after Rubens' original painting of the *Last Supper* in the Brera in Milan.

68. Excellent photographical documentation in: Martin Kuhn and Ingeborg Limmer, *Kloster Banz*, Freiburg i. Br., 1977.

69. O. A. Weigmann, *Eine Bamberger Baumeisterfamilie*, op. cit., p. 125, pl. 14.

70. O. A. Weigmann, op. cit., p. 122, note 3.

71. That Dientzenhofer's authorship of the original project is not endorsed by documents, as in Banz, cannot surprise: the original contract of 1700 envisaged that the sculptural and stucco decoration within the church were to be executed on the account of Dientzenhofer, "except for the altars, organ and confessionals." Frieda Dettweiler, (*Die Stuckarbeiten*, op. cit., pp. 10 ff) pointed out that only with regard to the sculptural decoration was the arrangement changed, and the payment made directly to the artists themselves, with Johann Baptista Artari as the major artist. He was responsible not only for all the statues in the nave but also for the two altars in the transept. Cf. O. A. Weigmann, op. cit., pp. 142 ff. Johann Neudecker the Elder, the sculptor of the statue of the Virgin Mary, also executed the alabaster reliefs adorning the altar of St. Boniface in the crypt (K. Freckmann, op. cit., pp. 35 ff, pls. 28, 30

ff; H. Retzlaff and E. Kramer, pls. 36 ff; Pralle, op. cit., Fulda, 1980, pls. on p. 48 ff). Our attribution of the scheme of the high altar in Fulda to Dientzenhofer is strongly supported by the fact that its configuration is much closer to the above-mentioned Roman prototypes than the former high altar in Würzburg Cathedral of 1701-1703 (lost in the second World War) by Johann Michael Riess and Balthasar Esterbauer (fig. 147). According to Max H. von Freeden, "Fuldaer Barock," in: *Fulda und die Rhön* (Special issue of "Bayerland," Munich, s.d., ca. 1956, p. 44) who, however, does not cite the pertaining documents, it served as a model for the high altar in Fulda, and the sculptor Neudecker was sent to Würzburg to study the altar. The structure in Würzburg consisted of four widely spaced columns on a simple concave curve which carried a monumental crown to allude to the Prince Bishop's worldly power. This arrangement is also connected with Fischer von Erlach's high altar in the Mausoleum church of Ferdinand II in Graz, and anticipated Balthasar Neumann's famous altars in Worms (1738), Brühl (1745), Bruchsal (1748), and Trier (1752), where as a variant of our type, only the central portion recedes in a semicircular curve. The high altar of the cathedral in Würzburg contained a crucifix in the center which Zacharias Junker had created in 1609 for the preceding high altar of the cathedral. The new altar received a painting in 1726 (St. Johann Nepomuk kneeling before a crucifix, by Clemens Lünenschloss; Fr. X. Himmelstein, *Der Kiliansdom in Würzburg*, Würzburg, 1889, p. 34; see Felix Mader, Die Kunstdenkmäler von Unterfranken und Aschaffenburg, XII, Stadt Würzburg, Munich, 1915, p. 48). The altar of the Würzburg cathedral which was dismantled in 1749 when the level of the choir was lowered, and recomposed afterwards, is known through photographs and the very detailed rendering on a painting by Rudolf Huthsteiner of 1910 in the Mainfränkiches Museum in Würzburg (fig. 147).

72.   The precise date of the construction and completion of the high altar in Weltenburg, which Gerhad Hojer (*Die frühe Figuralplastik Egid Quirin Asams*, Ph.D. diss. Munich, 1964 (1967), pp. 112-117) tried to establish between 1735-1736, is still a matter of debate. Berhard

Rupprecht (*Die Brüder Asam, Sinn und Sinnlichkeit im Bayerischen Barock*, Regensburg, 1980, pp. 88 ff) points out that part of the high altar structure seems to have been in place already in 1721, when the church was dedicated, and the payments were made in 1723-24 for the execution of the painting in connection with the high altar. However, Rupprecht admits that reliable stylistic criteria are missing for a precise chronology of Egid Quirin's works in the 1720s and 1730s.

73.   For a comparison with the *Assumption* in Fulda and that in Rohr, see K. Freckmann, op. cit., p. 34; and for the date, G. Hojer, *Die Frühe Figuralplastik*, op. cit., pp. 4-7; B. Rupprecht, op. cit., pp. 102 ff.

74.   For Cosmas Damian's participation in the competition of 1713 see Helene Trottmann, "Die Zeichnungen Cosmas Damian Asams für den Concorso Clementino der Accademia di San Luca von 1713," *Pantheon*, 38, 1980, pp. 158 ff; G. Hojer, "Der Fund barocker Aquarelle in der Accademia di San Luca," *Weltkunst*, 50, 1980, pp. 114 ff, 214 ff; B. Rupprecht, op. cit., p. 58.

75.   I. Lavin, op. cit., pp. 33-39.

76.   Bernhard Kerber, *Andrea Pozzo*, Berlin - New York, 1971, p. 84. The importance of Pozzo as a mediator between Bernini and the developments in Central Europe has recently been stressed by Karsten Harries, *The Bavarian Rococo Church. Between Faith and Aestheticism*, New Haven and London, 1983. See especially his chapter "Altar and Stage," pp. 126-138 and "Stages within Stage," pp. 138-144. However, Harries does not consider the role of Dientzenhofer in this process which is of concern to us. For a brief summary of the development of the high altar in the eighteenth century and the role of Dientzenhofer and the Asams see Pierre Charpentrat, *Living Architecture, Baroque Italy and Central Europe*, New York, 1967, pp. 137 ff.

77.   B. Kerber, op. cit., p. 86.

78.   I. Lavin, op. cit., pp. 85-91.

79.   For his illusionistic altar in the Gesú in Frascati, see B. Kerber, op. cit., p. 49, pl. 33; Allan Braham and Hellmut Hager, *Carlo Fontana. The Drawings at Windsor Castle*, London, 1877, pp. 66 ff.

80.   For a complete account of the perspective gallery (1652-1655), which was preceded by a painted one, and instead of the present statue showed a continuation of the perspective in a painted view of a garden by G. B. Magini, see Lionello Neppi, *Palazzo Spada*, Rome, 1975, pp. 146 f and especially chapter 3: "La Prospettiva," pp. 175-189; same author, "Punti di Vista sulla prospettiva Spada," *Bollettino D'Arte*, vol. 68, 1983, pp. 105-118. See also P. Portoghesi, *The Rome of Borromini. Architecture as Language*, New York, 1968, pl. LXXXVI.

81.   E. Coudenhove-Erthal, op. cit., p. 14, pl. 15. For a contemporary framed view of the fountain in the Palazzo Massimo see the engraving by Falda (Ugo Donati, *Artisti Ticinesi a Roma*, Bellinzona, 1942, pl. 250). For the altar in S. Spirito dei Napolitani see A. Braham and H. Hager, *Carlo Fontana*, pl. 100.

82.   Fontana may have been inspired by the original situation of the *Prospettiva* in the Palazzo Spada (see note 80). Even more important to him, however, was the view from the opposite vantage point within the garden, and in particular the view from the barrel vaulted loggia behind the rear front of the fountain. Fontana's opening, screened only by a low iron railing that projects forward, affords the spectator standing in the shadow of the hall a panoramic view across the city of Rome toward the Pincio, with SS. Trinità dei Monti and the Villa Medici as the major backdrops. For the modifications of the Fontana Paola under Alexander VIII (1689-1691) see E. Coudenhove-Erthal, op. cit., pp. 60 ff. Cf. Cesare D'Onofrio, *Acque e Fontane di Roma*, Rome, 1977, pp. 364 and pl. 431; for the history of the Fontana Paola and its urbanistic orientation see Christoph Heilmann, "Aqua Paola and the Urban Planning of Paul V Borghese," *The Burlington Magazine*, 112, 1970, pp. 656-683.

83.   A. Braham and H. Hager, *Carlo Fontana*, pp. 43 ff; H. Hager, "Un riesame di tre cappelle di Carlo Fontana a Roma," *Commentari*, 27, 1976, pp. 264, 266 ff, pls. 17 ff.

84.   For this much discussed drawing which was first published by Cesare D. Onofrio (*Le Fontane di Roma*, 2nd ed., Rome, 1962, p. 242, n. 44, pl. 211, with the erroneous attribution to Carlo Fontana) see H. Hager, "Puntualizzazioni su disegni scenici teatrali e l'architettura scenografica del periodo barocco a Roma," *Bollettino del Centro Internazionale di Studi di Architettura, Andrea Palladio*, 17, 1975, pp. 123; Sabine Jacob, *Italienische Zeichnungen der Kunstbibliothek Berlin*, Architektur und Dekoration 16. bis 18. Jahrhundert, Berlin, 1975, pp. 158 ff, no. 799. For a suggestion to move the dating of this drawing to 1705-1708, and to attribute it to Francesco Bizzacheri, see John Pinto, "The Trevi Fountain: Unexecuted projects from the Pontificate of Clement XI," *Projects and Monuments in the Period of the Roman Baroque*, Papers in Art History from The Pennsylvania State University, vol. I, 1984, pp. 102 ff; fig. 6-c. Because of the date 1700 inscribed on the drawing, however, it seems that we cannot place its origin beyond that year. For the establishment of the framed view into the space behind the colonnade in the history of projects for the Trevi Fountain, see William Eisler, in *Architectural Fantasy and Reality. Drawings from the Accademia Nazionale di San Luca in Rome. Concorsi Clementini 1700-1750*. Exhibition Catalogue, Museum of Art, The Pennsylvania State University, 1982, p. 59; and John Pinto, *The Trevi Fountain*, New Haven and London, 1986, p. 91. J. Pinto publishes a design by an anonymous architect who competed with Nicola Salvi in 1730, which, quite apropos, offers a scenographic view of a landscape with the ruin of a Roman aqueduct in the center which is viewed through a proscenium-like arch (op. cit., pp. 102 ff, pl. 70).

85.   Vincenzo Golzio, "Le chiese di S. Maria di Montesanto e di S. Maria dei Miracoli," Piazza del Popolo, *Archivi d'Italia*, VIII, 1941, pp. 139 ff, doc. 26B; H. Hager, "Zur Planungs-und Baugeschichte der Zwillingskirchen auf der Piazza del Popolo in

Rom," *Römisches Jahrbuch für Kunstgeschichte*, XI, 1967-1968, p. 251, note 131; 274 ff., pl. 199.

86.   Cf. D. de Rossi, *Architettura civile*, op. cit., III, 1721, pl. 31.

87.   B. Rupprecht, op. cit., pl. on p. 201.

88.   H. Hager, "La Cappella del Cardinale Alderano Cybo in S. Maria del Popolo," *Commentari*, 25, 1974, pp. 54 ff, pl. 4; cf. same author, "Un riesame," op. cit., *Commentari*, 27, 1976, p. 274, pl. 27 (reversed with pl. 28).

89.   Concerning the climactic importance of the framed view of the *Cathedra Petri* within the program envisaged by Pope Alexander VII for the pilgrims and other visitors to Rome, see Richard Krautheimer, *The Rome of Alexander VII, 1655-1667*, Princeton, 1985, pp. 137 ff. For the optical framing of the chair of St. Peter by the twisted columns of the *baldacchino*, see also Augusto Cavallari Murat, "Professionalità di Bernini quale urbanista: alcuni episodi e una confessione su Mirafiori," *Gian Lorenzo Bernini Architetto e l'architettura europea del Sei-Settecento*, A cura di Gianfranco Spagnesi e Marcello Fagiolo, Rome, 1983, pp. 354 ff.

90.   The term "light chamber" was coined by Paolo Portoghesi (*Borromini, Architettura come linguaggo*, Milan, 1967, pl. 225) to denote spaces in which the light is "collected" above certain areas, for example in the entrance vestibule of the Oratorio dei Filippini. For the employment of this device by architects of the Roman late Baroque, see H. Hager, "Un riesame," *Commentari*, 27, 1976, pp. 265 ff, p. 280 note 52. For the mode of employment of conducted light in Weltenburg, see K. Harries, op. cit., pp. 128 ff.

91.   For the dating and a description of the "Macchina," etc., see Nino Carboneri, *Andrea Pozzo*, Trento, 1961, pp. 15 ff, pl. 2; B. Kerber, op. cit., pp. 44, 98, 103 pls. 26 ff.

92.   Andrea Pozzo, *Prospettiva de Pittori e Architetti*, II, Rome, 1700, pl. 73. CF. K. Harries, op. cit., pp. 128, 131, pl. 97. For the

projects for the high altar in the Gesú and the execution of the no longer extant *altare maggiore* (reproduced in A. Pozzo, op. cit., II, pl. 81) 1697-1698, and removed in the nineteenth century, see N. Carboneri, op. cit., pp. 28 ff, pls. 10 ff; B. Kerber, op. cit., pp. 129 ff, (comparison with Bernini's Cappella Cornaro), pl. 77.

93.   Cf. K. Harries, op. cit., p. 126.

94.   According to G. Hojer (op. cit., p. 23 ff), there is no direct line of development leading from scenic altars in southern Germany which represent the Assumption of the Virgin, to the composition in Rohr.

95.   Cf. K. Harries, op. cit., p. 128.

96.   About this chapel and Juvarra's sojourn in Rome, see most recently Henry Millon, *Filippo Juvarra. Drawings from the Roman Period, 1704-1714,* part I, Rome, 1984, pp. 212-214, 307 ff.

97.   *Altari barocchi a Roma*, a cura di Emilio Lavagnino, et al., Rome, 1959, pl. on p. 201.

98.   A. Pozzo is dealing with a related problem, the creation of the illusion of an open space on a flat wall surface, in vol. I, pl. 1, which could have stimulated Johann Dientzenhofer's experiments.

99.   Margarete Baur-Heinhold, *Theater des Barock, Festliches Bühnenspiel im 17. und 18. Jahrhundert*, Munich, 1966, pp. 136, 284 pls. 196-199. Cf. K. Harries, op. cit., pp. 132-136. Richard Zürcher, *Die Kunstgeschichtliche Entwicklung an süddeutschen Barockaltären*, in: *Der Altar des 18. Jahrhunderts, Das Kunstwerk in seiner Bedeutung und als denkmalpflegerische Aufgabe, Forschungen und Berichte der Bau- und Denkmalpflege in Baden Württenberg*, vol. 5, Munich, 1978, pp. 59 ff, 65 ff. For a demonstation of the working method of the "Jesuit Perspective," see Jean Dubreuil, *La perspective pratique, troisieme et dernière partie*, Paris, 1649, p. 101, referred to by A. Hyatt Mayor, op. cit, pp. 12 ff, 36, pl. 29. The method of extension by the means of perspective has even been employed in garden

architecture. The painted avenues designed to extend the real ones mentioned by A. Hyatt Mayor (op. cit., p. 22) are lost. But a comparable example which is at least in principle close to Dubreuil's and Bernini's concepts (as well as the altar in Diessen when it is opened) survived in the gardens of Schwetzingen in the "Perspektiv" (also called "Ende der Welt") where the feigned landscape (ca. 1775) is visible at the end of a long "gallery" and painted as a fresco on the concave surface of a "broad screen" (Fig. 159) and receives its light from hidden, laterally arranged sources (see Kurt Martin, *Die Kunstdenkmäler des Amtsbezirks Mannheim, Stadt Schwetzingen*, Karlsruhe, 1933, pp. 268 f, pls. 246-249. Within the context of Roman palace architecture this mode of employing the means of perspective deception had of course long been anticipated in the Galleria Spada; see above notes 80 and 82.

100. See note 91 above.

101. For this altar (the statue of the Holy Virgin is an addition of the nineteenth century) see Miroslav Chalupnicek, *Praha Mesto Chiramu*, Prague, 1937, no. 55. For the building history of the church (1611-1616), which included a complete change of direction when the edifice, originally Lutheran, was assigned to the Carmelites (1624) after the victory at the White Mountain, see Oskar Schürer, *Prag*, 5th edition, Stuttgart, 1943, pp. 182 ff, 209 ff; Heinrich Gerhard Franz, op. cit., pp. 27, 31 ff, pls. 21, 24, 35.

102. Amedeo Bellini, *Benedetto Alfieri*, Milan, 1978. For the establishment of Alfieri's authorship and illustrations see pp. 25, 135 ff.

103. For Johann Dientzenhofer's development see H. G. Franz, op. cit., pp. 101-168; H. Reuther, op. cit., pp. 11-14.

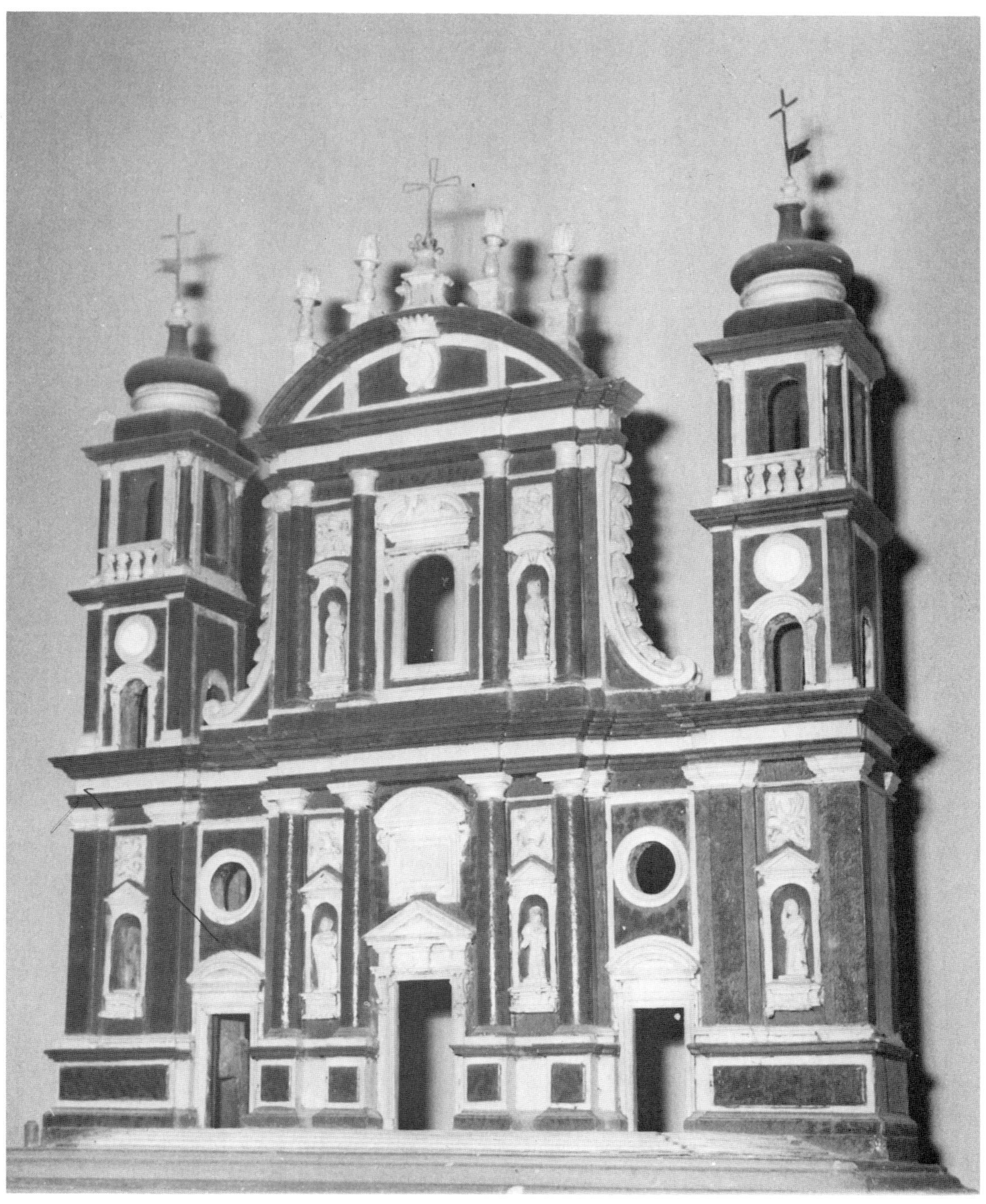

127.   Frascati, Cathedral, model for the façade (from Hager, in *Commentari*, 28, 1977).

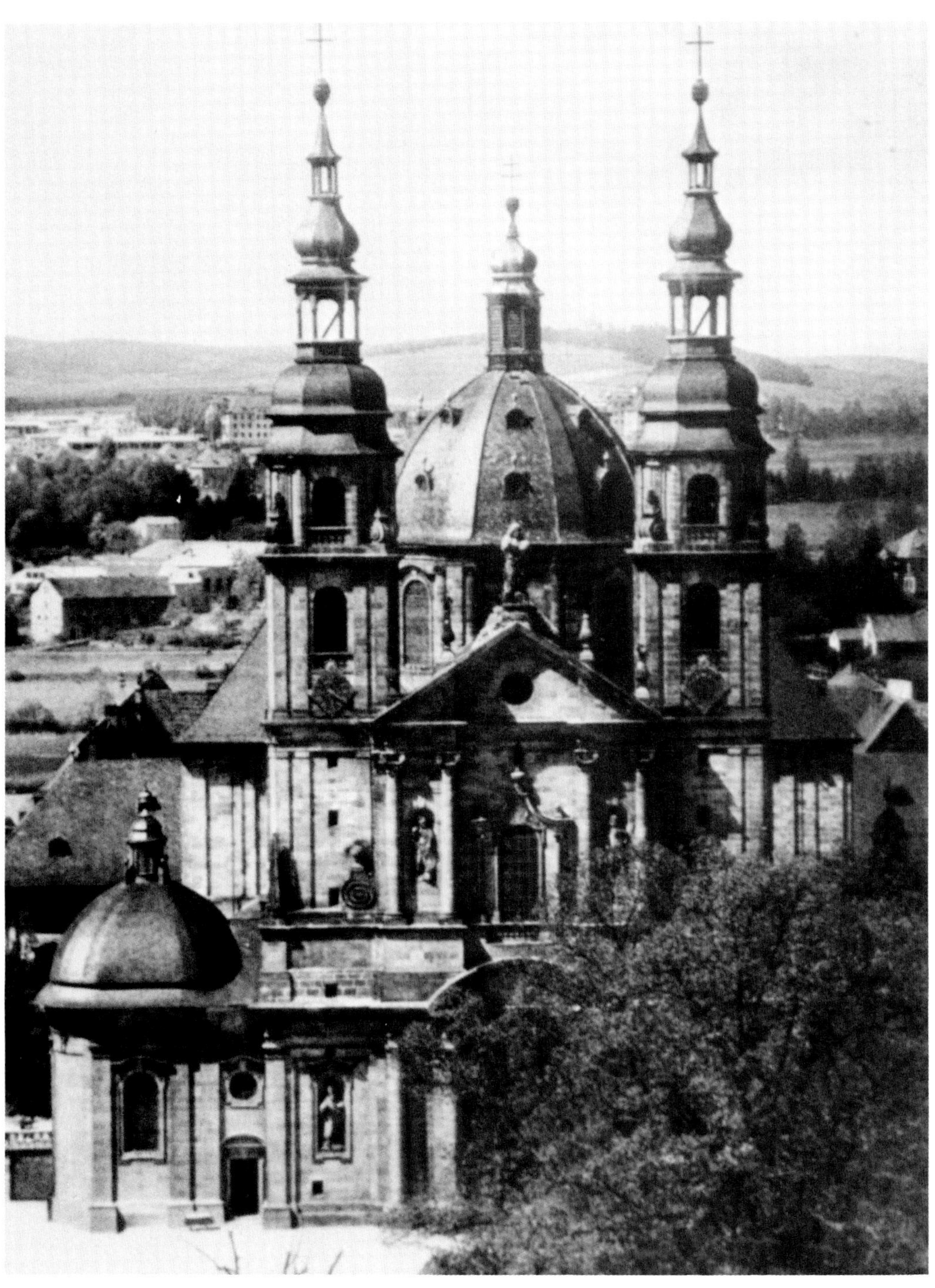

128.   Fulda, Cathedral, view of façade (from E. Kramer and H. Retzlaff, *Fulda*, Munich, 1964).

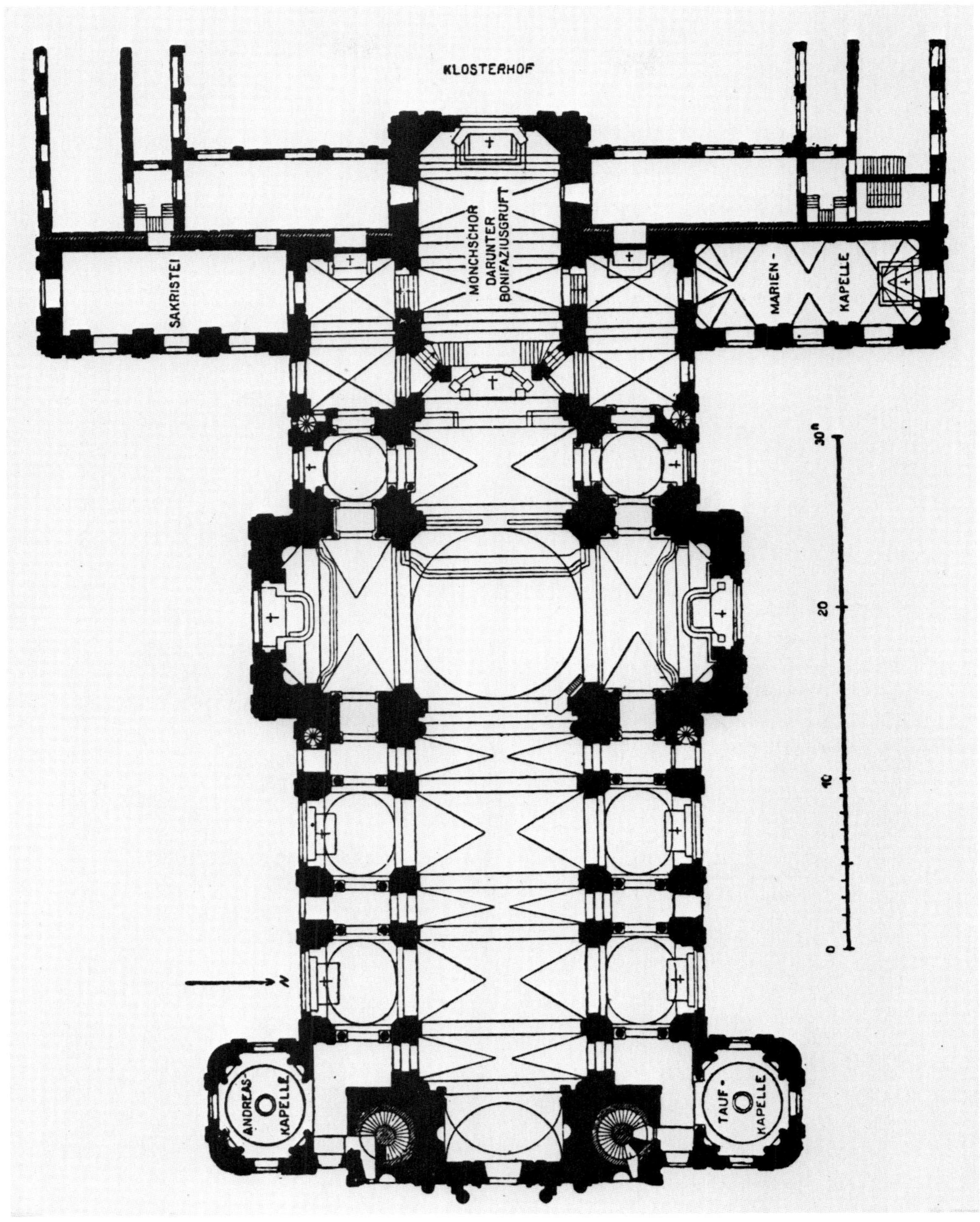

129.   Fulda, Cathedral, ground plan (after Freckmann; Bildarchiv Foto Marburg).

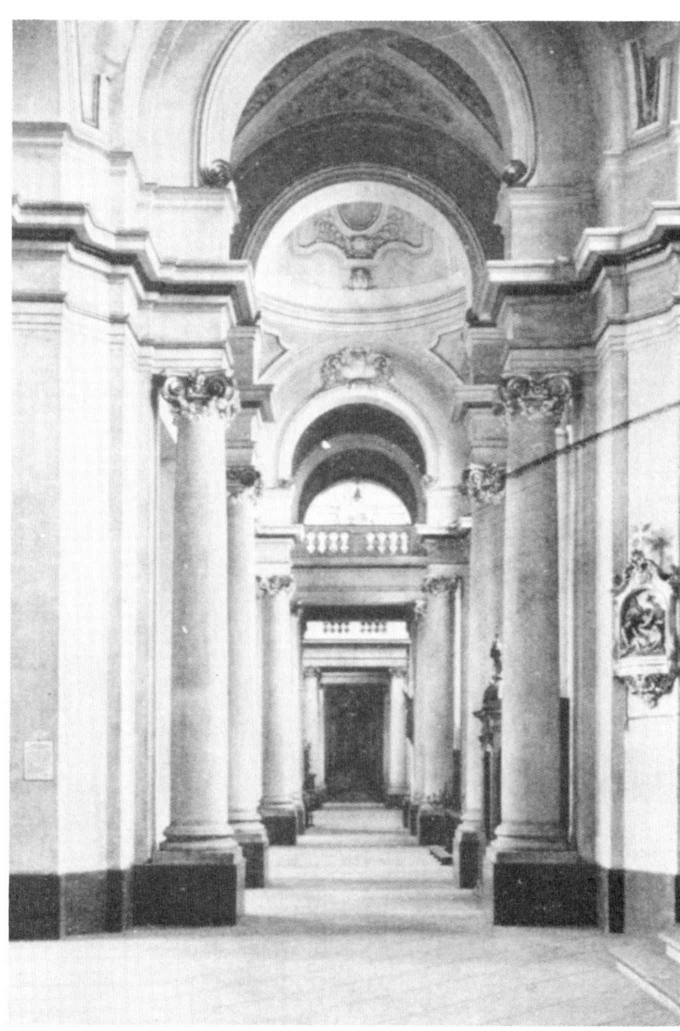

136.   Fulda, Cathedral, view along a side aisle
(from E. Kramer and H. Retzlaff, *Fulda*).

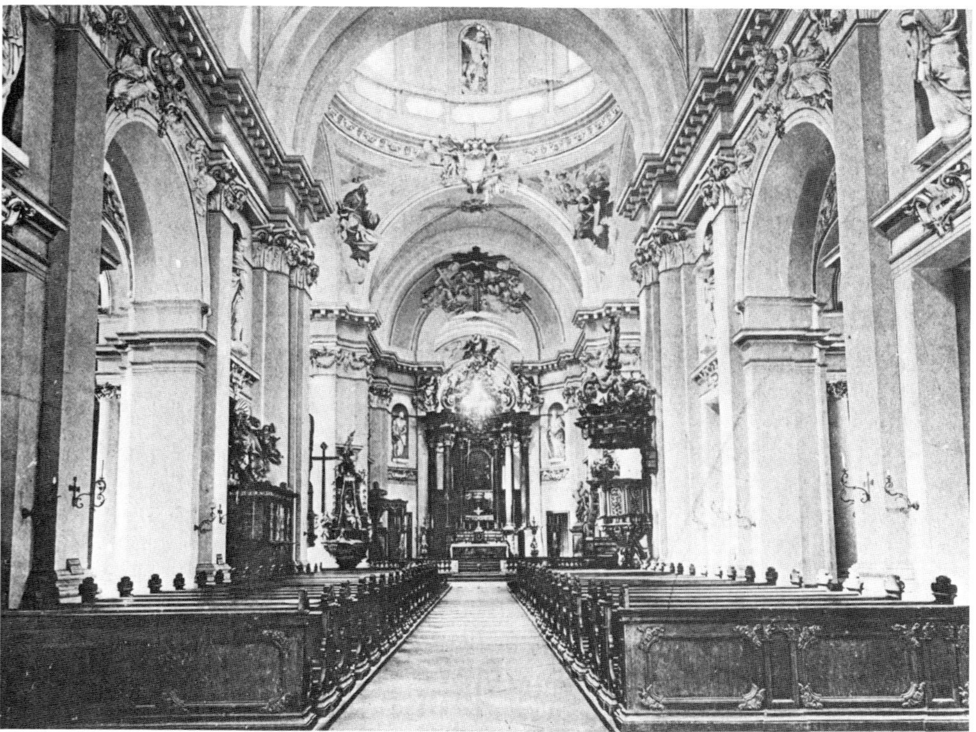

133.   Fulda, Cathedral, view towards main altar (photo: Knauff, Fulda).

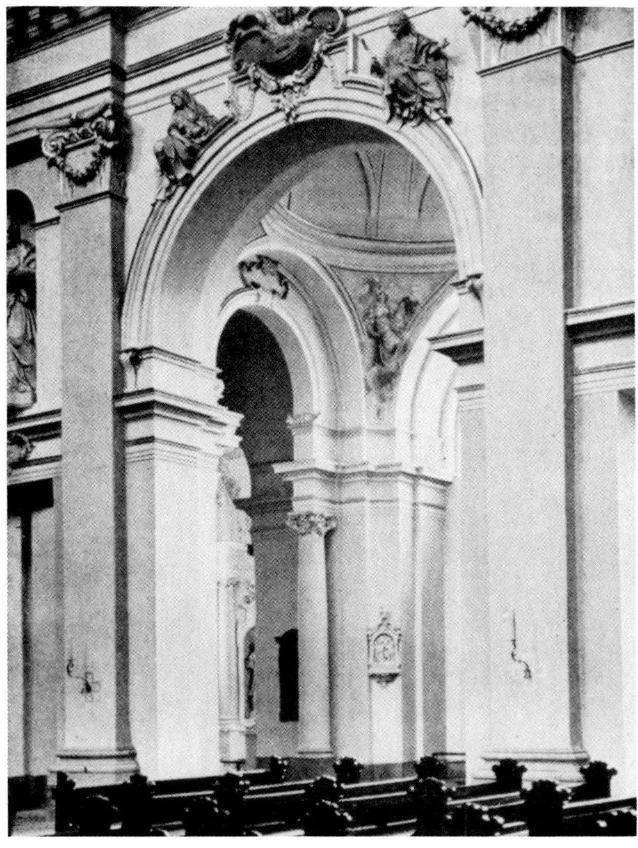

130. Fulda, Cathedral, view into the south side aisle (after A. Schmitt, *Der Dom zu Fulda*, 1964).

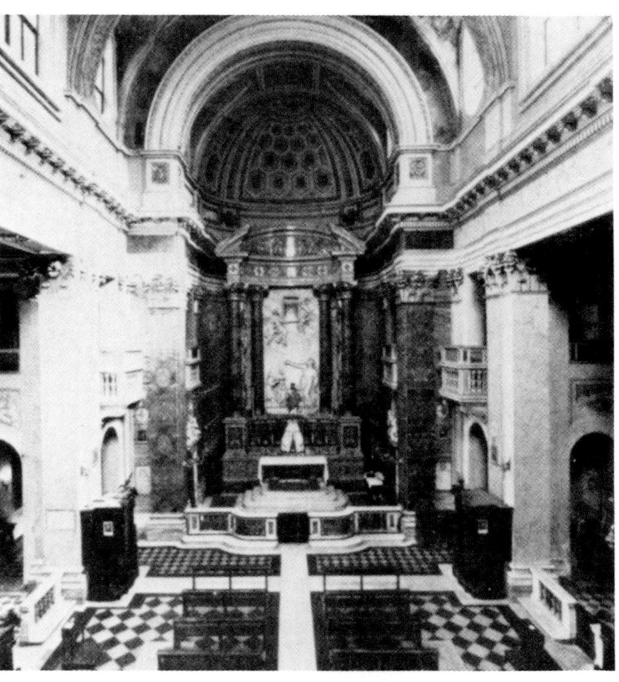

134. Rome, S. Pantaleo, view into the side chapels from the nave (from G. Spagnesi, *Giovanni Antonio de Rossi architetto romano*).

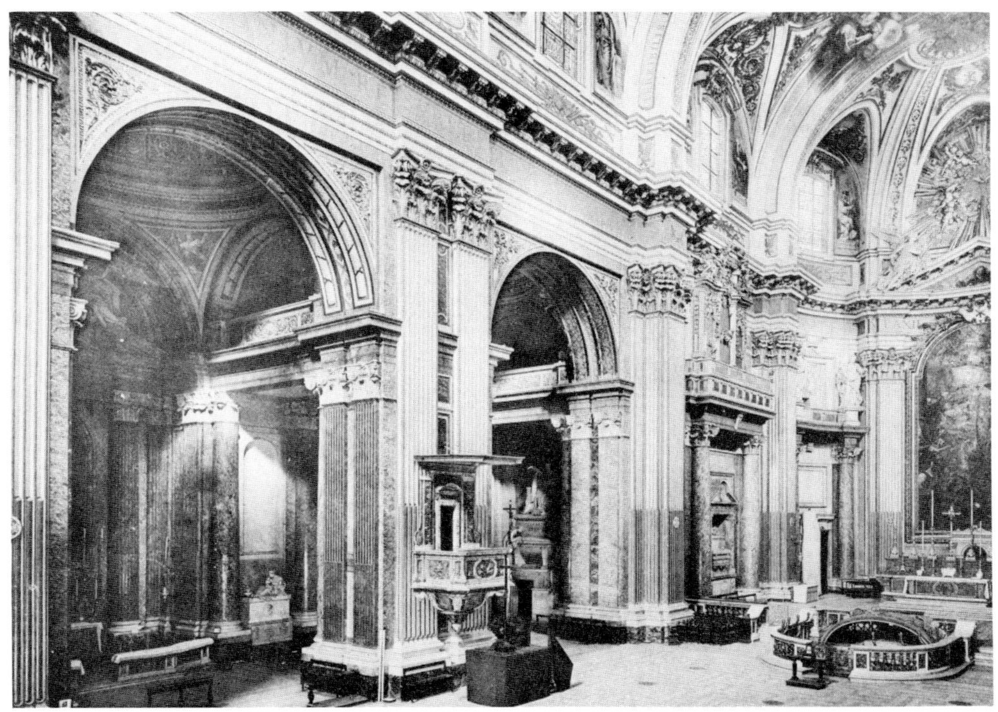

135. Rome, SS. Apostoli, view into the side chapels from the nave (from G. Magni, *Il Barocco a Roma*, I).

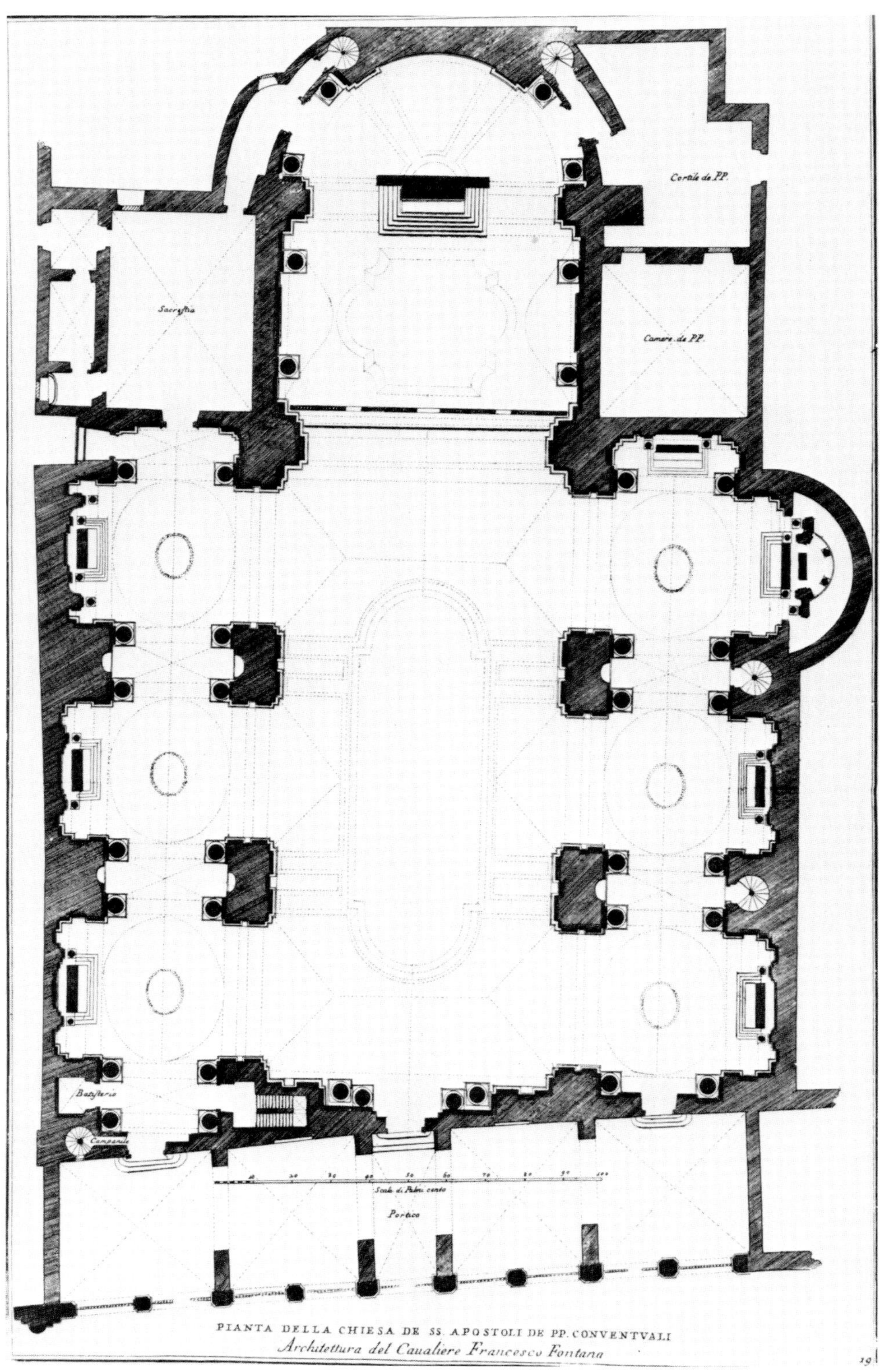

131.   Rome, SS. Apostoli, ground plan by D. de Rossi (*Architettura civile*, III, Rome, 1721).

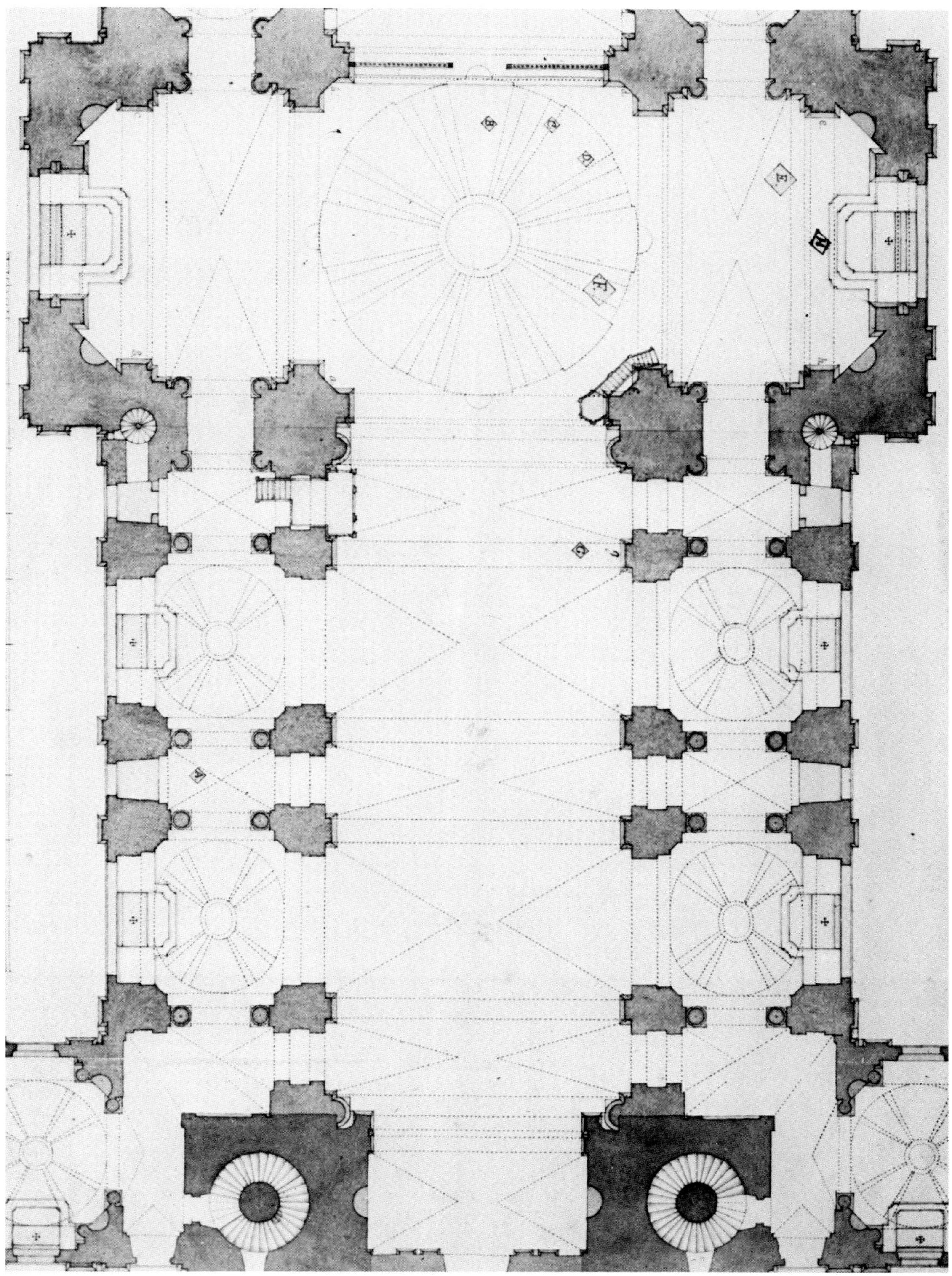

132.   Fulda, Cathedral, eighteenth-century plan (Hessische Landesbibliothek Fulda).

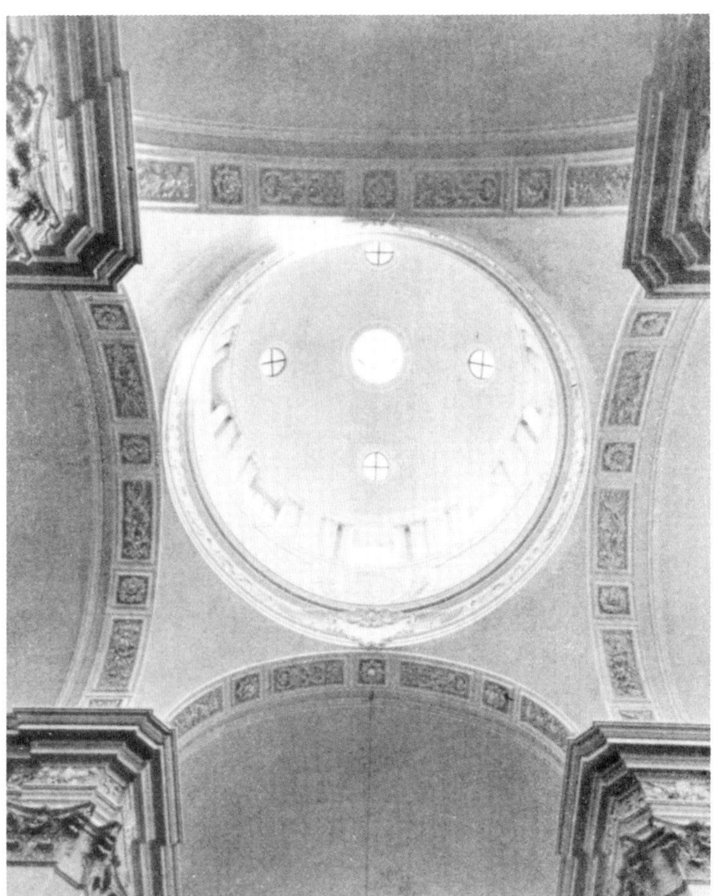

137.   Salzburg, Collegiate Church, view into
the dome (from F. Hagen-Dempf, *Die
Kollegienkirche in Salzburg*).

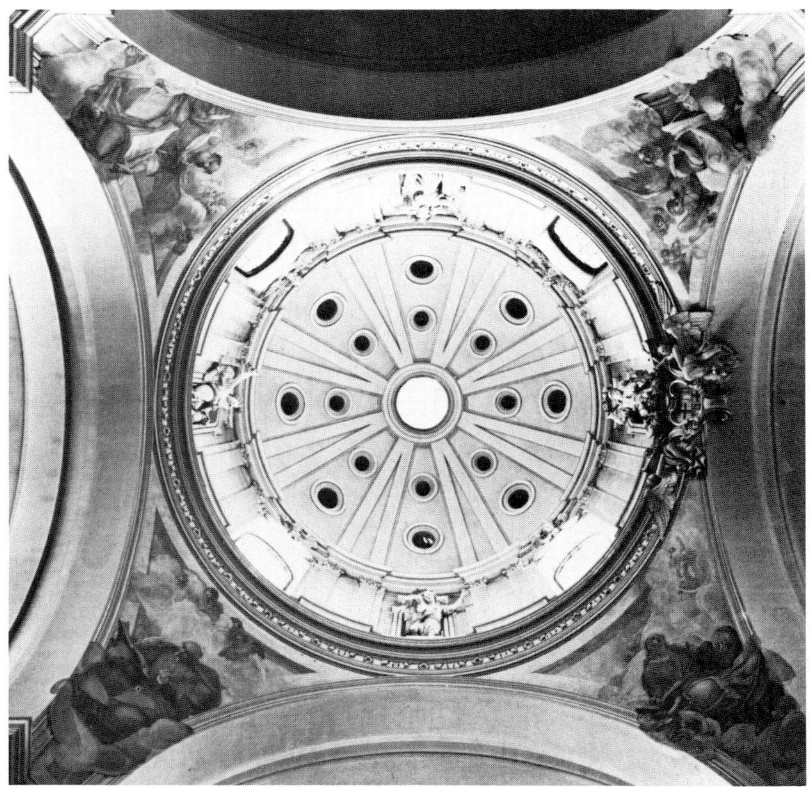

138.   Fulda, Cathedral, view into the dome (from L. Pralle, *Fulda Dom und Abteibezirk*).

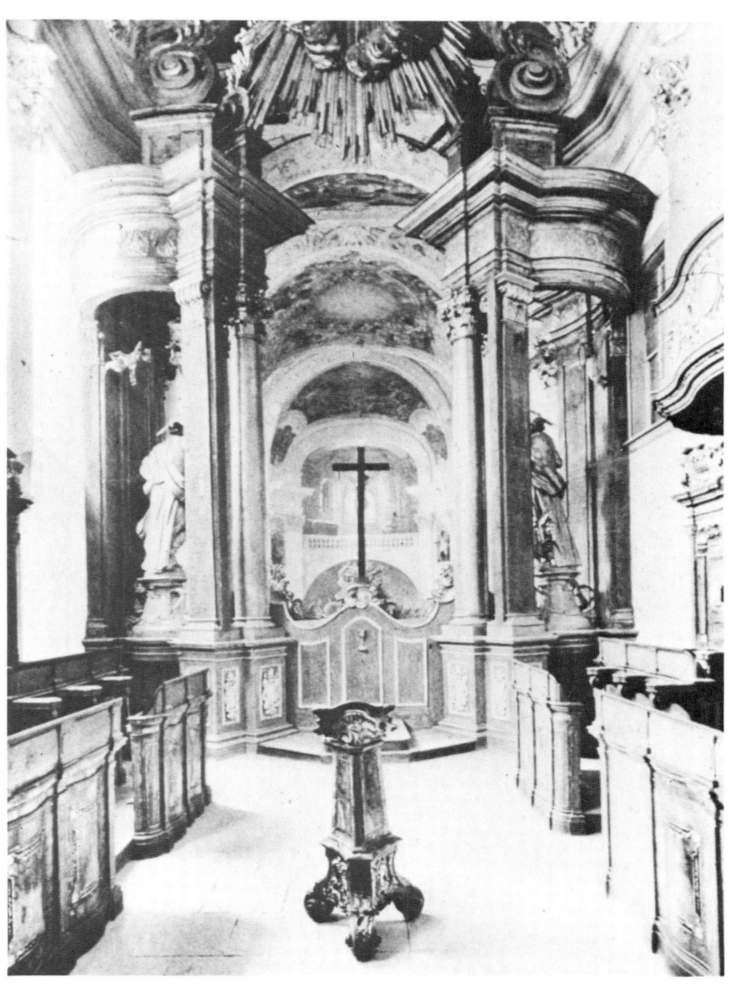

144.   Banz, Monastery Church, choir (from M. Kuhn
         and I. Limmer, *Kloster Banz*, Freiburg i. Br.).

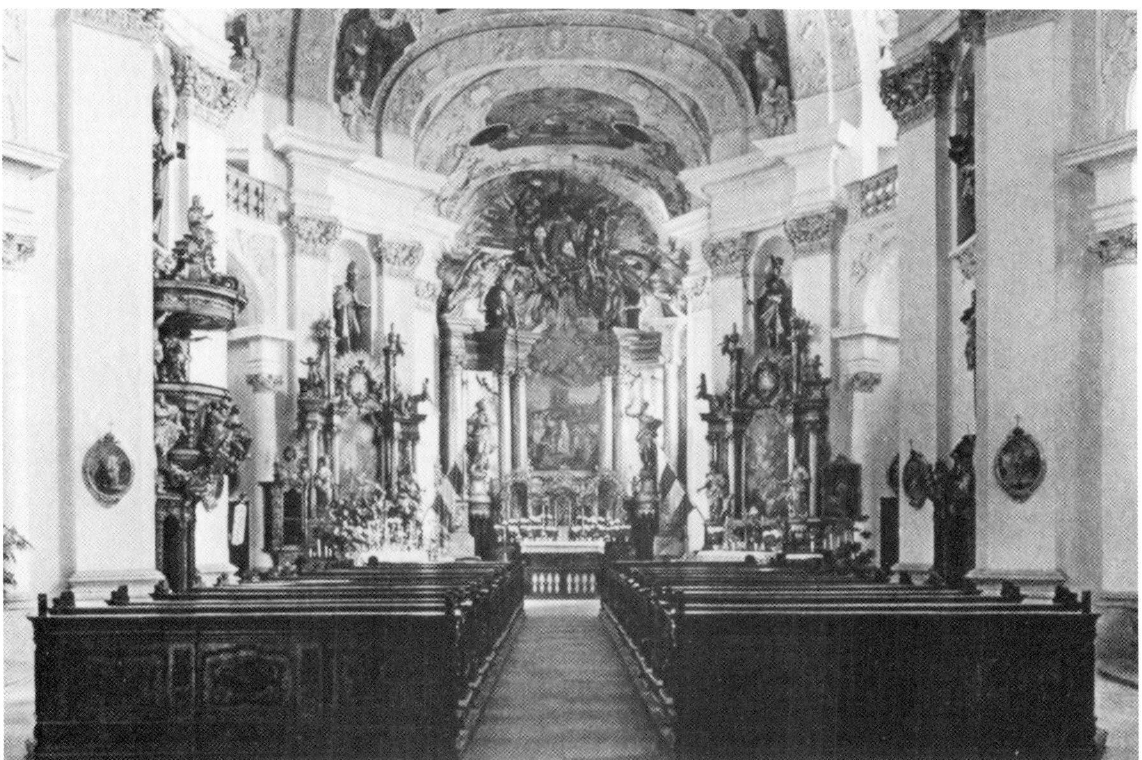

142.   Banz, Monastery Church, view towards the high altar (Bildarchiv Foto Marburg).

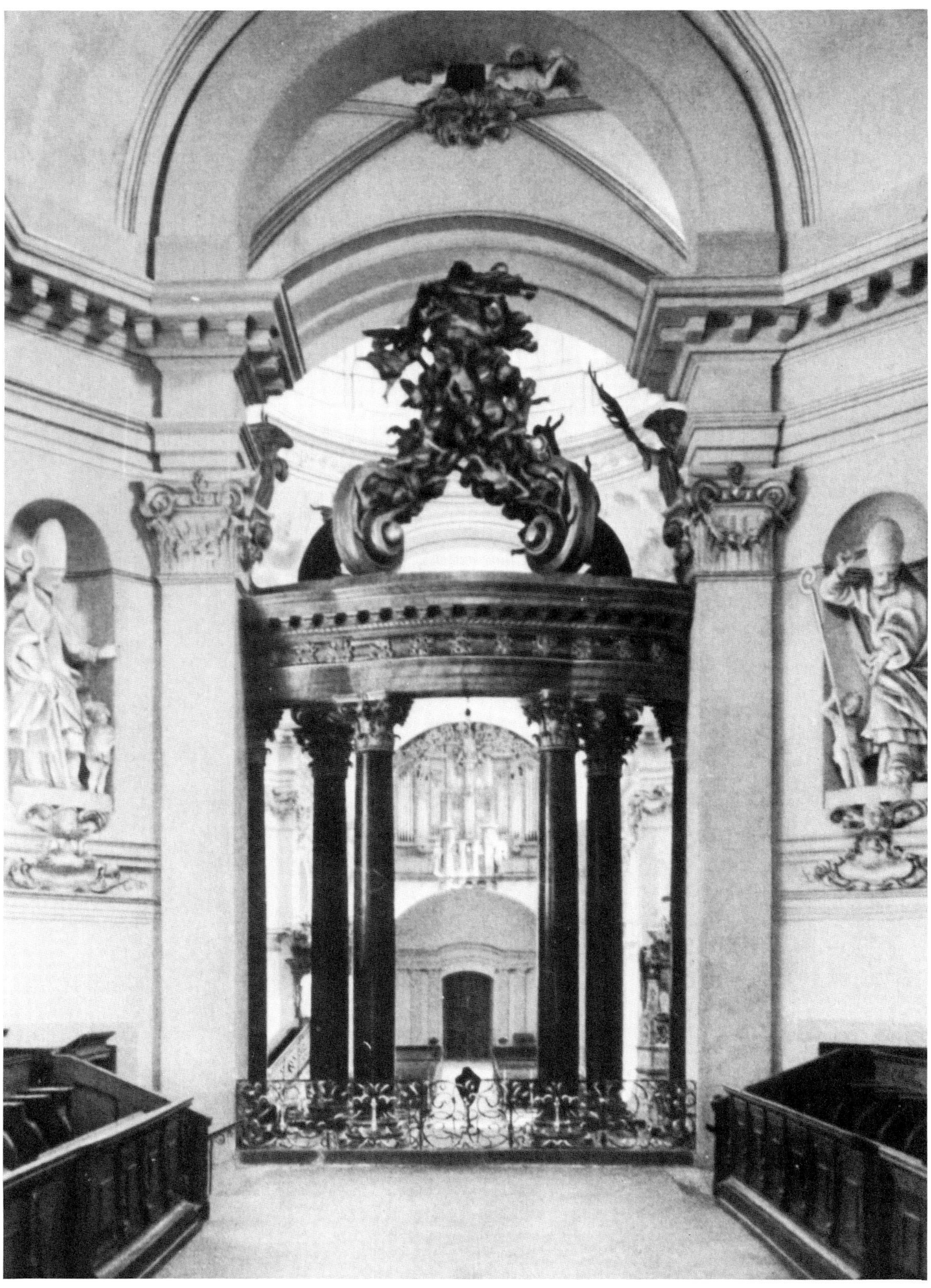

140b.   Fulda, Cathedral, view from the monks' choir into the nave (from E. Kramer and H. Retzlaff, *Fulda*).

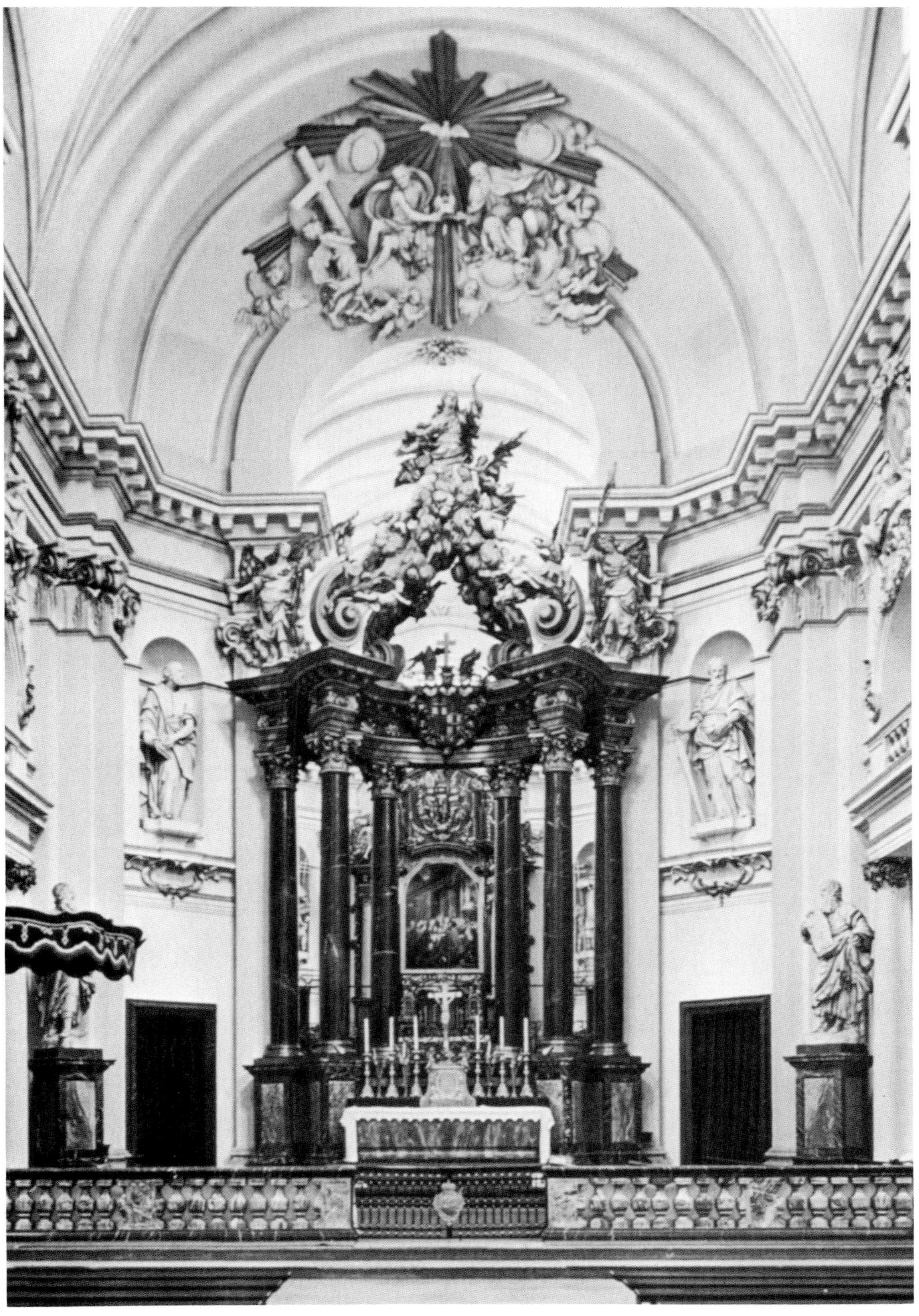

140a.   Fulda, Cathedral, high altar (photo: Gebrüder Metz, Tuüsngen).

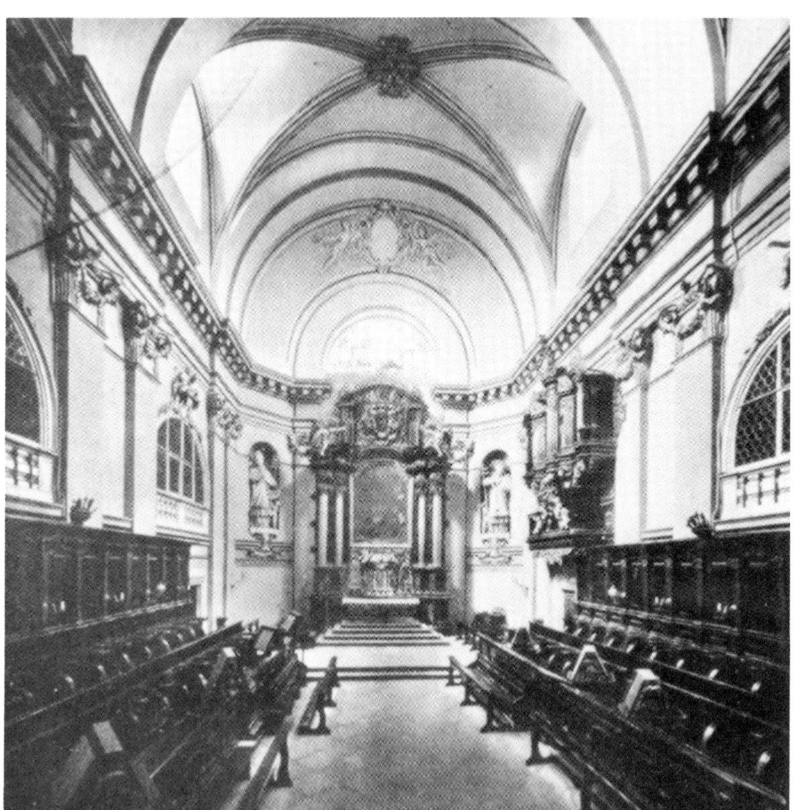

141.   Fulda, Cathedral, monks' choir (from
         E. Kramer and H. Retzlaff, *Fulda*).

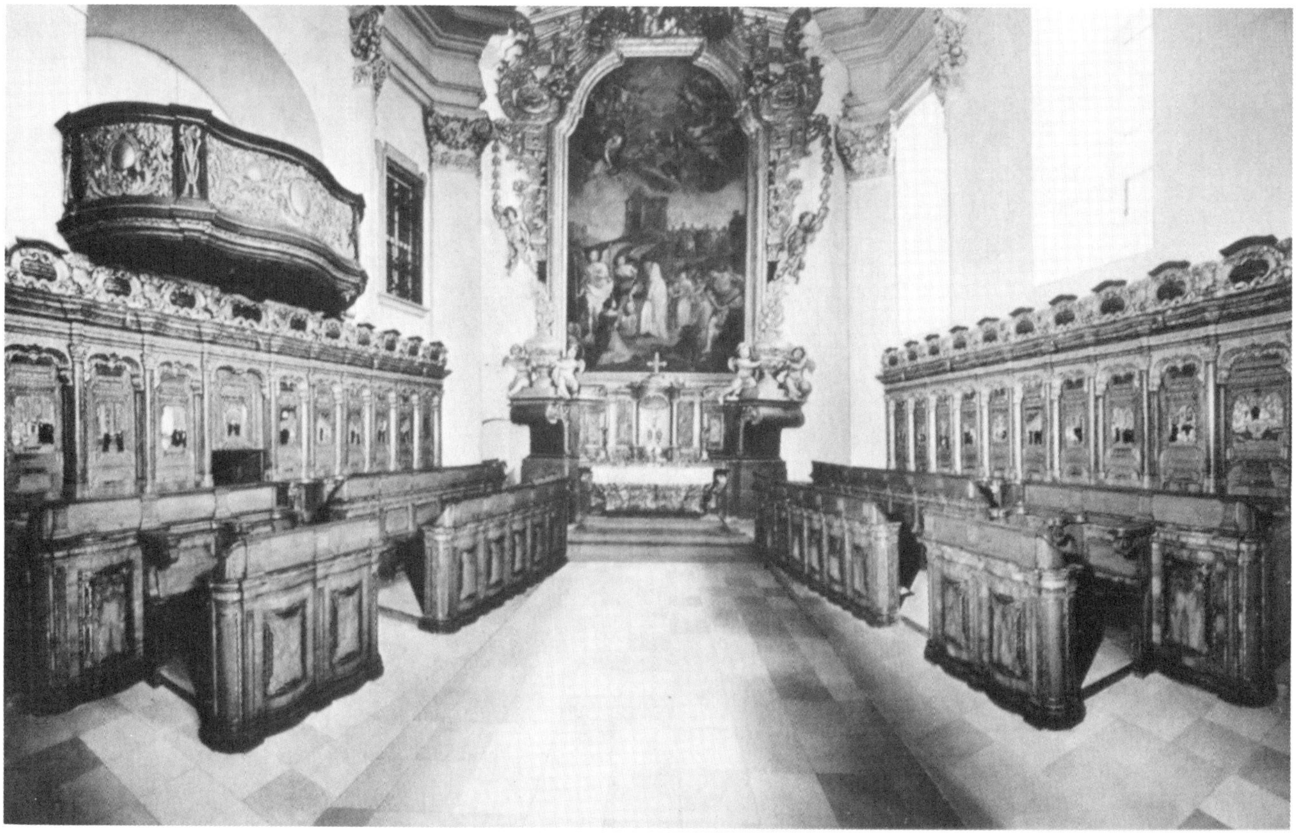

143.   Banz, Monastery Church, monks' choir (Foto - Bornschlegel, Staffelstein).

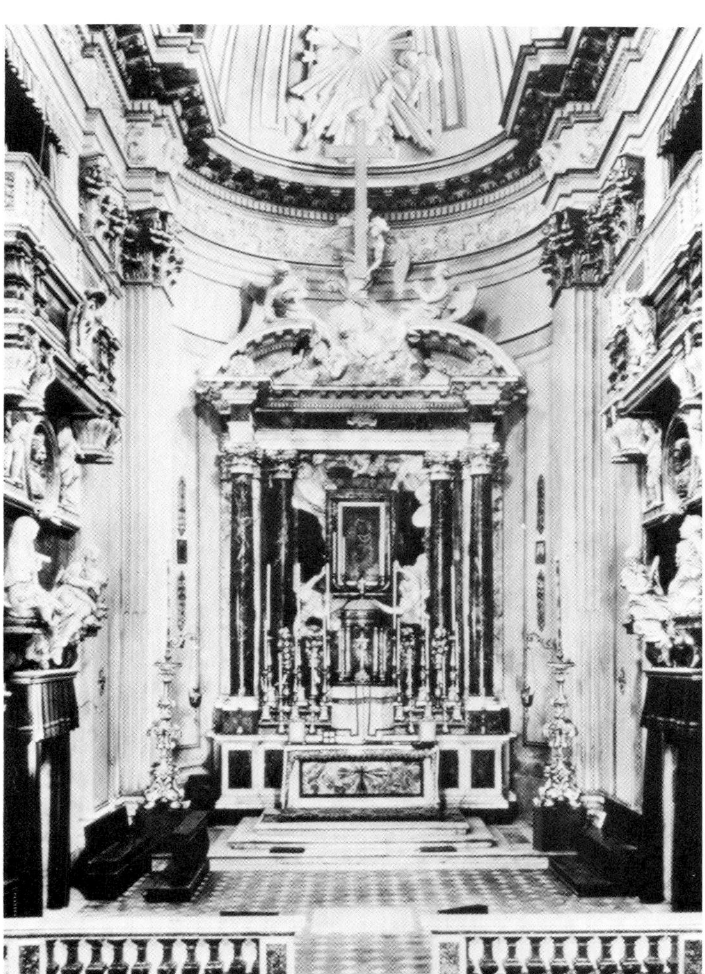

149. Rome, S. Maria dei Miracoli, view of high altar (from Hager, in *Römisches Jahrbuch für Kunstgeschichte*, XI, 1967-1968).

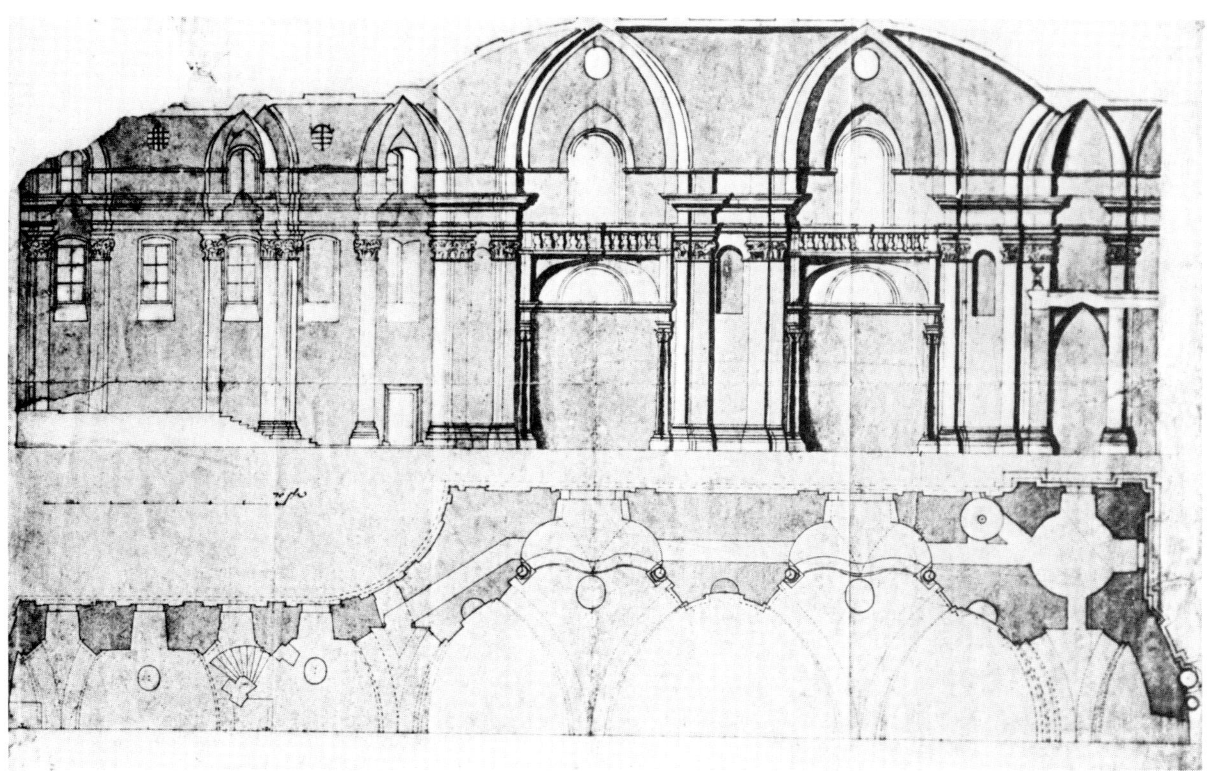

145. Banz, Monastery Church, ground plan and elevation (private collection; from O. A. Weigmann, *Eine Baumberger Baumeisterfamilie*).

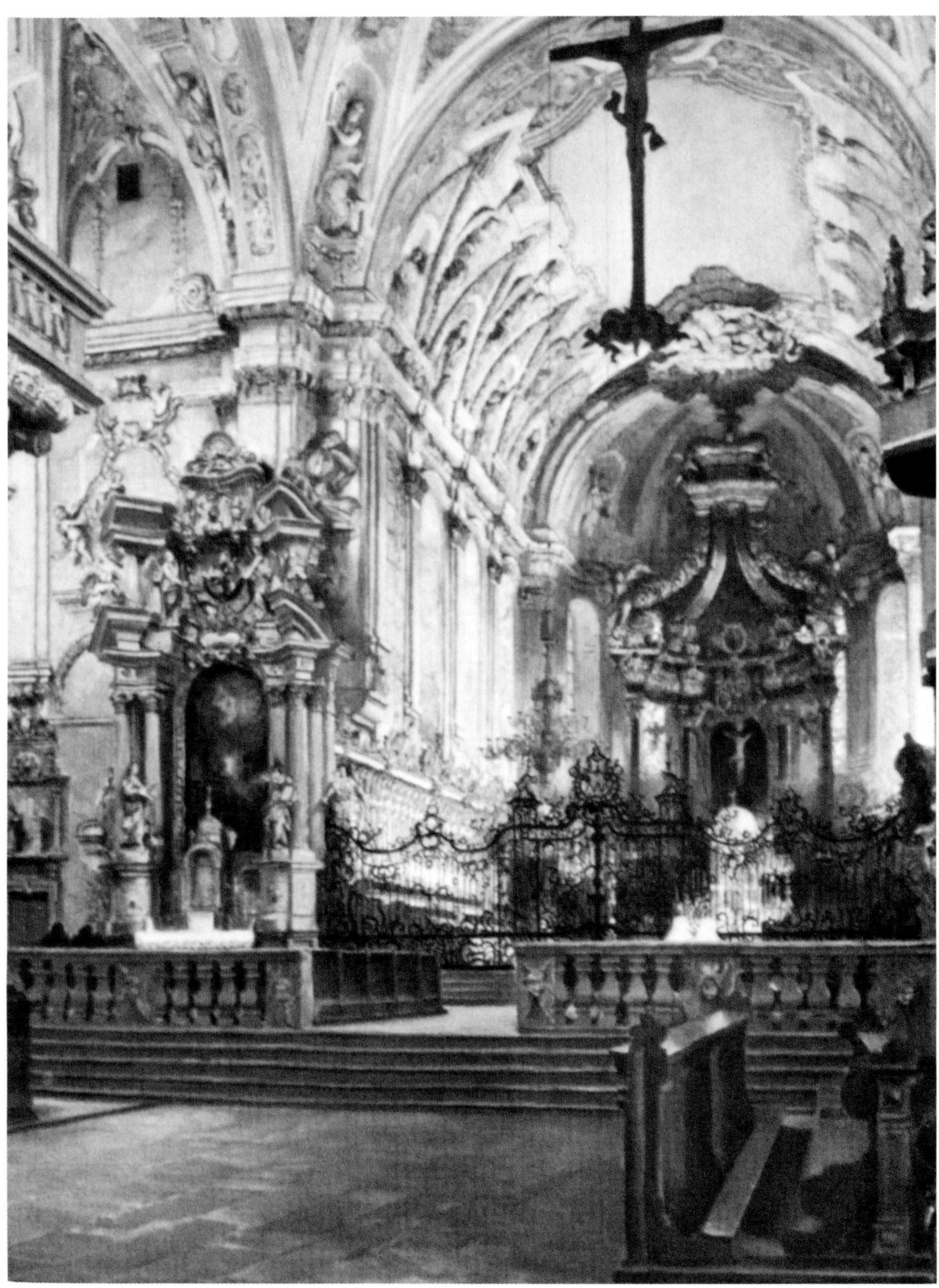

147.   Wurzburg, Cathedral, artist's view of the interior, 1910, Mainfränkisches Museum (postcard).

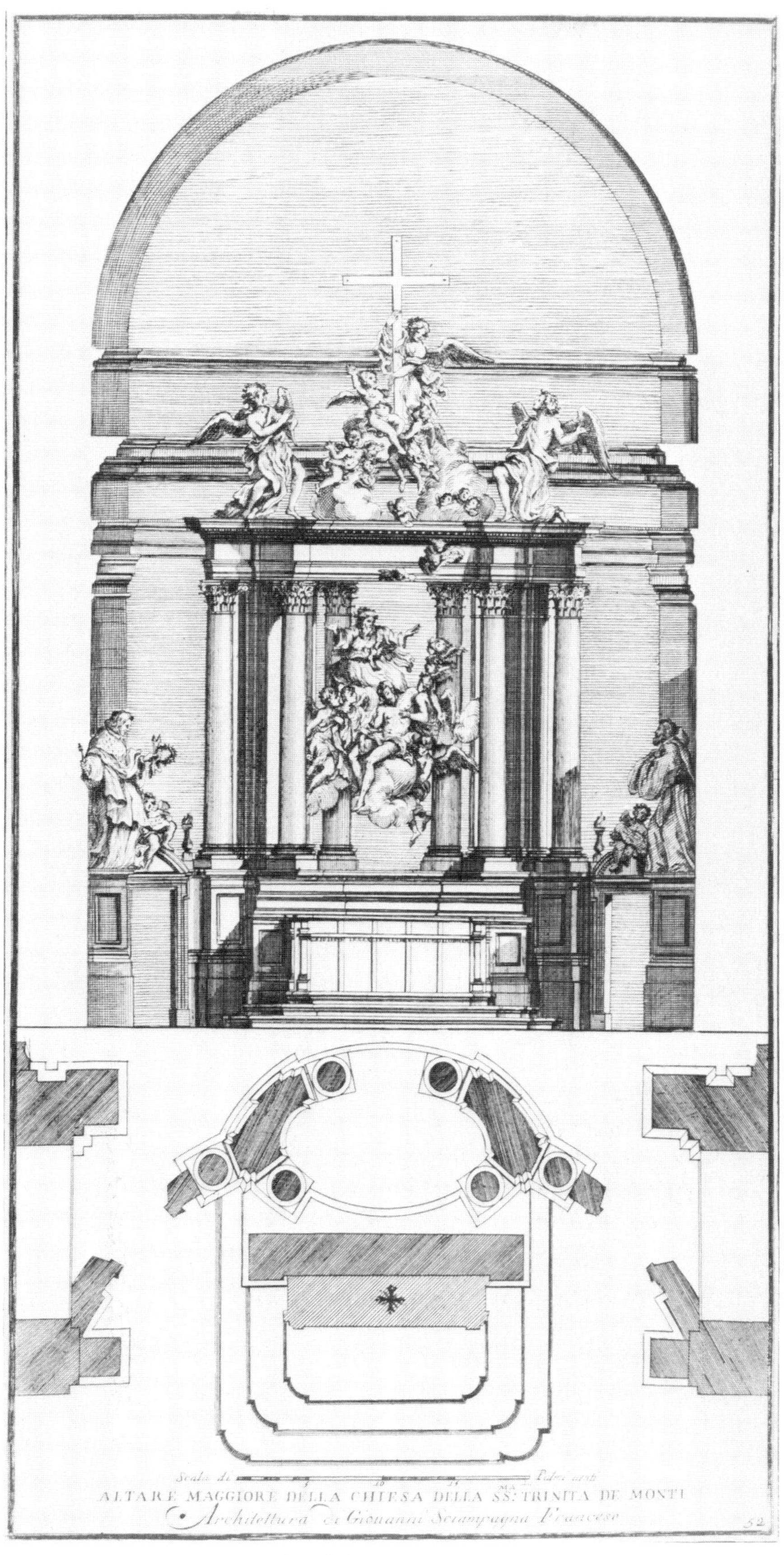

146.   Rome, S. Trinitá dei Monti, engraving of high altar by D. de Rossi (*Architettura civile*, III, Rome, 1721).

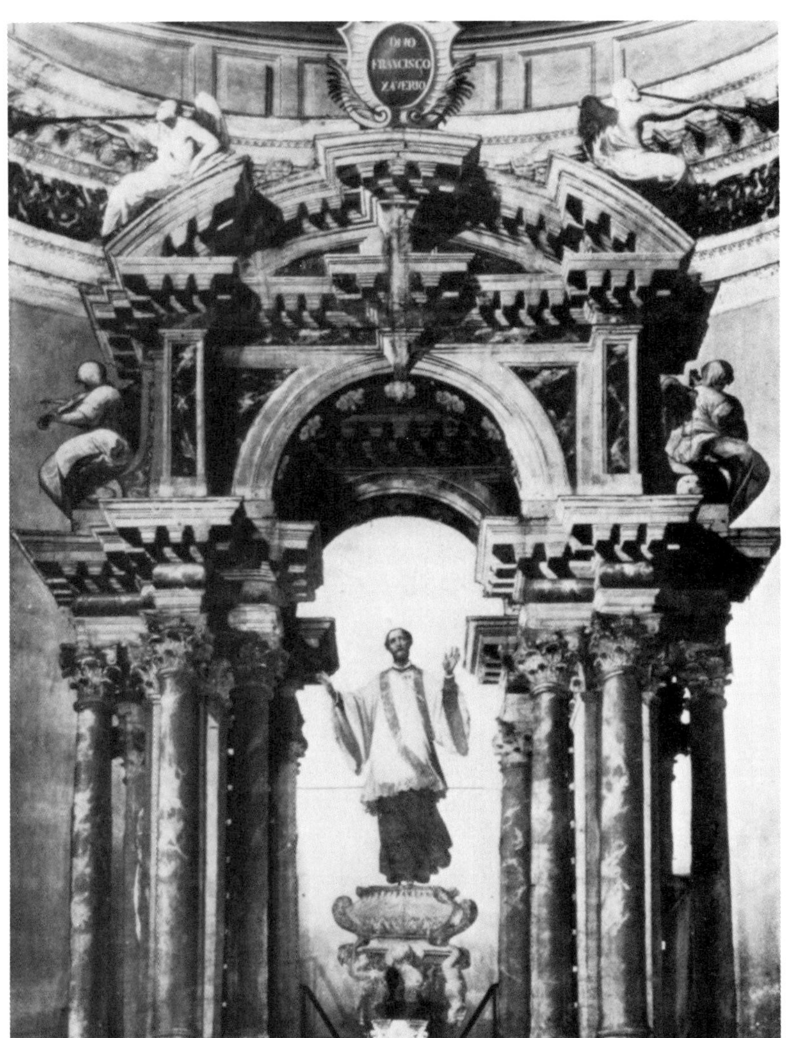

150.   Mondovi, S. Francesco Saverio, painted high altar by Andrea Pozzo (from B. Kerber, *Andrea Pozzo*).

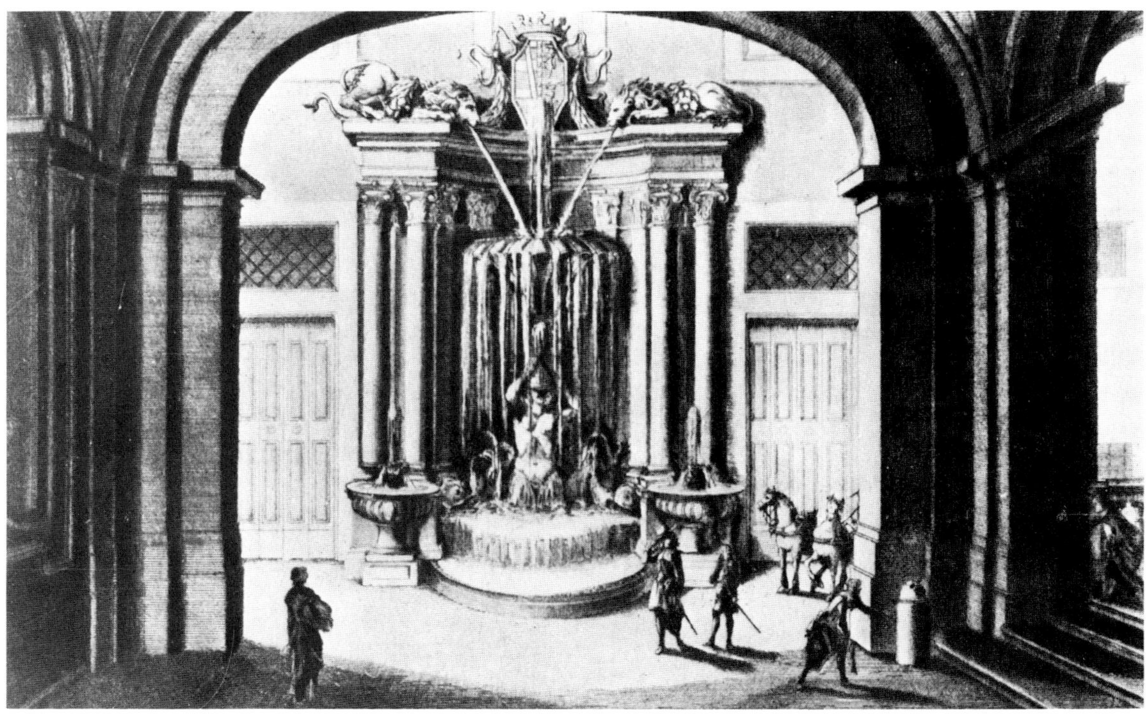

148.   Rome, Palazzo Massimo, courtyard, view by Giov. Batt. Falda (from U. Donati, *Artisti Ticinesi a Roma*).

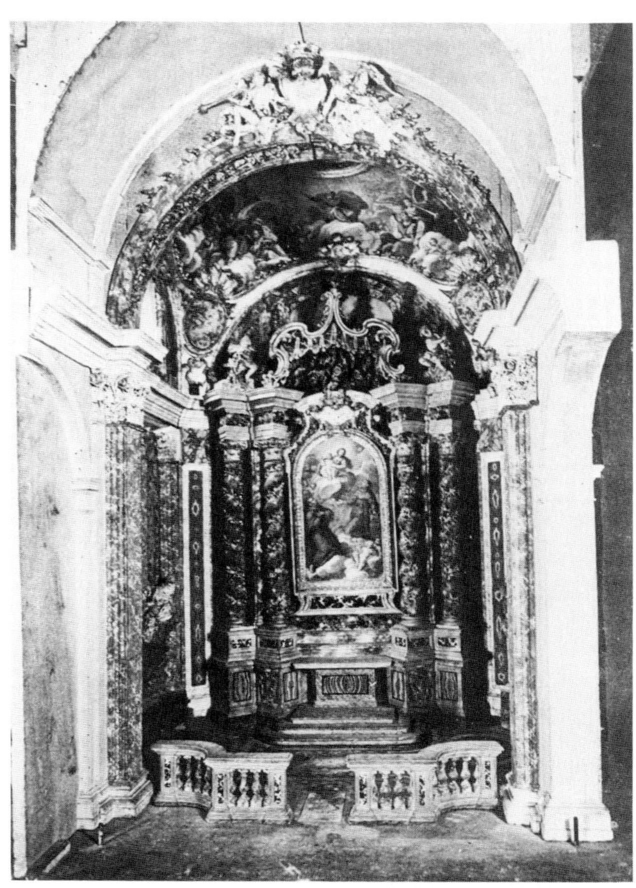

151.   Rome, S. Francesco a Ripa, Cappella Rospigliosi-
Pallavicini, model (from E. Lavagnino, et al., *Altari
barocchi a Roma*).

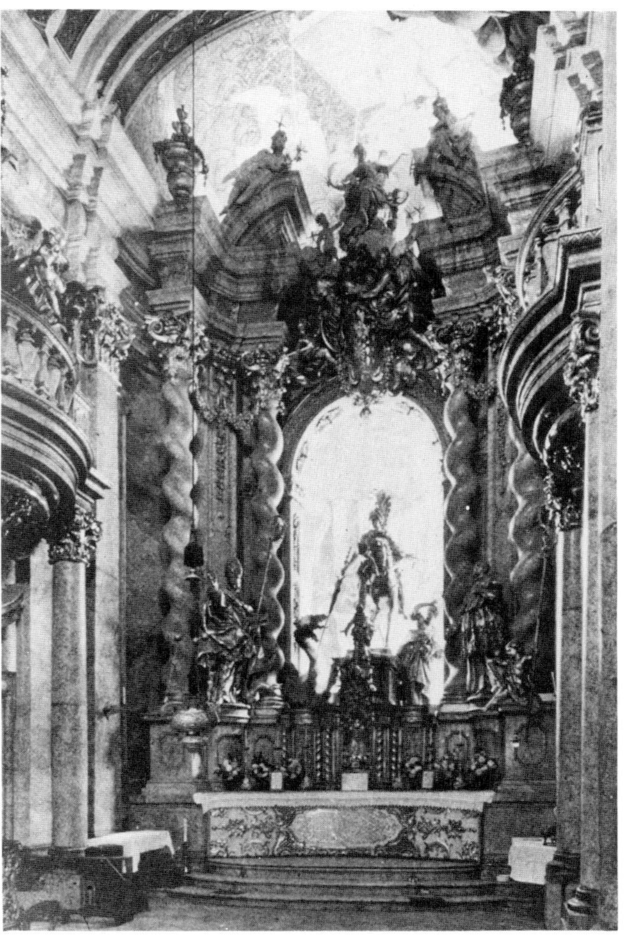

152.   Weltenburg, high altar (from M. Baur-Heinhold, *Theater
des Barock*).

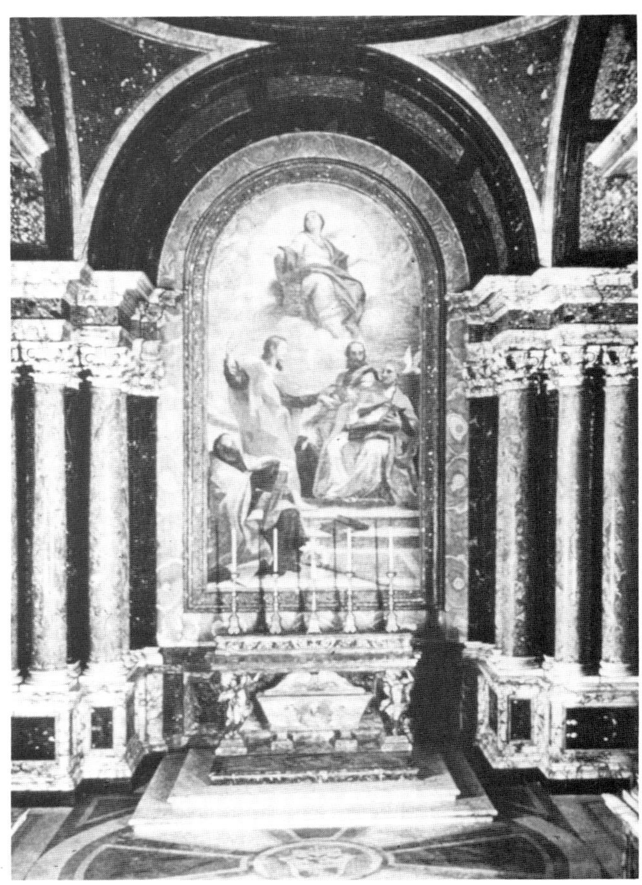

153.   Rome, S. Maria del Popolo, Cappella Cybo (from E. Lavagnino, et al., *Altari barocchi a Roma*).

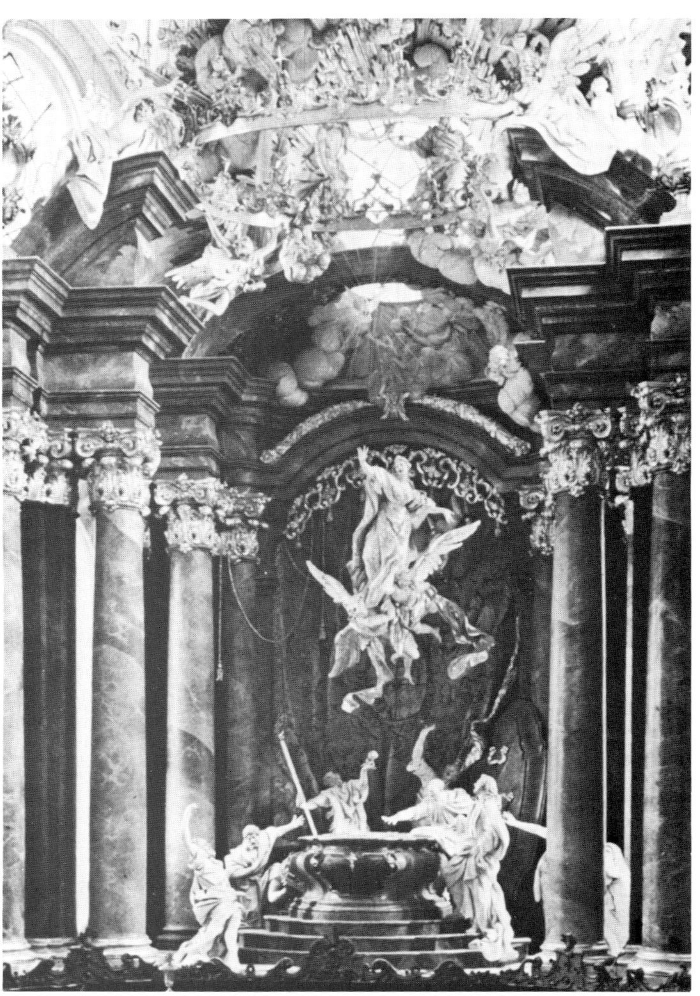

154.   Rohr, Cathedral, high altar (from M. Baur-Heinhold, *Theater des Barock*).

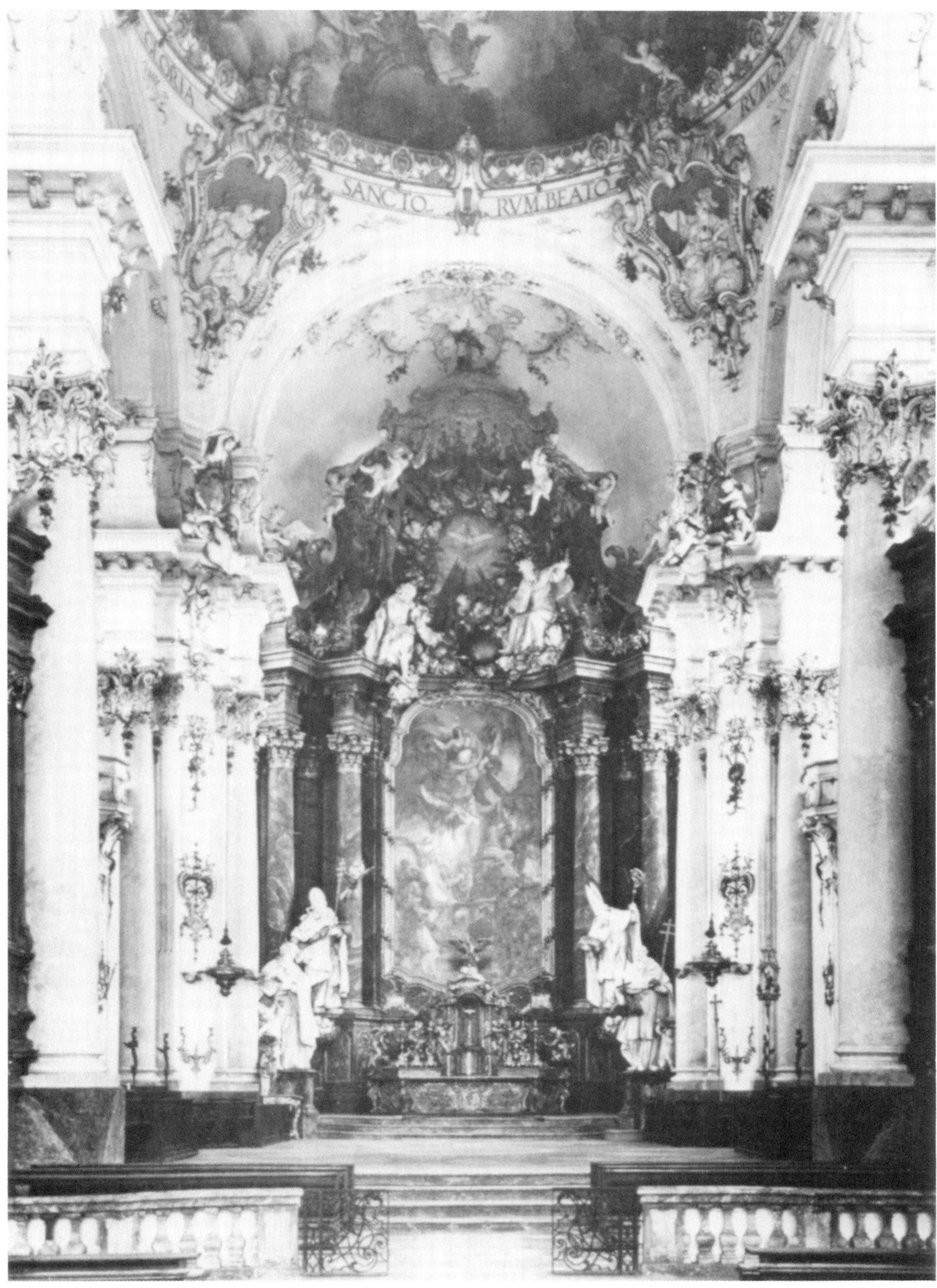

155.   Diessen, Priory Church, high altar (from K. Harries, *The Bavarian Rococo Church*).

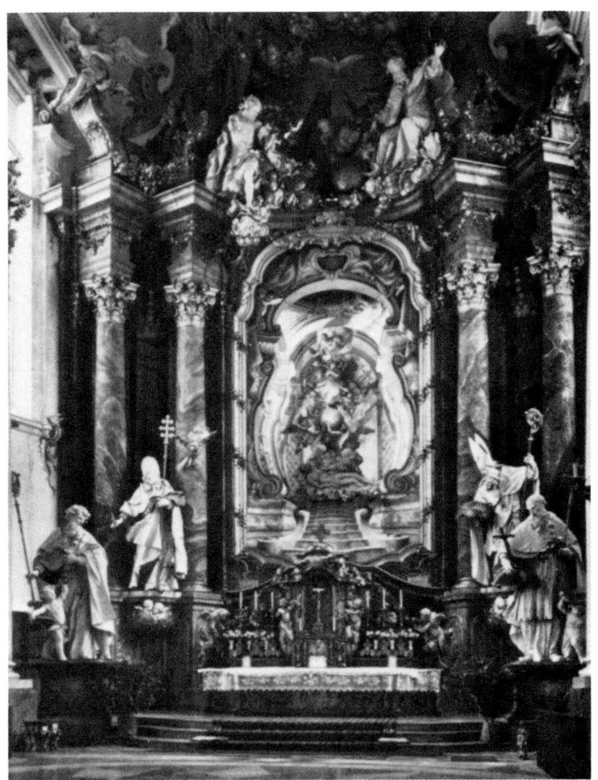

156.   Diessen, Priory Church, high altar with Christ in the Sepulchre (from M. Baur-Heinhold, *Theater des Barock*).

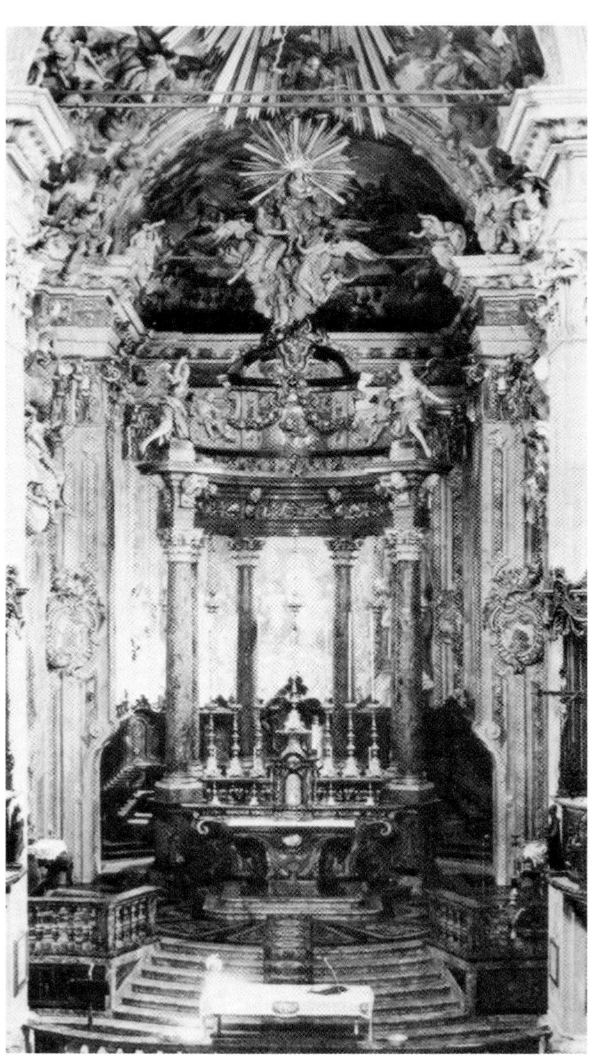

157.   Varallo, Sesia, Basilica of Sacro Monte, high altar by B. Alfieri (from A. Bellini, *Benedetto Alfieri*).

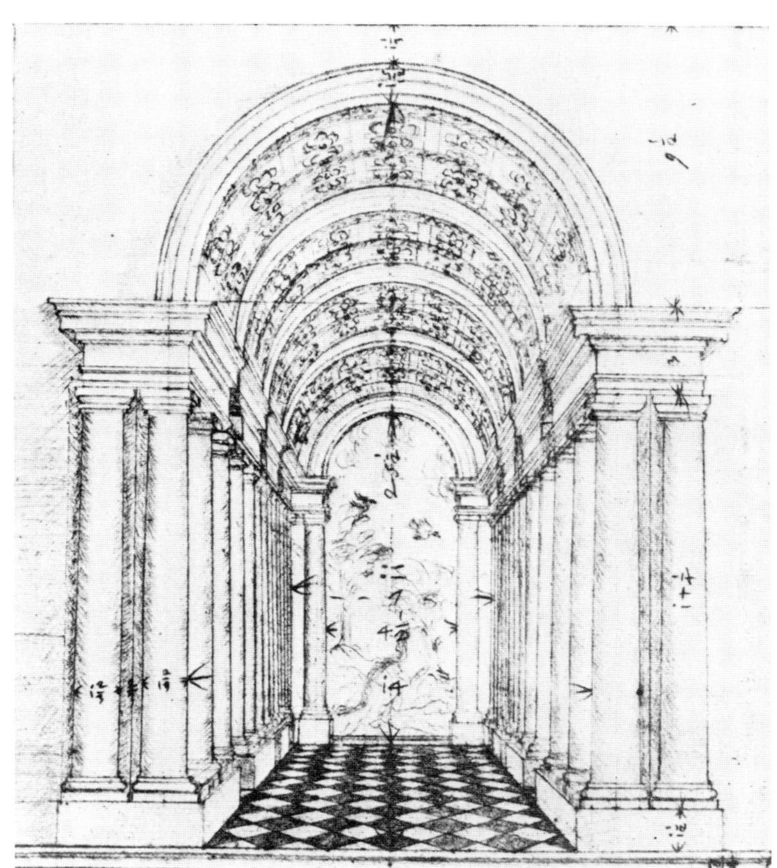

158. Rome, Galleria Spada, project by Borromini (from P. Portoghesi, *The Rome of Borromini*).

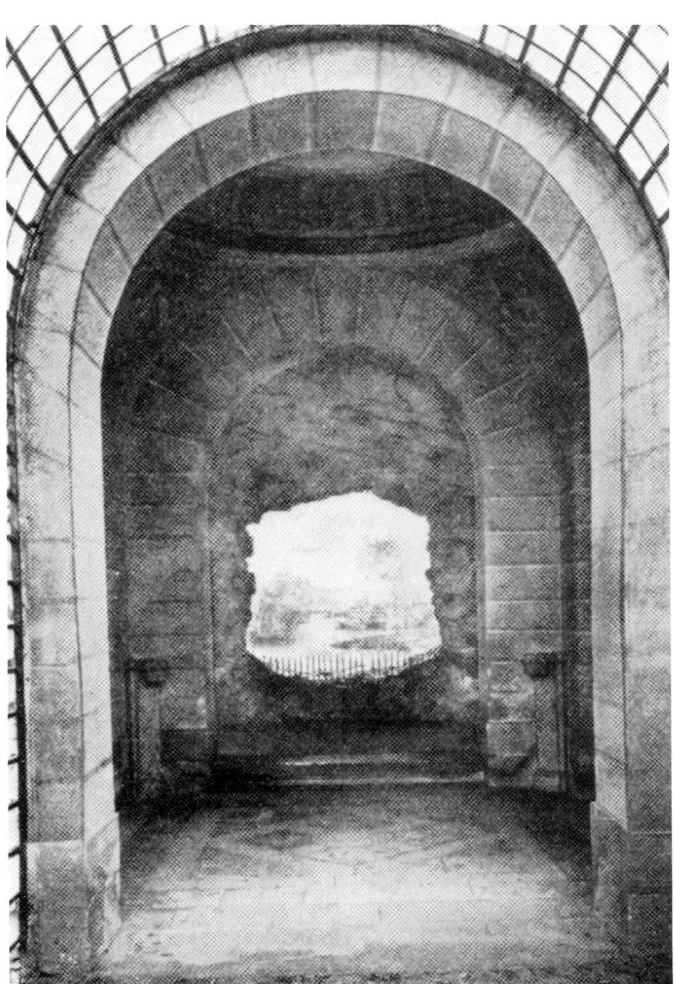

159. Schwetzingen, "Perspektiv" ("Ende der Welt"), feigned landscape fresco (from E. Martin, *Die Kunstdenkmaler des Amtsbezirks Mannheim, Stadt Schwetzingen*).

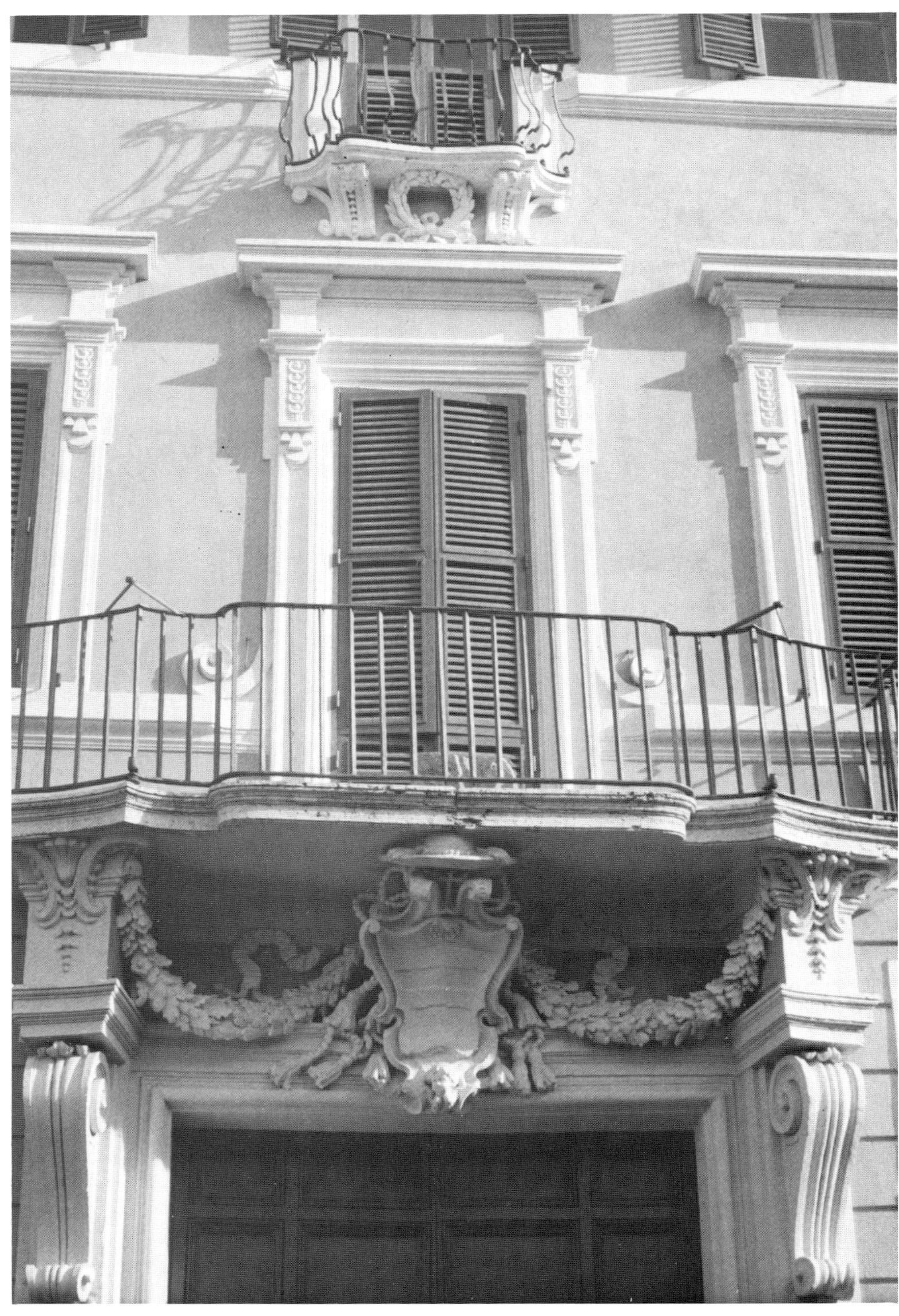

164.   Palazzo Lercari, façade, detail (photo: author).

Filippo Raguzzini, the Palazzo and Casino Lercari in Albano and the Neapolitan Ingredient in Roman Rococo Architecture*

9

On 29 January 1727, Cardinal Nicolò Maria Lercari left the city of Rome to hurry off to the mountain town of Albano in the Castelli Romani to supervise the preparation of his palace for the upcoming visit of Pope Benedict XIII Orsini (1724-1730).[1] Lercari's diligence as papal host would seem surprising. After all, Benedict XIII and his entourage did not arrive in Albano until the following March and, even then, they only stayed the night of March 24th, the first night out of Rome on the pope's spring trip south to Benevento.[2] But, Lercari's preparations involved more than mere housecleaning. In fact, he must have been nervously supervising the construction of a new portal for the palace leading into an entirely new and elegant atrium (figs. 160, 161). Two years later, in May 1729, the cardinal made a second and similar advance trip to his Albano residence to prepare for Benedict's second visit.[3] This time, Lercari watched over the final preparations of a new building designed and constructed with the pope foremost in mind (fig. 162). The Casino Lercari opposite the palace was readied for Benedict's arrival on 2 June 1729.[4] The pope remained for five days before returning to the Vatican and so ending his second and last spring sojourn in Benevento.

The core of the Palazzo Lercari, now the Palazzo Vescovile in Albano, almost certainly dates to the 17th century, but it was substantially enlarged and rebuilt once Lercari was elected to the College of Cardinals in December 1727.[5] The most important modification of the palace proper involved the construction of a main portal and atrium. The doorway is large and flanked by modified pilasters, each of which is topped with a great inverted scroll supporting a modified impost block with curvilinear and foliated decorations (figs. 163, 164). Visually, these form the support for a heavy swag which in turn leads to the large shield and arms of the cardinal centered over the entry. The pseudo-impost blocks also support a bold, if narrow, cornice which doubles as a balconied platform for a window of appearances above at the center of the *piano nobile*.

The decorative dressing of the portal contrasts with the simpler articulation of the palace façade. Indeed, the portal appears as an insert which leads the way into the grand ceremonial atrium behind (fig. 161). The atrium is relatively small, but in spite of its scale it is impressive. The major articulation is pushed away from the portal and so one sees the architecture before moving to it and through it. This far section is organized by two *Serliane*, one before the other. The structural elements describing the *Serliane* are carried out in dark grey stucco. Ovally shaped punctures open the vaults between the matching trabeated sections and these function to lighten the *Serliane*. The whole architectural program is backlit by the well of space and light defined by the unarticulated courtyard beyond. An enormous shell composition, here displaying the arms of Benedict XIII and an elaborate inscription, decorates the central arch of the first *Serliana* (fig. 165).[6] The *Serliane* present a spatial screen, but they also serve to define a cross axis at the rear of the atrium (figs. 166, 167, 168). The central bay is covered with a saucer dome ornamented with foliated stucco forms. The side bays, originally leading to stairways at either side, are barrel vaulted. The *Serliana* motif is also applied in plane to the side walls of the space (fig. 169). Here, the piers are converted into paired and bundled pilasters. The side bays frame square-headed doorways and the oval perforations above open shallow niches in the upper wall, while the central arches form niches decorated with stucco double-shell motifs above and full scale, free-standing antique statues below. In this space the vault is coved and the color coding of grey architectural elements and plain white vaulting with an ochre colored stucco for the walls is consistent with the principal section of the atrium beyond.

The Casino Lercari, opposite, is designed in response to the palace (figs. 162, 170). The width of the casino mirrors that of the palace and the full height of the casino is equal to that of the *piano nobile* of the palace. The casino is crescent shaped with the façade forming an exedra which steps back from the street and palace façade. In plan the sides and rear of the building are squared. The main façade is divided into two dwarfish stories organized into a series of bays which alternate in their design to form an apparently simple rhythmic traveé.

The outermost bays hug the street line and introduce the major bay type which is defined by square-headed entrance ways at ground level and large rectangular windows above (fig. 171). The entire bay unit is framed by pilasters. The secondary bay type is first introduced as the façade steps back from the street to form an open, semicircular space. These bays are organized on the basis of their fenestration and are articulated with round lights below and rectangular ones above; all are framed by elaborate curvilinear stucco surrounds. In addition to the fanciful fenestration, these bays carry decorative wall panels of roughened stucco.

All of these bays are defined by an extremely plain Doric order of pilasters which alternate as single or bundled units. Those bundled are plain, while the single pilasters read more exclusively as wall strips decorated with roughened stucco panels and, in the *piano nobile*, stucco disks. The bays and pilasters are given a continuity by a subtle but quite elaborate system of banding. The cornice dividing the two stories forms a thin but delicate band which responds only to the pilasters which support it. Above, the order supports a more demonstrative entablature that again breaks forward in response to the order. These, reinforced by the roofline podium and squat decorative baubles topping each pilaster, bind the pilasters together. The bays are girdled by two bands, both of which appear in the *piano nobile*. Here the upper and lower edges of the major rectangular windows continue beyond these major bay units, running under the pilasters and across the minor bays intersecting the curvilinear window units of these bays at the top and bottom. The lower wall bands here are marginally heavier and project forward slightly under the major windows. The upper band is more consistent in dimension, but more active, curving up and over the major lights to form modified segmental pediments and rippling forward to mark the tangency with the window frames in the alternate bays.

In all, there is a lively variety of syncopated rhythms. The traveés introduce a theme of alternating forms and functions for the bays. The pilasters themselves are alternately structural and decorative, and this rhythm reads just as strongly as does the beat of the wall bays between them. In fact, the pilasters and bays become consorts as the wall treatments of the secondary, decorative bays seem to flood over onto the pilasters adjacent. Then the more architectural themes reappear in the next bay and, in turn, capture the next pilaster. At the very center of the façade, the decorative strain of pilaster wins out (fig. 172). Here the modest arched entrance, only a slight variation on the major bay type, is flanked at either side by the decorated order, an arrangement that helps define the traveé theme of the bays, while also introducing another organizational scheme: the three central bays read as a larger unit, leaving two, two-bay units to either side and the single bays facing directly on the street around the bend. As with the bay units themselves, there is the implication of organization by function as well as by form. The two-bay units describe façades reminiscent in form, if not in decoration, of small *case*, while the central section becomes an expanded and more elaborate variant. The Casino Lercari was designed as a guest house for Pope Benedict XIII and his entourage, and one senses this in the sectioning of the façade and of the building behind. The effect is one of a small, rococo hospice. The pope's quarters were surely at the center of the exedra in the largest apartment and those officials of lowest rank, no doubt, were assigned the smaller, more remote units along the street.

Nicolò Maria Lercari (1675-1757) arrived in Rome from Benevento in the wake of Benedict XIII's election in 1724. While his initial assignment in the pope's administration was as *Maestro di Camera*, Lercari gained recognition rapidly. By June 1726, he was appointed Secretary of State, replacing Cardinal Fabrizio Paolucci at his death, and the following December he was elected cardinal.[7] Lercari's purchase of property in Albano has not been documented;

however, it seems unlikely that he owned the palace before his relocation to Rome in 1724. The documentation surrounding Lercari's projects for the palace and casino clearly imply that a palace already existed on the site before Lercari's ownership.[8] The building campaign involving the palace seems to have been two-fold. The portal and atrium were complete in time for Benedict's visit in March 1727. No documentation specifically for this work has come to light, but it appears that Benedict may have begun planning the Beneventan tour, which afforded the Albano layover, as early as late 1725.[9] The trip was not popular with Benedict's advisors, and at first efforts to abort the tour were somewhat successful. Nevertheless, the pope ordered the preparation of an itinerary in March 1726, although by April the trip had been postponed until October 1726.[10] While Benedict only announced his planned trip to the cardinals on 17 March 1727 (just one week before his departure), there is no question that Lercari was privy to the pope's plans with enough lead time to order and oversee the modification of his palace for his honored guest.[11] This scenario establishes a date for the portal and atrium architecture of between March 1726 and March 1727.

There is also evidence of a second building campaign at the palace. Records for this work, consisting largely of property valuations, exchange acts and payments, only begin to appear in February 1727. These continue without interruption through September and the scheduled deadline for the work was October 1727.[12] Given the types of documents and the descriptions of properties, this campaign evidently involved an enlargement of the palace by the addition of the northern wing (along the present Piazza della Rotonda and toward the church of S. Maria della Rotonda) and possibly additions around the courtyard as well.

Identification of the architect or architects of these two campaigns is difficult. The more pedestrian project of enlarging the palace can be associated with the Roman architect Tommaso de'Marchis (1693-1759) inasmuch as he is responsible for all of the *misure e stime* for the acquired properties and for a series of small property drawings accompanying these.[13] But, in lieu of any documentation for the architectural work on the portal and atrium, the stylistic aspects of this work remain the only possible key to the identity of the personality involved. Here the problem becomes especially teasing.

If de'Marchis can be associated with the enlargement of the palace, he may also be responsible for the treatment of the palace façade which is consistent on both the main street façade and on the added wing. The simple channeling of the base and the stucco window surrounds of the upper story are relieved by the more ornamented windows of the *piano nobile*. These more aggressive surrounds—panels at the side that grow into aedicules carrying heavier, flat lintels at the top—may well have been added to redress the façade, but whether they reflect the work of the same designer as that of the portal and atrium is yet another question. The language of the portal is considerably more decorative and the stucco work here leads naturally to the decoration of the atrium. The atrium itself seems rather distinctive in type as well as in detail.

There are occasional examples of some of the atrium forms in Roman architecture. The perforation of vaults, for example, can be found in the access corridor of the convent of the Maddalena (1680-1684) designed by Carlo Francesco Bizzacheri (1655-1721).[14] The use of stucco ornamentation, too, might be traced to Bizzacheri's decoration of the façade of S. Isodoro (1704-1705).[15] The lower story of this façade is also organized on the *Serliana*, although Bizzacheri inherited this motif from Domenico Castelli, the original architect of the church. The possible influence of Bizzacheri adds a wrinkle to the problem of the attribution of the portal and atrium in Albano inasmuch as he was the teacher of Tommaso de'Marchis. De'Marchis himself is something of a mystery; while he trained with Bizzacheri, his earliest documented work, the Palazzo Mellini on the Corso, dates to 1741 and is not closely related to the work at Palazzo Lercari.[16]

In type, the atrium at Palazzo Lercari is more convincingly related to architectural traditions in Naples. The organization of two separate staircases placed toward the rear of the *androne* or courtyard, as well as the type of screening of space and light that the double *Serliane* and consequent perforated vaulting introduce are both characteristics of Neapolitan architecture. The ensemble of portico and loggia with perforated walls and vaults is common in both church and palace architecture in Naples. In churches, this often forms a screen-like façade and vestibule to the nave with a loggia above, as in Cosimo Fanzago's S. Maria degli Angeli alle Croci (begun 1639) (figs. 173, 174), and in Marcello Guglielmelli's S. Giuseppe dei Ruffi (ca. 1715-1725).[17] In domestic architecture, this feature seems to grow into a more elaborate staircase structure for urban buildings and a more spacious, horizontal element for villa architecture, and while few of the villas are extant, the Palazzo Lercari design recalls the Villa Bisignano at Barra (fig. 175) and the Villa Menna at Portici.[18]

In detail as well, the work at Palazzo Lercari recalls southern Italian architecture. The stucco work applied to the dome, pendentives and vaults is similar to stucco ornamentation of these kinds of surfaces in Neapolitan buildings. And, too, the grey stucco architectural elements, especially those framing the stairway entries and oval vault perforations, are reminiscent of the strap-like work of early 18th-century Neapolitan designers.[19]

In sum, the Neapolitan sources for the portal and atrium of the Albano palace seem more comprehensive and complete than are the possible Roman sources. The sources can be traced both to traditions as well as to contemporary developments in Naples. In this, they are also more convincing. The references in architecture to Naples may not be entirely accidental. After all, Lercari, although Genoese by birth, served Benedict XIII before his election in Benevento. Furthermore, these modifications to the palace were in honor of the pope and may well have been tailored to Benedict's own known preference for Neapolitan and southern Italian architectural forms.[20]

The only architect working in and around Rome during the reign of Benedict XIII who was conversant with Neapolitan architectural developments was Filippo Raguzzini (ca. 1680-1771).[21] Like Lercari, Raguzzini had arrived in Rome in the service of the pope. By the time the alterations to Palazzo Lercari were begun in 1726, Raguzzini had already completed the Chapel of S. Domenico in S. Maria sopra Minerva for Benedict XIII; he was finishing Benedict's Holy Year project of 1725, the Ospedale di S. Gallicano, another markedly Neapolitan complex, and in October 1726 he was named papal architect.[22] The possible attribution of the portal and atrium to Raguzzini is given added force by the fact that he can be identified with certainty as the designer of the Casino Lercari, the next of the cardinal's Albano projects. And, by the 1730s, Raguzzini appears as the "Architetto d. D. Card.l Lercari" in various documents.[23]

The earliest documentation of work preparatory to the construction of the Casino Lercari dates to November 1728.[24] Four properties opposite the main façade of the palace were purchased between December 1728 and March 1729.[25] In February 1729, the Director of the Académie de France à Rome extolled Cardinal Lercari as a friend of the arts, especially since he had just acquired some French prints to decorate the "upper apartment" in his new house in Albano.[26] This reference would seem to be to the casino, but the work may not have been far enough along in February to worry over the appointments of the interior. In any case, the casino was complete in time for the pope's return visit in early June 1729. In the five days spent in Albano, Valesio reports that Benedict consecrated the altar of the chapel in Palazzo Lercari.[27] Chracas records Benedict XIII's visit one morning to Castel Gandolfo after which he returned to Albano where he delivered a benediction against a local infestation of insects from the balcony of the Casino Lercari.[28] There is no record of Benedict's delight with the guest accommodations, although in August 1729 he did issue a chirograph ordering the allotment of more water for the casino. Here he attests to the fact that he stayed in the casino and, therefore, can verify the need for more water.[29]

That Filippo Raguzzini is the architect of Casino Lercari is supported on the one hand by his role in the *misure e stime* for the properties (de'Marchis does not appear in these documents at all). But, more to the point is the fact that his authorship is undeniable on the basis of the casino architecture. Details of the casino such as the roughened stucco panels, their shapes, their use as an overlay on a pilaster order and the circular window shapes are directly related to Raguzzini's design for the main façade of the Ospedale di S. Gallicano (1725-1726) in Rome (fig. 176). The elaborate, if subtle, alternation of bays through variant treatments of the fenestration and the use of horizontal bands to girdle these bay systems recall Raguzzini's treatment of the elevations of the apartment buildings defining Piazza S. Ignazio, also in Rome (figs. 177, 178).

The architectural recipe for the details of Casino Lercari—part S. Gallicano, part Piazza S. Ignazio—is further supplemented by an ingredient of planning. The semi-circular or exedra plan of the casino has no exact precedent in Raguzzini's work. Rather, the form would appear to derive from Roman villa architecture, and specifically from nymphaea designs. To be sure, the casino did not function as a nyphaeum, but it shares this aspect both in plan and in elevation. The exedra shape as well as the series of bays divided by pilasters and the dwarfish scale all reinforce the villa/nymphaeum sources.[30] There is an element of logic here: the

Palazzo and Casino Lercari functioned as a second, rural residence for the cardinal and it was used for *villeggiatura*.

The planning element, the placement of the exedra opposite and on axis with Palazzo Lercari, is neither particularly elaborate nor especially successful. But, its basic motive of establishing a spatial dialogue between two unequally scaled structures is identical to the design problem and motive that Raguzzini faced in the Piazza S. Ignazio assignment.[31] In each case, the architect relies on two primary design devices. The simplest of these is the establishment of a link between the two opposing structures based on dimensions. At Piazza S. Ignazio, the entablature marking the division between the two stories of the façade of the church of S. Ignazio establishes the height of the five-structure ensemble defining the piazza in front. The width of the church façade determines the width of the piazza. For Casino Lercari, the height of the *piano nobile* of the palace determines the height of the casino, while the total width of the palace defines its width. This pairing of heights and widths is a simple device for relating two structures. But Raguzzini's planning solutions are also heavily dependent on the establishment of a spatial dialogue in which the shape and surface of the smaller structures are pitted against the mass and scale of the larger. At Piazza S. Ignazio the result is a delightful and rich orchestration of space. The open space invites exploration, and this promotes a sense of spaciousness in spite of the relatively small scale in real terms. In Albano, the result is less satisfying. The limitations of the site—of both the open space and of the casino—seem to deny a sense of space that is real and open. The corridor established by via Alcide de Gaspari (the former via del Plebiscito) overrides the little arena of space; the palace towers over the casino; and the diminutive scale of the casino heightens the sense of congestion between the two buildings. Raguzzini's involvement at Piazza S. Ignazio dates to March 1727, and although the work on the piazza continued into the 1730s, the eastern and central buildings were completed during 1729, the year of the Casino Lercari design.[32] Given the contemporaneity of the two projects, their conceptual relationship in terms of planning is hardly surprising. But what is remarkable is the startling difference in style between the two. Piazza S. Ignazio, to a certain extent, marks the Romanization of Raguzzini's architectural vocabulary. Casino Lercari shares none of this Roman flavor. Rather, it is marked by a strongly Neapolitan aspect. In style, it recalls the Chapel of S. Domenico (1724-1725) and the Ospedale di S. Gallicano. Given the rather harsh, at times

scathing, review of these works by the Roman audience, the style of the Casino Lercari would have been unthinkable in Rome as late as 1729.[33] Raguzzini was acutely aware of the criticism and responded by accommodating the style of his work in Rome to the Roman taste. The architectural detailing and surface handling of the Piazza S. Ignazio apartments, as well as his design for S. Maria della Quercia (1727-1731), provide ready testament to this change in style.[34]

The Neapolitan flavor of Casino Lercari, like the palace portal and atrium completed two years earlier, may reflect the taste of Cardinal Lercari. Indeed, the building was not for a Roman audience; it was for a client whose taste and sympathies lay in the very origins of Raguzzini's architectural style. Surely, the casino also satisfied the architectural appetite of Pope Benedict XIII. In the context of his return from southern Italy in June 1729, the Albano respite with the architectural setting of Casino Lercari must have functioned to prolong the pope's visit to his beloved Benevento.

The addition of Casino Lercari to Raguzzini's architectural production lends insight into the strength and tenacity of his Neapolitan roots.[35] It also suggests his attention to the client which, if apparent at the Ospedale di S. Gallicano and Piazza S. Ignazio, is given added force by the dramatic stylistic accommodation of the casino. And, if we can hypothesize his authorship of the portal and atrium of Palazzo Lercari on the basis of Neapolitan sources, the work in Albano also suggests a new versatility to Raguzzini as an architect.

Not too surprisingly, the Casino Lercari is without progeny in later 18th-century Roman architecture. But, the aspects of the portal and atrium of Palazzo Lercari do survive, and while Raguzzini's role must remain only hypothetical at this point, the Palazzo Lercari seems to have influenced the Roman architecture of Carlo de'Dominicis (1696-1758) and of Domenico Gregorini (1696-1758). De' Dominicis' association with Raguzzini began after Raguzzini arrived in Rome in 1724. The exact nature of this association is not entirely clear, but the two architects are closely related. By 1728, the year after the Palazzo Lercari alterations were carried out, de' Dominicis was living in Raguzzini's household in Rome. In fact, their relationship continued until 1731.[36] The aspects of the Palazzo Lercari work that continue in de'Dominicis' own independent architecture include specific aspects of the stucco decoration of both portal and atrium. These are most apparent in de'Dominicis' design for the church of Ss. Celso e Giuliano (1733-1736) in Rome where the scroll forms, swags and stucco shell arrangements are all strikingly similar to the Palazzo Lercari forms (fig. 179).[37] More intriguing is the possible argument that de'Dominicis developed a general predisposition toward Neapolitan architectural motifs under the influence of Raguzzini. For example, at Ss. Celso e Giuliano, the *coretti* over the corner chapels seem to derive from similar arrangements popular in Naples in 17th and early 18th-century church architecture. Examples of this include F. A. Picchiatti's chapel in the Monte della Misericordia (begun 1658 ; fig. 180) and the church of the Concezione a Montecalvario (1718-1724) by Domenico Antonio Vaccaro.[38]

In addition, Gregorini's design for the façade and portico of the Early Christian church of S. Croce in Gerusalemme (1741-1744) shares some of the characteristics of the Albano atrium.[39] At S. Croce, the space of the oval portico is activated by a running series of *Serliane* that form an inner screen repeating the oval plan (fig. 181). This device, with the open perforations over the trabeated passages, seems a most inventive and lively reinterpretation of the Palazzo Lercari atrium solution.

Clearly, a close examination of Palazzo Lercari as a vehicle for the dissemination of Neapolitan influence in later Roman architecture is beyond the scope of the present discussion. But, the suggestion seems plausible based on the later work of both de'Dominicis and Gregorini. In this light, the work for Cardinal Lercari in Albano might call for a significant reassessment of not only the role of Raguzzini and his influence on de'Dominicis and his other Roman colleagues, but also of the possible Neapolitan ingredient in Roman rococo architecture.

Dorothy Metzger Habel
University of Tennessee

Notes

*   Research for this paper was supported by a Research Grant awarded by the Samuel H. Kress Foundation in 1975-76 and by Faculty Research Awards granted by The University of Tennessee in 1982 and 1984. I would like to thank Professor John Pinto for suggesting that I visit the Casino Lercari.

1.   F. Valesio, *Diario di Roma (1700—1742)*, ed. G. Scano and G. Graglia, 6 vols., Milan, 1977-1979, IV, 772, 29 January 1727.

2.   L. von Pastor, *The History of the Popes*, 40 vols., London, 1894-1953, XXXIV, 171. The pope left Albano on 25 March and arrived in Benevento on 2 April, remaining until 12 May. He returned to Rome on 28 May 1727.

3.   Valesio, *Diario*, V, 64.

4.   Pastor, *History*, 173; G. F. Chracas, *Diario sia descrizione del viaggio della Santità di Nostro Signore Papa Benedetto XIII da Roma a Benevento, sua permanenza colà, e ritorno in Roma*, Rome, 1729, 74. This journey began 28 March and continued until the pope's return to Rome on 10 June 1729.

5.   Nicolò Maria Lercari (1675-1757) was made cardinal on 9 December 1726; Valesio, *Diario*, IV, 754 and Pastor, *History*, 131. See also G. Moroni, *Dizionario di erudizione storico-ecclesiastico*, 103 vols., Venice, 1840-1861, XXXVIII, 105. When he died, Lercari left the palace and casino to the bishopric of Albano which still owns the properties. For Lercari's testament, see Archivio del Palazzo Vescovile, Albano, Armadio P, Istromenti: 1753-1760, fols. 404r-415v and Archivio di Stato, Rome (hereafter ASR), Trenta Notai Capitolini, Ufficio 37, v. 392, fols. 225r-227v and 250r. Lercari's testament is dated 18 June 1753; he died 20 March 1757. The palace and casino are in via Alcide de Gaspari (formerly via del Plebiscito), 35-39 (palace) and 40-52 (casino).

6.   The inscription, which is dated 1727, reads: BENEDETTO   XIII   PONTIFICI.O.M./ ORDINI PRAEDICATORUM/ HISCE IN AEDIBUS/ BIS HUS HOSPITIO/ DUM INTER PURPURATOS PATRES ESSET/ -MOX ETIAM PONTIFICAE MAIESTATIS PRAESENTIA/   IN   SUO   AD BENEVENTANUM   ECCLESIAM/ DISCESSU REDITUQUE/ DECORATIS/ NICOLAUS MARIS CARD. LERCARIUS IANVENSIS/ SACRA PURPURA/ PRIMI ADMINISTRI MUNERE/ ALIISQUE INGEN-TIBUS BENEFICIIS/ AB EO MUNIFI-CENTISSIME AUCTUS/ HOC GRATI ET OBSEQUENTISSIMI ANIMI/   PERENNE

MONUMENTUN POSVIT/ AN. SAL. MDCCXXVII.

7. Pastor, *History*, 117, 129-131, 185.

8. For example, in Lercari's testament, the palace is described as having been "ampliato et ornato" under the cardinal's supervision; it also states here that Lercari spent 50,000 *scudi* on the work. Presumably, this figure included work on both the palace and the casino. Archivio del Palazzo Vescovile, Albano, Armadio P, "Istromenti: 1753-1760," fol. 405r.

9. Pastor, *History*, 170-171.

10. *Ibid*. The postponement apparently involved the slower than anticipated progress on the rebuilding of the church of S. Filippo Neri in Benevento, which was a project that Benedict had vowed to undertake at his own expense after the church was destroyed in the 1688 earthquake.

11. *Ibid.*, 171.

12. In all, six pieces of property were purchased; these were located north and east of what must have been the original palace block. The *misure e stime* begin to appear in February and March 1727; most of the parcels were acquired in May 1727. For complete documentation, see ASR, Trenta Notai Capitolini, Ufficio 37, v. 310, fols. 5r-17v and 19r-30v; fols. 35r-40v and 59r-63v; fols. 41r-46v and 53r-56v; fols. 213r-214r; fols. 320r-328r and 344r-351v; fols. 672r-677v and 705r-709r; v. 311, fols. 173r-181r and 183r-184v; ASR, Archivio Notarile di Albano, v. 266, fols. 127r-154r.

13. *Ibid*. The *misure e stime* are sprinkled throughout the documents cited above; in a few cases, de'Marchis is not the only architect involved, but he is always identified as the architect representing Lercari's interests. Francesco de'Sanctis, Filippo Barigioni and Carlo Stefano Maderno also signed *misure e stime* for some of these properties. The de'Marchis plans are found in ASR, Trenta Notai Capitolini, Ufficio 37, v. 311, fols. 180v-181r and ASR, Archivio Notarile di Albano, v. 266, fols. 134v-147r.

14. N. A. Mallory, with J. L. Varriano, "Carlo Francesco Bizzacheri (1655-1721)," *Journal of the Society of Architectural Historians*, XXXIII, 1, 1974, 29-30.

15. *Ibid.*, 37.

16. *Ibid.*, 28; see also P. Portoghesi, *Roma barocca*, trans. B. LaPenta, Cambridge, Ma., 1970, 544.

17. This type of porticoed façade first appears in late 16th-century Naples. For these and other examples, see A. Blunt, *Neapolitan Baroque and Rococo Architecture*, London, 1975, 68-69; 105; 107; pls. 71, 156, 161.

18. For the development of this in urban palaces, see Blunt's chapter on Ferdinando Sanfelice's palaces (*Neapolitan Baroque*, 129-158). The villas outside of Naples are especially difficult to study. Only a limited number survive and these have not been well researched and photographed. For these two villas, see Blunt, *Neapolitan Baroque*, 152, pl. 258 (Villa Bisignano, Barra) and 107 (Villa Menna, Portici). See also R. Pane, *Ville visuviane del settecento*, Naples, 1959, 56, 138, 148-149 and V. Gleijeses, *Ville e palazzi vesuviani*, Naples, 1980 which does include photographs of Villa Menna, 80/81, 219-225. Villa Bisignano was begun in the 17th century. The Villa Menna has been identified as the work of Muzio Nauclerio and appears to date from 1742.

19. For a discussion of the decorative stucco work in Naples, see Blunt's chapter on Domenico Antonio Vaccaro, *Neapolitan Baroque*, 110-128, in particular 124-125. G. Bonelli, "Il rococo napoletano," *Napoli nobilissima*, 3rd ser., XVIII, 1979, 201-219 presents a general discussion of the rococo style in Neapolitan architecture and decoration.

20. Benedict's taste for a southern style was made apparent early in his reign, in part by his summons of Raguzzini and a group of either Beneventan or Neapolitan workmen and by his immediate commission of Raguzzini's Chapel of S. Domenico in S. Maria sopra Minerva in 1724.

21. Raguzzini's birth and family roots were first hypothesized as Neapolitan by M. Rotili, *Filippo Raguzzini e il rococò romano*, Rome, 1951, 11-12; 23-24, nos. 7-8. These have now been confirmed; see my own "Piazza S. Ignazio, Rome, in the 17th and 18th Centuries," *architectura*, 11, 1981, 55, n. 102. For a more recent discussion of this issue, see Rotili's, *Filippo Raguzzini nel terzo centenario della nascita*, Studi e testi di storia e critica dell'arte, XV, Naples, 1982, 13-16.

22. For the Chapel of S. Domenico and the work of S. Gallicano, see Rotili, *Raguzzini* (1951), 30-32; 34-37 and Rotili, *Raguzzini* (1982), 17-19. Raguzzini was elected papal architect on 31 October 1726; Rotili, *Raguzzini* (1951), 110, no. 7.

23. For example, ASR, Notai dell'Acque e Strade, v. 146 (1738), fols. 124r-v.

24. The earliest *misura e stima* of the property acquired for the casino is dated 28 November 1729; ASR, Trenta Notai Capitolini, Ufficio 37, v. 314, fols. 667r-v- 678r.

25. *Ibid.*, v. 314, fols. 664r-669r and 680r-681r fols. 691r-692v and 695r-697r; v. 315, fols. 3r-17r and 22r-31r; fols. 411r-414v and 417r-418r; v. 317, fols. 341r-342v and 353r-354v.

26. A. de Montaiglon and J. Guiffrey, *Correspondance des directeurs de l'Académie de France à Rome avec les Surintendents des Bâtiments*, Paris, 1887-1908, VIII, no. 3218, 4 February 1729.

27. Valesio, *Diario*, V, 67, 6 June 1729. I have not been able to gain admittance to the papal chapel, although it does apparently still exist and is located in the new north wing of the palace.

28. Chracas, *Diario o sia descrizione*, 74, 8 June 1729.

29. Archivio del Palazzo Vescovile, Albano, Armadio I, "Bullarium ad anno 1741 usque 1781," [sic], fol. 554, 27 August 1729.

30. For a discussion of the ancient nymphaea, see A. G. McKay, *Houses, Villas and Palaces in the Roman World*, Ithaca, 1975, especially 126-128; for the form in Renaissance villa architecture, see D. R. Coffin, *The Villa in the Life of Renaissance Rome*, Princeton, 1979 and for the early 17th-century developments of the nyphaeum as the *teatro d'acqua*, see R. M. Steinberg, "The Iconography of the Teatro d'Acqua at the Villa Aldobrandini," *The Art Bulletin*, XLVII, 4, 1965, 453-463 and K. Schwager, "Kardinal Pietro Aldobrandinis Villa di Belvedere in Frascati," *Römisches Jahrbuch für Kunstgeschichte*, IX-X, 1961-1962, 379-382.

31. For a more detailed discussion of the design problems and restrictions, see my own, "Piazza S. Ignazio," 31-33; 49-56.

32. *Ibid.*, 52.

33. Consider, for example, Pier Leone Ghezzi's caption to his caricature of Raguzzini identifying him as "Il Cav.re Raguzzini Architetto Gotico e Beneventano il quale a rovinato Roma con il suo Architettura . . .;" Biblioteca Apostolica Vaticana, Ottob. lat. 3116, fol. 179r.

34. The history of the 18th-century rebuilding of S. Maria della Quercia is discussed in detail in my own "The Church of S. Maria della Quercia, Rome by Filippo Raguzzini (c. 1680-1771)," *Storia dell'arte*, in press. Mallory was the first to recognize the Romanization of Raguzzini's style; N. A. Mallory, *Roman Rococo Architecture from Clement XI ti Benedict XIV (1701-1758)*, Columbia University, 1965, published by Garland Press in the Outstanding Dissertations in the Fine Arts series, 1977, 21-22, n. 18.

35. There are building records from Benedict's reign that suggest that Raguzzini made frequent trips to Naples to obtain marble and other building materials for papal projects in Rome; for example, ASR, Camerale I, v. 1071, fol. 652 (1726); v. 1689, fol. 146 (1727).

36. F. Fasolo (*Le Chiese di Roma nel '700*, Rome, 1949, 67, n. 9) was the first to find documentation supporting a formal relationship

between the two architects in a document dated to 1733 in which de'Dominicis is referred to as the *giovane* of Raguzzini. Mallory (*Roman Rococo Architecture*, 131, n. 3) suggests that de'Dominicis apprenticed under Raguzzini before 1733, perhaps as early as 1728. M. G. Gargano ("Carlo de'Dominicis," *Storia dell'arte*, XVII, 1973, 86) hypothesizes that their relationship may have begun as early as 1724 and continued until 1733 when de'Dominicis launched his own independent career. In the spring of 1728, de'Dominicis is listed as resident in Raguzzini's household, which was located in one of the houses in front of S. Ignazio which was destroyed in 1730. While Raguzzini and his family are listed in this location from 1728 until 1730, de'Dominicis' name appears only in 1728; Archivio del Vicariato, Rome, S. Marcello: Stati d'anime, v. 76, fols. 42r-v.

37. For Ss. Celso e Giuliano, see G. Segui, C. Thoenes and L. Mortari, *Ss. Celso e Giuliano*, Le chiese di Roma illustrate, 88, Rome, 1966 and Gargano, "Carlo de'Dominicis," 94-106.

38. This arrangement is discussed in Blunt, *Neapolitan Baroque*, 95.

39. For a discussion of Gregorini, see Mallory, *Roman Rococo Architecture*, 145-162 and E. A. Plummer, "The Eighteenth-Century Rebuilding of S. Croce in Gerusalemme in Rome," Ph.D. dissertation, The University of Michigan, Ann Arbor, 1983. Gregorini's authorship of the work and his project for the façade are discussed in detail in E. A. Plummer, "S. Croce in Gerusalemme, Rome: A Drawing and An Attribution," *Journal of the Society of Architectural Historians*, XLII, 1984, 356-363.

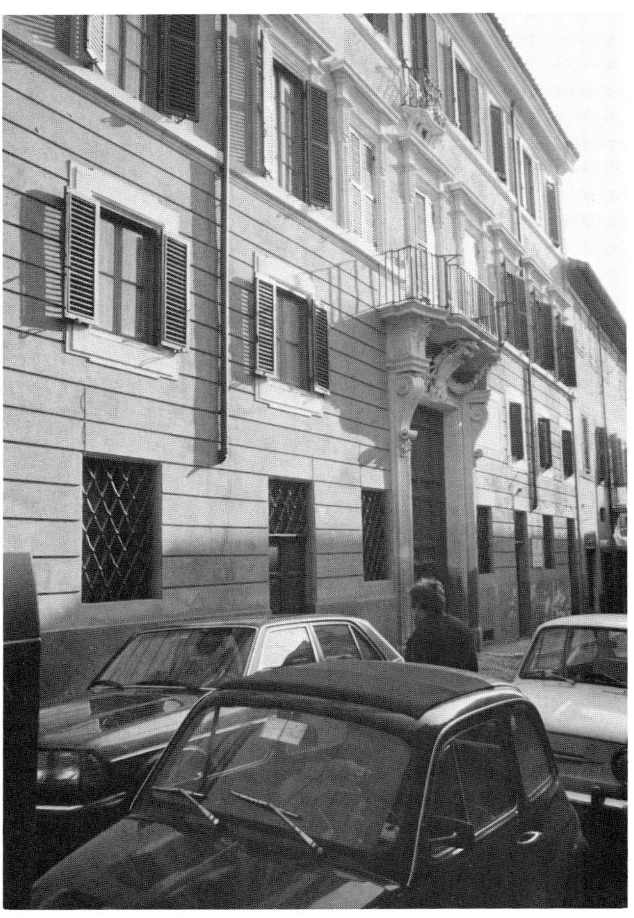

160.   Albano, Palazzo Lercari, façade (photo: author).

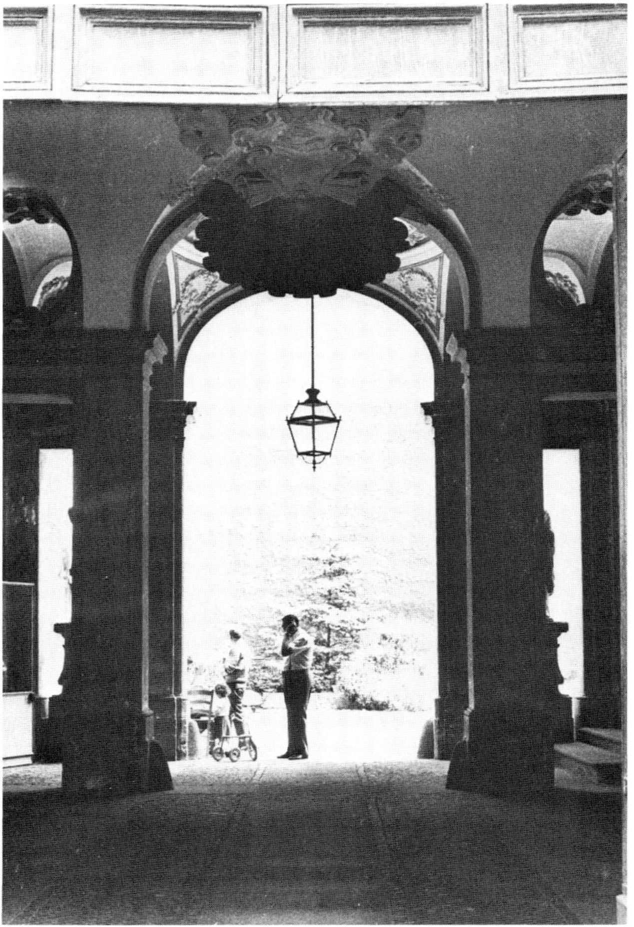

161.   Palazzo Lercari, atrium, 1726-1727 (photo: author).

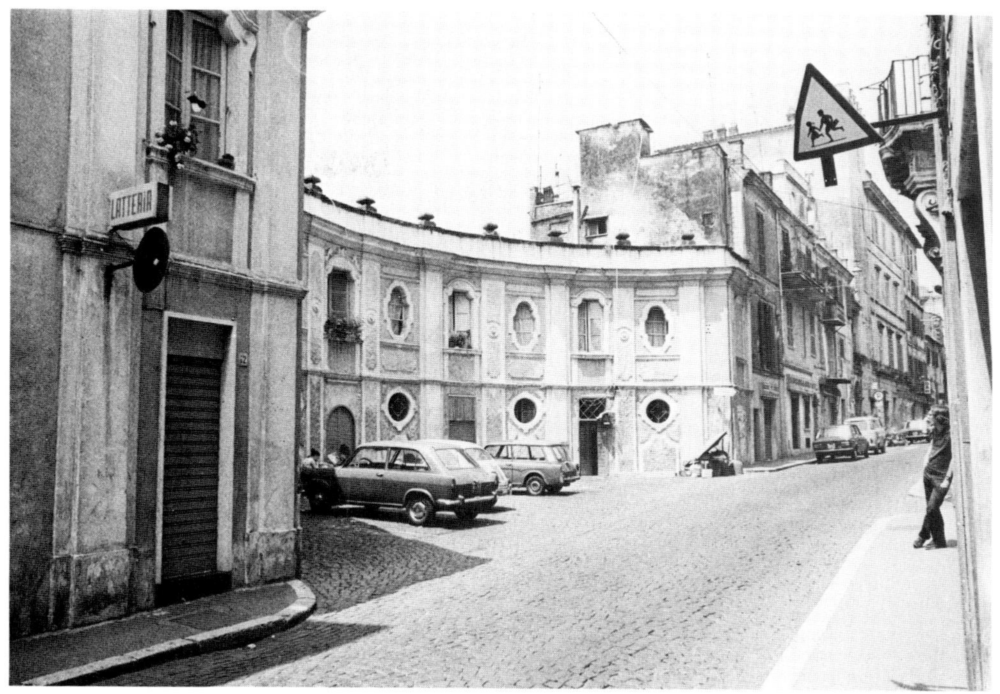

162.   Albano, Casino Lercari, 1728-1729 (photo: author).

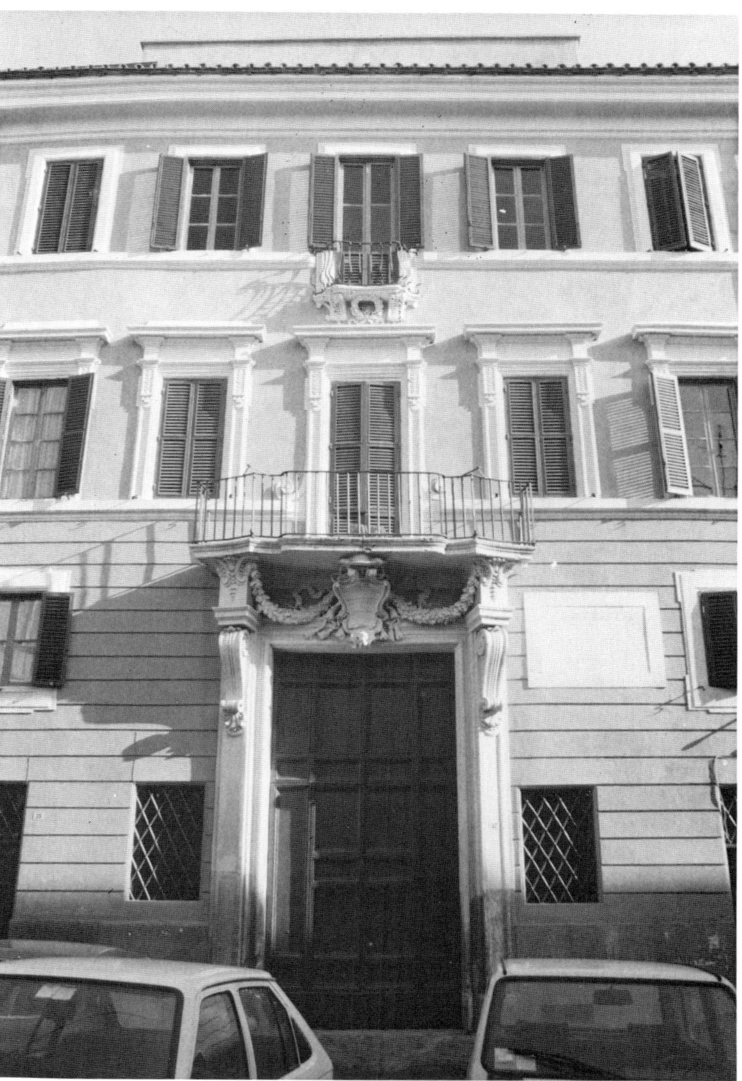

163.   Palazzo Lercari, façade, detail (photo:
author).

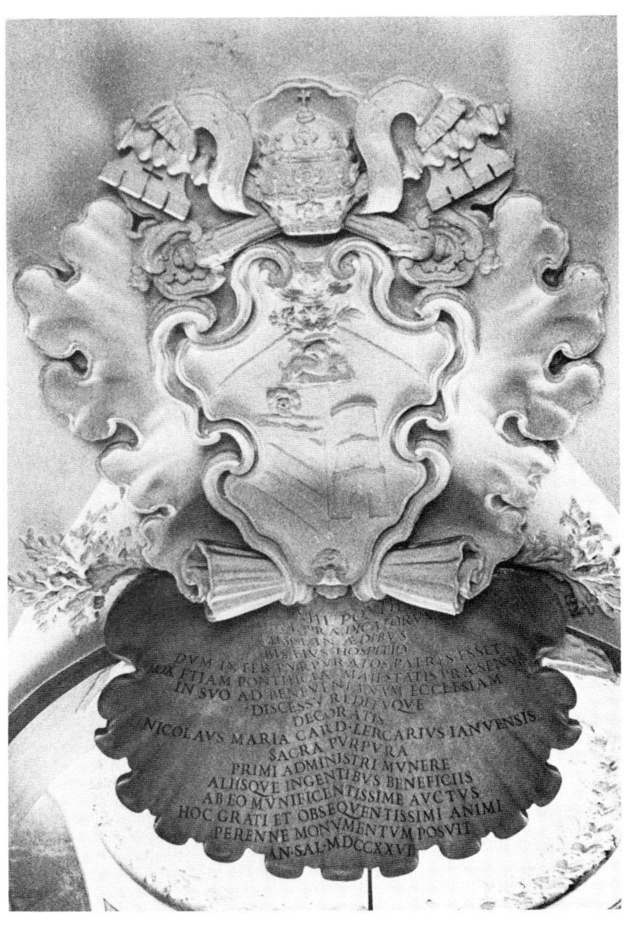

165.   Palazzo Lercari, atrium decoration (photo: author).

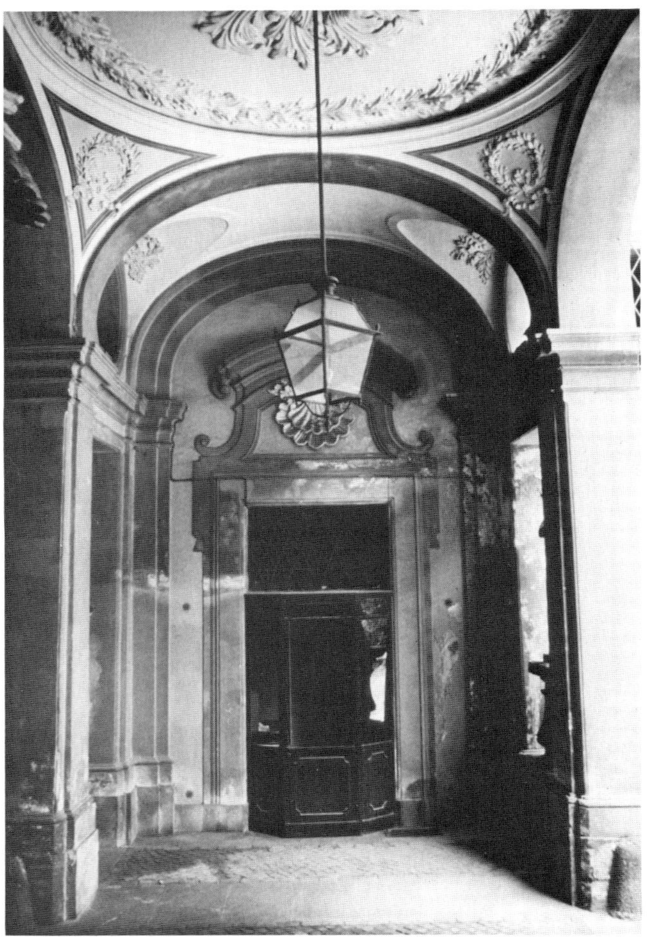

166.   Palazzo Lercari, atrium (photo: author).

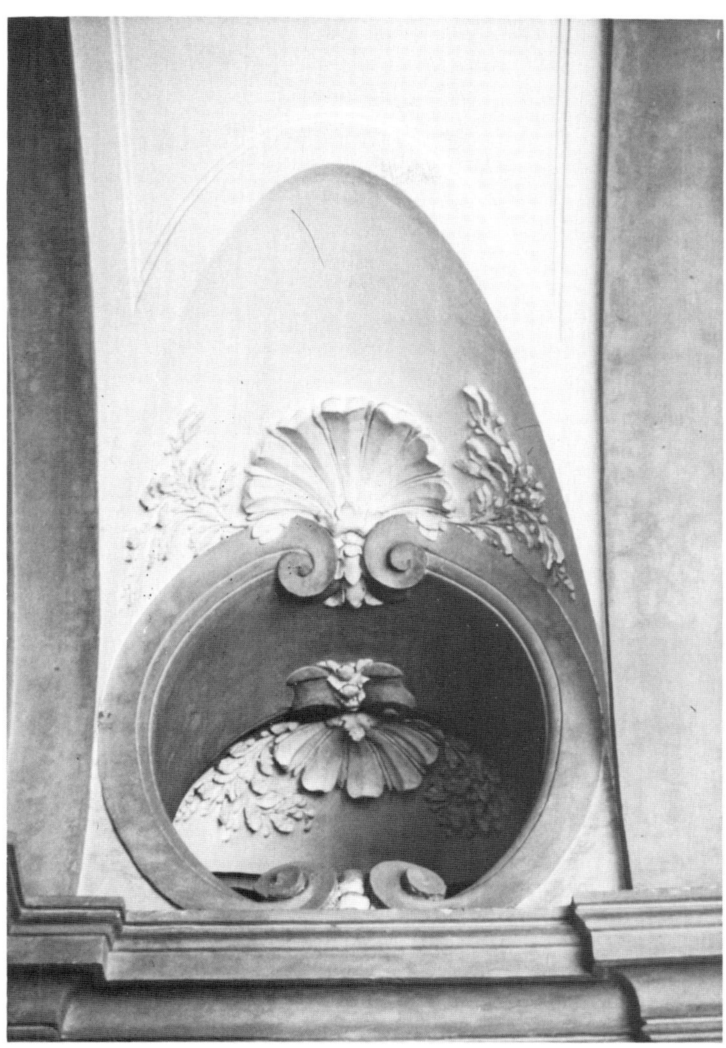

167.   Palazzo Lercari, atrium, detail (photo: author).

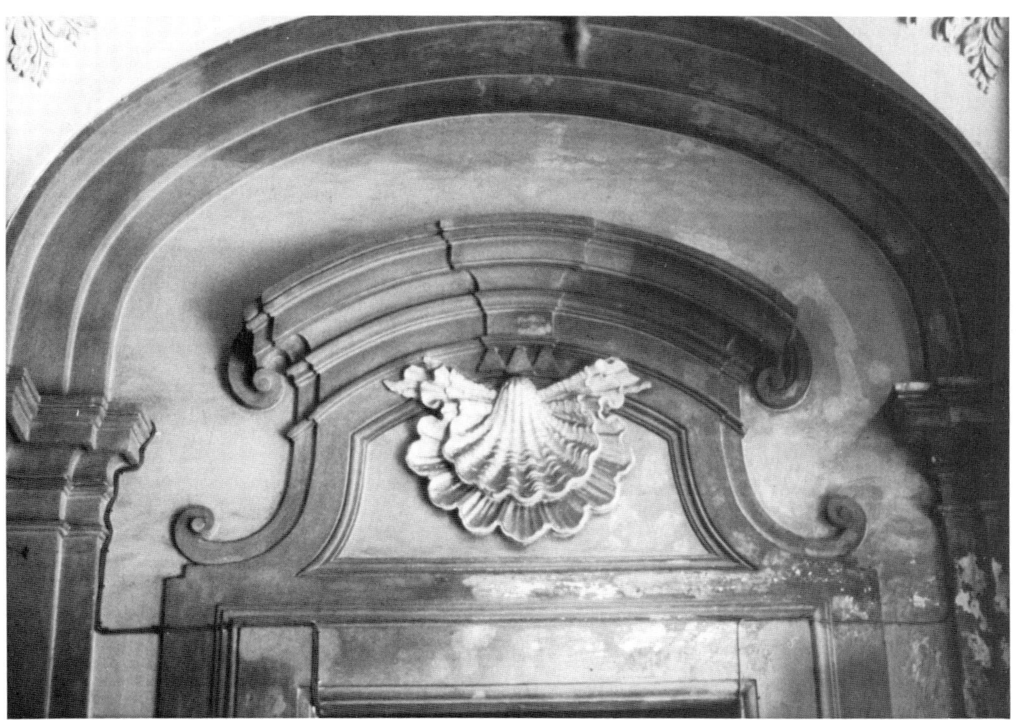

168.   Palazzo Lercari, atrium, detail (photo: author).

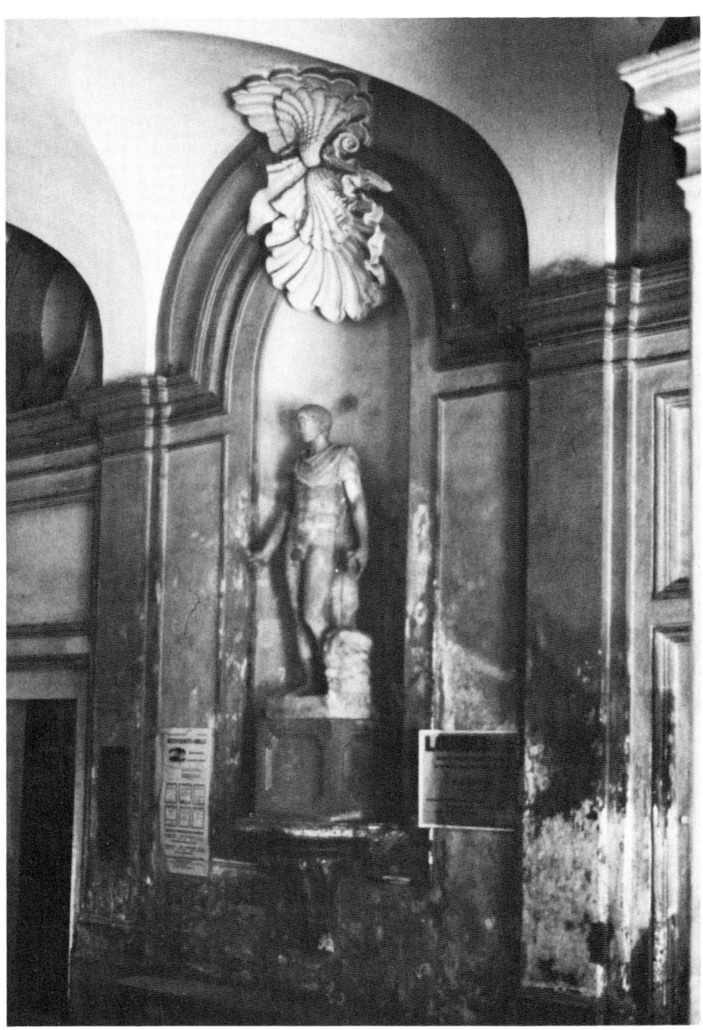

169.   Palazzo Lercari, atrium (photo: author).

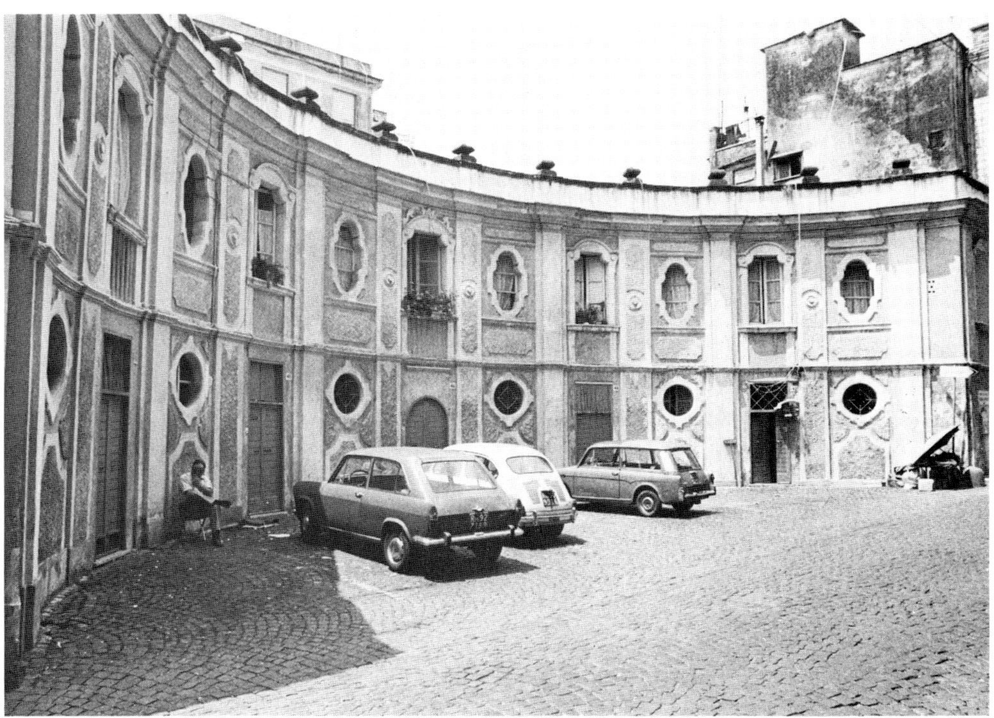

170.   Filippo Raguzzini, Casino Lercari (photo: author).

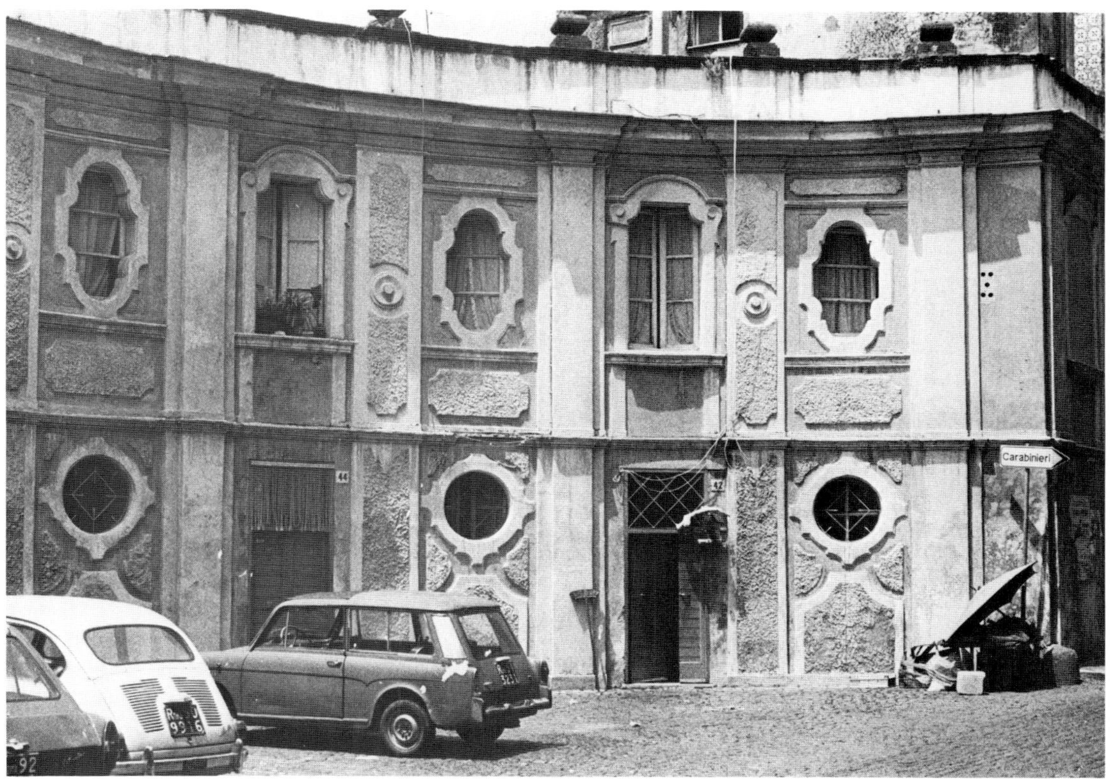

171.   Casino Lercari, detail (photo: author).

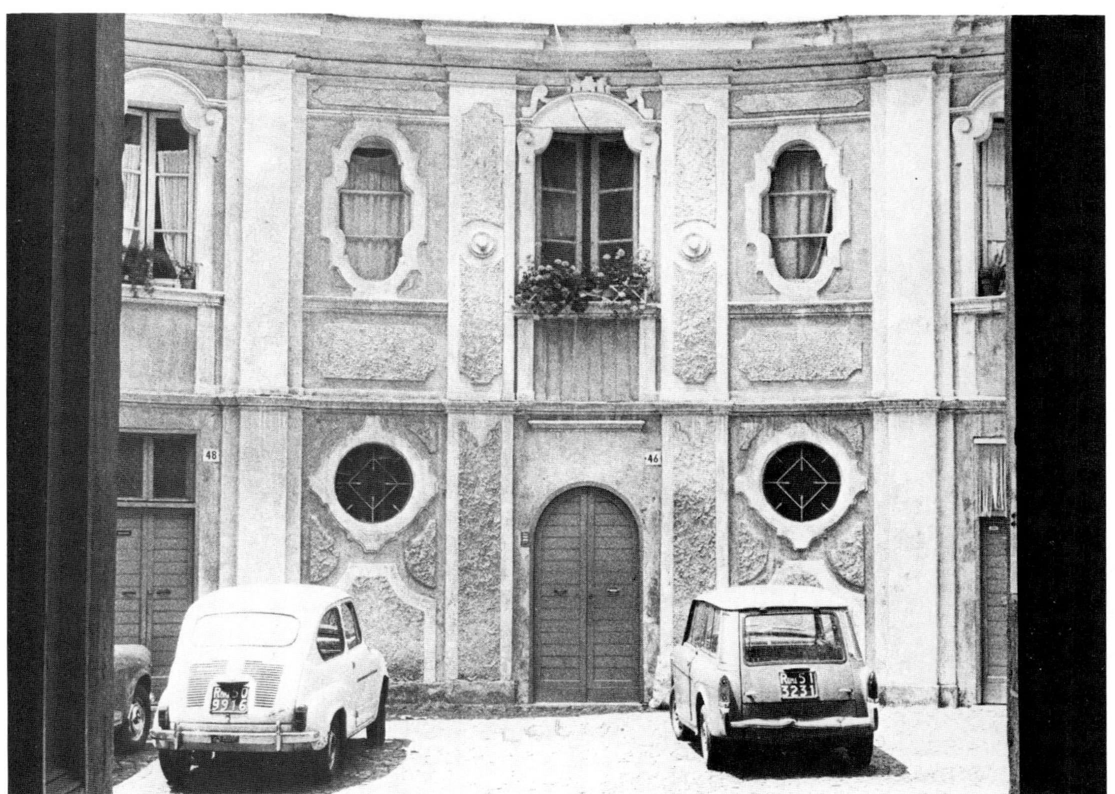

172.   Casino Lercari, main entrance (photo: author).

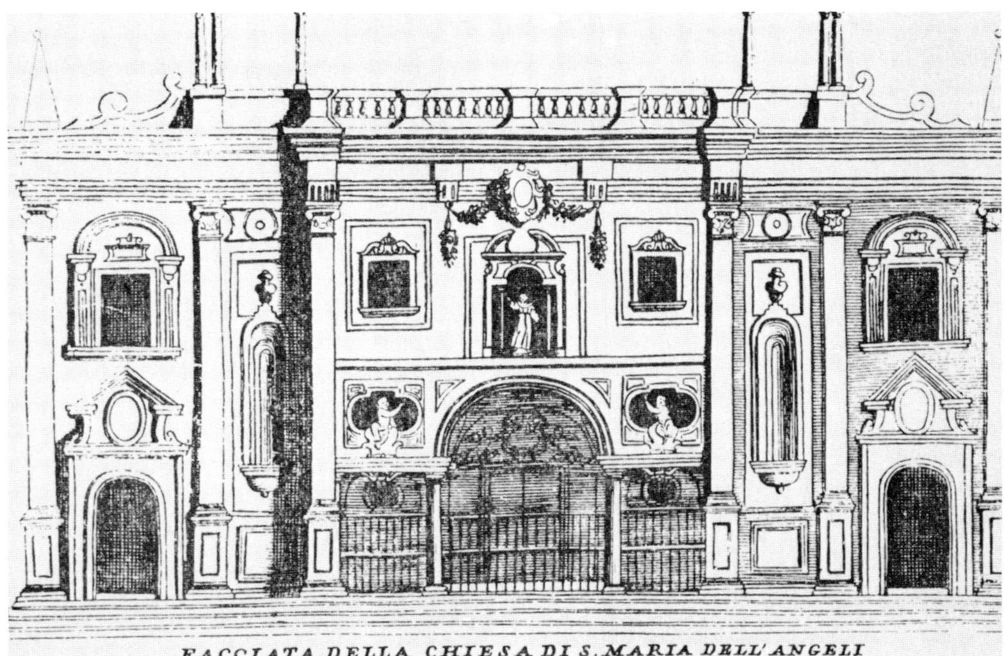

173.   Cosimo Fanzago, S. Maria degli Angeli alle Croci, Naples, façade, after an engraving by Petrini (after
A. Blunt, *Neapolitan Baroque and Rococo Architecture*; photo courtesy of Tim Benton, London).

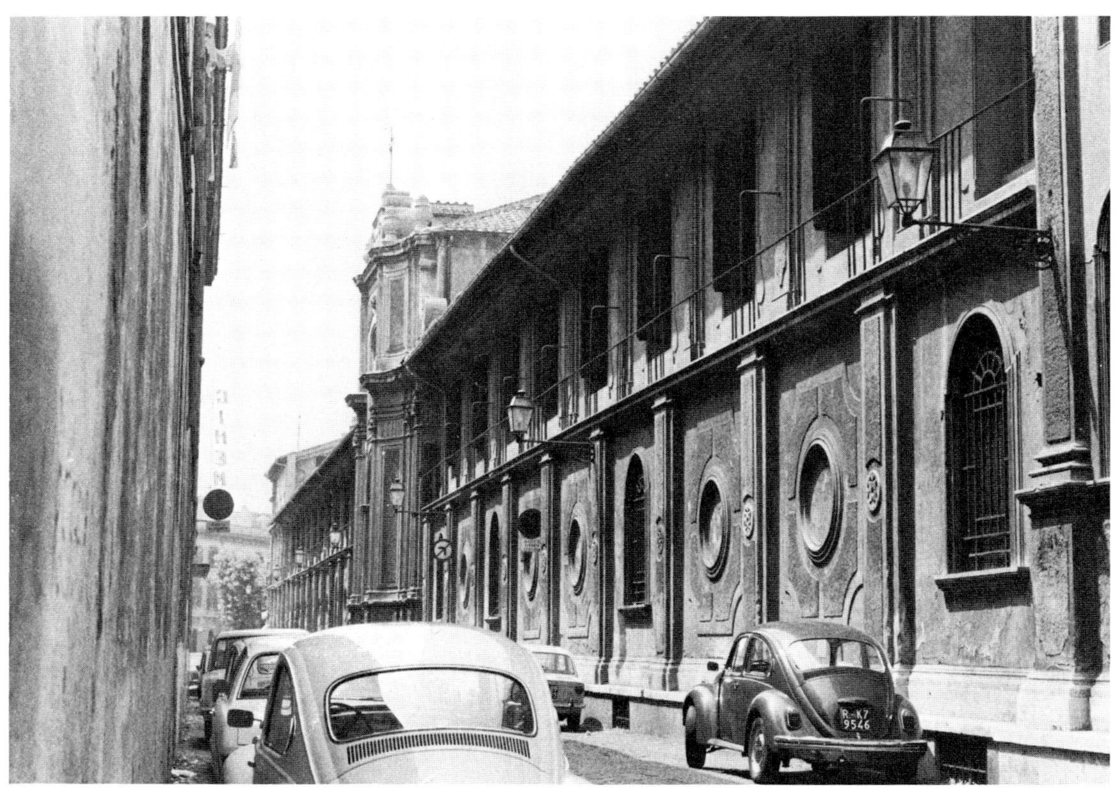

176.   Raguzzini, Ospedale di S. Gallicano, Rome, 1725-1726, façade (photo: author).

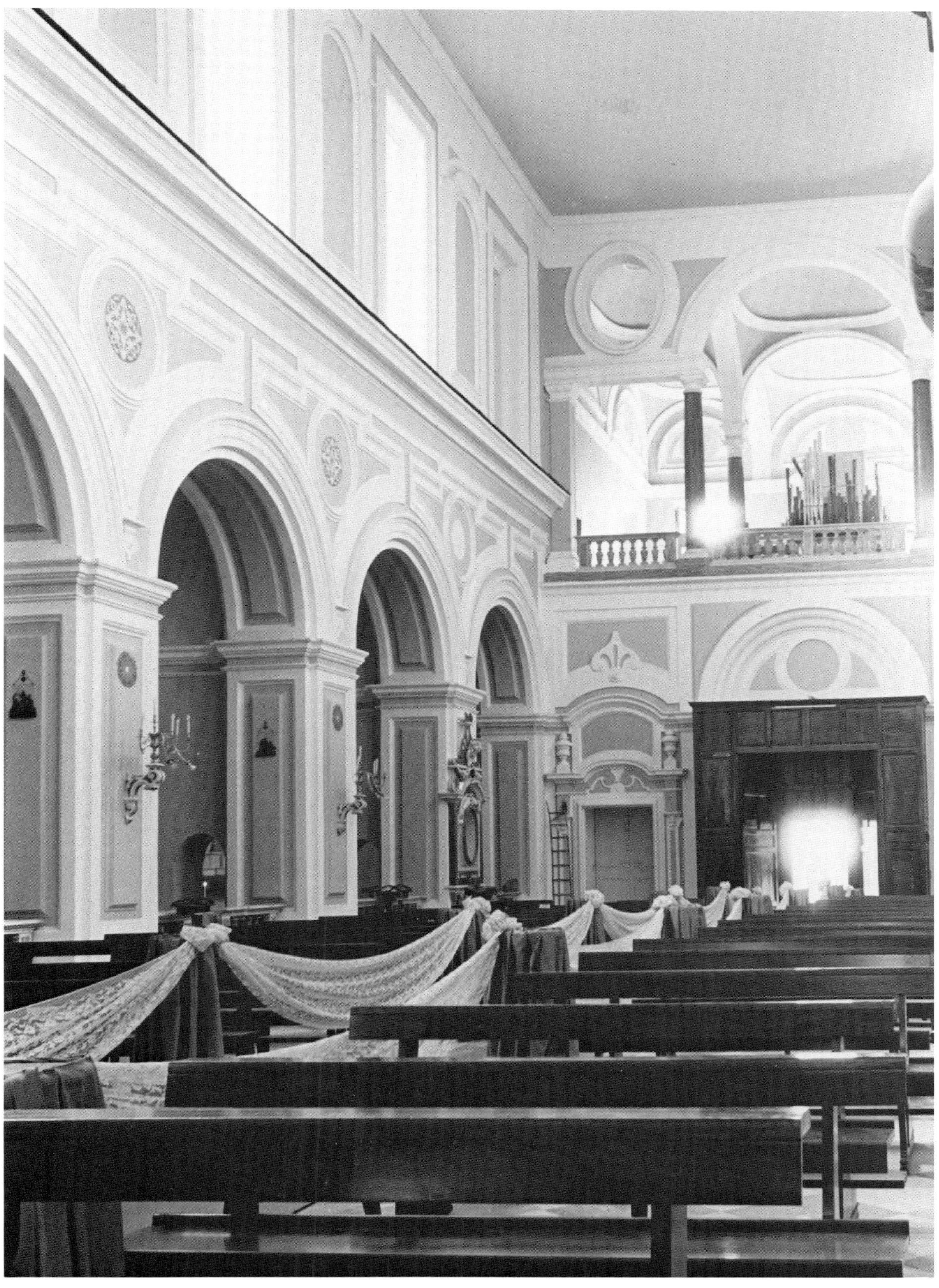

174.   Naples, S. Maria degli Angeli alle Croci, interior with upper story loggia over vestibule (after A. Blunt, *Neapolitan Baroque and Rococo Architecture*; photo courtesy of Tim Benton, London).

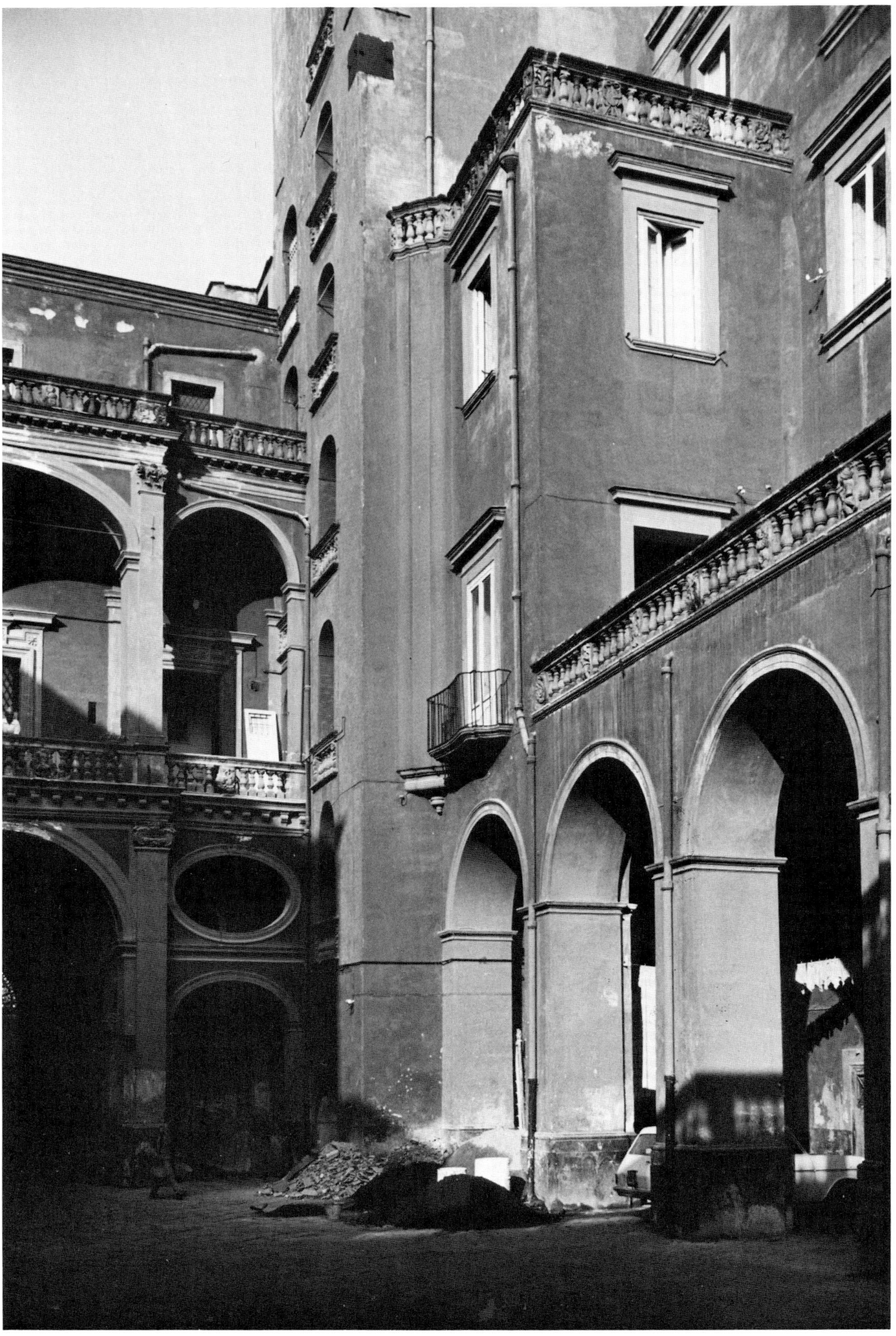

175.   Barra, Villa Bisignano (after A. Blunt, *Neapolitan Baroque and Rococo Architecture*; photo courtesy of Tim Benton, London).

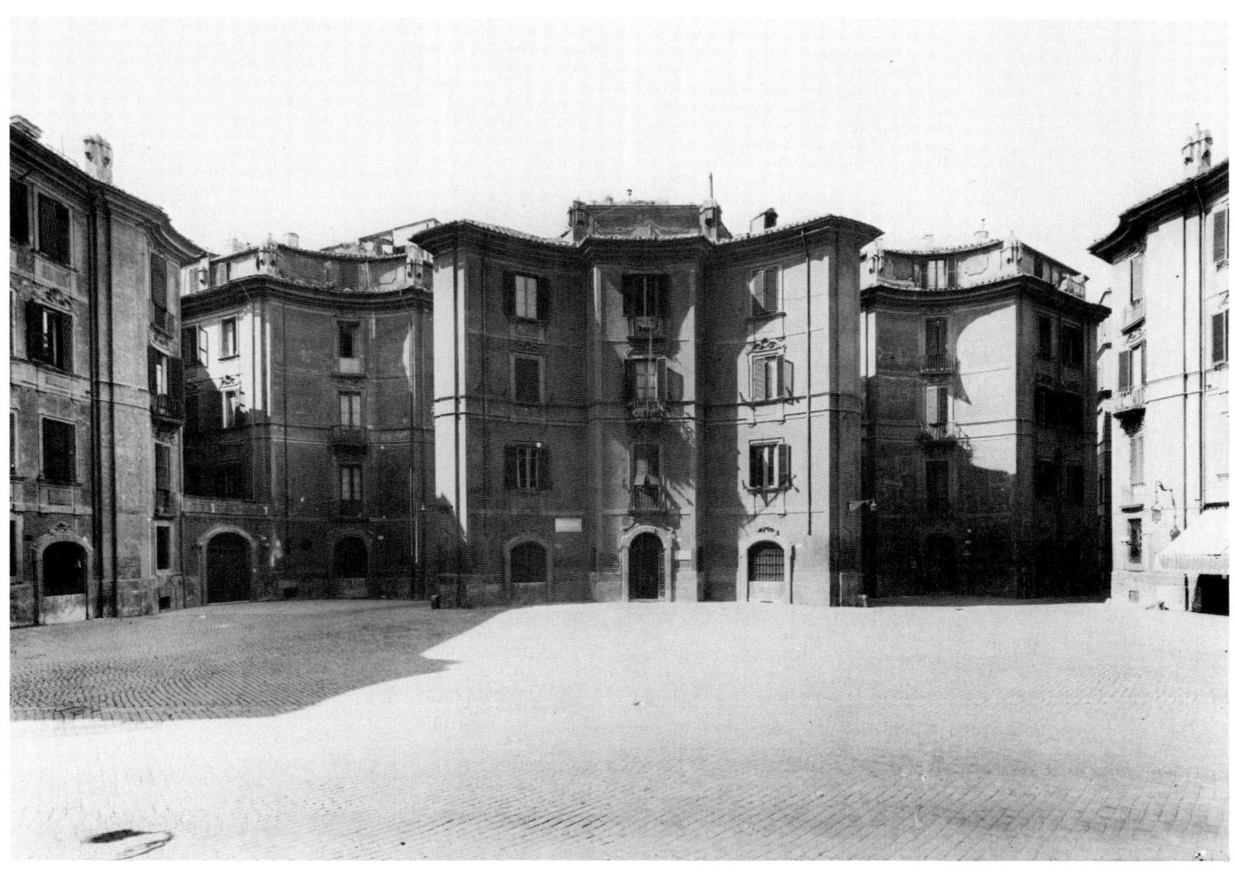

177.   Raguzzini, Piazza S. Ignazio, Rome, 1725-1736 (photo: Marburg).

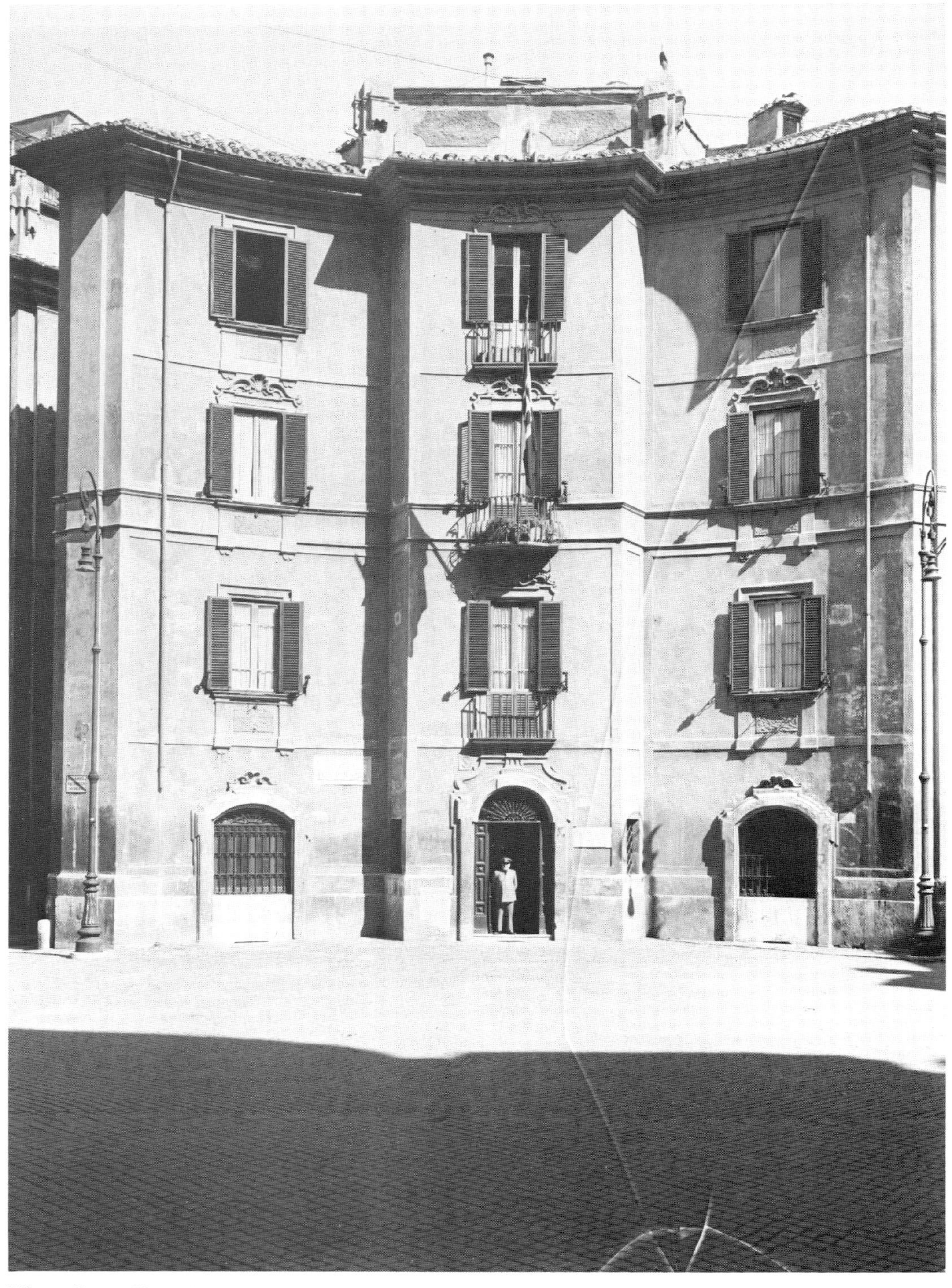

178.   Rome, Piazza S. Ignazio, central building, 1727-1729 (photo: Soprintendenza ai Monumenti del Lazio).

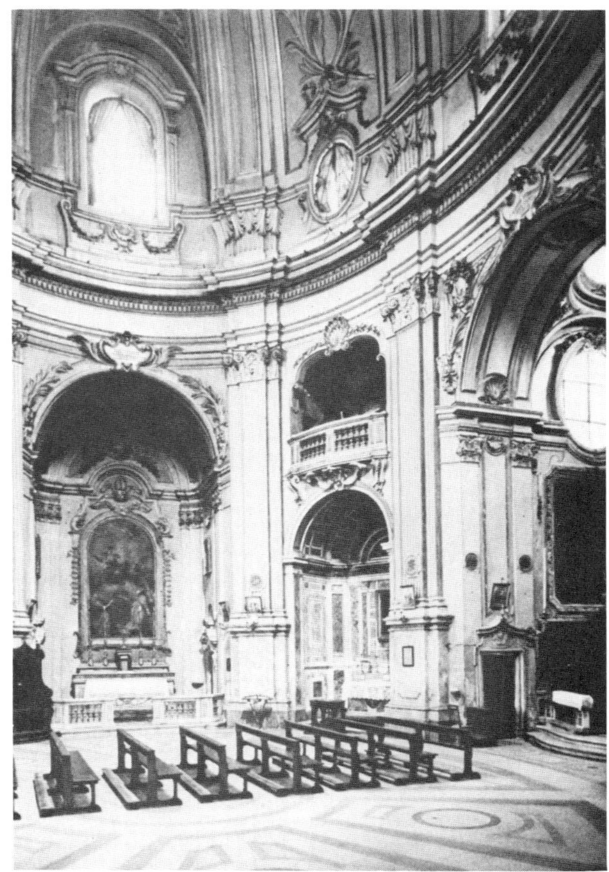

179.   Carlo de'Dominicis, Ss. Celso e Giuliano, Rome, 1733-1736, interior (after P. Portoghesi, *Roma barocca*).

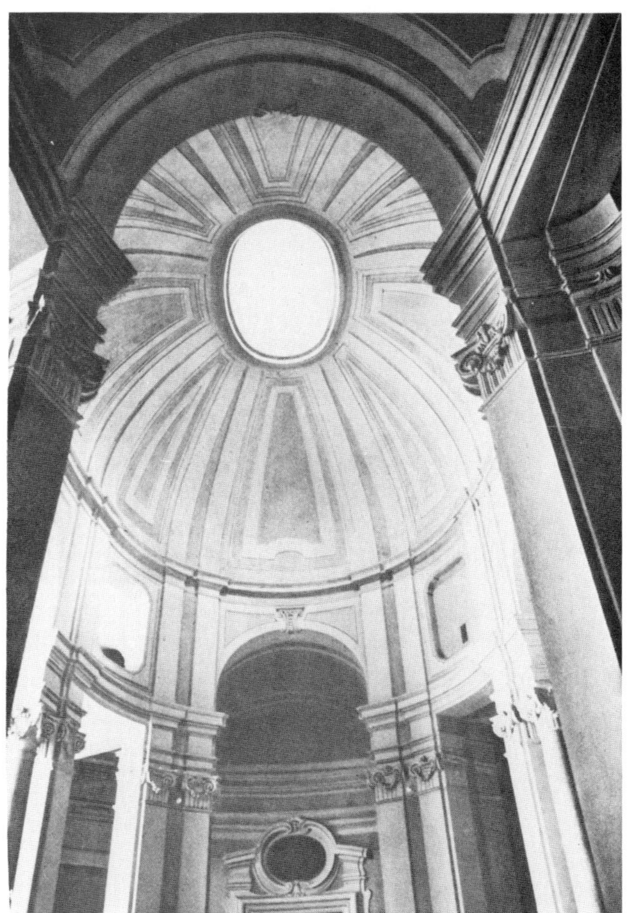

181.   Domenico Gregorini, S. Croce in Gerusalemme, Rome, 1741-1744, portico (after P. Portoghesi, *Roma barocca*).

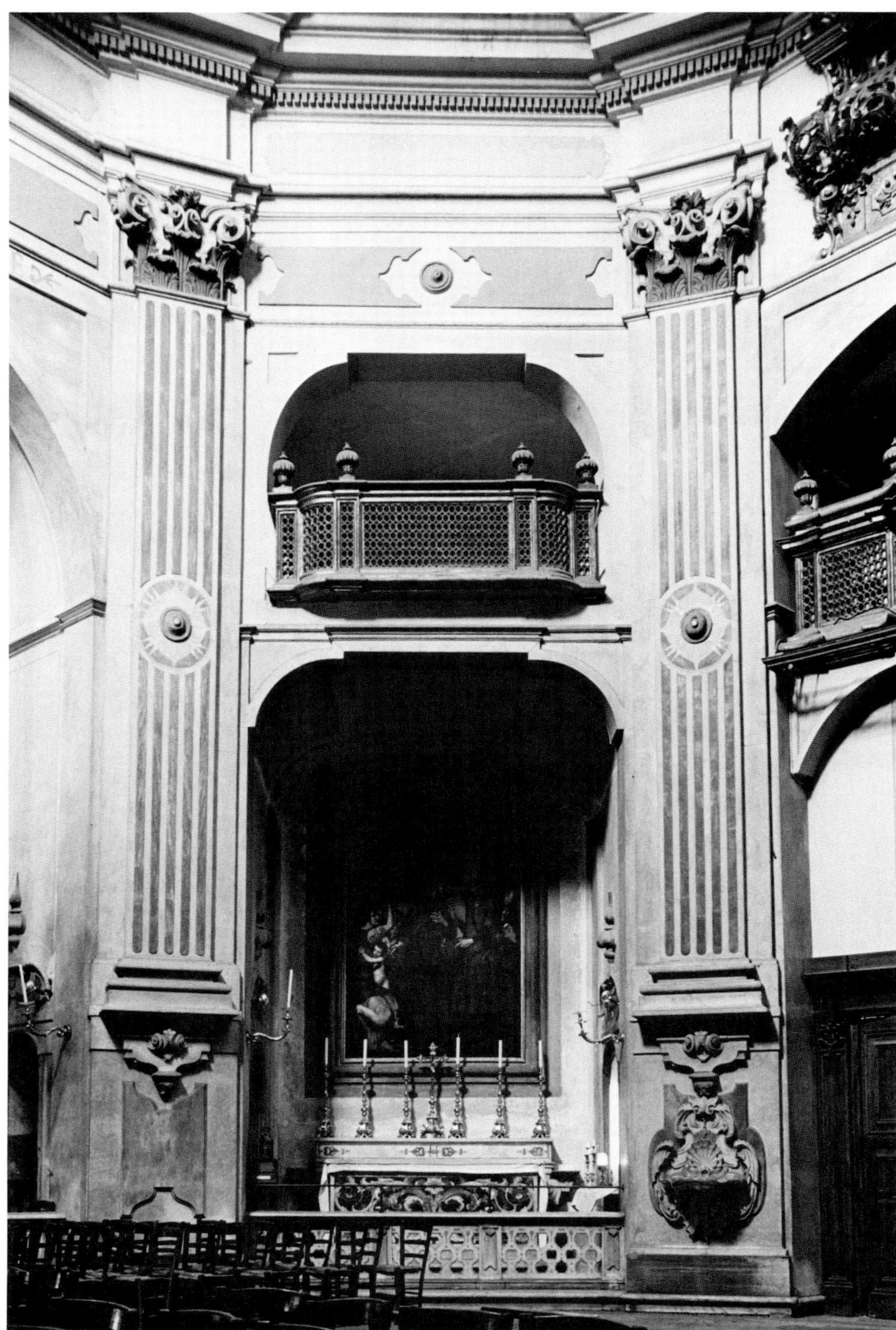

180.   F. A. Picchiatti, Chapel, Monte della Misericordia, Naples, begun 1658, interior (after A. Blunt, *Neapolitan Baroque and Rococo Architecture*; photo courtesy of Tim Benton, London).

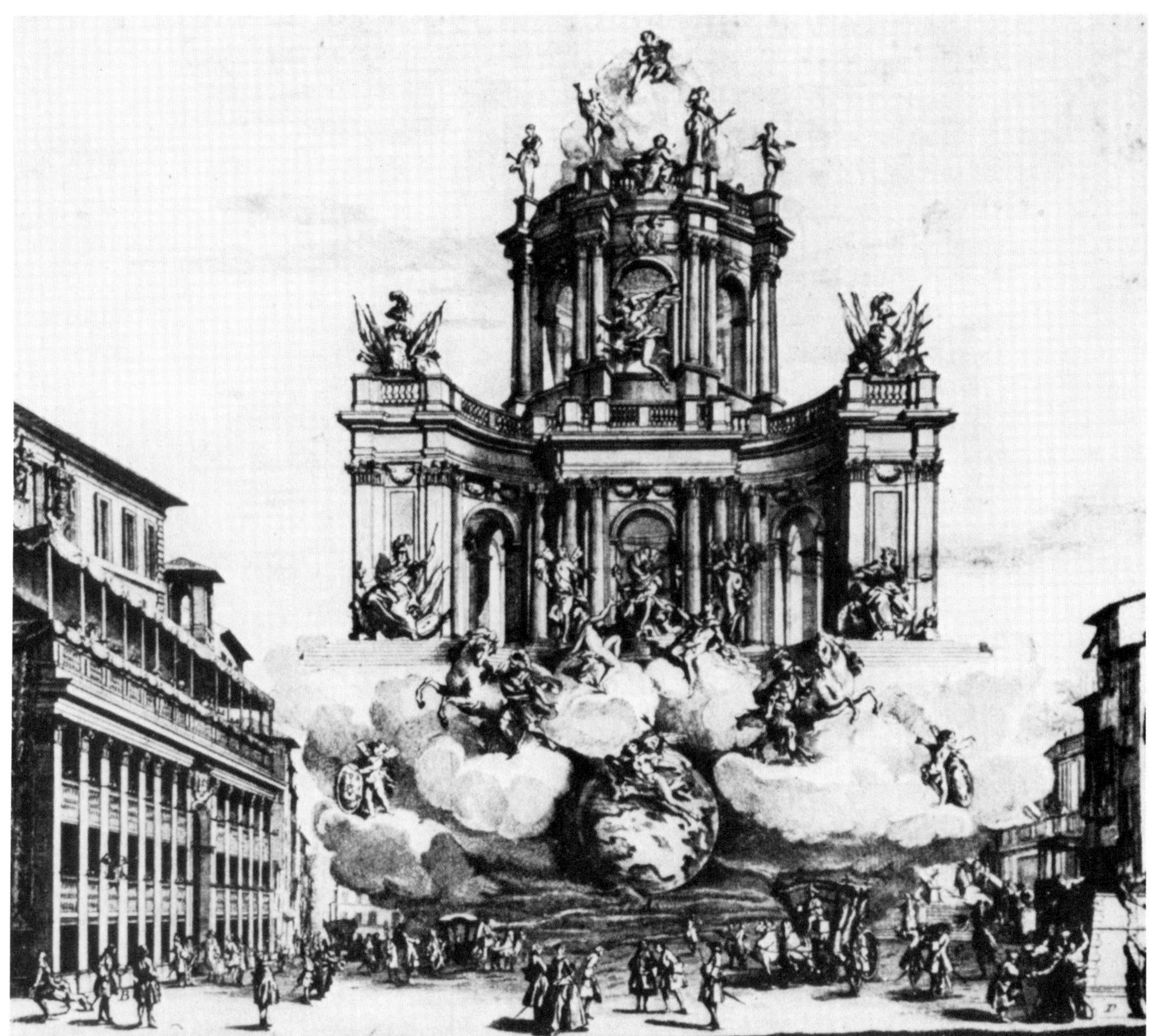

183.   Nicola Salvi, festival structure for the Piazza di Spagna, 1728. Rome, Gabinetto Nazionale delle Stampe (after A. Schiavo, *La Fontana di Trevi*).

Rome in 1732: Alessandro Galilei, Nicola Salvi, Ferdinando Fuga*

10

"L'Etruria esulta e ride," Tuscany rejoices and laughs, Filippo Juvarra wrote in April 1732 from Rome to Turin.[1] The most famous Italian architect, who had been summoned to Rome on behalf of Cardinal Alessandro Albani to build a new sacristy for St. Peter's, had been rejected due to a report by the unknown Florentine architect, Alessandro Galilei.[2] When Juvarra, deeply humiliated and hurt, left Rome in late August 1732, Galilei had just been declared winner of the competition for the Lateran façade. Two weeks later, Nicola Salvi was commissioned to execute the Fontana di Trevi, and in October 1732 Ferdinando Fuga began building the Palazzo della Consulta on the Quirinal Hill, the third great papal building commission ordered in that year.[3]

The coincidence of Juvarra's definite parting from Rome with the appearance of three newcomers—Galilei, Salvi and Fuga—is not incidental, and it implies more than a mere shift of generations or personal animosities. The year 1732 was indeed a signal for the transition from Roman late Baroque to Neoclassicism.

Juvarra's expression "Etruria" (Tuscany) referred not only to Alessandro Galilei, but included the entourage of Pope Clement XII and his nephew and secretary of state, Neri Corsini.

The pope, formerly Cardinal Lorenzo Corsini, was descended from an old and rich Florentine family.[4] As a cardinal, he had been renowned for his uncorrupt handling of administrative positions in the papal curia, and his interest in literature and music was well known. Montesquieu described him in his memoirs as one of the most brilliant and educated cardinals.[5] But it is his nephew, Neri Corsini, who became the key figure of the ten-year Corsini pontificate between 1730 and 1740.[6]

Neri Corsini began his career as cardinal secretary of state, and was responsible for the inner and foreign affairs of the papal states, with a determined reform program that included economics as well as the arts. Corsini had a background different from that of most of his fellow cardinals. A former ambassador of the Tuscan court, he had lived for many years in Paris and London and had travelled in central Europe as well. In Florence, Neri Corsini had grown up in a highly intellectual climate, dominated by strong patriotic feelings. Florentine scholars understood themselves as the intellectual executors of Galileo Galilei's philosophy, and as the preservers of the Italian language of Dante and Bocaccio, were deeply convinced that it fell to Tuscany to act as a promoter in every kind of progress because of her superiority over the other Italian regions.[7] Galileo Galilei's new scientific standards were preserved: the critical-rational treatment of phenomena, the empirical argumentation, perception based on evidence proved by experiment instead of adapting ideas to pre-determined patterns. This new approach occurred in most European countries at the end of the seventeenth century, but met with greater difficulties in Italy than in the Northern countries. At the end of the seventeenth century, also, these new criteria for unprejudiced analysis found their way into Italian philosophy, which added a strong anti-baroque tendency. Some time before the Roman "Arcadia" was founded in 1690 as a society for the reformation of language, the so-called "Pre-arcadia Toscana" had just established a reform program to abolish the baroque pathos and the excessive use of metaphors. The "oscurità e falsità barocca" was confronted with new demands for "evidenza e chiarezza" (evidence and clarity), to give way to elegance of language through simplicity and purity.[8]

It was Ludovico Antonio Muratori, librarian to the Duke of Modena, who introduced this reform program into historical science.[9] He recognized that Italy could no longer claim to have a leading position in the sciences, due to the political weakness of a nation which was splintered up into dozens of little states, mainly governed by foreign rulers. The political and economical rise of France and England had set Italy aside, and her former predominance in the sciences was lost forever. Only one thing, perhaps, was left that could be restored to its former glory: Italy's leading position in the arts. Muratori complained of the sale of irreparable evidence of her glorious past. He proposed to collect the documents illustrating Italian history, for the purpose of conservation as well as transmission, and to challenge contemporary Italian art by confronting it with the high standards of former times. Muratori's idea to establish an all-Italian academy, a "Repubblica Letteraria," which could act as a corporation comparable to the French Academy in Paris and the Royal Society in London was announced in 1705.[10] Muratori wanted the famous antiquarian and physicist Giuseppe Bianchini as president, but Bianchini refused this position. It was in Florence that Muratori's ideas met with enthusiastic approval. The Florentine scholar, Antonio Maria Salvini, became a leading figure in the Italian "Repubblica Letteraria."[11] Henceforward, major research in the natural sciences and humanities was centered around Florence. A culture free of prejudices and dogma was to be created, evidence to be obtained by exploiting and analyzing documents as bearing witness of their time, and Muratori not only referred to the written documents (*Rerum Italicarum Scriptores*), but to works of art as documents, too. The great achievements of Florentine scholarship in the first half of the eighteenth century have to be valued as a systematic contribution to the "Repubblica," to discover and safeguard pieces of evidence which prove the grandeur and predominance of Italian (Tuscan) art. Among these achievements were the introduction of Etruscan archaeology, in history of literature the rediscovery of Dante, new editions of Bocaccio, the completion of the "Vocabulario della crusca" (Dictionary of the Italian Language); in the history of Florence and her art, a re-evaluation of medieval art,

and a rediscovery of Brunelleschi and the early Renaissance.[12]

The deliberate Florentine contribution toward the reconstruction and revitalization of Italian history and Italian grandeur has to be taken into account to understand the art patronage of Neri Corsini between 1730 and 1740. The *magnificenza* and *grandezza romana* was to be preserved—thus the foundation of the first European museum, the Capitoline, in 1733—and restored; therefore, the great undertakings in architecture. To promote this new approach, Neri Corsini did not engage Juvarra or one of the Roman architects, but summoned the Florentine court architect Alessandro Galilei to Rome.

Galilei (1691-1737), a distant relative of Galileo Galilei, had studied mathematics and physics.[13] In 1714, the British envoy to the Tuscan court, John Molesworth, invited Galilei to accompany him to London, where he was to spend the next five years. In 1718, he met with Neri Corsini, who persuaded him to return to Florence and procured the position of court architect for him. These years, 1719 to 1731, gave Galilei almost no opportunity to build, due to the unfortunate economic and political situation under the last Medici grand dukes. Galilei, therefore, was not well known when he arrived in Rome in December of 1731 to build the Corsini family chapel in the Lateran basilica.

In 1730, fifty years after the death of Bernini, Roman architecture was still dependent on its great Baroque heritage. "Berninisti" and "Borroministi" — as Milizia called them — were the protagonists, and the personal controversy of the last century was repeated, although on a different level. The rise of the "Borrominismo," one of the most interesting phenomena of the early eighteenth century in Rome, is not yet fully explained.[14] The "Berninismo" creates fewer problems, deriving from Carlo Fontana and his studio. In 1714, Fontana had died and Filippo Juvarra, who had been able to blend and integrate both tendencies, had left for Turin.[15] Obviously due to these two facts, the Baroque heritage disintegrated and in the twenties the "Borrominismo" became more and more dominant.

To illustrate the "Borrominismo," I will confront two festival decorations. One was made to decorate the front of the Lateran basilica in 1729 for a canonization by the Roman architect, Ferdinando Reif (fig. 182).[16] The other "Berninesque" is Nicola Salvi's *macchina* erected in the Piazza di Spagna in 1728 to celebrate a Royal marriage in Madrid (fig. 183).[17]

Reif's design displays several superimposed orders, rich convex-concave movements of the wall surface and an illusionistic crowning feature. At the same time, it is revealing how far this instrumentation is from Borromini's. The movement of the wall, the contrapost of convex-concave are decorative and almost mechanically used, as quotations, but not the result of a consistent process of design and invention. Reif's façade is elegant and gracious, but it was its "prettiness" that the "Berninisti" opposed.

Salvi's *macchina*, a domed centralized structure with projecting convex-curving wings on all four sides, suggests consciously tectonic and spacious implications. The controlled movement is not applied to the surface, but results from the architectural form. The position of the "Berninisti" is more abstract, more normative.

This was the artistic ambiente in Rome when Galilei arrived in December 1731. The foundation stone of the Cappella Corsini was laid in May 1732, the finished chapel was consecrated in January 1735.[18]

Galilei planned the chapel as a domed structure over a Greek cross with very short arms (fig. 184). The semicircular niches in the "transept" enclose the funerary monuments to the pope and his uncle, Cardinal Neri Corsini the Elder. The articulation of the walls was conditioned by the existence of the arch which formed the entrance from Borromini's aisle (fig. 185). Galilei repeated the arch in the arms of his cross as frames for the tombs in the side bays and for the altar in the end one. All the walls are articulated by Corinthian pilasters, set on a high base which runs around the entire chapel, and capped by an unbroken entablature. Barrel vaults with light coffering cover the side bays. The drum of the dome rises from a strongly profiled circular moulding. The hemispherical coffered dome culminates in a lantern with eight windows. The simplicity of the design brings out by contrast the richness of the extravagantly luxurious marble revetment. Pilasters, arches, statues, and reliefs are in white marble which forces a strong contrast with the flat panels of many-colored marbles. These are dominated by violet, green, and red marbles, as well as porphyry. Combined with the gilded stuccoes of the vaults and dome, these form a cool, subtle and elegant color harmony, which never becomes garish, but gives the chapel the luminous quality of a precious casket.

It remains an open question whether Galilei himself sympathized with the rich sculptural program. There is a significant passage in his contract with the sculptors, who had to pledge themselves to keep exactly to the measurements for the reliefs in the lunettes, and not to allow a single hand or an attribute to extend beyond these limits.[19] The sculptures are remarkably uniform in character and create a homogeneous whole, but their relation to the architecture is less harmonious as they are not completely in step with Galilei's severe manner.

On the Pope's request, the Cappella Sistina in S. Maria Maggiore (fig. 186), which is in fact the first papal funerary chapel, provided the model for the Cappella Corsini.[20] In contrast to Domenico Fontana's architecture Galilei uses an order of fluted pilasters set on an unbroken base nearly two meters high, and carrying an unbroken entablature. The decorative elements are strictly subordinated to this articulation and are kept within a narrow range of motifs. The barrel vaults and the dome are without ribs and are uniformly coffered. The monuments in the side bays do not determine the form of these bays, but are absorbed into them. Galilei uses fully three dimensional forms—a hemispherical dome and niches crowned by half-domes—and yet the chapel seems to be developed from the walls rather than moulded in space. The emphasis on verticals in the chapel depends not so much on the pilasters, but on the correlation of the "transept" and the dome. But this upward movement is counterbalanced by the horizontals of the base and the entablature, and even the coffering of the dome. Since the barrel vaults of the transept do not have ribs, the order of pilasters cannot establish a continuous movement running right through to the top of the dome, but remains a flat network articulating the walls. It is an elegant, almost pretty feature rather than a powerful element which binds together different parts of the design. Spatially, the chapel consists of a collection of independent units which form a whole partly through the uniformity of their decoration (symetria), but above all through their carefully calculated proportion in relation to each other. Wittkower's phrase about the tendency of neoclassical architects to create "isolated balanced surface patterns" could be applied to this forerunner of the movement.[21]

The reasoned basis of the whole design is spread out before us. The carefully thought-out proportions, the simplicity of the ornamentation, the symmetry of the whole, and the richness of the marbles with their subtle gradations of color were Galilei's contribution, and they reflect his conception of "truly good architecture" as he had formulated it in 1723: "Simplicity and solidity, embellished only by rightness of proportion and with decoration suitable to the order."[22] The unity of the arts, that great aim and creation of the High Baroque, is suspended. Architecture tends to autonomy. Painting and sculpture are no longer equal companions, but are subordinated, have to respect their given frames and are not even necessary. There is no place for allusion—no capital displays the pope's arms—and there is no place for illusion.

In the Corsini chapel, Galilei left contemporary Roman architecture behind him and moved further toward neoclassical forms than would be possible again in Rome for many decades (fig. 187).[23] Contemporary comments are more enthusiastic about the richness of the decoration than about the design. Valesio found the chapel "dry and boring," the general reaction was more puzzlement than approval.[24]

Galilei's next commission, however, the façade of S. Giovanni in Laterano, caused a scandal, and the puzzlement changed into fury and disgust.

The Lateran basilica, still within the city walls, but far away from the actual city-center, had been partly remodeled by Borromini for the Holy Year of 1650.[25] The vaulting of the main nave and the building of a new façade toward the city gate was suspended because of a lack of money and time. In 1732, therefore, the main façade of the papal basilica was still as it was left by Borromini in 1650 (fig. 188). In 1723, drawings for the façade turned up from Borromini's heirs, and they were bought by Cardinal Benedetto Pamphily, archpriest of S. Giovanni in Laterano.[26] Their authenticity was doubted, but Pamphily commissioned a model built after the designs and was determined to have it executed. The drawings and the model have disappeared. They evidently represented a design with several stories articulated with small columns, and it is possible that Ferdinando Reif's decoration of the Lateran façade, created in 1729 for the canonization of S. Giovanni Nepomuceno, reflects the so-called "Borromini design" (fig. 182).[27] At the end of 1729, the beginning of the execution was imminent, when Cardinal Pamphily died. His successor, Cardinal Pietro Ottoboni, caused the designs to be brought to him. At about the same time, the site for the Cappella Corsini had been given to the pope and Neri Corsini now became interested in the building of the façade as well. In November 1731, it was decided

to abandon the idea of building according to Borromini's project and to request new designs for which the architects would be allowed complete freedom. As soon as Galilei arrived in Rome in December 1731, he began to work on a design for the façade as well as on that for the Corsini chapel.

In March 1732, the number of designs, which Juvarra had referred to as "endless" had grown more numerous, and the attempts to influence the commission more intense so that the pope found himself compelled to announce in April 1732 a public competition, the first of this kind ever to happen.[28] In the first week of June, all the designs and models which had been submitted were exhibited in the gallery of the Quirinal Palace. At the end of June, an expert commission composed of eight members of the Accademia di San Luca were to deliver their judgment. They gave first a verbal report, then submitted their vote in written form. Four of these votes were solidly for Galilei's model, whereas the others gave their support to various other designs. Given this narrow majority, the congregation decided to hold another competition between Galilei, Ludovico Rusconi Sassi (the next most favored model) and Vanvitelli, and stipulated that Vanvitelli should produce a model—he had submitted two drawings—so that all the competitors should have presented the same evidence and the comparison would be more fairly balanced. These decisions were submitted to the pope. But the pope declared Galilei the winner of the competition, as he had been placed first by four votes, and the pontiff did not want further delay of the building.[29]

The decision disturbed the Roman architects as nothing had ever before. Valesio makes the interesting comment that the judges from the Academy had ensured that Vanvitelli's design should be given preference over Galilei's, but the reports were reversed.[30] So two judges had preferred to keep silent about their decisions. Roman architects wrote to the pope, demanding a new competition due to the manipulation of the first one, and accused Galilei of ignorance and complete incapability of handling the commission.[31] Apart from envy and Roman-Florentine mutual dislike, it is evident from the reports of the judges that two fundamentally different views of architecture had been confronted, and there was no way of reconciliation.

Galilei's and Rusconi Sassi's models are thesis and antithesis of this confrontation, Galilei's representing a new, Sassi's a traditional Roman rendering. Galilei's model is lost; there is a sketch in Paris (fig. 189).[32] Sassi's model was rediscovered by Hellmut Hager in the Fabbrica di San Pietro (fig. 190).[33]

Galilei's façade is a blocklike screen with two porticoes framed by a composite order of giant pilasters. The proportion of height to length is 1 to 2. The central bay projects slightly and carries a pediment. The design is a grid of vertical and horizontal lines, the function of the upper portico, which serves as a Benediction Loggia, is clearly visible.

Sassi's model incorporates features of the Borromini model. The surface is projecting in convex and concave curves, the effect enhanced by the increasing salience of the order, from pilasters to columns and the overwhelming crowning top.

Sebastiano Conca, one of the judges who preferred Sassi's model, described Galilei's design as "molto andante e scarso, e non secondo il buon costume Romano che richiede ornato di colonne e maggiori aggetti" (very pedestrian and poor, and not in accordance with the best tradition of Roman architecture which demands the use of columns and more projections).[34] Pannini, another member of the jury, remarked on Galilei's model: "Idea assai facile e semplice, un contorno troppo quadro, e senza interrompimento o risalto" (a very easy and simple idea . . . too square and without breaks or projections),[35] criticizing the very hard effect of Galilei's design. Of all Galilei's supporters, only the French architect Antonio Derizet spoke in favor of the model without qualification.[36] He explicitly selected the severe and simple form without projections, solely articulated by giant pilasters as providing the only solution suitable to the building, and attacked the "good Roman tradition" as a "wild and unreasonable compilation of pilasters and columns and unnecessary projections." "Andante, semplice, sodo," are his expressions for noble simplicity, clearness and pure design, according to the best rules of architecture. This is a fundamental dispute on the principles of architecture, and no longer a discussion of fashion. The Roman sense of superiority was shaken and challenged.

Vanvitelli's first design took over the scheme emphasized by his colleague, but he made characteristic changes (fig. 191).[37] The emphasizing of the middle section by means of columns, and the breaking forward of the entablature over the coupled pilasters at the end weakens the linear effect of Galilei's model, and the absence of pedestals reduces the emphasis of the vertical. The choice of a fluted order and the addition of swags to the frieze give the design a more serene and less austere character. Vanvitelli takes the sharp edges off Galilei's much more severe design and makes it conform more closely to traditional models. The emphasis on the wall surface takes away the open, skeletal character; it appears lighter and richer, though the giant order allows it to retain its monumental rendering. It is a transformation of the Florentine model in the best tradition of Roman architecture.

Galilei had been informed in time about the greatest faults of his design: not enough projection and the absence of a suitable terminating feature. Thus, he obligingly changed his pilasters in the middle section for Vanvitelli's columns and offered to heighten the top-balustrade and the statues, and submitted this solution as a drawn alternative to his model.[38] It was this compromise that was eventually executed, though the façade seems to be top-heavy, a fact that damages the effect of the whole (fig. 187).

How strictly Galilei followed his perception that every detail had to obey the same rules as the whole, is demonstrated here with doorframes and niches in the lower portico (fig. 192). No invention, no fanciful play with papal arms, emblems or allusions, but every line developed from the order, strictly architectonical and every decorative part such as the soffitte of the arches or the lunette, derived from antique models (figs. 193, 194). All are to be found in Desgodets' *Edifices de Rome* of 1685, a book that was in Galilei's library.

Galilei's façade, though, met with complete disapproval by almost all his Roman colleagues because it was not "alla Romana." In the intention of its architect and his patron Neri Corsini, however, it was an example of "nobile, maestosa e sul buon gusto antico eretto" architecture.[39]

In the opinion of most Roman art critics and architects, this judgment referred rather to the Fontana di Trevi. Clement XII had at once suspended a project for the fountain just under construction after he had been elected, and had asked for new designs.[40] Most of the projects submitted in 1731 are similar to the one in the Kunstbibliothek Berlin (fig. 195),[41] where the fountain is placed between the two wings of the Palazzo Poli, the architectural background either projecting convexly or concavely with its appropriate crowning features.

A design once in the Archivio Bracci and now in Montreal, usually attributed to Luigi Vanvitelli, can — I think — be regarded as one of Salvi's first designs for the Trevi fountain (fig. 196).[42]

The monumental *final* design that covers the whole palace behind blends the great achievements of Baroque architecture—the air of "performance," the festive richness of allusions, the allegorical messages — with a rigorous and severe architectural system (fig. 197). The sculpture is still an inseparable part of the whole, equal in right with the architecture. The joy of illusion, the pretended existence of nature in the rocks, animals, plants—the transitory element of the water, all compose a great allegory of the water, "la visible immensa mole dell'aqua" (Salvi).[43]

The severe architectural background is linked through the illusionistic rocks to the performance without interrupting the context. The middle section projects and is crowned by an attic, subordinating the lateral parts. Compared with the "first" design, it is apparent that the spaciousness of the concave exedra in the center, linking the accompanying wings, is reduced to a mere niche, set tightly in the triumphal arch-like center. The strict grid of vertical elements (pilasters) and horizontals (bands, missing in the first design) produces a system of coordinated parts that is evidently near to Galilei's components of the Lateran façade design. Salvi's *macchina* of 1728 and the "first" Trevi design show similarities, and the change to the more rigid executed version of the Trevi is, I think, a repercussion of Galilei's contemporary designs for the Lateran and the Cappella Corsini.

But, unlike Galilei, Salvi was able to integrate the new rigorous theories with the Roman Baroque heritage. He fused "grandezza romana" and "sodezza," achieving thus a balance between tradition and innovation. The Roman Salvi, who admired Bernini, succeeded in the position Carlo Fontana and Filippo Juvarra had held before. He acted as an intermediate between the Berninesque and Cortonesque heritage of Roman Late Baroque and the new demands for reason, that were hostile to fantasy and invention. Salvi's work influenced French architects like Soufflot considerably.[44]

Ferdinando Fuga's work reflects the pragmatic reaction to the challenge the Corsini pontificate provoked. Fuga, a Florentine, had been trained at the Accademia di San Luca in Rome.[45] His early projects—a design for the Lateran façade of 1722 and one for the Fontana di Trevi of 1723[46]—demonstrate his abilty to design either Borrominisque projects or those in the Late Baroque taste of the Academy. His "easy virtuosity"[47] enabled him to change his style like a chameleon without ever lacking in consistency or falling into mere caprice.

Fuga became papal architect in 1731. His first project was the design of the Palazzo della Consulta on the Quirinal Hill, an administration building for two secretaries of state and official residence of Neri Corsini.

His first design, dated 1731, is Fuga's ambitious contribution to the new monumentality of Roman architecture (fig. 198).[48] The façade opens to the piazza and the Quirinal Palace. Ground floor and *piano nobile* have a proportion of 1 to 1. The characteristic element of the ground floor is the use of rustication. Interesting is the variety of movement—the center section projects in a convex move, not very strong, but distinctive, breaking in height through the balustrade, thus creating a crowning feature. The window bays of the *piano nobile* and the wall between them project and recess in a rhythmic sequence. The recessed, rusticated parts seem to move back far deeper than they actually do, creating a surface play of shadow and light. Window and doorframes are fancifully stuccoed. The design combines—typical of Fuga—manneristic and baroque elements and Florentine and Roman reminiscences, also. But it was refused. The pope requested a "simple, plain" design,[49] and Fuga designed a second façade from which all movement is eliminated, straight lines run through without interruption, no projections but a plain surface, some appropriate ornamental decoration reserved for doors, and no crowning feature except the pope's coat of arms (fig. 199). Fuga had switched, smoothly, easily, and convincingly, to the "Corsini style"

The formation of the neoclassical style in art and architecture in the eighteenth century is usually defined as of French and English origin. John Harris proved in 1967 that it was, in fact, the fellows of the French Academy in Rome who introduced the new way of art in architectural designs around 1740 in Rome.[50] Thus, the origin of neoclassicism was at least linked to Italy — but without the participation of the Italians.

I think that the intellectual circle around Neri Corsini and Alessandro Galilei led the path the young French artists were to follow only a few years later. The intellectual preparation and the new buildings begun in Rome between 1730 and 1740 were the Italian answer to a desire for change to nature, truth and ratio, which Italy could only fulfill to a certain point, because the Italian artists lacked that sense of emotion in confrontation with antiquity which in the end proved to be the starting point for neoclassicism.

The importance of Galilei lay in the fact that he tried to find by way of abstraction an objective, rational rule for architecture based on natural laws. When architecture turns to autonomy, the pure form of the structure shall be visible like a smaller image of the inner law of the world. The rigorous morality,[51] the deep sincerity which accompanied this concept excludes all joy of movement, or ornamental invention, of show. As an English traveller remarked in 1733: "The present pope's architect (A. Galilei) has with success imitated the noble simplicity to be met with in the works of the ancient, which gives a lustre and grandeur to his performances, above those of his contemporaries."[52]

Galilei had no followers. His "Vitruvian" architecture is definitely no longer part of the Baroque, but not yet neoclassical. He stirred up and irritated. Because of his contribution, Nicola Salvi was able to blend Roman tradition with Florentine challenge. It was Salvi, in whom some of the Roman architects saw the restorer of ancient grandeur. The Fontana di Trevi was, as Salvi's biographer remarked with deep satisfaction: "fatto alla Romana."[53]

Between 1730 and 1740, Rome was presented with the great parallel variety of styles, provided a challenge and controversy about the principles of architecture, and became a fascinating center of inspiration for contemporary architecture — alas, for the last time.

Elisabeth Kieven
Bibliotheca Hertziana, Rome

Notes

*   This paper was presented at the 1984 annual meeting of the Society of Architectural Historians in Minneapolis, when I was a fellow at the Center for Advanced Studies in the Visual Arts, the National Gallery of Art, Washington, D.C. It is the enlarged English version of an earlier paper given at the Deutscher Kunsthistorikertag 1982 in Kassel (summary in *Kunstchronik*, 36 (1983), pp. 40-41) and at the University of Tübingen in December 1983.

1.   L. Rovere, V. Viale, A. E. Brinckmann, *Filippo Juvarra*, Milan, 1937, p. 96.

2.   A. Telluccini, "Alla Biografia di D. Filippo Juvarra architetto messinese," *Archivio storico siciliano*, XXXIV (1909), pp. 357-384.

3.   For the history of the *concorso* and the art patronage of Clement XII, see Ludwig von Pastor, *Geschichte der Päpste seit dem Ausgang des Mittelalters*, Vol. XV, Freiburg-Br., 1930, pp. 733-754; A. Schiavo, *La Fontana di Trevi e le altre opere di Nicola Salvi*, Rome, 1956, pp. 45 ff; H. Hager, "Il modello di Ludovico Rusconi Sassi del concorso per la facciata di S. Giovanni in Laterano ed i prospetti a convessità centrale durante la prima metà del Settecento in Roma," *Commentari*, 22 (1971), pp. 36-67.

4.   Pastor, op. cit., pp. 607 ff; A. Caracciolo, *ad vocem* in *Dizionario Biografico degli Italiani*, vol. 26, Rome, 1982, pp. 320-328.

5.   R. Shackleton, *Montesquieu. A Critical Biography*, London, 1961, p. 98.

6.   M. Caffiero, *ad vocem*, *Dizionario Biografico degli Italiani*, vo. 29, pp. 651-656; Pastor, op. cit., pp. 632-633.

7.   F. Conte Algarotti, "Saggio sopra il Cartesio," in: *Saggi Francesco Algarotti*, Bari, 1963, pp. 405-431 (Scrittori d'Italia 226); G. B. C. Nelli, *Vita e commercio letterario di Galileo Galilei*, 2 vols., Lausanne, 1793; G. Costa, "Un avversario di Addison e Voltaire: John Shebbeare alias Battista Angeloni S. J., Contributo allo studio dei rapporti italo-britannici da Salvini a Baretti," *Atti dell' Accademia delle Scienze di Torino, II Classe di Scienze morali, storiche e filologiche*, 99 (1964-1965).

8.   W. Binni, *Storia della Letteratura Italiana, Il Settecento*, Milan, 1968 (vol. 6), pp. 326 ff. (with further bibliography); I. Carini, *L'Arcadia dal 1690 al 1890. Memorie Storiche*, Rome, 1891.

9.   A. Vecchi, "La Nuova Accademia Letteraria d'Italia," *Atti del Convegno Internazionale di Studi Muratoriani*, Modena, 1972, vol. 5: *Accademie e cultura, Aspetto storici tra sei- e settecento*, Florence, 1979, pp. 39-72.

10.   Muratori's ideas were first formulated in 1703 and made public in 1705 (Vecchi, op. cit., pp. 61-63).

11.   His name is published in the 1708 list of members of the "Repubblica Letteraria," added to Muratori's anonymously (under the name of Lamindo Pritanio) published in *Riflessioni sopra il buon gusto intorno le scienze e le arte*, Venice, 1708. For Salvini see further: M. G. Morei, *Le Vite degli arcadi illustri*, Rome, 1751, V, pp. 85-100; C. Cordaro, *A. M. Salvini, Saggio criticobiografico*, Piacenza, 1906.

12.   G. Pignatelli, A. Petrucci, *ad vocem* "Bottari," in *Dizionario Biografico degli Italiani*, vol. 13, Rome, 1971, pp. 409-418; Costa, op. cit., E. Cochrane, *Tradition and Enlightenment at the Tuscan Academies, 1680-1800*, Chicago and London, p. 973; Marco Dezzi Bardeschi, "Archeologismo e neoumanesimo nella cultura architettonica fiorentina sotto gli ultimi Medici," *Die Kunst des Barock in der Toskana, Studien zur Kunst unter den letzten Medici*, Munich, 1976, pp. 245-267 (*Ital. Forschungen*, 3. Folge, Band IX).

13.   I. Toesca, "Galilei in Inghilterra," *English Miscellany*, vol. 3 (1952), pp. 189-220; H. Colvin, *A Biographical Dictionary of English Architects, 1660-1840*, vol. 2, London, 1978, pp. 324-325; E. Kieven, *ad vocem* in : *Macmillan's Encyclopedia of Architects*, vol. 2, New York, 1982, pp. 145-149.

14.   P. Portoghesi, *Roma Barocca*, Rome, 1966; N. Mallory, *Roman Rococo Architecture, 1700-1758* (Ph.D. diss. 1965), New York, 1978; C. Kelly, "Ludovico Rusconi Sassi and Early Eighteenth-Century Architecture in Rome," (Ph.D. diss. 1980), The Pennsylvania State University, University Park, Pennsylvania.

15.   H. Millon, "Filippo Juvarra and the Accademia di San Luca in the Early Eighteenth Century," *Projects and Monuments in the Period of the Roman Baroque*, Papers in Art History from The Pennsylvania State University, vol. I, 1984 (ed. by Hellmut Hager and S. Scott Munshower), pp. 13 ff; H. Millon, *Filippo Juvarra. Drawings from the Roman Period, 1704-1714*, part I (*Corpus Juvarrianum*, 1), Rome, 1984, XXII-XXV, XXXVIII.

16.   Vienna, Graphische Sammlung Albertina, Historische Blätter Rom. (E. Kieven, "Revival del Berninismo durante il pontificato di Clemente XII," *Gian Lorenzo Bernini Architetto e l'architettura europea del Sei-Settecento*, Atti del convegno, 1981, ed. by G. Spagnesi and M. Fagiolo, Rome, 1984, vol. 2, pp. 459-468; Chracas, *Diario Ordinario*, 49, no. 1815, 25/3/1729).

17.   A. Schiavo, op. cit., fig. 6.

18.   F. Caraffa, "La Cappella Corsini nella Basilica Lateranense (1731-1799)," *Carmelus*, 21 (1974), pp. 281-338.

19.   Florence, Archivio di Stato, Carte Galilei, filza 14, fasc. 1, fols. 49-50 (will be published in E. Kieven, *Alessandro Galilei*, London, 1986).

20.   A. de Montaiglon, ed., *Correspondance des Directeurs de l'Acadèmie de France à Rome*, vol. VIII, n. 3524, pp. 322-323.

21.   F. Saxl and R. Wittkower, *British Art and the Mediterranean*, London, 1948, p. 54.

22.   I. Toesca, "Un parere di Alessandro Galilei," *Paragone*, 4 (1959), n. 39, pp. 53-55.

23.   It is interesting to compare a typical "established" Roman work of that period, Carlo De Dominicis's church of SS. Celso e Giuliano, begun in 1732, with the Cappella Corsini, to mark the difference.

24.   F. Valesio, *Diario di Roma* (ed, G. Scano and G. Graglia), Milan, 1979, V, p. 758.

25.   For the history of the rebuilding of the façade of San Giovanni in Laterano, cf. H. Hager, op.

cit.; A. Schiavo, op. cit., pp. 37-62; S. Jacob, "Die Projekte Bibienas und Doris für die Fassade von S. Giovanni in Laterano," *Zeitschrift für Kunstgeschichte*, 35 (1972), pp. 100-117.

26. V. Golzio, "La facciata di S. Giovanni in Laterano e l'architettura del Settecento," *Miscellanea Bibliothecae Hertzianae*, Munich, 1961, pp. 450-463.

27. This will be discussed in the author's forthcoming monograph on Alessandro Galilei.

28. A. Schiavo, op. cit., 41 ff; Hager, op. cit., pp. 37 ff.

29. Vanvitelli's statement that he had won the competition was first published by Milizia (*Memorie degli architetti antichi e moderni*, Bassano, 1785, II, p. 264). Though not quite to the point, it has since been taken for granted.

30. Valesio, op. cit., V, p. 496.

31. ASV, Fondo Bolognetti, Misc. vol. 270, c. 4-15v: "Memoriale in forma di scrittura mandato alla Santità di Nostro Sig.re Papa Clemente XII. Dalli virtuosi Architetti di Roma quali hanno operato in dare alla luce i loro disegni per la Facciata di S. Giovanni Laterano." (This document was kindly pointed out to me by John Pinto.)

32. Paris, Archive of the Ministry of Foreign Affairs, Affairs étrangers, Rome, t.735, f.293.

33. H. Hager, op. cit.

34. F. Cerroti, *Lettere e memorie autografe ed inedite di artisti tratte da manoscritti della Corsiniana*, Rome, 1860, p. 23.

35. Cerroti, op. cit., p. 36.

36. Cerroti, op. cit., pp. 30-33.

37. A. Schiavo, op. cit., pp. 50-53, figs. 8 and 9 (Rome, Museo di Roma, Gabinetto comunale delle stampe, N. 06028).

38. Cerrotti, op. cit., pp. 35, 40.

39. Francesco Scotto, *Itinerario d'Italia*, Rome, 1747, p. 364. This edition of Scotto was written by Galilei's friend, Ridolfo Venuti, and finished about 1739, though published only ten years later.

40. A. Schiavo, op. cit., p. 118; H. L. Cooke, "The Documents Relating to the Fountain of Trevi," *The Art Bulletin*, 38 (1956), pp. 149-173; C. D'Onofrio, *Acque e Fontane di Roma*, Rome, 1977, pp. 526-563; and most recently, John A. Pinto, *The Trevi Fountain*, New Haven and London, 1986.

41. S. Jacob, *Italienische Zeichnungen der Kunstbibliothek Berlin*, Berlin, 1975, pp. 158-160.

42. Montreal, Canadian Centre for Architecture, Drawing Collection, DR 1966:001:102. This drawing was first published by C. Gradara (*Pietro Bracci*, Milan, s.a. (1922), tav. XXIX, pp. 77-78). Thereafter, the whereabouts were unknown for about fifty years and the design was, following Gradara's attribution, always regarded as a project by Vanvitelli (see L. Bianchi, "Disegni del Vanvitelli e del Fuga al Gabinetto nazionale delle stampe," *Atti dell' 'VIII. convegno nazionale di storia dell'architettura* (Caserta, 1953), Rome, 1956, pp. 115-125; Cooke, op. cit., figs. 16-19; M. Rotili, "I projetti di L. Vanvitelli per la Fontana di Trevi," *Studi Romani*, 21 (1973), pp. 314-331. I referred to the then lost drawing—with a point of interrogation—as Vanvitelli, too (Bernini *Atti*, op. cit.), but now, after having found the drawing, I feel sure in attributing it to Salvi. The drawing itself is not by Salvi's hand, but is a copy, with the matching ground plan, formerly in the Bracci-Archive and now in the Roman Gabinetto nazionale delle stampe e dei disegni, F.N.32057 (Cooke, op. cit., p. 156). I am indebted to Pierre du Prey for pointing out to me the existence of the Bracci-Archive in Montreal). John Pinto and Jörg Garms agree with my attribution.

43. Cooke, op. cit., p. 169.

44. I shall return to that in an article on Salvi's influence on European architecture.

45.   R. Pane, *Ferdinando Fuga*, Naples, 1956: G. Matthiae, *Ferdinando Fuga e la sua opera romana*, Rome, s.a. (1952).

46.   J. Pinto and E. Kieven, "An Early Project by Ferdinando Fuga for the Trevi Fountain," *The Burlington Magazine*, 125 (1983), n. 969; pp. 746-749.

47.   R. Wittkower, *Art and Architecture in Italy, 1600-1750*, Baltimore and Harmondsworth, 3rd edition, 1973, p. 382.

48.   L. Bianchi, *Disegni di Ferdinando Fuga e di altri architetti del Settecento*, Rome, 1955, n. 5, pp. 26-27, fig. 3.

49.   Florence, Archivio di Stato, Med. 3458, "avviso" 30/8/1732.

50.   J. Harris, "Le Geay, Piranesi and International Neoclassicism in Rome 1740-1750," *Essays in the History of Art Presented to R. Wittkower*, London, 1967, vol. II, pp. 189-191.

51.   Neri Corsini, G. Bottari and A. Galilei were Jansenists.

52.   E. K. Waterhouse, "Rome in 1733," *Italian Studies*, 17 (1962), pp. 49-51.

53.   Biblioteca Apostolica Vaticana, *vat. lat.* 8235, fol. 3.

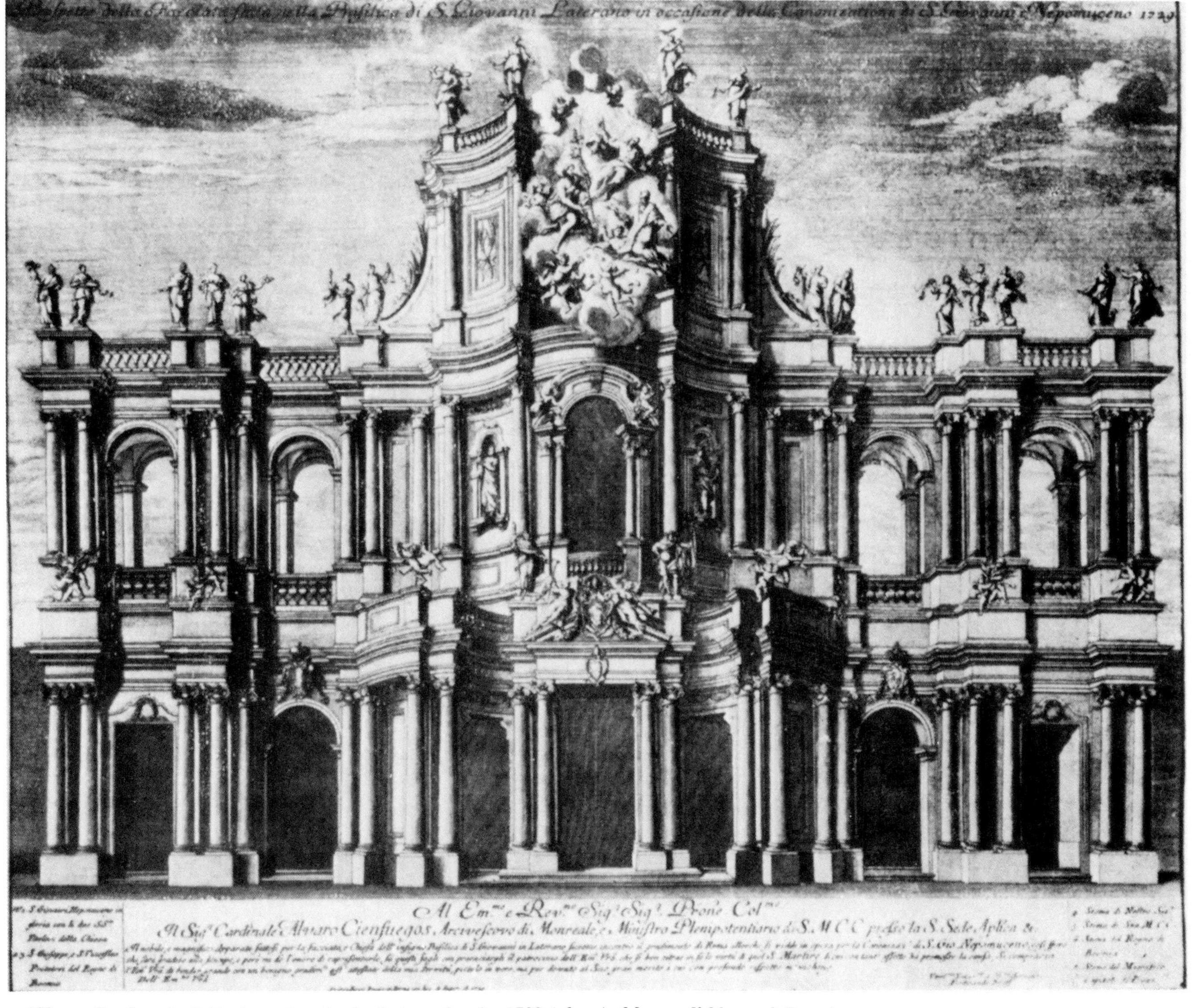

182.   Ferdinando Reif, decoration for the Lateran façade, 1729 (after A. Munoz, *Il Museo di Roma*).

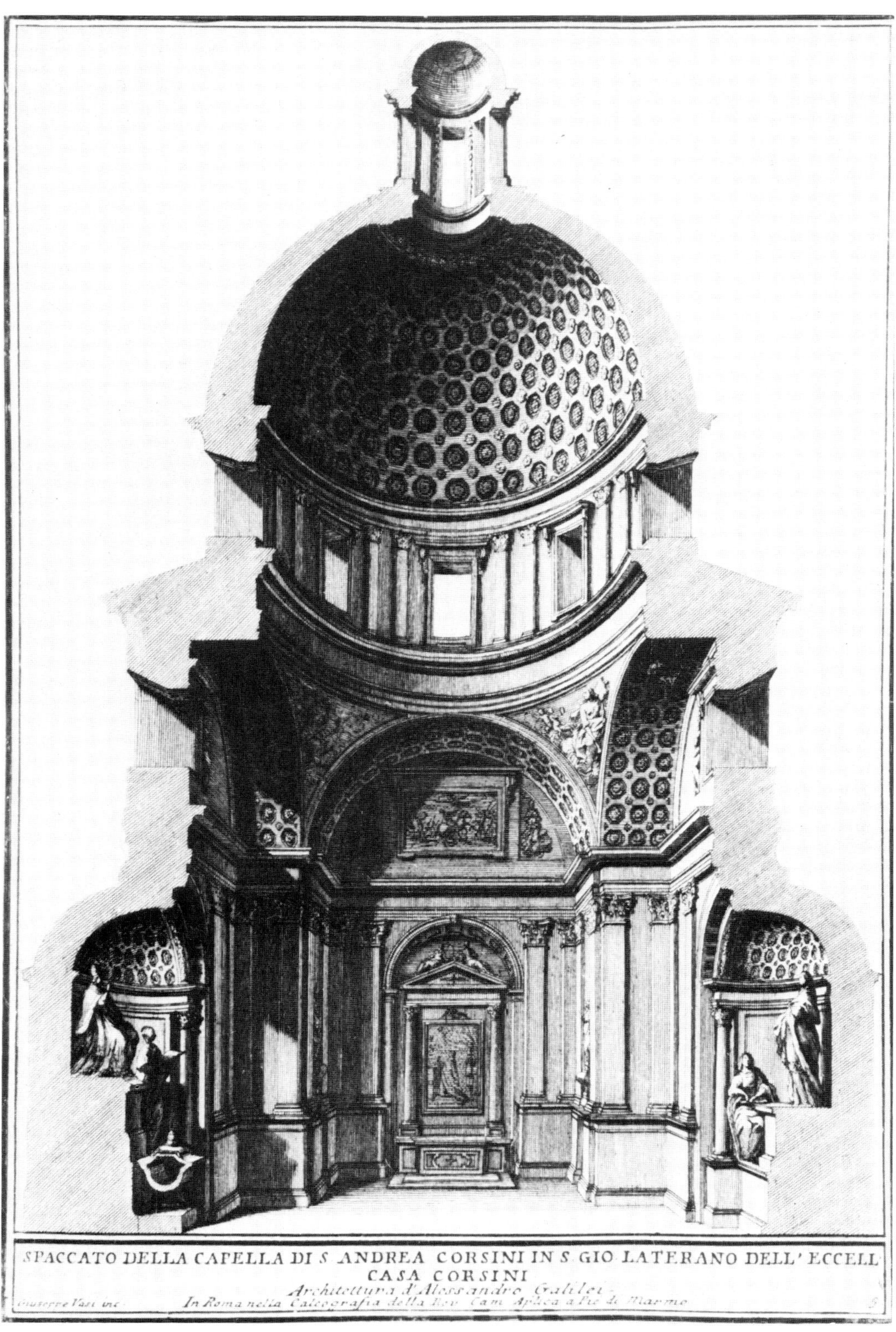

184.   Rome, S. Giovanni in Laterano, Cappella Corsini (engraving from *Quinto Teatro*, 1739).

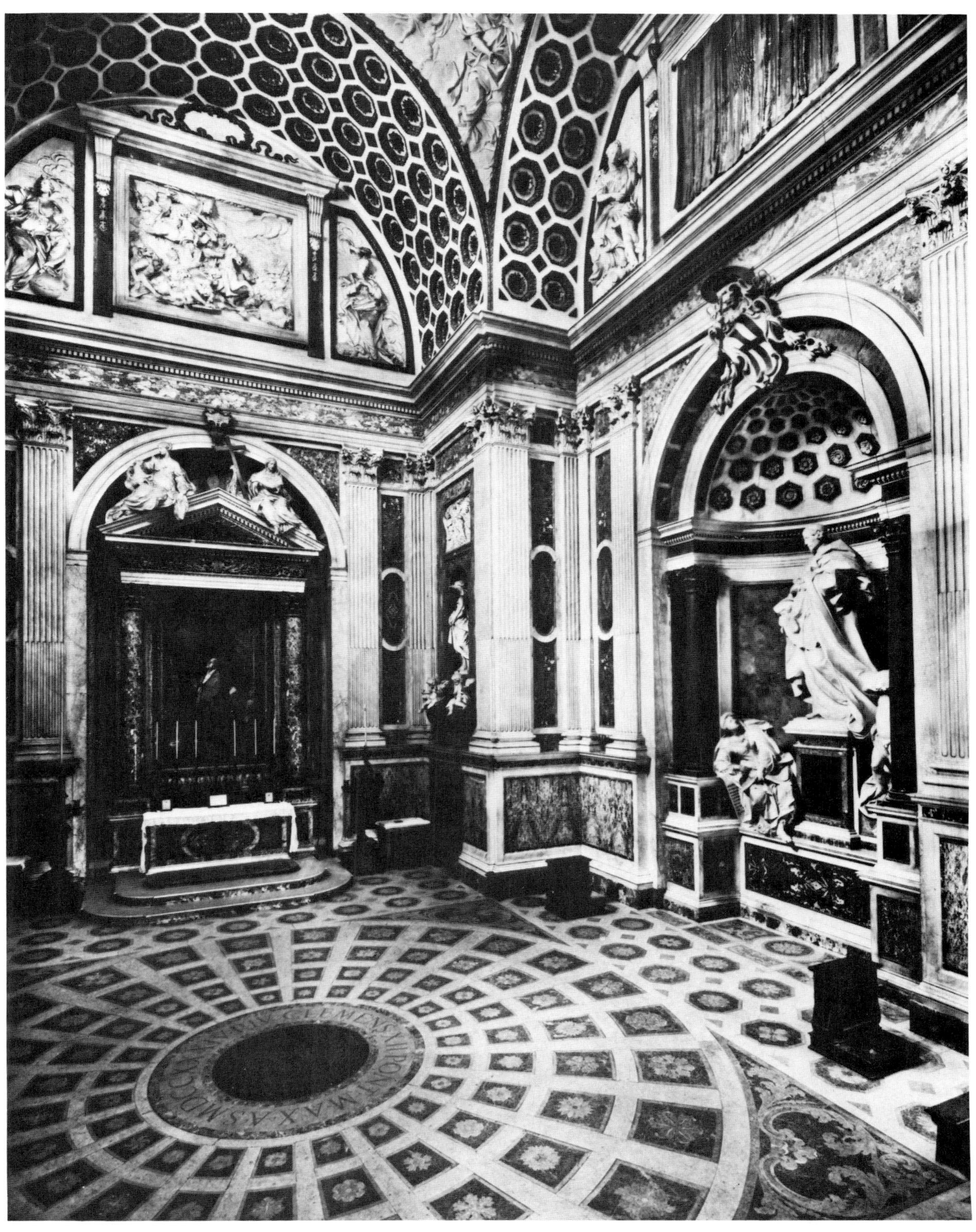

185.   Rome, S. Giovanni in Laterano, Cappella Corsini (photo: Alinari).

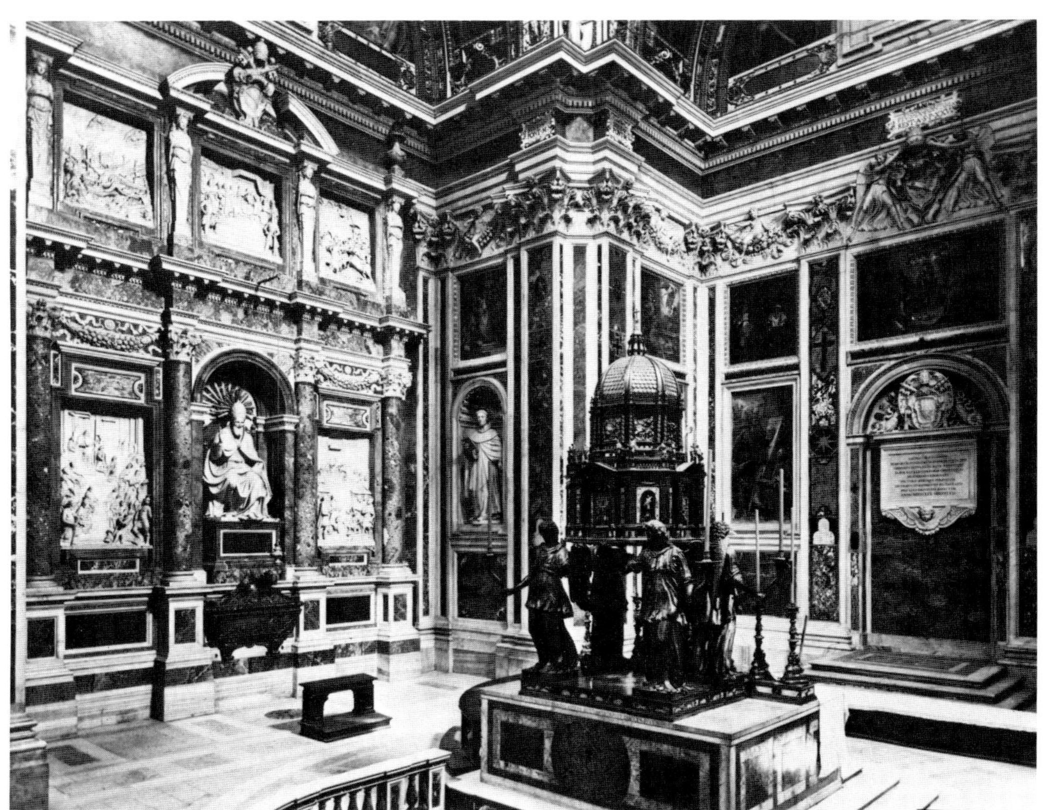

186.   Rome, S. Maria Maggiore, Cappella Sistina (photo: Alinari).

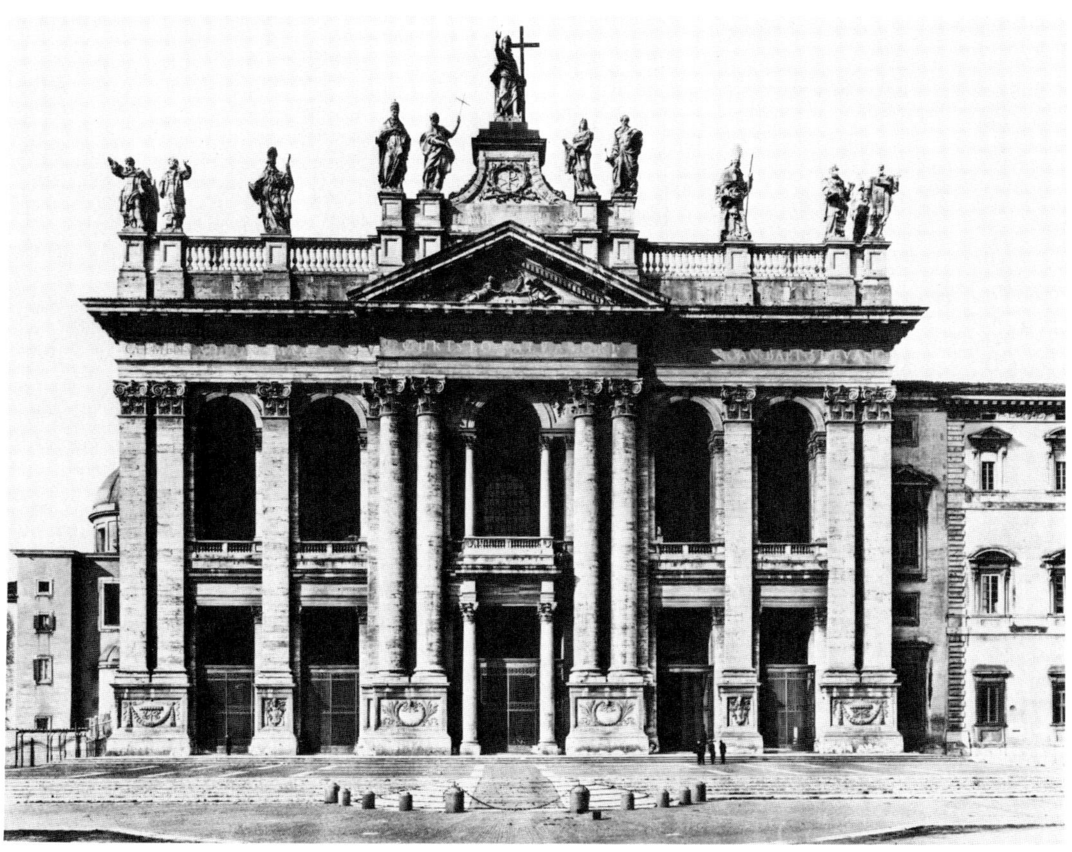

187.   Rome, S. Giovanni in Laterano, façade by Alessandro Galilei.

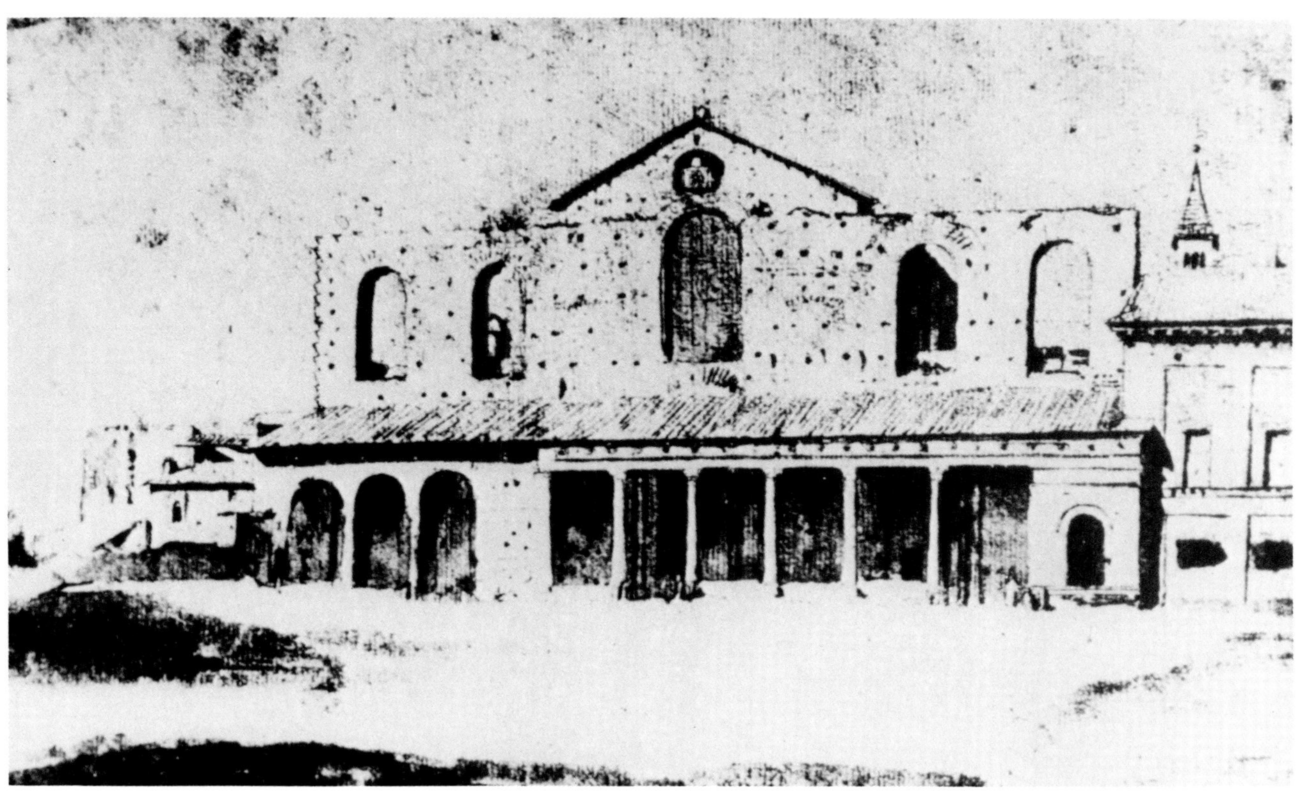

188.   Rome, S. Giovanni in Laterano, state of façade in 1650 (Berlin, Kupferstichkabinett und Sammlung der Zeichnungen; photo after V. Hoffmann, *Römisches Jahrbuch für Kunstgeschichte*, 1978).

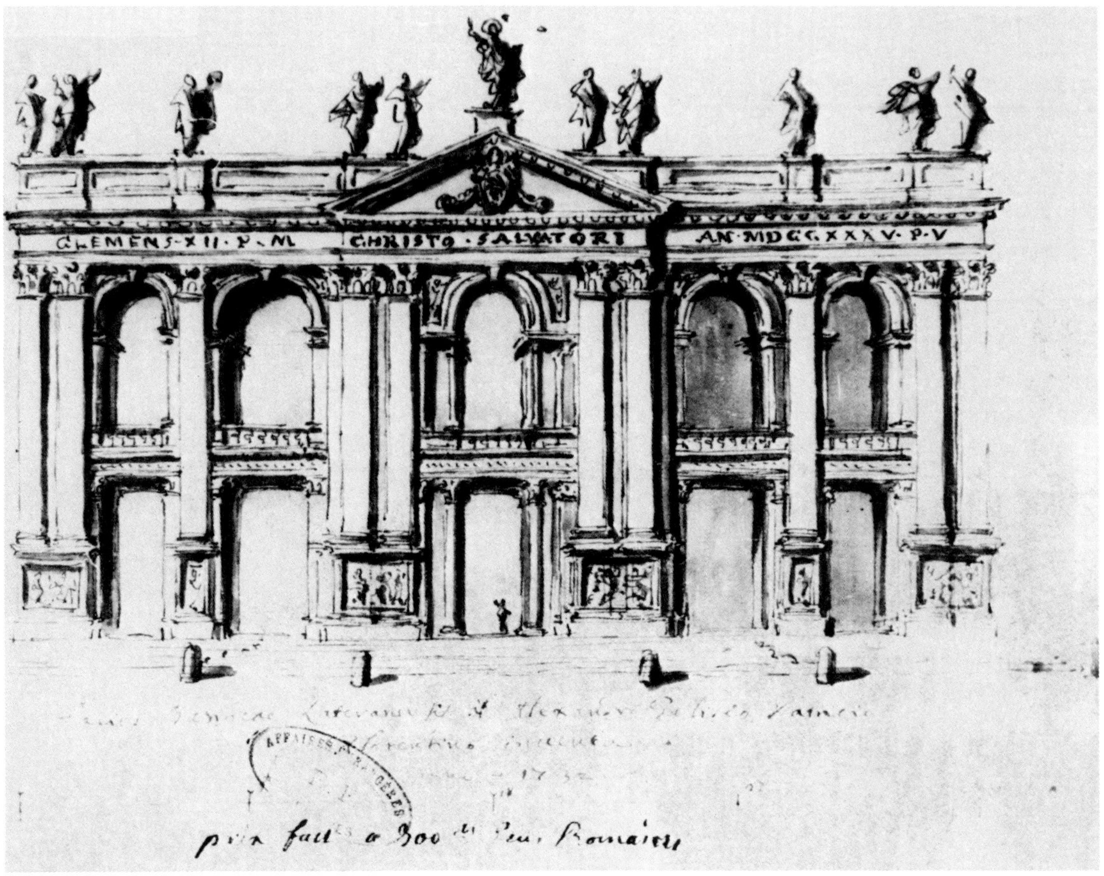

189.   Anonymous sketch after Galilei's model of S. Giovanni in Laterano (Paris, Ministry for Foreign Affairs).

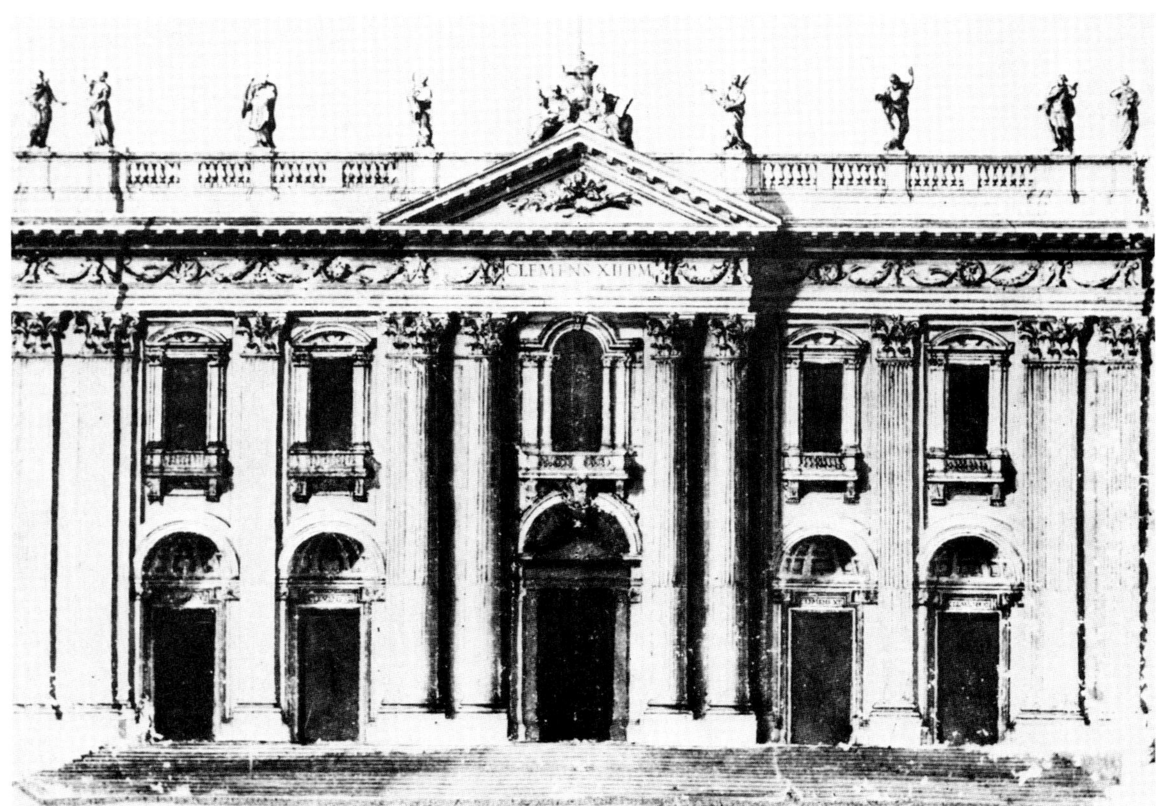

191.   Luigi Vanvitelli, drawing for the façade of S. Giovanni in Laterano, competition of 1732 (disegno X, GFN n1022; Museo di Roma).

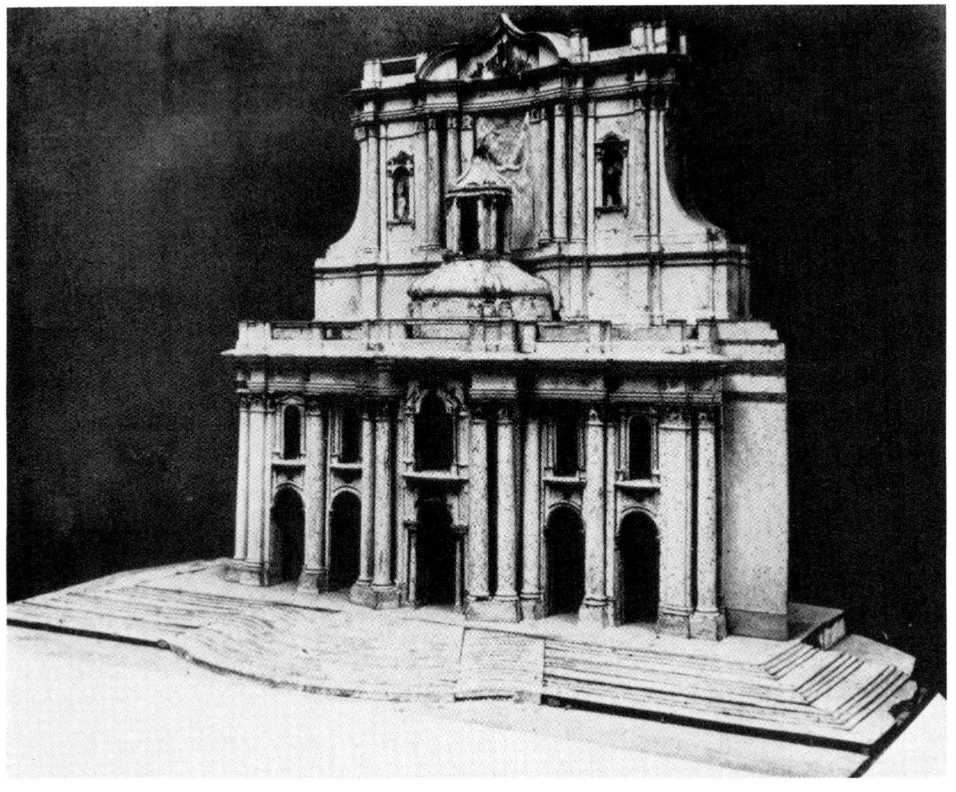

190.   Ludovico Rusconi Sassi, model for the façade of S. Giovanni in Laterano, competition of 1732 (after H. Hager, *Commentari*, 1971).

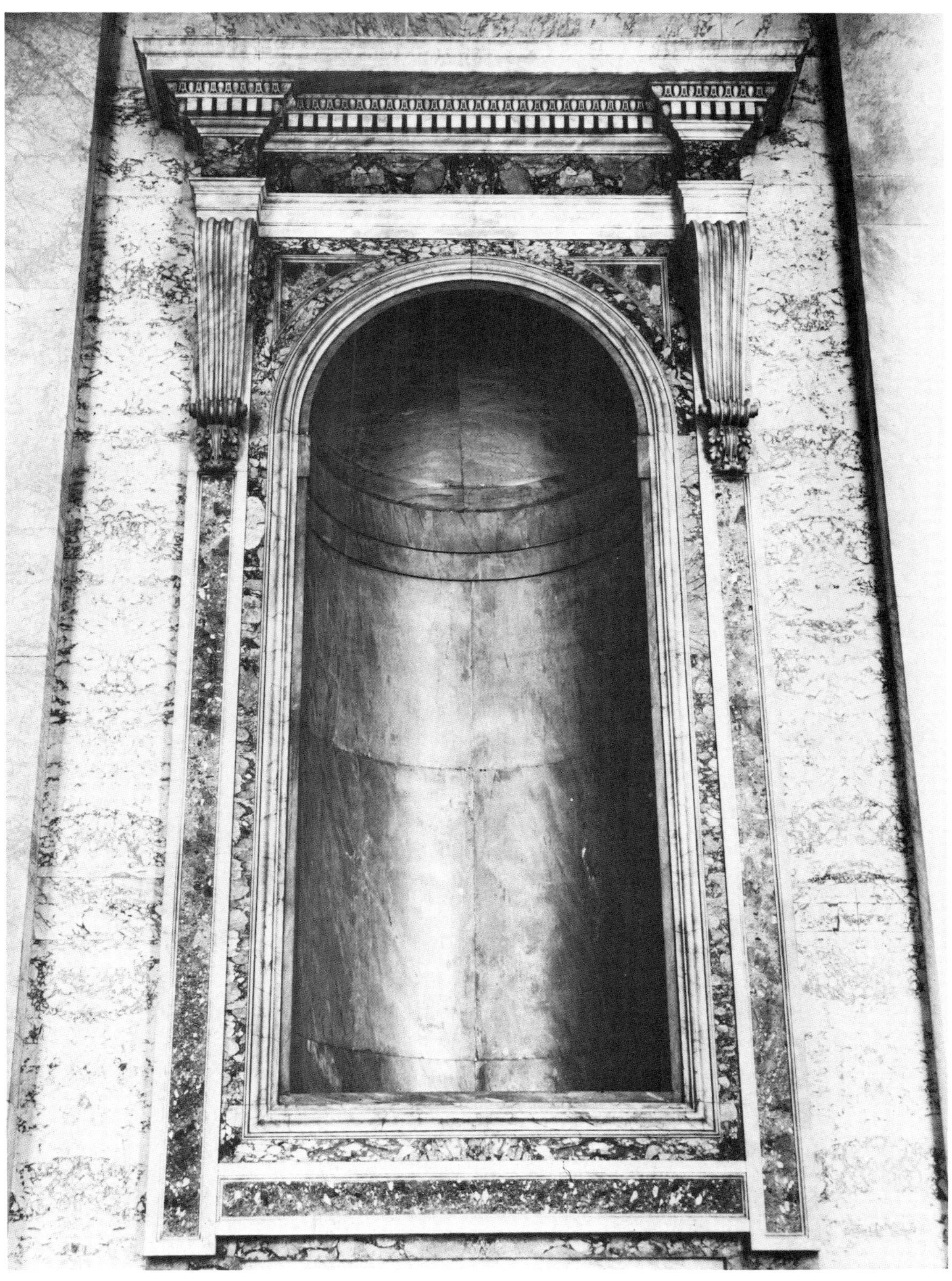

192.   Alessandro Galilei, portico of S. Giovanni in Laterano, niche (photo: Bibliotheca Hertziana, Rome).

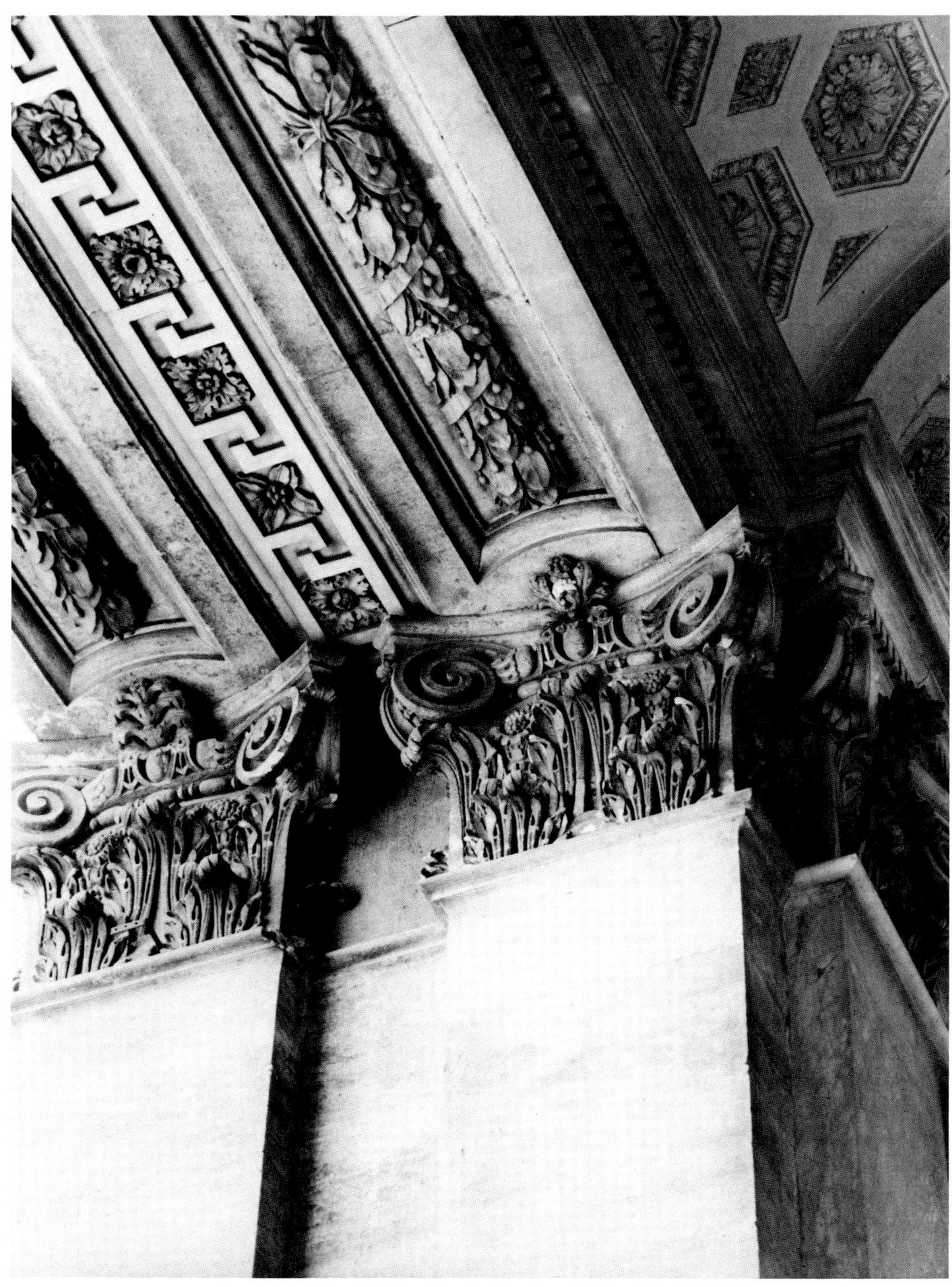

193.   Galilei, portico of S. Giovanni in Laterano, soffittes (photo: Bibliotheca Hertziana, Rome).

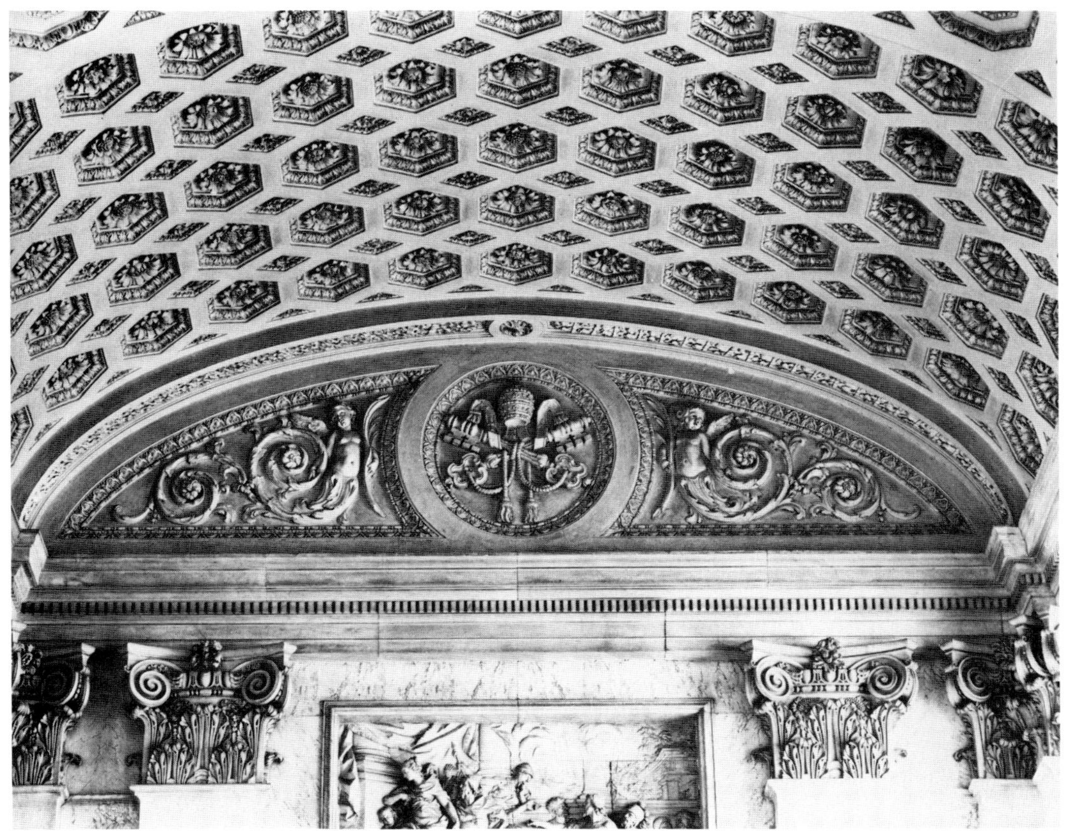

194.   Galilei, portico of S. Giovanni in Laterano, lunette (photo: Bibliotheca Hertziana, Rome).

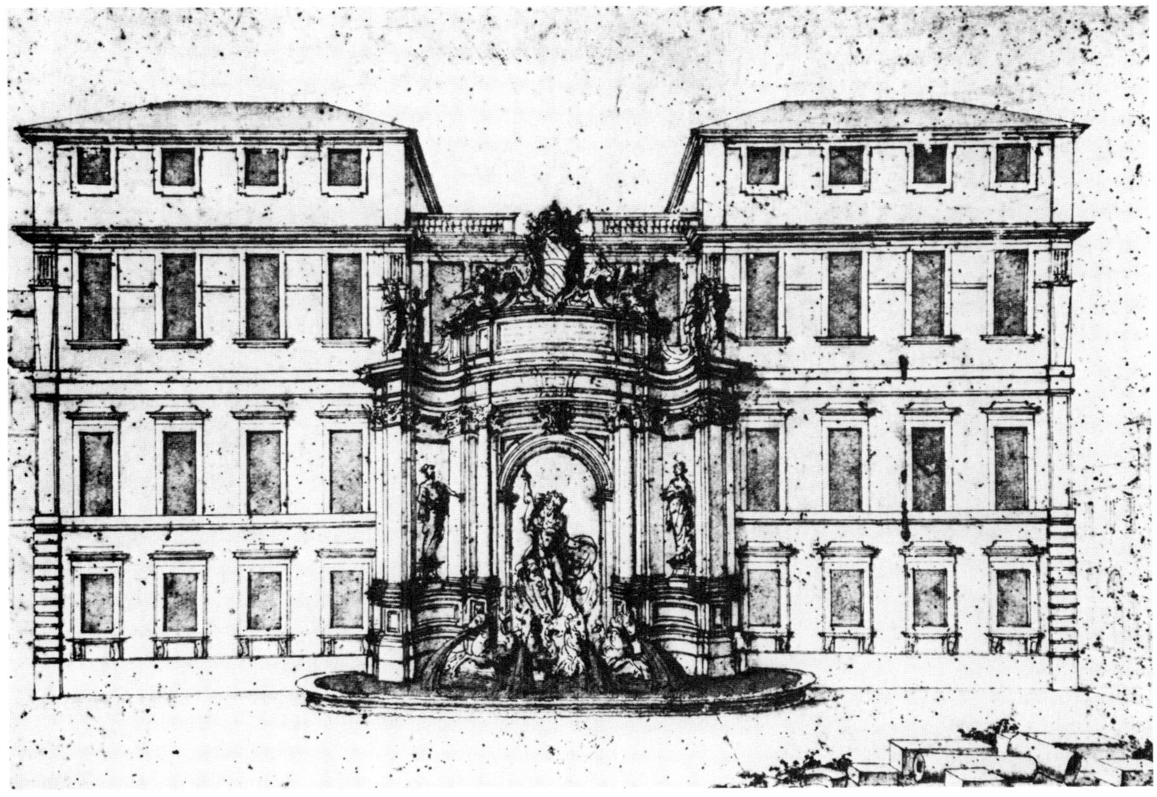

195.   Anonymous architect, project for the Trevi Fountain, 1730-1731 (photo: Berlin, Kunstbibliothek).

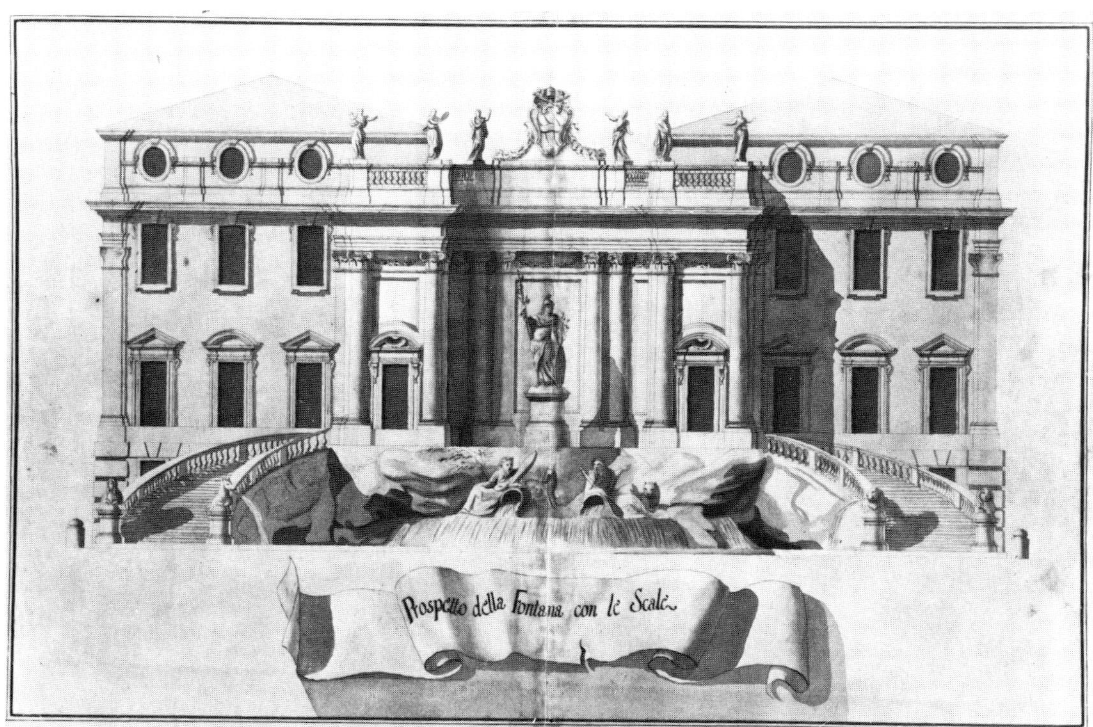

196.   Nicola Salvi, project for the Trevi Fountain, 1732 (Montreal, Canadian Centre for Architecture).

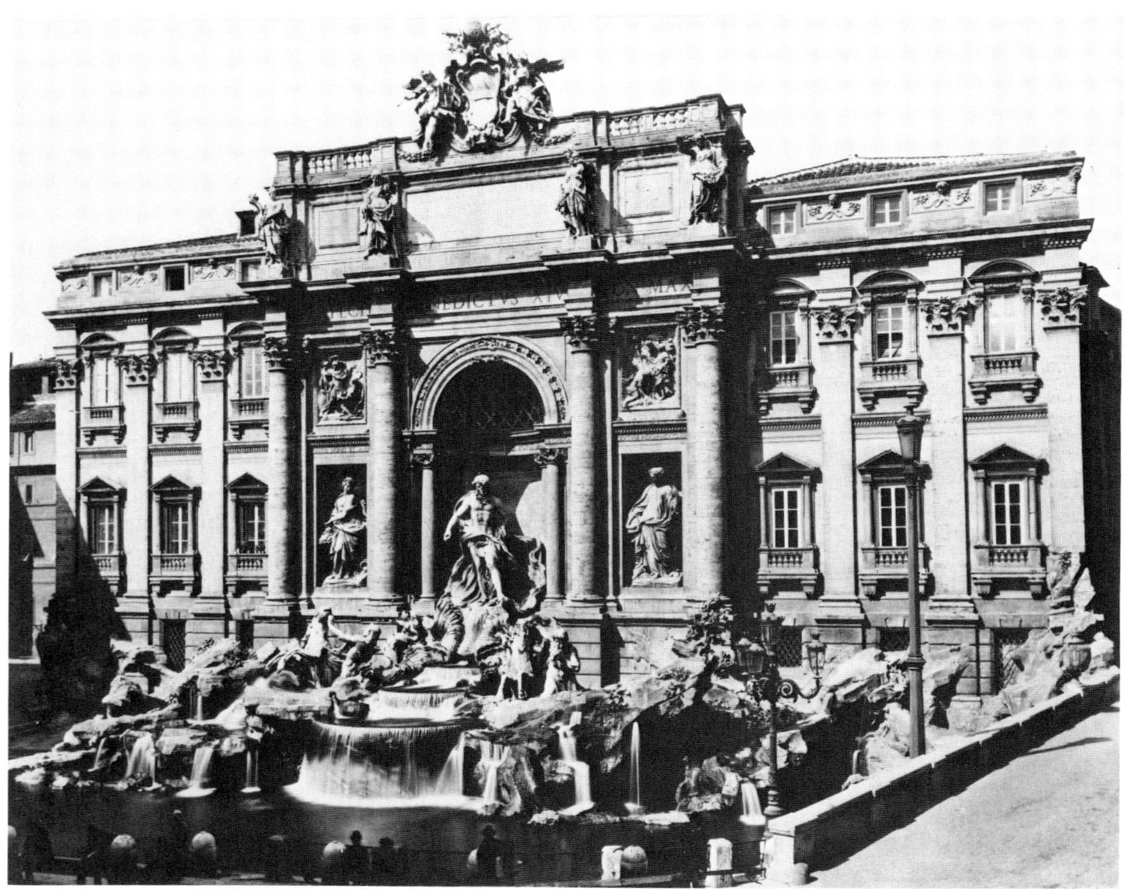

197.   Nicola Salvi, The Trevi Fountain (photo: Anderson).

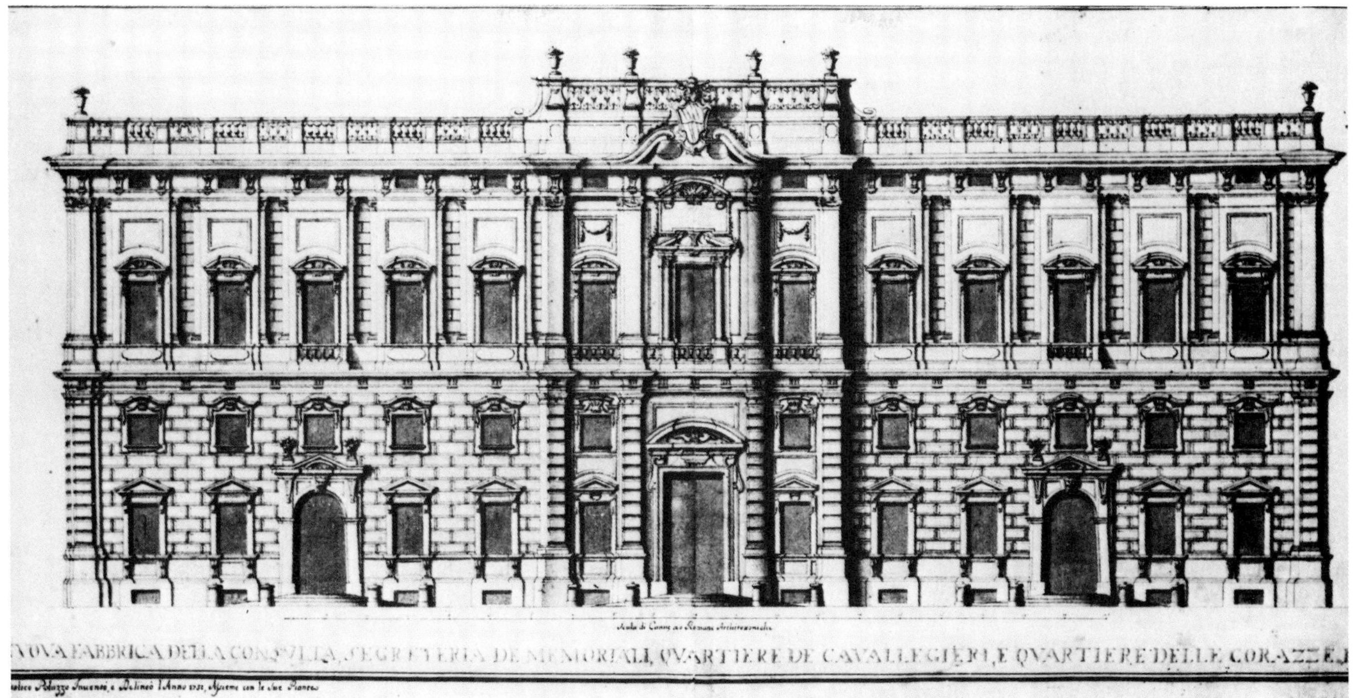

198.   Ferdinando Fuga, project for the Palazzo della Consulta, 1731 (GFN; Museo di Roma).

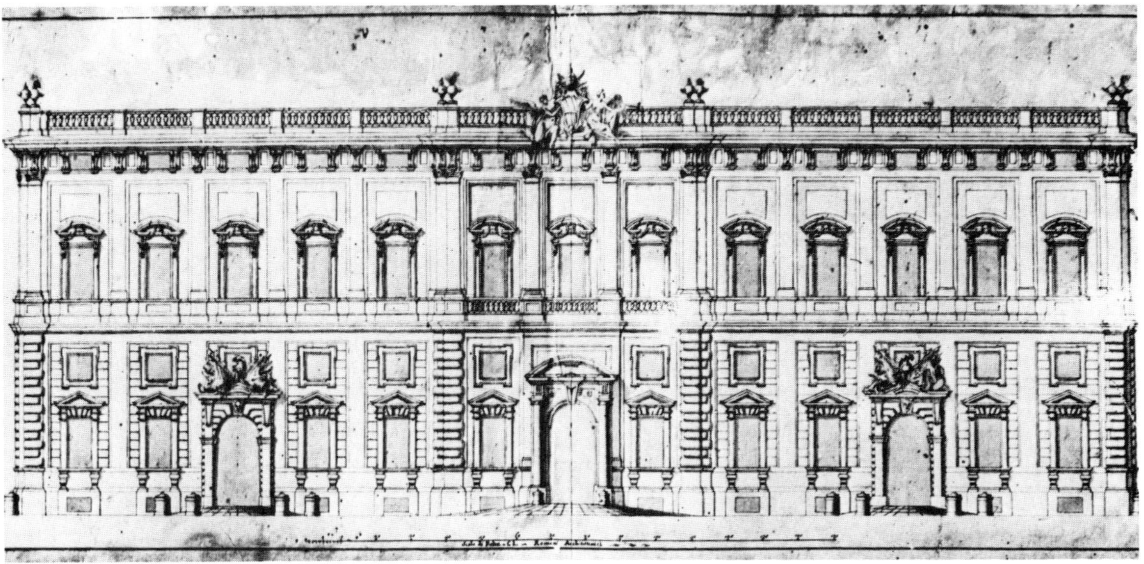

199.   Ferdinando Fuga, Palazzo della Consulta, final project (GFN; Museo di Roma).

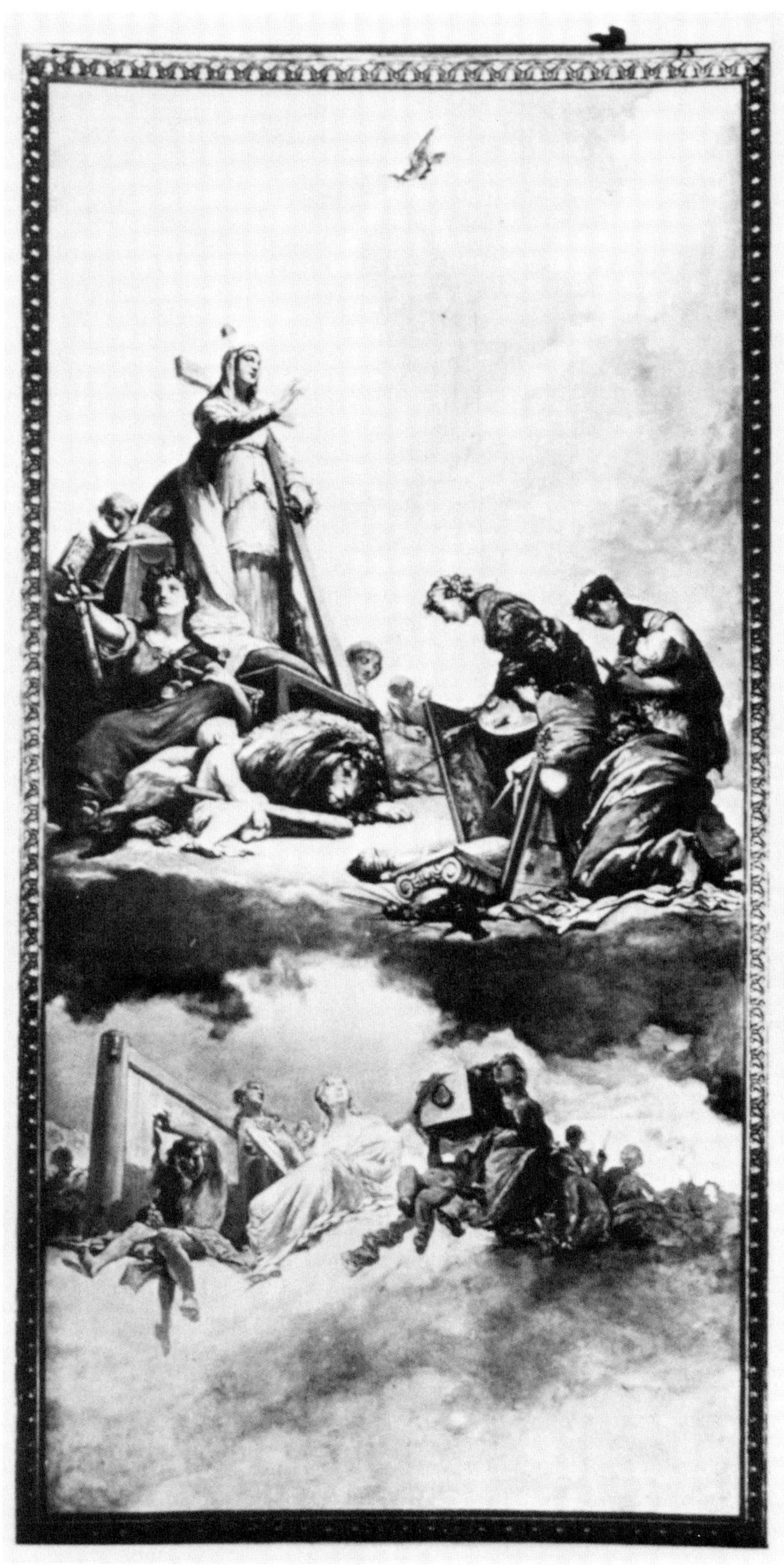

200. Attributed to Domenico Torti, fresco on the ceiling of the Galleria dei candelabri, Vatican.
Commissioned by Pope Leo XIII between 1883 and 1887 (Direzione Generale dei Musei Vaticani).

Roman Antiquities in Early Photography*

11

INTRODUCTION

Amidst the glories of Rome, in the company of Michelangelo, Raphael, Bernini and Fontana, photography might be thought of as a very humble art, but its credentials are in fact well established in the very heart of the Eternal City itself.[1] Figure 200 is a painting which comes from the ceiling of the Galleria dei Candelabri in the Vatican, a painting which was designed, amongst several other things, to honor photography. *Religion* stands upright on her throne, blessing *Painting, Sculpture* and *Architecture*; in a position only slightly less exalted, we find *Photography* (in uneasy partnership with *Carpet-weaving*, as it happens). The child and the lion symbolize peace in general, and not merely, as enthusiasts might be tempted to assume, a final reconciliation between the new art and the old. Pope Leo XIII commissioned the painting[2] in the early 1880s, and did so because he was himself a photographic enthusiast, and no one could wish for a more agreeable and potent source of respectability.

This overview begins with the year 1839, which is, as far as photography is concerned, a year to be remembered, when the invention of photography was publicly announced in France and England. By that time Rome had already been in existence for a while, and it would be fair to admit that the foundations of the Eternal city were not shaken by the discovery of the new graphic art. For the unfortunate multitudes who were unable to go there and see for themselves, the image of the city had been shaped for centuries by paintings and drawings; after 1839 it was shaped in the main by photography. Actual travel was mind-expanding for the few who could afford it; armchair travel from the safety of their homes had to do the same kind of service for those who could not.

Rome had always been the artist's city, and it was to be expected that the announcement of Daguerre's invention should have been greeted there with special interest and enthusiasm. Daguerre's discovery was first reported quite briefly by a Turin newspaper in February 1839. In December of that year a more complete description of the process appeared[3] in a Neapolitan weekly, *Poliorama pittoresco* (fig. 201). By February 1840, an announcement had been made in Rome, and by April of that year a poem in praise of the daguerreotype had been read in public at the Academia Tiberiana, not exactly a masterpiece of the poetic muse, but a sincere tribute nevertheless.[4] Daguerre's own handbook was by then available in Italian translation.[5]

When Daguerre, in one of his first attempts, photographed some statuary, his interest was neither artistic nor archeological. What he was most concerned with was to find some pleasing objects that would stay put in front of the camera during the long exposure, and carved stone fulfilled that role admirably. At about the same time, Fox Talbot in England had the same needs while experimenting with *his* photography on light-sensitive paper. He likewise took photographs of art objects that did not move, and he wrote at length about the fact that photography would turn out to be a remarkable medium for the recording of such objects, and of architecture too. In due course, he bequeathed to generations of art historians-to-be the magic wands of their profession, the photograph on paper and the transparency in the projector.

The present survey will confine itself to Rome, and to the earliest period, and just for once there is no problem of definitions. The "earliest period" ends some time in the 1870s. In 1870 itself, Rome became the political capital of a united Italy, and from then onward its character began to change. Much has been written about this change, from a sleepy papal seat to a busy political and business center and, of course, the setting in which Rome's antiquities found themselves changed also. New avenues were being laid out, threatening to damage the archeological record and, at times, destroying it. At the same time, a great deal of misguided "restoration" was also undertaken. Ruskin visted Rome in 1874 and sent a vivid description of the state of things to Thomas Carlisle:

> Any thing so dismal as the state of transitional and galvanized Rome I never saw. Two kinds of digging go on side by side - antiquaries' excavations and foundations of factories and lodging houses. The ground, torn newly up in every direction, yawns dusty and raw round the feet of Imperial, that is to say clumsy, monstrous and even dying Rome.[6]

It all happened within very few years, after a period of virtual stagnation, virtual, because nothing ever stands *completely still*. Figure 202 shows an 1857 photograph of the Piazza del Popolo, looking south. The details are not easily seen, but the street on the right is still lit by oil lamps fixed to the sides of houses, the street in the middle by self-supporting gas lamps installed from 1853 onward. Of course, changes of that kind had been going on all the time.[7]

All this would be enough to justify our cut-off date, but there is actually another reason. Before the mid-1870s or so, photography was an activity indulged in by a few enterprising and dedicated men; later, with the arrival of dry plates, it became a hobby pursued by everybody and his brother. Professionals and serious amateurs deeply resented this influx of mindless button-pushers, but they could not stop it. A photographic era came to an end when the multitudes poured in.

PANORAMAS

The notion that photography might record the world's *man*-made as well as *natural* beauties came to people very quickly, and did not actually grow in a vacuum. Indeed, photography was the heir of an interest created much earlier by painters and sketch artists, and also by the purveyors of popular entertainments like Panoramas and Dioramas. So, for instance, Thomas Edward Barker (son of Robert Barker, who had pioneered panoramas as an entertainment) set up his own establishment in the Strand in London in 1801 or 1802, and soon afterwards (1804) showed a painted panorama of Rome, important enough to be reviewed in print by Constable (who, however, did not like it). Other shows of this kind were to follow, notably one by John Burford in 1839, devoted to the Coliseum, and the skyline of Rome soon became something that everyone living within a few miles of the Strand and Leicester Square was able to see and get acquainted with.[8] Of course, Rome, as a subject, always had to face tough competition for top billing from the Middle East, which shared the same unbeatable combination of classical and Christian heritage.

After 1837, London boasted another great attraction, located in the Surrey Gardens on the South Bank, where there was not only a zoo to rival the one in Regents Park, but a huge set of free-standing panoramas. In 1841 those showed the "Colossal Pictorial Typorama, or Modelled View of Rome", as it was called (fig. 203). It was indeed a huge affair, on which the cross of St. Peter's was 97 feet off the ground. The river Tiber was represented by a real lake which happened to be conveniently in that park, and the bridge as well as the Castel Sant' Angelo actual structures built to scale. The Castello had a balcony from which privileged spectators could watch the fireworks.[9] "Beyond comparison", wrote one of the critics, and we can only hope that he meant it kindly. One night, the whole thing burned down, torched, presumably, by a latter-day Nero who had not been allowed to play his violin. No matter, within a very short time, the glory that was Rome in the Surrey Gardens was forgotten, and a new "Typorama" of Indian temples was quickly built in its place.

ARTISTS AS REPORTERS

The Typoramas were paintings, of course, but were loved as entertainments, as focal points of a spectacle. Nobody regarded them as fine works of art, and in that sense they did not compete with the pictures and drawings that notable artists made in Rome itself. Of course, there were large numbers of those. People always held them in high esteem, but knew well enough that they could not always rely on them for accurate information about the buildings and scenes they depicted. Two such artist's impressions will serve as examples. Figure 204 shows a gigantic but totally imaginary ruin by Jerome Cock (of Antwerp), an etching dating from 1551.[10] That was romantic enough and might actually have existed somewhere in Rome, but did not, and that was something designed to make people highly suspicious of such offerings. The technical term for such a work is a "capriccio", and many artists made them. Figure 205, for instance, is one by Giovanni Paolo Pannini, 18th century, showing not exactly Rome, but the distilled essence of Rome, poetically correct but topologically misleading, to say the least.[11]

The suggestion has been made that such pictures were composed to serve the interests of underprivileged travellers, who lacked the means to buy separate paintings of each hallowed Roman sight, but one might legitimately doubt whether social altruism was the motivating force behind them.

In contrast, one might refer to Piranesi's 1758 etching of the Temple of Antoninus and Faustina (fig. 206), and this time there is no question as to whether the building actually existed; it certainly did and does.[12] The question is, does it really look like this, and what, indeed, do we mean by "really"? Piranesi's building is highly theatrical in character and somehow vast in size. Fox Talbot went there also, some time in the 1840s, with his camera and made a calotype of the same building (fig. 207), which now looks humdrum and prosaic in comparison. As Hyatt Mayor put it in his book *Prints and People*, the early photographers, who had not yet learned to make the camera lie as blandly as the brush, undid Piranesi's magic, just as photographers of royalty undid the court painter's flattery by exposing wrinkles and bunches.[13] It is instructive to refer to a passage from George Stillman Hillard in 1853:

Nor does the first aspect of most of the ruins satisfy the longings of the heart. In all probability, the visitor will have formed some notion of these or, at least, the most prominent of these, from engravings, and those are rarely true. "To lie like an engraving" would be as good a proverbial expression as "to lie like a bulletin" Not that the size, dimensions and character of the object delineated are falsified, but liberties are taken with all that is in immediate proximity of it. Many of [the] Roman ruins are thrust into unsightly neighborhoods . . . surrounded by decay which has no dignity, and by offensive objects which are like discordant notes in a strain of music. All these are swept away by the engraver.[14]

These practices yield, Hillard says, "untruth enough to excite vexatious disappointment" To illustrate Hillard's point concerning squalor, figure 208 represents a daguerreotype by Achille Morelli, showing the church of Santa Maria Maggiore, as it looked in 1841.[15]

When the first photographers came, they mostly saw Rome with the eyes of painters and etchers, but could not quite make their cameras register the awe that they themselves experienced. It took a while for them to learn how to lie with the camera and, of course, they have since learned how to do just that, but in the early 1840s Rome became the first city to be extensively scrutinized by the remorseless lens.

Fox Talbot was not, of course, the only photographer to be attracted by the temple of Antoninus and Faustina (or the church of S. Lorenzo in Miranda that it had become). Figure 209 shows another picture of it, one by an unknown photographer, dated circa 1847. He put the building somewhat in its context, which Fox Talbot had failed to do, and he included a top-hatted man at the bottom left who is actually identified.[16] He was a rope-maker, and had a business in one corner of the Forum Romanum, as shown on the right in figure 210, and that itself gives us some idea of how the antiquities of Rome were used and abused. This photograph is by a Frenchman, Frederic Flanchéron, and dates from 1850. Flachéron had taken up photography only one year earlier. Here we have no embellishment; the scene shown is as squalid as it really was.[17] The citizens of Rome did not seem to care much about their heritage.

However this may be, photographers held from the very start conflicting views of their task. There were those who considered, explicitly or implicitly, that their role was to continue in the tradition of painting and sketching and, at the lowest level, this meant finding the most favorable view, the most attractive composition. Others considered themselves not as artists, but as archeologists and scientists. Their purpose was to catalog architectural detail in the ·most straightforward way, without reference to composition and without frills. They did not aim to make pictures for display; they made photographic records. This diversity of purpose certainly runs through the photographs here reproduced.

There are even examples of photographers with a split personality, who sought to combine these two conflicting missions. We have a splendid example (fig. 211) by Charles Smeaton, probably from the late 1860s, which shows, amongst other things, the catacomb of S. Domitilla, taken by magnesium light.[18] This technique represented the very beginning of photography by artificial light, and in its use Charles Smeaton was obviously a pioneer, indeed a rival of Piazzi Smyth, who photographed chambers in the Pyramids in the same way, also in the 1860s. In figure 211, left of center, we have a measuring rod, cool and scientific, like the one used by land surveyors. In the middle, we have a photographic *vanitas*, a photographic version of the age-old meditation on mortality and impermanence. The pensive hero holds a skull in the approved manner, but is crowned with an incongruous top hat. We have some notion of what the wearer is supposed to be thinking, but what the photographer was thinking about when he took this picture is much harder to fathom.

EXCURSIONS DAGUERRIENNES

It must not be imagined that the preoccupation with travel in general and with travel to Rome in particular was a purely English interest; the same desires and tastes prevailed in France and, indeed, it was the French who, during those very early years, led the world in photographic exploration. The invention of photography was announced on August 19, 1839, and by the 15th of December the prominent Paris optician N. P. Lerebours had daguerreotypes on view in his shop that had been taken to his orders in Italy and Corsica, and we have every reason to believe that one by Appert (fig. 212) was among them, showing Rome from the Palatine. In the following year a portfolio of engravings, called *Excursions Daguerriennes*, was

published, with images based on daguerreotypes made expressly for Lerebours in many places around the Mediterranean. The images themselves concentrated on ancient monuments, but by the time the engravers had finished with them they were often embellished. Figure 213 is an example, based on a daguerreotype by Martens, which illustrates the sort of things that happened.[19] The Temple of Vesta is real enough, but the men who are so anxious to get away from it come entirely from the engraver's fertile imagination. This is not an isolated case; it happened everywhere, not only for the sake of embellishment, but because engravers felt that they *ought* to make a personal contribution to the work as a whole, without which they would be degraded into mechanical craftsmen.

The publication of the complete *Excursions Daguerriennes* took about two years, and by then interested people knew that this kind of reportage was no mere fantasy; it could be done, and the public was eager to see more work along those lines.

THE CULTIVATED TRAVELLER

The cultivated traveller in Italy in the 1840s still moved in the Grand Tour tradition, and planned to take home with him paintings and prints of the great sites he had visited, bought from an army of professionals. Sometimes, he succumbed to the urge to play the role of picture supplier himself, and joined their ranks as an amateur, with varying degrees of success.

The great cities of Italy - Venice, Florence, Rome - had swarmed with artists for centuries, and so it comes as no surprise at all to find their ranks swelled by the addition of photographers right from the earliest years of the new art. In one sense, at least, photographers were just like any other tourists, they tended to go to the principal sights first, the Coliseum, the Forum, St. Peter's, the Spanish Steps, and so on. The Spanish Steps were indeed the traditional place where artists found and hired their models every day. The present survey will have to follow a similar regime, concentrating on very few of Rome's sights, and leaving a great deal unsaid about the less obvious tourist attractions.

A great many Britishers travelled to Italy in those early years and took photographs there, including Fox Talbot himself (who visited Pompeii) and, notably, a medical man by the name of Dr. Alexander John Ellis, who photographed mostly in Florence and Rome. He did so because he could not obtain engravings of Rome that he could trust, and he went on to make scathing remarks about "the rage for embellishment implanted in every artist" Figure 214 shows his view of the Forum, more specifically of the Temple of Saturn, taken from the church of SS. Luca e Martina in 1841.[20] It is a whole-plate daguerreotype, and was not only a photographic achievement, but (since daguerreotypes are photographs on *silver*) a great plate-polishing achievement as well. Dr. Ellis took, or had taken for him, 158 such pictures, which are now in the Science Museum in London, all framed, under glass, and neatly stacked in a cupboard built for this purpose.

It should be borne in mind that 1841, only two years after the initial announcement of the daguerreotype, was incredibly early for an adventure of the kind undertaken by Ellis. In particular, it was before Fox Talbot's *Pencil of Nature* (the first photographically-illustrated book) had appeared, and before Fox Talbot himself had made his pronouncements about the role of photography as a record maker.

Dr. Ellis had planned to make engravings from his daguerreotypes and to issue them in the form of a monthly periodical, but the idea was abandoned. Dr. Ellis explained that he did not have time to make all the photographs himself, and found that those made for him by other people did not quite come up to his standards. Had he nevertheless proceeded, his name would now be as famous as Lerebours'. Still, he left to the Science Museum a pile of hand-written notes in which he recorded the exposure times of the pictures he did take, and much else.[21] Around mid-day (when, alas, the shadows were least interesting) those times were 6-10 minutes, but in the late afternoon his plates demanded exposures of 25-30 minutes. He made as many as nine exposures a day, and together with the cleaning, polishing and sensitizing of the plate (which had to be done immediately before each exposure) this represents a hard day's work. Figure 215 is another daguerreotype by Ellis, in this case of an exceedingly messy Piazza Navona, also taken in 1841.[22]

As time went on, daguerreotype photography gave way to photography on paper, and figure 216 shows a waxed salt print made from a paper negative by another Britisher, namely Thomas Sutton, dating from 1853.[23] This was also a large picture, and the fact that it shows elements of deliberate composition is obvious enough.

Ten years later, photographers enjoyed the benefits of a great deal of technical progress. Robert MacPherson's albumen print of the Forum (fig. 217) was made from a collodion wet plate in 1863, and is likewise carefully composed. The excavated foreground structure is not simply included for information; it fulfills an aesthetic function in the picture, and the degree of detail shown is remarkable.

Robert Macpherson was no mere tourist. He had been a medical student in Edinburgh in the early 1830s, but moved his residence to Rome in 1840 and became a landscape painter there. He also delighted his Roman friends by continuing to wear his kilt, which must have created quite a sensation as he swaggered through town. Thackeray wrote about him, and found him very irritating. The chances are that the strength of his personality was greater than its charm. MacPherson did not take up photography until 1851, and then did so because he needed a profession that he thought of as more reliable than painting to support his family. His views of Roman antiquities were made for sale, and within a few years he had hundreds of them on his list. In 1862 he held a large public show of architectural photographs in London, and *The Athenaeum* praised it lavishly: "Subjects chosen with fine taste, and pictures executed with skill and delicacy." Remarkable as it may seem, MacPherson also continued to paint, and the National Gallery in London bought one of his works for 2000, which was a fortune. MacPherson was also a collector of "old masters", and was in the habit of referring to them as his "nest egg", not entirely the terms a *pure* art lover would use. He was right, though, because that collection was also sold to the National Gallery, at a handsome profit.[24]

Figure 218 shows a very different sort of picture, by an unknown photographer, which must have been taken before 1860. The building on the left, thoughtlessly erected by some misguided entrepreneur, was a grain store, which was demolished in 1860. It is on the basis of such facts, when they are known, that photographs can be dated.[25]

Figure 219, also by an anonymous photographer, shows the Forum Romanum south of the Via del Campidoglio about 1855. Trees were planted in 1857 and, as yet, these are nowhere to be seen. The raised Via del Campidoglio was actually removed in 1900 and replaced by a new north-south artery called the Via del Foro Romano.[26]

Figure 220 is a more dramatic picture, likewise by an unknown, and dating from about 1857. The man in the foreground is a teacher, identified as such by his hat. The antique cobblestones which can here be seen are now under the Via del Foro Romano.[27]

Whatever grounds the archaeologist gained from the people of Rome, the people of Rome recaptured every wash day. This can be seen in figure 221, an 1854 picture by the Luswerghs, Angelo and Giacomo, a father and son team that issued a splendid catalog of photographs for sale.[28] Nor did photographers have only laundry to cope with. Then, as now, Rome had a traffic problem (fig. 222), and that managed to get in the way of all scholarly and touristic activities.[29] In passing, figure 223 shows the researchers at work, bringing a statue of Hercules to light in 1864.[30] It was found in the garden of the Palazzo Pio and dates from the second century A.D. According to a contemporary inscription, it had been ceremoniously buried on that spot, having been struck by lightning during the previous night.

Lastly, a photograph (fig. 224) by Altobelli taken in the 1860s, from a platform behind the Portico of the Twelve Deities, the pediment of which can be seen in the foreground. Many people had written about the charms of Rome by night, but actual photography by moonlight was not yet feasible with the available plates. Altobelli obliged, nevertheless, by using well-known darkroom tricks.[31]

It may be that the popularity of such pictures inspired Henry James' ingenuous American tourist, *Daisy Miller*, in the 1870s, with the determination to see the Coliseum by moonlight. Against everybody's advice, she went and sat in the romantic shadows which, unfortunately, were popular not only among tourists, but amoung dangerous germs as well. Daisy caught typhoid, and the last scene of her story is set in Rome's Protestant cemetery. Had Daisy lived long enough to read the 1886 edition of Baedeker's *Rome*, she might have profited from its sober advice. Says Baedeker: "Even persons of robust health will do well to remember the Roman Proverb: Dove non va il sole, va il medico."

The Coliseum received the same sort of treatment from photographers as the Forum. Figure 225 represents a large daguerreotype taken in 1841 by Lorenzo Suscipj, who was also for a time in Alexander Ellis' employment. He was one of the earliest Italian practitioners, though his name suggests that he may have been Albanian. Ellis himself took another daguerreotype (fig. 226) on June 8 of that year, between 5:24 and 5:36 p.m., to be precise (12 minute exposure).[32] From a few years later, we have a calotype (fig. 227) by Robert MacPherson, taken in 1850, distinctly before the days when the structure came to be surrounded by the permanent traffic jam that is now so characteristic of it.[33] From the same year, there is an internal view (fig. 228) by Sir James Francis Dunlop, who was astute enough to include a person to convey a sense of scale.[34] The side lighting gives a sculptured effect and, in comparison, the MacPherson photograph is quite flat. And so, while we are only in the mid-19th century, we are already confronting the dilemma and central problem of architectural photography. Is it the architectural photographer's obligation to show buildings with clinical precision, or should he try to romanticize them, to make them pretty, to make them impressive, to show them in a good light, or, more complicated still, should he seek to impress his own tastes and personality upon the finished work? If that was a problem in 1849, it has remained one to this day. A photographer wants to be known by his style, by the personal imprint he leaves on his pictures, but when he photographs a building, he is inevitably competing with an architect, and victory is not pre-ordained for either of the two. Even so, one generally wins, though there are occasions when both manage to lose.

Figure 229 shows another picture of the Coliseum, and stylistically a thousand miles away from the last one. It is an albumen print by an unknown photographer, which found its way into the Parker collection, of which more below.[35] Nothing clinical here, nothing scientific, but a composition which may well have been inspired by one of Piranesi's *carceri*.

COLLECTIONS AND COMMERCE

It did not take long for the photography of Rome to become a thriving tourist business. At the lower end, the motivation was, as so often, to make a fast buck, and many a fast buck was in fact made, though some travellers actually testified to the fact that photographs were cheap in Rome. One visitor wrote: "For three scudi you can acquire a view of the temple ruins of the Forum nearly a yard-and-a-half long and half a yard high." At the upper end of the scale the motivation was more complex, not entirely disinterested in profit, but otherwise mixed.

The enterprises of Ellis and MacPherson have already been mentioned; another prominent operator from the British sphere was John Henry Parker, incidentally the founder of Parker's Bookshop in Oxford, now a part of Blackwells. Parker himself took photographs in Rome, and had many others taken for him. Parker was not only a bookseller, but also keeper of the Ashmolean Museum of History and Archaeology; altogether a major personality in nineteenth century Oxford, which was not short of major personalities at the time. He set himself the task of preparing a text for students of architecture which would, as he put it, "differ from any other work on the architecture of Rome in being entirely grounded on the existing remains, and written on the spot after careful examination of these remains" This work was begun in 1865, only just within our period. By the time Parker died in 1884, thirteen volumes had been issued.

Parker's collection of photographs came to be owned by his company, Parker & Son, and in 1925 Francis Kelsey, who was Professor of Latin at the University of Michigan, noticed an advertisement which offered that collection for sale. He began the necessary fund-raising campaign, and in December of the year the collection was in fact sold to the University of Michigan for the princely sum of 60. This must surely go down as the Bargain of the Century in Ann Arbor, and as the Folly of the Century in Oxford. The negatives had been mostly destroyed by a Rome fire in 1893, which makes the Parker Collection all the more valuable now. The individual photographs in it are not unique, but it is probably the most complete set there is. Parker had six Italian photographers as helpers, as well as Charles Smeaton, whose exploits with magnesium light were mentioned above. Figure 230 is an example of a photograph from the Parker Collection, a fragment of a statue found in the Terme di Caracalla in 1868.[36]

Then, of course, there were the makers of photographic souvenirs. Figure 231 shows an album cover by Michele Danesi, dated 1871, in which views of Rome are reproduced by photo-lithography. Fox Talbot was the first to suggest this method. We do not know exactly how Danesi did it, but whatever his procedure may have been, he got there, as he wrote, "dopo lunghi studi ed esperimenti" The front cover is once again a photograph of the Piazza del Popolo, but not the MacPherson photograph of fig. 202, though a very similar one.[37]

Prints could be bought from any one of Rome's many bookstores, either in large formats suitable for framing or in the form of *cartes-de-visite*, suitable for albums or else for sending home in a letter. With the development of card photography, collecting became a possibility even for interested people who were not rich. Such cards were often chosen and carefully annotated on their backs as records of a once-in-a-lifetime European tour.

Most of the card photographers were anonymous, but here and there well-known names turn up, including Altobelli and Molins, to whom we owe a splendid view of Santa Maria Maggiore (fig. 232), much loved by photohistorians because it shows an elegant, top-hatted photographer with his heavy equipment, and a carriage to take him to his next assignment. We can see that this picture, like many others, was taken on a wash day.[38]

Another name that has to be mentioned is that of the Alinari brothers, photographers based in Florence, though they worked all over Italy.

There was, however, another way of buying such photographs. Books on Roman themes, fiction and non-fiction, were printed with many pages left blank, and onto those thin albumen prints could then be glued from a selection provided by the book stores, to suit the purchaser's own taste. Many such books have survived and no two are exactly alike. A good example is the Tauchnitz edition of *The Marble Faun* by Nathaniel Hawthorne, sometimes bound in leather, sometimes in simulated vellum, depending on the customer's purse. As a matter of fact, certain bookstores in Rome were known for their bookbinding services, as well as for the photographs they offered for sale. In the 1890 Baedeker, Olivieri is listed under both headings. One can easily guess how much these books were treasured after they had been "personalized" in this way.

MEETING PLACES

Illustrations of the kind here shown could be multiplied manyfold, and in this way we could gently walk around Rome, visiting major and minor sights, maybe with an enjoyable side-excursion down the Via Ostiense (fig. 233) to see the Pyramid of Caius Cestius,[39] or maybe down the Via Appia (fig. 234), which also attracted many early photographers.[40] We could return by moonlight (albeit with caution), and could do it all in air-conditioned comfort, without a single squirt of the insect spray that our nineteenth-century predecessors so sadly lacked.

If we were actually undertaking our walk around Rome in the nineteenth century, we might very well pause for a while at the Albergo dell'Orso, the Bear Tavern (fig. 235). A century earlier, it was reputed to be one of Rome's finest hostelries, but by the time this photograph was taken in 1868 it had come down in the world, and was mainly used by cabmen and postillions.[41] Today, a luxury restaurant once again occupies the site, eloquent testimony to the fact that benevolent forces are at work in shaping human destiny. In the mid-nineteenth century, one would not perhaps go there to eat, but to enjoy some local color and atmosphere.

If one wanted to eat or, even more important, to meet kindred photographic souls, then one might very well go the the Café Lepre, or else to the Café Greco, close to the Spanish Steps, which was, indeed, the principal meeting point of photographers (fig. 236). The Café Greco was, and is, immediately on the left of this picture, and a little behind the viewer.[42,43] There we would almost certainly meet Monsieur Flachéron at some time of the day, and many others of those who took the pictures here shown. We have this on excellect authority, from a letter to *The Art Journal*, sent in by Mr. Richard W. Thomas, chemist, of 10, Pall Mall, London. He was himself a photographer and, judging by his letter, a charming man:

Sir,

It occurs to me that some few facts respecting the state of Photography in Rome may not be without interest to those of your readers who take a delight in this beautiful branch of Art, and as many of my photographic acquaintances have frequently expressed a wish that I would publish the method I adopted for making negatives during a four month's residence in the Eternal City, I have thought it best to forward a letter on the subject for insertion in your journal, should you deem the communication of sufficient importance.[44]

This was printed long before the days when ruthless editors began to insist on short crisp sentences. Thomas then recommends the two cafés, and suggests that people go to the Greco, especially, to single out a bearded habitué, namely a Mr. Robinson, who appears to have been the doyen of the photographic community. Meeting him would undoubtedly lead to other introductions, and thus to an entry into the clique, as Mr. Robinson called it, founded by M. Flachéron in 1850. We know what the Café Greco looked like (fig. 237), but though Mr. Robinson may have had the finest connections, he himself remains a totally enigmatic figure; not a single crumb of information about him has come to light - so far.

Thomas then proceeds to describe his method (he took calotypes like Fox Talbot), and we can only marvel at his dedication, and at the sheer effort that went into the making of all the serene, timeless pictures we have been looking at. Through Thomas' eyes, the whole scene becomes alive, and we cease to be mere beneficiaries of those exertions; in a most pleasing sense, we become bystanders, albeit more than a century removed. But then, what is a mere century in the life of the Eternal City?

Heinz K. Henisch
The Pennsylvania State University

Notes

*   I should like to express my indebtedness to Professor H. Hager and Professor George Mauner for their unstinting support, over many years, in the development of photo-historical studies at The Pennsylvania State University, and for the generous way in which they and, indeed, all my colleagues, have welcomed this discipline into the Art History Program. Thanks are also due to Bonny Farmer, Inge Miller and Bridget Henisch for their invaluable help in the preparation of this paper.

1.   Benjamin Spear, *History of Photography*, Vol. 3, issue 1, Jan., 1979, frontispiece.

2.   E. Stenger, *Die Photographie in Kultur und Technik*, Seeman, Leipzig (1938).

3.   Piero Becchetti, *Fotografi e fotografia in Italia*, Edizione Quasar, Rome (1978).

4.   Piero Becchetti and Carlo Pietrangeli, *Roma in dagherrotipia*, Edizione Quasar, Rome (1979).

5.   *Ibid.*

6.   Judith Keller and Kenneth A. Breisch, *A Victorian View of Ancient Rome*, Kelsey Museum of Archaeology, University of Michigan, Ann Arbor, Michigan (1980).

7.   Dyveke Helsted, *Rome in Early Photographs; the Age of Pius IX*, The Thorvaldsen Museum, Copenhagen (1977).

8.   Richard D. Altick, *The Shows of London*, The Belknap Press of Harvard University Press, Cambridge, Massachusetts (1978).

9.   *Ibid.*

10. A. Hyatt Mayor, *Prints and People*, The Metropolitan Museum of Art, New York (1971).

11. Clovis Whitfield and J. G. Liuks, *Views from the Grand Tour*, Colnaghi, New York (1983).

12. A. Hyatt Mayor, *loc. cit.*

13. *Ibid.*

14. George Stillman Hillard, *Six Months in Italy* (2 vols.), Tickno, Reed and Fields, Boston, Massachusetts (1953).

15. Piero Becchetti and Carlo Pietrangeli, *loc. cit.*

16. Dyveke Helsted, *loc. cit.*

17. *Ibid.*

18. Judith Keller and Kenneth A. Breisch, *loc. cit.*

19. Piero Becchetti and Carlo Pietrangeli, *loc. cit.*

20. Robert Hershkowitz, *The British Photographer Abroad; the First Thirty Years*, Robert Hershkowitz Ltd., London (1980).

21. Thanks are due to Dr. D. B. Thomas and Mrs. John Ward of the Science Museum, for their generous help in connection with this article.

22. Piero Becchetti and Carlo Pietrangeli, *loc. cit.*

23. Robert Hershkowitz, *loc. cit.*

24. D. B. Thomas, "Early English Daguerreotypes", London, no date, and *The Science Museum Photography Collection*, London (1969).

25. Dyveke Helsted, *loc. cit.*

26. *Ibid.*

27. *Ibid.*

28. Piero Becchetti, *loc. cit.*

29. Dyveke Helsted, *Loc. cit.*

30. *Ibid.*

31. *Ibid.*

32. Piero Becchetti and Carlo Pietrangeli, *loc. cit.*

33. Robert Hershkowitz, *loc. cit.*

34. *Ibid.*

35. Judith Keller and Kenneth A. Breisch, *loc. cit.*

36. *Ibid.*

37. Piero Becchetti, *loc. cit.*

38. *Ibid.*

39. Dyveke Helsted, *loc. cit.*

40. George Dimok, *Caroline Sturgis Tappan and the Grand Tour*, Lennox Library Association, Lennox, Massachusetts (1982).

41. Dyveke Helsted, *loc. cit.*

42. George Dimok, *loc. cit.*

43. Georg Poensgen, *C. Ph. Fohr und das Café Greco*, F. H. Kerle Verlag, Heidelberg (1957).

44. Richard W. Thomas, "Photography in Rome", *The Art Journal*, London (May 1852).

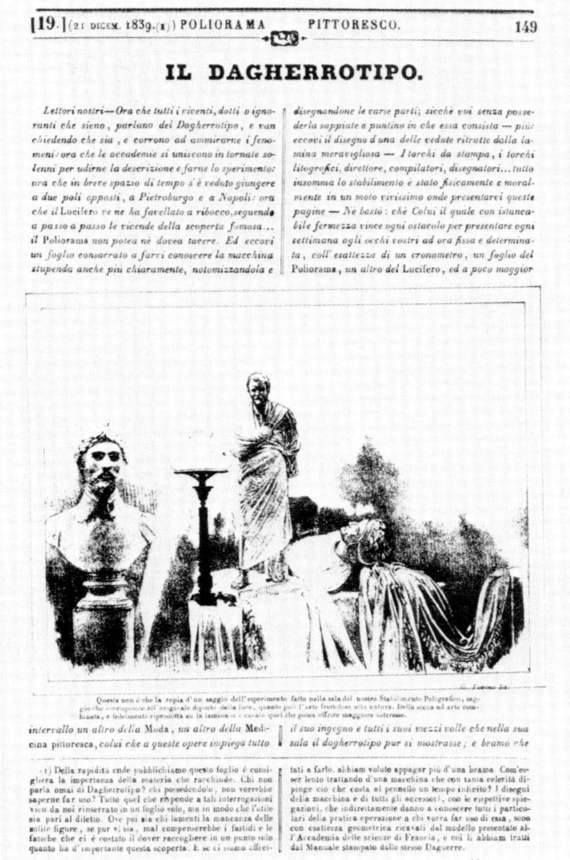

201.   Announcement of the daguerreotype in *Poliorama pittoresco*, December 1, 1839 (after P. Becchetti, *Fotografi e fotografia in Italia*).

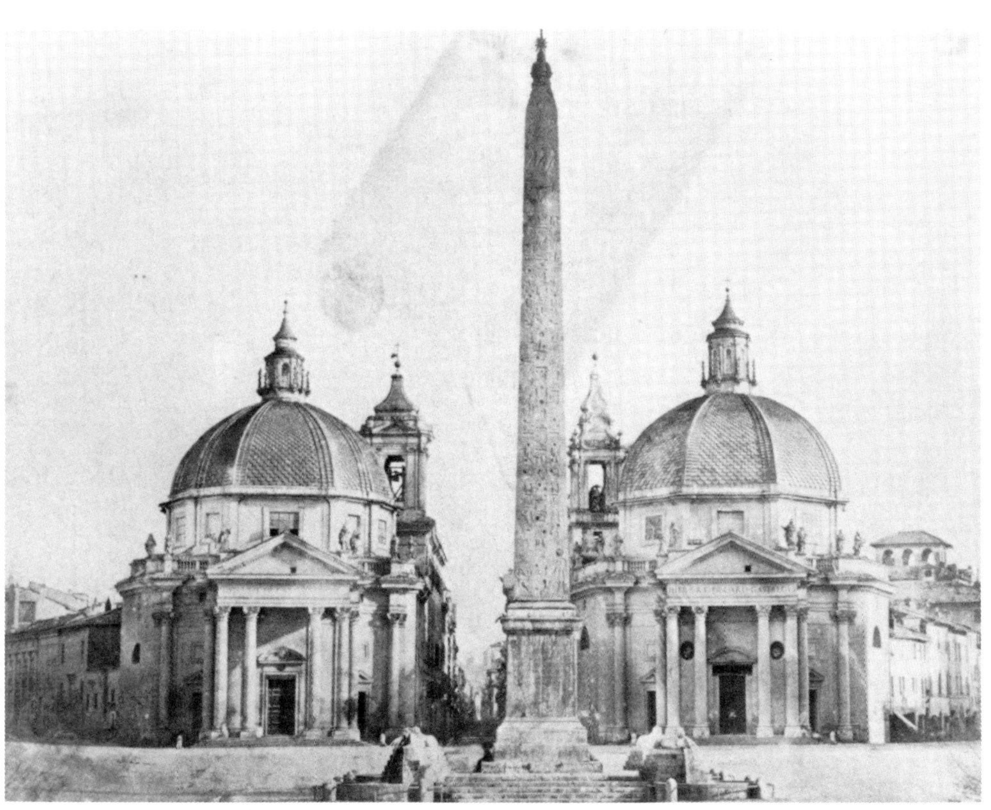

202.   Robert MacPherson, Piazza del Popolo, 1857. Becchetti Collection, Rome.

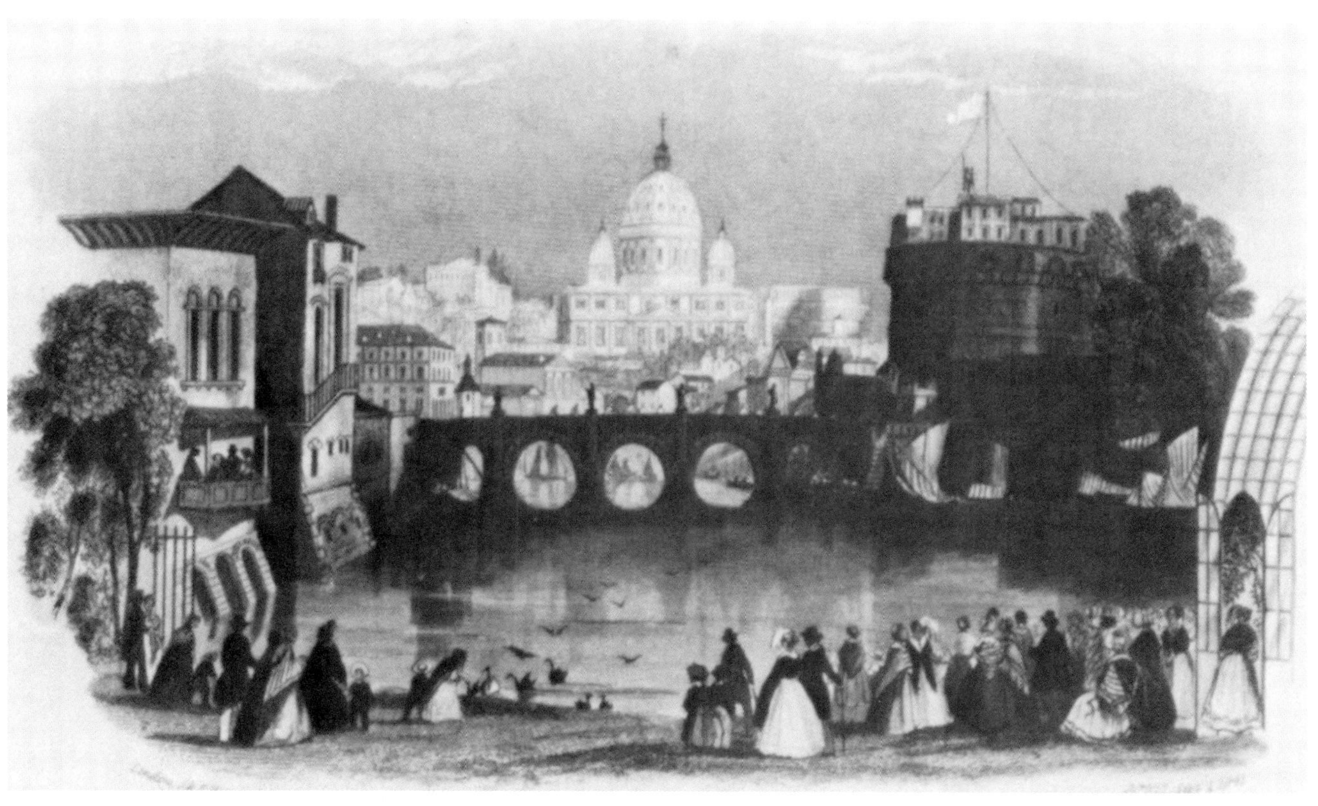

203.   The "Colossal Pictorial Typorama, or Modelled View of Rome". Surrey Gardens, London, 1837 (from R. D. Altick, *The Shows of London*).

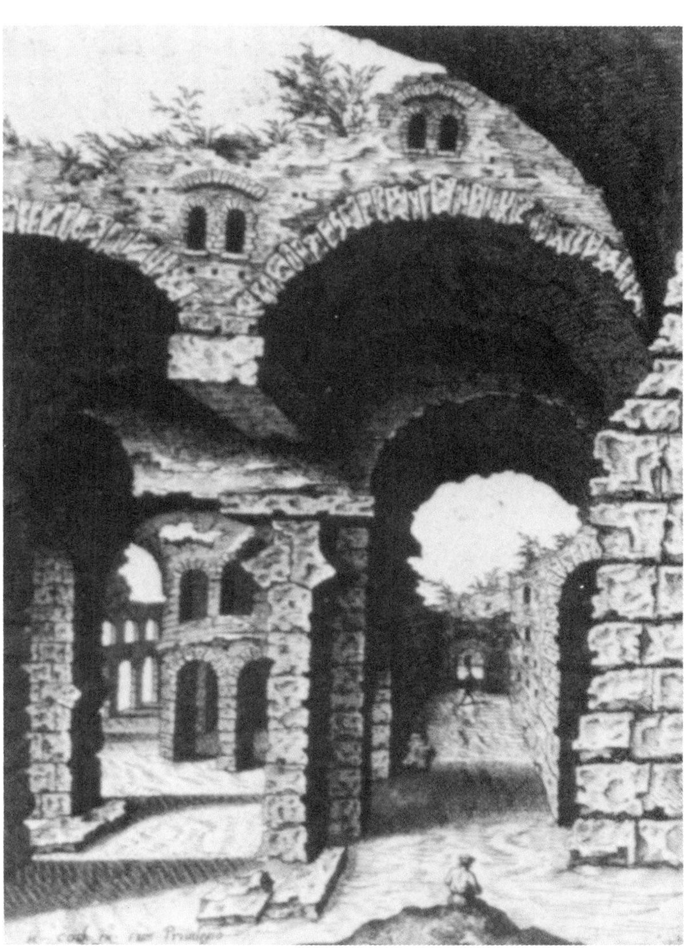

204.   Jerome Cook (1551), Antwerp, etching: *capriccio* (from A. Hyatt Mayor, *Prints and People*).

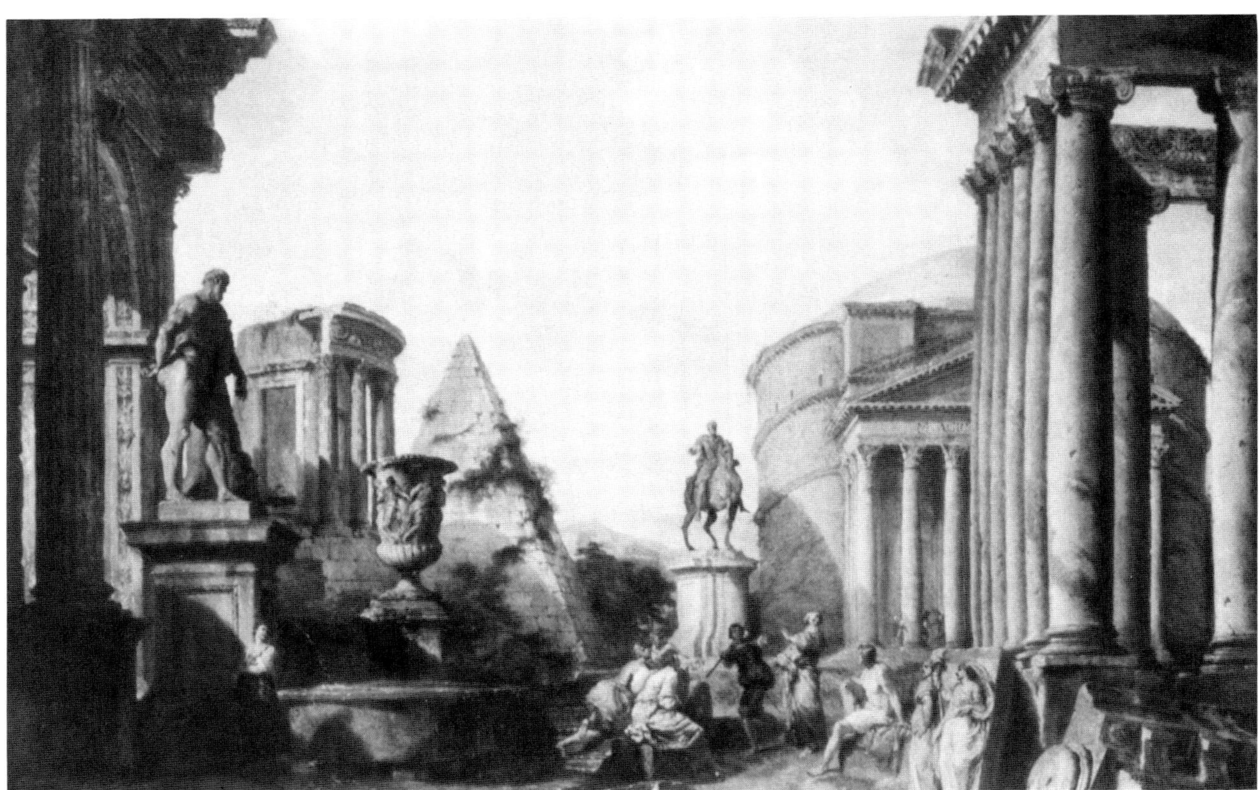

205.   G. P. Pannini (1712-1765), oil, *capriccio* with Pantheon, the famous Hercules, the statue of Marcus Aurelius, and the Pyramid of Caius Cestius background (from C. Whitfield and J. G. Liuks, *Views from the Grand Tour*).

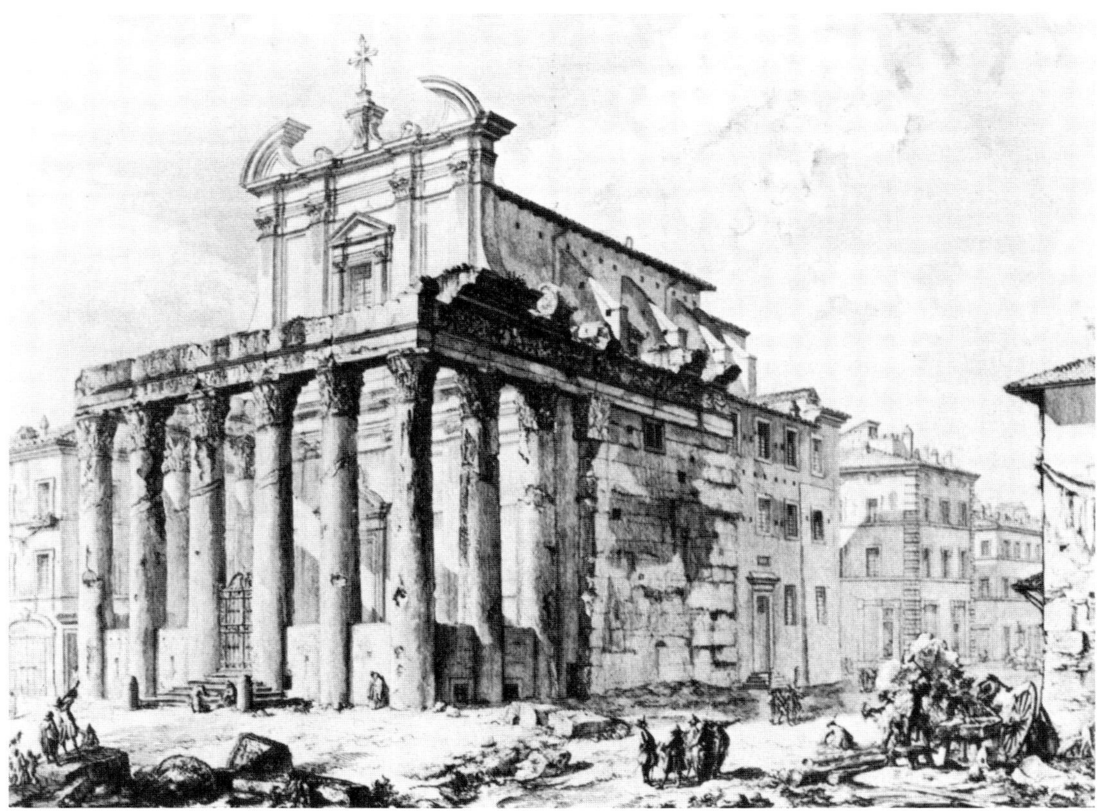

206.   G. B. Piranesi, etching (1758): Temple of Antoninus and Faustina (from A. Hyatt Mayor, *Prints and People*).

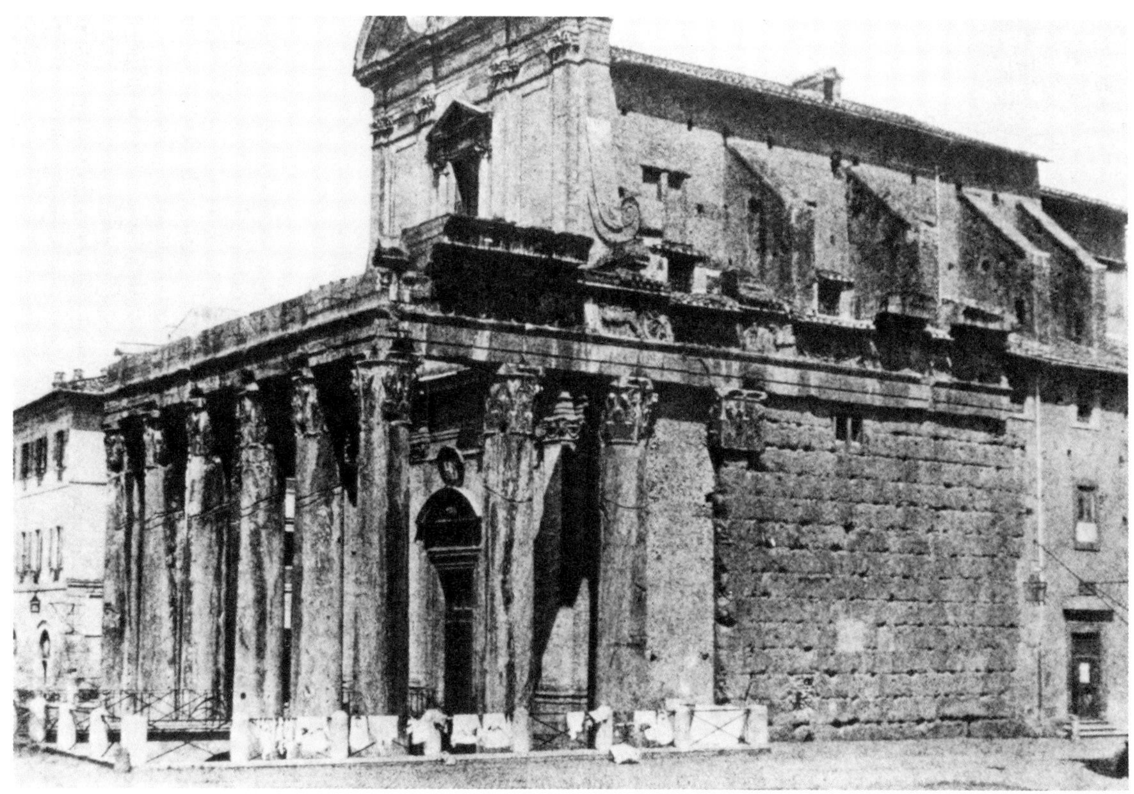

207. William Fox Talbot, calotype, 1840s; Temple of Antoninus and Faustina (from A. Hyatt Mayor, *Prints and People*).

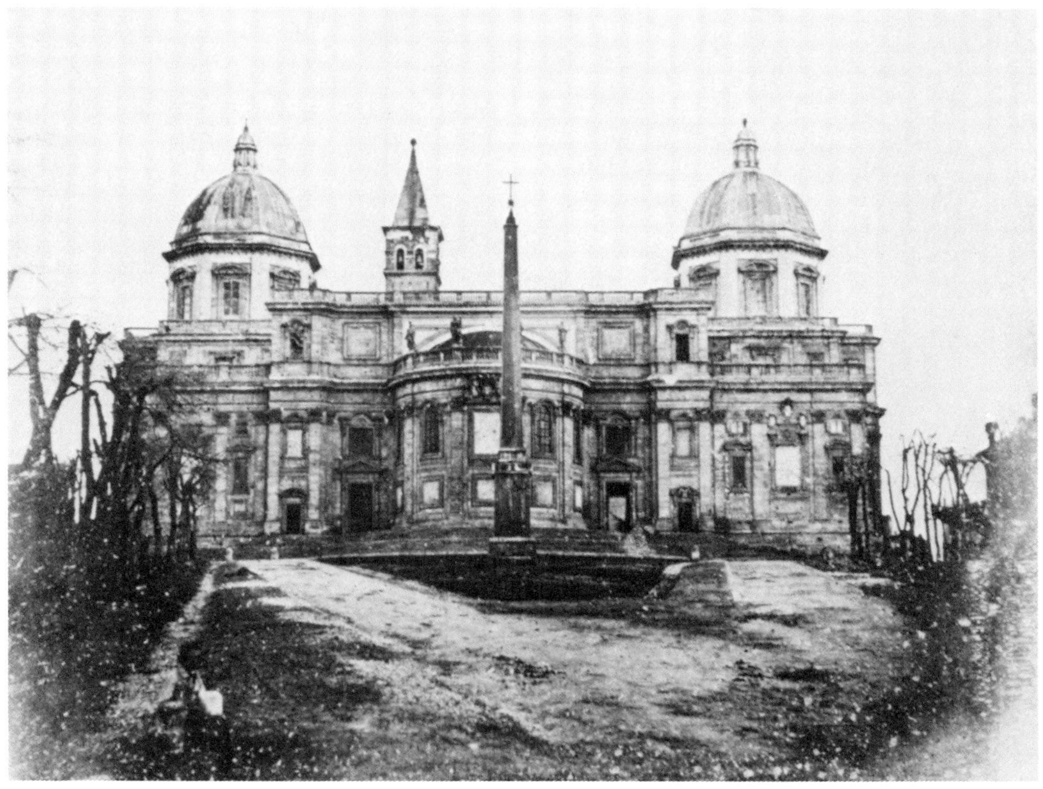

208. Achille Morelli, daguerreotype, 1841; Basilica of S. Maria Maggiore (from P. Becchetti and C. Pietrangeli, *Roma in dagherrotipia*).

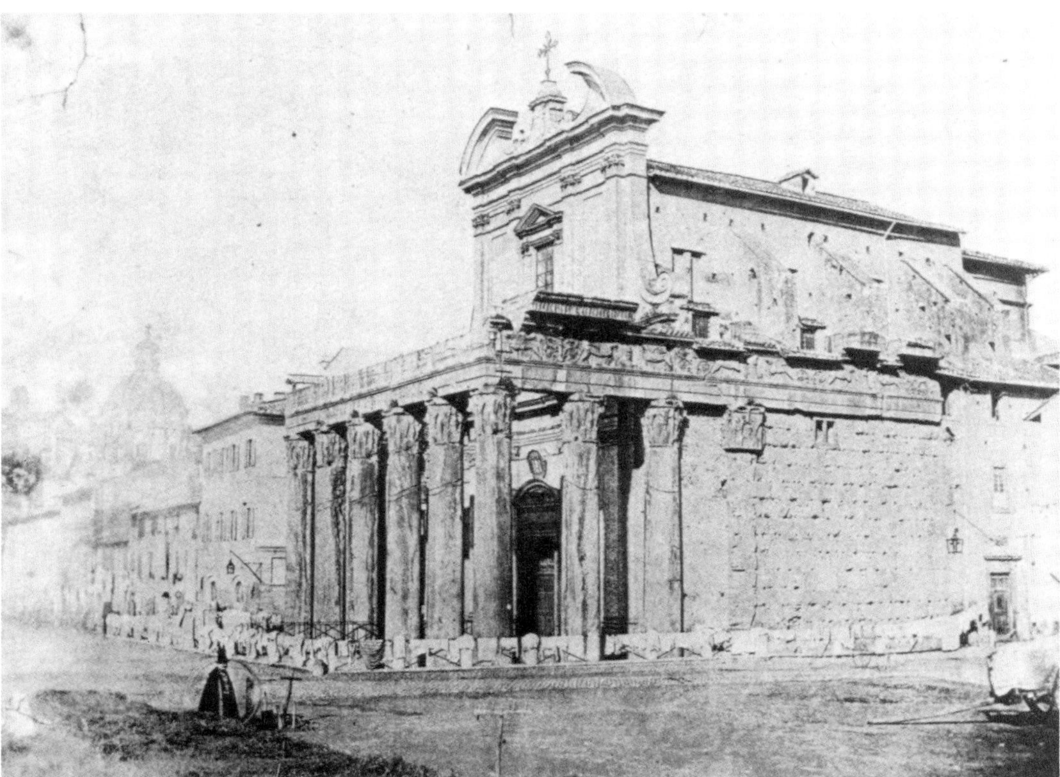

209.   Unknown photographer, calotype, 1850; Temple of Antoninus and Faustina (S. Lorenzo in Miranda; from D. Helsted, *Rome in Early Photographs*).

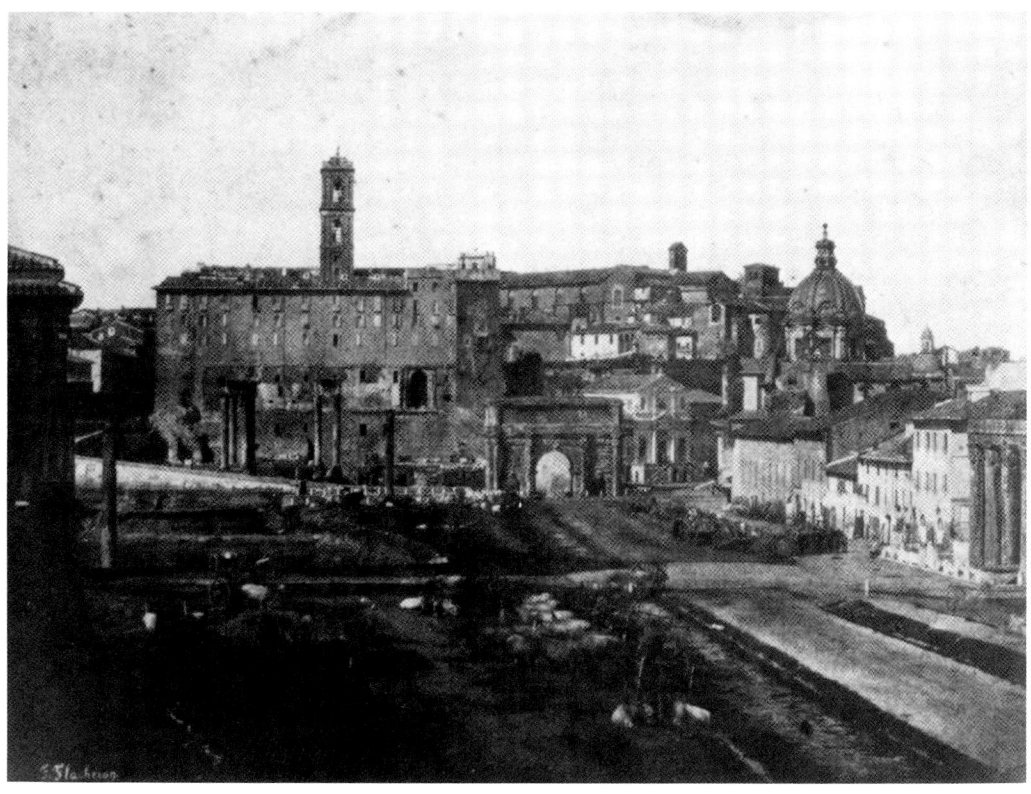

210.   Frederic Flachéron, calotype, 1850. The Roman Forum, looking towards the Capitol (from D. Helsted, *Rome in Early Photographs*).

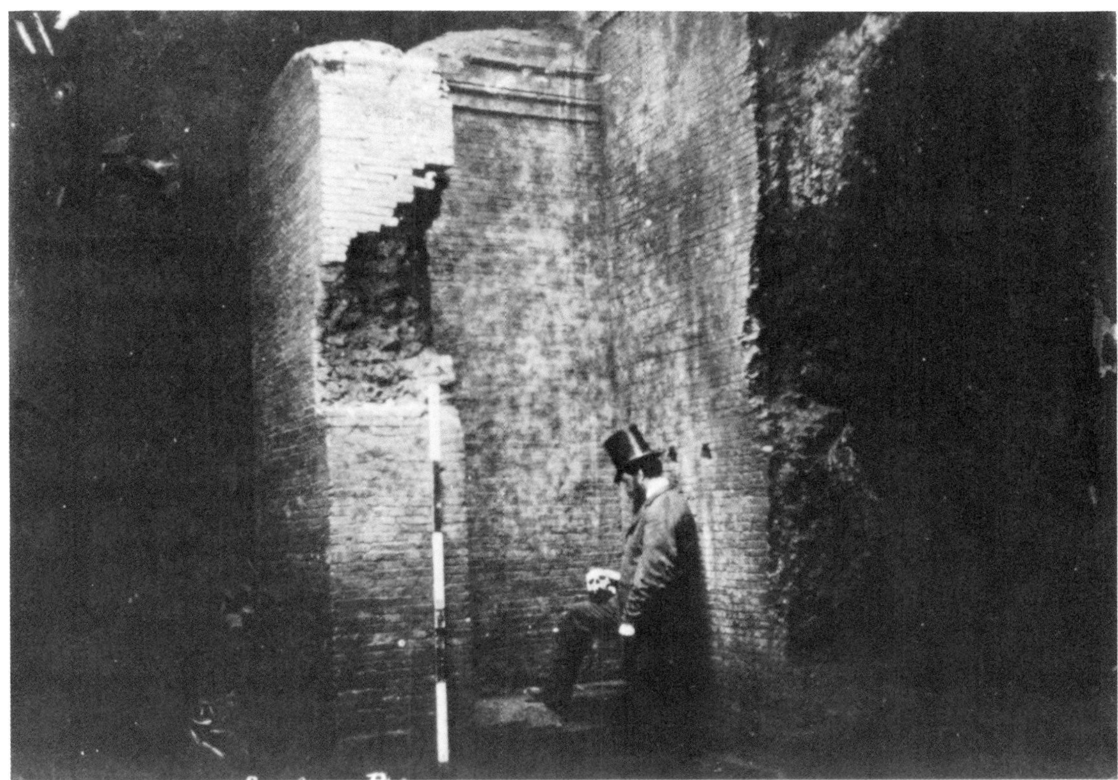

211.   Charles Smeaton, calotype, late 1860s. Catacomb of S. Domitilla, photographed by magnesium light. (Parker Collection; photograph from J. Keller and K. A. Breisch, *A Victorian View of Ancient Rome*).

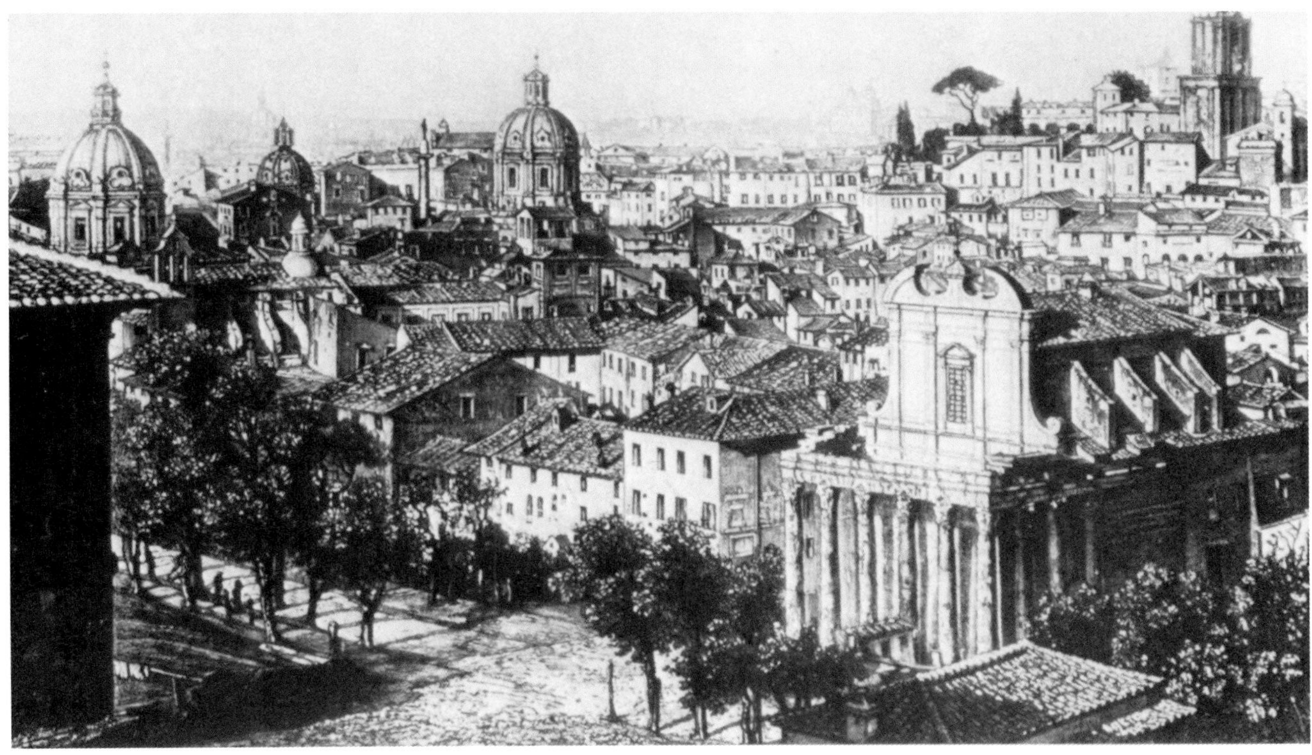

212.   A. Appert, engraving after a daguerreotype, 1840. View of Rome from the Palatine. (From *Excursions Daguerriennes*; photograph from P. Becchetti and C. Pietrangeli, *Roma in dagherrotipia*).

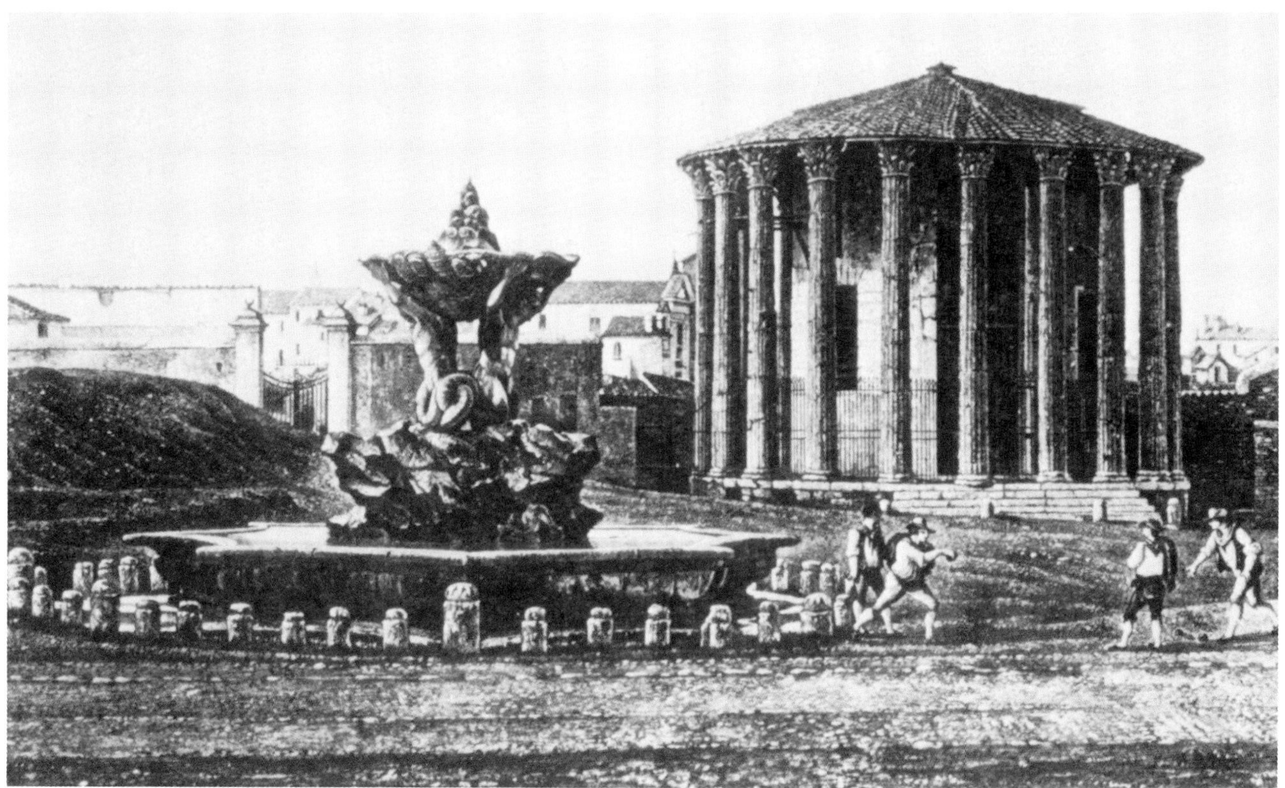

213.   Martens, engraving after a daugerreotype, 1840. Temple of Vesta. (From *Excursions Daguerriennes*; photograph from P. Becchetti and C. Pietrangeli, *Roma in dagherrotipia*).

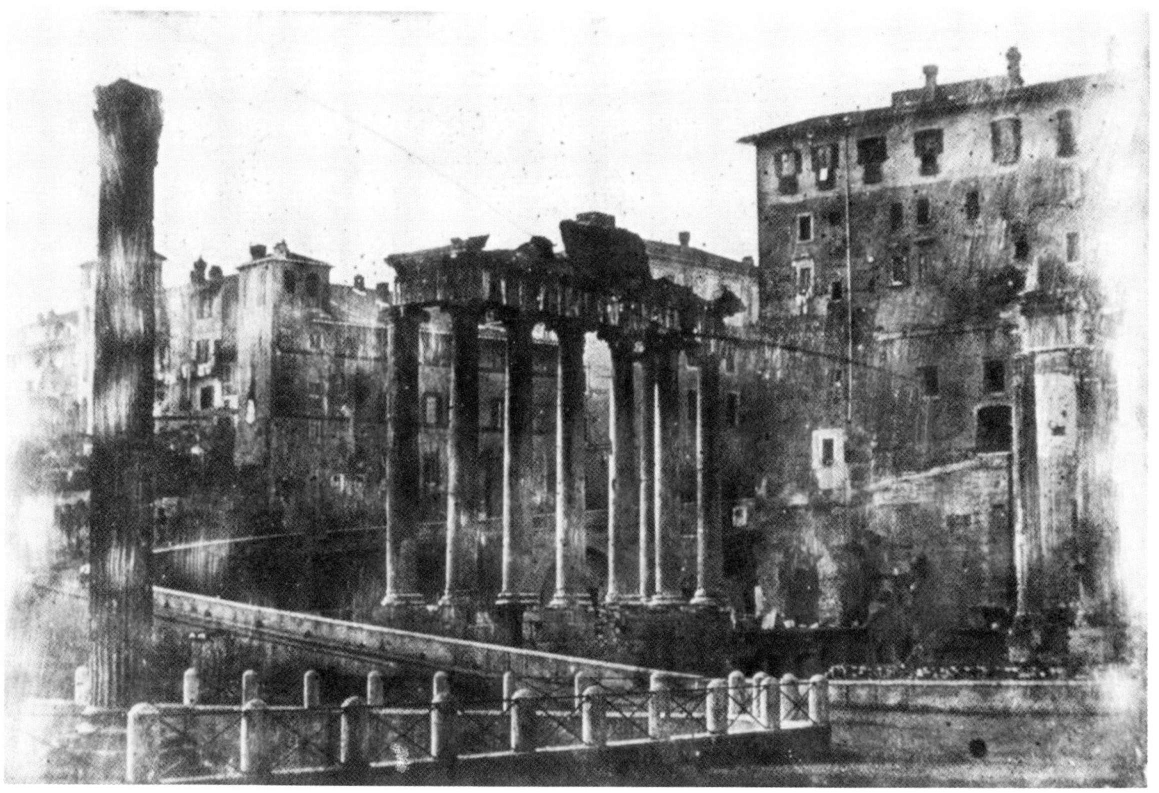

214.   Alexander John Ellis, daguerreotype, 1841. Temple of Saturn, photographed from the church of SS. Luca e Martina (from R. Hershkowitz, *The British Photographer Abroad; the First Thirty Years*).

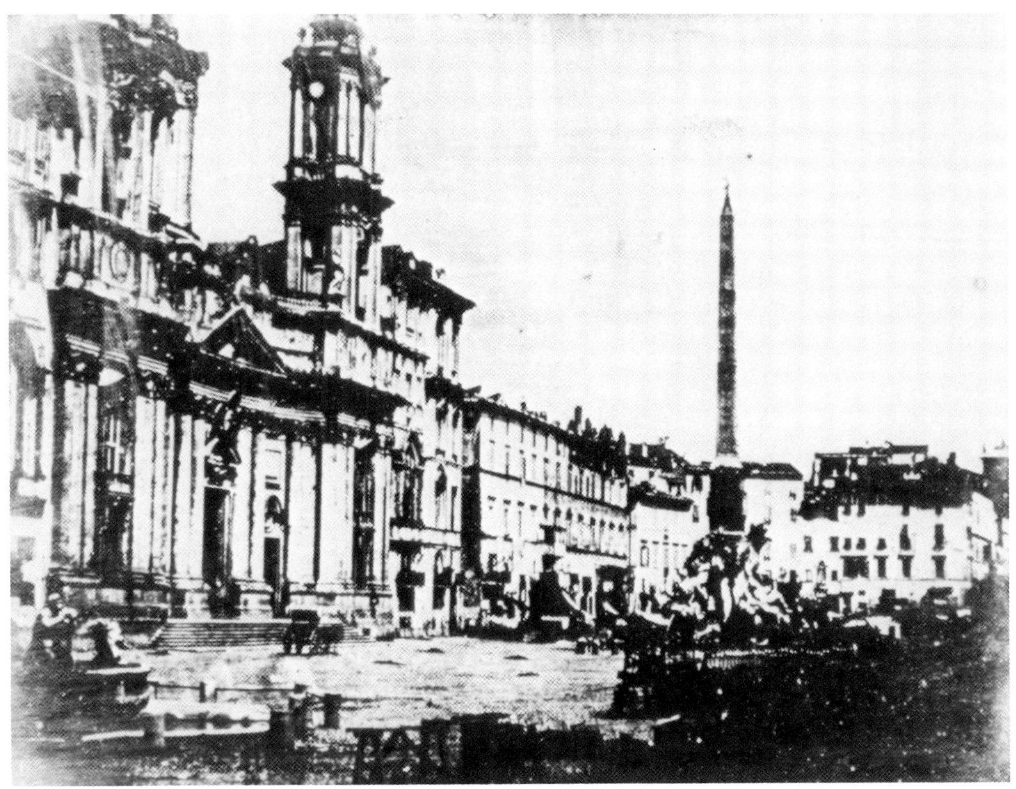

215.   Alexander John Ellis, daguerreotype, 1841. Piazza Navona (from P. Becchetti and C. Pietrangeli, *Roma in dagherrotipia*).

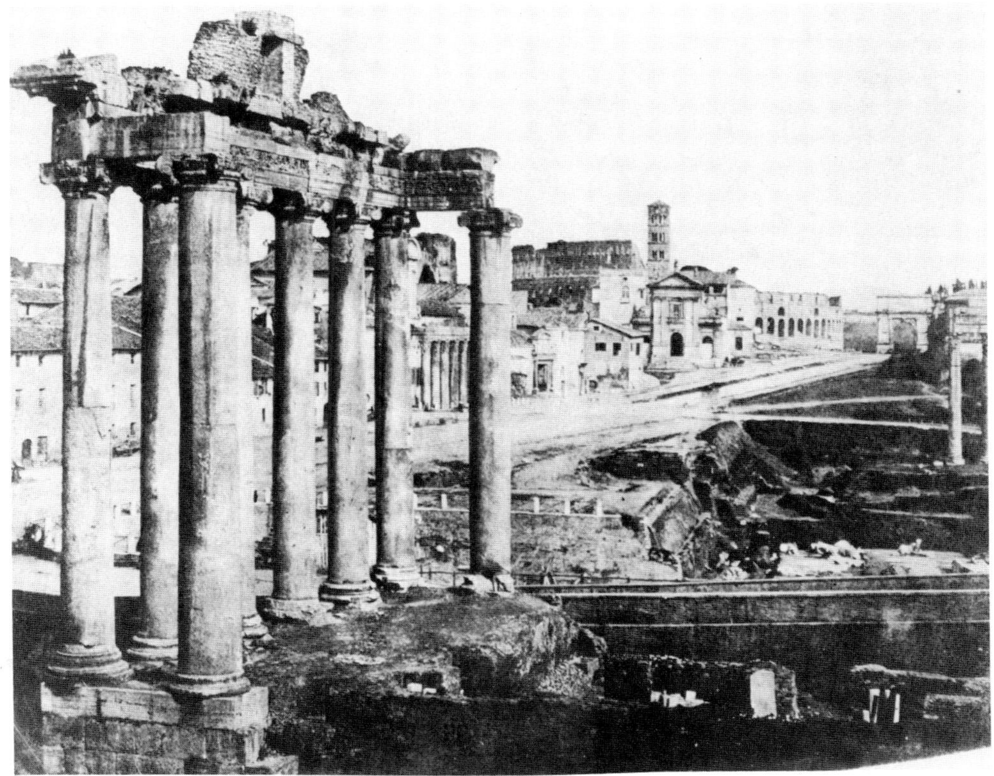

216.   Thomas Sutton, waxed salt print, 1853. The Roman Forum (from R. Hershkowitz, *The British Photographer Abroad*).

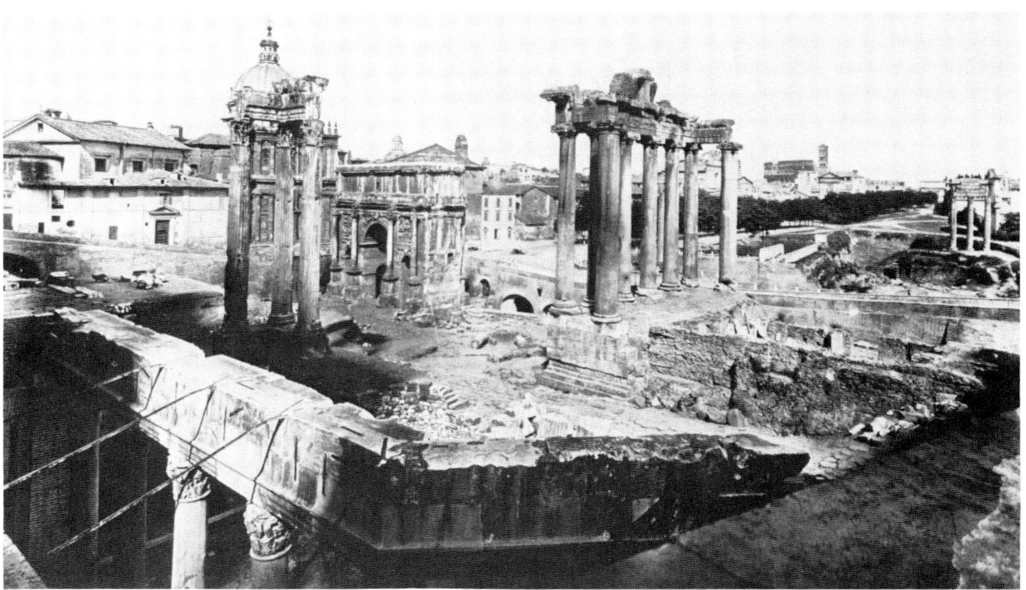

217.   Robert MacPherson, albumen print, 1863. The Roman Forum (from P. Becchetti and C. Peitrangeli, *Roma in dagherrotipia*).

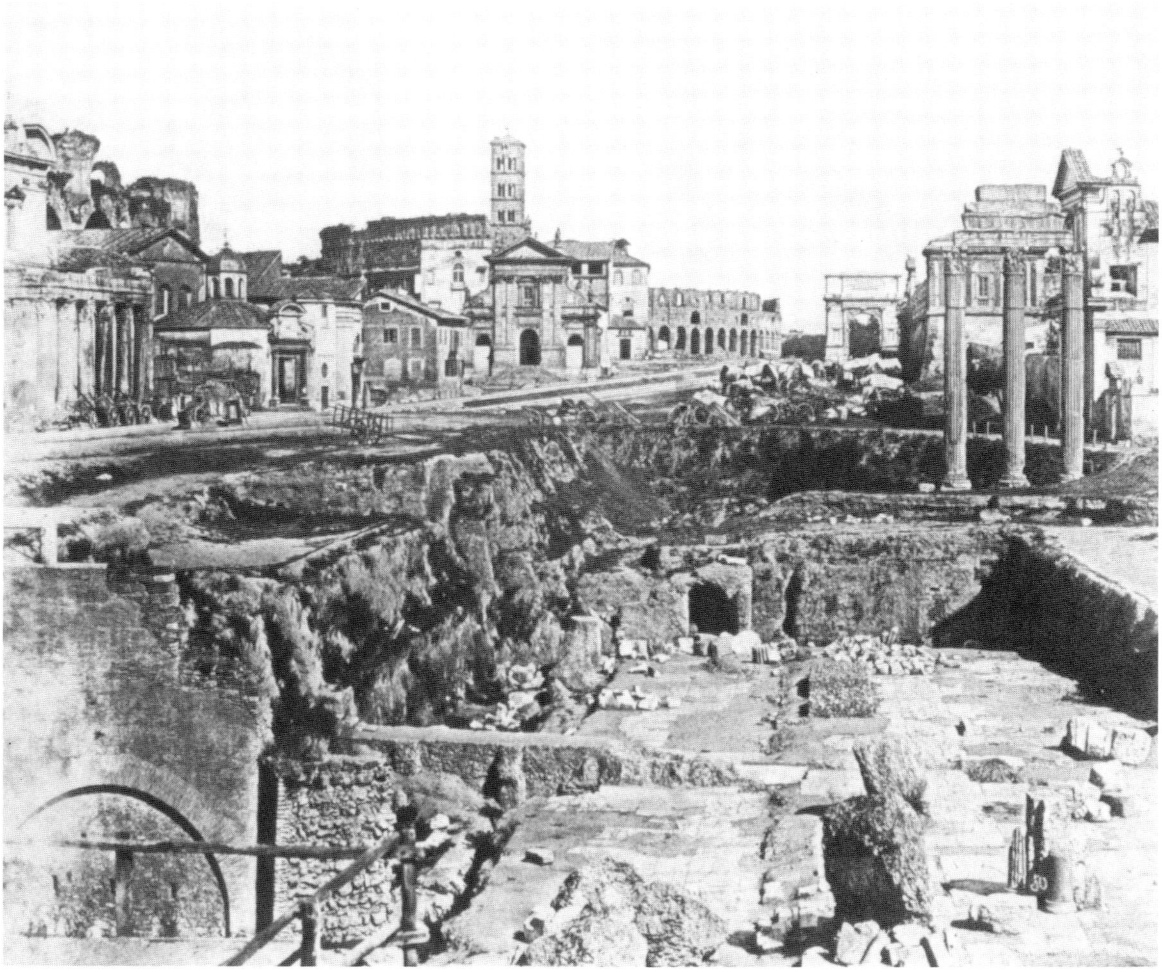

219.   Unknown photographer, albumen print, c. 1855. The Forum, south of the Via del Campidoglio (from D. Helsted, *Rome in Early Photographs*).

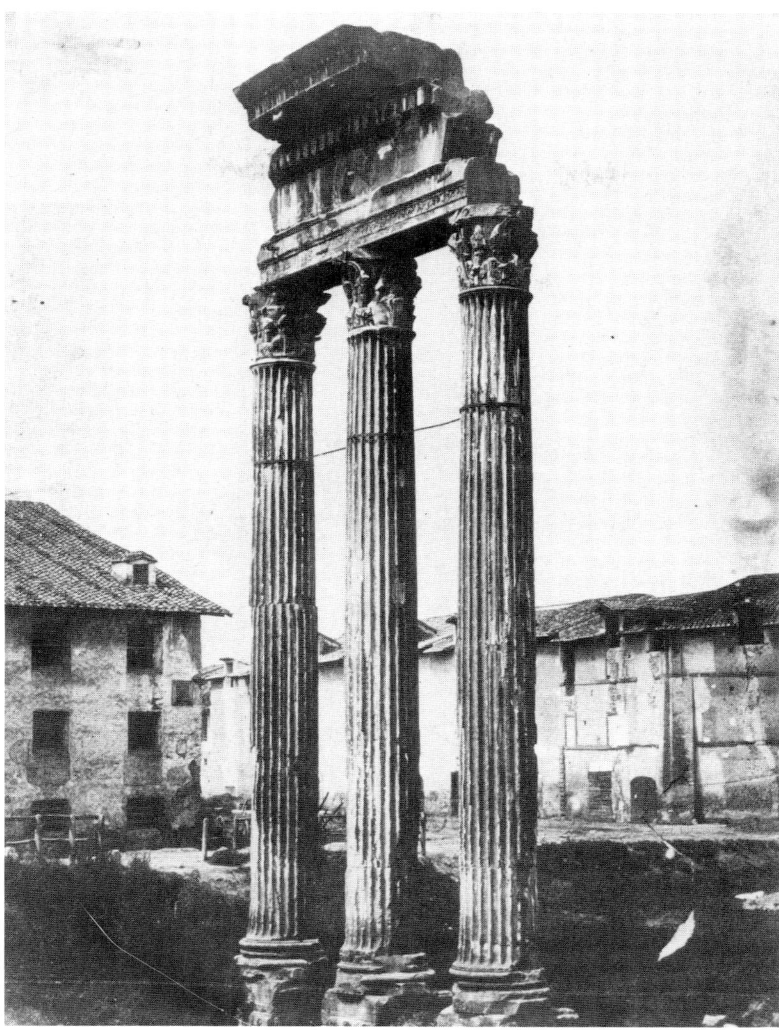

218.   Unknown photographer, albumen print, before 1860. Temple of Castor, seen from the east (from D. Helsted, *Rome in Early Photographs*).

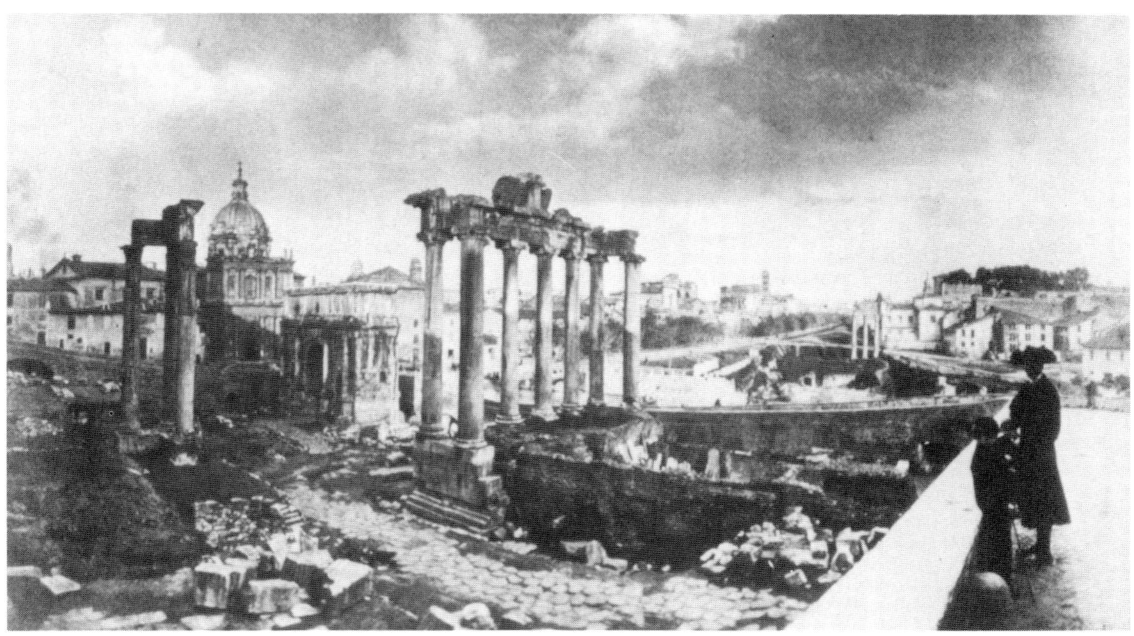

220.   Unknown photographer, albumen print, c. 1857. View over the Forum from the Via del Campidoglio (from D. Helsted, *Rome in Early Photographs*).

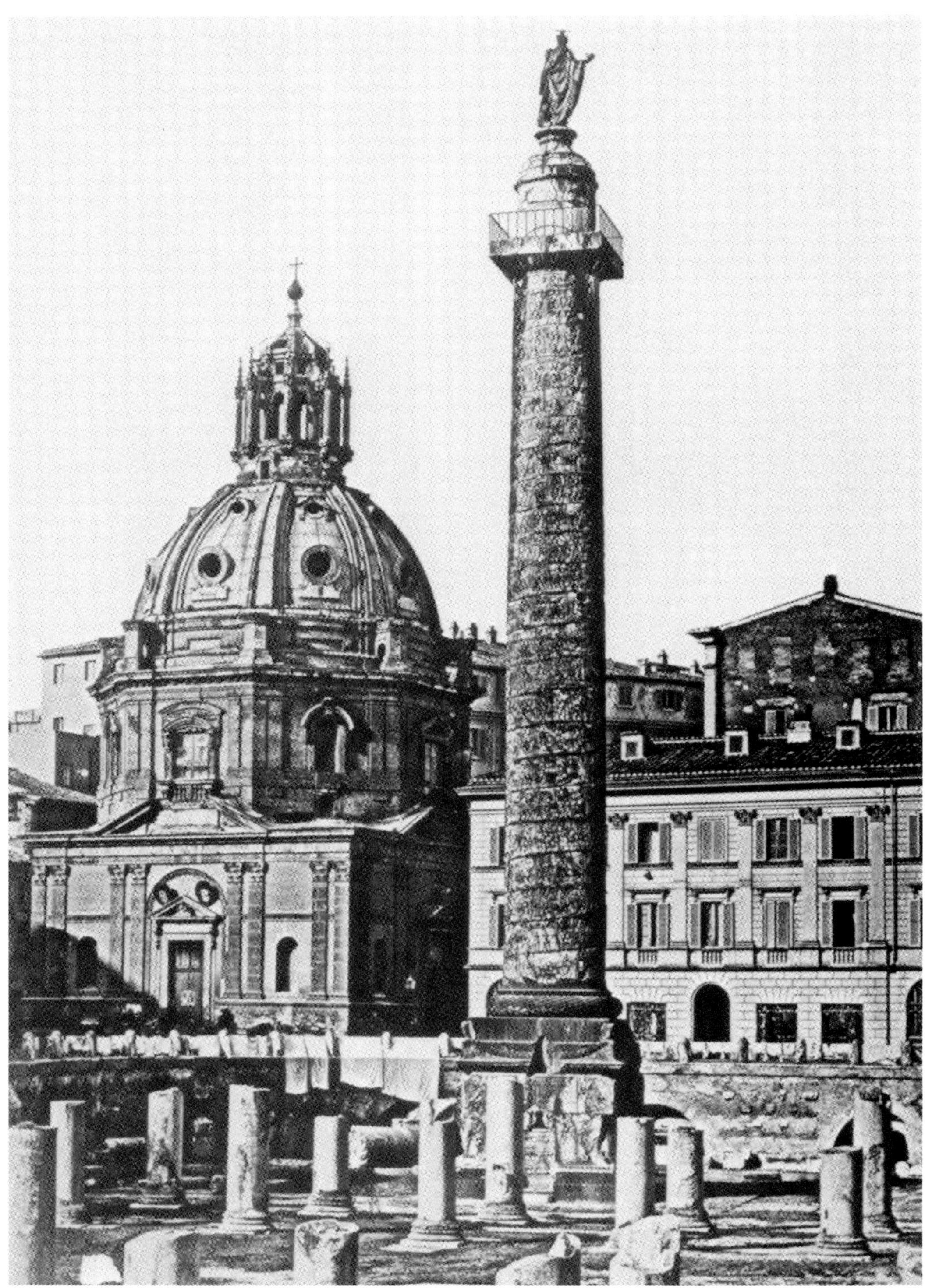

221.   A. and G. Luswergh, albumen print, 1854. The Forum of Trajan (from P. Becchetti, *Fotografi e fotografia in Italia*).

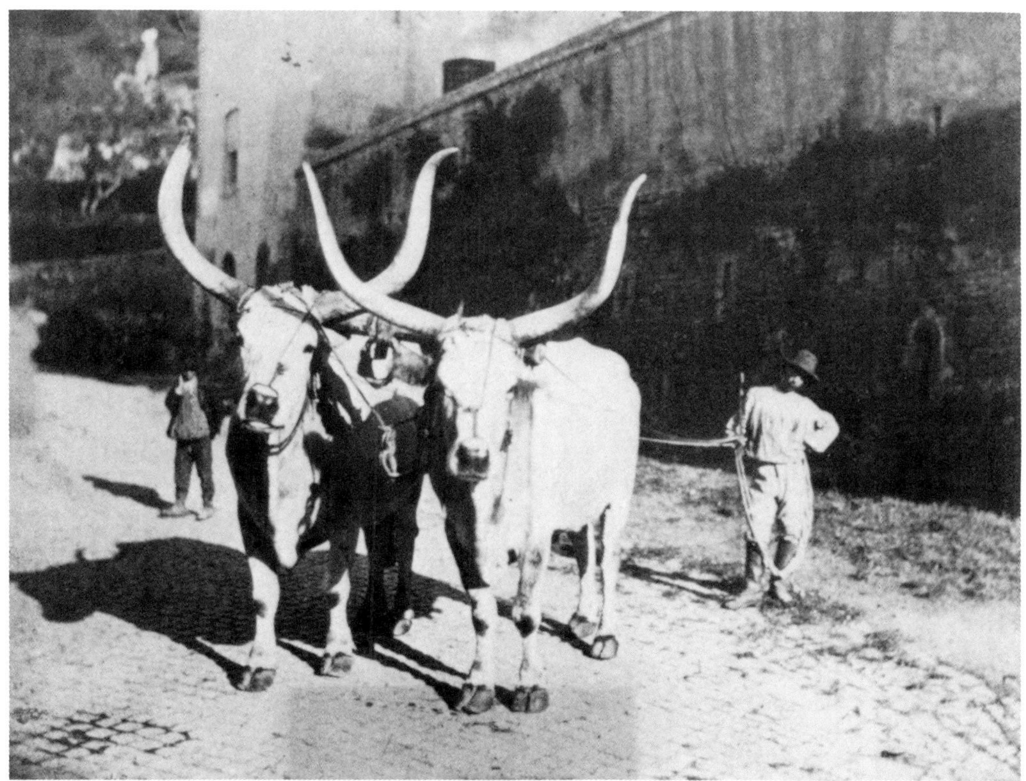

222. Unknown photographer, c. 1870. Traffic in Rome (from D. Helsted, *Rome in Early Photographs*).

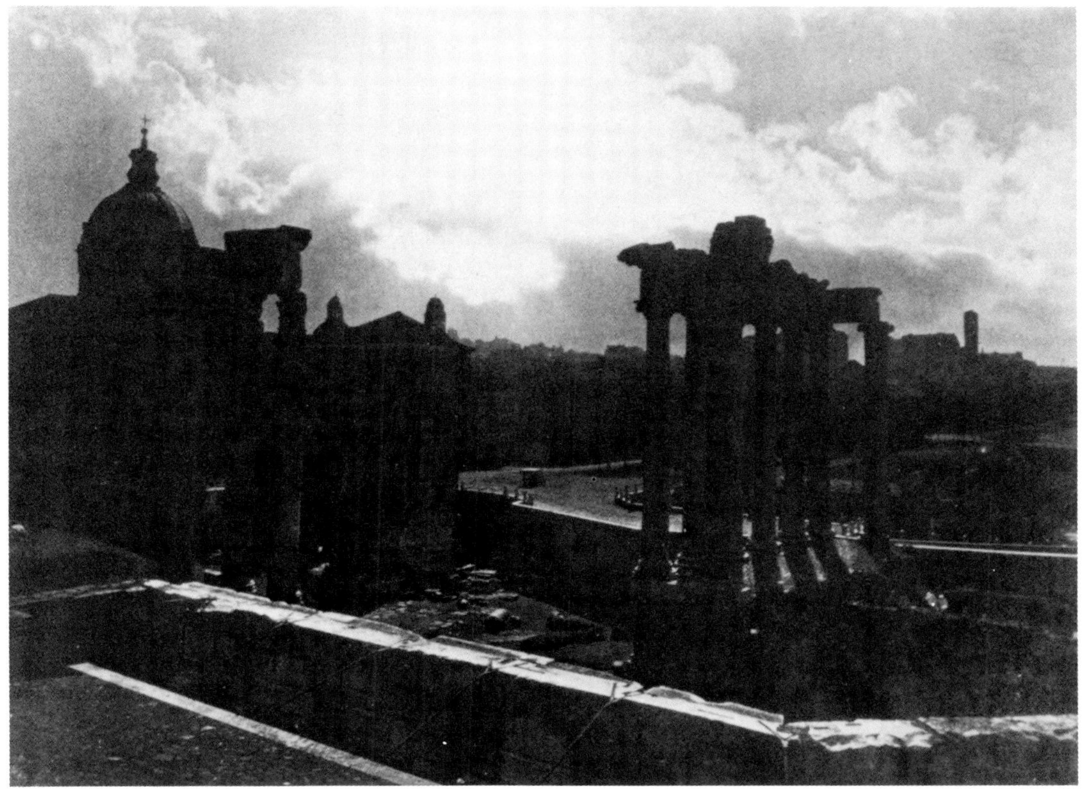

224. Altobelli, c. 1866. View of the Forum; simulated moonlight (from D. Helsted, *Rome in Early Photographs*).

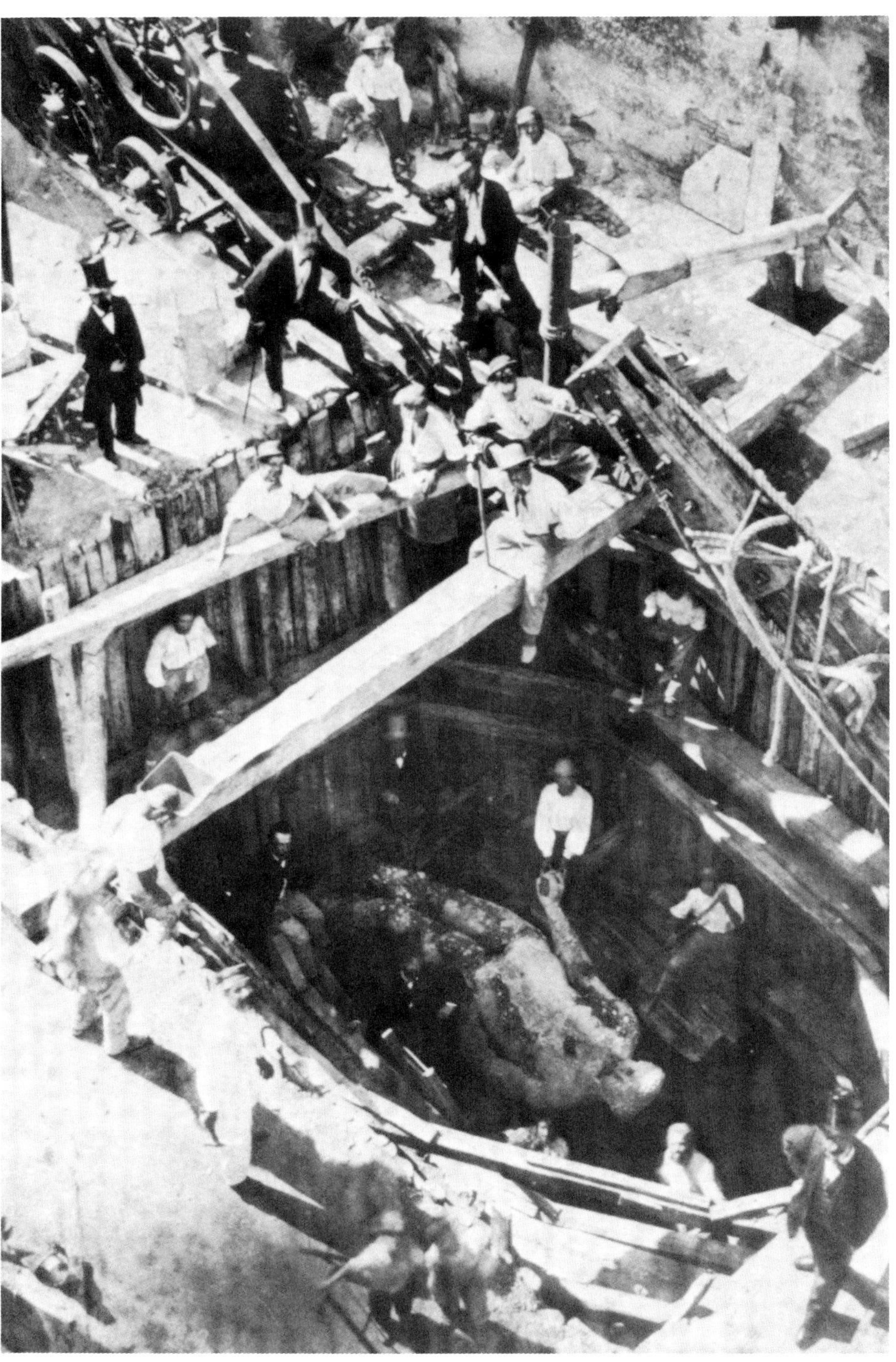

223.   Unknown photographer, 1864. The excavation of the Hercules Master (from D. Helsted, *Rome in Early Photographs*).

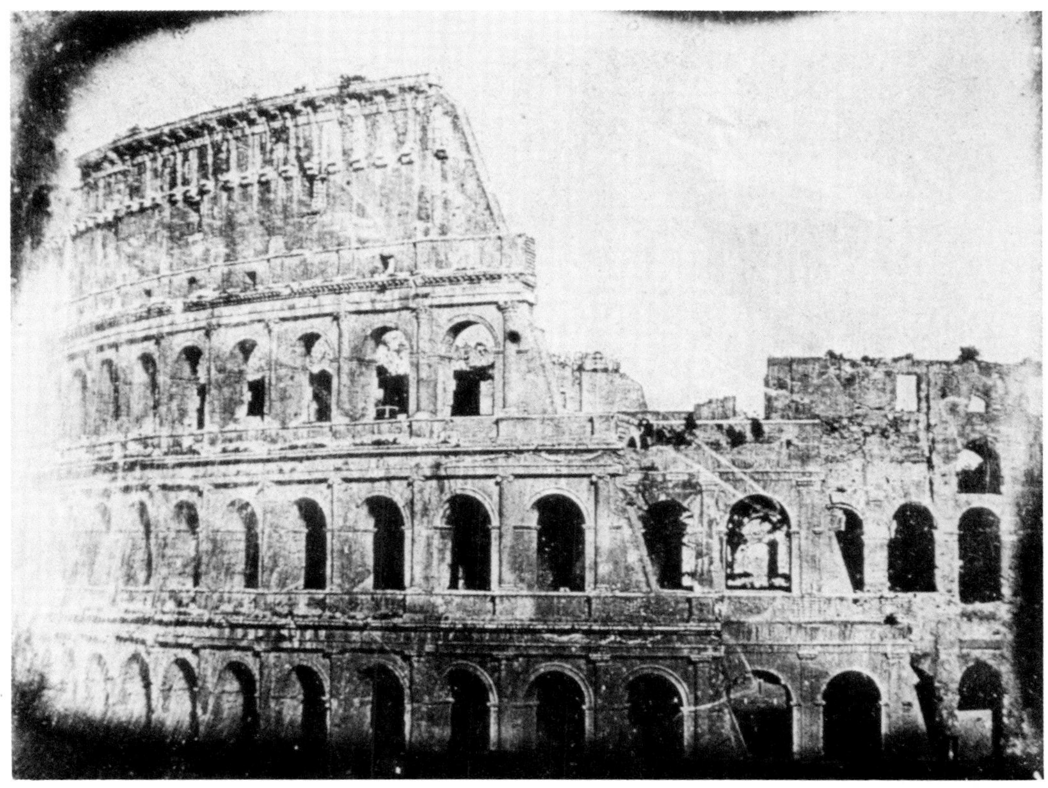

225.   Lorenzo Suscipij, daguerreotype, 1841. The Coliseum (from P. Becchetti and C. Pietrangeli, *Roma in dagherrotipia*).

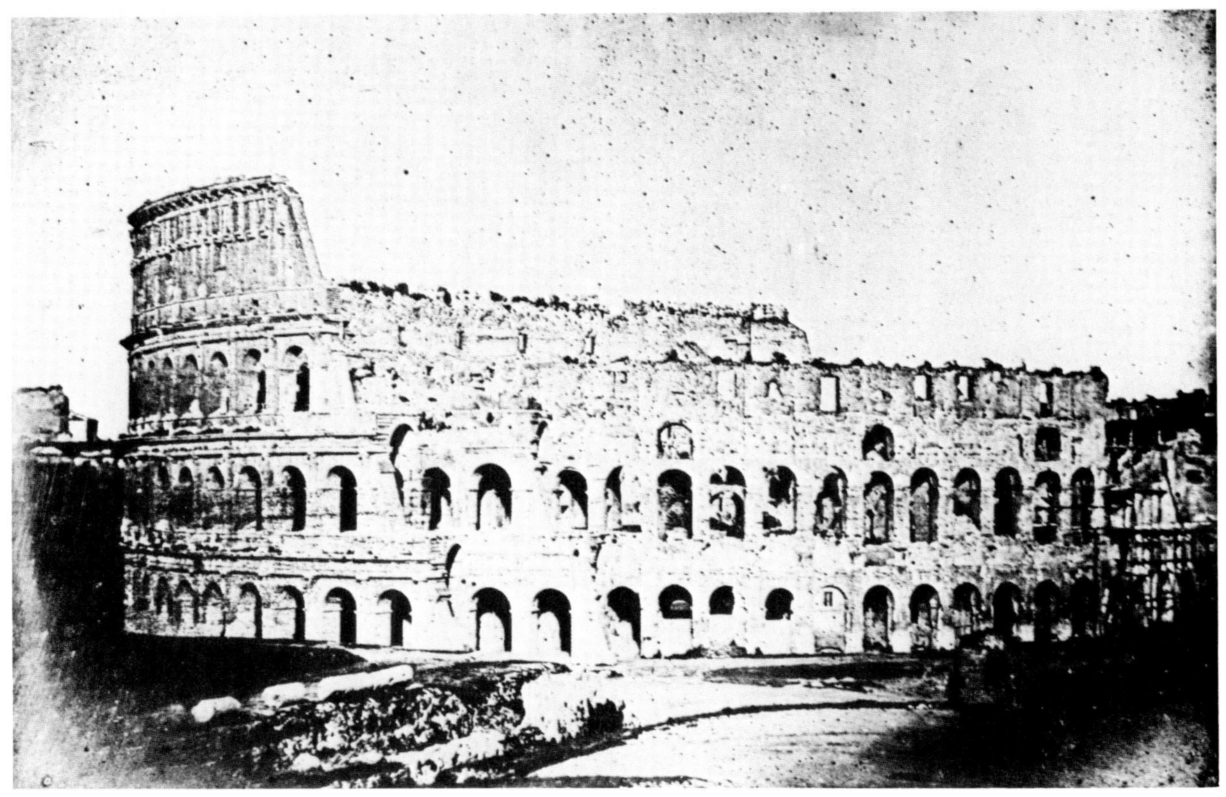

226.   Alexander John Ellis, daguerreotype, 1841. The Coliseum (from P. Becchetti and C. Pietrangeli, *Roma in dagherrotipia*).

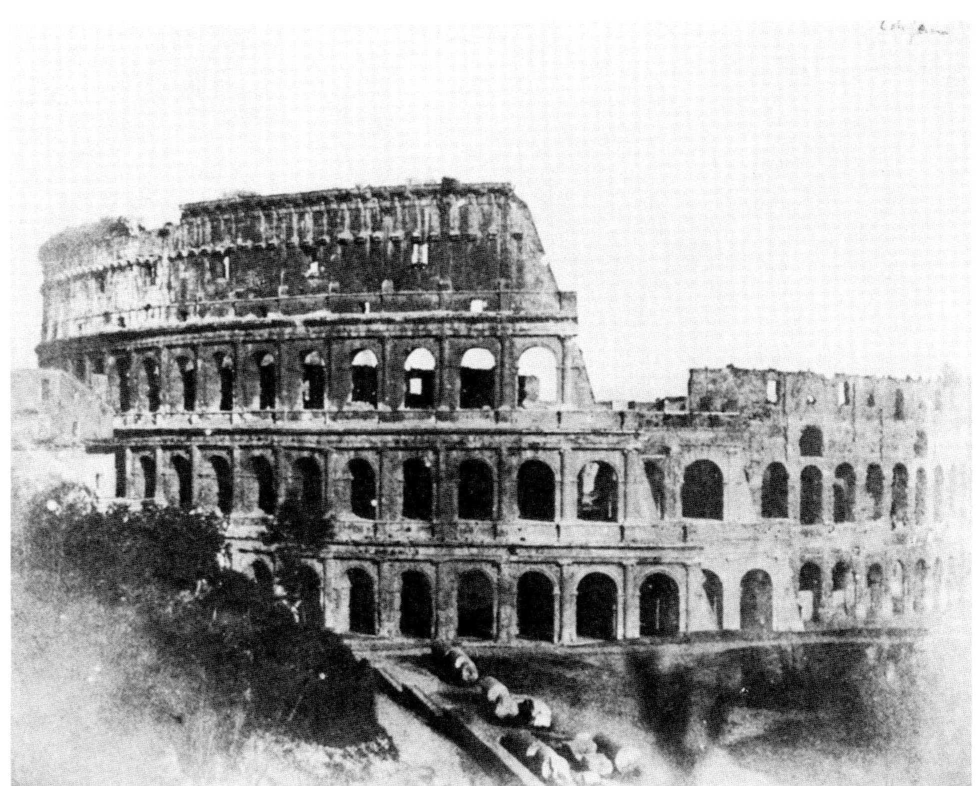

227.   Robert MacPherson, calotype, c. 1850. The Coliseum (from R. Hershkowitz, *The British Photographer Abroad*).

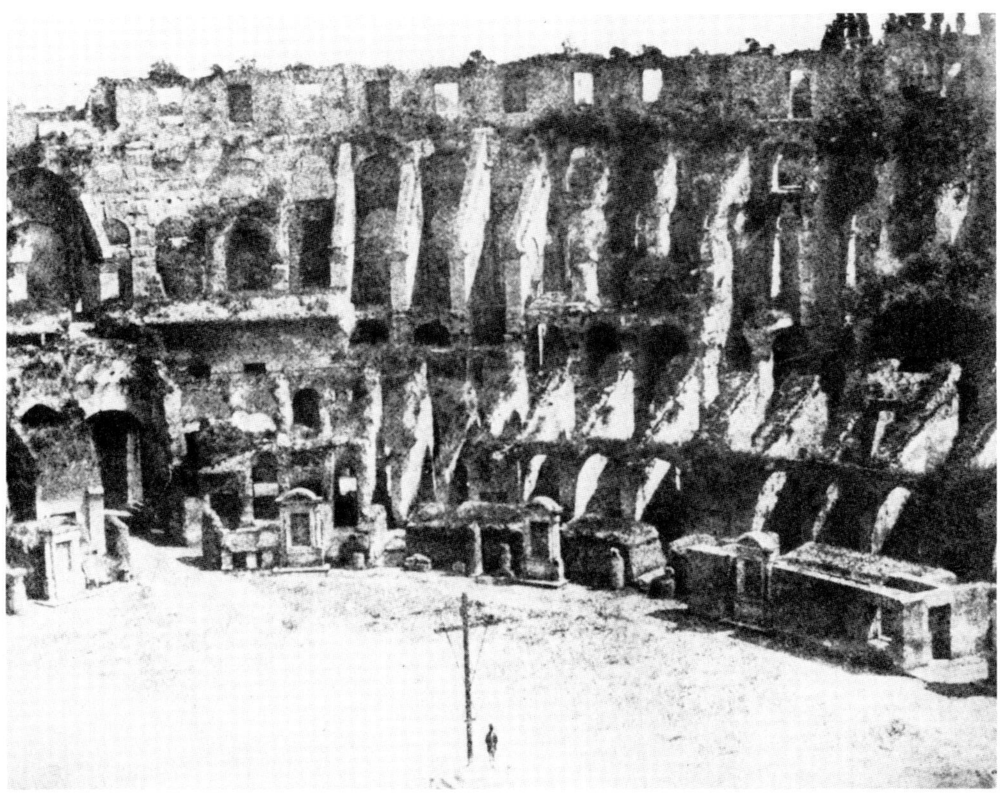

228.   James Francis Dunlop, calotype, c. 1850. Interior of the Coliseum (from R. Hershkowitz, *The British Photographer Abroad*).

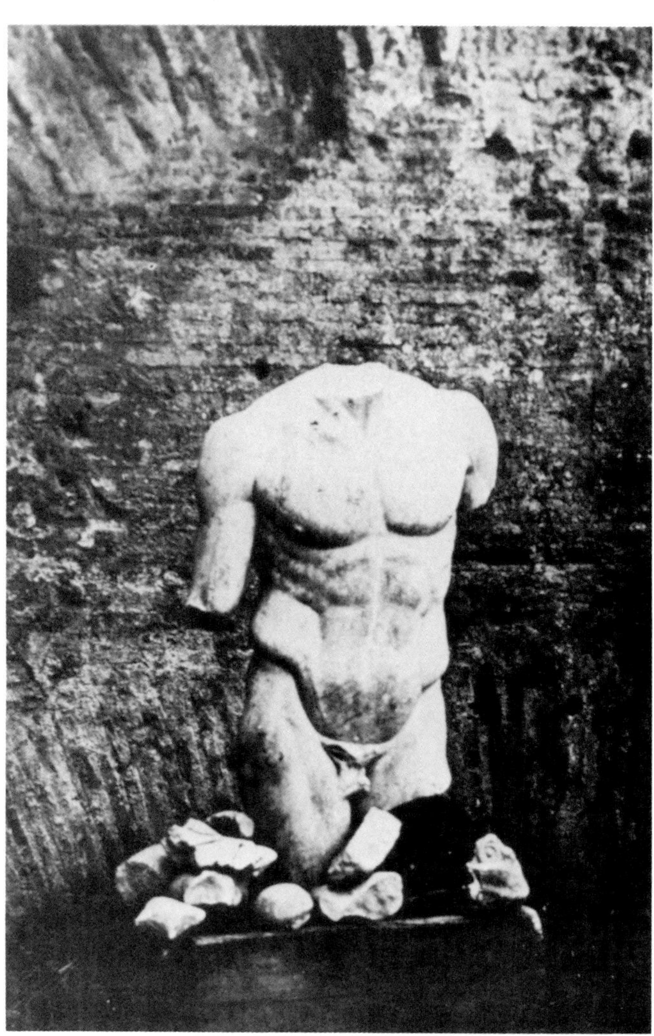

230. Unknown photographer, 1868. Fragment of a statue found in the Baths of Caracalla (from J. Keller and K. A. Breisch, *A Victorian View of Ancient Rome*).

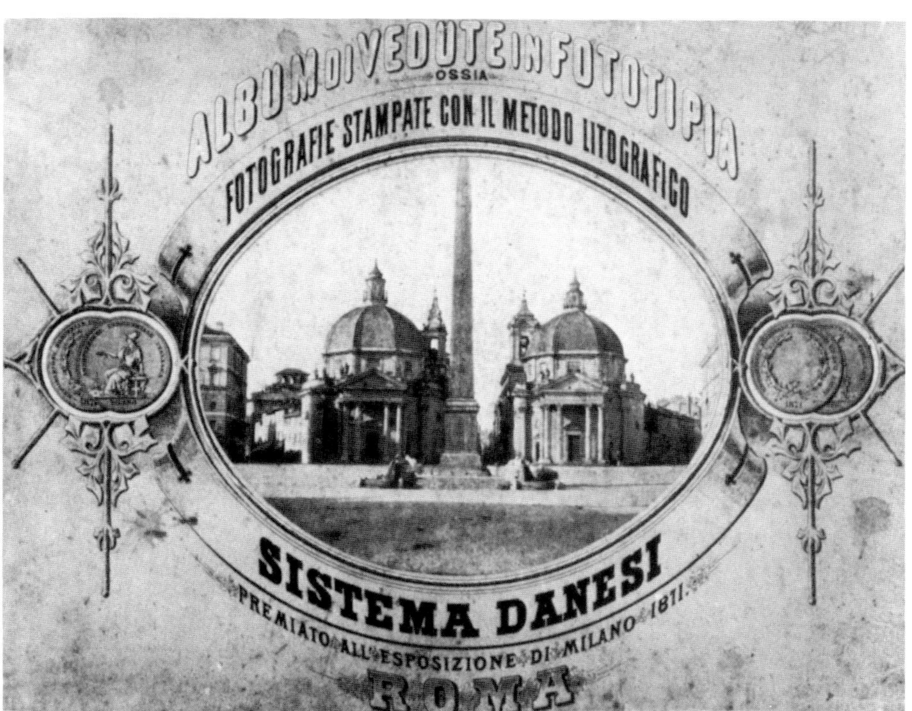

231. Michele Danesi, 1871. Album cover (from P. Becchetti, *Fotografi e fotografia in Italia*).

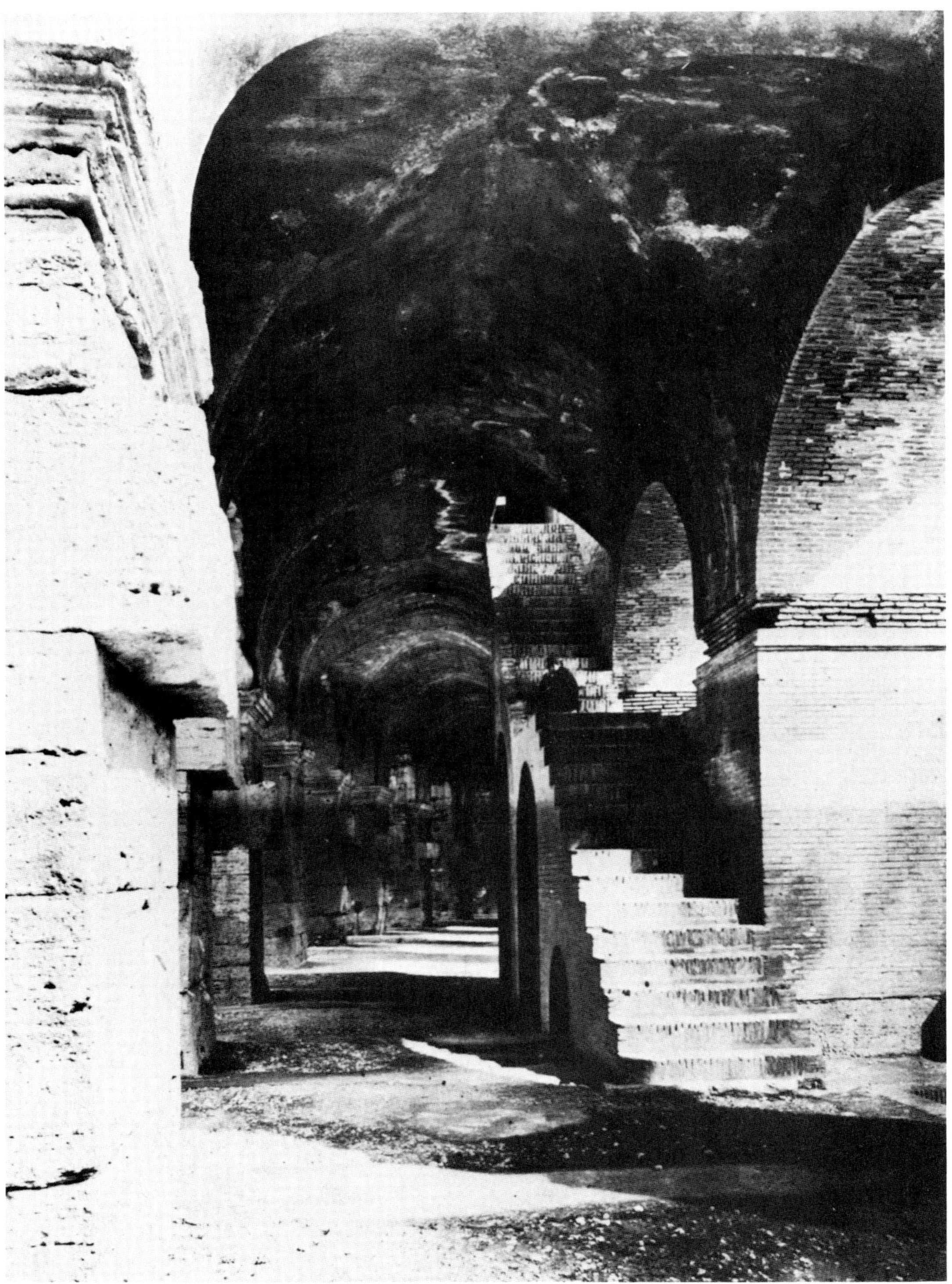

229.   Unknown photographer, undated. Coliseum, view of one of the Vomitoria. (Parker Collection; from J. Keller and K. A. Breisch, *A Victorian View of Ancient Rome*).

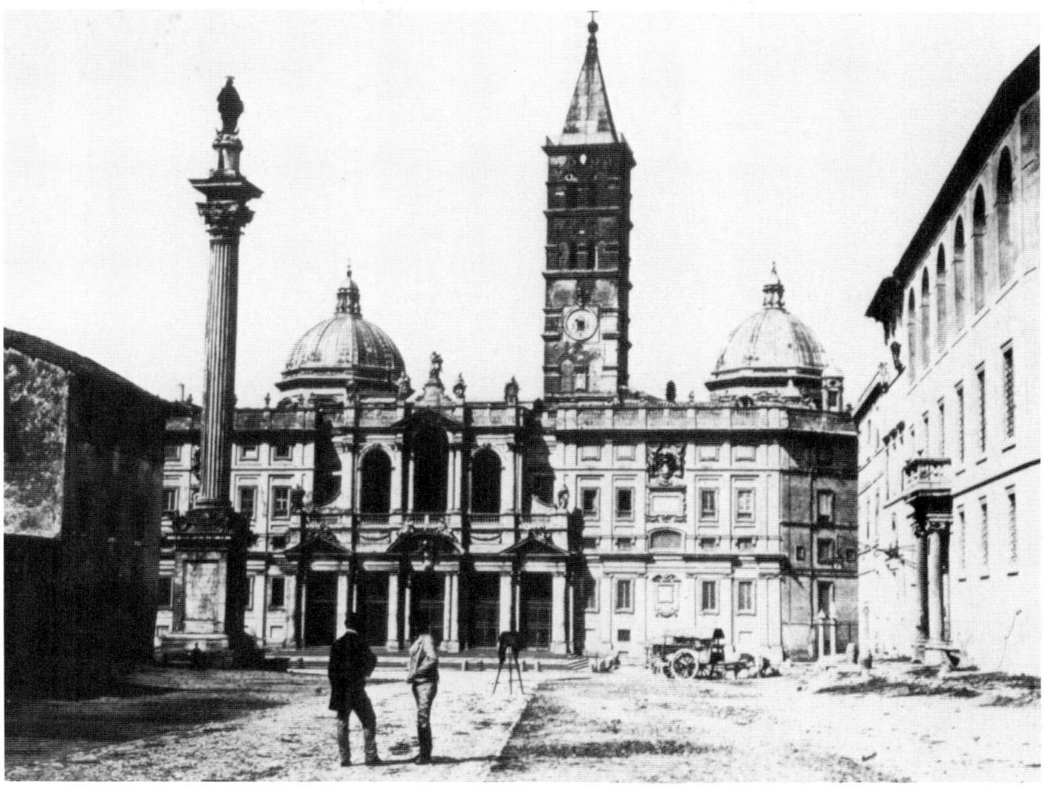

232. G. Altobelli and P. Molius, collodion plate, c. 1860. Piazza of S. Maria Maggiore (from D. Helsted, *Rome in Early Photographs).*

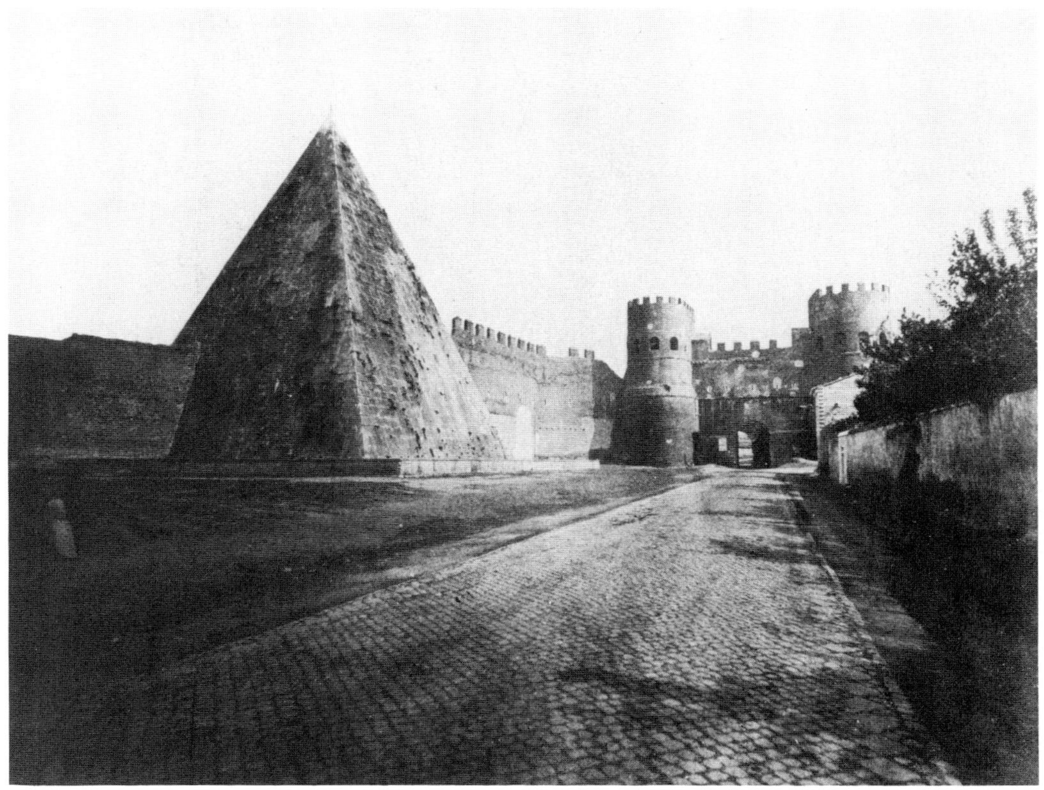

233. Unknown photographer, c. 1865. Via Ostiense, Pyramid of Caius Cestius (from D. Helsted, *Rome in Early Photographs).*

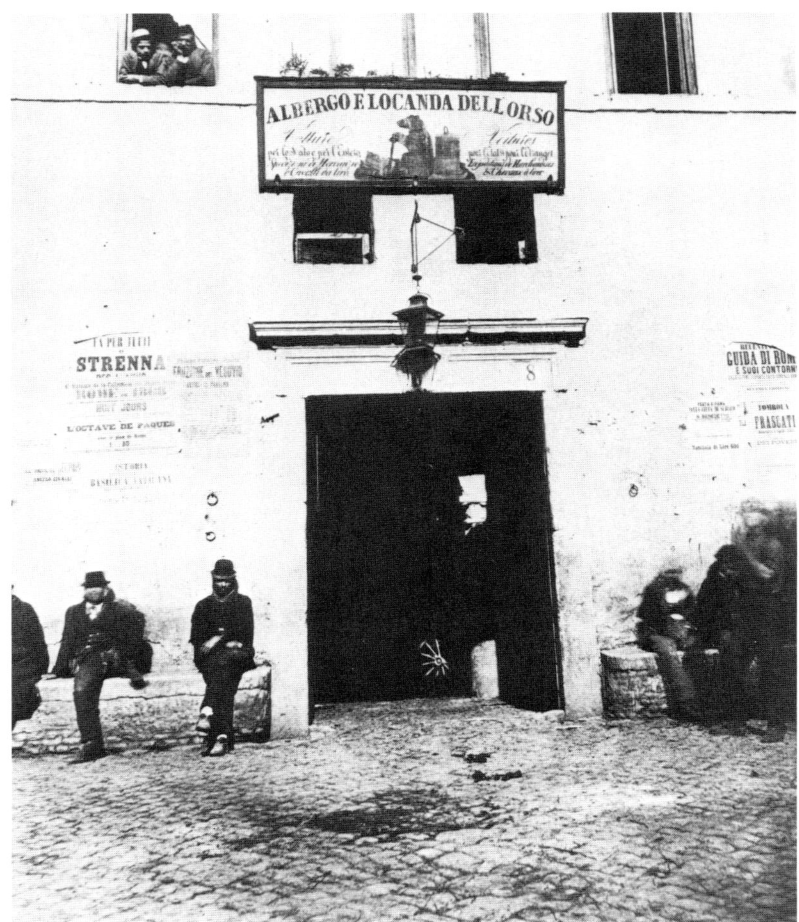

235.   Unknown photographer, 1868. Albergo dell'Orso (from
D. Helsted, *Rome in Early Photographs*).

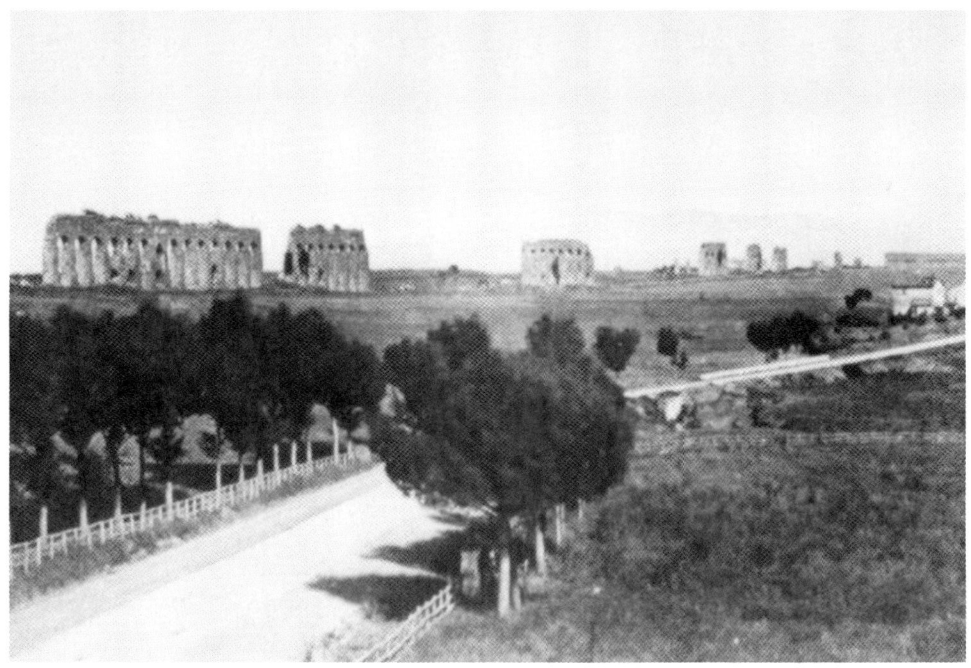

234.   Joseph Spithone, 1860s. The Appian Way (from G. Dimok, *Caroline Sturgis Tappan and the Grand Tour*).

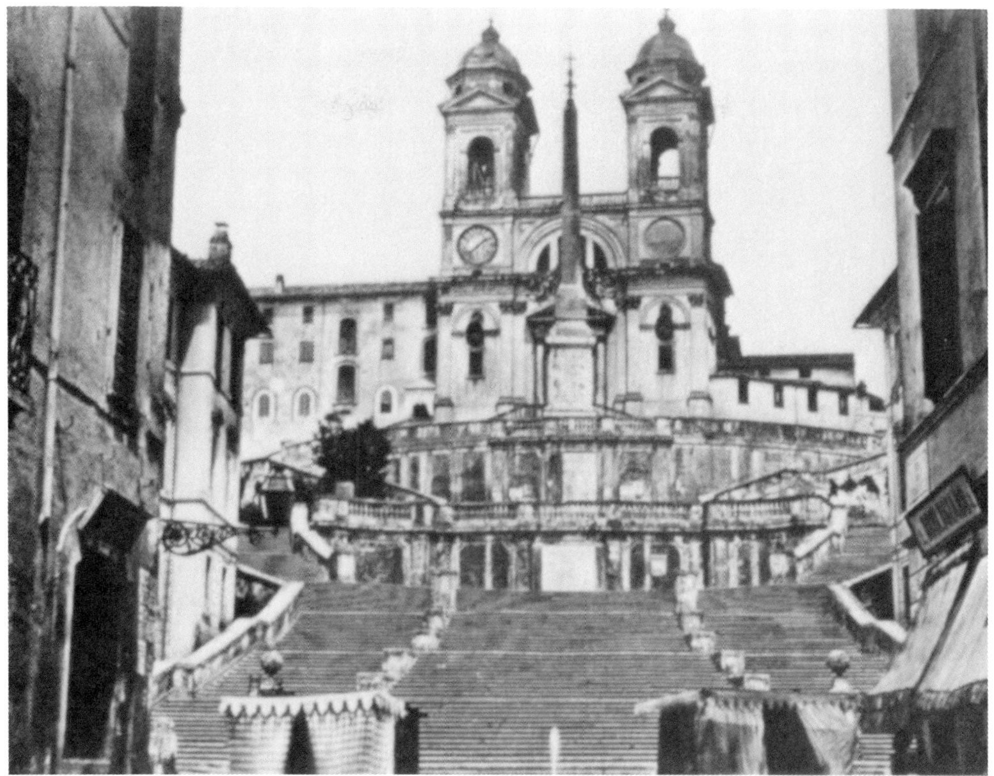

236.   Robert MacPherson, 1850s. Spanish Steps and SS. Trinità dei Monti (from G. Dimok, *Caroline Sturgis Tappan and the Grand Tour*).

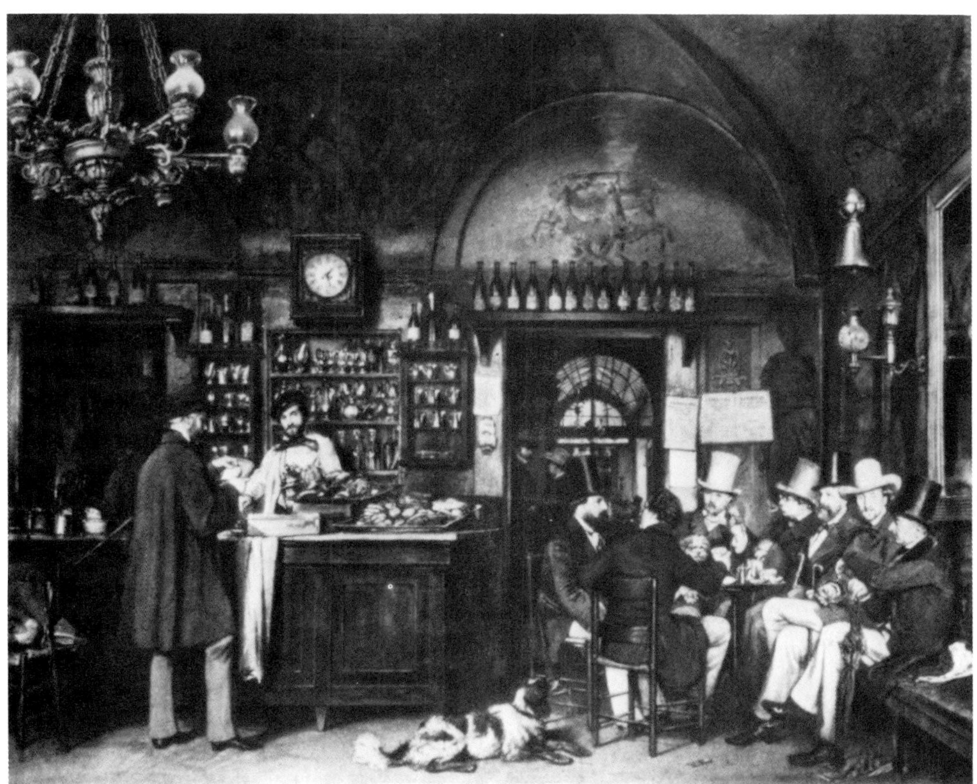

237.   Ludwig Passini, water color, c. 1850. Café Greco; Hamburg, Kunsthalle (from G. Poensgen, *C. Ph. Fohr und das Café Greco*).

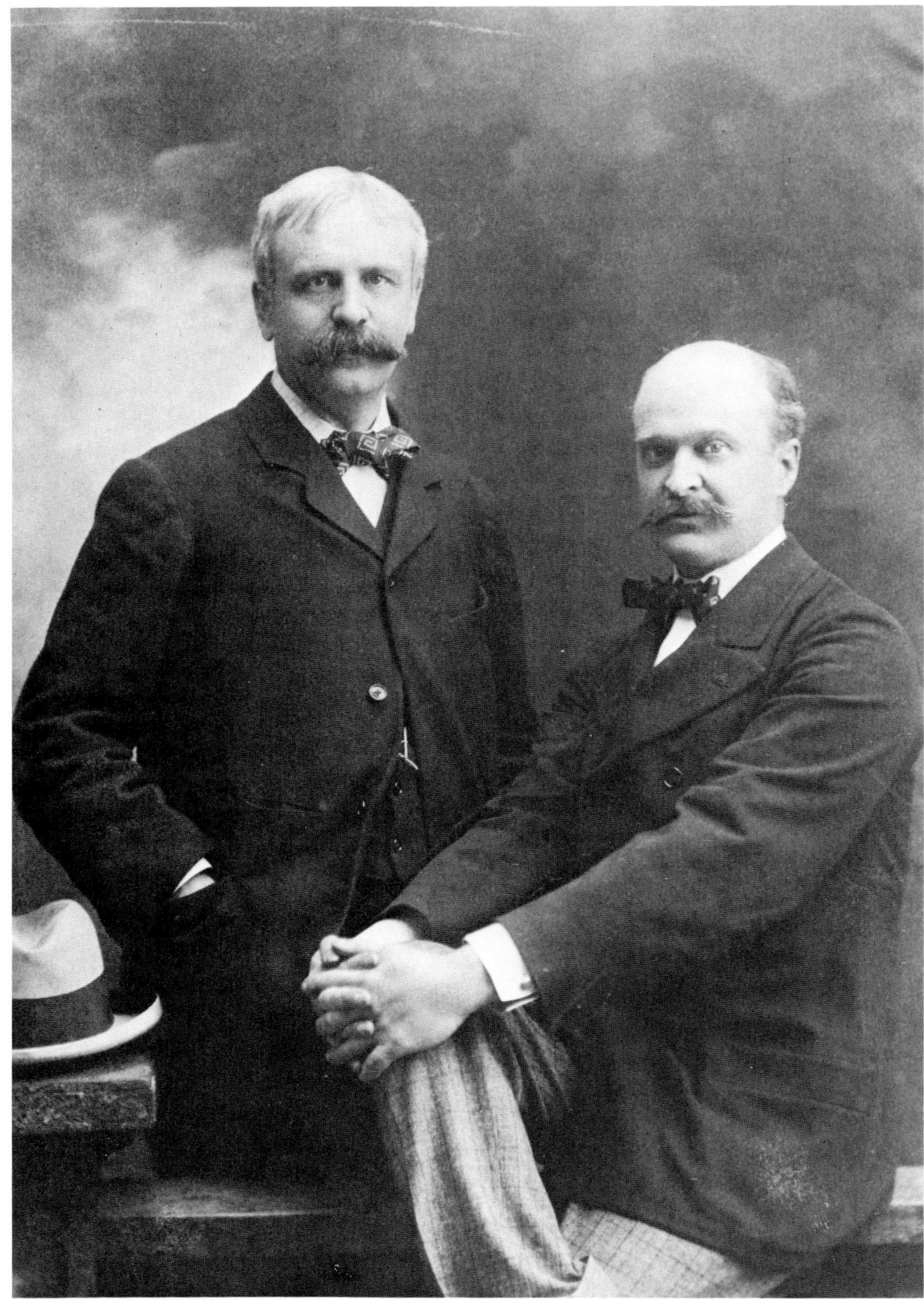

238.   William R. Mead and Charles F. McKim (left and right), c. 1896-97, (Manuscripts Department, Library of Congress).

Charles F. McKim and the Foundation of the American Academy in Rome

12

Thirteen years after the American Academy in Rome's establishment in 1894, William Rutherford Mead wrote a discouraging assessment of its future prospects to his partner, Charles Follen McKim: "Don't make the mistake of thinking there is a universal interest in the Academy in Rome—it is confined to you and a few others and if you dropped out nobody would take it up..."[1] From the outset, the Academy was a controversial issue in the American architectural community and a financially troubled undertaking. It was hampered by bitter arguments over Rome's suitability as a location for such a program, a general lack of students, a vague and ill-defined course of study, and an erratic cash flow.

Yet the Academy did survive and celebrated its ninetieth year in 1984. Its survival during these troubled early years of its history was due, in large part, to Charles McKim's efforts. As Mead had observed in 1907, his partner was the organization's driving force. It was McKim who convened a group of prominent architects at his townhouse in the spring of 1894 to discuss the possibility of founding an architectural studio in Rome.[2] Designed to function in much the same capacity as the Ecole des Beaux-Arts' Villa Medici in Rome, the program accepted only advanced students in architecture and was first known as the American School of Architecture in Rome. When mural painters and sculptors were admitted as fellows in 1897, the name was changed to the American Academy in Rome. Until his death in 1909, McKim played the leading role in the Academy's councils. He organized its program of study, vigorously defended the choice of Rome as its site, selected the first fellows, solicited donors for its endowment, and ultimately contributed over \$29,000 of his own funds.[3] Just as the University of Virginia is identified with one man, Thomas Jefferson, the American Academy is linked to Charles McKim (fig. 238).

McKim, Mead and White, Architects, was one of America's leading architectural firms by the end of the nineteenth century. By the early twentieth century Europeans had acknowledged its prominence; the Royal Institute of British Architects awarded its gold medal for achievement to McKim in 1903. The firm was an innovator in its adaptation of vernacular forms for domestic work and classical and Renaissance architecture for modern urban building types. Commissions included such works as Columbia University's Morningside Heights campus, the Rhode Island State Capitol, the Pennsylvania Railroad Station, and a remodeling of the White House interiors. For over thirty years, the office was the largest architectural practice in the world. It also nurtured successive generations of important American architects. John M. Carrère, Thomas Hastings, Cass Gilbert, John Galen Howard, Henry Bacon, and John Mead Howells all worked for McKim, Mead and White.[4]

Apart from his buildings, McKim exerted an influence on American architecture through his professional activities. He served as editor of the *New York Sketchbook* from 1874 until 1876 and as president of the American Institute of Architects from 1902 until 1903, established traveling fellowships for young architects at Columbia and Harvard, presided over an atelier at Columbia and, as we have seen, founded the American Academy in Rome.

By virtue of McKim's involvement alone, the American Academy must be considered a touchstone of late nineteenth-century architects' ideals and aspirations for American design. This essay will explore the role that McKim envisioned for the Academy in the creation of a modern style that was both appropriate to American conditions and also rooted in architectural tradition. Furthermore, by recounting the controversy that arose over the Academy's establishment, insights into the profession's views on such issues as the use of precedent, the Ecole des Beaux-Arts' influence on American architecture, and the direction of architectural education will be gained.

The Chicago World's Fair of 1893 has always been considered the inspiration for the American Academy's foundation.[5] It was only a few months after the exposition closed in the autumn of 1893 that McKim gathered together his fellow architects and artists from the Fair to broach the idea of an advanced school of architecture in Rome. Among those invited were Richard M. Hunt, Daniel H. Burnham, Robert S. Peabody, and Augustus Saint-Gaudens. In a May 22, 1894, letter to the latter, McKim outlined the basis for the American program:

> The plan is to take one or two rooms in Rome and to compel the scholarship men who at present go abroad without limitations to follow a course of study resembling that of the French Academy in the Villa Medici...Of course, if the Atelier proves successful it will mean that one day we too will have a Grand Prize of Rome.[6]

Established as the headquarters for the French Academy in Rome in 1666, the Villa Medici received Ecole students in painting, sculpture, and architecture after they had won a rigorous design competition, the *Grand Prix de Rome*. A *Prix de Rome* man was awarded four years of state-sponsored study in Rome, with excursions to the rest of Italy, Sicily, and Greece permitted during the final three years.[7] Upon his return to France, he received the most prestigious government commissions. For architects, the course of study at the Villa Medici consisted of measuring and drawing antique structures with more limited attention paid to Renaissance buildings. The fourth and final year was devoted to the preparation of restoration drawings of an ancient building or site in Italy, Sicily or Greece. As foreigners, American students at the Ecole were automatically barred from participating in the *Prix de Rome* competitions.

The French Academy was clearly on McKim's mind the year before the American School of Architecture in Rome was established. He patterned the New York State Pavilion at the Chicago Fair after the Villa Medici (fig. 239). As with all his designs, McKim adapted, he did not revive, the historical prototype. Since the Fair building was intended as "a convenient and comfortable club house for New Yorkers," McKim reasoned that the Villa Medici's "broader treatment, more festal and palatial characteristics and grander proportions of the Italian Renaissance in which the use of Allegory and Symbol is possible, adapt it admirably to all requirements."[8] Yet McKim regularized and simplified the original building's forms, plan and ornament so that they accorded with the lay-out and bleached classicism of the exposition buildings on the Court of Honor (fig. 240).

As Henry Van Brunt, one of the participating architects at the Fair, explained, the Chicago exposition buildings gathered around the Court of Honor were all designed as variants on the classical theme for two reasons: one, to serve as an object lesson for this country's architects and two, to demonstrate to foreign observers that the United States, the youngest of nations, was capable of working within the European architectural tradition. Van Brunt elaborated on these issues in two articles written between 1892 and 1893:

> It was considered that a series of pure classic models, in each case contrasting in character according to the personal equation of the architect, and according to the practical conditions to be accommodated in each, but uniform in respect to scale and language of form, all set forth with the utmost amount of luxury and opulence of decoration permitted by the best usage, and on a theatre of unprecedented magnitude, would present to the profession here an object lesson so impressive of the practical value of architectural scholarship and strict subordination to the formulas of the schools, that it would serve as a timely corrective to the national tendency to experiment in design...There are many uneducated and untrained men practising as architects...men who have never seen a pure classic monument executed on a grand scale...To such it is hoped that these great models, inspired as they have been by a profound respect for the masters of classic art, will prove such a revelation that they will learn at last that true architecture cannot be based on undisciplined invention, illiterate originality, or indeed, upon any audacity of ignorance...(1892)

It was evident that the great court wherein the guests of the nation were to be received, and where they should be welcomed with stately ceremony, should be surrounded by buildings of a style most associated with modern civilization...By this decision it was not proposed that the architects of our country were to pose before the world as the conservators of tradition, but to show that the youngest of nations respects and understands the past and acknowledges its fundamental indebtedness to classical art...and that our civilization does not affect to be independent of the experience of mankind in history. (1892-1893)[9]

Although Van Brunt denied that the Fair buildings were intended to spark a classical revival in American architecture, others welcomed just such an occurrence. Daniel H. Burnham, supervising architect of the exposition, envisioned reshaping America's cities in the Fair's image. As Frank Lloyd Wright recalled in his autobiography, Burnham's enthusiasm was unbounded:

The Fair, Frank, is going to have a great influence on our country. The American people have seen the classics on a grand scale for the first time. You've seen the success of the Fair and it should mean something to you. We should take advantage of the Fair...I can see America constructed along the lines of the Fair, in noble and dignified classic style. The great men of the day all feel that way about it—all of them.[10]

The Chicago Exposition has been identified as a manifestation of the so-called American Renaissance, the late nineteenth- and early twentieth-century classical resurgence in this country. The terms Renaissance and American Renaissance appear frequently in the literature of the 1880s and 1900s to describe contemporary painting, sculpture, architecture, and decorative arts. No less an authority than Bernard Berenson, as Richard Guy Wilson has noted, commented on the affinities between fifteenth-century Italy and late nineteenth-century America:

Every generation has an innate sympathy with some epoch of the past wherein it seems to find itself foreshadowed...We ourselves because of our faith in science and the power of work, are instinctively in sympathy with the Renaissance... Our tasks are more difficult because our vision is wider, but the spirit which animates us was anticipated by the spirit of the Renaissance: and

more than anticipated. That spirit seems like the small rough model after which ours is being fashioned.[11]

McKim, Mead and White was certainly associated with this Renaissance movement. McKim was called the Bramante of the firm, and a former assistant recalled that the office "seemed to breathe the spirit of the fifteenth century."[12] Not surprisingly, this spirit enfolded the American Academy. McKim wrote to Saint-Gaudens that the fellows were:

to occupy their time in close contact with the great examples of Greece and Rome and the early Renaissance under the direction of a qualified pilot who has been over the ground and who will see to it that they spend their time on the greatest examples and are not allowed to foolishly spend their prize money over their own immature selections.[13]

Prospective Academy patrons were also urged to cast themselves in the Renaissance mold. Daniel Burnham tried to persuade Charles Crocker, the California millionaire, to pledge $100,000 to the Academy endowment with the following words:

If moved by the desire to record one's family name forever, this is the opportunity and Rome is the place. This is not an unworthy motive, as the Medicis and Dorias and many other Italian families perceived—families whose names are known entirely through their connection with the fine arts.[14]

Crocker, however, declined this chance for immortality as a modern-day Medici; he preferred to fund undertakings closer to his California home.[15]

As Richard Longstreth has pointed out, the Renaissance movement was not exclusively confined to this country. A similar classical resurgence developed more or less concurrently in Europe and was influenced on both sides of the Atlantic by Beaux-Arts theory and design.[16] Stylistic considerations aside, certain attitudes were unique to the American Renaissance and can be appreciated only through reference to this country's architectural development in the nineteenth century. The American Academy, we will see, was but another manifestation of these attitudes.

Arrogance was certainly one of the American Renaissance movement's attributes. Berenson's likening of the Italian Renaissance spirit to a "small rough model" after which this country's was being fashioned is typical. A corollary of the United State's burgeoning political and economic power, the American Renaissance was predicated on the idea of a civic function for the fine arts. Artists such as Edward Moran paid tribute to such American imperialistic ventures as the Spanish-American War in works like *Return of the Conquerors, September 29, 1899* (fig. 241).

The American Academy in Rome's establishment was proof that the United States had attained its majority culturally as well as politically and economically and could now take its place alongside France, Germany, Spain, and Belgium, all countries with their own academies in Rome. Published as part of a 1902 fund-raising effort, an Academy pamphlet proclaimed:

> American schools now stand firmly on their own feet, and have obtained an excellence which justifies the establishment of a National Academy of Fine Arts in Rome. The United States must give to its students opportunities equal to those enjoyed by the French students to study the fundamental principles of art where best exemplified.[17]

Although the American Renaissance was predicated on a knowledgeable use of European artistic and architectural traditions, it was believed that this country, and not Europe, would mold these past styles into an appropriately modern expression. This attitude is quite pronounced in two letters F. D. Millet, an American painter and Academy trustee, penned to McKim about his search for a building in Rome to house the Academy. On July 12, 1906, Millet wrote:

> I had a change of heart in Rome and now am down on old palaces...if we could ever build our own building and show these Dagos what architecture is...what an object lesson it would be to Italy and to other nations. Show these Johnnies how much better we have taken to heart the lessons of the past than they have, show them what we can do and how we can be modern and not forget the masters of the past. Show them that all the improvements of Science need not destroy beauty of line, proportion and mass; show them it isn't necessary for an architect to have dirty lines or an artist dirty fingernails. Show them in fact that we are *it*.[18]

And again on July 24, 1906:

> What I would like to see in Rome would be a group of buildings, or, rather a number of buildings properly placed, designed by American architects and provided with every reasonable convenience and comfort. This would at once be a great object lesson. The buildings of modern Rome are, as a rule, beneath contempt, even the Romans confess this...I am sure we could teach them a great and salutary lesson, and we, would profit by it...Why desire an old historic Palace...Why not have the best modern thing we can get? *The idea of Rome must be adapted to modern conditions.* [italics author's][19]

The acquisition of a suitably imposing building for the American Academy seemed to occupy an inordinate amount of the trustees' time and energy. Real estate matters dominated the Academy meetings while discussion of the students and their program of study was less frequent. Millet wrote to McKim for information, explaining that:

> I am continually annoyed, and I daresay other members of the Board of Trustees have the same experience, at my utter inability to answer any questions in regard to the work of the Academy. I do not even know the number of students.[20]

Characteristically, Millet's request for information arose from his attempt to solicit pledges of $100,000 for the Academy; he discovered then that he could tell prospective patrons little of substance about the Academy programs.

When Millet wrote to McKim that "we can be modern and not forget the masters of the past," he articulated the central issue of American architecture in the late nineteenth and early twentieth centuries.[21] This period was just as stylistically eclectic as the earlier decades of the nineteenth century. While there was a decided preference for ancient and Renaissance prototypes, especially for public buildings, this did not drive out all other stylistic references. Designs predicated on the Byzantine, Romanesque, Gothic, Tudor, and Spanish Mission styles coexisted with the classicizing tendencies of the American Renaissance. What was unique about the late nineteenth and early twentieth centuries was the insistence that all historical styles be used knowledgeably and appropriately. Richard Longstreth has seen this academic approach to eclecticism as the leitmotif of the period and explains it as follows:

The approach taken by architects during this period [the late nineteenth and early twentieth centuries] can be more accurately described as academic eclecticism and the cause they championed as the academic movement. This nomenclature focuses on aim, method, and origins, not style. The movement emphasized fostering the art of design through a scholarly knowledge of the past. The method was academic in the importance given to formal education as a means of acquiring that knowledge.[22]

In the late nineteenth century, American architects consistently denounced their immediate past. Architecture in the United States, it was believed, had fallen on dark days after the Civil War. Alexander J. Davis stated that only a search through Rabelais or Dante would yield terms adequate to describe the "licentiousness and depravity" of American architecture after 1865.[23] Disseminated through the house pattern books that first appeared in the 1840s, the picturesque movement had destroyed classicism's hegemony and opened a Pandora's box of styles. Architects and builders alike were no longer innocent; they were burdened by a modern self-consciousness of historical styles. Writing in 1893, H. Langford Warren, a Boston architect and later Harvard professor, explained the modern architect's dilemma:

Until the present century, was there ever any doubt as to the architectural language which the builder at any given time and place would use to express his thoughts? That he used simply and naturally the style of his own time and country in erecting a building was as much a matter of course as that he used his tongue in speech: and just as the languages gradually and continuously developed from each other, so...through the modifications brought about by actual circumstances and the imperceptible changes of ideals, did architectural styles...There is now no style which is our natural language...[24]

What resulted in the mid-century from the breakdown of the classical language was an architecture universally condemned as bizarre and extravagant beginning in the late 1870s. As Ernest Flagg asserted, Victorian design had "reached probably the lowest state of debasement and degradation ever known in a civilized country."[25] Specifically, the sins of post-Civil War architecture were seen as a lack of coherence, homogeneity, skill, knowledge, and refinement of detail; the American taste for eclecticism

led to a disturbing looseness and discursiveness in design which expressed itself in "countless angles, bays, dormers, and peaks" (fig. 242).[26] American architecture was not faulted for its want of originality, but rather for an overabundance of it. Such boisterous inventiveness led to vulgarity and extravagance. Professional education was seen as the panacea. As William Robert Ware, founder of the first program in architecture at an American university, expressed it, good building was possible without formal instruction, but good architecture was not.[27] In 1868, there was only one academic course of study in architecture—Ware's curriculum at the Massachusetts Institute of Technology—but there were eleven such programs at American universities by the end of the nineteenth century.[28]

American architects turned to the Ecole des Beaux-Arts as the model for professional education. Beginning with Richard M. Hunt in 1846, increasing numbers of young Americans went to Paris to study architecture in the second half of the nineteenth century. It was believed that their work, regardless of the style chosen, was rationally and coherently designed. With a curriculum based on the classical tradition, the Ecole inculcated qualities, in the words of one architectural journalist, of "sobriety, dignity, elegance, and good composition."[29] Henry Van Brunt, an architect and astute critic of American work, observed that training at the Ecole equipped designers to work knowledgeably and sensitively in any architectural style:

It has been remarked that graduates of the Ecole des Beaux-Arts who have come to this country to practice, so far from being cramped in their methods by the classic limitations of their studies, adapt themselves to their new circumstances, and express themselves in any architectural language, whether classic or Gothic, brick or stone, or even in our wooden vernacular, with a facility, freedom, and correctness, a grace and an elegance, beyond the reach of any who have not enjoyed similar advantages.[30]

The Ecole also appealed to Americans because of its emphasis on architecture as a fine art studied in the same curriculum as painting and sculpture. In this country architecture had always been regarded as more of a craft or trade than an art. The profession of architecture emerged only in the second half of the nineteenth century; builders and carpenters, who had previously dominated design and construction, were unwilling to surrender their control. American architects waged a protracted and bitter struggle to secure recognition as professional practitioners and artists throughout the late nineteenth century. Thus, the Ecole's approach was a source of solace and vindication to them. A. L. Brockway, a student in Paris in 1888, explained the Ecole's appeal to his countrymen:

> The result in the mind and heart of the student is an uplifting one, a loftier conception of architecture results, a devotion to one's chosen work is aroused, an increase of thoughtfulness, and the memory is stored with experiences to be drawn upon later. One realizes that architecture is a fine art.[31]

Given late nineteenth-century American architects' fervent belief in education in general and the Ecole in particular, one would have expected McKim's plans for an American atelier in Rome patterned after the Villa Medici to receive their unqualified support. Such was not the case. Opposition to the American school developed almost immediately after the first public announcements of its foundation. Ironically, McKim found that the young architects who had attended the Ecole and even worked in his office were the proposed Academy's harshest critics. The Society of Beaux-Arts Architects spearheaded the drive against the Roman school. Also founded in 1894, the Society was composed of architects who had studied at the Ecole; McKim was, in fact, one of the organization's charter members.[32] The Society argued that Paris, and not Rome, provided the best training for young American architects. The student's work at the Ecole actually revolved around the ateliers presided over by the most important architects of the day, usually former Villa Medici *pensionnaires* themselves. John M. Carrère argued the Society's case in a July 18, 1894, letter to McKim:

> It seems to me that Rome, at the present, is the center of archaeological research; and represents the past while I believe, Paris is the center of modern architecture representing both the present and the future.[33]

John Galen Howard, another Beaux-Arts member, further elaborated the Society's objections to an American school in Rome:

> Shall we send boys to Rome to make dainty drawings of elevations and details before they understand the principles and needs of which these are mere clothing and expression: or shall we send them to Paris, first to learn the why and how by exercising their own powers and developing them to the utmost.[34]

As Howard had warned McKim, the Society of Beaux-Arts Architects publicly stated its opposition to the Rome program. In August of 1894, it published a resolution applauding McKim's and his associates' generosity in attempting to establish an American school in Rome but also condemning such an undertaking as "unnecessary and unjudicious."[35]

Criticism of the Academy came also from within its own Board of Managers. Although William Robert Ware served as this board's chairman, he was troubled by McKim's unwillingness to open up the program to all young American architects traveling abroad. McKim insisted that Academy fellows either be drawn from the ranks of holders of university scholarships or be winners of a special competition modeled after the *Prix de Rome*. Writing to him on December 21, 1894, Ware warned:

> I have not met a single person who...does not cry out against what he regarded as the narrow, illiberal, exclusive, undemocratic, unAmerican character of our rules.[36]

Despite these criticisms, McKim prevailed: an advanced architectural program was established in Rome for a select group of students in the fall of 1894.

McKim was adamant in his contention that Rome rather than Paris was the proper training ground for young American architects. In an April 7, 1894, letter, he wrote:

> Do I think it wise to spend so much time in Rome? I think it would be wise to spend a whole lifetime in Rome. As between Rome and all other Italian cities, give me Rome—not that I care less for Florence or Venice, but more for Rome, since it contains for the architect the greatest number of typical examples. Still you must go to Paestum, and to Pompeii and steep yourself in the Naples Museum: and again Venice claims you without dispute for a time at least. And when you get through with all these go back to Rome—Rome and the surrounding countryside.[37]

McKim studied at the Ecole from 1867 until 1869, but as Robert S. Peabody, a friend and fellow

Ecole élève, later recalled: "He [McKim] never really liked modern French taste and he was in fact more close to Rome than to Paris."[38] In the firm commissions he was responsible for, such as the Boston Public Library, Columbia's Low Library, and the Pennsylvania Railroad Station, he invoked the chaste classical forms of ancient Rome or the High Renaissance. Leland Roth, author of the definitive monograph on the firm, contrasts the artistic temperaments of McKim and his partner, Stanford White, as follows:

McKim's own work tended increasingly toward abstract order, to parallel that of Alberti or Bramante with an assertiveness studied from Roman monuments, while White...was caught up in exploring the flexibility and freedom possible in the Renaissance idiom; his work was marked by richly textured surfaces and ornament which increased in extravagance...[39]

McKim cast the modern architect's task in Renaissance terms. Like Bramante, he studied the remains of antiquity not in order to reproduce them, but as the basis of inspiration for new forms. H. Langford Warren also perceived the parallels between the fifteenth-and nineteenth-centuries' attitudes toward the past as the basis of modern architectural consciousness:

The first conscious looking to precedent came with the Renaissance, and it is to Renaissance thought and work that we owe the essential characteristics of modern conditions. It was the Renaissance which created the art of architecture and gradually brought about the separation between the architect and craftsman by consciously turning to precedent, and so requiring in the architect the training... of the scholar in place of the...practical knowledge and manual skill of the builder.[40]

McKim echoed Warren's emphasis on the contemporary American architect as scholar in a 1902 address he delivered at the annual convention of the American Institute of Architects:

great opportunities demand thorough training. Confidence comes not from inspiration but from knowledge. The architect who would build for the ages must have the training of the ages that are past.[41]

In sending students to Rome rather than Paris, McKim was grooming a select group of architects.

Like their Villa Medici counterparts, these men were to return home to undertake the most important public commissions. A 1902 publication on the American Academy made this purpose quite clear:

This country is now engaged in building in marble at its capital, a city that will be filled with monuments far exceeding in grandeur and beauty the perishable ones of the Chicago Fair...the work was begun by the founders of government, Washington and Jefferson...they believed they were laying the foundations of the capital city for a nation that should be as great and as enduring as Rome. In their wisdom, they took as models the works of antiquity that had stood the test of time. They believed they had no right to inflict on posterity their personal idiosyncracies or the fashions of the moment...The nation will demand that the work shall be completed in the spirit in which it was begun...To afford these opportunities is the object of the American Academy.[42]

McKim was especially concerned with how young American architects would grapple with the task of designing these large public buildings. In 1893, the year before the Academy's foundation, he had lobbied Congress for the passage of the Tarsney Act, which would authorize the federal government to establish open competitions for its building commissions. In 1901, McKim served as a member of the McMillan Commission which called for a return to L'Enfant's plan for the city of Washington. An ambitious undertaking, the commission recommended that classical precepts of style and organization be used to create an uninterrupted vista from the Capitol to the Washington Monument, to expand the White House, and to construct monuments, museums, government office buildings, and a parkway system.[43] Surely McKim saw the American Academy training the architects, sculptors, and mural painters necessary to carry out the Tarsney Act's and McMillan Commission's provisions. "You will find opportunities awaiting you that no other country has offered in modern times," he wrote to Lawrence Grant White (son of his partner, Stanford White) in 1909, "the scale is Roman and it will have to be sustained."[44]

By virtue of the fact that the Academy fellows would be engaged in such monumental projects, it was imperative that they study in Rome rather than Paris. Still defending the selection of Rome, several Academy trustees addressed the 1903 convention of the American Institute of Architects on this subject; Austin W. Lord, who had supervised the first fellows in Rome from 1894 until 1896, spoke on Rome's importance to the architect, while Augustus Saint-Gaudens and Edwin H. Blashfield discussed its significance for the sculptor and mural painter respectively. Blashfield made very clear why the Academy sent its fellows to Rome rather than Paris:

> The lesson of Rome and Italy is more useful because it is broader, it is less tumultuous and more serene, because instead of emphasizing sharply one phase of thought, it offers the development of a chain of thought. Above all, because it enables the pupil to realize that the present is not the ultimate thing which it has seemed to him; that not the art which dazzles, but the art which shines enduringly is to be sought...This confrontation of the pupil with the best art of all times, together with his sequestration from the ephemeral...is the prize object of the Academy...Sequestration from the ephemeral has, in the idea of the founders of the American Academy in Rome, been almost as important as access to the best examples of work....In Paris, too, there is a splendid background...but, and here is the relative disqualification, the background in Paris is confused by the foreground. We have said that the horizon in Rome is wider; it is above all clearer; in Paris the clouds that pass across it often pass rapidly and sometimes dissolve under our very eyes.[45]

Thus, it was the enduring and timeless in architecture that the Academy sought to provide exposure to in Rome rather than the fleeting fashions of Paris. Yet students were not to imitate mindlessly Roman forms, but distill their essence and adapt them to American needs and conditions. An 1895 memorandum set out the founders' purpose:

> The school is not, primarily, one of design, nor...is it one of copying, in the sense of storing the mind with the 'motifs' of old masters to be reproduced with pedantic exactness at home. It is rather to educate the tastes and thoroughly to impress upon the mind by daily contact with the great monuments those principles which are essential to the enduring quality in Architecture, be the style what it may.[46]

The measurement and drawing of ancient monuments required of the American Academy fellows, it was believed, were essential in revealing certain architectural virtues of scale, mass, proportion, and line. Austin W. Lord explained this aspect of the Academy curriculum as follows:

> These things are presented to his [the young architect's] study in all the austerity and simplicity which comes from a complete elimination of trivial details or utilitarian accessories...In the varying degrees of decay that mark the ruins of ancient Rome, he learns to what a slight extent these monuments depend for their majesty upon the particular details he has been brought to regard as their most distinguishing characteristics. He realizes as never before that what we call scale, the adequate expression of the bigness of things is a quality inherent in the proper proportioning of masses, and has an existence entirely independent of the details and accessories which are too frequently employed in modern buildings to supply by means of their size and position the lack of quality itself.[47]

These, then, were the ideas and attitudes that shaped the American Academy in Rome. Yet what was the reality of its first fifteen years? William Robert Ware wrote that he found "a curious air of hollowness and unreality" about the Academy "as if calling things so made them so."[48] The enterprise's unreal quality stemmed from its general lack of funds and students. McKim had launched the Academy at a most unpropitious moment, in the midst of the financial depression that followed the panic of 1893. Burnham and McKim were able to raise about fifteen thousand dollars in the spring of 1894, which was sufficient to implement a limited program the following fall.[49] Yet there were no funds to endow a fellowship for the first year, and McKim had to persuade other traveling scholarship committees to send their men to Rome. That first winter and spring in Rome, there were only three students: Harold van Buren Magonigle, holder of the Rotch Scholarship, and Seth Justin Temple and George B. Page, recipients of travel funds from the architectural programs at Columbia University and the University of Pennsylvania respectively. Magonigle and Temple arrived in Rome during the winter of 1894, while Page did not turn up until the new year. Since these students were not indebted to the Roman school for their funds, they were resistant to the founders' edicts to spend almost all of their time abroad in Rome measuring and drawing ancient buildings.[50] Rather than stay a full year in Rome, they all three bolted after only four or five months there.[51] There was also no real director in Rome. McKim sent Austin Lord, an assistant from his office, to preside over the American school.[52] According to one eyewitness, Lord, barely older than his charges, encountered a chilly and skeptical reception in Rome:

> Mr. Lord has not provided himself with credentials so that no one knows who he is or what sort of school he is starting, and people are naturally inclined to sneer at a school which has no apparent backing and but two scholars.[53]

By January of 1895, the situation had improved somewhat. Sufficient funds had been secured to offer a fifteen hundred dollar *Prix de Rome* in architecture. Through a competition, John Russell Pope, a student at Columbia University, was selected; Pope was to spend ten months in Rome and another eight months in travel mutually agreeable to him and the School's founders. The *Prix de Rome* was awarded again in 1896, but was then suspended until 1907. During the intervening years, students from other university programs were coaxed into spending a few months at the Academy in order to maintain some sort of a presence in Rome. A succession of directors followed Lord's departure in 1896, but their tenures were brief and troubled.[54] At one point, Will S. Aldrich, a student, ran the program from 1896 until 1897. William M. Kendall, an associate from McKim's office, wrote in 1904:

> I wish the Academy were in better condition....In Rome there is nothing but mutual criticism among those directly connected with the School. The general public either know nothing about it, or, if they do, show a decided distrust in its usefulness. They need to be reassured by the presence of numerous students and of a Director.[55]

McKim held the Academy together during these difficult early years. When the Academy could not offer its own fellowships, he persuaded the universities to send their scholarship men to Rome for at least a few months. He devoted much of his time to soliciting $100,000 donations to establish an endowment. When these funds fell short, he advanced his own money to keep the Academy open. He presided over its transition from the American School of Architecture in Rome to the American Academy in Rome in 1897 and lobbied strenuously for its incorporation as a national institution by Congress in the 1900s.

McKim also tried to direct the architectural fellows' work. Naturally, he wanted them to concentrate on ancient Roman monuments with some attention to the Renaissance. The first fellows dutifully measured and drew the Baths of Caracalla, the Theatre of Marcellus, Hadrian's Villa, the Palazzo Cancelleria, and the Palazzo Farnese under Lord's supervision.[56] Other antique structures studied are recorded in Magonigle's line drawing of a rosette from the Temple of Vespasian and Pope's measured drawing of the Erechtheum and its details (figs. 243 and 244). Yet McKim could not completely curb the American penchant for the decorative and picturesque. Magonigle succumbed to the charms of the Doge's Palace, while Pope was intrigued by the cathedral at Orvieto (figs. 245 and 246). Ware reported, no doubt somewhat gleefully, to Burnham that the fellows did not like following the committee's prescribed course of study: "they are grown men and know what they want."[57]

McKim's efforts were finally vindicated. By 1907, the Academy's endowment was sufficient to resume the *Prix de Rome* competitions and three fellows in architecture, painting, and sculpture were sent to Rome for a course of study lasting three years.[58] The Academy had also acquired a permanent home, the Villa Mirafiori, in 1906.[59] Millet's dream of a building designed by an American architect was also eventually realized. In 1912, three years after McKim's death, the Academy began construction of a building on the Janiculum appropriately designed by the firm of McKim, Mead and White (fig. 247).[60]

John Russell Pope later recalled that his year at the Roman school was "the cream of it all."[61] In spite of their complaints about the restrictive course of study, the fellows did fulfill McKim's hopes for them. Pope and Magonigle, for example, returned to the United States to design monumental buildings in the classical style. Pope, most fittingly, was responsible for such Washington commissions foreseen in the McMillan Commission's recommendations as the National Gallery of Art and the Jefferson Memorial. Magonigle developed a specialty, worthy of any Villa Medici *pensionnaire*, in public monuments such as the Maine Monument in New York. Like the French Academy, the American program in Rome did provide a group of architects able to design large scale public structures in an enduring architectural style.

The ascendancy of European modernism in twentieth-century architecture meant that institutions such as the American Academy in Rome and the works of such architects as Charles McKim, John Russell Pope, and Harold van Buren Magonigle were abruptly dismissed as examples of American architects' inability to deal with the realities of modern life. It is perhaps fitting, then, that Robert Venturi and Michael Graves, two architects instrumental in dethroning the modern movement, were both fellows at the American Academy.[62] McKim would surely have understood and encouraged their attempts to reconcile architectural tradition with contemporary needs and conditions.

Mary N. Woods
Department of Architecture
Cornell University

Notes

1. Mead to McKim, Oct. 14, 1907. Charles F. McKim Papers, Manuscript Division, Library of Congress, Washington, D.C.

2. Memorandum of July 10, 1894. American Academy in Rome Papers, Archives of American Art, Washington, D.C.

3. Memorandum on Credits and Debits of the American Academy in Rome, June 9, 1902. McKim Papers, Library of Congress.

4. Carrère and Hastings were the architects for the New York Public Library; Cass Gilbert designed the Minnesota State Capitol and the Woolworth Building; John Galen Howard was professor of architecture at the University of California, Berkeley; Henry Bacon designed the Lincoln Memorial; and John Mead Howells was architect of the Chicago Tribune Tower.

5. In a speech, McKim referred to F. D. Millet's remark that the Academy was a "male child born at Jackson Park on the banks of the lake in '93." Millet was a mural painter and secretary and trustee of the Academy from 1905 until his death in 1912. See TS (1908?) speech, McKim Papers, Library of Congress. For other associations of the American Academy with the Chicago World's Fair of 1893, see Charles Moore, *Daniel H. Burnham*, I (Boston and New York: Houghton Mifflin, 1921), and *The Life and Times of Charles Follen McKim* (Boston and New York: Houghton Mifflin, 1929), pp. 53-58 and 123, and Lucia and Alan Chester Valentine, *The American Academy in Rome 1894-1969* (Charlottesville, Virginia: University Press of Virginia, 1973), pp. 1-6.

6. McKim Papers, Library of Congress.

7. After meeting with the director of the French Academy in Rome, Austin W. Lord, the American Academy's first director, wrote McKim that the Villa Medici *pensionnaires* devoted their first year in Rome to studying and drawing the classical orders, the second year to Renaissance work, the third year to ancient Greek work, and their fourth year to restoration of an ancient building or site. See Lord to McKim, Jan. 7, 1895. Academy Papers, Archives of American Art. The French students were allowed to travel outside Italy to Greece and Asia Minor only after 1845. See *Paris-Rome-Athens: Travels in Greece by French Architects in the 19th and 20th Centuries* (Houston: Museum of Fine Arts, 1983), pp. xviii-xix.

8. Moore, *Charles Follen McKim.* pp. 117 and 121. The pavilion was not on the Court of Honor.

9. "Architecture at the World's Columbian Exposition" and "Historic Styles, Modern Architecture" (1892 and 1892-93) reprinted in *Architecture and Society: Selected Essays of Henry Van Brunt*, ed. William A. Coles (Cambridge: Belknap Press, 1969), pp. 233-34 and 300.

10. Frank Lloyd Wright, *An Autobiography* (1932: reprint, New York: Horizon Press, 1977), p. 150. For Van Brunt's remark, see Coles, p. 234.

11. *The Venetian Painters* (1894) reprinted in *Italian Painters of the Renaissance* (New York: Phaidon, 1952), p. iii. For Wilson's commentary see his "Architecture and the Reinterpretation of the Past in the American Renaissance," *Winterthur Portfolio*, 18 (Winter 1983), 69.

12. William Boring to Charles Moore, n.d. (ca. 1927), Charles Moore Papers, Manuscript Division, Library of Congress. Harold van Buren Magonigle, who entered the office as White's draftsman in 1887, was rather disdainful of McKim's scholarly approach to design. Magonigle recalled that [McKim] "felt & talked his way toward the solution of a problem. It seemed to take forever and yet the job got done somehow. He anxiously consulted the books, and had his assistants spend hours looking up data for him, particularly Letarouilly, which was kind of the office Bible—if you saw it in Letarouilly it was so! and if he could not find, somewhere, authority for a certain combination of mouldings or other elements he desired to make, he would give it up and use something else for which he could find a precedent. He was the most convinced authoritarian I have ever encountered." See his "Half a Century of Architecture," *Pencil Points*, 15 (March 1934), p. 116. The reference to Letarouilly is to Paul Marie Letarouilly's *Edifices de Rome Moderne* (1840-1857), which Leland Roth notes McKim may have brought back from France in 1870. See his *McKim, Mead and White, Architects* (New York: Harper and Row, 1983), p. 88 n. 74.

13. May 22, 1894 Letter. McKim Papers.

14. June 26, 1905 Letter. McKim Papers.

15. Crocker to Burnham, July 14, 1905. McKim Papers.

16. Richard W. Longstreth, "Academic Eclecticism in American Architecture," *Winterthur Portfolio*, 17 (Spring 1982), p. 56.

17. *The American Academy in Rome*, 1902 pamphlet in McKim Papers.

18. July 12, 1906 Letter. McKim Papers.

19. July 24, 1906 Letter. McKim Papers.

20. Millet to McKim, June 26, 1905. Academy Papers, Archives of American Art. McKim wrote to Samuel Abbott, who was to become the director of the Academy in 1897: "We only want better times to purchase a habitat on the plan of that of France [the Villa Medici]." Oct. 9, 1894 Letter, McKim Papers.

21. July 24, 1906. See also Longstreth, pp. 56-57.

22. *Ibid.*

23. Davis's comment is written on his calling card pasted in a scrapbook of the New York Chapter of the American Institute of Architects. By virtue of its placement near other items from 1866, I would tentatively date it from this period as well. The scrapbook is in the collection of the American Institute of Architects Archives, Washington, D.C.

24. H. L. Warren, "The Use and Abuse of Precedent," *Architectural Review*, 2 (Feb. 13, 1893), p. 11.

25. "Influence of the French School on Architecture in the United States," *Architectural Record*, 4 (Oct.-Dec. 1894), p. 214. Flagg had attended the Ecole des Beaux-Arts and was architect of the Singer Tower in New York.

26. "Architectural Students - VIII" and "Our Abuses of Boldness in Design," *American Architect and Building News*, 2 (Feb. 24, 1877 and Aug. 25, 1877), pp. 58 and 270.

27. *Outline of a Course of Architectural Instruction* (Boston: 1866), p. 19.

28. Massachusetts Institute of Technology, 1868; University of Illinois at Urbana, 1870; Cornell University, 1871; Syracuse University, 1873; University of Pennsylvania, 1874; Columbia University, 1881; George Washington University, 1893; Armour Institute of Technology, 1895; Harvard University, 1895; University of Notre Dame, 1898; and Ohio State University, 1899.

29. "Architectural Students - V," *American Architect and Building News*, 1 (Nov. 18, 1876), p. 371.

30. "Delicacy of Perception Dependent upon Study," *American Architect and Building News*, 2 (Aug. 11, 1877) p. 254. The article ran unsigned but according to editor William

Rotch Ware's annotated copy of the journal, now in the collection of Loeb Library at the Harvard Graduate School of Design, Van Brunt was the author.

31.   "Influence of the French School of Design upon Architecture in America," *Proceedings of the 33rd Annual Convention of the American Institute of Architects* (1899), p. 64.

32.   "Formation of Beaux-Arts Society in New York" *American Architect and Building News*, 43 (Feb. 23, 1894) p. 49.

33.   Letter. Academy Papers, Archives of American Art.

34.   July 23, 1894 Letter to McKim. Academy Papers, Archives of American Art.

35.   Society of Beaux-Arts Architects Resolution, Aug. 9, 1894. Academy Papers, Archives of American Art. The Society eventually experienced a change of heart; the April 22, 1907 minutes of the Academy's Executive Committee noted that the Society had donated one thousand dollars to the Academy. See McKim Papers.

36.   Academy Papers, Archives of American Art. Ware and McKim later clashed over the direction of Columbia's architectural program, which Ware had headed since 1881. McKim and other prominent New York architects complained that Ware's liberal arts course of study at Columbia did not prepare students to work as draftsmen or superintendents in the architectural offices. They lobbied for the adoption of a program more closely patterned after the ateliers of the Ecole des Beaux-Arts. Ware was forced to resign in 1903 and by 1905 two ateliers, one under McKim and the other under Thomas Hastings, had been established at Columbia. See "School of Architecture at Columbia University," *American Architect*, 88 (Dec. 30, 1905), pp. 212-13; A. D. F. Hamlin to William Robert Ware, June 21, 1904. Ware Papers, Massachusetts Institute of Technology Archives; William T. Partridge, "Reminiscences of William Robert Ware," Ware Papers, Avery Library, Columbia University; and Steven M. Bedford and Susan M. Strauss "History II- 1881-1912," in *The*

Making of an Architect, ed. Richard Oliver (New York: Rizzoli, 1981), pp. 36-44.

37.   April 7, 1894 Letter to John Galen Howard, McKim Papers.

38.   "A Tribute to Charles F. McKim," *The Brickbuilder*, 19 (Feb. 1910), p. 55. Others shared McKim's concern about contemporary French architecture's effect on American design. F. W. Chandler, then head of M.I.T.'s architecture program, wrote McKim the following: "I am sure that Paris and France are overdone and that there is more architecture to the square inch in Italy than to the square mile in France. I fully appreciate the training at the Beaux-Arts but there is an immense amount of artificialness through it all which can't be otherwise because it's French - the Roman school [the American Academy] should have infinitely more humanity about it and appeal...I have from the beginning held it up to my boys as the place to strive for." See his January 6, 1895 Letter, Academy Papers.

39.   Roth, *McKim, Mead and White*, p. 174.

40.   Warren, "Use and Abuse," p. 11. In her article on American country houses, Mariana van Rensselaer stressed that this country's architects must be independent but scholarly in their approach to design. See her "American Country Dwellings III," *Century*, 32 (July 1886), p. 426.

41.   Reprinted in the *American Architect and Building News*, 78 (Dec. 20, 1902), pp. 91-92.

42.   *The American Academy in Rome*, pamphlet in McKim Papers. F. D. Millet reported to William R. Mead that "one firm told me that if one of their men could go to the academy for a year they would guarantee to raise his present salary of $20 a week to $40 a week on his return." See his letter of Dec. 30, 1909, Academy Papers.

43.   Roth, p. 252.

44.   Quoted in Roth, p. 335.

45.   "Rome as a Place of Schooling for the Decorative Painter," *Proceedings of the 37th*

Annual Convention of the American Institute of Architects (1903), pp. 64-65. Blashfield made clear that these remarks applied not only to the Academy's program in mural painting but also to those in architecture and sculpture.

46. Feb. 20, 1895 Memorandum. Academy Papers.

47. "Significance of Rome to the American Architectural Student," reprinted in the *American Architect and Building News*, 82 (Nov. 7, 1903), p. 45. An 1876 article in the same journal had faulted American draftsmen for their inability to subordinate detail to mass and the resulting lack of unity and breadth of effect in their work. See "Architectural Students - VI." 1 (Nov. 25, 1876), p. 379.

48. Feb. 6, 1895 Letter to Daniel Burnham. Academy Papers. Ware had previously written to McKim: "We have no villa and few students and the course of study has no definite shape." See his July 14, 1894 Letter, Academy Papers.

49. See McKim to Saint-Gaudens, May 22, 1894. McKim Papers.

50. Magonigle, one of the first students at the then American School of Architecture in Rome, complained: "I have not found except in Bramante's work the things I hoped to find in profusion [in Rome]...I can and try to find good in everything, and I find many unexpected excellencies horribly overlaid with brutalities." See his letter of Nov. 25, 1894 to C. H. Blackall. Academy Papers.

51. When Magonigle found out that Temple and Page planned to stay in Rome only four to five months, he also resisted spending a full year there. See Austin W. Lord to McKim, Dec. 26, 1894. Academy Papers.

52. Lord graduated from the M.I.T. architectural program in 1888. He worked for several years in Boston firms and won the Rotch Traveling Fellowship, which Magonigle was later to hold. He worked in McKim's office and was dispatched to Rome as the first head of the American School of Architecture. In 1912 he became director of Columbia's architectural program. He also established a New York practice with James Hewlett.

53. Marcus T. Reynolds to William Robert Ware. Nov. 26, 1894. Academy Papers. Reynolds was a student of Ware's at Columbia.

54. Lord served as head of the Roman program from 1894 until 1896. Will S. Aldrich, a Rotch Scholar at the Academy, served as a caretaker until 1897 when Samuel Abbott became director. Abbott was a cousin of Julia Appleton, McKim's second wife, and had worked with him on the Boston Public Library as head of that institution's Board of Trustees. Abbott was forced out in 1903. Henry S. Mowbray, a mural painter, then served as director until 1906. George Breck, another mural painter and former fellow at the Academy, was director from 1906 until 1909. See Valentine, pp. 154-55, 159, 181.

55. May 22, 1904 Letter to McKim. Academy Papers. Millet wrote to the Academy's Board of Trustees: "The American Academy in Rome had no students of its own until the present year [1907]. It provided a home for others. Late last autumn the executive committee awarded three fellowships for three years' study in Rome." Dec. 11, 1907 Letter, McKim Papers.

56. The list of projects is contained in a letter from Lord to McKim, May 30, 1895. Academy Papers.

57. Letter to Daniel Burnham, Feb. 6, 1895. Academy Papers. Ware further reported that the fellows did not like following the board's prescribed course of study.

58. Director's Report for the Year Oct. 1, 1907 through September 30, 1908, submitted by George Breck, October 10, 1908. McKim Papers.

59. Valentine, pp. 39-41.

60. *Ibid.*, p. 60.

61. Pope to Charles Moore, Sept. 20, 1926, Charles Moore Papers, Manuscript Division, Library of Congress. I am indebted to Steven Bedford of Columbia University, who is completing a dissertation on Pope, for this reference.

62.   Venturi and Graves were holders of the Academy's *Prix de Rome* in architecture from 1954-1956 and 1960-1962 respectively.

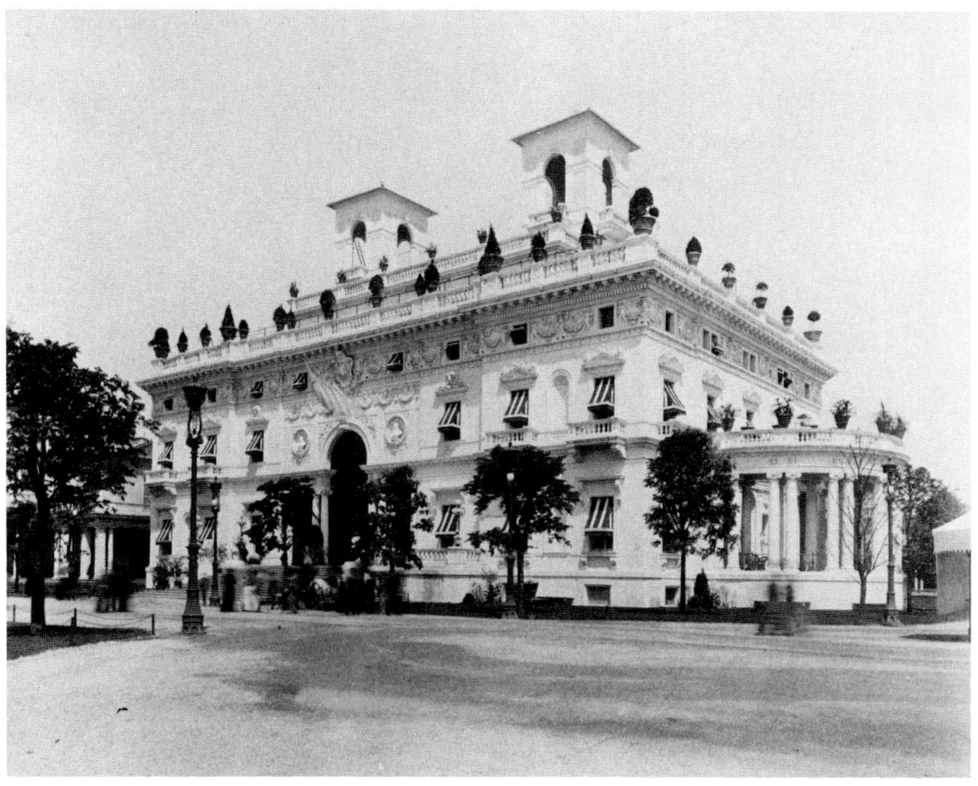

239.   Charles F. McKim, New York State Pavilion, Chicago World's Columbian Exposition, 1893 (The Art Institute of Chicago).

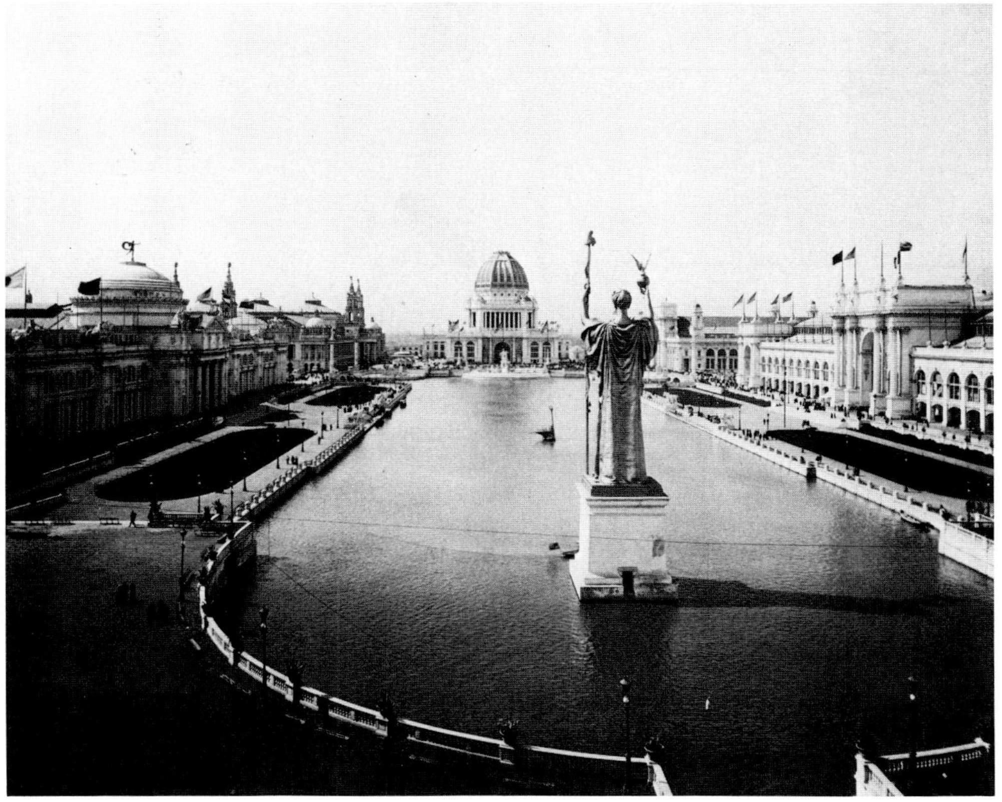

240.   Court of Honor, Chicago World's Columbian Exposition, 1893 (The Chicago Historical Society).

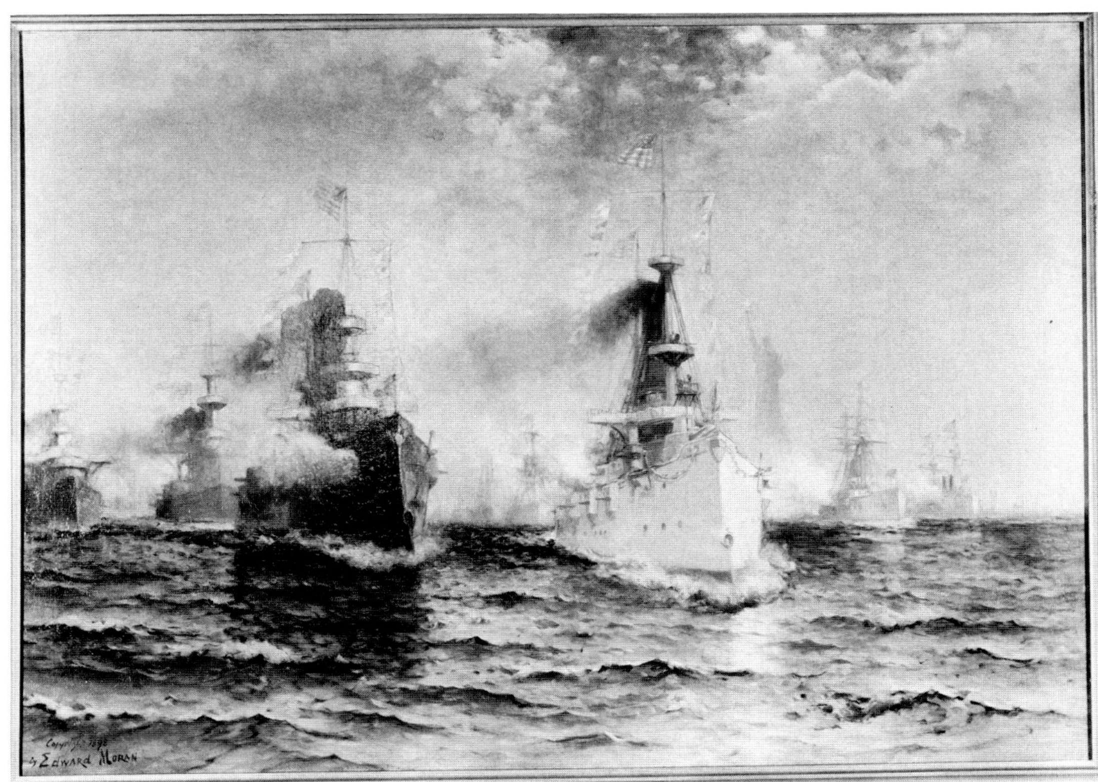

241.   Edward Moran, *Return of the Conquerors, September 29, 1899*, 1899 (United States Naval Academy Museum collection).

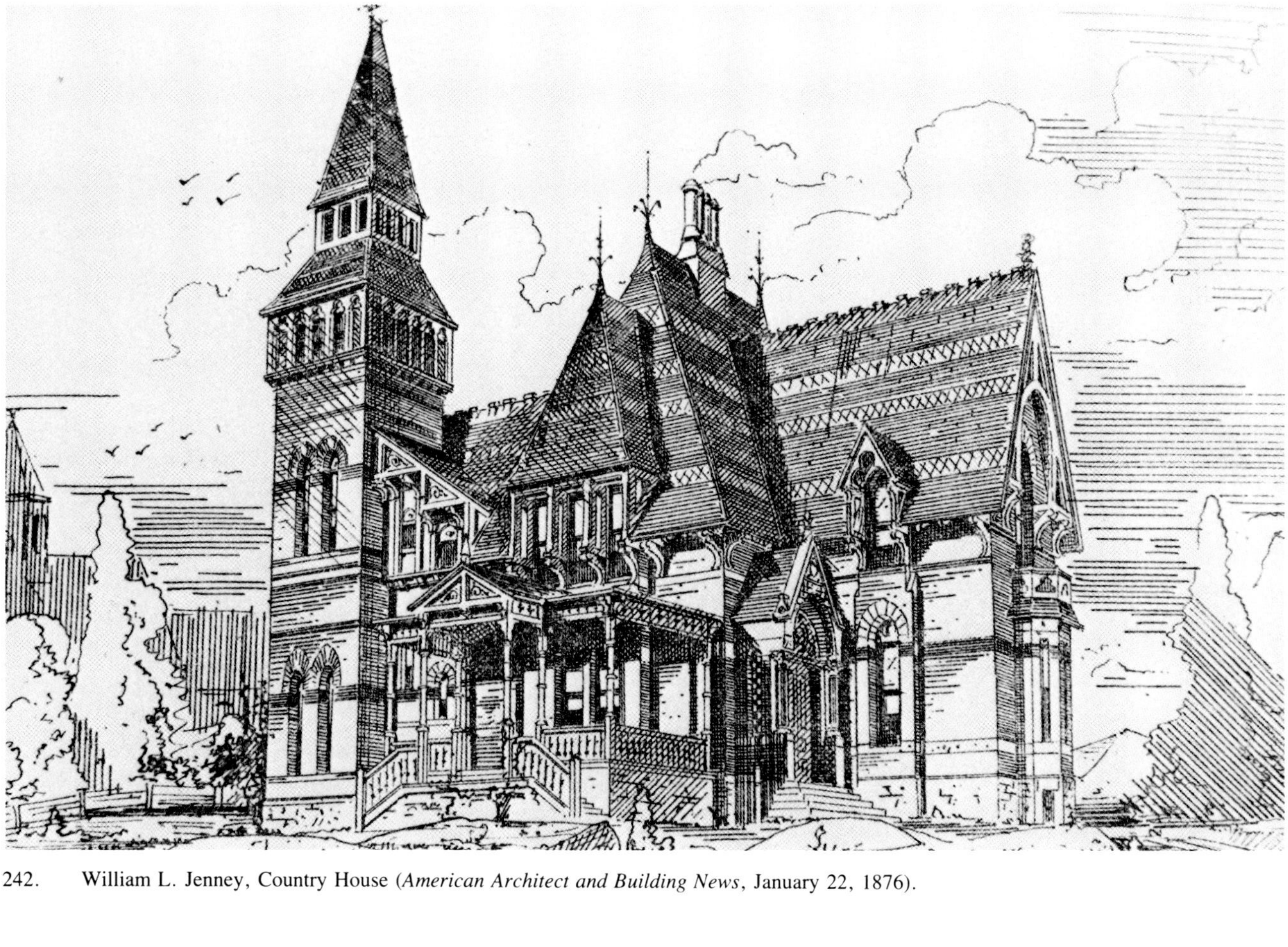

242.   William L. Jenney, Country House (*American Architect and Building News*, January 22, 1876).

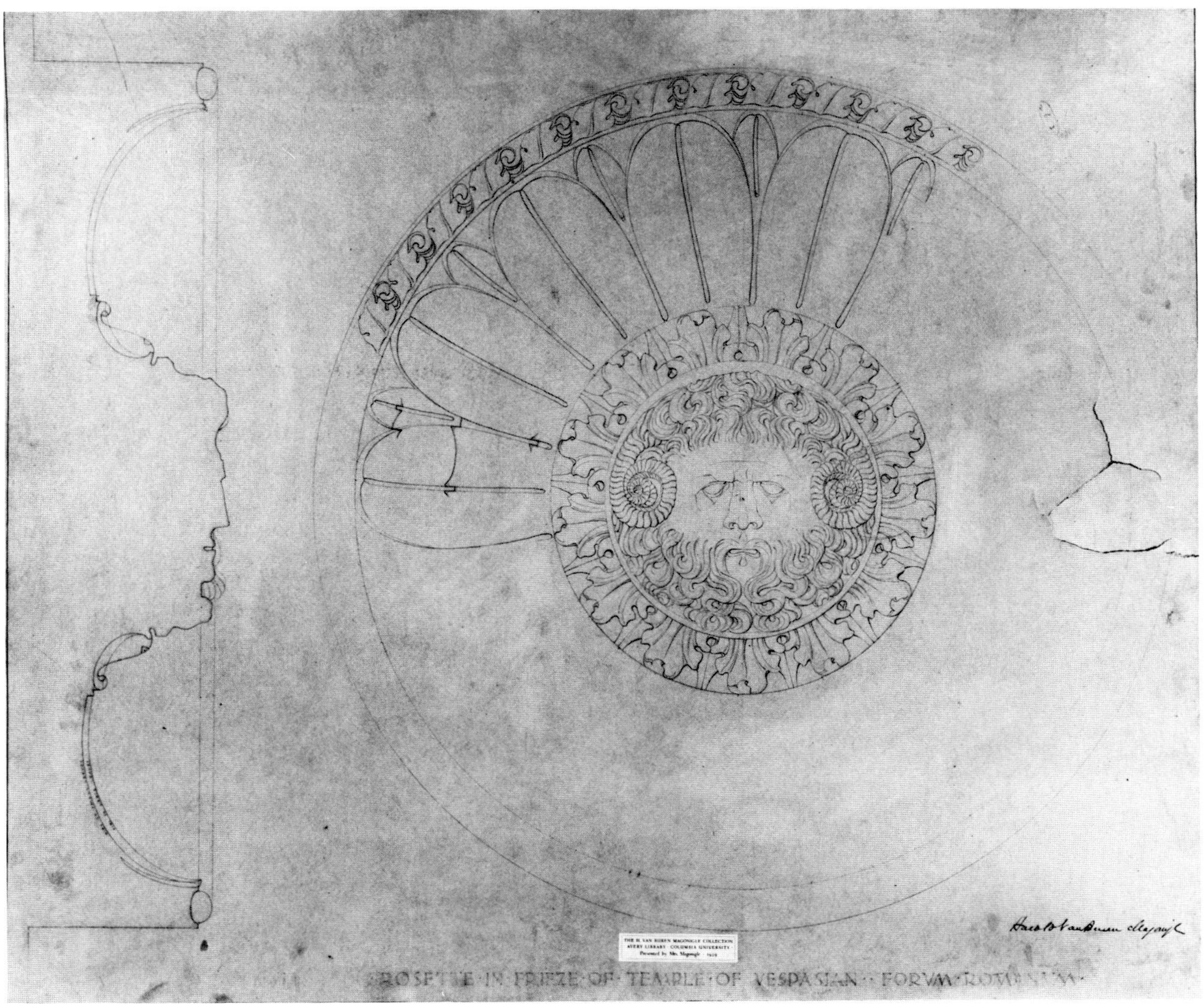

243.   Harold van Buren Magonigle, Drawing of a Rosette from the Frieze of the Temple of Vespasian, Rome, 1894-95 (H. van Buren Magonigle Collection, Avery Library, Columbia University).

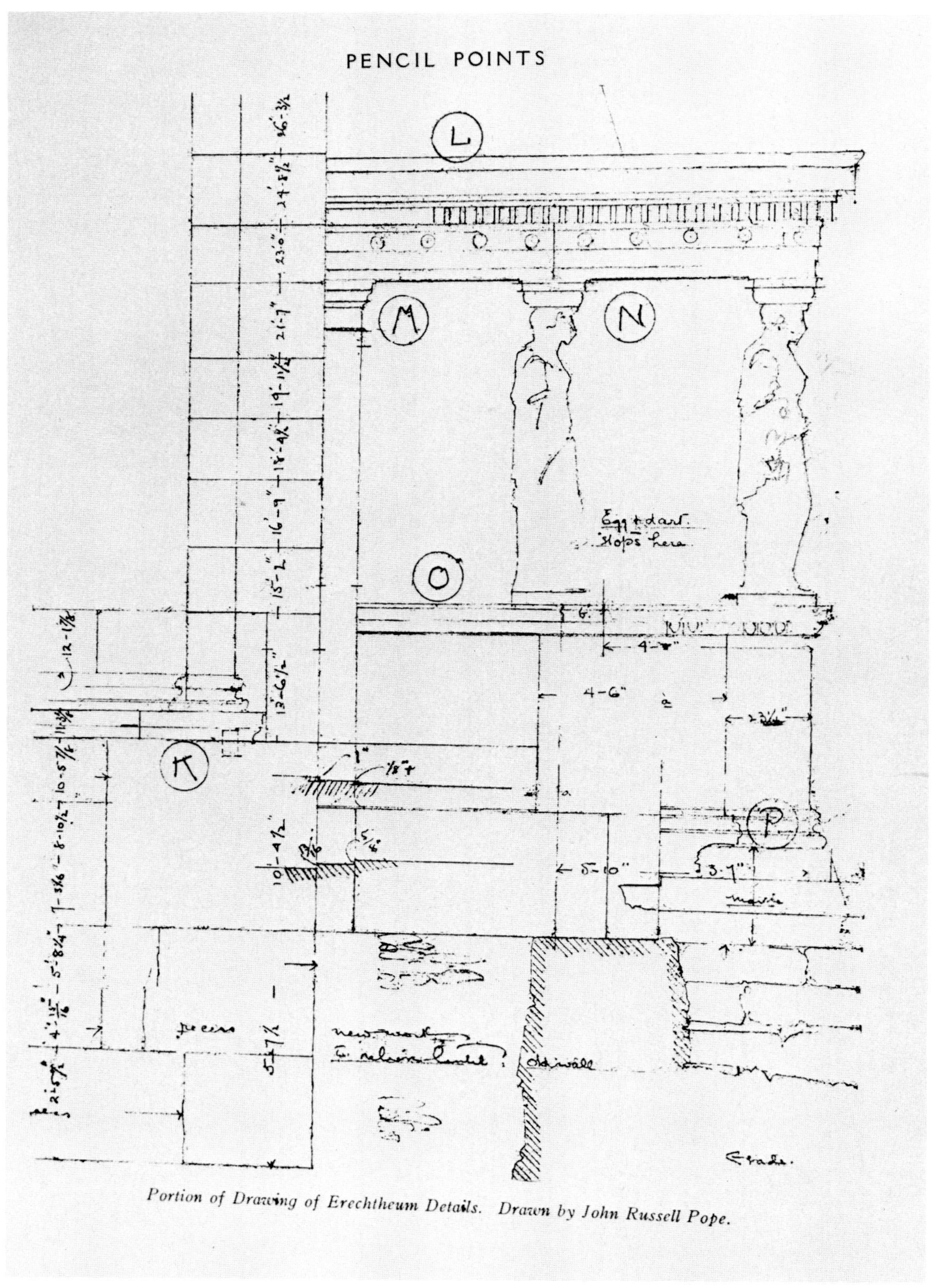

244.   John Russell Pope, Portion of a Drawing of Details from the Erechtheum, Athens, 1896 (*Pencil Points*, December 1924).

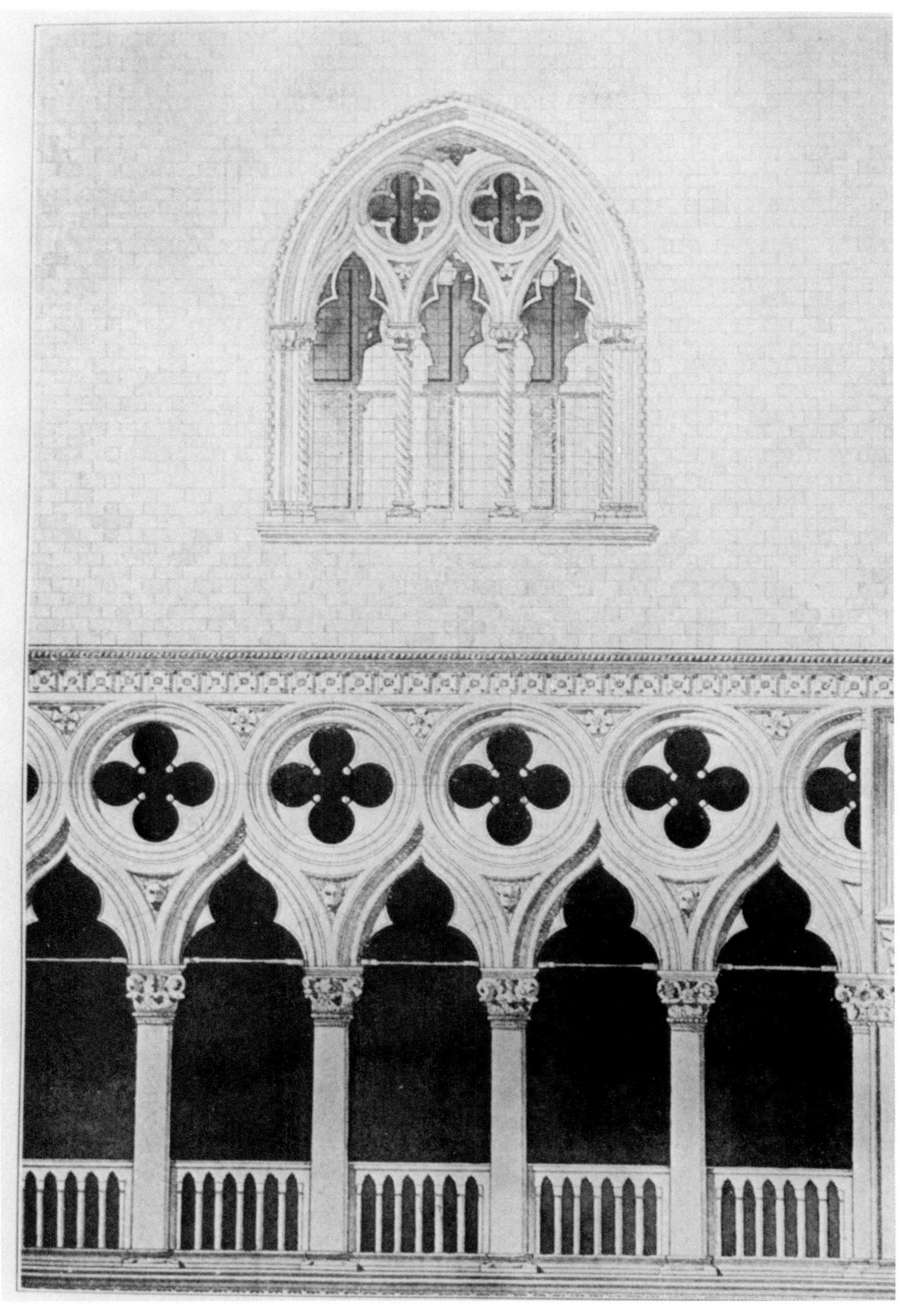

245.   Harold van Buren Magonigle, Portion of the Doge's Palace, Venice, 1894-95 (*Pencil Points*, March 1925).

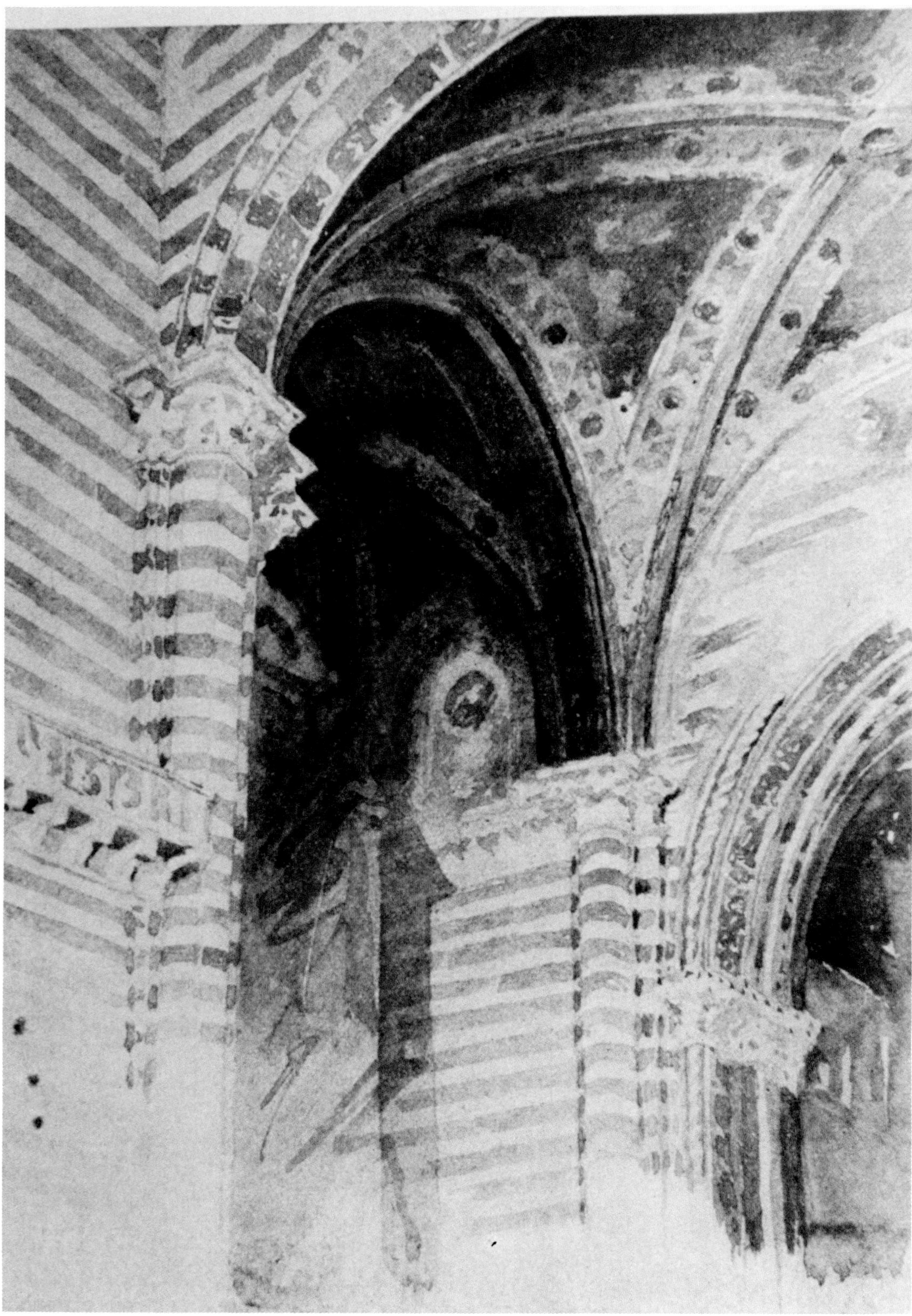

246.   John Russell Pope, Watercolor Study of the Cathedral at Orvieto, 1896 (*Pencil Points*, December 1924).

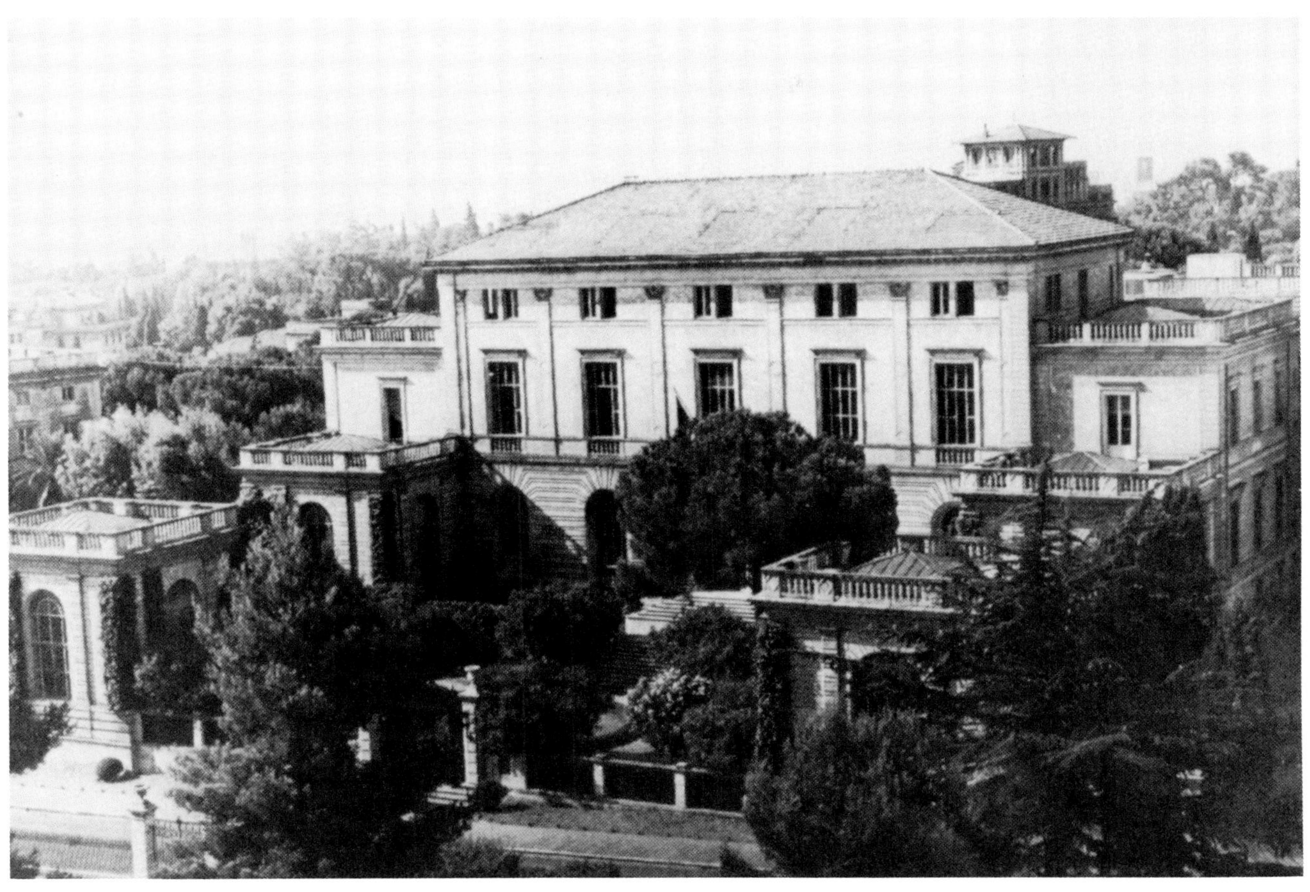

247.   McKim, Mead and White, The American Academy in Rome, 1912-13 (The New-York Historical Society).

List of Illustrations

49. Caravaggio, *Entombment of Christ*, Rome, Vatican Museums (from Hibbard, *Caravaggio*).

50. Raphael, *Transfiguration*, Rome, Vatican (from Oskar Fischel, *Raphael*).

51. Raphael, *Transfiguration*, detail.

52. Caravaggio, *Conversion of St. Paul*, Rome, S. Maria del Popolo, Cerasi Chapel (from Hibbard, *Caravaggio*).

53. Raphael, *Transfiguration*, detail.

54. Caravaggio, *Entombment of Christ*, detail, Rome, Vatican Museums (from Hibbard, *Caravaggio*).

55. Raphael, *Transfiguration*, detail.

56. Caravaggio, *Doubting Thomas*, Potsdam, Staatliche Schlösser und Garten (from Hibbard, *Caravaggio*).

57. Leonardo, detail from the *Treatise on Painting* (from L. Goldscheider, *Leonardo da Vinci*).

58. Annibale Carracci, *Assumption of the Virgin*, Rome, S. Maria del Popolo, Cerasi Chapel (from Hibbard, *Caravaggio*).

59. Caravaggio, *Crucifixion of St. Peter*, Rome, S. Maria del Popolo, Cerasi Chapel (from Hibbard, *Caravaggio*).

60. Caravaggio, *Death of the Virgin*, Paris, Louvre (from Hibbard, *Caravaggio*).

61. Caravaggio, *Resurrection of Lazarus*, Messina, National Museum (from Hibbard, *Caravaggio*).

62. Titian (?), *Portrait of Philip II*, Cincinnati (Ohio), Museum of Art.

63. Anonymous artist, *Sacrifice of Isaac*, Boal Collection, Boalsburg, Pennsylvania.

64. Columbus Chapel, exterior. Boal Mansion, Boalsburg, Pennsylvania.

65. Columbus Chapel, interior. Boal Mansion, Boalsburg, Pennslvania.

66. Columbus Chapel, interior. Boal Mansion, Boalsburg, Pennsyslvania.

67. Palacio de Colón, Llamas del Mouro (Asturias), Spain.

68. Palacio de Colón, exterior of chapel. Llamas del Mouro (Asturias), Spain.

69. Colón Family Tree (after Garner and Henderson, *Columbus and Related Family Papers*).

70. Sierra Sarria Salcedo Family Tree (after Garner and Henderson, *Columbus and Related Family Papers*).

71. Caravaggio, *Sacrifice of Isaac*, 1603 (Florence, Uffizi).

72. Anonymous artist, *Sacrifice of Isaac* (Formerly Como, Italy: Collection of Prof. Luciano di Bona).

73. Anonymous artist, *Sacrifice of Isaac* (Duomo, Castellamare di Stabia).

74. Anonymous artist, *Sacrifice of Isaac* (Alcalá de Henares, Convent of St. Ursula).

75. Anonymous artist, *Sacrifice of Isaac* (Madrid, Confederación de Cajas de Ahorros).

76. Jean Charles Le Vasseur, copy of lost *Sacrifice of Isaac* attributed to Caravaggio (Boston, Museum of Fine Arts).

77. Anonymous artist (Giuseppe Vermiglio?), *Sacrifice of Isaac* (Stockholm, Rapp Collection).

78. Anonymous artist, *Sacrifice of Isaac* (Jaen, Collection Ramirez).

79. Anonymous artist, *Sacrifice of Isaac* (Madrid, En Comercio, M. Gonzalez).

80. Valentin de Boulogne, *Sacrifice of Isaac* (Montreal, Museum of Fine Arts).

81. Francesco Guarino (attributed by G. Ortolani), *Sacrifice of Isaac* (Salerno, Private Collection).

108. Filippo Juvarra, project for a public forum with church and hospital, sketch. Turin, Collection of Adriano Tournon (Millon, *Filippo Juvarra*).

109. Ange-Jacques Gabriel, project perspective for *Place Louis XV* (now *Place de la Concorde*), engraving. Paris, Bibliothèque Nationale (Kalnein and Levey, *Art and Architecture of the Eighteenth Century in France*).

110. Emmanuel Héré de Corny, project plan for the *Place Royale*, Nancy (Patte, *Monumens érigés en France à la gloire Louis XV*, 1765).

111. Nancy, Place du l'Intendance (now Palais du Gouvernement), view (Brinckmann, *Platz und Monument*).

112. Carlo Fontana, project plan for the Piazza S. Pietro, Rome (Fontana, *Il Tempio Vaticano*, 1694).

113. Luigi Vanvitelli, project plan for the Palazzo Reale, Caserta (Vanvitelli, *Dichiarazione dei disegni del real palazzo di Caserta*, 1756).

114. Luigi Vanvitelli, project perspective for the Palazzo Reale, Caserta (Vanvitelli, *Dichiarazione dei disegni del real palazzo di Caserta*, 1756).

115. Robert de Cotte, project plan for Buen Retiro. Paris, Bibliothèque Nationale (Bottineau, *L'art de cour dans Espagne de Philippe V*).

116. Naples, San Francesco di Paola, aerial view (*Napoli e il suo Golfo*).

117. Leningrad, plan of Nevsky Prospekt (Egorov, *The Architectural Planning of St. Petersburg*).

118. Leningrad, Cathedral of the Virgin of Kazan, view from the north (Hamilton, *Art and Architecture of Russia*).

119. Giuseppe Valadier, project for the Piazza del Popolo, ca. 1815. Rome, Gabinetto Nazionale delle Stampe (*Valadier, segno e architettura*, Rome, 1986).

120. The Val-de-Grâce, Paris. Plan of church and convent (from Ruprich-Robert, *L'Eglise et le monastère du Val-de-Grâce,* Paris, 1875).

121. The Val-de-Grâce, Paris. High Altar (photo N. D. Roger-Viollet).

122. Michel Anguier, *Nativity*. Paris, St. Roch (photo N. D. Roger-Viollet).

123. G. L. Bernini, *Nativity*. Berlin, Kupferstichkabinett (museum photo).

124. Pietro da Cortona, Project for the High Altar of S. Giovanni dei Fiorentini, Rome. Windsor Castle, Royal Library (reproduced by Gracious Permission of Her Majesty Queen Elizabeth II).

125. S. Nicola da Tolentino, Rome. High Altar (photo Bibliotheca Hertziana).

126. S. Tomaso da Villanova, Castel Gandolfo. High Altar (photo Alinari).

127. Frascati, Cathedral, model for the façade (from Hager, in *Commentari*, 28, 1977).

128. Fulda, Cathedral, view of façade (from E. Kramer and H. Retzlaff, *Fulda*, Munich, 1964).

129. Fulda, Cathedral, ground plan (after Freckmann; Bildarchiv Foto Marburg).

130. Fulda, Cathedral, view into the south side aisle (after A. Schmitt, *Der Dom zu Fulda*, 1964).

131. Rome, SS. Apostoli, ground plan by D. de Rossi (*Architettura civile*, III, Rome, 1721).

132. Fulda, Cathedral, eighteenth-century plan (Hessische Landesbibliothek Fulda).

133. Fulda, Cathedral, view towards main altar (photo: Knauff, Fulda).

134. Rome, S. Pantaleo, view into the side chapels from the nave (from G. Spagnesi, *Giovanni Antonio de Rossi architetto romano*).

135. Rome, SS. Apostoli, view into the side chapels from the nave (from G. Magni, *Il Barocco a Roma*, I).

136. Fulda, Cathedral, view along a side aisle (from E. Kramer and H. Retzlaff, *Fulda*).

169. Palazzo Lercari, atrium (photo: author).

170. Filippo Raguzzini, Casino Lercari (photo: author).

171. Casino Lercari, detail (photo: author).

172. Casino Lercari, main entrance (photo: author).

173. Cosimo Fanzago, S. Maria degli Angeli alle Croci, Naples, façade, after an engraving by Petrini (after A. Blunt, *Neapolitan Baroque and Rococo Architecture*; photo courtesy of Tim Benton, London).

174. Naples, S. Maria degli Angeli alle Croci, interior with upper story loggia over vestibule (after A. Blunt, *Neapolitan Baroque and Rococo Architecture*; photo courtesy of Tim Benton, London).

175. Barra, Villa Bisignano (after A. Blunt, *Neapolitan Baroque and Rococo Architecture*; photo courtesy of Tim Benton, London).

176. Raguzzini, Ospedale di S. Gallicano, Rome, 1725-1726, façade (photo: author).

177. Raguzzini, Piazza S. Ignazio, Rome, 1725-1736 (photo: Marburg).

178. Rome, Piazza S. Ignazio, central building, 1727-1729 (photo: Soprintendenza ai Monumenti del Lazio).

179. Carlo de'Dominicis, Ss. Celso e Giuliano, Rome, 1733-1736, interior (after P. Portoghesi, *Roma barocca*).

180. F. A. Picchiatti, Chapel, Monte della Misericordia, Naples, begun 1658, interior (after A. Blunt, *Neapolitan Baroque and Rococo Architecture*; photo courtesy of Tim Benton, London).

181. Domenico Gregorini, S. Croce in Gerusalemme, Rome, 1741-1744, portico (after P. Portoghesi, *Roma barocca*).

182. Ferdinando Reif, decoration for the Lateran façade, 1729 (after A. Munoz, *Il Museo di Roma*).

183. Nicola Salvi, festival structure for the Piazza di Spagna, 1728. Rome, Gabinetto Nazionale delle Stampe (after A. Schiavo, *La Fontana di Trevi*).

184. Rome, S. Giovanni in Laterano, Cappella Corsini (engraving from *Quinto Teatro*, 1739).

185. Rome, S. Giovanni in Laterano, Cappella Corsini (photo: Alinari).

186. Rome, S. Maria Maggiore, Cappella Sistina (photo: Alinari).

187. Rome, S. Giovanni in Laterano, façade by Alessandro Galilei.

188. Rome, S. Giovanni in Laterano, state of façade in 1650 (Berlin, Kupferstichkabinett und Sammlung der Zeichnungen; photo after V. Hoffmann, *Römisches Jahrbuch für Kunstgeschichte*, 1978).

189. Anonymous sketch after Galilei's model of S. Giovanni in Laterano (Paris, Ministry for Foreign Affairs).

190. Ludovico Rusconi Sassi, model for the façade of S. Giovanni in Laterano, competition of 1732 (after H. Hager, *Commentari*, 1971).

191. Luigi Vanvitelli, drawing for the façade of S. Giovanni in Laterano, competition of 1732 (disegno X, GFN n1022; Museo di Roma).

192. Alessandro Galilei, portico of S. Giovanni in Laterano, niche (photo: Bibliotheca Hertziana, Rome).

193. Galilei, portico of S. Giovanni in Laterano, soffittes (photo: Bibliotheca Hertziana, Rome).

194. Galilei, portico of S. Giovanni in Laterano, lunette (photo: Bibliotheca Hertziana, Rome).

195. Anonymous architect, project for the Trevi Fountain, 1730-1731 (photo: Berlin, Kunstbibliothek).

196. Nicola Salvi, project for the Trevi Fountain, 1732 (Montreal, Canadian Centre for Architecture).

197. Nicola Salvi, The Trevi Fountain (photo: Anderson).

198. Ferdinando Fuga, project for the Palazzo della Consulta, 1731 (GFN; Museo di Roma).

199. Ferdinando Fuga, Palazzo della Consulta, final project (GFN; Museo di Roma).

200. Attributed to Domenico Torti, fresco on the ceiling of the Galleria dei candelabri, Vatican. Commissioned by Pope Leo XIII between 1883 and 1887 (Direzione Generale dei Musei Vaticani).

201. Announcement of the daguerreotype in *Poliorama pittoresco*, December 1, 1839 (after P. Becchetti, *Fotografi e fotografia in Italia*).

202. Robert MacPherson, Piazza del Popolo, 1857. Becchetti Collection, Rome.

203. The "Colossal Pictorial Typorama, or Modelled View of Rome". Surrey Gardens, London, 1837 (from R. D. Altick, *The Shows of London*).

204. Jerome Cook (1551), Antwerp, etching: *capriccio* (from A. Hyatt Mayor, *Prints and People*).

205. G. P. Pannini (1712-1765), oil, *capriccio* with Pantheon, the famous Hercules, the statue of Marcus Aurelius, and the Pyramid of Caius Cestius background (from C. Whitfield and J. G. Liuks, *Views from the Grand Tour*).

206. G. B. Piranesi, etching (1758): Temple of Antoninus and Faustina (from A. Hyatt Mayor, *Prints and People*).

207. William Fox Talbot, calotype, 1840s; Temple of Antoninus and Faustina (from A. Hyatt Mayor, *Prints and People*).

208. Achille Morelli, daguerreotype, 1841; Basilica of S. Maria Maggiore (from P. Becchetti and C. Pietrangeli, *Roma in dagherrotipia*).

209. Unknown photographer, calotype, 1850; Temple of Antoninus and Faustina (S. Lorenzo in Miranda; from D. Helsted, *Rome in Early Photographs*).

210. Frederic Flachéron, calotype, 1850. The Roman Forum, looking towards the Capitol (from D. Helsted, *Rome in Early Photographs*).

211. Charles Smeaton, calotype, late 1860s. Catacomb of S. Domitilla, photographed by magnesium light. (Parker Collection; photograph from J. Keller and K. A. Breisch, *A Victorian View of Ancient Rome*).

212. A. Appert, engraving after a daguerreotype, 1840. View of Rome from the Palatine. (From *Excursions Daguerriennes*; photograph from P. Becchetti and C. Pietrangeli, *Roma in dagherrotipia*).

213. Martens, engraving after a daugerreotype, 1840. Temple of Vesta. (From *Excursions Daguerriennes*; photograph from P. Becchetti and C. Pietrangeli, *Roma in dagherrotipia*).

214. Alexander John Ellis, daguerreotype, 1841. Temple of Saturn, photographed from the church of SS. Luca e Martina (from R. Hershkowitz, *The British Photographer Abroad; the First Thirty Years*).

215. Alexander John Ellis, daguerreotype, 1841. Piazza Navona (from P. Becchetti and C. Pietrangeli, *Roma in dagherrotipia*).

216. Thomas Sutton, waxed salt print, 1853. The Roman Forum (from R. Hershkowitz, *The British Photographer Abroad*).

217. Robert MacPherson, albumen print, 1863. The Roman Forum (from P. Becchetti and C. Peitrangeli, *Roma in dagherrotipia*).

218. Unknown photographer, albumen print, before 1860. Temple of Castor, seen from the east (from D. Helsted, *Rome in Early Photographs*).

219. Unknown photographer, albumen print, c. 1855. The Forum, south of the Via del Campidoglio (from D. Helsted, *Rome in Early Photographs*).

220. Unknown photographer, albumen print, c. 1857. View over the Forum from the Via del Campidoglio (from D. Helsted, *Rome in Early Photographs*).

221. A. and G. Luswergh, albumen print, 1854. The Forum of Trajan (from P. Becchetti, *Fotografi e fotografia in Italia*).

222. Unknown photographer, c. 1870. Traffic in Rome (from D. Helsted, *Rome in Early Photographs*).

223. Unknown photographer, 1864. The excavation of the Hercules Master (from D. Helsted, *Rome in Early Photographs*).

224. Altobelli, c. 1866. View of the Forum; simulated moonlight (from D. Helsted, *Rome in Early Photographs*).

225. Lorenzo Suscipij, daguerreotype, 1841. The Coliseum (from P. Becchetti and C. Pietrangeli, *Roma in dagherrotipia*).

226. Alexander John Ellis, daguerreotype, 1841. The Coliseum (from P. Becchetti and C. Pietrangeli, *Roma in dagherrotipia*).

227. Robert MacPherson, calotype, c. 1850. The Coliseum (from R. Hershkowitz, *The British Photographer Abroad*).

228. James Francis Dunlop, calotype, c. 1850. Interior of the Coliseum (from R. Hershkowitz, *The British Photographer Abroad*).

229. Unknown photographer, undated. Coliseum, view of one of the Vomitoria. (Parker Collection; from J. Keller and K. A. Breisch, *A Victorian View of Ancient Rome*).

230. Unknown photographer, 1868. Fragment of a statue found in the Baths of Caracalla (from J. Keller and K. A. Breisch, *A Victorian View of Ancient Rome*).

231. Michele Danesi, 1871. Album cover (from P. Becchetti, *Fotografi e fotografia in Italia*).

232. G. Altobelli and P. Molius, collodion plate, c. 1860. Piazza of S. Maria Maggiore (from D. Helsted, *Rome in Early Photographs*).

233. Unknown photographer, c. 1865. Via Ostiense, Pyramid of Caius Cestius (from D. Helsted, *Rome in Early Photographs*).

234. Joseph Spithone, 1860s. The Appian Way (from G. Dimok, *Caroline Sturgis Tappan and the Grand Tour*).

235. Unknown photographer, 1868. Albergo dell'Orso (from D. Helsted, *Rome in Early Photographs*).

236. Robert MacPherson, 1850s. Spanish Steps and SS. Trinità dei Monti (from G. Dimok, *Caroline Sturgis Tappan and the Grand Tour*).

237. Ludwig Passini, water color, c. 1850. Café Greco; Hamburg, Kunsthalle (from G. Poensgen, *C. Ph. Fohr und das Café Greco*).

238. William R. Mead and Charles F. McKim (left and right), c. 1896-97, (Manuscripts Department, Library of Congress).

239. Charles F. McKim, New York State Pavilion, Chicago World's Columbian Exposition, 1893 (The Art Institute of Chicago).

240. Court of Honor, Chicago World's Columbian Exposition, 1893 (The Chicago Historical Society).

241. Edward Moran, *Return of the Conquerors, September 29, 1899*, 1899 (United States Naval Academy Museum collection).

242. William L. Jenney, Country House (*American Architect and Building News*, January 22, 1876).

243. Harold van Buren Magonigle, Drawing of a Rosette from the Frieze of the Temple of Vespasian, Rome, 1894-95 (H. van Buren Magonigle Collection, Avery Library, Columbia University).

244. John Russell Pope, Portion of a Drawing of Details from the Erechtheum, Athens, 1896 (*Pencil Points*, December 1924).

245. Harold van Buren Magonigle, Portion of the Doge's Palace, Venice, 1894-95 (*Pencil Points*, March 1925).

246. John Russell Pope, Watercolor Study of the Cathedral at Orvieto, 1896 (*Pencil Points*, December 1924).

Photographic Credits

The Age of Caravaggio. Exhibition Catalogue, The Metropolitan Museum of Art, New York, 1985: 40.

R. D. Altick, *The Shows of London*, Cambridge, Massachusetts, 1978: 203.

American Architect and Building News, January, 1876: 242.

Margarete Baur-Heinhold, *Theater des Barock. Festliches Bühnenspiel im 17. und 18. Jahrhundert*, Munich, 1966: 154, 156.

G. Beard, *The Work of Christopher Wren*, Edinburgh, 1982: 95, 96.

Piero Becchetti and C. Pietrangeli, *Roma in dagherrotipia*, Rome, 1979: 208, 212, 213, 215, 217, 225, 226.

Piero Becchetti, *Fotografi e fotografia in Italia*, Rome, 1978: 201, 221, 231.

Amedeo Bellini, *Benedetto Alfieri*, Milan, 1978: 157.

M. Birindelli, *La macchina heroica: il disegno di Gianlorenzo Bernini per Piazza San Pietro*, Rome, 1980: 90.

Anthony Blunt, *Neapolitan Baroque and Rococo Architecture*, London, 1975 (photos courtesy of Tim Benton, London): 173, 174, 175, 180.

Y. Bottineau, *L'art de cour dans l'Espagne de Philippe V, 1700-1746*, Bordeaux, n.d.: 115.

Allan Braham, *The Architecture of the French Enlightenment*, Berkeley and Los Angeles, 1980: 104.

A. E. Brinckmann, *Platz und Monument als Künstlerlisches Formproblem*, Berlin, 1963: 111.

David A. Brown, *Leonardo's Last Supper: The Restoration*, National Gallery of Art, Washington, D. C., 1983 : 39.

Elisa Debenedetti, ed., *Valadier, segno e architettura.* Exhibition Catalogue, 1985-1986 (Rome, 1985): 119.

G. A. Dell'Acqua, *I pittori bergamaschi dal XIII al XIX secolo*, Bergamo, 1975: 25, 27, 28, 29, 41.

George Dimok, *Caroline Sturgis Tappan and the Grand Tour*, Lennox Library Association, Lennox, Massachusetts, 1982: 234, 236.

Ugo Donati, *Artisti Ticinesi a Roma*, Bellinzona, 1942: 148.

Kerry Downes, *English Baroque Architecture*, London, 1966: 97.

Luitpold Dussler, *Raphael. A Critical Catalogue of His Pictures, Wall Paintings, and Tapestries*, London and New York, 1971: 43.

I. Egorov, *The Architectural Planning of St. Petersburg*, Athens, Ohio, 1969: 117.

M. Fagiolo dell' Arco and G. Spagnesi, eds., *Gian Lorenzo Bernini architetto e l'architettura europea del Sei-Settecento*, Rome, 1983: 92.

Mercedes Viale Ferrero, *La scenografici del '700 e i fratelli Galliari*, Turin, 1963: 103.

Oskar Fischel, *Raphael*, Berlin, 1962: 50, 51, 53, 55.

Karl Freckmann, *Der Dom zu Fulda*, Augsburg, 1928: 129.

Richard Garner and Donald C. Henderson, *Columbus and Related Family Papers, 1451-1902*, University Park and London, 1974: 69, 70.

L. Goldscheider, *Leonardo da Vinci*, 3rd edition, London, 1948: 35, 57.

Felicitas Hagen-Dempf, *Die Kollegienkirche in Salzburg*, Vienna, 1949: 137.

Hellmut Hager, in *Commentari*, 1971: 190.

Hellmut Hager, in *Commentari*, 1977: 127.

G. Hamilton, *The Art and Architecture of Russia*, Baltimore and Harmondsworth, 1975: 118.

Karsten Harries, *The Bavarian Rococo Church. Between Faith and Aestheticism*, New Haven and London, 1983: 155.

Dyveke Helsted, *Rome in Early Photographs; the Age of Pius IX*. The Thorvaldsen Museum, Copenhagen, 1977: 209, 210, 218, 219, 220, 222, 223, 224, 232, 233, 235.

K. Herding, *Pierre Puget, Das bildnisches Werk*, Berlin, 1970: 98.

R. Hershkowitz, *The British Photographer Abroad; the First Thirty Years*, London, 1980: 214, 216, 227, 228.

Howard Hibbard, *Caravaggio*, New York and London, 1983: 30, 31, 32, 33, 34, 36, 37, 42, 44, 45, 46, 47, 49, 52, 54, 56, 58, 59, 60, 61.

Volker Hoffman, in *Römisches Jahrbuch für Kunstgeschichte*, 1978: 188.

W. Kalnein and M. Levey, *The Art and Architecture of the Eighteenth Century in France*, Baltimore and Harmondsworth, 1972: 109.

J. Keller and K. A. Breisch, *A Victorian View of Ancient Rome*, Kelsey Museum of Archaeology, University of Michigan, Ann Arbor, Michigan, 1980: 211, 229, 230.

Bernhard Kerber, *Andrea Pozzo*, Berlin and New York, 1971: 150.

Timothy Kitao, *Circle and Oval in the Square of St. Peter's: Bernini's Art of Planning*, New York, 1974: 91.

E. Kramer and H. Retzlaff, *Fulda*, Munich, 1964: 128, 136, 140b, 141.

Martin Kuhn and Ingeborg Limmer, *Kloster Banz*, Freiburg, i. Br., 1977: 144.

E. Lavagnino, et al., *Altari barocchi a Roma*, Rome, 1959: 153.

P. Lavedan, *Histoire de l'urbanisme*. Vol. II, *Renaissance et temps modernes*, Paris, 1941: 93, 94.

Giulio Magni, *Il Barocco a Roma nella architettura e nella scultura decorativa* I, *Chiese*, Turin, 1911: 135.

P. Marconi, A. Cipriani, E. Valeriani, *I disegni di architettura dell' archivio storico dell' Accademia di San Luca*, II, Rome, 1974: 99, 100.

Kurt Martin, *Die Kunstdenkmaler des Amtsbezirks Mannheim Stadt Schwetzingen*, Karlsruhe, 1933: 159.

A. Hyatt Mayor, *Prints and People*, The Metropolitan Museum of Art, New York, 1971: 204, 206, 207.

Henry Millon, *Filippo Juvarra. Drawings from the Roman Period, 1, 1704-1714*, Rome, 1984: 108.

Alfred Moir, *Caravaggio*, New York, 1982: 26.

A. Munoz, *Il Museo di Roma*: 182.

Napoli e il suo Golfo, Naples, n.d.: 116.

Pencil Points, December, 1924: 244, 246; March, 1925: 245.

Piranese et les Français 1740-1790, Exhibition Catalogue, Rome, Académie de France, Rome, 1976: 105.

Georg Poensgen, *C. Ph. Fohr und das Café Greco*, Heidelberg, 1957: 237.

Paolo Portoghesi, *Roma Barocca*, trans. B. LaPenta, Cambridge, Massachusetts, 1970: 179, 181.

Paolo Portoghesi, *The Rome of Borromini. Architecture as Language*, New York, 1968: 158.

Ludwig Pralle, *Fulda, Dom und Abteibezirk*, Königstein im Taunus, 1980: 138.

Ruprich-Robert, *L'Eglise et le Monastère du Val-de-Grâce*, Paris, 1875: 120.

Armando Schiavo, *La Fontana di Trevi e le altre opere di Nicola Salvi*, Rome, 1956: 183; cover illustration.

Anton Schmitt, *Der Dom zu Fulda. Grabeskirche des heiligen Bonifatius*, Fulda, 1964: 130.

G. Spagnesi, *Giovanni Antonio de Rossi architetto romano*, Rome, 1964: 134.

John Spike, *Italian Still Life Painting from Three Centuries*. Exhibition Catalogue, Centro Di, National Academy of Design, Old Masters Society of New York, 1983: 38.

O. A. Weigmann, *Eine Bamberger Baumeisterfamilie um die Wende des 17. Jahrhunderts. Ein Beitrag zur Geschichte der Dientzenhofer*, Strassburg, 1902 (2nd ed. 1979): 145.

Harold E. Wethey, *The Paintings of Titian*, II, *The Portraits*, New York and London, 1971: 62.

C. Whitfield and J. G. Liuks, *Views from the Grand Tour*, New York, 1983: 205.

Rudolf Wittkower, "Palladio e Bernini," *Bollettino del Centro Internazionale di studi di Architettura: Andrea Palladio*, VIII, 1966: 101.